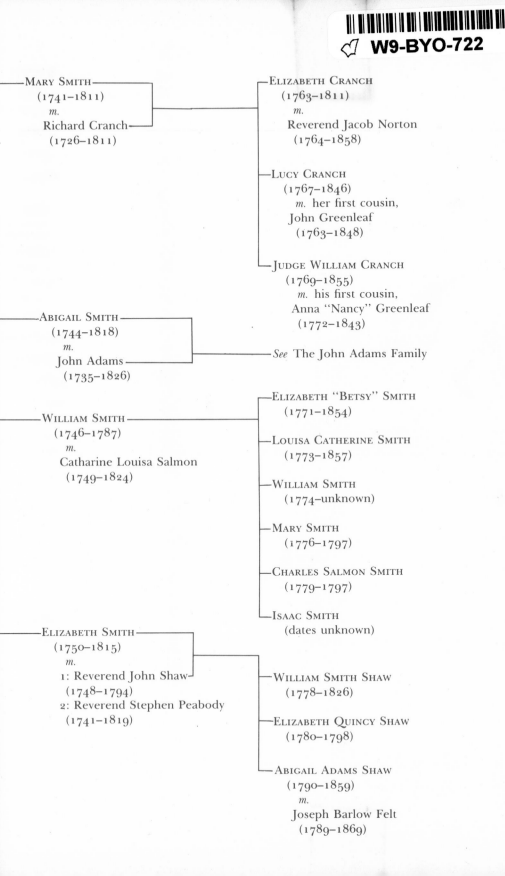

MARY SMITH
(1741–1811)
m.
Richard Cranch
(1726–1811)

ELIZABETH CRANCH
(1763–1811)
m.
Reverend Jacob Norton
(1764–1858)

LUCY CRANCH
(1767–1846)
m. her first cousin,
John Greenleaf
(1763–1848)

JUDGE WILLIAM CRANCH
(1769–1855)
m. his first cousin,
Anna "Nancy" Greenleaf
(1772–1843)

ABIGAIL SMITH
(1744–1818)
m.
John Adams
(1735–1826)

See The John Adams Family

WILLIAM SMITH
(1746–1787)
m.
Catharine Louisa Salmon
(1749–1824)

ELIZABETH "BETSY" SMITH
(1771–1854)

LOUISA CATHERINE SMITH
(1773–1857)

WILLIAM SMITH
(1774–unknown)

MARY SMITH
(1776–1797)

CHARLES SALMON SMITH
(1779–1797)

ISAAC SMITH
(dates unknown)

ELIZABETH SMITH
(1750–1815)
m.
1: Reverend John Shaw
(1748–1794)
2: Reverend Stephen Peabody
(1741–1819)

WILLIAM SMITH SHAW
(1778–1826)

ELIZABETH QUINCY SHAW
(1780–1798)

ABIGAIL ADAMS SHAW
(1790–1859)
m.
Joseph Barlow Felt
(1789–1869)

ABIGAIL ADAMS

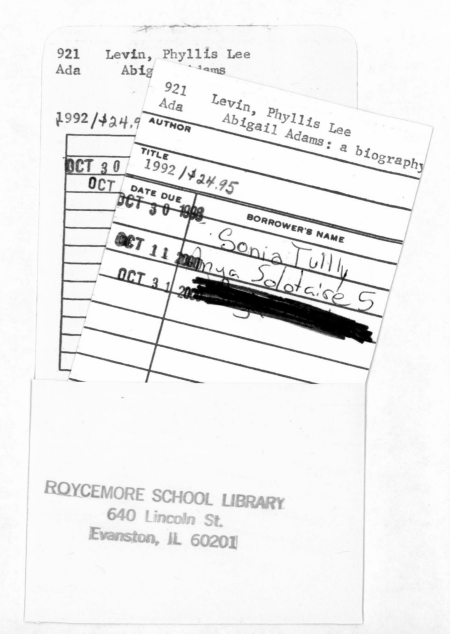

ABIGAIL ADAMS

a biography

Phyllis Lee Levin

St. Martin's Press/New York

A Thomas Dunne Book

Library of Congress Cataloging-in-Publication Data

Levin, Phyllis Lee.
    Abigail Adams: a biography.

    1. Adams, Abigail, 1744-1818.   2. Adams, John,
1735-1826.   3. Presidents—United States—Wives—
Biography.   I. Title.
E322.1.A38L48   1987   973.4'4'0924   86-27889
ISBN 0-312-00007-3

First Edition
10   9   8   7   6   5   4   3   2   1

For my husband;

for my children and theirs.

I know the voice of Fame to be mere weathercock,

unstable as Water and fleeting as a Shadow.

Yet I have pride, I know I have a large portion of it.

—ABIGAIL ADAMS[1]

Contents

A section of photographs follows page 288.

Preface

On a June day in 1960, *The New York Times* carried the
not-so-summery news that former coeds were finding that family
routine was stifling them, that "The road from Freud to Frigidaire,
from Sophocles to Spock, has turned out to be a bumpy one." The
problem was not a new one, the article noted, but it had reached
boiling point. "Suddenly everyone is talking about the problem," the
then president of Barnard College, Mrs. Millicent C. McIntosh, admitted. The descent from ivory tower to park playground was a
tedious adjustment for the young woman who had once speculated
on whether architecture was frozen music and now brooded about
frozen-food plans, who had once penned thoughts about "grave-
yard" poets and now wrote notes to the milkman. The *Times* article
also remarked that it was only since 1945 that women could earn
admission to Harvard Medical School, and merely since 1920 that
they had won the right to vote. Modern woman was only forty years
old then, and probably ought to show more patience.[2]

It was Thomas C. Mendenhall who tried to clarify women's obviously perplexing position by attempting to reaffirm the purpose of
education at Smith College, of which he was then president. "Our
main aim," said Mendenhall, "is to turn out women who can apply
a trained intelligence to the problem of daily living and whose intellectual resources can enrich their lives and those of their children."
Another educator thought workshops might help undergraduates
prepare for the transition from intellectual to domestic life. It was the

sociologists who were the seers. Several who were interviewed suggested that the picture was shifting, that homemaking and child-rearing were not lifetime propositions, with life expectancy extended as it now was.[3]

The article, of which I was the author, reflected my own awareness, of course, of the puzzle of being a woman, of my own need to explore the predicament of my friends, among them one with a doctorate in biophysics from the Massachusetts Institute of Technology, another with a medical degree from Harvard University. In both cases, their research in those days was confined to hunting up their offsprings' uncatalogued shovels in the rummages of Central Park's congested sandboxes.

I thought of my article as an exploration, a recognition of a situation, not a call to action. When a *Times* editorial assistant implied that she saw little need for my piece, that it did not seem very representative, I was half injured, half sympathetic. When several publishing houses asked me to enlarge on the article, I wrote back appreciatively but definitively: I had nothing more to say on the subject. Not because I didn't care how my friends resolved their careers, or I my own (if it could be called such, having as much symmetry as an itinerant dockworker's), but because I saw little hope for a solution to an existing dilemma. It remained for Betty Friedan in another year to write the declaration of women's independence. I would wait many years to broach the subject again, and then only because of a chance meeting with a colonial housewife, Abigail Adams.

I first met Abigail in December of 1969, when I was writing a book about historic houses in America, fifty houses in all. I had agreed to do that book if I was permitted to concentrate on the people who lived in the houses, rather than on the curtains they hung. As the particular house I was writing about at that time was that of the Adams family in Quincy, Massachusetts, I asked my son John if he would look in the library at Columbia University to see if there was anything about Abigail, judging hers to be the domestic responsibilities, while her husband attended to his duties as a statesman. Late that afternoon John produced two thin, withered volumes of the *Letters of Mrs. Adams,* and I was committed to Abigail even before I finished reading the first volume, edited so protectively by her grandson Charles Francis Adams.[4]

By 1973, commitment had turned to confrontation; Abigail's persistence could not be ignored. She was a fiercely proud woman who had earned her own biography, if for no other reason than to expose others to her unique and visionary ambitions for women. I thought it remarkable that the prim design of her early years did not stifle her sensitivity or her dreams, but fostered instead a universal understanding of women's timeless dilemma. How "miserable" must that woman be, Abigail supposed, who allowed herself to be confined to a narrow circle of domesticity with no higher sites in mind. More to be pitied, however, was the woman of both genius and taste who could not "cheerfully" leave her intellectual pursuits to tend to the daily cares of the prudent housewife. But Abigail understood the rigorous demands on the gifted and ambitious. "Such talents and such devotion of time and study," she said, "exclude the performance of most of the domestic cares and duties which exclusively fall to the lot of most females in this country."[5]

Another reason for writing about Abigail was to satisfy the curious, in these times of frail family ties, about her role as founder of an amazing and America's most enduring dynasty. Abigail's husband, John, an "Awakener" of the Republic, helped to draft its Declaration of Independence and served as its first minister to England, its first Vice-President, and its second President. Their eldest son, John Quincy Adams—Harvard rhetorics professor; minister to Prussia, Holland, Russia, England; Secretary of State; sixth President of the United States; senator and representative early and late in life—sired a son, Charles Francis, who was ambassador to Britain, legislator, historian, Fellow at Harvard. The line has persevered, despite its share of casualties, with politicians and financiers, bibliophiles and philosophers, noble eccentrics, eccentric artisans, writers. To be an Adams seems synonymous with being a writer, almost always of some merit, and, in the case of Henry Adams, of sweeping acclaim.[6]

A third reason for a book about Abigail Adams is to recognize her talents as a journalist who left behind a poignant report of the American Revolution. It is her letters that are her bequest; they document the colonial era with sewing-circle intimacy and honesty, as they also plumb the depths of her own resourceful mind. John Adams fondly appreciated the contribution of his "best, dearest, worthyest, wisest friend," along with those of several women with whom he corresponded: "In Times as turbulent as these, commend me to the Ladies for Historiographers. The Gentlemen are too much engaged in Action. The Ladies are cooler Spectators. . . ." He singled out Abigail in particular when he added: "There is a Lady at the Foot of Pens Hill, who obliges me, from Time to Time with clearer and fuller Intelligence, than I can get from a whole Committee of Gentlemen."[7]

I have, in the mounting years since I began documenting Abigail's life, been privileged to share in her amazingly prodigious wealth of letters at libraries in Washington, Worcester, Boston, Philadelphia, and New York. I have read some of the books she valued that are keepsakes of the British Museum; seen glorious maps at the Bibliothèque nationale in Paris that reveal the pastoral landscape of Auteuil where she lived in reunion with her husband and two children for a fleeting eight months. I have stood in Grosvenor Square imagining Abigail's adjustment to the fine stone mansion that was the first American embassy in Great Britain, and I have walked the craggy four miles, with my daughter Emme, from Auteuil to the Place de l'Opéra, to understand why Abigail's friends found her house too remote to visit, which she claimed they did.[8]

All these years, and all the hundreds of pages of manuscript later, my admiration and affection for Abigail are intact. Yet her story is not without problems for me, reminiscent of E. B. White's appraisal of Thoreau's *Walden:* "not a simple and sincere account of a man's life . . . [but] a journey into the mind." To write her biography justly is to recognize that for the first forty years of her life she journeyed but a few dusty miles from her fireside; traveled mostly between parlor and field; chatted, in the main, with the farm hands, her children's tutors, and a handful of relatives. Her most daring and valuable excursions originated at her writing table in the candlelit quiet of infinite solitary nights. Neither artist nor actress, musician nor courtesan, she is simply a woman whose claim to immortality is based on a flair for independence, a gift for language, extraordinary intellect, the capacity to love.[9]

I think of Harold Pinter writing the screenplay of a Proust work and saying that in no sense could he rival the word, but he could be true to it. In a sense, her letters are Abigail's biography. My contribution, I would hope, is perspective, along with preservation. As I type, I recall the portrait Gilbert Stuart painted of her, a portrait of age, though it was begun in 1800. The Abigail that Stuart introduces to us appears to be swathed in a sheer handkerchief, from which scarcely a handful of curls protrude, the whole riveting the viewer's attention to the sitter's precise mouth, firm chin, thrifty facial planes, and Mona Lisa gaze, as inscrutable as it is intolerant of compromise. If I am to be true to Abigail I must discern her message, however subtle. I must recognize that her life illustrates feminism in the most comprehensive, Websterian significance of that electrifying word. Abigail did, indeed, have the vision to support (if not invent) the principle that women should have "political, economic, and social rights equal to those of men." She was also the embodiment of that rarer but valid definition of feminism, a woman of "feminine qualities," such as "gentleness, weakness, delicacy, modesty."[10]

But there is still greater depth to Abigail's story. Ultimately, I am convinced that to write her life is to write of a partnership, again in the most specific connotation. In sum, her biography turns out to be as much John's as Abigail's, because Abigail's life was inseparable, emotionally and philosophically, from her husband's private and public pursuits, and as much the story of early America, because her country was as a "secondary God" to her.[11]

Abigail and John were "partner" to one another, "the Dearest of friends" and "the best of friends," united in dedication to the struggle of forming a new nation, rearing a family, and, not least, nurturing their extraordinary romance over fifty-four years of marriage. Thinking about them, as I sit at my desk, I am amazed at how relevant their challenges remain and how immediately their eighteenth-century lives transcend the centuries.[12]

New York City, 1986

PART ONE

ONE

In Youth the Mind Is Like a Tender Twig

In 1744, the year Abigail Adams was born Abigail Smith on November 11, a comet kindled the New England sky on a number of evenings. It was slow-moving and in part of hazy color, the *Boston Weekly News* reported, with a nucleus "like a dim star of the first Magnitude." A telescope clarified details: the comet was "small at the Beginning; and from thence stretches Several Degrees and spreads regularly wider." Like the comet, Abigail reached ever widening horizons, only faintly imagined in the sky-bound seaport town of Weymouth, Massachusetts.[1]

Under the spartan roof of her family's immaculate cupboard of a house, life in Weymouth meant upright thoughts and chairs; pristine church at the crest of the winding road; sister Mary, born in 1741; brother William, born in 1746; sister Elizabeth, born in 1750; father, the Reverend William Smith; mother, Elizabeth Quincy Smith; and a "steady adherence to the Path of Duty, however rigorous."[2]

Summer at home was a celebration of bright skies, singing birds, white sails billowing in a blue bay, and sheep grazing over verdant fields that rolled skyward into the hilly distance. Inevitably, these sun-dappled days peaked to a florid brilliance, then muddied and froze into ominous, vindictive winter grays, and then, just as predictably, revived to a joyous green, gaudy with golden daffodils. All in all, it was a challenging atmosphere in terms of weather and family, which seemed to inspire young Abigail with a sense of passing time and a nervous need to acquire valuable knowledge before it eluded her reverent grasp.[3]

One month before her seventeenth birthday, Abigail, tall, slender, her grave beauty fired with "keen, penetrating" black eyes, wrote wistfully of her aspirations and frustrations. She hoped she wouldn't be thought a stupid girl, apologized for being a "very incorrect writer" (Pope was a better "moddle" by far), and affirmed that the reason she entered into correspondence with friends was not merely for entertainment but for "instruction and edification."[4]

Abigail speculated at length about disappointments, accepted dutifully the responsibility for somehow having created her own failures, for believing that much unhappiness arose from forming false notions of things and persons. "We strangely impose upon ourselves; we create a fairyland of happiness," she wrote her friend Hannah Lincoln on October 5, 1761:

> Fancy is fruitful and promises fair, but, like the dog in the fable, we catch at a shadow, and when we find the disappointment, we are vexed, not with ourselves, who are really the imposters, but with the poor, innocent thing or person of whom we have formed such strange ideas.

Clearly, Abigail knew disappointments, took their measure with a wounded hand, but also faced their inevitability with common sense. That person who could not bear disappointments must not live in a world as changeable as hers; disappointments being a person's lot, they must be accepted with patience. "Daily experience" had taught her these truths.[5]

On the record, there are few explanations for Abigail's bitter wisdom. One, perhaps, was her ambition for an education and her crushing disappointment at its unavailability—according to her rigorous standards. A perfectionist, instilled with formidable goals, Abigail yearned to study with the "greatest Masters" who taught the male members of her family. Convinced that women played no less a role than men in the "Great Theater" of life, being responsible for the care and early instruction of their children, she mourned their lack of training for this "Trust."[6]

Instead, Abigail's quest for more challenging instruction, beyond the usual arithmetic, reading, music and dancing, Irish and ten-stitch embroidery, was richly, if extemporaneously fulfilled by a subtle osmotic process. A "kind hand" here and there introduced her to the poetry of Milton, Pope, and Thomson, to Shakespeare and to the novels of Samuel Richardson. One person mentioned on several occasions in connection with her education is Richard Cranch, who married her sister, Mary, in 1762. He was an émigré from Devon, England, a graduate of Harvard, a sometime glass manufacturer, watch repairer, farmer, and judge to whom she was thankful for teaching her to cultivate habits that afforded her "rational pleasure and satisfaction." Somehow Abigail acquired "some small acquaintance" with the French language and the sensitivity to know that it was impossible for her to translate works in French—though she tried—without a deep familiarity with that tongue. Undoubtedly, her knowledge of history and government broadened during discussions with educated, courageous, and visionary family members. Her attendance at these privileged seminars was her inheritance.[7]

In Abigail's girlhood, on her maternal side, the Quincys were already rooted in American soil five generations deep, four claiming diplomas from Harvard. The first émigré from Northamptonshire, England, in 1633, the prosperous Edmund Quincy, with six servants, had married Joanna Hoar, a widow with five children from Gloucester. Edmund was elected a representative of the town of Boston in the first General Court ever held in Massachusetts. Edmund's grandson, Abigail's grandfather, John, was a colonel in the militia, Speaker of the House of Representatives, negotiator of Indian treaties.[8]

John Quincy and his wife, Elizabeth Norton, a minister's daughter, lived in Braintree in a spacious house crowning Mount Wollaston. A brief four-mile carriage ride transported Abigail into her grandparents' rarefied world, where literate country gentry tended their broad acres as well as their hilly politics, mindful of the "Oath of Free Man," so gratefully pledged by members who had preceded them to the Massachusetts Bay Colony.[9]

Abigail, who claimed her share of "early, wild and giddy days," paid lengthy visits to the Quincys, and was on especially affectionate terms with her "merry and chatty" grandmother, who knew how to discipline with justice and dignity. Her grandfather's sense of public service and of active concern for the commonwealth helped to crystallize Abigail's fundamental values and ideas. Melded with her commitment, undoubtedly due to her preacher father's teachings that "nothing bound the human mind but religion," and her mother's model of strenuous goodness and tireless devotion to God and family, Abigail's credo would govern her future family until her last breath, and even theirs. Her principles, first codified for her younger cousin Isaac Smith's benefit, when she hoped he might "daily grow in virtue and useful Learning, and be a bright Orniment in Church or State," resound in her voluminous correspondence with her children and her grandchildren.[10]

Fortunately, Abigail was not the only young person in her circle who hungrily sought intellectual fulfillment. Invitations to correspond on literary and political as well as social matters were customary; they were formally requested and respectfully acknowledged. It was, however, rare that a male relative or friend initiated such an exchange, as did the exceedingly precocious thirteen-year-old Isaac Smith. Abigail's solemn acceptance was gracious:

> As to your request of entering into a correspondence with me, I freely consent to it,—there was no need of my cousin of a complement to intice me into what I was before so well inclin'd to. . . .

Riddled with the sense of lost opportunity and in consideration of Isaac's "growing genious," she lovingly but firmly advised:

> Youth is the best season wherein to acquire knowledge, tis a season when we are freest from care, the mind is then unincumbered & more capable of receiving impressions than in an advanced age—in youth the mind is like a tender twig, which you may bend as you please, but in age like a sturdy oak and hard to move.

In her early wisdom and, perhaps, disillusionment, she concluded that without a "good foundation" intellectually and, undoubtedly, morally, no "permanent satisfaction" was to be expected.[11]

Another reason for Abigail's lengthy discourse on the subject of disappointment might be her conviction that her lack of wealth accounted for her lack of a "spark."* Friends, such as Mrs. Lincoln, might suppose that young men were "as plenty as herrings," but alas! there was as great a scarcity of them as there was of justice, honesty, prudence, and many other virtues, in Abigail's opinion.[12]

Concerning this very subject, on the verge of the new year of 1762, Abigail's life took a momentous turn. She could claim a "spark" of her own. Her sister Mary's fiancé, Richard Cranch, must somehow have been responsible for her reintroduction to John Adams, a twenty-seven-year-old lawyer and graduate of Harvard College. The

---

*According to Webster, a beau or lover.

couple's earlier meeting, when Abigail was fifteen, had gone disas-
trously, judging from John's comments. At that time John, in love
with a riper young woman, Hannah Quincy, had been uncomfortable
with Abigail's father, thinking him a "crafty, designing Man." John
had even suspected that Parson Smith, who could afford a Negro
servant named Tom, a chaise, and a fine personal library, concealed
his wealth from his parishioners that they might send him presents.[13]

As for Abigail and her sisters, John conceded that they were
"Wits," but wondered about their other attributes. He spelled out his
doubts in his diary: "Are S girls either frank or fond or even candid?"
He abruptly concluded the negative. The "S girls" did not measure
up: "Not fond, not frank, not candid." His superficial judgment
would probably not have surprised the sisters. Certainly the youngest, Elizabeth, was aware of their shortcomings. Years of discipline
had inhibited any genuine display of emotion. Wistfully she recognized that they were beings who felt vastly more than they could
express, "whether it be Joy or Grief, Love, or any other Passion."[14]

Two years later, John's opinion of Abigail had altered almost miraculously. On December 30, 1761, John wrote to Mary, asking her to
deliver a prophetic though cryptic message to Abigail, referred to
therein as Mrs. Nabby. "My—I don't know what to Mrs. Nabby. Tell
her I hear she's about commencing a most loyal subject to young
George—and altho my Allegiance has been hitherto inviolate I shall
endeavour, all in my Power to foment Rebellion."[15]

John's teasing about Abigail's loyalty to the Crown belied the gravity of John's sentiments. Only superficially did he conceal his disen-
chantment with young George III, King of England since the previous October, or a deepening relationship with Abigail. John's
commitments, as definitive as they were life-lasting, had been resolved upon by emotional and intellectual contortions of extraordinary intensity. A profound understanding of their meaning would be
fundamental to any projection of the future of the young woman he
was courting.

In appearance, Abigail's spark was not by any imaginative process
a romantic figure. Pigeon-breasted, a lumpy bundle of a man, with
protruding eyes and sensuous lips, he claimed, somewhat whimsi-
cally, to be five feet seven or nine inches tall, "I really don't know
which." Not even his most youthful portrait would intimate his allure
for Abigail, who soon proclaimed openly and with tender sincerity

the investment of her whole heart, her hopes and wishes in the bosom of this "dearest friend" and "beloved partner." Nine years apart in age, with strikingly different educational backgrounds—his as rigorous as hers was a matter of bits and pieces—theirs, they recognized, was an explicit, passionate love. John, signing himself "Lysander" very often, dreamed of "Miss Adorable, of Dr. Miss Jemina," of his Aurora and Diana (she was Portia only after marriage), dreamed of her morning presence, of her kisses. Abigail, in turn, was devoted, proud, and shy.[16]

At his father's death, the previous spring, John had inherited his parents' house and barn, ten acres of adjoining land, and thirty acres of neighboring orchard, pasture, and woodland. Also there was the understanding that his father wished that he would "never forget this nation, but . . . stand by the Law, the Constitution, and the real Welfare and Freedom of this Nation vs. all Temptations."[17]

Though Abigail insisted that she and John were both cast in the same mold, it was John who was emphatic about the differences in their heritage. If the Quincys were gentry, the Adamses were aspiring yeoman, English émigrés to Massachusetts Bay in 1639, humbly ascending from constable to field driver to fence viewer to surveyor to tithingman to selectman. John's grandmother, Hannah Bass, however, was descended from the Honorable John Alden, who sailed to Plymouth on the Mayflower in 1620. John's mother, Susanna Boylston Adams, was a niece of Zabdiel Boylston, who introduced the practice of inoculation for smallpox to the British Empire. His father, John Adams, a cordwainer, was, in family tradition, a constable, tithingman, ensign in the militia, selectman, and church deacon. His younger brothers were Peter Boylston, whom John spoke of as neighbor and friend, and Elihu, a captain in a company of militia stationed in Cambridge, Massachusetts, who would die of dysentery the summer of 1775. John was the family's first graduate of Harvard, the only one of three brothers.[18]

John had grown up in a frequently troubled household, often governed by "Passion, Accident, Freak Humour." At times when his mother fretted and scolded, when her "rages, raves" with his father over money made it seem as though "all was breaking into flame," John would run from the room, fright knotted deep inside him, to try to read in hope of composing himself.[19]

While he pitied his mother, was even angered by her, he also credited her with teaching him to read and with supervising his education. As an athletic child, he had loved to ice skate, wrestle, and swim, to sail boats and fly kites, and had wanted to be a farmer. Instead, he was tutored for Harvard. Once admitted, his incessant self-search for his place in the "starry worlds" outside, for a "new, grand, wild yet regular thought" that might make him famous, intimated all that he was to be as a husband, father, statesman. A man of passion, intellect, and vanity, he had unlimited need for approval and recognition.[20]

John taught for a year in Worcester, Massachusetts, after graduation from Harvard in July 1755. Then he contracted to stay on to study law and was not completely surprised, with the entire town immersed in the subjects of government and war, that he had "turned politician." In the next years and after he had returned to Braintree, his birthplace (later called Quincy), in 1760, aware of the acute issues and looming choices he faced as an American, he was inspired by James Otis, Jr., an impassioned thirty-six-year-old student of constitutional rights, a Harvard graduate and lawyer. Thick set, with narrow, brooding eyes and an irascible spirit, Otis termed Britain's newly imposed writs of assistance nothing more than disguised search warrants, authorizing royal customs collectors to break open ships, shops, cellars, and houses to search for goods on which taxes had not been paid, especially those made of prized molasses.[21]

John's destiny as a patriot would be influenced just as surely by his second cousin, Samuel Adams, the class of 1740 at Harvard, whose masterful conception of the so-called Committees of Correspondence was responsible for publicizing the cause of the colonies from town to town. When John looked back on the series of events leading to the revolution, he would find himself telling Abigail that Britain had been "filled with Folly, and America with Wisdom."[22]

The incipient politician, zealous student of the Scriptures, of English and Latin authors, had, however, to face up to what he considered a personal weakness—his enjoyment of the society of females "engaged" him too much. So much so that on several occasions he recorded in his diary what amounts to an exhaustive primer on his ideal female. His description of her role in society is prescient. To one day produce "an Hero or a Legislator, a great Statesman or Divine or some other great Character that may do Honour to the World"—this, in John's opinion, was "the Highest Pinacle of Glory to which a Woman can in Modesty aspire."[23]

Despite his first impressions, John had found a remarkable semblance to this ideal woman in young Abigail Smith. Her appearance and temperament possibly even exceeded his most stringent standards. Plans for their marriage were cruelly interrupted by a terrifying epidemic of smallpox so rampant that on March 3, 1764, Boston voted to allow the extreme measure of private arrangements for inoculation. John arranged to board at the home of his uncle, James Cunningham, on Washington Street in the South End of Boston, with Dr. Nathaniel Perkins scheduled to perform the inoculation. On Saturday, April 7 he left behind an anxious Abigail, whose brother, William, would endure the same ordeal at this same period.[24]

As John was required to spend the next three or four weeks "in an absolute Vacation of Business and Study," he was readily able to attend to a request from Abigail. As a critic, Abigail said she feared John more than any other person on earth, and she wished for his truthful estimation of her thoughts and deeds. John's response provides an unexpectedly delightful portrait of Abigail during their courtship. It animates another, painted two years later by Benjamin Blyth, in which Abigail appears thoughtful, composed, pristinely groomed. Her dress is classic—pearls, an embroidered white lace collar, her hair drawn immaculately into a tidy bow.[25]

Answering Abigail, John noted that her habit of reading, writing, and thinking made her head hang like a bulrush. She did not play cards or sing or dance. She walked as though she were parrot-toed, and crossed her legs to the ruination of her posture. But she blushed and smiled easily, her eyes sparkled, and all the rest, he assured her, appeared to be "bright and luminous."[26]

Abigail read John's description of her faults as cheerfully as another person would read of her perfections. Obviously not too damaged by his sketch, which included examination and review of "all the Spotts," she admitted to her neglect of singing, explaining that she had a voice "harsh as the screech of a peacock."[27]

When both mothers had been won over to the couple's intentions —to their immense relief—a wedding was plotted in detail and scheduled for Thursday, October 25, 1764. A "neat and clever girl" named Rachel Marsh was hired for £1 6s. 8p. "lawful money" for a quarter's wages, and a man named Brackett was to help Abigail pack her belongings. John left for Plymouth with a foul stomach, a distaste for his impertinent and stingy clients, and an anxious heart. Old doubts about his life's work and success surfaced. By September 30, John admitted that a month or more separated from Abigail would make him the most insufferable cynic in the world.[28]

Before their marriage, however, John, with "Prophetick Imagination," discerned the pivotal role Abigail would fill with supreme tenderness in his long and accomplished life. On September 30, 1764, he wrote:

> you have always softened and warmed my Heart, shall restore my
> Benevolence as well as my Health and Tranquility of mind. You
> shall polish and refine my sentiments of Life and Manners, banish
> all the unsocial and ill natured Particles in my Composition, and
> form me to that happy temper, that can reconcile a quick
> Discernment with a perfect Candour.[29]

Years before meeting Abigail, John had understood his problem, which his marriage would solve to a dramatic degree: "Ballast is what I want. I totter, with every Breeze. My motions are unsteady." Abigail would be that "ballast" he sought on his long and difficult journey.[30]

Mountains Arise
to Hinder Me

Abigail and John married on Thursday, October 25, 1764,
the fourth anniversary of George III's accession to the throne of
England. Within a scant nine months their daughter, also named
Abigail, and always called Nabby, was born, on July 14, 1765. The
twenty-one-year-old bride's life fell swiftly into place. She was quite
settled on the Adamses' family property, in the farmhouse built almost catercorner to her husband's birthplace, on the road from
Plymouth to Boston, framed by field and farmland. In a front room
remodeled into a law office by replacing a window with a door, John
went about expanding his law practice. He also continued to spend
Thursday evenings at "Sodalitas, A Clubb of Friends," lawyers dedicated to studying such authors as Cicero and Tully and debating on
such subjects as feudal law. A third interest directly involved Abigail.[1]

Working the land was as much a matter of sustenance, survival, and
pride for Abigail as for John; his enthusiasm and dedication were
contagious. As though it were a calling, an art form, John thrived on
the beauty and challenges of his land. By contrast, he despised
crowded, noisy Boston, the "rattle gabble" of its chimney sweeps,
wood carriers, merchants, priests, horses and carts, market men and
women who crowded the narrow cobblestone streets carved into the
hilly terrain. And though he had close to forty cases listed in the city
in the year of 1764, he returned home to Braintree, to his orchards,
pastures, and swamps as a soldier escaped from enemy territory. By
far, he preferred to spend his time pruning his apple trees, digging

stones, mending and building fences, or, depending on the season, ploughing the uplands with six yoke of oxen, sowing onions, planting crab and English grasses. Not a ginger bush, dogwood, elm, ash, oak, or birch escaped his eye or axe.[2]

No wonder that Abigail would be unable to spend Thanksgiving with her sister Mary's family in Salem, what with court cases that came "so thick upon us," and her deep involvement in farming. Abigail's early concern for the Adams property was to be lasting, though its appeal probably differed from that of her husband's. It was always the peach, pear, and "plomb" trees, the peas "to stick," the maple sugar and asparagus on which she seemed to focus especially loving attention, as well as the daffodils of what she called the "renovating" season.[3]

John was an exhaustive teacher and Abigail his equal as a pupil. He even professed jealousy that her wise and prudent management might cause neighbors to think their affairs more discreetly conducted in his absence. For her part, Abigail was grateful for John's approval. His praise, she said, spurred her on to discharge her duties as efficiently as possible in the absence of her dearest friend.[4]

Still another subject preoccupied Abigail and John with equal intensity. This was the "Contest" in which they were inexorably involved between America and England. It would be impossible to overstate John's influence on Abigail's evolution from housewife to patriot. In the early years of their marriage John was, undeniably, Abigail's eyes and ears, her main witness and principal delegate and scribe in matters relating to the revolution. He was a charter member of radical groups such as the Sons of Liberty, founded in 1765 to oppose the Stamp Act, and of the Committees of Correspondence, the town meetings organized by his older cousin, Samuel Adams. He would call James Otis, Samuel Adams, and the merchant John Hancock the three "most essential characters," in his opinion, of the whole revolution. He was entirely sympathetic to Abigail's "ten thousand questions," and such an informed participant that he would, though he teased Abigail, most studiously try to quench her "Eveship's" thirst for "retailed Politicks."[5]

As resourceful as she was inquisitive, when she herself turned home-front reporter during John's absences, Abigail would fill the gaps in news by keeping contact with statesmen as well as relatives, friends, and her children's tutors, at home and abroad. But even while John was nearby and Abigail on only a brief visit to her family in Weymouth, she was unable to stifle her curiosity. She wrote her husband: "If you have any news in Town, which the papers do not communicate, pray be so good as to Write it."[6]

Abigail's mention of newspapers as a source of information is not incidental. That she and John were habitual readers of the *Boston Gazette* ("Containing the Freshest Advices Foreign and Domestick"), published by Benjamin Edes and John Gill, next to the prison house on Queen Street, is evinced in the liberal quotations of this newspaper in letters. The moment her "good Man" arrived home with the *Gazette,* to which he contributed articles, Abigail would put an end to even her most avid correspondence. She could hardly have missed a column signed "Mentor" about "an unjust and too violent authority in Kings" or on how "Nothing threatens so fatal a fall, as an authority that is strained too high; it is like a bow too much bent."[7]

The British dominion now reached from sea to sea. England had won Canada, Florida, Louisiana as far west as the Mississippi, and islands in the West Indies. It also owned Acadia, Cape Breton and its dependent islands, and fisheries in which France would retain some share. Louisiana west of the Mississippi, and the island of New Orleans were ceded to Spain by France. In Asia, the victories of Clive at Plassey, of Coote at the Andiwash, of Waton and Pococke on the Indian Seas gave England unquestioned ascendency in the East Indies and the promise "without end" of more conquests.[8]

Unfortunately, England's bills were also without end. The national debt in 1764 rose to £140,000,000; to maintain 10,000 troops in America cost more than £300,000 per year. Thus far, expert smugglers and indifferent tax collectors had permitted a pittance, only £1,800 per year, to trickle into the British treasury. This seemed an outrageous inequity to Britain's Secretary of the Treasury, the pragmatic George Grenville. His solution, an American Revenue Act, more widely known as the Sugar Act, was a more or less updated version of the thirty-year-old and useless Molasses Act. Though logical, it was catastrophic.[9]

Before long, according to Grenville's proposition, the navy would patrol the Atlantic waters rigorously, and governors and agents were to report on smugglers relentlessly. The accused would be tried in admiralty courts without juries. The fact that British customs duties had been conceived to regulate the flow of trade, rather than to channel revenue into the British treasury, was to be ignored. Now, though duties on molasses were cut in half, those on refined sugar were raised. Fresh duties on Madeira (especially popular with the colonists) and Canary Island wines eradicated old and comfortable arrangements between Portugal and the colonies. The new duties on lumber prohibited delivery anywhere but to England; the purchase of British linens was mandatory.[10]

One year later, on March 22, 1765, the Stamp Tax, proposed by George Grenville, which required the stamping of fifteen classes of court documents, as well as college diplomas, real-estate certificates, newspapers, and even playing cards, was passed by royal assent by commission, the King being too ill to sign the fateful document himself. Even the mere hint of another tax incited Sam Adams to full and urgent voice. "There is no room for delay," he cautioned fellow colonists. "Those unexpected proceedings may be preparatory to more extensive taxation; for, if our trade may be taxed, why not our lands and everything we possess?" To Sam Adams, taxes in any form, without legal representation, meant diminution of the individual from free subject to the miserable state of tributary slave, meant the annihilation of the charter right of colonists to govern and tax themselves. "We claim British rights, not by charter only; we are born to them," he insisted.[11]

Predictably, James Otis rose to the challenge. Supreme power lay with the people, he said, and the people never "freely, nor can rightly, make an unlimited renunciation of this divine right." Otis spoke twelve years before the Declaration of Independence was written, yet the heart of that superb document had begun to beat. The first principle and great end of government being to provide for the best good of all the people, Otis would not tolerate putting the powers of all into the hands of one or some few. Seeming to impart a succinct summary of the messages of both Sam Adams and James Otis, the *Gazette* predicted, with mordant accuracy, that the passage of the Stamp Act was likely to produce "very little more than disgust, trouble and oppression to the colonies." But the fifty-nine-year-old Benjamin Franklin, already famous as a scientist and inventor, and now joint postmaster for the colonies (with William Hunter), seemed to think the Stamp Tax inevitable. "We might as well have hindered the sun's setting," he said.[12]

The consequences of the Stamp Act gave John much to brood about. The courts were shut, business was at a standstill, his law practice halted. He and Abigail would have to cut down on their expenses, and their future seemed bleak just when he had gained, after thirty years of groping in "dark Obscurity" a "small degree of Reputation." The Stamp Tax had been perpetrated the precise month he had been chosen as one of the surveyors of highways in Braintree, as well as a member of the committee to lay out the North Commons in lots for sale.[13]

John did have the time, however, to write an essay that was published in four parts in the *Gazette*, over August and September of 1765, which heightened his recognition in the community. What he called a "speculation" or even a "rhapsody," nameless at the start and later entitled *A Dissertation on the Feudal and Canon Law*, was his heartfelt exploration of the reasons the colonists had established themselves in America. John's next written work that year was an official document, the "Instructions of the Town of Braintree to Their Representative." At the town meeting on September 24, he read the "Instructions," which would be adopted by forty towns without a dissenting voice. Its first paragraph summed up the dilemma of a loyal people who wished to be a free people who "In all the calamaties which have ever befallen this country" had never felt "so great a concern, or such alarming apprehensions, as on this occasion."[14]

John, the reluctant, tormented patriot, spoke for Abigail and for countless others who insisted that their loyalty to the King, their "veneration" for both houses of Parliament, their "affection" for fellow subjects in Britain accounted for their extreme sensitivity concerning the late acts of Parliament. In the final paragraph of the "Instructions" reprinted in the *Gazette* that October 14, in brave and moving words, John Adams recommended "the most clear and explicit assertion and vindication of our rights and liberties to be entered on the public records, that the world may know, in the present and all future generations, that we have a clear knowledge and a just sense of them, and with submission to Divine Providence, that we never can be slaves."[15]

Probably, in recognition of John's "Instructions," he learned on a clear winter day, Thursday, December 19, that he had been voted unanimously, along with two others, Jeremiah Gridley and James Otis, to appear before His Excellency the Governor in support of the petition that the law courts of the province be opened. John admired Otis and had much in common with Gridley, Harvard, class of 1725, a leading lawyer in Boston. He too taught school before studying the law, cared about words (he had edited the *Weekly Rehearsal*), and was interested in maritime affairs (he founded a club of shipmasters), as was John, who would help to initiate the American navy. John was pleased that the town of Boston had shown him such respect and friendship. He also wondered about the possibility that Braintree would elect him to the General Court the next May.[16]

On Christmas day of 1765, just before a snowfall, John and Abigail had tea with Abigail's grandparents, the Quincys, and then dined home alone. The evening by the fireside found John "thinking, reading, searching, concerning Taxation without Consent, concerning the great Pause and Rest in Business." He had reached an uneasy conclusion: "A person ought to be very cautious what kinds of fewell he throws into a fire."[17]

March 28, 1766, brought most welcome news from England. William Pitt, "The Genius, and Guardian Angel" of Britain and British America, had, in the House of Commons, declared himself in favor of repeal of the Stamp Act on principle. He had called it the "most impolitic, arbitrary, oppressive and unconstitutional Act" that was ever passed. The House of Commons granted taxes in its representative capacity, not in its legislative capacity, and therefore, he concluded, Parliament had no right to tax the colonies.[18]

On Monday, May 19, there were, at last, "Rejoicings" over the repeal of the Stamp Act, signaled by clanging bells, erupting cannon, drumbeats, and houses illuminated from attic to parlor windows— except, it seemed, in Braintree, where John could not remember a "duller" time. Abigail and the baby were ill with whooping cough, which ruined their plans to go to Boston to celebrate. Besides, John had to attend the Superior Court at Plymouth on the very day that the town of Braintree was "insensible to the Common Joy."[19]

But, in truth, nothing could mar the satisfaction of having the era of the Stamp Act over and done with. Even when John learned that he had not been elected a representative to the General Court, but that the incumbent, Ebenezer Thayer, hardly a favorite, a tavern keeper who dabbled in politics, had been kept in office, he was not displeased. With courts of law open and business thriving, he could once more pursue the goal that was always at the nub of his ambition —to earn enough money to support his family, pay his bills, and give him peace of mind concerning his finances. By the end of June 1766

John confided to Richard Cranch that he was amazingly changed since the Stamp Act had been repealed. Now he was "at perfect Ease about Politicks." He cared not a shilling who was in or out of office or favor. He insisted, "I have no Point, that I wish carried."[20]

His self-portrait in this letter to his brother-in-law was charmingly inaccurate. John Adams, contented and relaxed citizen, devoted husband and father, could now plan a visit to the Cranches, who had moved to Salem after failing at business ventures in Weymouth and Germantown. He felt compelled, in order that the brushstrokes be consistent, to emphasize that his brother-in-law's habit of rising at 4:00 A.M. was quite out of keeping with his own schedule. "Before I venture to Salem you must write me express Leave to lye abed till Eight o'clock in the morning absolutely, and till 9 upon Condition I shall find it necessary." He complained about the lazy town of Boston and about how his "squeamish" wife, keeping the shutters closed, had put him in the vile habit of dozing in the morning. But all of this banter was, in fact, just that.[21]

Abigail's life might now have swerved in an opposite path had she married a man who could close the shutters not only on early-morning light but on the politics of the day. The portrait John had painted for his brother-in-law was the essence of wishful thinking. In truth, John, for better or for worse, was a slightly more mature version of the younger, vainer, more ambitious, learned, affectionate, and dedicated John of courtship days. Even as he protested lack of interest in any political point, he was writing constantly on facets of that very subject for publication under signatures such as "Clarendon" and "Misanthrop" and "Humphrey Ploughjogger."[22]

John's portrait of his squeamish wife was just as fanciful as his self-description. His squeamish wife was consumingly in charge of their daughter, whom everyone called Nabby, "fat as a porpouse," coughing and cutting teeth. As the farm expanded, so also did Abigail's responsibilities. The farm now included two horses, three cows, two yearlings, twenty sheep, and one cock. Besides feeding her animals, it seemed to her that she was feeding half, if not all, of the influential colonists who came to call.[23]

Fortunately, Abigail and John's hospitality was reciprocated and perhaps, for the last time until their retirement, they enjoyed the semblance of an ordinary couple's social pastime. They were able to savor wild goose and cranberry sauce with Abigail's uncle, Dr. Cotton Tufts, and his wife, the former Lucy Quincy, and to visit John's cousins, the Nicholas Boylstons, said to have the richest furnishings in North America. Abigail and John were awed by the Boylston establishment. With its spacious gardens, Turkey carpets, painted hangings, marble tables, crimson damask curtains, and magnificent clock, theirs was a seat for a "noble Man," for a prince. Abigail and John probably spent their carriage ride home counting up its cost, said to be a thousand pounds sterling just for the furniture.[24]

Finally, on July 15, 1766, Abigail was able to write her sister Mary that the week after the Superior Court sat, and after the Inferiour Court was adjourned, she hoped she could plan a visit to Salem—that no longer would "Mountains arise to hinder me. Mole hills," she told her sister, "I always Expect to find, but them I can easily surmount." She also warned Mary that the weather would be so hot she could not think of bringing Nabby with her. The poor "Rogue" had been very poorly the past three or four days, cutting teeth. Her cough, too, was bad again.[25]

Abigail and John did manage two visits to the Cranch family in Salem in 1766. In mid-August, on their outing from Salem to Marblehead, John rode a single horse while the sisters went in a chaise. On their second visit, the first week that November, John was content to sit and hear "the Ladies talk about Ribbon, Catgut and Paris net, Riding hoods, Cloth, Silk and Lace." Then Cranch, presumably tending his watch-and-clock business, returned and the two couples enjoyed "a very happy Evening."[26]

Abigail's reaction to her first visit was almost to seem sadder than happier for having made it. She was broadly sentimental about Mary's daughter Betsy:

> . . . what would I give to hear her prattle to her Cousin Nabby, to see them put their little arms around one an others necks, and hug each other, it would really be a very pleasing Sight, to me.

But, she added, to leave those charmers for a moment, she wished to speak further of Mary's Salem acquaintances, in whom she found "a very odd kind of politness." By what she heard of them, they had well learned the lesson of Iago to Roderigo, to "put money in thy purse." It was in the character of the whole people that she found fault, in their attitude of "get what you can, and keep what you have got." As a result, Abigail told Mary, "My advice to you is among the Romans, do as the romans do." Nor had Abigail finished. She reflected with startling cynicism:

This is a selfish world you know. Interest governs it, there are but
very few, who are moved by any other Spring. They are Generous,
Benevolent and Friendly when it is for their interest, when any
thing is to be got by it, but touch the tender part, their Interest,
and you will immediately find the reverse, the greater half the
World are mere Janases.[27]

In June of 1767, just fourteen months after the repeal of the Stamp
Act, Parliament passed a set of duties, alerting the colonists to the
presence of a new political villain. His name was Charles Townshend,
the ambitious Chancellor of the Exchequer, a rousing orator (especially under the influence of champagne), also known as "the Weathercock" because of his fickle politics. Duties on glass, painter's oils
and colors, tea and wine, known as the Townshend Acts, followed by
the establishment of a board of customs and the legalization of general writs of assistance, plunged the colonists into a fresh siege of
soul-searching.[28]

John Adams, evaluating the consequences of Townshend's measures, predicted they would excite a "great fermentation." The Gazette published numerous editorials on the issues at stake. It went to
the length of reprinting the content of the Bill of Rights, acutely
relevant at this time: "No taxage or aid shall be laid or levied by the
King or his heirs in this realm, without the good will and assent of
the archbishops, bishops, earls, knights, burgesses, and other than
the freemen of the commonalty of this realm." Further, the Gazette
called attention to the "precedent" of 1688 that gave the crown to
William and Mary, and with it the charter and birthright entitling all
Englishmen, mainland and colonial, to certain rights and customs.[29]

In view of mounting rejection of British authority by the colonies,
Governor Francis Bernard reported to the Crown that there never
were people "more divided in opinions, hopes and fears, than those
of Boston now are." In his estimation, the minds of the common
people had been poisoned to a great degree. It was his melancholy
consideration that the rich and populous town was disgraced by a set
of "desperadoes (perhaps even a dozen), whose own ruined or insignificant fortunes make the distruction of the country a matter of
indifference to them."[30]

After just a few years of marriage, both Abigail and John seemed
already to cherish their brief past, as though the elements of happiness it had afforded them were forever beyond reach. John reminded
Cranch of the "still pleasanter Times of courtship at Weymouth."

Abigail, even at twenty-two, seemed sadly aged when she said that a letter from Mary gave "new Spring to my nerves and a brisker circulation to my Blood." Resigned, desolate, she told affectionately of her "Good Man" who was such an "itinerant" that she had but little of his company. Summing up her life after two years of marriage, she wrote: "We do pretty much as We used to of old. Marry and give in Marriage, encrease and multiply all in the old fashioned way."[31]

Abigail's consolation over John's absences was undoubtedly rooted in her understanding of their economic necessity. John traveled in heat and cold, from town to town and court to court, for the reason he repeated constantly: "Nothing but the Hope of acquiring some little Matter for my dear Family, could carry me, thro these tedious Excursions." In one instance, traveling from Martha's Vineyard to Boston to Taunton to Barnstable to Concord to Salem to Cambridge to Worcester, he seriously questioned his life apart from his family, his life of "Here and everywhere" to use the expression, he said, that Desdemona's father applied to Othello.[32]

A poignant view of Abigail on a Sunday evening in Weymouth, September 1767, during a two-day visit with her parents, is prophetic of times to come. Nabby is rocking the cradle of her two-month-old brother, John Quincy, born that July 11 (and named after his great-grandfather who died two days later). She is singing, "Come pappa come home to Brother Johnny." The song reinforces Abigail's sense that Sunday seems a more "Lonesome Day" than any other day on which John is absent. "For tho I may be compared to those climates which are deprived of the Sun half the Year," she writes, "yet upon a Sunday you commonly afforded us your benign influence." On her return home from visits like this one, she is pathetically grateful to be gladly received "even by one's Servants," in the absence of her "Dearest of Friends and the Tenderest of Husbands."[33]

Whatever the depths of her loneliness, Abigail wryly admitted to the surprising pleasure to be found in the company of one's own children. She who had always felt "vex'd" hearing parents relate their children's "chit-chat"—regarding this as a weakness in people whose good sense in other instances she had not doubted—was astonished at how every word and action of her own children "twines round ones heart." Still, she hoped that in company she would not be guilty of the error of repetition.[34]

Snow blocked the roads by the second week of January 1767. This meant that Abigail was more or less housebound, cut off from visits to her parents in Weymouth, to her sister in Salem. It would be May before she saw Mary again. She scanned the public papers for political news, but learned nothing conclusive. With the future unpredictable, she tended to look back on the past with "painful pleasure." Those relatively uncomplicated days that afforded moments for gossip and tea, "alas where are they?" she asked. She knew the answer too well: fled "in the Dark backward, and abyss of time." The era of Diana the moon goddess and her Spartan general, Lysander, was eclipsed forever.[35]

THREE

An "Eaqual" Share
of Curiosity

In April 1768, Abigail prepared to move the family from Braintree to Boston. For frequently mentioned but unspecified reasons of health, John was determined to "hazard the experiment" of leaving native ground. He declined election as one of Braintree's selectmen and moved, with Abigail and their two children, into the rented White House, as it was called, in Brattle Square. John considered it a good omen that its former owner had lived there for many years. Unfortunately, the omen proved misleading.[1]

On October 1, 1768, in official obedience to His Majesty's commands, regiments of redcoats had disembarked from the Long Wharf and from Wheelwright's Wharf, which jutted out into Boston's vulnerable harbor, to march their way uphill to King Street, and over to the once-innocent grassy Common. By December, their artillery was strategically focused on the Town House, where the courts met and the legislature held its sessions. With the awesome knowledge of additional troops no farther away than Castle William (on Castle Island in the Boston harbour), with the unquestionable presence of British men-of-war moored just beyond the wharves, there was only one way for the patriots to describe their beloved Boston: "Our town is now a perfect garrison."[2]

As for Abigail and John, the serenity they so earnestly sought never materialized. Instead, the family was driven out of bed in early morning to the insistent beat of fife and drums. They were indignant beyond consolation at the intrusion. Just the sight of the redcoats was a flag of danger—strong proof, John said, that Great Britain's determination to subjugate the colonists was "too deep and inveterate" ever to be altered. When John was named to the committee to prepare instructions for the Boston representatives to the General Court for the second time, in May 1769 (the first being June, 1768), concern was marked over the unfriendly presence of British troops, as well as the formidable power of the admiralty courts.[3]

A second daughter, Susanna, was born in the White House on December 28, 1768, and baptized on New Year's Day by Dr. Samuel Cooper at the Brattle Street Church. The White House, however, was soon up for sale. Because John hadn't sufficient confidence "in the Stability of any Thing," he refused to buy it. This meant that he was obliged to relocate, and an exhausting, seesawing period was begun in terms of the family's housing. The next move was to a home on Cole Lane, a street that ran northward from Hanover Street to the Mill Pond. By the next spring the family was back in Brattle Square.[4]

The months of February and March 1770 sealed Abigail and John's decisive commitment to the cause of the colonists. Life was increasingly threatening, and already difficult enough for Abigail, pregnant again and mourning the death on February 4 of the fourteen-month-old Susanna, whom they had called Suky. Only fragmentary records of the infant remain for posterity, as a letter in which her father asks her mother "to kiss my little Suky for me." John also mentions in his autobiography the loss of "a Child a Daughter, whose name was Susana." Abigail was silent about this baby, with probably one exception. When she later attempted to comfort her daughter-in-law, Louisa Catherine, John Quincy's wife, despairing the loss of an infant child, she admitted a similar loss.[5]

February's military unrest did not come as a surprise. John had feared what Sam Adams called the "merry-andrew Tricks" of the troops of redcoats. Sunday was a day for worship, for family meetings, not for horseracing on the Common, not for military parades, Dr. Cooper complained. Other grievances went unheard, such as those of men, women, and children, uneasy at the sight of the redcoats and their sticks, clubs, and cutlasses, and resentful of the idle pokes of their bayonets.[6]

On February 22, the tense relationship between the British and the colonists blistered into tragedy. A group of boys demonstrated against a merchant who violated the non-importation agreement not to carry British goods until taxes were rescinded. They next marched on the home of Ebenezer Richardson, ridiculing the customs employee, who retaliated by shooting one of the demonstrators, Christopher Snider, who was about eleven years old. John reported to Abigail that he had never beheld such a funeral, such a procession as this one, which extended farther than one could have imagined. Reaction to the child's death triggered further bloodshed two weeks later and proved to be a prelude to what would be known as the Boston Massacre.[7]

On March 5, 1770, Abigail, seven months pregnant, was at home with Nabby, Johnny, and the servants. John was at Henderson Inches's house in the South End of Boston when he and his fellow club members heard bells ringing with such urgency—a sure signal of fire or friends in danger—that they snatched their hats and coats and raced outdoors to navigate the treacherous ice underfoot. The conflagration, they quickly realized, was a matter of personalities, not flames. In the swiftly crowding streets, they learned of bloodshed, of a captain taunted by a barber's apprentice for not paying for the dressing of his hair, and of a sentinel answering back with a crashing blow that made the apprentice cry out.[8]

Converging from Murray's Barracks, from Royal Exchange Lane, a mob clustered onto King Street, where a tearful boy pointed to the sentinel, who was now loading his gun. Sides were drawn, and snowballs, cheers, whistles, dares, and oaths filled the frosty air. The officer of the day, Captain Thomas Preston, shouted for the protection of more soldiers. A stick struck one of the crowd, bayonets wavered in the air, muskets fired. Suddenly five were dead, six more wounded. Drums droned, church bells crashed, word was out that "the troops had risen on the people."[9]

John missed the initial physical conflict, but he did not misinterpret its threat. He rushed home to Abigail, apprehensive about her state. Once Abigail's mind was at ease, at least about her husband's safety, there was nothing more to be said or done—nothing, John said, but to recognize that "this was the Explosion."[10]

By morning, the involvement of the British was no longer a matter of rumor. Asked to defend Captain Preston, John accepted the case, hazarding his popularity in the belief that "Council ought to be the very last thing that an accused Person should want in a free Country." John won the case with the assistance of Abigail's cousin, Josiah Quincy, on the basis of doubt as to whether Preston had given orders to kill. One year later, the Boston Massacre, termed the "horrid Massacre" would be celebrated "as a Solemn and perpetual Memorial of the Tyranny of the British Administration of Government."[11]

On June 6, 1770, when John was elected a representative to the General Court from Boston, he once again had to face the fact that to serve in public office would entail sacrifice of personal ambition and fortune. He had, he calculated, more business than any man in the province, and he believed he would be trading in bright prospects for endless labor and anxiety—"if not infamy and death." That evening he confided his doubts to Abigail. Flooded with tears, that "excellent Lady" who had always encouraged him said she was very sensible of all the danger to him, to her, and to their children. But he had done as he ought, she told him, adding that she was "very willing to share in all that was to come and place her trust in Providence."[12]

In April of 1771, John complained of a pain in his breast and in his lungs, which he believed was life-threatening. He decided to maintain his office in Boston, but to return with his family to Braintree, where he spoke of being restored by the healing air—the fine breezes of the sea on one side and the rocky hills of pine and cedar on the other—as well as the daily rides on horseback, the amusements of agriculture, even a journey to drink the mineral waters at Stafford Springs in Connecticut. But with the most optimistic motives, John did not solve his problems. Again overwhelmed with work, he found the commute too much and decided to move back to Boston after roughly nineteen months in Braintree. On a late-summer day, August 21, 1772, he paid one Shrimpton Hunt £533 6s. 8d. for a brick house and lot in South Queen Street, opposite the courthouse and near his business.[13]

This transaction, at age thirty-seven, to his bitter regret, left him with only three hundred pounds in his pocket. He also felt his health as well as his funds exhausted, and made the "fixed Resolution" not to meddle with public affairs. He had already served his country and was determined to devote himself wholly to his law office and farm, and to laying a foundation for a better fortune for his children and a more serene life than had been his thus far.[14]

On Tuesday, November 24, 1772, Abigail arrived at the Queen Street house with Nabby, aged seven, John Quincy, five, Charles (born May 29, 1770), and the two-month-old infant, Thomas Boylston (born September 15, 1772), cradled in her arms. Abigail was twenty-eight years old and had been married for eight years. John was once again heard to say that he hoped to live in the house on Queen Street as long as he had any connections with Boston.[15]

Compared to that of her husband, who left behind a vivid and detailed map of his life, Abigail's early record is parsimonious. By inference we learn about her; her correspondence, especially with her cousin Isaac, immediately before and after her marriage, mirrors her mental and intellectual state with prophetic accuracy. As did her sister Elizabeth, Abigail maintained a respectful and affectionate relationship with Isaac. Her letters, written in the "Spirit of real Friendship," are full of purposeful advice on morals and integrity, and provide an invaluable record of her own aspirations. Impervious to John's teasing about her "Instructions and Exhortations," Abigail solemnly cautioned Isaac to be superior to temptation, warned him against vice and imprudence (too frequently the inseparable companions of youth), and passed on the excellent advice, twenty lines' worth, of Polonius to his son, Laertes, ending:

> This above all, to thine own self be true
> And it must follow as the Night the Day
> Thou canst not then be falce to any man. [16]

Isaac could not have expected less from a disciplined, dutiful Abigail, but he might have been surprised by the breadth of her horizons. A worldly puritan, she did not disdain ambition or deny curiosity. She was a child of her father's ministry, but also of the Age of Reason and the Enlightenment. She prized learning perhaps a shade less than morality; she was persuaded that "this passion of Ambition," when centered in an honest mind, did service to the world.[17]

Thus she would wish Isaac to make improvements equal to his prudence; ultimately she expected that his contribution might be of global importance. She was ingenuous as she implored her cousin to report the "curious or remarkable" in the course of his travels. In the light of this last request, Abigail's wistful words of approval of Isaac's intended voyage to England are those of a prematurely burdened young woman:

> Now is the best Season of Life for you to travel; Ere you have
> formed connection which would bind you to your own little Spot.[18]

Abigail enlarged on this theme subsequently. Isaac's report of his travels in England—of that antique and curious object, Canterbury Cathedral; of that vast magnificence, St. Paul's Cathedral; of visits to the opera, to theaters, to the Tower—evoked her candid thoughts on the distinct limitations imposed on women. "Bear with me Sir," she pleaded. "From my Infancy I have always felt a great inclination to visit the Mother Country as tis call'd and had nature formed me of the other Sex, I should certainly have been a rover." The obstacles to this course, however, seemed insurmountable.

> Women you know Sir are considered as Domestick Beings, and altho they inherit an Eaquel Share of curiosity with the other Sex, yet but few are hardy eno' to venture abroad, and explore the amaizing variety of distant Lands. The Natural tenderness and Delicacy of our Constitutions, added to the many Dangers we are subject too from your Sex, renders it almost impossible for a Single Lady to travel without injury to her character. And those who have a protector in an Husband, have generally speaking obstacles sufficient to prevent their Roving.[19]

Abigail's analysis of travel, and women's limited opportunities to do so, was without self-pity. Indeed, Abigail demonstrated much partisan interest in the achievement of her sex. The celebrated English historian Catharine Sawbridge Macaulay, mentioned in Isaac's letter, caught her attention. As Isaac had met her, Abigail hoped he could satisfy her great desire to be acquainted with Mrs. Macaulay's history. One of her own sex, so eminent in a tract so uncommon, Abigail explained, raised her curiosity.[20]

It was revealing of Abigail's intellectual gifts that at one of the most intensely domestic and transient periods of her life, she was able to reach beyond the nursery, kitchen, and field and sequester time to explore the outside world. Though she betrayed instances of frustration—having a protector begot "obstacles" that prevented her from being "a rover"—it was left to sister Elizabeth, as an unmarried observer of the Adams household, to speak of brains "all roiled," of being "almost crazed" in coping with the "natural Blessings of Matrimony."[21]

Abigail's marked interest in the writings of exceptional women, or in sympathetic works by men on the subject of women, implies an acute sensitivity to the special condition of being born female. In this regard, she was fascinated by the work of the flamboyant Reverend James Fordyce, D.D., whose *Sermons to Young Women* were written out of an "unfeigned regard for the Female Sex." The minister, an acquaintance of Samuel Johnson, wrote in this and a later work about the "softer sex," who were not always treated with the charity and justice they deserved, or recognized for their virtues and talents. Abigail thought enough of the *Sermons* to forward a copy to her sister Mary.[22]

Another author who won Abigail's attention, with his *Letters on the English Nation,* was supposedly a Jesuit named Batista Angeloni, shortly discovered to be the English political writer John Shebbeare. He wrote about the inhuman tyranny of barring women from the privileges of education. It was ignoble cowardice, he said, to disarm them and not allow them the same weapons men used, as their senses were generally as quick as men's, their reason "as nervous," their judgment as mature and solid. Abigail was intrigued not only by Shebbeare's thoughts on women, but also on religion. Fearful that her own people considered religion a "negative virtue," she learned from Shebbeare that the situation was far more crucial in London, where religion was periodical, like an "ague" that only returned once in seven days, and then attacked the inhabitants "with the cold fit only."[23]

It was Mercy Otis Warren who initiated the correspondence with Abigail. Abigail sincerely welcomed the arrangement: "Thus imbolden'd I venture to stretch my pinions," she thanked Mercy on July 16, 1773. Mercy, with her vigilant eyes, set jaw, and pursed mouth, was sixteen years older than Abigail, and though their literary styles differed measurably—Mercy's was baroque, prickly, guarded; Abigail's was reportorial, poetic, guileless—they shared brilliant intellects and almost identical concerns about female circumstances. It was with Mercy that Abigail revealed her most feminine and feminist thoughts. Together they were able to "visit" about writers, politics, children, and fashion—they regularly bartered yards of ribbons, laces, and fabrics—as well as the roles thrust upon their husbands.[24]

The body of letters they produced during their lifelong, though flawed, friendship established Abigail as the equal of the older and acknowledgedly more learned woman, but Abigail always deferred to Mercy. Not even in old age would Abigail make any pretentions to the character of an educated woman. There were so few women who really could be called learned, she said, that she did not wonder they were considered "black swans." To be one required such talents and such devotion of time and study as to exclude the performance of most domestic cares and duties, which fell exclusively, in her opinion, to the lot of most females. Her lot, apparently, would always exclude her from this prestigious membership. Yet Mercy, who attempted poetry as well as writing plays and history, respected Abigail's own literary gifts, urging her to write "very long letters" giving all the intelligence she could, "and dont be ceremonious." In turn, Abigail told her "Worthy Friend": "I love characters drawn by your pen."[25]

Early letters between the two women regarding the worth of Molière, for example, were characteristic. Abigail admitted immediately that she could not be brought to like that author. There was a general "Want of Spirit" about his work that caused disappointment with the closing of each story. Further, his characters appeared unfinished, and he seemed to ridicule vice without engaging his readers in virtue. Molière might have drawn many pictures of real life, yet all pictures of life, Abigail said, "are not fit to be exhibited upon the State."[26]

Mercy's response was candid, her arch style marking the dramatic difference in the personalities of the two women:

> As I am Called upon both by Mr. and Mrs. Adams to give my opinion of a Celebrated Comic Writer: silence in me would be inexcusable; tho, otherways my sentiments are of little Consequence. . . . The solemn strains of the tragic Muse Have been generally more to my taste than the lighter Representations of the Drama. Yet I think the Follies and Absurdities of Human Nature Exposed to Ridicule in the Masterly Manner it is done by Molière may often have a greater tendency to reform Mankind than some graver Lessons of Morality.[27]

But the subject of Molière was only a peripheral distraction from the subject of tea, "that bainful weed" lingering in the harbor, the subject of escalating negotiations. Abigail referred Mercy to the *Gazette* for details. The November 29, 1773, edition reported:

> Yesterday morning, Captain Hall, in the ship *Dartmouth*, came to anchor near the castle, in about eight weeks from London. On board it is said, are one hundred and fourteen chests of the so-much-detested East-India Company's tea, the expected arrival of which pernicious article has for some time past put all these northern colonies in a very great ferment. Friends! Brethren! Countrymen! that worst of Plagues the detested Tea shipped for this Port by the East-India Co. is now arrived—the Hour of Destruction or manly opposition to the Machination of Tyranny stares you in the face.[28]

With the arrival of the tea in port, members of the Committees of Correspondence resolved to pitch all the chests overboard. Bells tolled day and night. The evening of the twenty-ninth, in the Old South Meeting House, thousands of colonists from Dorchester, Roxbury, Brookline, Cambridge, and Charleston, as well as Boston, denounced the tea commissioners as more obnoxious to their countrymen than even the stamp masters. Facing up to the "last, worst, and most destructive measure of the administration," they extracted a promise from the owner of the *Dartmouth,* anchored at Griffin's Wharf, not to dock in the harbor until Tuesday. They hoped that by then the owner, Francis Rotch, would obtain permission from the customs collector to return his goods to Britain, thereby avoiding a disastrous confrontation.[29]

Negotiations were unsuccessful. Abigail was in anguish. She wrote to Mercy on December 5: "The flame is kindled and like Lightning it catches from Soul to Soul. Great will be the devastation if not timely quenched or allayed by some more lenient Measures." She was prepared, however, to face the ultimate, tragic challenge:

Altho the mind is shocked at the Thought of sheding Humane Blood, more Especially the Blood of our Countrymen, and a civil War is of all Wars, the most dreadful Such is the present Spirit that prevails, that if once they are made desperate Many, very Many of our Heroes will spend their lives in the cause, With the Speach of Cato in their Mouths, "What a pitty it is, that we can die but once to save our Country."[30]

Abigail confided to Mercy that she trembled at the thought of the "firefull concequences" right there in Boston. Her heart beat at every whistle she heard; she did not dare openly express half her fears. She wished "Eternal Reproach and Ignominy be the portion of all those who have been instrumental in bringing fears" upon her.[31]

The letter, explaining that she was only partially recovered (enough to leave her room some of each day) from a fever and illness more severe than she had known in years, verged on hysteria. Mercy's reply was discerning: "By the stile and spirit of yours of the 5th December one would judge you was quite as much affected by the shocks of the political as the Natural Constitution."[32]

After almost a week of somewhat eerie quiet, Abigail would call the rainy December 16, "the most momentous" in Boston's annals, a day she seemed to both dread and welcome. By ten o'clock in the morning, two thousand people had gathered in the Old South Meeting

House; by evening the crowd seemed more like seven thousand. "Who knows how tea will mingle with salt water?" someone asked. Sam Adams's oblique answer assured the gathering that "this meeting can do nothing more to save the country." The cause was desperate, the measures radical.[33]

Shouts and war whoops signaled the rush of men into the moonlight (the figure in history books varies from thirty to sixty, the Dartmouth log says one thousand). The strange group, with Indian headdresses and painted faces, swathed in blankets and brandishing hatchets, had emerged from a room in the rear of Edes and Gill's printing office. Throngs joined them as they passed by the Old South, marching directly to Griffin's Wharf, where the three ships lay that contained the tea. A guard of twenty-five men boarded the *Dartmouth.* They warned the ship and customs-house officers out of the way and methodically tended their quarry. They undid the hatches, went down to the hold, hoisted to deck 340 chests of tea and in less than three hours had cut them up, and systematically and quietly (except for an occasional supposedly Indian sound) tossed the pieces overboard into the bay.

Afterward, it was "as if it had been a holy time." John, so moved by the event, readily recognized the destruction of the tea as "so bold, so daring, so firm, intrepid and inflexible" and its consequences "so lasting" that he wrote on December 17 to James Warren, Mercy's husband: "The die is cast. The people have passed the river and cut away the bridge . . . The sublimity of it charms me."[34]

For all his pride in the daring of his countrymen, John's lawyerly instincts provoked questions. As the destruction of the tea was "but an Attack upon Property," another, similar "Exertion" of popular power might effect the event he feared mightily, the destruction of lives. But then the risk seemed inevitable when he thought about the "malicious Pleasure" of Governor Thomas Hutchinson, and the customs officers who stood by as the colonists struggled to return the tea to London before deciding to destroy it. "Amazing," he found, that there were "Persons so hardened and abandoned" and, he might have added, so lacking understanding. Hutchinson's earlier delivery of "general instructions" to end "irregularities" and "introduce tranquillity," had only unnerved the colonists further.[35]

Governments established in the "Plantations," Hutchinson had said, which, due to their separate and remote situations required more general and extensive powers of legislation, were subject to all

such laws of the kingdom as "immediately respect them or are designed to extend to them." Also, those who claimed exemption from
acts of Parliament by virtue of their rights as Englishmen should
consider that it was impossible that the rights of English subjects
should be the same "in every respect" in all parts of the Dominions.[36]

Hutchinson, attempting to be as conciliatory as possible, succeeded only in being provocative as he reached the last of his arguments on behalf of the Crown. "Without its protection," he asked,
"should we not become the prey of one of the Powers of Europe,"
and further, was there "anything which we have more reason to dread
then Independence?"[37]

Hutchinson's interpretation of the state of government affairs only
multiplied Abigail's fears of imminent war. Yet by late February she
was collected enough to apologize to Mercy for her last letter, which
"abounded with so many terrors." She explained that she was not
naturally of a gloomy temper, or disposed to view objects "upon the
dark Side only." She even found she could rejoice that no blood had
been spilled in the tea incident. Despite her efforts to be cheerful, the
remainder of the letter was the effort of a troubled woman.[38]

Abigail did not, though she wished she might, respond positively
to Mercy's suggestion that there was hope that they might both see
the colony's "Beautiful Fabrick" repaired and reestablished so firmly
that the "Venal and narrow hearted on Either side of the Atlantic,"
would be powerless "to break down its barriers." Instead, Abigail was
obsessed by the ravages of "that restless ambition" that had "broken
this people"—herself included, of course—into factions. In itself,
ambition in a person of honest mind and great ability might lead, and
had led, to eminent service to the world, she readily conceded. But
ambition could also pervert a person to "very base purposes," to
eradicate every principal of humanity and benevolence.[39]

"Every day more and more" Abigail felt that she had further cause
to deprecate the "growing Evil" that threatened all the precepts she
lived by. "This party Spirit ruins good Neighbourhood, eradicates all
the Seeds of good nature and humanity," Abigail told Mercy. "It
sours the temper and has a fatal tendancy," she continued, "upon the
Morals and understanding and is contrary to that precept of christianity thou shallt Love thy Neighbour as they self." Abigail was obviously thinking of the English King George when she mentioned
Alexander, the Greek conqueror who would certainly have achieved

much greater glory, in her opinion, by a wise government of his conquered kingdoms than by "childishly blubering" after new worlds.[40]

A bill to regulate the government of the province of Massachusetts Bay, regarded by John Adams as the "last Effort of Lord North's Despair," was presented to Parliament on March 14, signed March 31, and printed in Boston papers on May 10, effective June 1. The Boston Port Bill was initiated to punish Boston by closing its port to all commerce until the East India Company was repaid for the destruction of the tea. There would be no landing or shipping of merchandise within the Boston harbor. An army was on its way; British ships would soon blockade the town.[41]

Not unexpectedly, reaction was instant and dramatic. The seat of government was moved to Salem. The Committees of Correspondence, led by Dr. Joseph Warren, Mercy's brother-in-law, invited eight neighboring towns to a conference on the critical state of public affairs. Agreement was unanimous that the bill was one of injustice and cruelty, repugnant to law, religion, and common sense. The outcome was a joint resolution by the colonists to stop all trade, both importation and exportation, with Great Britain and the West Indies, until the Port Act was repealed.[42]

Another bill read before the House of Commons, on April 15, compounding the colonists' misery, appeared to be designed to alter the charter of the province of Massachusetts and thereby its government. Without warning, town meetings were to be abolished, the Crown was to be in charge of appointing and removing sheriffs (formerly chosen at a convention), and trial by jury was to become trial by Crown-appointed sheriffs. Should any of the Crown appointees, magistrates, revenue officers, or soldiers be brought up for charges, their trials would be held in Nova Scotia or Great Britain.[43]

Another measure legalized the quartering of troops within the town of Boston. Another abolished the writ of habeus corpus. Still another shattered charters and rights not only of Massachusetts, but of Connecticut, New York, and Virginia, by spreading the new boundaries of Quebec to the Ohio and Mississippi rivers and over the region that encompassed, besides Canada, what would be the states of Ohio, Michigan, Indiana, Illinois, and Wisconsin.[44]

To students of colonial justice it was emphatically apparent that all power was to stem from the royal government. The rights and liberties of colonists, renewed in charter from the time of William and Mary, and observed by the people of Massachusetts for the past eighty years, were abolished. Benjamin Franklin shrewdly observed that "the Army of Boston cannot answer any good purpose, and may be infinitely mischievous." The French, appraising conditions in America, thought it "plain enough the King of England is puzzled between his desire of reducing the colonies and his dread of driving them to separation."[45]

The arrival of General Thomas Gage on May 13, to enforce the "Coercive Acts" and the closing of the port pending on June 1— Governor Hutchinson having sailed for England—dramatized the realities of the new era. John could find no peace when he thought of its prospects. Besides, he and Abigail were both in poor health. Abigail was visiting in Weymouth, and her father's reports on her "Disorder" worried John. He suspected she had taken cold; he also wrote from Boston of efforts to subdue his own cold, the most obstinate and threatening one he could remember. Besides walks in the fresh air, he constantly plied himself with teas and Abigail's "Specific," about which there are no further details.[46]

Gage's arrival, Abigail's infirmities and his own, and the public news all at once challenged John's "Utmost Phylosophy."

> We live my dear Soul, in an Age of Tryal. What will be the Consequence I know not. The Town of Boston, for ought I can see, must suffer Martyrdom: It must expire: And our principal Consolation is, that it dies in a noble Cause. The Cause of Truth, of Virtue, of Liberty and of Humanity: and that it will probably have a glorious Reformation, to greater Wealth, Splendor and Power than ever.

The last paragraph held out hope, however. "Don't imagine from all this that I am in the Dumps." Far otherwise. He would no more be defeated by the oncoming events, he promised, than he had been in "The Project of the Tea."[47]

On June 17, John, with four other men, was elected by the General Court in Salem to be a delegate to America's first Continental Congress. Besides John, the other delegates included Thomas Cushing, Sam Adams, and Robert Treat Paine. James Bowdoin was "indisposed" due to family problems. John wrote with pride and awe three days later, on Monday, June 20:

This will be an assembly of the wisest Men upon the Continent, who are Americans in Principle, i.e. against the Taxation of Americans, by Authority of Parliament. . . . I feel myself unequal to this Business. A more extensive Knowledge of the Realm, the Colonies, and of Commerce, as well as of Law and Policy, is necessary, than I am Master of.[48]

John's election to Congress marked the beginning of a new era for Abigail as well. John was absent from Braintree, touring the Eastern Court circuit in Maine for the tenth and last time, and in the course of his fifteen letters written in less than a month's time, from June 23 to July 9, 1774, before leaving for Philadelphia, he set out the principal roles Abigail would assume for the next ten years of her life.[49]

In order for him to serve his country—"Swim or sink, live or die, survive or perish with my country, is my unalterable determination" —John created a partnership with Abigail. His letter from York, Maine, written on July 1, might be regarded as a directive couched as an invitation, begging Abigail to dedicate herself to a joint endeavor. It would prove to be a masterful summation of her life's work:

I must entreat you, my dear Partner in all the Joys and Sorrows, Prosperity and Adversity of my Life, to take a Part with me in the Struggle. I pray God for your Health—intreat you to rouse your whole attention to the Family, the stock, the Farm, the Dairy. Let every Article of Expense which can possibly be spared be retrench'd. Keep the Hands attentive to their Business, and [let] the most prudent Measures of every kind be adopted and pursued with Alacrity and Spirit.[50]

John was already nostalgic for the present, let alone the past. In Maine, in the heat, with little work to do, he was aware that this was no ordinary interval of absence from his family but rather the prelude to his first lengthy physical separation from them. But it was not only the imminent parting that John found painful. He was suffering "unutterable anxiety" about forthcoming duties, "too grand, and multifarious" for his comprehension. "We have not Men, fit for the Times, We are deficient in Genius, in Education, in Travel, in Fortune—in every Thing," he complained. Overcome with a sense of inadequacy, his own mostly, but his friends' as well, he prayed: "God grant us Wisdom, and Fortitude!"[51]

By the time of the last of his letters to Abigail before his return to Braintree, John seemed to have resolved his reasons for making the costly choice of serving his growing nation.

I have a Zeal at my Heart, for my Country and her Friends, which I
cannot smother or conceal: it will burn out at Times and in
Companies where it ought to be latent in my Breast. This Zeal will
prove fatal to the Fortune and Felicity of my Family, if it is not
regulated by a cooler Judgment than mine has hitherto been.[52]

On Wednesday, August 10, a hot, dry, dusty day, Abigail and her
four children—Nabby was nine, Johnny seven, Charles four, Tommy
two—waved good-bye to John, who had promised to meet the three
other delegates to the first Continental Congress at Thomas Cushing's by eleven o'clock in the morning. Abigail would be thirty on her
next birthday. Aware that uncertainty and expectation left the mind
great scope, she could not have known that her farewell wave to the
"very respectable parade" of the passing coach-and-four, bound for
Philadelphia, also signaled the start of a turbulent decade in which
the family would grow increasingly fragmented and their lives as
separate as Braintree was from St. Petersburg, Russia, let alone
Philadelphia.[53]

Whatever else Abigail sensed, she already knew loneliness and
seems to have been born with an acute sense of time lost—past,
present, future. She had yet to learn that the pending political and
intellectual revolution would drastically and intimately affect her entire family's moods, personalities, fortunes. Still, horrified as she was
to think about the possibility of bloodshed, she was wholehearted in
her decision to join John as partner on behalf of their country. She
would shoulder her responsibilities; she was quite ready for John to
assume his. On August 19, when a twelve-hour rain had greatly
revived the parched garden as well as her spirits, she told John:

> I long impatiently to have you upon the Stage of action. The first
> of the month of September, perhaps may be of as much
> importance to Great Britain as the Ides of March were to Caesar. I
> wish you every Publick as well, as private blessing, and that wisdom
> which is profitable both for instruction and edification to conduct
> you in this difficult day.[54]

The Die Is Cast

"I dare not trust myself with the thought of how long you may, perhaps, be absent," Abigail wrote John on September 16. A blue vein of pathos marked her letters; a hunger for reassurance —"I had rather give a dollar for a letter by the post, tho the consequence should be that I Eat but one meal a day for these 3 weeks to come"—spelled fear of the unknown. "Rocks and quick Sands" appeared to her on every side; anxiety for her country, her husband, and her family had changed her life, making her days "tedious" and her nights "unpleasant." As she acknowledged to John: "What course you can or will take is all wrapt in the Bosom of futurity. Uncertainty and expectation leave the mind great Scope. Did ever any Kingdom or State regain their Liberty, when once it was invaded without Blood shed? I cannot think of it without horror."[1]

Abigail's letters, in the next weeks, months, and up to ten years, might vary in information, views, tenderness, but never in thoughtfulness. She might be distraught emotionally, but she was always intellectually keen, turning to other examples and histories to reason out the proliferating drama of her own era. She was eclectic in her research, combing Greek and French as well as English and American references, ancient and contemporary, as though, by examining every leaf in the maze, she might comprehend its ultimate design.

America's cause was affirmed, in her judgment, by the Greek historian Polybius's ancient premise that peace, however desirable when founded in justice and honor, was shameful when attained by "bad" measures, and purchased at the price of liberty. The reprint in Boston of the Bishop of St. Asaph's speech, declaring North America "as the only great nursery of freemen now left upon the face of the earth," was additional reinforcement at this crucial political hour. The bishop, an Englishman born Jonathan Shipley, had voted in the House of the Lords against the bill to alter the Massachusetts Charter; his opinion, said Abigail, "meets, and most certainly merits the greatest encomiums."[2]

Still another insight into contemporary problems was afforded by reading Charles Rollin's *Ancient History*. In her new "recluse" life, Abigail found pleasure, entertainment, and relevance in the work of the eighteenth-century French historian, former Professor of Eloquence and Rector of the University of Paris. Rollin wrote of the Egyptians, Carthaginians, Persians, and Greeks; a page or two of the seven-volume series, read aloud to her by Johnny, not only afforded her the pleasure of her son's company, she said, but a chance to examine the methods by which empires were founded, by what steps they rose to an "exalted" pitch of grandeur and true glory, and the cause for their decline and fall. John, immensely pleased to learn of this practice, though casual in his evaluation of its significance, wrote back directly that he was "charmed" by her amusement with their little Johnny: "Tell him I am glad to hear he is so good a boy as to read to his Mamma, for her Entertainment, and to keep himself out of the Company of rude Children."[3]

Abigail's portrait of reclusive domesticity is relieved by occasional visits to her parents' house in Weymouth, or from her mother-in-law or John's brothers. Uncle Norton Quincy appears frequently on a special mission—to enjoy an hour of "sweet communion" with his niece on the specific subject of politics. She was admittedly less lonely, too, because of the company of the two young clerks who had settled over John's office. One was Nathan Rice, the other her cousin John Thaxter, both recent graduates of Harvard College. At mealtimes they made a "table full"; otherwise the two spent their time in the office. There were never two people, Abigail said, who gave a family less trouble, and apart from enjoying their company, she found it especially helpful to send Johnny to be tutored by Mr. Thaxter. Abigail's comment to John on the law clerk, who would play a substantial role in their lives in a short while, is of somewhat shaded enthusiasm, but reveals her demanding standards. She intended to consult with John on his return concerning their son's education.

Meanwhile, she was certain that if Johnny "does not get so much good, he gets less harm." As she explained to her husband:

> I have always thought it of very great importance that children should, in the early part of life, be unaccustomed to such examples as would tend to corrupt the purity of their words and actions that they may chill with horror at the sound of an oath and blush with indignation at an obscene expression. These first principal[s] which grow with their growth and strengthen with their strength neither time or custom can totally eradicate.[4]

In the very first letter John wrote to Abigail on his way to Philadelphia he outlined precisely the primary areas of responsibility in their partnership, which he would constantly redefine during his absences. Essentially, these were the supervision of their farm and of the education of their children, duties she accepted without hesitation, doubting only her ability to discharge them. From time to time Abigail would speak of herself as the directress of husbandry and farming, of her hopes to build a reputation of being as good a farmeress as her partner was a statesman.[5]

Warned by John about checking the proper time to get the freights of marsh mud or creek mud to lay by the wall to ferment as they were mixed with dust and dung, she was also instructed to see that her tenants and farm hands performed. "You must take Care my Dear, to get as much Work out of our Tenants as possible," John would insist. Specifically, Abigail was to note that "Belcher is in Arrears. He must work. Hayden must work. Harry Field must work, and Jo. Curtis too must be made to settle. He owes something." Others were not to be forgotten: "Jo. Tirrell too, must do something—and Isaac. I can't loose such Sums as they owe me—and I will not," John added firmly.[6]

Drilled as she was in the need for "Frugality, Industry and economy" (the alternative was to see their "small Boat" suffer shipwreck), Abigail's inspired management of their expanding property was relayed to John by James Warren, who predicted that "Mrs. Adams Native Genius will Excel us all in Husbandry." Very likely, Abigail was spurred on in her duties by John's vision of a larger vessel than their own small boat: "Our Expences, in this Journey, will be very great—our only Reward will be the consolatory Reflection that We toil, spend our Time, and tempt Dangers for the public Good." Sustaining their plural involvement, the dual nature of their mutual enterprise, John assured Abigail it would be "happy indeed, if we do any good."[7]

When John did permit himself to wander from politics or farming, in the early years of their separate lives, he would land full strength on the subject of his children's education, which, he said bluntly, was "never" out of his mind. The role of "school mistress" was one that he assured Abigail she was well qualified to fill. His affectionate respect for her intelligence and adequacy to the task, considering his elaborate curriculum and nagging regard for learning, and Abigail's totally homemade education, was exceedingly complimentary. "No doubt you are well qualified," he flattered her. He wrote her that an English gentleman who had visited in Braintree pronounced her the most accomplished lady he had seen since he left England. "You see," he wrote from Philadelphia, "a Quaker can flatter, but dont you be proud."[8]

John must have been impressed, though he tried to make light of the compliment to Abigail, for he dealt with it more than once. Two days before writing to Abigail, he had already recorded it in his journal, which he fully expected her to read as her "Entertainment" in lieu of the "Particulars" he either had no time to relay or feared to commit to paper for security's sake. Possibly the letter was unplanned when he wrote in his diary:

> One Thing he [Stephen Collins] told me, for my Wife, who will be peeping here, sometime or other, and come across it. He says when he call'd at my House, an English Gentleman was with him, a Man of Penetration, tho of few Words. And this silent, penetrating Gentleman was pleased with Mrs. Adams, and thought her, the most accomplished Lady he had seen since he came out of England. —Down Vanity, for you don't know who this Englishman is.[9]

John was nothing if not imposing in his demands of Abigail. The grandeur of his pronouncements on education was nearly as intimidating as his "conferences" on the subject were interminable. Education made greater differences between man and man than nature made between man and brute, he thought. And further, the virtues and powers to which men might be trained by early education and constant discipline were truly sublime and astonishing, he said, citing Newton and Locke as examples of the deep sagacity to be acquired by long habits of thinking and study. It should be Abigail's care and his, therefore, to

> elevate the minds of our children and exalt their courage; to accelerate and animate their industry and activity; to excite in them an habitual contempt of meanness, abhorrence of injustice and inhumanity, and an ambition to excel in every capacity, faculty, and virtue. If we suffer their minds to grovel and creep in infancy, they will grovel all their lives.[10]

He had not finished. A significant facet of his program was left to be fulfilled. Nourishing the children's minds was mandatory, but their bodies must be hardened, and their souls exalted: "Without strength and activity and vigor of body, the brightest mental excellencies will be eclipsed and obscured.[11]

Theories on learning, behaving, thinking—commandments to live by —were issued by John from York, Maine, and Philadelphia, Pennsylvania, as well as from Holland, England, and France. Concerns with "great and solid objects," with ambition and decency, grace and honesty, industry and virtue, as opposed to uselessness, frivolity, and vice that was "shameful and unmanly," did not, however, exclude a pragmatic interest in writing and French, subjects on which he was obsessive.[12]

With regard to French, John was convinced that learning the language was a necessary accomplishment of American gentlemen and ladies. And also of politicians. He would blame the lack of this facility as the reason he was not chosen to join Benjamin Franklin in a committee to journey to Canada, where troops were led by General Benedict Arnold. John insisted it was well within Abigail's power to teach their children French, and he prayed she would not suffer them to feel a pain of inferiority similar to his. He even requested the name of the author of her thin French grammar, which gave her the pronunciation of the French words in English transliteration. As a result of efforts to master the language during his first ocean crossing, he would leave behind long sheets of strenuously tabulated French verbs in all their myriad tenses.[13]

In contrast to his need for a textbook for his French studies, John virtually wrote his own on the subject of writing. Referring to Cicero and Pliny, Pope and Swift, considering the varieties of expression, John informed Abigail that the epistolary style was essentially different from the oratorical and historical style. Oratory abounded with figures; history was simple but grave, majestic, and formal; letters, like conversation, should be free, easy, and familiar, a concept both he and Abigail mastered with exhilaration. John's need to define Abigail's teaching program so scrupulously might be thought arrogant, except that he took care to explain his peering over Abigail's shoulder. His advice was not only one way of compensating for his feelings of "banishment" from the family, but also of avoiding the pitfalls of his own education. As he reasoned: "I never had a regular Tutor, I never studied any Thing methodically, and consequently never was compleatly accomplished in any Thing. But as I am conscious of my own Deficiency, in these Respects, I should be the less pardonable, if I neglected the Education of my Children."[14]

Timing was also a factor in John's approach to learning; early youth was the period to form taste and judgment, before any unchaste sounds had fastened on children's ears, and before any affectation or vanity was settled on their minds. Music, he added, was a great advantage, for style depended in part on a delicate ear. Discipline was still another essential factor, the taskmaster insisted: "The Faculty of Writing is attainable, by Art, Practice, and Habit only. The sooner, therefore the Practice begins, the more likely it will be to succeed. Have no Mercy upon an affected Phrase, any more than an affected Air, Gate [gait], Dress, or Manners."[15]

Consistent with John's striving nature, it never occurred to him that any one of their four children would be less than equal to or surpassing the others in ability. He assured Abigail that "your Children have Capacities equal to any Thing. There is a Vigor in the Understanding, and a Spirit and Fire in the Temper of every one of them, which is capable of ascending the Heights of Art, Science, Trade, War, or Politicks."[16]

John was hardly casual in his conclusions about their children. He had, in his opinion, studied them carefully. He had decided that John had genius, and so had Charles. It was up to their mother to safeguard these two, to cultivate their minds, inspire their hearts, raise their wishes. "Fix their Attention upon great and glorious Objects, root out every little Thing, weed out every meanness, make them great and manly," he instructed Abigail. But her duties hardly ended there. "Teach them to scorn Injustice, Ingratitude, Cowardice, and Falsehood." Speaking as a perfect puritan and patriot, he added,

"Let them revere nothing but Religion, Morality and Liberty."[17]

Nor were Nabby and Tommy forgotten by their father. The first, by reason of her sex, required a different education from the boys, he said, but he left its components to Abigail. However their schedules might vary, if they did at all, the four understood the gravity of their father's concern for learning. When Abigail, at John's request, made separate inquiries as to the present each might like, a book was the answer of all. Only Tom wanted a picture book; Charles, the histories of kings and queens. It was natural for the children to think of books; as one of them observed, they were the only presents their papa ever gave them.[18]

That Abigail's aspirations and standards for her children were nearly indivisible from John's would account, of course, for their extraordinary collaboration, which willed greatness on their descendants. When Abigail returned from an early visit to Mercy Warren, in Plymouth, she wrote to tell her friend that she so admired Mercy's little offspring that she must beg her to communicate the happy art of "rearing the tender thought, teaching the young Idea how to shoot, and pouring fresh instruction o'er the Mind." And while on the subject of children, she mentioned her interest in a series of letters by the English writer Juliana Seymour, the pseudonym of John Hill, *On the Management and Education of Children.* She was forwarding these to Mercy, not because Mercy stood in need of any assistance, but because Abigail wished to know her sentiments on this book and whether it corresponded with Mercy's own system in which she had "so happily" succeeded. "I am sensible I have an important trust committed to me," she wrote, "and tho I feel myself uneaquel to it, tis still incombent upon me to discharge it in the best manner I am capable of."[19]

To Mercy, Abigail expressed the longings and goals of a "young and almost inexperienced Mother in this Arduous Business," that the tender twigs allotted to her care might be so cultivated as to do honor to their parents and prove blessings to the rising generation. Abigail concluded her letter—a glossary of her conception of parental duties —with a poem declaring her wish to imitate the

> *Parent who vast pleasure finds*
> *In forming of her children's minds*
> *In midst of whom with vast delight*

She passes many a winters Night
Mingels in every play to find
What Bias Nature gave the mind
Resolving thence to take her aim
To Guide them to the realms of fame
And wisely make those realms the way
To those of everlasting day.

Each Boisterous passion to controul
And early Humanize the Soul
In simple tales beside the fire,
The noblest Notions to inspire.
Her offspring conscious of her care
Transported hang around her chair. [20]

A crusty Mercy dismissed Mrs. Seymour's treatise as "of very little Consequence," but empathized with Abigail's sense of purposeful parenthood and feelings of inadequacy to the task, touching lightly on the daring subject of feminism in the latter regard. As one "yet looking for Every foreign aid to Enable her to the discharge of a duty that is of the utmost importance to society," Mercy bemoaned the fact that the education of children should, for such a number of years, be left almost wholly to their "uninstructed sex." She also confirmed Abigail's sense of momentous challenge in her parental role by espousing an equally ambitious credo. She would esteem it a happiness indeed if she could acquit herself of the "important Charge (by providence devolved on Every Mother.)" Continuing, Mercy said it would be a "noble pleasure" if she and Abigail had the conscious satisfaction of having exerted their utmost efforts to "rear the tender plant and Early impress the youthful mind" so that, when out of their hands, it might be useful on the present theater of action and "happy forever when . . . introduced into more Enlarged and Glorious scenes."[21]

John's main reason for moving Abigail and the children back to Braintree in June of 1774 was to spare them anxiety, to prepare the family for the "Storm that was coming on." Toward the end of a parched September, it was certain their anxieties were dismally justified but also far too narrowly gauged. It was terribly true that Boston was now a place of unceasingly warlike preparations, with the governor mounting cannon, digging entrenchments, throwing up breastworks, and encamping regiments in increasing numbers. But it was naïve to think that what happened in Boston did not affect citizens outside the "Metropolis." As a pebble dropped in a pond induces ripples to its outer edge, so a letter found on a Boston Street on August 27 shattered any hopes that Abigail, in Braintree, would be able to fulfill John's wishes that she make herself "as easy and quiet as possible," while concentrating on the farm and the children.[22]

When the colony's brigadier general, William Brattle, of Cambridge, wrote to Britain's General Thomas Gage to warn him that orders were out for men "to meet at one Minute's Warning, equipt with Arms and Ammunition," and that stocks of powder were being withdrawn from the provincial arsenal in Quarry Hill, his letter was intercepted and Brattle had to run for his life. The governor's reaction to Brattle's information was swift: on September 1, his men seized both powder and weapons from Quarry Hill. The colonists' response was *not* to resort to bloodshed and bombardment, as was sensationally rumored, but to play the governor's game. Abigail was sure that John would receive "a more particular account" from the public papers, she wrote him, but she did think she could fill in what he might not learn from any other person concerning details of the events of the night of September 11.

> In consequence of the powders being taken from Charlestown, a general alarm spread thro many Towns and was caught pretty soon here. The report took here a fryday, and a Sunday a Soldier was seen lurking about the common. Supposed to be a Spy, but most likely a Deserter. However inteligence of it was communicated to other parishes, and about 8 o'clock a Sunday Evening there passed by here about 200 Men, preceded by a horse cart, and marched down to the powder house from whence they took the powder and carried [it] into the other parishes and there secreted it. I opened the window upon there return. They pass'd without any Noise, not a word among them till they came against this house, when some of them perceiveing me, asked me if I wanted any powder. I replied not since it was in so good hands. The reason they gave for taking it, was that we had so many Tories here they dare not trust us with it.[23]

Judging by Abigail's reaction to Sunday evening's "errand," it is possible she was more fearful of the underlying question of loyalty triggered by Brattle's deceit than by the seizure of the powder and arms. The awareness that a people "all in flames" in a town as "high" as one could imagine, might soon be in arms was a probability she faced with pain. Choices had to be made; the incident of the powder illuminated the personal tragedies of a people divided against one another, of parents and children, husbands and wives, cousins and friends, parted over political incompatibility. In this fearful time one could not trust one's general or even one's parson. "Not a Tory but hides his head," Abigail noted. When the church parson had thought the colony's soldiers were after him, he had run up to his garret; another had jumped out of his window and hidden in the corn; gossip had the third crouching below his wooden fence, telling his beads.[24]

The question of loyalty was of vibrant concern when Abigail dined with the brothers Samuel and Josiah Quincy and their families. "A little clashing of parties you may be sure," Abigail reported to John. "Mr. Sam's wife said she thought it high time for her Husband to turn about, he had not done half so clever since he left her advice." It had apparently gone unheeded, for, the following year, when her husband sailed for England, Hannah Quincy, the former Miss Hill, sister-in-law of John Adams's early love of the identical name (who married Bela Lincoln and then Ebenez Storer), chose to remain at home in Massachusetts. Though "defections" were noted and agonized over repeatedly by Abigail, one above all, that of her cousin Isaac Smith, was a source of greatest disillusionment and concern to Abigail and her family.[25]

It was Abigail's sister, Mary Cranch, who chose to delve into rumors concerning the young minister Smith's allegiances. This tense, opinionated woman did not mince words: "Tho you should preach like an angel if the People suppose you unfriendly to the country and constitution and a difender of the unjust, cruil and arbitrary measures that have been taken by the ministry against us, you will be like to do very little good."[26]

It was Mary's hope that Cousin Isaac did not deserve this criticism, but such was the opinion of many who twelve months ago had applauded him in admiration and who now left the meeting house the moment he entered it.

Isaac Smith's answer was thoughtful and honest. On October 20 he wrote to explain that he was not indifferent to the good opinion of those around him, but that he could not in complaisance to others, even to those for whose understanding he had a much higher veneration than for his own, give up the independence of his own mind. He politely told his cousin that he thought her opinions were founded on misinformation. He tried to explain that he had, admittedly, not exclaimed so loudly against the cruelty, the injustice, the arbitrary nature of the late acts of Parliament as others, but that his age, his particular profession in life, and his connections with a seminary of learning, the seat of liberal inquiry, had forbidden him to do so. He ended his letter with an eloquent if flawed summation of his position, not unlike that of many other Tory sympathizers:

> I must freely own, that I had rather calmly acquiesce in these, and
> an hundred other acts, proceeding from a British Legislature (tho'
> we need not even do this), than be subject to the capricious,
> unlimited despotism of a few of my own countrymen, or behold the
> soil, which gave me birth, made a scene of mutual carnage and
> desolation.[27]

Had Cousin Isaac been called to name the "few" he was accusing of unlimited despotism, of caprice, he would have had to list Abigail's name with the radical handful. Her commitment was now complete. She was ready to sacrifice for the cause of her "much injured Country." If she could not have her wish to be a "fellow Traveller" to Congress, she could support, proudly, John's work in Congress, as of Friday, October 14, helping to adopt a Declaration that twelve of the colonies (Georgia had not joined) might explore the proper means to pursue the restoration of their rights. Abigail could also derive satisfaction from a friend who described the minds of the colonists as being "firm as Rocks," who spoke rousingly of their anticipation of a "glorious Restoration of American Liberty." As far as she could see, and judging from all she heard, Boston to her was "Boston Garrison," a place of such misery that she found herself at a loss to picture adequately the complex miseries and distresses she was witness to. "Suffice it to say," she wrote in one of her rare letters to Catharine Macauley,

> we are invaded with fleets and armies, our commerce not only
> obstructed, but totally ruined, the courts of Justice shut, many
> driven out from the Metropolis, thousands reduced to want, or
> dependent upon the charity of their neighbors for a daily supply of
> food, all the Horreurs of a civil war threatening us on one hand,
> and the chains of Slavery ready forged for us on the other.[28]

Yet, for all the chains that were choking colonial liberties, Abigail was heartened by signs of colonial muscle, of willingness to break traditional links and to fight back—with words, at least. For every chain forged, a new committee seemed to be formed, a resolution made, a protest registered, a petition drafted. Abigail had witnessed all the steps along the way that propelled county meetings into provincial meetings, and a convention into the First Continental Congress, which John was now attending.

Abigail was back in Braintree for only two months before she learned that, given the mood of the times, in city and country, everywhere, people waited in "longing expectation." In Cambridge, on September 3, four thousand men had met, "composed as if they were at a funeral," demanding, among other things, that the sheriff, David Phips, ask pardon for his role in removing the powder, and that he swear to take no hand in executing the tyrannical Parliamentary edicts.[29]

At Dedham, on September 6, Braintree's representatives to the Suffolk Convention were empowered to act on all such matters as they might judge of "public utility" in this time of general stress. In an attempt, perhaps, to soften the burden of her news, but also indicative of her preoccupation with the gravity of the issues, Abigail took to equating this strangely arid time of waiting, guessing, and formulating strategy with the harsh Indian-summer drought that was so punishing to her livestock. The cows would certainly be proferring a petition, she warned John in her third letter to him since his departure for Philadelphia. They would be setting forth their grievances to inform him that they had been deprived of their ancient privileges. They desired these privileges restored, she said, especially as their living, by reason of the drought, was taken from them, and their property caused to decay.[30]

Lightly or severely couched, stealthily or boldly executed, the terms used to plead the cause for independence by no means warranted Cousin Isaac's use of the word *capricious*. Ingrained allegiances lingered; Sam Adams spoke for John and Abigail as well when he said: "Nothing is more foreign to our hearts than a spirit of rebellion. Would to God they all, even our enemies, knew the warm attachment we have for Great Britain, notwithstanding we have been contending these ten years with them for our rights."[31]

Dr. Joseph Warren, statesman and Adams family physician, who served as a kind of director-general of the Suffolk meeting during Sam Adams's absence in Philadelphia, was equally cautious about separation proceedings with the Mother Country. He denounced routs, riots, or "licentious" attacks upon the properties of any person as being subversive of all order and government. Instead, he sought "a steady, manly, uniform and persevering opposition to convince our enemies, that, in a contest so important, in a cause so solemn, our conduct shall be such as to merit the approbation of the wise, and the admiration of the brave and free of every age and of every country."[32]

Abigail could only have welcomed Warren's temperate approach equally as much as she must have despaired over Isaac's demeaning description of her involvement. "Capricious" was an insulting way to describe the thoughtful agony of her political choice, and equally inappropriate in relation to her private loss of John's company. "I find I am obliged to summon all my patriotism to feel willing to part with him again," she wrote Mercy Warren in August of 1775. "You will readily believe me when I say that I make no small sacrifice to the public."[33]

In most times of crisis in Abigail's life, even the ones she tended to play down—as in her description of John's absences as "tedious"—she adapted to any reasonable solution to her problems with relative grace. With regard to her sacrifice, she soon discovered that John's letters afforded her at least some approximation of their devoted relationship, revealing, in her appreciation of the "frequent tokens of remembrance," both the heartwarming and heartbreaking aspects of their dependent love. Letters from John made her heart "as light as a feather," set her spirits "dancing," stirred her to tears:

> How they rouse every tender sensation of my Soul, which
> sometimes find vent at my Eyes nor dare I discribe how earnestly I
> long to fold to my fluttering Heart the dear object of my warmest
> affections. The Idea sooths me, I feast upon it with a pleasure
> known only to those whose Hearts and hopes are one.[34]

Abigail, whose pen was frequently, by her own admission, her "only pleasure," and writing to John "the composure of my mind," might very well have had to put up with a husband too preoccupied with pressing affairs of the day to find the time to sustain a correspondence. But, on the contrary, John seemed to accept his share as his duty and he was thoroughly apologetic when he did not keep up his end of the bargain fully. He recognized also that health, children, farm, and affirmation of affection were desirable subject matter, but that he owed Abigail more. He must write her as husband, lover, father of her children, farmer, and lawyer, but also as informant. He respected this role as he respected their partnership. He was willing to recognize his wife as his equal, and said as much. He paid her the compliment of telling her that her "Sentiments of the Duties We owe to our Country, are such as become the best of Women, and the best of Men." They were collegial patriots, and though he sometimes teased her about how she loved "to pick a political bone," he seriously reviewed his observations and opinions for her benefit ("under the rose" at times)—surprisingly so, considering the hazards of spies and the pressure of his duties. Nor did he refute her reference to Elizabeth Adams, Sam's wife, as a "Sister Delegate," suggesting that the two women had formal roles in governmental proceedings.[35]

Remarkably, the life-sustaining properties of their correspondence were to be a two-sided affair. John, who virtually dictated Abigail's roles as educator and farmer, viewed with selfless admiration what probably was the third major aspect of their partnership, her role as a writer and reporter. From the very beginning, her display of extraordinary gifts for portraying her personal life and public times would evoke his grandest compliment. "I really think that your Letters are much better worth preserving than mine," he would tell her, treating her literary output as an unexpected windfall, an inexhaustible dowry that enriched his life.[36]

Abigail's written words, for the next ten years especially, would be his primary link with family and farm, as well as home-front politics. Her shrewd gifts of perception, observation and curiosity molded the modest housewife into a respected historian. Able to convey her thoughts with candor, tenderness, and wit—"my pen is always freer than my tongue," she recognized—her worth was immediately appreciated by John. A "delicious" letter from you, he told Abigail, is "worth a dozen of mine."[37]

Until John's departure for Philadelphia, Abigail's letters to him during his circuit-riding days were primarily love letters and family letters. Still, they were tinged with concern and the desire for any news apart from that available to her in the newspapers and journals she read during John's absence. Once he was on the road to Philadelphia, she was very firm about her expectations of being informed in all matters, personal or otherwise. There was a precedent, she pointed out; as John had "indulged her so much in that Way" during his previous absences, especially during the July days in Falmouth, she made the outright claim that she had a "right" to hear as often from him as he had leisure and opportunity to write.[38]

By her own admission, Abigail was hard-pressed to explain her greedy appetite for news of the "doings" of the Congress via Paul Revere or William Tudor or any other courier-friends or the "title Tattle" of neighbors and relatives. She knew she ought not to grumble when John's writing was scant, considering that his labors must be great and his mouth closed, yet she could not restrain herself from pleading: "All you may communicate, I beg you would. . . . There is a pleasure I know not whence it arises nor can I stop now to find it out, but I say there is a degree of pleasure in being able to tell new's —especially any which so nearly concerns us as all your proceedings do."[39]

John's first words from Philadelphia arrived on the evening of September 16, 1774. Abigail was so affected she did not fall asleep until one o'clock in the morning. On the whole, his trip to Philadelphia (he was forty-two miles short of the city in this first letter, dated August 28, from Prince Town, New Jersey) had been most agreeable, affording him opportunities to see the world and to form acquaintances with the most eminent and famous men in the colonies he had passed through, where he reported that he was treated with unbounded "Civility, Complaisance and Respect." He observed that in New York, for all the opulence and splendor of the city, very little good breeding was evident; though he and his party were treated with assiduous respect, he did not see one real gentleman, one well-bred man, during his visit. At the entertainments, he found no conversation that was agreeable, no modesty, no attention to one another. The men talked very loud, very fast, and all at once. If they asked a question, before one could utter three words in answer, they would break upon one again, and talk away. He did, however, find his visit to Princeton to his liking, and was politely treated at Nassau Hall College by the scholars, tutors, professors, and president. He had expected to reach the theater of action, Philadelphia, the next day. The people, wherever he had been, he reported further, seemed to be of very favorable spirit and universally considered the colonies' cause as their own, expressing the firmest resolution to abide by the determination of the Congress.[40]

Abigail might complain from letter to letter—in truth, none of John's would ever be full enough, particular enough—but she was always made to comprehend the gravity and splendor of his mission. The scene was almost too tender for his "State of Nerves"; he was dazzled by the prospect ahead:

> The Art and Address, of Ambassadors from a dozen belligerant Powers of Europe, nay of a Conclave of Cardinals at the Election of a Pope, or of the Princes in Germany at the Choice of an Emperor, would not exceed the Speciments We have seen. —Yet the Congress all profess the same political Principles. . . . They all profess to consider our Province as suffering in the common Cause, and indeed they seem to feel for Us, as if for themselves. We have had as great Questions to discuss as ever engaged the Attention of Men, and an infinite Multitude of them.[41]

At one early point, so much was happening so fast that John wished he had the time to write Abigail a dozen letters every day. But his business was arduous: he had the characters and tempers, the principles and views of fifty gentlemen, total strangers, to study, and the trade, policy, and whole interest of a dozen provinces to learn. And there were pamphlets, newspapers, private letters to read. Happily, he could report a "great Spirit" in the Congress; he added grimly, however, in the very next sentence: "But our People must be peaceable." It was all right for their people to exercise every day of the week —the more the better. Let them furnish themselves with artillery, arms and ammunition. Let them follow the maxim that Abigail had already said they had adopted: "In Times of Peace, prepare for War." Above all, "Let them avoid War, *if possible, if possible* I say."[42]

In a short time, John, having studied their tempers, views, characters, and designs, was alternately impressed and impatient with his colleagues. John Dickinson, the author of fourteen essays in the form of "Letters from a farmer in Pennsylvania to the British Colonies," was troubled with hectic* complaints. John found him "shadow tall, slender as a Reed, pale as ashes." At first sight he did not suppose he would live a month; "Yet upon a more attentive Inspection," John concluded, "he looks as if the Springs of Life were strong enough to last many Years." John described the Virginian, Peyton Randolph, president of the Congress, as "a large, well looking man," and found Richard Henry Lee a tall, spare man. He thought the struggling Patrick Henry a man of "high Notions" who was impatient with many, including the Rutledge brothers, lawyers from Charleston, South

---

*"Fever accompanying wasting diseases, esp. tuberculosis," according to Webster.

Carolina, whom Henry categorized as "horrid." John was only slightly more pleasant about these gentlemen. Edward Rutledge, he reported, was "sprightly but not deep" and had the most indistinct, inarticulate way of speaking—through his nose. How he would shine in public, John could not conceive, though he seemed good-natured but conceited. The older brother, John Rutledge, with his "Air of Reserve, Design and Cunning," was coupled with other undesirables such as James Duane and Joseph Galloway.[43]

Taken altogether, this was an assembly like no other that ever existed, John reported to Abigail on October 9.

> Every Man in it is a great Man—an orator, a Critick, a statesman, and therefore every Man upon every Question must shew his oratory, his Criticism and his Political Abilities. . . . The Consequence of this is, that Business is drawn and spun out to an immeasurable Length. I believe if it was moved and seconded that We should come to a Resolution that Three and two make five We should be entertained with Logick and Rhetorick, Law, History, Politicks and Mathematicks, concerning the Subject for two whole Days, and then We should pass the Resolution unanimously in the Affirmative.

Besides, he added, his patience was further tried by the perpetual round of feasting on the likes of whipped syllabubs, flummery, jellies, trifles, melons "fine beyond description," and excellent pears and peaches. Also, nothing less than the very best of burgundy, claret, and Madeira. He admitted to drinking the latter "at a great Rate and found no Inconvenience in it."[44]

By way of impressing Abigail with the diverse character of the members of the new Congress, despite its theoretically unified purpose, John chose to elaborate on the difficulty of their settling on an opening ceremony. When the Congress first met, he explained, the motion that it should be opened with prayer was opposed by some on the grounds that the division in religious sentiments—some members being Episcopalians, some Quakers, some Anabaptists, some Presbyterians, some Congregationalists—precluded joint worship. Then Sam Adams rose and said he was no bigot and that he could hear a prayer from a gentleman of piety and virtue who was at the same time a friend to his country. He said, further, that he had heard that Mr. Jacob Duché, assistant rector of Christ Church and St.

Peter's in Philadelphia, deserved that character, and therefore he moved that the Episcopal clergyman be "desired" to read prayers to the Congress the next morning.[45]

The motion was seconded and passed; Mr. Duché read several prayers and the Thirty-fifth Psalm and John said that, Episcopalian though he was, he had never heard a better prayer, or one so well pronounced. By comparison, he had to admit Boston's Dr. Samuel Cooper, the Episcopalian minister of the Brattle Street Church, a renowned orator, had not prayed "with such fervor, such Ardor, such Earnestness and Pathos, and in Language so elegant and sublime— for America, for the Congress, for The Province of Massachusetts Bay, and especially the Town of Boston." John concluded with satisfaction: "It has had an excellent effect upon every body here."[46]

In a sense, John's impartiality lasted a mere three weeks. By October 9 he confided to Abigail that he was not fond of the Presbyterian meetings in Philadelphia, and that he preferred his own church.

> We have better Sermons, better Prayers, better Speakers, softer, sweeter Musick, and genteeler Company. And I must confess, that the Episcopal Church is quite as agreeable to my Taste as the Presbyterian. They are both Slaves to the Domination of the Priesthood. I like the Congregational Way best—next to that the Independant.

Still exploring the kinds and places of worship, John, led by curiosity and good company, strolled over, one early autumn afternoon, to what he called the "Mother Church, or rather Grandmother Church, I mean the Romish Chappell," which was St. Mary's Church on Fourth Street, in Philadelphia. There he heard a solid, moral essay on the duty of parents to their children to take care of their interests, temporal and spiritual. The afternoon's "Entertainment," as he described it to Abigail, was, however, "most awfull and affecting":

> The poor Wretches, fingering their Beads, chanting Latin, not a Word of which they understood, their Pater Nosters and Ave Maria's. Their holy Water—their Crossing themselves perpetually— their Bowing to the Name of Jesus, where ever they hear it—their Bowings, and Kneelings, and Genuflections before the Altar. The Dress of the Priest was rich with Lace—his Pulpit was Velvet and Gold. The Altar Piece was very rich—little Images and Crucifixes about—Wax Candles lighted up. But how shall I describe the Picture of our Saviour in a Frame of Marble over the Altar at full

Length upon the Cross, in the Agonies, and the Blood dropping and streaming from his Wounds.[47]

Given the setting—adding organ music, the nearly constant chanting and singing, "most sweetly and exquisitely," except at sermon time—in which there is everything to lay hold of the "Eye, Ear, and Imagination," everything to "charm and bewitch the simple and ignorant"—John could not help but wonder how Luther ever broke the spell. John sounded almost seduced, but, of course, was not. Nor was he irreligious—only puritanical. He, and Abigail as well, were uncomfortable with, though not unadmiring of, tangible signs of opulence, whether in church or in a friend's house.[48]

For both, who cherished a "primitive Simplicity" of manners, who were skeptical of too many "high sounding words," religion was to be adorned only by the splendor of perfect faith. Faith made their sacrifice possible, even plausible. Resignation to the will of Heaven was their only resource in dangerous times, as prudence and caution should be their guides, Abigail said. At the very start of the Revolution, Abigail made her pact in these words: "If the Sword be drawn I bid adieu to all domestick felicity, and look forward to that Country where there is neither wars nor rumors of War in a firm belief that thro the mercy of its King we shall both rejoice there together." Furthermore, patriotism and religion were inextricably allied; the one without the other was "as an honest Man without the fear of God." The Scriptures, as she interpreted them, told her "righteousness exalteth a Nation."[49]

It was pouring rain when John Adams left "polite" Philadelphia on Friday, October 28, 1774. He left in an affable mood, grateful for the "Civilities" accorded him, and with some sense of accomplishment; despite the tiresome "nibbling and quibbling" of Congress, some decisions had been made. On October 20, the nonimportation, nonconsumption, nonexportation agreement, called the Continental Association, had been adopted by the first Continental Congress. Two days later, arrangements had been made for the printing of a congressional journal. A resolution was passed that same day that another Congress would meet on the tenth day of May, unless redress of grievances was made before that date. Philadelphia was recommended again as the best meeting place. John reached home the second week in November; on December 2 the Provincial Congress, sitting in Cambridge, reelected him and his three colleagues to the next Congress, substituting John Hancock for James Bowdoin, who had never been able to attend in the first place.[50]

By January 1775, Abigail was beginning to sound resigned to a more strenuous position regarding Great Britain. As she had written Catharine Macaulay: "Tender plants must bend, but when a Government is grown to strength like some old oak rough with its armed bark it yealds not to the tug, but only nods and turns to sullen state." Abigail spoke also of the "pandoraen Box," and its fatal ingredients, wantonly and cruelly scattered by the British. In another impassioned letter she called her friend Mercy Warren's attention to the "cunning and chicanery" of the writing of the execrable "Massachusettensis," (the pen name of the loyalist lawyer Daniel Leonard), in Margaret Draper's *Massachusetts Gazette and Boston Weekly News-Letter.* * In answer to this "Sly undermining Tool," John had published in the *Boston Gazette,* over a period of twelve weeks, under the signature "Novanglus," a fervent rebuttal.[51]

Point by point, John had fenced with Draper's writer, restating his belief that the destruction of the tea had been just, that the Committees of Correspondence were intended by Providence for great events, that Britain could restore harmony by desisting from taxing the colonies and interfering with their internal concerns. Fundamental to the patriots, he continued, was the principle that all men were by nature equal, and that kings were but the ministers of the people, holding delegated power. As forcefully as he stated his position, John sounded better-humored than his wife: Abigail said she would not think it "unlikely" that "Massachusettensis" received a share of the money sent, according to rumor, to bribe the leaders of the pro-British faction.[52]

By early February, Abigail had committed herself yet again to separation. "The die is cast," she wrote to Mercy Warren the day after she read George III's speech at the opening of Parliament on November 20, published in the *Massachusetts Spy* on February 2, 1775. The King, Abigail ascertained, was determined to execute "the acts passed by the late Parliament, and to Maintain the authority of the Legislature over all his dominions." The reply of the Houses of Commons and Lords showed, as far as she could determine, that the most "wicked and hostile" measures would be pursued against the Americans, without permitting them the opportunity for self-defense. George's speech had left one option to "Friends of Liberty":

*After Richard Draper's death in 1774, his widow Margaret continued as publisher.

to die [the] last British freemen, than bear to live the first of
British Slaves, and this now seems to be all that is left to americans
with unfeigned and penitant suplications to that Being who delights
in the welfare of his creatures, and who we humbly hope will
engage on our side, and who if we must go forth in defence of our
injured and oppressed Country will we hope deliver us from the
hands of our enemies and those that persecute us.

Heaven only knew what was to take place next, but as far as Abigail
was concerned, "The Sword is now our only, yet dreadful alternative,
and the fate of Rome will be renued in Brittain." With prayerful
thought she added that if "the war should rise against us, in this will
we be confident, that the Lord reigneth. Let thy Mercy o Lord be
upon us according as we hope in thee."[53]

Abigail was alone at the time she read the King's speech. With
heart "tremblingly anxious" she indulged herself in the wisp of a
hope that John might bring different news with him from Boston. On
the other hand, she did not want anyone to think she would give up
"one Iota" of their rights and privileges to have the situation al-
leviated, for with "maturest deliberation" she could say that "dreadful as the day would be," she would rather see the sword drawn. She
refused to be entirely pessimistic, and seemed buoyed by her decision, saying, "We know too well the blessings of freedom, to tamely
resign it—and there really seems to be a ray of light breaking thro
the palpable darkness which has for so long a time darkened our
hemisphere and threatened to overwhelm us in one common ruin."
She could not help but hope, with her friend Mercy Warren, for
"more favorable Scenes, and brighter Days."[54]

On April 5, three weeks before John's scheduled departure for
Philadelphia, General Gage had given orders to seize any cannon,
small arms, or military stores secreted by the patriots. Two weeks
elapsed before details were known as to how the British planned to
execute Gage's orders. Then, at 10:00 P.M. the night of April 18,
Joseph Warren charged Paul Revere with the crucial duty of warning
both John Hancock and Sam Adams that eight hundred grenadiers
and light infantry had embarked in long boats on the Charles River
at the foot of the Boston Common, crossed, and were heading toward
Concord on a secret expedition to destroy their stores and capture
both men.[55]

By noon the next day, on the sloping countryside, with its secret
curves and silent thickets, 4,000 worn Americans confronted 1,800

British regulars and triumphed: 73 redcoats were dead, 174 wounded, 26 missing. The Americans counted 49 dead, 39 wounded, 4 missing. The events begun in Concord and decided a few miles beyond, in Lexington, and heralded on that damp spring night by ringing church bells and roaring cannons, would be judged crucial by John Adams. The battle of Lexington, on the nineteenth of April, he said, had changed, with doomful finality, "the Instruments of Warfare from Penn to the Sword."[56]

Abigail, too, sensed "Great Events are most certainly in the womb of futurity." She prayed for the deliverance of the people of Boston as for the children of Israel—not by miracles but by the interposition of heaven in their favor. John had already reached New York City on his way to Philadelphia when she wrote of the desperate plight of family and friends:

> There are but very few who are permitted to come out in a day.
> They delay giving passes, make them wait from hour to hour, and
> their counsels are not two hours together alike. One day they shall
> come out with their Effects, the next Day merchandise are not
> Effects. One day their household furniture is to come out, the next
> only wearing apparel, and the next Pharaohs heart is hardned, and
> he refuseth to hearken unto them and will not let the people go.

Everything was so uncertain; rumors flew about those on the "black list," those implicated in dumping the tea and therefore judged "obnoxious." One such was Benjamin Edes, who was said to have escaped from Boston on May 6 in a small boat, and to have been fired upon, but turned up safe in Braintree, twenty-four hours later.[57]

On May 22, Abigail wrote to Edward Dilly, the London bookseller, regarding some transactions that John had not had time to complete before leaving town. She did not spare him the details of the plight of the Bostonians, or shade her disdain for his countrymen:

> So brutal are they as to take away even to a Bisquit if they find it
> by their inhumane searches, or a little chocolate does not escape
> even tho in the pockets of the distressed women. Those who
> receive the mighty boon of bringing out a little household furniture
> must turn it down in the Street, Exposed to the inclemancy of the
> weather.

But words only faintly described the woes, Abigail continued, especially of men and women with their little ones in tow, following their property as though they were in funeral procession.[58]

As Abigail sat at her writing desk on Sunday, May 21, it was no longer a question of imagining danger; she could hear it, see it, had only to lean out of her window to touch it. The colony's soldiers were thumping the warm spring earth (the meadow was almost fit to mow), responding to drumming, bells, and actual gunfire. She had risen at six that morning; in answer to her worried message she learned that the British troops, about three hundred men, arriving in three sloops and one cutter, had dropped anchor just four miles from her house, just below the Great Hill, and that all was confusion and terror. People from the ironworks had run in terror, and Parson Smith's house had emptied in moments. Aunt Tufts was so distressed that she threw herself into a cart and summoned a boy to drive her off to Bridgewater. Once the colonists, about two thousand strong and crowding the water's edge, realized that the British were in search of hay and bound for Grape Island, not for Germantown or Weymouth, a small band of them jumped on board a sloop and beat the British to the quarry, setting fire to nearly the entire cache, which some thought amounted to eighty tons' worth.[59]

After the Grape Island episode, Abigail seemed resigned; she could only be certain of the uncertainty of the future. "We know not what a day will bring forth, nor what distress one hour may throw us into," she warned John. Until then, in late May, she felt she had been able to maintain a calmness and presence of mind, but now she knew change was imminent. A farmhand, Isaac, was talking of going into the army. Nathan Rice, who she did not believe would be a very hardy soldier, had military prospects in mind, and Mr. Thaxter had already gone; both young lawyers were discouraged by the lean prospects of ever being able to practice. As for the house, ever since the alarms, she could only describe it as a "Scene of confusion," milling with soldiers coming in for lodging, breakfast, supper, and drink, and with weary refugees from Boston hunting asylum for a day or a night or a week. She could only think that John would find it hard to imagine how she was existing:

> Yet to the Houseless child of want
> our doors are open still.
> And tho our portions are but scant
> We give them with good will. [60]

"We must Expect continual allarms, and prepair ourselves for them," was Abigail's stance from here on. How long it would be before she was driven from her "yet quiet cottage" was a guessing matter. It was a strange time. Abigail's mood was a match for the weather, which was very dry—not a rainy day in more than five weeks —with the English grass not expected to yield half as much as the previous year. Yet the fruit was promising, though the caterpillars were innumerable—a nettlesome situation Abigail understood perfectly: "Courage I know we have in abundance, conduct I hope we shall not want, but powder—where shall we get a sufficient supply?"[61]

On June 17, at three o'clock on Saturday morning, cannonfire announced "the day,—perhaps, the decisive day" Abigail had anticipated for weeks. Of Boston's many hills—Copp's Hill, Breed's Hill, Dorchester Hill, Penn's Hill—the British warships chose to fire on the imperfect breastwork thrown up the previous night on the crest of Bunker's Hill. On Sunday, thirty-six hours later, at three in the afternoon, Abigail wrote to John that her "bursting heart must find vent at my pen." She had just heard that their dear friend Dr. Warren had died. A dreadful battle was expected that night; how many had already fallen was unknown. If she found herself unsafe, she had the option of going to her brother-in-law Elihu, who had offered her family part of his house. She could hardly compose herself as she prayed: "The race is not to the swift, nor the battle to the strong, but the God of Israel is he that giveth strength and power unto his people. Trust in him at all times, ye people pour out your hearts before him. God is a refuge for us."[62]

By Tuesday, despite ten thousand rumors "vague and uncertain as the wind," she could not contradict the report on Dr. Warren, the remarkable man whose courage, John said, would have been rash absurdity, had it not been tempered by self-control. The losses on that hottest of summer nights were comparatively few, but this one in particular was almost too much to bear. It was the "lamentable Truth," that the beloved physician, who had once saved young Johnny's fractured forefinger from amputation, had died at the age of thirty-four, his fine clothes soaked with blood, beheaded, according to whispered accounts. A widower, he was the father of four.[63]

With Johnny, on that clear June day of intense heat, Abigail had made the sorrowful climb up the giant slabs of rock to the top of Penn's Hill to stare in horror across the blue bay and into the black, smoking mass that was all that was left of Charlestown. Tears blurred her eyes, but not her memory of the poem by William Collins that she had been teaching Johnny that spring and early summer, as though keeping herself, and her child, in readiness for the tragedy of Warren's death:

> How sleep the Brave who sink to rest,
> by all their Country's wishes blest?
> When Spring with dew'ey fingers cold
> Returns to deck their Hallowed mould
> She their [there] shall dress a sweeter Sod
> Than fancy's feet has ever trod.
> By fairy hands their knell is rung
> By forms unseen their Dirge is sung
> Their [there] Honour comes a pilgrim grey
> To Bless the turf that wraps their Clay
> And freedom shall a while repair
> To dwell a weeping Hermit there. [64]

It was months before Abigail could even resign herself to Warren's death. "We wanted him in the Senate, we want him in his Profession, we want him in the field. We mourn for the citizen, the senator, the physician and the Warriour," she wrote to John on July 5, still brooding over the report, that seemed to confirm that the doctor had been beheaded and savagely dumped into a hole on the battlefield. It was only a year later that Abigail found some peace regarding the "Worthy General Warren," when his body was dug up and carried into Boston, attended by a procession of Masons, prayed over by Dr. Cooper, and praised by the orator Perez Morton. At last, people were reminded of Warren's heroism and the noble cause for which he was martyred, as well as their own sufferings and injuries. The proceedings made Abigail think of a passage in *Julius Caesar*:

> Woe to the Hands that shed this costly blood;
> A curse shall light upon their line;
> Domestick fury, and firce [fierce] civil strife
> Shall cumber all the parts of Britton. [65]

At a time of devastating apprehension and loss, Abigail thought herself "very brave upon the whole," though if danger touched her dwelling, she supposed she would "shuder." Somewhat ambivalent, however, about recognition of her plight, she insisted she would not have John distressed about her, yet bothered to drill him about how much Congress knew about Boston and its sufferings. "Does every Member feel for us? Can they realize what we suffer? And can they believe with what patience and fortitude we endure the conflict—nor," she added, "do we even tremble at the frowns of power."[66]

Abigail had need of support and sympathy. Her problems were multiple, both with and without solutions. She and John both suffered from minor complaints about their health. John's eyes were worrisome; the middle finger of Abigail's right hand was so sore she could not hold her pen for three weeks. Nor was there comfort to be found at Weymouth; her father's hurt expression told the sad story of his family birthplace, Charlestown, consumed by fire. Housing was another problem. Abigail's lone tenant would not give up his quarters, though she asked him to do so "handsomely," that she might move a dispossessed friend and his family in with her. She faced a grain shortage and the possible disappearance of coffee, sugar, and pepper. Pins and needles were in pressing demand but short supply, and were essential if stocking weaving was to continue.[67]

Only when Abigail referred to the children did she seem able, at this time, to lighten the burden of her news. Abigail assured John that the children wished to see their father, and that Charles asked, whenever she received mail from Philadelphia, "Mar, what is it any good news?" And "Who is for us and who against us?" was the habitual inquiry. John would laugh, she said, to see the children run at the sight of his letters—"like chickens for a crumb, when the Hen clucks."[68]

John, keenly aware of the trials of Boston, could not have been surprised by his children's involvement. They lived from hour to suspenseful hour; their household was thick with strangers, plans and plots, hearsay and heresies, their bodies tense from the din of cannonfire ripping the neighboring sky. Besides, their mother was like a beacon in her self-appointed role of co-delegate, and they had no choice but to bask in the light that radiated from her and attracted news of the cause of the colonists.[69]

In his letter of June 10, John had explained that "in Congress We are bound to secrecy: But, under the Rose, I believe, that ten thousand Men will be maintained in the Massachusetts, and five thousand in New York at the Continental Expence."[70]

The day after receiving this news, Abigail wrote two letters. One, to James Bowdoin, was a general roundup of several of John's past letters, in which she informed Bowdoin

that the Congress are determined to support the Massachusetts—
that there is a good Spirit among them, and that they have an
amazing Field of Business before them—that it is extensive,
complicated and hazardous, but their Unanimity is as great as
before—that they have a Number of new and ingenious Members—
that the military Spirit which runs thro' the Continent is truly
amazing. The City of Philadelphia turns out 2000 Men every Day.
Mr. Dickinson is a Coll., Mr. Reed a Lt. Coll., Mr. Mifflin a
Major.[71]

The same day Abigail wrote to Mr. Bowdoin, she also sent off a
letter to John. She did not specifically mention passing on the critical
information gathered "under the Rose," but took care to note Mr.
Bowdoin's being "very inquisitive of every person with regard to the
times," and how he begged her to let him know "of the first intelligence" she received from John. Perhaps she justified her confidences
to Bowdoin with the thought the poor gentleman was so low that she
was sure he was "hastning to an house not made with Hands."[72]

One other public responsibility shouldered by Abigail—this one not
assumed but rather imposed in recognition of John's official position
—was that of semiofficial hostess. In this role, Abigail said she was
dedicated to "receive and entertain in the best Maner I am capable
of" gentlemen who had generously preferred their service to the
army, or to the government in general. One who fit this description
admirably, and who had intrigued her for some time, was an army
officer, Colonel George Washington. His "Experience and Abilities
in military Matters" John had mentioned to her in late May, and he
believed Washington would be of "much use" to Congress.[73]

Not quite a month later he had written again to tell her that Congress had made the choice on June 15, 1775, of the "modest and
virtuous, the amiable, generous and brave" George Washington to
be the General of the American Army, and that he was to repair as
soon as possible to the camp in Boston. John was impressed by
Washington's "reticence," and the humility with which he had accepted his nomination as Commander-in-Chief, allowing that he
thought himself launched into a wide and extensive field "too boundless" for his abilities and "far, very far" beyond his experience.[74]

Subsequently, Abigail assured John that both Washington's promotion to commanding general and that of Charles Lee to major
general gave "universal satisfaction." Soon after the pair's arrival in

Boston she was able to tell John that she was nothing less than "struck with General Washington. You had prepaired me to entertain a favorable opinion of him, but I thought the one half was not told me. Dignity with ease, and complacency, the Gentleman and Soldier look agreeably blended in him. Modesty marks every line and feture of his face." Lines of John Dryden "instantly" occurred to her on meeting the stately forty-three-year-old Virginian:

> *Mark his Majestick fabrick! he's a temple*
> *Sacred by birth, and built by hands divine*
> *His Souls the Deity that lodges there.*
> *Nor is the pile unworthy of the God.* [75]

General Lee's fate, at Abigail's hands, was less splendid. Like a "careless hardy Veteran," his appearance brought to her mind his namesake Charles XII, King of Sweden: "The Elegance of his pen far exceeds that of his person."[76]

On the subject of pens, and in answer to John's regrets over their disuse by friends, Abigail asked, "May not I in my turn make complaints?" Without stopping for an answer, she proceeded to tell him just where his letters fell short.

All the Letters I receive from you seem to be wrote in so much haste, that they scarcely leave room for a social feeling. They let me know that you exist, but some of them contain scarcely six lines. I want some sentimental Effusions of the Heart. I am sure you are not destitute of them or are they all absorbed in the great publick. Much is due to that I know, but being part of the whole I lay claim to a Larger Share than I have had. You used to be more communicative a Sundays. I always loved a Sabeth days letter, for then you had a greater command of your time—but hush to all complaints.[77]

Abigail was as good as her admonition. It was mid-July, and possibly because of plentiful showers, the prospect of Indian corn and English grain gave cause for optimism. "Be not afraid," Abigail wrote, "ye beasts of the field, for the pastures of the Wilderness do spring, the Tree beareth her fruit, the vine and the olive yeald their increase." Everything might yet be perfect; "Every thing at present looks blooming," she promised John. Everything depended on the answer to a prayer: "O that peace would once more extend her olive Branch."[78]

Intellectually, Abigail puzzled over the fact that she had little reason to sound as hopeful as she did, except perhaps that she was hopeful by instinct. As she explained to Mercy Warren, who kindly inquired about her health:

I sometimes wonder at my-self, and fear least a degree of stupidity or insensibility should possess my mind in these calamitous times or I could not feel so tranquil amidst such scenes, and yet I cannot charge myself with an unfealing Heart. I pitty, commisirate and as far as my ability reaches feel ready and desirous to releave my fellow creatures under their distresses. But I am not naturally (tis no virtue acquired in me) of that rastless anxious disposition.[79]

If she was completely honest with herself, Abigail might have attributed her "good flow of spirits" to "the most Leasurely and therefore the most Sentimental" letter Abigail had received in a while, In return, Abigail promised on July 25 to take back her complaints if only John would continue his "obliging favours" whenever time would allow. Among other things, John had called her a "Heroine" and described her soul "as pure, as benevolent, as virtuous and pious," He had also said he hoped it would not be more than a month before he was able to return to Braintree.[80]

Ten Thousand Difficulties

The morning of August 11, 1775 was a time to sing of "Mercies and judgments," a mixture of joy and grief. It marked John's return after four months' absence, and the death of his brother Elihu, after a week's suffering from dysentery. By September Abigail was swept with melancholy—John had begun his journey back to Philadelphia on a rain-cleansed August 27 to participate in a third Congress—and she could only write what she called "a bill of Mortality." Eight neighbors had been buried in one week alone; some poor parents mourned the loss of three, four, and five children; some families were stripped of every member. Tommy lay ill; she had sent Charles and Johnny out of the house in hope they would remain free of disease. Dr. Tufts was tending to sixty or seventy cases of distemper in Weymouth; four Sabbaths had passed without any meeting because their minister, Reverend Wibird, was so ill he could hardly walk a step.[1]

Abigail was almost apologetic about her "doleful tale." Characteristically, she studied the remotest corners of her mind and heart, trying reason as well as faith for answers that might help her govern her emotions. Momentarily, her grip was tenuous. If it weren't for the "tender connections" that bound her, would she wish to live on? Were she to lose those she loved, could she relish life any longer? Or wish to be "Wedded to the World?" Almost immediately, as though realizing the futile indulgence of questioning her lot, she reworked her thoughts. She talked now about self-deception and her failure to recognize that her path was not chosen but forever ordained, and that "To Bear and Suffer is our portion here." Once again she affirmed that "Unto him who mounts the Whirlwind and directs the Storm I will cheerfully leave the ordering of my lot, and whether adverse or prosperous Days should be my future portion I will trust in his right Hand to lead me safely thro, and after a short rotation of Events fix me in a state immutable and happy."[2]

Abigail, supplicant that she seemed, sincere as she professed her readiness to be led, also proposed very definitely to meet her destiny on her own two feet. Being devout did not mean being devoid of responsibility and motivation. She defined her role staunchly in words that might come to haunt her in view of her mother's illness: "God helps them that help themselves as King Richard said and if we can obtain the divine aid by our own virtue, fortitude and persever-ance we may be sure of releaf."[3]

On September 25, Abigail wrote John that "Woe follows Woe and one affliction treads upon the heal of an other." She had not felt well earlier, was exhausted from caring for Tommy, and welcomed her mother's daily visits to both of them. Now her mother lay ill, and was not expected to live. Abigail commuted between two beds, the one in her own home holding Patty, her servant, whom Abigail thought such a "putrid mass" that it was scarcely possible to take care of her, and the other, that of her own mother, with whom she stayed for twelve hours at a time. She could only think that until now she had tasted a small portion of the "Bitter Cup," in comparison with many others. But presently, she feared, "a large draught" was being pre-pared for her. She prayed to be able to submit "with patience and resignation to the rod and him who had appointed it, knowing it is directed by unerring wisdom." She reminded herself that the conso-lations of religion were the only "sure comforters in the day of affliction."[4]

On the morning of October 1, Abigail brought her mother tea, raised her head so that she might swallow a few drops, heard her gasp, saw her look up at her—"It was the eagerness of a last look" —and recognized "the last sad silence of a Friend." Elizabeth Smith died at five o'clock that afternoon; by chance, it was the communion day on which Reverend Smith was welcoming his granddaughter, Betsy Cranch, into the church. "I know I wound your Heart," Abigail wrote John, after pouring out her grief. "Ought I to give relief to my own by paining yours?" she worried.[5]

There seemed to be no choice. Her heart would burst if she could not give vent to her feelings. Having witnessed more than one death, she explained, "My Heart is made tender by repeated affliction. It never was a hard Heart. The death of Patty came very near me, having lived four years with me, under my care." Responsibility for others was a great trust. Daily she felt the weight and importance of it, she said, and of her own inability to cope. She wished more assistance from her "dearest Friend," regretting the perilous times that swallowed him up. She pleaded for his understanding: "My pen is always freer than my tongue. I have wrote many things to you that I suppose I never could have talk'd."[6]

John's response to Abigail was all she could have hoped for, considering their separation. His letters were a comfort to her "wounded Heart," as well as a tender appreciation of her woes: "If I could write as well as you, my sorrows would be as eloquent as yours," he told her, "but upon my Word I cannot."[7]

John's appreciation of Elizabeth Smith, this "valuable ancestor," was astonishingly sensitive. His affectionate criticism of her left no doubt as to his expectations of the women he respected—and where Mrs. Smith fell short of them—but in no way tempered his feeling that her death was a loss not only to Abigail but to himself and to their children. In a special letter of condolence to Nabby, he reminded his daughter that Grandmother Smith had been an excellent instructress to her, a bright example of every amiable virtue. Her piety and benevolence, her charity, prudence, patience, and wisdom, would have been, if it had pleased God to spare her life, an admirable model for Nabby to copy. Now he hoped Nabby would remember a great deal of her grandmother's advice, and be careful to heed it. Also, he urged her to be more attentive than ever to the instructions and examples of her mother and her aunts. They would give her assistance in forming her heart to "goodness" and her mind to "useful knowledge," as well as to those other accomplishments that were "peculiarly necessary and ornamental" in her sex.[8]

John's letter to Tommy, the only one who did not attend his grandmother's funeral, was firmer in tone, though kind. John was glad that Tommy was recovered from his illness, hopeful that he would imitate his grandmother's goodness, and cautionary that he be dutiful and obedient. The ultimate message, however, had more to do with John Adams than with Grandmother Smith: Tommy was to mind his books, because "it is only from your Books and the kind Instructions of your Parents that you can expect to be useful in the World."[9]

Meanwhile, Abigail wrote freely to John about her mother, the stoic woman who had neither smiled nor wept during her illness, though she had continued to dispense advice "where she thought it necessary." Abigail was preoccupied with memories of her mother's kindness and tenderness, her watchfulness in Abigail's infant years, her great care and "assiduity" in instilling religious principals into her children early on. This example, which Abigail followed with obvious faithfulness in rearing her own children, had probably been shaped even a generation earlier. In a rush of nostalgia, Abigail vigorously affirmed John's belief in parental and grandparental powers:

> The instructions of my own Grandmamma are as fresh upon my mind this day as any I ever received from my own parents and made as lasting and powerful impressions. Every virtuous example has powerfull impressions in early youth. Many years of vice and vicious examples do not erase from the mind seeds sown in early life. They take a deep root, and tho often crop'd will spring again.[10]

Although when he wrote to his children on the subject of Grandmother Smith he showed only deep regard and affection for her, it was to Abigail that John delicately broached the subject of what was, in his opinion, his mother-in-law's single failing. The "Thing" he was talking about was public service, and he openly solicited Abigail's support for the "exact values" that would be thought of as "distinctly branding" future generations of Adamses. With regard to her mother, John asked Abigail:

> Were not her Talents, and Virtues too much confined, to private, social and domestic Life. My Opinion of the Duties of Religion and Morality, comprehends a very extensive Connection with society at large, and the great Interest of the public. Does not natural Morality, and much more Christian Benevolence, make it our indispensible Duty to lay ourselves out, to serve our fellow Creatures to the Utmost of our Power, in promoting and supporting those great Political Systems, and general Regulations upon which the Happiness of Multitudes depends.[11]

The rest of John's letter extended the most thoughtful possible welcome to women to participate in the world at large. Remarkably, John harbored aspirations for women that would not be thought of, let alone achieved, for generations. He envisioned a boundless horizon, and he told Abigail so exactly:

The Benevolence, Charity, Capacity and Industry which exerted in private Life, would make a family, a Parish or a Town Happy, employed upon a larger Scale, in Support of the great Principals of Virtue and Freedom of political Regulations might secure whole Nations and Generations from Misery, Want and Contempt.

He did not distinguish between male or female when he concluded that "public Virtues, and political Qualities therefore should be incessantly cherished in our Children."[12]

By deep autumn, Abigail's immediate sadness was blunted slightly, faded into resignation and the feeling that "Life is a poor play." She mourned for her mother, for Patty, for her brother-in-law Elihu and his baby, dead six weeks after her father, and for countless others; she was also worried that both her sisters were sickly. Letters from John offered some diverting moments, but it was an invitation to dine with Dr. Benjamin Franklin on October 27 that actually extracted the "nun" from her cloister, as she described her situation. It also allowed her to observe the highly regarded statesman firsthand—and to enlist him as a courier of her letters to John. Abigail's interest in Franklin was long-standing and, judging from her report of their first meeting, it would seem improbable that anything but goodwill could ever mark the relationship between her or John and the elder statesman whom Abigail had been taught to venerate, she said, from infancy.[13]

The "ingenious and worthy Dr. Franklin," after ten years in England, had sailed for America on the Pennsylvania packet, docking in Philadelphia on May 5, 1775. Not three weeks later, Abigail was writing of how Franklin's arrival afforded reason to "rejoice greatly," as he must certainly be able to inform "very particuliarly" of the situation in England. As Franklin had been chosen a delegate to the Second Continental Congress one day after his arrival in Philadelphia, Abigail must have assumed that John and he would meet, and that John would learn some vital news to share with her. Her instructions in this regard were specific: "Be as particuliar as you may, when you write—every one here abouts comes to me to hear what accounts I have."[14]

By July, when she had received no answer, Abigail nudged John: "You scarcely make mention of Dr. Franklin. Surely he must be a valuable member." This time, John tried to satisfy Abigail's curiosity. "You have more than once in your Letters mentioned Dr. Franklin," he wrote on July 23, "and in one intimated a Desire that I should write you something concerning him." Apparently with a great deal of thought, John crafted a painstakingly judicious portrait:

> Dr. Franklin has been very constant in his Attendance on Congress from the Beginning. His Conduct has been composed and grave and in the Opinion of many Gentlemen very reserved. He has not assumed any Thing, nor affected to take the lead; but has seemed to choose that the Congress should pursue their own Principles and sentiments and adopt their own Plans: Yet he has not been backward: has been very useful, on many occasions, and discovered a Disposition entirely American. He does not hesitate at our boldest Measures, but rather seems to think us, too irresolute, and backward. He thinks us at present in an odd State, neither in Peace nor War, neither dependent nor independent. But he thinks that We shall soon assume a Character more decisive.[15]

In other words, Franklin was optimistic about America's future, in John's opinion. He was encouraging the colonists to think they had the power of preserving themselves—even if they should be driven to the "disagreeable" necessity of assuming total independence and setting up a separate state. And, while Franklin could not be credited with leadership in the implementation of what was to happen, he could certainly be counted as an advocate of the colonists' cause. The subject of credit was apparently of vital concern to John; repeatedly he sought to analyze, with studious accuracy, precisely how much was owed Franklin.

> The people of England, have thought that the Opposition in America, was wholly owing to Dr. Franklin: and I suppose their scribblers will attribute the Temper, and Proceedings of this Congress to him: but there cannot be a greater Mistake. He has had but little share farther than to cooperate and assist. He is however a great and good Man. I wish his Colleagues from this City were all like him, particularly one, whose Abilities and Virtues, formerly trumpeted so much in America, have been found wanting.[16]

By November 5, Abigail could speak for herself on the subject of Franklin—he called on her at her home; they dined together at Colonel Quincy's—and add some flattering highlights to John's cameo. Innocent of the future, fretful, sometimes bitter, often infuriated reactions to the elder statesman's politics, morals, fresh-air theories,

French grammar, French friendships, and the behavior of his son and grandson, Abigail was full of praise for Franklin:

> I found him social, but not talkative, and when he spoke something usefull droped from his Tongue; he was grave, yet pleasant, and affable. —You know I make some pretensions to physiognomy and I thought I could read in his countenance the Virtues of his Heart, among which patriotism shined in its full Lustre—and with that is blended every virtue of a christian, for a true patriot must be a religious Man.[17]

Franklin must have appealed to Abigail for purely personal reasons. She seemed quite ready to accept his invitation to spend the winter in Philadelphia—she was miserably lonely—unless John should return to Braintree. In response, John said he hoped to be excused from going to Philadelphia again, at least until others had taken their turns. In any case, he would never go without her, if he could persuade her to come with him. He even elaborated: "Whom God has joined together ought not to be put asunder so long with their own Consent." He proposed that Abigail's father and her sister Betsy keep their house in Braintree, and that she bring Johnny with her—both to "have" the smallpox in Philadelphia, that is, to be inoculated against the disease—and he promised her, "We will be as happy, as Mr. Hancock and his Lady."[18]

For the time being, however, John seemed to be writing only to placate Abigail. He had no precise "Thoughts of it," and he wrote telling her as much on December 3. Affairs were in a critical state and "important Steps" were being taken every day. John's plans were not surprising to Abigail. Colonel Warren had already "damp'd" her spirits by telling her that John's stay had been prolonged. Physically she was not in the best of condition, either. Jaundice, rheumatism, and a violent cold from which she had suffered late in November had been relieved only after her taking a "puke." She was hardly alone with her ailments. She felt that the "great and incessant" rains all that autumn might have occasioned the present illnesses that felled many others. It was now Abigail's hope that the frigid weather ("as cold as January") and the snowfall that had followed the rains would purify the air. Abigail also lamented the loss of hundreds of bushels of apples, spoiled by the unseasonable weather, that would cost her family alone five barrels' worth of cider.[19]

Having tabulated her woes in some detail, and vented her disappointment that John would not be joining her, Abigail almost abruptly disallowed another moment of complaint or regret. "Tis in vain to repine," she sighed, hoping the public would "reap what I sacrifice." She knew that "mighty things were fabricating," and it was to those things that she now turned her attention.[20]

Abigail's correspondence with John in the last days of 1775 and the spring of 1776 delineates with amazing intensity the agonizing issues crucial to the construction of what she called the "Great Empire." Her decision, arrived at with the greatest deliberation possible, was absolutely clear-cut. She might have been pounding her fist on her desk as she wrote. As staunch a "delegate" as America would ever nurture, her farewell to England was unequivocal: "Let us separate, they are unworthy to be our Breathren. Let us renounce them and instead of suplications as formerly for their prosperity and happiness, Let us beseach the almighty to blast their counsels and bring to Nought all their devices."[21]

Her problem was not with the decision to reach for Independence, but how to arrive at this desperately desired goal with thought and in peaceful order. In her opinion, "ten thousand Difficulties" were bound to arise; the reins of government had been slackened for so long she feared the people would not quietly submit to the restraints necessary for the peace and security of the community. Intermittently, consoling herself that "great difficulties may be surmounted, by patience and perseverance," she worried that "if we separate from Brittain, what Code of Laws will be established. How shall we be governed so as to retain our Liberties? Can any government be free which is not administered by general stated Laws? Who shall frame these Laws? Who will give them force and energy?"[22]

Abigail, wandering about her "Labyrinth of perplexities," was preoccupied not only with the form of government, but just as much with the form of the governors. In one of her most anxious moments of skepticism, she said she was more and more convinced that man was a dangerous creature and that power, whether vested in many or few, was "ever grasping." She had reached the opinion, she continued, that "great fish swallow up the small," and that he who most championed the rights of the people, when vested with power, was as eager after the prerogatives of government. As for those who favored ancient customs and regulations, they made her more anxious for the fate of the monarchy or democracy, or whatever was to take place. Witheringly, she dismissed these people as "a little of the Spanel kind. Tho so often spurned still to fawn argues a meanness of Spirit that as an individual I disclaim, and would rather endure any hardships than submit to it."[23]

In her exhaustive examination of the components of the future "Empire," Abigail was not about to overlook economic as well as legislative questions. "As I have been desired to mention to you some things I shall not omit them," she wrote John, by way of attracting his attention to her thoughts about a tax on liquor. As it was, with Massachusetts paying the tax—while the other colonies paid little or none—trade was drawn away from her state. And though she foresaw objections to her plan, she thought all the colonies ought to be taxed, not only in the interests of fairer trade, but because, she said, "too frequent use of Spirit endangers the well being of Society."[24]

Another issue, called to John's attention by Abigail, concerned the loss of silver and gold that was poured into the West Indies in payment for molasses, coffee, sugar, and other commodities. As a result of this daily occurrence, Abigail could tell John that a dollar in silver was a great rarity, and that traders would give a hundred pounds of paper for ninety of silver, or about that proportion. Abigail's remedy was ingenuous: "If any trade is alloud to the West Indias would it not be better to carry some commodity of our own produce in exchange?"[25]

Communication between Abigail and John was by no means one-sided at this time. His wish was equal to hers to share a "compleat History from the Beginning to the End of the Journey." What he had no time to write about, he promised to tell her at a future time. Guarded though he was—"Pimps destroy all freedom of Correspondence," he wrote—he seemed, nevertheless, to write amply about the climate, food, characters, and work he encountered in Philadelphia. "No Mortal Tale could equal it," he insisted, mincing no words about "the Fidgets, the Whims, the Caprice, the Vanity, the Superstition, the Irritability of some of us. . . ."[26]

In spite of the complexities of the gathered assembly, John was intrigued from the beginning by such prospects as establishing monetary and postal systems, and consideration of Dr. Franklin's draft of the "Articles of Confederation and Perpetual Union." Alternately burdened and inspired, John defined for Abigail the breathtaking scope of the work ahead:

> The Business I have had upon my Mind has been as great and important as can be intrusted to [One] Man, and the Difficulty and Intricacy of it is prodigious. When 50 or 60 Men have a Constitution to form for a great Empire, at the same Time that they have a Country of fifteen hundred Miles extent to fortify, Millions to arm and train, a Naval Power to begin, an extensive Commerce to regulate, numerous Tribes of Indians to negotiate with, a standing Army of Twenty seven Thousand Men to raise, pay victual and officer, I really shall pity 50 or 60 Men.[27]

After an unexpected visit home—contrary to his earlier word, he had requested leave on December 8 because he was "worn down with long and uninterrupted Labour"—John took his seat in Congress two months later, on Friday, February 9. Once again the established routine was observed, with John packing newspapers and pamphlets along with his letters, which were more reticent and less frequent, but, if anything, more eagerly sought by Abigail. On February 18, 1776, he wrote of sending her a recently published pamphlet he thought written in "Vindication of Doctrines" to which they were both committed. The pamphlet, Thomas Paine's *Common Sense: Addressed to the Inhabitants of America,* published anonymously, was significant to Abigail and John on several counts.[28]

At the time of the publication of *Common Sense,* on January 10, 1776, Independence was still a matter of theory and even dispute, though John saw "no Prospect, no Probability no Possibility" for an alternative. He could only despise credulous minds that expected an honorable peace. He detested the hypocritical hearts, he said, that pretended to expect it, when in truth they did not. The pamphlet, which included fifty pages of "simple facts, plain arguments, and common sense," according to its author—"conceived to challenge even the warmest advocate of reconciliation to show a single advantage that America could reap by being connected with Great Britain" —added another block of votes, or would when it achieved its full readership, to the cause of Independence.[29]

Abigail agreed. She was much obliged for the pamphlet, though its author was unknown to her at the time. It was highly prized around Boston, she said, and carried conviction wherever it was read, and she tried to spread it around as much as she could. "Everyone assents to the weighty truths it contains," she said, and she could only wish it could gain credit enough in John's assembly, to be "carried speadily into Execution." Her personal assessment was a complete endorsement:

> I am charmed with the Sentiments of Common Sense; and wonder how an honest Heart, one who wishes the welfare of their country, and the happiness of posterity can hesitate one moment at adopting them; I want to know how those Sentiments are received in Congress? I dare say their would be no difficulty in procuring a vote and instructions from all the Assemblies in New England for independancy. I most sincerely wish that now in the Lucky Minuet it might be done.[30]

A few weeks later, on March 19, John answered Abigail's query on how Congress felt about *Common Sense.*

> Sensible Men think there are some Whims, some Sophisms, some artful Addresses to superstitious Notions, some keen attempts upon the Passions, in this Pamphlet. But all agree there is a great deal of good sense, delivered in a clear, simple, concise and nervous Style. . . . His Sentiments of the Abilities of America, and of the Difficulty of a Reconciliation with G.B. are generally approved. But his Notions, and Plans of Continental Government are not much applauded. Indeed this Writer has a better Hand at pulling down than building.[31]

John added one other stunning bit of information to his provocative appraisal—there were many who thought *he* was the author of the pamphlet, an opinion he could not accept as a compliment. While he could not have written anything in so "manly and striking a style," he flattered himself, he said, that he should have made a "more respectable figure as an Architect." And further, the writer seemed to him to have "very inadequate Ideas of what is proper and necessary to be done, in order to form Constitutions for single Colonies, as well as a great Model of Union for the whole."[32]

For the time being, John's differences with the author of *Common Sense,* the Englishman Thomas Paine, were entirely intellectual. Paine, who would be known variously as "pamphleteer laureate" of America, propagandist, opportunist, meddler, and gadfly, was introduced to the colonies by Benjamin Franklin as an "ingenious worthy young man"; his recognition by Thomas Jefferson would one day imperil the latter's friendship with John, and therefore with Abigail.

A Quaker, a student of Newtonian science, the son of a corset maker, Paine was said by the painter John Trumbull to be a dull companion until after a bottle, which helped him talk, to everyone's surprise, like an "oracle."[33]

The complexities of Thomas Paine's personality and contribution were, however, for the spring of 1776, future history. But John was stirred to write an anonymous reply, called *Thoughts on Government,* to what he thought were Paine's naïve notions about prospective new governments in America. *Thoughts* (published in Philadelphia by John Dunlap on April 22, 1776), synthesized John's lengthy studies of British law, of the principles of Aristotle and Plato, of Livy and Cicero, of Sidney, Harrington, and Locke. It concluded that all men by nature were equal, that kings had only delegated authority. *Thoughts* concentrated on the goals of American Independence as John saw them: "The happiness of society is the end of government . . . the happiness of the individual is the end of man . . . the form of government which communicates ease, comfort, security, or in one word, happiness, to the greatest number of persons, and in the greatest degree is the best. . . ." As a representative assembly, John envisioned one "in a miniature an exact portrait of the people at large. It should think, feel, reason, and act like them."[34]

On May 9, Abigail commented on *Thoughts,* which she had received two days before its publication date.

> Upon reading it I some how or other felt an uncommon affection for it; I could not help thinking it was a near relation of a very intimate Friend of mine. If I am mistaken in its descent, I know it has a near affinity to the Sentiments of that person, and tho I cannot pretend to be an adept in the art of Government; yet it looks rational that a Government of Good Laws well administered should carry with them the fairest prospect of happiness to a community, as well as to individuals.[35]

By the end of May, in response to Abigail, John maintained a modest or perhaps apologetic stance on the subject of *Thoughts.* It was best to say little about it, he cautioned Abigail. It was a "hasty hurried Thing of no great Consequence, calculated for a Meridian at a great Distance from N. England." It had one merit that he had to acknowledge: if it had done no good, it would do no harm, he said, and did accomplish something. It set people thinking. Since the publication of the letter, the "Manufactory of Governments" had been as much talked of "as that of salt Petre was before."[36]

In the third week of February 1776, Abigail explained to John that she had not written because she had nothing worth saying. Except for the burning of some houses on Dorchester Neck, it had been a "dead calm of dull repose." It was true that preparations were increasing, that something great, something "terible" was predicted daily. On Saturday evening, March 2, she seemed almost despondent: "It has been said to morrow and to morrow for this month, but when the dreadful to morrow will be I know not." She had to stop writing at this point; her house was shaking. She ran to her door to learn from a passerby that the army had begun to fire, and the remaining militia was ordered to report within forty-eight hours. There was no sleep for Abigail that night. And if there was none for her, free of guilt for whatever was to happen—and she did presume that something would take place—she could hardly think that the "misirible wretches," the "procurers of this Dreadfull Scene," would rest easy, burdened with the "load of guilt" they bore upon their souls.[37]

That Saturday night Abigail's pen kept pace with the cannonfire, as did her heartbeat, she assured John. Sunday was fairly quiet, but she was apprehensive. On Monday, the militia marched past her house at 3 P.M. (though they did not have to report until 8 P.M.), fortified with three days' provisions. She had climbed the giant slabs of stone to the top of Penn's Hill to look across the harbor, awed by the meaning of the evening's sights and sounds of shells and cannon, meant to harass the enemy and divert their attention from the plans to fortify Dorchester Neck. "The sound I think is one of the Grandest in Nature and is of the true Species of the Sublime. Tis now an incessant Roar. But O the fatal Ideas which are connected with the sound. How many of our dear country men must fall?"[38]

What happened to Dorchester Hill mattered crucially. The only hill not fortified by the British, it was mounted with cannon that General Knox and his men had hauled hundreds of miles, over ice and snow and frozen rivers, 43 cannon and 16 mortars, 5,500 pounds in all, from Fort Ticonderoga. There was hope that the British, who had made Bunker's Hill impregnable, would be vanquished—a hope miraculously fulfilled, with the evening's help of a wild storm. By six o'clock on Tuesday morning, March 5, all was quiet, and Dorchester Hill was considered the colony's once more.[39]

By Sunday, March 17, Abigail finally had a subject "worth writing upon." She proudly informed John of movements among the "Ministerial Troops," and that General William Howe, possibly sensing he had been outmaneuvered, thought Boston's troops had done more work in one night than the British had done in three months. She did not think this a bit of exaggeration, considering that two forts and long breastworks had sprung up almost instantly, besides a number of barracks, and that in the dark, foggy evening, an estimated four thousand men had dedicated themselves to backbreaking work with "good Hearts."[40]

The enemy was quitting at last, and Abigail thought the American generals could say with Caesar, "veni vidi et vici." Monday, March 18, was a fine, quiet night—no alarms, no cannons—an ideal time to mull things over. Abigail was frankly amazed by General Howe's decision, on March 7, to evacuate Boston, leaving behind such a harbor, such fortifications, such entrenchments. Most of all, she could not comprehend his reason for leaving the Americans in "peaceable" possession of a town that hadn't cost them a drop, let alone the river, of the blood they had anticipated losing. By March 26, Howe, all his troops, and 1,000 Loyalists would set sail for Halifax. "Shurely it is the Lords doing and it is Marvelous in our Eyes," she said contentedly. "Every foot of Ground which they obtain now they must fight for, and may they purchase it at a Bunker Hill price," she told John.[41]

Abigail confronted the changing aspect of the war with guarded elation. She was relieved that Boston was not destroyed, and hoped it would be so secured and guarded as to baffle all future attempts against it. Still, she did not see that the enemy quitting Boston was the solution to the problem; rather, "tis only lifting the burden from one shoulder to the other which perhaps is less able or less willing to support it." She sensed some "very important Crisis" near at hand:

> Perhaps providence see's it necessary in order to answer important ends and designs that the Seat of War should be changed from this to the Southern colonies that each may have a proper sympathy for the others, and unite in a separation. The Refuge of the Believer amidst all the afflictive dispensations of providence, is that the Lord Reigneth, and that he can restrain the Arm of Man.[42]

Just two weeks made the most extraordinary difference in Abigail's outlook. Like a butterfly freed from an intolerable cocoon, on winged spirits, Abigail soared to heights of optimism at which she could not help but marvel. "I feel a gaieti de Coar [*sic*] to which before I was a stranger," she said, almost bemused by her findings that the sun looked brighter to her, birds sang more melodiously, nature put on a more "cheerful countanance." She felt a temporary peace with the world and even a tentative sense of security—as though she and all those about her "might sit under our own vine and eat the good of the land." It had all been so different under the British, she wrote: "We knew not then whether we could plant or sow with safety, whether when we had toild we could reap the fruits of our own industry, whether we could rest in our own Cottages, or whether we should not be driven from the sea coasts to seek shelter in the wilderness. . . ."[43]

Under the now more promising circumstances, Abigail could think about reclaiming the house in Boston. Because she was afraid of smallpox, she sent someone else to inspect it. To her relief, she learned it was very dirty but not damaged, the way General John Burgoyne, that man of "dark" designs and "Horrible wickedness," had left Samuel Quincy's house. There, it was reported by a neighbor, mahogany tables had been ruined by hacking raw meat on their surfaces, and superb damask curtains and cushions had been exposed to the rain as if they had no value at all. Abigail, elated at the prospect of retrieving her household, regarded it as a new acquisition that she could not have realistically valued at a single shilling just weeks before, and could, "with pleasure," have seen it go up in flames in the colony's cause.[44]

Also in the interests of the cause, Abigail continued to make soap, manufacture clothing for her family ("which would else be naked"), and considered experimenting with saltpeter. She had recently seen a small manuscript describing the proportions for the various sorts of powder fit for cannon, small arms, and pistols, and would have it transcribed, she wrote to John, if it was of any "Service" down his way. Though it seemed at times as if all of Abigail's energies were confined to practical and immediate issues, such was hardly the case.[45]

Abigail remained consistent in her pursuit of Independence; her bold concept of its horizons was singular. By March 31, 1776, in a letter to John, she had launched, unwittingly, the timeless campaign for women's rights. Accustomed to John's "indulgence," she had always written truthfully her thoughts about people, speeches—"tis a heavy unelegant verbose performance," she reported about one that did not strike her fancy at all—and places. "Tis a liberty I take with you," she admitted to John. Risking his finding her "saucy," Abigail proceeded:

> I long to hear that you have declared an independency—and by the way in the new Code of Laws which I suppose it will be necessary for you to make I desire you would Remember the Ladies, and be more generous and favourable to them than your ancestors. Do not put such unlimited power into the hands of the Husbands. Remember all Men would be tyrants if they could. If perticuliar care and attention is not paid to the Ladies we are determined to foment a Rebelion, and will not hold ourselves bound by any Laws in which we have no voice, or Representation. . . . That your Sex are Naturally Tyrannical is a Truth so thoroughly established as to admit of no dispute, but such of you as wish to be happy willingly give up the harsh title of Master for the more tender and endearing one of Friend. Why then, not put it out of the power of the vicious and the Lawless to use us with cruelty and indignity with impunity. Men of Sense in all Ages abhor those customs which treat us only as the vassals of your sex. Regard us then as Beings placed by providence under your protection and in immitation of the Supreme Being make use of that power only for our happiness.[46]

The breadth of Abigail's concept was undoubtedly enhanced by the mounting possibilities of its realization. Still, the subject was of continuing interest to her, and she had already alerted John to the universality of her views of independence. She had written to him in September, 1774, of a cumbersome situation in which Negroes agreed to fight for the Governor if he would arm them and then liberate them if his side won. "You know my mind upon this Subject," she had said. "I wish most sincerely there was not a slave in the province. It allways appeared a most iniquitious Scheme to me—fight ourselves for what we are daily robbing and plundering from those who have as good a right to freedom as we have.[47]

Again, in the summer of 1775, Abigail intimated a sense of deprivation regarding the subject of Independence, but this time in a highly personal way. She and her sister, Mary Cranch, had driven their chaise eleven miles to Dedham to hear the Reverend Jason Haven, and to spend time with Mrs. Samuel Adams. In reporting the pleasant

events of July 25, Abigail referred to Mrs. Adams as her "name sake
and Sister Delegate," living with "patience, perseverance and fortitude" in a little country cottage. Somewhat defensively, Abigail explained the honorific she conferred on Elizabeth Adams: "Why
should we not assume your titles when we give you up our names."[48]

John, who fretted about finding a way for two "friendly Souls" to
"converse" together, although the bodies were four hundred miles
apart, appeared to experience no difficulty unburdening himself as
to precisely what he thought about Abigail's letter, with its brave
declaration of independence for the ladies. While excusing the brevity of his letters because of the "critical State of Things and the
Multiplicity of Avocations," he responded, on April 14, in ample
detail, more indulgently than condescendingly:

> As to your extraordinary Code or Laws, I cannot but laugh. We
> have been told that our Struggle has loosened the bands of
> Government every where. That Children and Apprentices were
> disobedient—that schools and Colledges were grown turbulent—
> that Indians slighted their Guardians and Negroes grew insolent to
> their Masters. But your Letter was the first Intimation that another
> Tribe more numerous and powerful than all the rest were grown
> discontented.—This is rather too coarse a Compliment but you are
> so saucy, I won't blot it out.[49]

Having acknowledged Abigail's argument on behalf of her sex,
John, by way of an elaborate and affectionate rebuttal, insisted that
Abigail overstated her case and that it was really the men, rather than
the women, who were threatened. To enforce his point, he even left
out the onerous word.

> Depend upon it, We know better than to repeal our Masculine
> systems. Altho they are in full Force, you know they are little more
> than Theory. We dare not exert our Power in its full Latitude. We
> are obliged to go fair, and softly, and in Practice you know We are
> the subjects. We have only the Name of Masters, and rather than
> give up this, which would compleatly subject Us to the Despotism
> of the Peticoat, I hope General Washington, and all our brave
> Heroes would fight. I am sure every good Politician would plot, as
> long as he would against Despotism, Empire, Monarchy,
> Aristocracy, Oligarchy, or Ochlocracy.—A fine Story indeed. I
> begin to think the Ministry as deep as they are wicked. After
> stirring up Tories, Landjobbers, Trimmers, Bigots, Canadians,
> Indians, Negroes, Hanoverians, Hessians, Russians, Irish Roman

Catholicks, Scotch Renegadoes, at last they have stimulated the
to demand new Priviledges and threaten to rebell.[50]

Either Abigail had received no response from John as yet, or she
chose to ignore it, in her determination to make her thesis emphatic.
She had rephrased her initial pronouncement in her letter of May 7,
but the message was whole, and almost threatening:

> I cannot say that I think you very generous to the Ladies, for whilst
> you are proclaiming peace and good will to Men, Emancipating all
> Nations, you insist upon retaining an absolute power over Wives.
> But you must remember that Arbitrary power is like most other
> things which are very hard, very liable to be broken—and
> notwithstanding all your wise Laws and Maxims we have it in our
> power not only to free ourselves but to subdue our Masters, and
> without violence throw both your natural and legal authority at our
> feet

> *"Charm by accepting, by submitting sway*
> *yet have our Humour most when we obey."*[51]

One person with whom Abigail discussed thoroughly the subject of
women's independence, and her exchange with John, was Mercy
Warren. The two women's correspondence was already a thriving
success. No matter how careworn she was, no matter how she might
complain of the "multiplicity" of concerns, Abigail always rallied.
"Let your letters be of the journal kind," she enthusiastically urged
Mercy. "I could participate in your amusements, in your pleasures,
and in your sentiments which would greatly gratify me, and I should
collect the best of inteligence."[52]

True to character, then, Abigail interrupted her preoccupation
with her family, farm, country, and particularly her thoughts on the
ramifications of independence long enough, in the spring of 1776, to
inquire about a recent resident of Boston. "How do you like Mrs.
Washington?" she asked Mercy. "Any other person you have seen,
and *noticed* should be glad of your opinion," she added.[53]

Mercy responded obligingly. She would endeavor to gratify her
friend, as her "Curiosity seems to be awake with Regard to the Company I keep and the Manner of spending my time." She had met with
Mrs. Washington in Cambridge one April morning at eleven o'clock,
as well as with her son and his wife. She had been received with that

politness and Respect shewn in a first interview among the well bred and with the Ease and Cordiallity of Friendship of a much Earlier date. . . . If you wish to hear more of this Ladys Character I will tell you I think the Complacency of her Manners speaks at once the Benevolence of her Heart, and her affability, Candor and Gentleness Quallify her to soften the hours of private Life or to sweeten the Cares of the Hero and smooth the Rugged scenes of War.[54]

Mercy seemed equally impressed by John Parke Custis, whom she described as "A sensible Modest agreable young Man." His wife, Eleanor Custis, received a more equivocal tribute:

His Lady a Daughter of Coll. Calvert of Mariland, appears to be of an Engaging Disposition but of so Exstrem Delicate a Constitution that it Deprives her as well as her Friends of part of the pleasure which I am perswaded would Result from her Conversation did she Enjoy a Greater share of Health. She is prety, Genteel, Easey and Agreable, but a kind of Languor about her prevents her being so sociable as some Ladies. Yet it is Evident it is not owing to that want of Vivacity which Renders youth agreable, but to a want of health which a Little Clouds her spirits.[55]

As a result of Mercy's account of the members of the Washington family, Abigail said she should "most certainly" be tempted (if coveting her neighbor's goods was not prohibited by sacred law), to envy her friend the happy talent she possessed—"above the rest of her Sex"—of adorning with her pen even trivial occurrences, as well as dignifying the most important.[56]

Abigail's compliment, one of many she bestowed on Mercy, was returned in kind and quantity. Furthermore, however much they deferred to one another, however much Mercy insisted she fell short of Abigail "in many Female accomplishments," she did believe they were on equal footing in one quality. She was speaking of curiosity, consigned to them "so Generously" by the other sex for no other reason, she supposed, but that men had opportunities of indulging their "inquisitive Humour to the utmost in the Great school of the World," while women, on the other hand, were confined to the "Narrower Circle of Domestic Care." But Mercy insisted she was not defeated on this score. It afforded them "yet one Advantage peculiar to ourselves," she told Abigail with mischievous pleasure:

If the Mental Faculties of the Female are not improved it may be Concealed in the Obscure Retreats of the Bed Chamber or the kitchen which she is not often Necessitated to Leave. Whereas Man is Generally Called out to the full display of his Abilities but how often do they Exhibit the most Mortifying instances of Neglected Opportunities and their Minds appear Not with standing the Advantages of what is Called a Liberal Education, as Barren of Culture and as Void of Every useful acquirement as the most Triffling untutored Girl.[57]

Given their special relationship, their binding persuasions, Abigail was at ease discussing her recent exchange with John. On April 27, 1776 Abigail confided to Mercy that John had been "very sausy" to her in return for a "List of Female Grievances" she had transmitted to him. She thought she would ask Mercy to join her in a petition to Congress, as it was very probable that their wise statesmen would erect a new government and form a new code of laws. "I ventured to speak a word in behalf of our Sex," she explained to her friend, "who are rather hardly dealt with by the Laws of England which gives such unlimited power to the Husband to use his wife Ill." Repeating her extraordinary plan to establish some laws in favor of women on "just and Liberal principals," she also mentioned John's wishfully conciliatory reply. "So I have help'd the Sex abundantly," she had concluded.[58]

On the whole, Abigail was probably more effective than she realized. On May 26, in a letter to Brigadier General Joseph Palmer, Mr. Cranch's brother-in-law, John discussed his ideals of government and who had the right to vote, and under what circumstances. He was certain in theory that the only moral foundation of government was the consent of the people; his question was to what extent this principle could be carried out. "Shall we say, that every Individual of the Community, old and young, male and female, as well as rich and poor, must consent . . . to every act of Legislation?" And if this was impossible, as he judged Palmer would say, then what about the "Right of Man to govern women without their consent," John probed, or the "Right of the Old to bind the young without theirs?"[59]

John labored specifically over his presumption that Palmer would exclude women from voting because it was the obligation of the minority to obey and because their delicacy rendered them unfit for the hardy enterprises of war, as well as for the cares of state, and besides, nature had made them "fittest" for domestic cares. "But will not these reasons apply to others?" John insisted.[60]

Men who were destitute of property, for example, were also too infrequently associated with public affairs, too dependent upon other men, to have a will of their own. If, therefore, every man was given a vote without regard to property ownership, then, by the same reasoning, ought not women and children be entitled to vote? After all, he reasoned, men who were destitute of property were "to all intents and purposes" as much dependent on others to feed, clothe, and employ them as women were "upon their husbands, or children on their parents."[61]

It is impossible to disassociate John's final paragraph to the general from Abigail's threatened rebellion. It was as though he had her letter open before him when he wrote: "Depend on it, Sir, it is dangerous to open so fruitfull a source of Controversy and altercation, as would be opened by attempting to alter the Qualifications of Voters. There will be no end to it—New claims will arise—Women will demand a Vote. . . ."[62]

Just two months after the evacuation from Boston, Abigail's silken spirits were frayed by impatience and disappointment. Parliament had passed the American Prohibitory Act as of December 22, 1775, declaring all American ships and goods subject to British seizure, an act John regarded as "the last Stretch of Oppression." He assured Abigail that they were "hastening rapidly to great Events," but hardly rapidly enough for her. In her opinion, the eyes of their rulers were closed, and a lethargy had seized almost every member. She feared that a fatal sense of security had taken possession: "Whilst the Building is on flame they tremble at the expence of water to quench it," she complained to John. She was distressed that Boston's Harbor lay unprotected: "Tis a Maxim of state That power and Liberty are like Heat and moisture; where they are well mixt every thing prospers, where they are single, they are destructive."[63]

By May 9, Abigail could at last report the awakening of "the Spirit of fortification." Fort Hill, the Castle, and Dorchester Point were almost completed; a committee had been sent down to Nantasket; orders had been given to protect Moon and George's Island. Still, a government of more stability was much wanted in the colony; people were waiting expectantly for direction from Congress. As she was already inclined to making "Maxims of State," she added another. It was possible, she said, "that a people may let a king fall, yet still remain a people, but if a king let his people slip from him, he is no longer a king."[64]

John's letter of May 17 bolstered Abigail's hope for decisive action. Great Britain, he reported, had "at last" driven America to the final step, "a compleat Separation from her, a total absolute Independence, not only of her Parliament but of her Crown, for such is the Amount of the Resolve of the 15th." John was referring to the preamble, adopted on May 15, to a resolution voted after a debate of May 10, recommending to the assemblies and conventions of the individual colonies that they "adopt such government as shall, in the Opinion of the Representatives of the People, best conduce to the Happiness and Safety of their Constituents in particular, and America in general." Though ostensibly the work of a committee of three, including Edward Rutledge and Richard Henry Lee, the preamble was written by John, whose strong recommendation for separation from Great Britain was objected to by conservatives as "a Machine to fabricate independence."65

John was not unaware of his responsibility. He was also humbled by his decisive role:

> When I consider the great Events which are passed, and those
> greater which are rapidly advancing, and that I may have been
> instrumental of touching some Springs, and turning some small
> Wheels, which have had and will have such Effects, I feel an Awe
> upon my Mind, which is not easily described.

Despite the particular "Flickerings of Parties," he was optimistic about the future. He had reason to believe that any colony that assumed a government "under the People" would never give it up. With vision, he realized that "there is something very unnatural and odious in a Government 1,000 Leagues off. An whole Government of our own Choice, managed by Persons whom we love, revere, and can confide in, has charms in it for which Men Will fight."66

Abigail, too, was vigorously persistent in the belief in eventual Independence, even as she allowed that the "dissagreable News" from Quebec was a "great damper" to their spirits. "But shall we receive good and not Evil?" she reasoned. At a time like this, she relied on the wisdom of one of John's favorite writers, Maximilien de Béthune, the Duc de Sully. The seventeenth-century Frenchman had taught Abigail the importance, "in bold and difficult enterprizes," of subduing one obstacle at a time, and of not being "deprest by their Greatness and their Number." Paraphrasing Béthune, Abigail's message to John was decisive and hopeful:

We ought never to despair of *what has been once accomplished.* How many things have the Idea of imposible been annexed to, that have become easy to those who knew how to take advantage of Time, opportunity, lucky Moments, the Faults of others, different dispositions and an infinite Number of other circumstances.

Furthermore, it was a sincere wish, she admitted, that they might be fortunate enough to have the "Spirit of Sully animaeting our counsels."[67]

Abigail was able to write, on May 27, "My Heart is as light as a feather and my Spirits are dancing." She had received John's "fine" parcel of letters, a "feast" for her. She was also pleased that she had been able to hire a "Negro fellow" for six months, at ten pounds less than she had expected to pay, and that her farmhand Belcher was "exceeding assiduous" (and should he "purloin a little" she would look the other way). She even managed, on June 17, to spend "a remarkable day"—her first away from Braintree since John's departure—at Plymouth. There, with her sister Betsy, and with Mercy, she had been entertained aboard the brig *Defence,* where she had admired its captain, learned of its nine sea engagements, viewed a mock engagement, sipped tea, and observed dancing on the quarterdeck to violin and flute music. Her departure with her party at day's end was heralded by gunfire—an honor that Abigail said she could have dispensed with "readily."[68]

Having enjoyed one excursion, Abigail planned another, of a drastically different sort. Anxious over the disastrous news from Canada that smallpox had been one of the main reasons for the precipitous retreat from Quebec ("The Small Pox is ten times more terrible than Britons, Canadians and Indians together," John said), Abigail made definitive plans to remedy her family's vulnerability. On July 7 she invited John Thaxter—he had always expressed a desire to have the smallpox with her family—to join her the following Thursday. Those in her party would include the Cranches and their children, her sister Betsy, Cotton Tufts, Jr., a maid, and an elderly nurse.[69]

If Thaxter chose to enter as part of the family, at the cost of eighteen shillings weekly, he also needed to be prepared to pay his doctor for inoculation—a guinea per week was the cost, she had heard. She promised to find a bed and a bedstead for him, but said she would appreciate his bringing along two pairs of sheets and a counterpane. She was also taking a cow, hay, and wood from Braintree. If all went well, they might return in three weeks. "If you conclude to go, be at our House a wednesday Night," she added.[70]

When word of Abigail's plans reached John, he wrote back almost immediately to tell her that he was happy to find her "resolved" to be with the children in the first group of patients to be received by Dr. Thomas Bulfinch. It was not until Sunday, July 14, however, that Abigail was able to reply—her eyes were so badly inflamed—to comment on the "Spirit of inoculation" that pervaded the town and every house in it, drawing not less than thirty people from Braintree to Boston.[71]

That Sunday, Abigail felt well enough not only to write about family news, but to pay attention to the world beyond her sickbed. She could report that she was not only recovering, but actually happy. John's letters never failed to give her pleasure, whatever the subject. But these, dated July 3 and 4, that "heightened" the prospect of the future happiness and glory of her country, were especially prized. They brought her the momentous news she longed for. On July 3, John had written from Philadelphia:

> Yesterday the greatest Question was decided, which ever was
> debated in America, and a greater perhaps, never was or will be
> decided among Men. A Resolution was passed without one
> dissenting Colony "that these united Colonies, are, and of right
> ought to be free and independent States, and as such, they have,
> and of Right ought to have full Power to make War, conclude
> Peace, establish Commerce, and to do all the other Acts and
> Things, which other States may rightfully do.

He also promised Abigail: "You will see in a few days a Declaration setting forth the Causes, which have impell'd Us to this mighty Revolution, and the Reasons which will justify it, in the Sight of God and Man. A Plan of Confederation will be taken up in a few days."[72]

John's obvious elation over the news of independence dispelled tedium, discomfort, even doubts, momentarily. Acknowledging his inadequacies, proud of his responsibilities, humbly determined to do as well as he could, and make "Industry supply, in some degree the place of Abilities and Experience," he was inspired by the achievement.

> When I look back to the Year 1761, and recollect the Argument
> concerning Writs of Assistance, in the Superior Court, which I have

hitherto considered as the Commencement of the Controversy, between Great Britain and America, and run through the whole Period from that Time to this, and recollect the series of political Events, the Chain of Causes and Effects, I am surprised at the Suddenness, as well as Greatness of this Revolution. Britain has been fill'd with Folly, and America with Wisdom, at least this is my Judgment.—Time must determine. It is the Will of Heaven, that the two Countries should be sundered forever.[73]

At this moment of euphoria, even as he wistfully considered that an earlier Declaration would have advanced foreign alliances and might have achieved possession of Quebec, John recognized the positive values in the delay. Waiting had, in his opinion, "gradually and at last totally extinguished" hopes for reconciliation. Time had allowed for the "whole" people to consider maturely the "great Question of Independence," and to ripen their judgments, dissipate their fears, and "allure their Hopes," so that they had adopted it as their own act. He concluded, "This will cement the Union, and avoid those Heats and perhaps Convulsions which might have been occasioned by such a Declaration Six Months ago."[74]

Having yearned and worked for the concept of Independence, John understood its startling significance and envisioned its enduring brilliance.

The Second Day* of July 1776, will be the most memorable Epocha, in the History of America.—I am apt to believe that it will be celebrated, by succeeding Generations, as the great anniversary Festival. It ought to be commemorated, as the Day of Deliverance by solemn Acts of Devotion to God Almighty. It ought to be solemnized with Pomp and Parade, with Shews, Games, Sports, Guns, Bells, Bonfires and Illuminations from one End of this Continent to the other from this Time forward forever more.[75]

The significance of the Declaration, so grandly defined, did not obliterate knowledge of its price. John was full of apprehension. The new governments would require a "Purification" from their vices and an "Augmentation" of their virtues, or there would be no blessings. The people, too, presented problems. As they were extremely addicted to "Corruption and Venality," he would submit all his hopes and fears to an "overruling Providence, in which, unfashionable as the Faith may be," he believed firmly. He hoped Abigail's brother

---

*July 2 was the day Congress actually voted for Independence.

and his would serve their country "at this critical Period of its Distress." His words were both ominous and splendid at once as he wrote Abigail:

> You will think me transported with Enthusiasm but I am not. I am
> well aware of the Toil and Blood and Treasure, that it will cost Us
> to maintain this Declaration, and support and defend these States.
> —Yet through all the Gloom I can see the Rays of ravishing Light
> and Glory. I can see that the End is more than worth all the
> Means. And that Posterity will tryumph in that Days Transaction,
> even although We should rue it, which I trust in God We shall
> not.[76]

With the Declaration, Abigail seemed to forget the eye inflammation that had prevented her from writing to John for nearly a month. The news seemed to soothe her many cares, particularly over her children's recovery from their inoculations. She was thrilled not only by the actual event, but by the fact that a person "so nearly connected" with her had the honor of being a "principal actor" in laying a foundation for her country's "future greatness. May the foundation of our new constitution, be justice, Truth and Righteousness," she wrote to John. Craving permanence, she added: "Like the wise Mans house may it be founded upon those Rocks and then neither storms or tempests will overthrow it."[77]

Abigail did not speak of John's coming home, and she promised to write very often. She asked to be informed "constantly" of every important transaction. And she reaffirmed his place in her life. All expressions of tenderness were invaluable, each a "cordial" to her heart. Unimportant as they might be to the rest of the world, to her, she emphasized, "they are *every Thing.*"[78]

To Rob Me of All My Happiness

In London, in March of 1777, people were saying that a country dance, known as "Lord Howe's jigg" ("cross over, change hands, turn your partner, foot it on both sides"), caught to perfection the rhythm of the present relationship between America and Great Britain. Abigail could certainly vouch for this. Her correspondence with John, spanning those frustrating months, delineates the enigmatic movements of the enemy leader with a kind of stubborn agility.[1]

The past September of 1776, John, with Benjamin Franklin and Edward Rutledge—a committee of three appointed by Congress—had conferred with His Lordship, Admiral Richard Howe. John, traveling on horseback, Franklin and Rutledge on chairs, had transferred to Howe's barge which His Lordship met as it touched the shores of Staten Island. Howe had guided the party past lines of guards who looked as fierce as "ten furies," into a house as dirty as a stable, except for the "wholesome but romantically elegant" conference room. Ingeniously, his Lordship had carpeted the floor with moss and green sprigs; he had enhanced the atmosphere further by offering the committee good claret, good bread, cold ham, tongues, and mutton. John's flattering notations ended here.[2]

Much to John's disappointment, Howe was only permitted to deal with the members of the congressional committee as private people, not as official representatives of Congress. He might converse, confer, consult, and advise, but he had no official power to deal with the subject of peace. Accordingly, Howe had lost caste, if he had ever had much in the first place. Though the admiral was "well-bred," John believed he could name many Americans in his own neighborhood whose "Art, Address, and Abilities" were greatly superior. Shatteringly, John added, "His head is rather confused, I think."[3]

Subsequent events did nothing to elevate Howe or his brother General William Howe; the latter's advance through the Jerseys John regarded as a "rash Step." It was also an inconvenient one, causing Congress to adjourn from Philadelphia to Baltimore for safety's sake. By March, though resigned to the fact that the Quakers, "dull as Beetles," remained "a kind of neutral tribe," John thought it probable that if the colonies could collect an army of twenty thousand men by April 1, Howe could "scarcly" cross the Delaware River that year, and New Jersey might still be the Englishman's tomb.[4]

The sense of optimism was not confined to challenges on the domestic front. Franklin, Deane, and Lee, according to latest reports, had had a promising audience with the Count Charles Gravier de Vergennes, the French secretary of state and minister of foreign affairs, concerning the proposed Treaty of Commerce. A similar consideration was hoped for with the Spanish. There was reason for John to insist that "The Hearts of the French are universally for Us, and the Cry is strong for immediate War with Britain." The French had offered a loan without interest, to be repaid when the United States was settled in peace and prosperity, no conditions or securities required. And, assuming that Abigail's "political Curiosity" extended itself all over Europe, John reported that the agent of the King of Prussia often made proposals of a commercial nature to the American agents in France. However, they could not depend on the Dutch—Amsterdam being the "Treasury of Europe"—to trade directly with America.[5]

The vicissitudes of change—they lived in an "Age of political Experiments"—were hardly news to Abigail; John's dedication to satisfying her "goust" for politics was a source of satisfaction and pride. Still, she was both "happy and unhappy" as she considered her lonely winter; her choice of John's honor and reputation over her own pleasure and happiness she found "cold comfort in a winters Night."[6]

John had correctly observed that his return home, in late fall of 1776, would put her "Ladyship" in the "twitters." Even the *Boston Gazette* heralded the arrival, on November 4, of the "Honorable John

Adams, one of the members of the grand American Congress . . . at his seat in Braintree." When he left, two months later, on January 9, Abigail admitted that no separation was "ever so painful" as this last. Many circumstances accounted for this; of hazards real or imagined, there was one, in particular, that she especially tried to avoid thinking about. Other issues had to be faced immediately.[7]

First, she was finding just the routine of feeding and clothing her family a critical challenge. A so-called "regulating bill," meant to fix wages for labor and prices of both domestic and imported commodities, was anything but helpful. "The merchant scolds, the farmer growls," Abigail complained. Sugar, molasses, rum, cotton, wool, coffee, and chocolate were virtually unavailable. Some days Abigail shopped fifteen to twenty butchers who could easily supply her with meat, provided she was willing to pay fourpence a pound, and half again as much for delivery (which she was not). As for clothing, she was constantly worrying about finding wool and flax to make her own. She wouldn't dream of buying any, she said, even if the alternative meant she and the children "were to live like Adam and Eve in innocence." Another grating worry was the house on Queen Street. It was advertised for rent, which meant she had to hire someone to scrub the dirt-filled, coal- and poultry-scented rooms and repair the mildewed floors, the sagging ceilings. But she really did not have to look further than her immediate dwelling for problems. Her farmhand Prince, who refused a salary of eight dollars monthly, had been bribed back with the promise of twelve, a firm offer for six months.[8]

Life without John, at this juncture, weighted Abigail's frail shoulders with care: aged parents, ailing relatives, monetary struggles, and, perhaps most crucial of all, the nurturing of the children to achieve what both parents saw as their awesome potential. For them to enjoy "happy, usefull and honourable Days" was only the first step. The parent who thought "a deficiency of ambition is as criminal and injurious as an excess of it," as John insisted, had clearly laid down the gauntlet, which he expected to be picked up in vigorous challenge. As his children were "blessed with excellent Parts," he prayed they would never dishonor themselves by anything "unworthy" of them. John sought to define and clarify their goals in his precise way.[9]

"A Taste for Literature and a Turn for Business, united in the same Person, never fails to make a great Man," he had informed Johnny. As for Tommy, his father would make a physician of him, reminding him of his maternal great-great-grandfather, the surgeon and apothecary who had emigrated from London in 1656, and for whom he was named. Would Charles, the thoughtful child, be a lawyer, a divine, a physician, a merchant, a mechanic, or what? Noting Nabby's "remarkable Modesty, Discretion, and Reserve," her father expressed interest in her proficiency in handwriting, and also her "turn of Thinking," cautioning her that to be good and to *do* good was all there was to do. Abigail, having been over all this ground before, and no less aspiring than John, was far more of a fatalist and, at the same time, more of a realist. To predict the lives their children might live caused her to suffer "Heartake." The delicacy involved in probing the unknown made her sigh at the condition of "short sighted mortals." And something within her made her gratefully welcome this provocative boundary:

> O Blindness to the future kindly given
> that each may fill the circle marked by Heaven. [10]

As often as she was able, in odd corners of her day, when her work was done and the house was still, Abigail basked in John's companionship, reading his letters until they were almost memorized, or writing her own to him. A most poignant instance—it had almost made her period of recuperation from her vaccination seem rewarding—was her time in Boston, at the end of August, when she wrote of spending three days almost "intirely" with John. The weather was stormy; she and the children had triumphed over a frightening period in their lives. Perhaps both emotional and physical climates accounted for Abigail's rare expression of her private tastes and needs, which would be echoed by centuries of women.

> I have possession of my Aunts chamber in which you know is a
> very convenient pretty closet with a window which looks into her
> flower Garden. In this closet are a number of Book Shelves, which
> are but poorly furnished, however I have a pretty little desk or
> cabinet here where I write all my Letters and keep my papers
> unmollested by any one. I do not covet my Neighbours Goods, but
> I should like to be the owner of such conveniences. I always had a
> fancy for a closet with a window which I could more peculiarly call
> my own.

Sustained by the solitude, Abigail movingly affirmed her love:

Here I say I have amused myself in reading and thinking of my
absent Friend, sometimes with a mixture of paine, sometimes with
pleasure, sometimes anticipating a joyful and happy meeting, whilst
my Heart would bound and palpitate with the pleasing Idea, and
with the purest affection I have held you to my Bosom till my
whole Soul had dissolved in Tenderness and my pen fallen from
my Hand.[11]

Abigail's pen was, at times, her "only pleasure." There was no
longer need for John to ask her, in the winter of 1777, to write in
"Hieroglyphicks" about her "Circumstances." By April, her figure
was so clumsy that even ten-year-old Johnny was prompted to tell
her: "Mar, I never saw any body grow so fat as you do."[12]

This pregnancy at thirty-two—the baby was due in July—was her
most difficult of all; she almost wallowed in apprehension. So languid
that she could hardly manage her daily duties, she wrote indulgently
about spring unstringing her nerves, and about south winds affecting
her as certain winds affect Sicilians, blowing away all gaiety and spirit.
June heat left her sleepless, mysteriously unwell, and hardly able to
walk. She longed for John, and pitied herself for being cut off from
the privilege that some of "brute creation" enjoyed, that of having
their mates sit by them with anxious concern during "their solitary
confinement."[13]

The night of July 8 she had reason to think she had lost her baby,
her body shook so fiercely. Forty-eight hours later, on Thursday,
despite her doctor's reassurances, Abigail prepared for the worst.
Though she tried to distract herself, and John, by speculating about
Howe's retreat, expressing her fear for Ticonderoga and her curiosity over Congress's dealings, she could not numb her pain and sense
of imminent crisis. Nor did she see how she could last till Monday.[14]

Tragically, Abigail had sensed her situation exactly. On July 13,
John Thaxter wrote to John Adams: "The day before Yesterday Mrs.
Adams was delivered of a daughter; [but] it grieves me to add, Sir,
that it was still born. It was an exceedingly fine looking Child."
Thaxter added that Mrs. Adams was as comfortable as could be
expected and in a "good Way." Abigail's own letter, written three
days later, was both sad and consoling. Though she was extremely
disappointed at the loss of their baby, she knew John would be
grateful that her own life had been spared. She had set her heart on
a daughter, and had felt strongly that her desire would be granted.
John had suggested calling the infant Elizabeth, after her grandmother and aunt.[15]

It was twelve days before the dismal news reached John. He was almost apologetic about his sense of loss. "Is it not unaccountable," he asked Abigail, "that one should feel so strong an Affection for an Infant, that one has never seen, nor shall see?" Yet he confided that "the Loss of this sweet little Girl, has most tenderly and sensibly affected me." When, in August, Abigail attended the christening of her brother-in-law Peter Boylston Adams's infant, she faced up to her loss in "all its poignancy," perhaps more critically than in any previous time. Her questions echoed John's as she asked him:

> Do you feel in your own Breast any Sentiments of tenderness for one you never knew, for one who could scarcely be said ever to have had an existance? The loss occasions very different Sensations from those I once before experienced, but still I found I had a tenderness and an affection greater than I imagined could have possess'd my Heart for one who was not endeared to me by its smiles and its graces.

But John was Abigail's great consolation. She explained: "The Parent is dear to me, dear to me beyond the power of words to discribe."[16]

August 5 found Abigail doing some simple mathematics and some obvious rationalizing. On Wednesday, August 10, it would be three years since John had stepped into the coach at Thomas Cushing's door and, in some respects, out of Abigail's life. They had been married thirteen years; it seemed as though they hadn't had the happiness of living together for half that time. She regretted the "unfealing world" that might not appreciate her sacrifice and that of her children, who were practically fatherless at a time when they were in need of him.[17]

On the positive side, she could report fine crops: the promise of two hundred bushels of corn, 150 weight of flax, and plenty of beef, vegetables, and pork. There was no sugar, tea, coffee, or molasses, but a system of manufacturing molasses syrup was successfully under way; several mills were already at work turning cornstalks into that most essential ingredient of all hardy liquors.[18]

Even more ingenuity was displayed in the way a "New Set of Mobility" solved the lack of coffee and sugar. According to Abigail, they were "not your Maggys" who set about righting matters, but reputable, clean women, some even dressed in silks, who decided that certain merchants would no longer be permitted to hoard desirable supplies. With relish, for John's entertainment, Abigail recounted the rousing incident regarding his miserly bachelor cousin, Thomas Boylston.

> It was rumored that an eminent, wealthy, stingy Merchant . . . had a Hogshead of Coffe in his Store which he refused to sell to the committee under 6 shillings per pound. A Number of Females some say a hundred, some say more assembled with a cart and trucks, marchd down to the Ware House and demanded the keys, which he refused to deliver, upon which one of them seazd him by his Neck and tossed him into the cart. Upon his finding no Quarter he deliverd the keys, when they tipd up the cart and discharged him, then opend the Warehouse, Hoisted out the Coffe themselves, put it into the trucks and drove off.

Abigail wound up her tale by reporting that a large number of men had "stood amazd silent Spectators" during this whole transaction. But she inferred that she doubted stories suggesting that Mr. Boylston had also received a spanking from the women.[19]

Other news, not so local, was less entertaining, more urgent. On August 29, 1777, General Washington reported that militia from four states were joining him at Wilmington and John passed this news on to Abigail the next day. He also belittled the enemy's claim to an army of eighteen thousand strong, said it was like General John Burgoyne's "Make Believes," probably not amounting to even ten thousand in reality. A few days later the British situation worsened. It was rumored that Howe's army was in a "very unwholesome Situation," that its water was brackish and that its men suffered fevers caused, it was suggested, by the frequent morning and evening fogs. On October 17, Burgoyne surrendered at Saratoga. A letter from Washington dated October 24 confirmed news of the bitter and victorious fighting on October 21 and 22, to keep control of Forts Mifflin and Mercer on the Delaware.[20]

John was ebullient at what he regarded as the "Glory of turning the Tide of Arms." He was also transparent in his seemingly sudden betrayal of Washington. Congress, he hoped, would appoint a day of Thanksgiving, he told Abigail, not only because of the recent military victories, but also because they were not "immediately due to the Commander in Chief, nor to southern Troops." Had the situation been otherwise, "Idolatry, and Adulation would have been unbounded," so excessive as to endanger their liberties, as he recognized them. "We can allow a certain Citizen to be wise, virtuous, and good," he added, "without thinking him a Deity or a saviour."[21]

There was reason now for Abigail to rejoice that "the Sunshine from the North gilds the dark Clouds of the South." General Burgoyne and his vanquished troops would arrive in Cambridge with vain hopes of repatriation; General Howe and his army would soon be captives. But John had made some private decisions before these remarkable public events occurred. Voted a leave of absence at his request on November 7, as was Samuel Adams, the two men did not even wait for the completion of the Articles of Confederation, which Congress had been agonizing over since the past April. Instead, on November 11, five days short of the final draft of November 15, they were bound for Massachusetts. John arrived at Braintree on November 27, a homecoming that was unknowingly a prelude to still another wrenching parting. The distance of three hundred miles, to which Abigail and John adjusted with reasonable grace, was to multiply to three thousand by a vote taken by Congress on November 28, the date John Adams was elected a commissioner at the court of France "in the room of S. Deane esqr."[22]

News of John's appointment reached Braintree while John was trying a case in Portsmouth, New Hampshire, unaware of the "plot" against him. On December 15, just three weeks after John's return, it was Abigail who opened the letter, addressed to John, that was contrived, she said, "to rob me of all my happiness." The letter was written by James Lovell:

> I am charged by all those who are truly anxious here for the best prosperity of our affairs in France to press your acceptance of the Commission which has this day been voted you. The great sacrifices which you have made of private happiness has encouraged them to hope you will undertake this new business. As one I hope that you will not allow the consideration of your partial defect in the Language to weigh any thing, when you surmount others of a different nature. Doctor Franklin's Age allarms us. We want one man of inflexible integrity on that Embassy. . . . You see I am ripe in hope about your acceptance, however, your dear amiable Partner may be tempted to condemn my Persuasions of you to distance yourself from her farther than Baltimore or York Town.[23]

One of the intriguing aspects of Lovell's letter was his consideration of Abigail, his recognition of the unique bond between wife and
husband. While living with the family of the affluent landowner Daniel Roberdeau in York, when Congress had fleetingly moved there
under dire threat from Howe, John must have talked to more than
one person of the deprivation he felt in living apart from his wife. The
precise day of John's election to the commission, the genial Roberdeau, a brigadier general in the Pennsylvania militia, wrote a telling
letter to his fellow delegate in which he said:

> Your domestick views of happiness was not consulted on this
> occasion, but the necessity of your Country for your Talents, which
> being devoted to her service, I expect a chearful acquiescence with
> a call so honorable, which I doubt not will prove a lasting honor to
> you and your Connections as well as a blessing of these States.[24]

Abigail did not hesitate to reply to both Lovell and Roberdeau,
though neither had written to her directly. To Roberdeau she expressed her polite thanks for housing her husband so hospitably. She
also reassured him that both she and John knew about public duty.
"Taught both by his precept and example to sacrifice every private
view to the publick good," she feared her husband would not be able
to withstand the solicitations of his friends, even at the expense of her
present tranquility and happiness. Though she admitted this was the
hardest conflict of the many she had endured thus far, she vowed to
resign herself to her husband's absence, for she did not wish to
embarrass him. "I shall endeavour," she promised, "as much as
possible to leave him free to act [for himself] as he thinks best."[25]

Abigail's letter to James Lovell was more revealing. She was not
unappreciative of the honor to her husband, nor was she unaware
that his appointment to such an important embassy was "grateful
proof to me of the esteem of his Country." But there were other
considerations. Though she did not wish John to be less deserving,
she admitted that she was almost selfish enough to wish her husband's abilities confined to private life—a wish that was his as well,
at times. On behalf of her children and also herself, she explained:

> I have often experienced the want of his aid and assistance in the
> last 3 years of his absence and that Demand increases as our Little
> ones grow up 3 of whom are sons and at this time of life stand
> most in need of the joint force of his example and precepts. . . .
> And can I Sir consent to be seperated from him whom my Heart

esteems above all earthly things, and for an unlimited time? My life will be one continued scene of anxiety and apprehension, and must I cheerfully comply with the Demand of my Country?[26]

Abigail knew Lovell's answer; she knew he would not have been "accessary" to the nomination, had he thought otherwise. She ended her letter by assuring Lovell that she would discipline herself, though at the expense of food and rest, to bear the prospect of her husband's departure. She also apologized for writing so freely, explaining that it had been a relief "to drop some of my sorrows through my pen," which she would otherwise have "poured" on her husband, had he been present.[27]

Among others with whom Abigail discussed John's new prospects, it was Mercy Warren who confirmed what Abigail knew must be inevitable. Though Mercy said that she wept with Abigail over the prospect of John's leaving behind his beloved wife and little "brood," she also congratulated Abigail for being so "nearly connected with a Gentleman Whose Learning, patriotism And prudence qualify Him to Negotiate at Foreign Courts at this Very Critical period." But all of this was academic. John had written his formal acceptance of his appointment as joint commissioner to France on December 23. It was read in Congress on January 19, 1778.[28]

Initially, Abigail and the children—there seemed to be a question whether the two eldest or all four would go—intended to travel abroad with John. But when that plan was dismissed as "too hazardous and imprudent," ten-year-old John Quincy, at his request, was the only family member to accompany his father. Feverish preparation resulted in mounting baggage that included two fat sheep, two hogs, one barrel of apples, five bushels of corn, some chocolate, rum, sugar, eggs, a double mattress, comforter and pillow, two quires of paper, quills, and ink. There was also a French grammar, as it was John's intention of overcoming his "Partial defect". He faced the fact, however, that his age, forty-three, was an "advanced" one for acquiring a speaking knowledge of French.[29]

Father and son boarded the ship *Boston* on February 13. John wrote Abigail two notes that day, one at 11:00 A.M. and one at 5:00 P.M., the latter reassuring her of their safe passage from the barge they had boarded at Hough's Neck, to the ship, where, despite sea spray and chilling winds, they arrived dry. "Tomorrow Morning We Sail—God

Bless you, and my Nabby, my Charley, my Tommy and all my Friends, Yours, ever, ever, ever yours."[30]

At home by her fireside, Abigail tried to sort out her feelings. It was bad enough to be "Bereft" of her "better Half;" to part with her son was like having a limb "lopt off." She tried to conceal her anguish; the world might talk of honor, and the ignorant multitude of profit, but she had resigned her own "personal felicity" for one reason alone. This was her conviction, she confided to John Thaxter, that her husband's abilities and integrity might be "more extensively useful to his Country in this Department" at this time than at any other. Therefore, she added, she knew she had once more discharged her duty to the public.[31]

Abigail had had roughly one month to adjust to the idea of this formidable separation. Cruel as it was, she was determined to make the best of it. She devised one scheme that offered her some consolation; her proposal, under Thaxter's auspices, to James Lovell, was almost coquettish. She had a bargain to "compound" with him for the robbery he had perpetrated. She recognized her large share of "Grandmother Eves curiosity," and, being deprived of a very indulgent partner, she claimed some small right of knowledge from others. Her proposition, then, was that Lovell permit John Thaxter, now in New York, to communicate to her all the news and intelligence from his quarter that might be told to a *"Woman."* The quixotic Lovell seemed to relish his end of the bargain. He begged Abigail to count him among her "affectionate humble Servants(s)." Thus began a supportive, entertaining, and surprisingly flirtatious correspondence that would last several years and have a bittersweet bouquet of its own.[32]

SEVEN

A Call So Honorable

"I asked not my Heart what it could, but what it ought to do," was the way Abigail explained her consent to John's first call to France. Still, for all her noble theories, her studied resignation to a "negative kind of happiness," she was desolate. Her "Most Forlorn and Dismal of all states" she considered "widowhood"; she waited four months and was on the verge of panic before receiving John's first two letters. Reports of the assassination of Dr. Benjamin Franklin in his bed, and the description of his lingering death from stab wounds in his ribs, though discredited after a month, prepared her, if anything could, for the even more threatening news that followed shortly. Rumors that the *Boston* had been captured meant only one thing—imprisonment of a husband and son.[1]

During the next twenty-one months of spartan communication, Abigail would weep with relief when John's first letter assured her of his safety, scold at another's brevity, and eventually conclude bitterly that writing was not "A La mode de Paris." She began to wonder if John had changed hearts with some frozen Laplander, and threatened, even though she knew she was being unfair, to adopt his "concise" method. Relenting in almost the same breath, she explained that her "Friend" had left a "Craveing void," that she missed him for reasons ranging from the mighty to the mundane, including her need for advice about paying taxes (supporting an army was costly), as well as the "important weight" of educating their children.[2]

Charles was her main concern at this time. A puzzling, thoughtful

child, given to meditating on "some deep thing or other," Charles
eluded definition and categorization. It was one thing for his parents
to think about his future and another to settle him for the present.
It was Abigail's lonely decision, to make up her mind—as no instruction was available in Braintree—whether to board Charles with her
sister Betsy, now married to the Reverend John Shaw, in Haverhill,
where he might attend a "very good School."[3]

Inflation was another gnawing worry. It seemed to her that people
were more "extravagant, selfish, oppressive" than ever, and a year's
budget was easily exhausted in a month. The challenge for her of
"studying frugality and economy" meant renting out half of the farm
to tenants, and importing goods (with John's cooperation) that her
cousin William Smith, partner in the Boston mercantile firm of Cod-
man & Smith, might help her turn at profit. It also meant abandoning
thoughts of buying a new carriage—three hundred pounds for this
"light commodity" was beyond reason—when she was already committed to spending $150 for a fence, and sixty dollars more for a pair
of cartwheels. To add to her problems, the scorching months of July
and August 1778 ruined the corn and potatoes and smothered Abigail's hope of turning out even a single barrel of cider. In a fatalistic
mood, she consoled herself that at least she was not alone. Everyone
was embarked, she said, on the same voyage; if the country sank, "we
must sink with it."[4]

Fortunately, Abigail was not only burdened by care during this period of her life, but also swayed by curiosity. She craved to know a
"thousand circumstances" about her family's life abroad and was
able, in the course of nine months, three letters, and two teatime
guests, to patch together a reasonably accurate account of her family.
The reports of two visitors from France, Sir James Jay and Mr.
George Diggs, both "very social and communicative," dispelled her
fears as to their safety and even amused her, initially.[5]

On the whole, Abigail could assume that her husband and son had
survived their arduous journey with "utmost firmness." At times,
however, John, she would later learn, was horrified by the filth of the
ship and the cursing seamen, annoyed by the cook for not having his
meals ready punctually, distressed by the amputation of a limb, and
the subsequent death, of a fellow passenger. Thunderous gales,
waves, winds, and the stench of putrid water and smoking coal provoked intermittent seasickness. Lightning struck one seaman and

split the mainmast; as they were chased by enemy ships and gave chase, it was not at all clear in the father's mind that it was his duty —as he had been led to believe—to expose his child to all that had to be endured.[6]

It was six weeks between the time they boarded the *Boston,* on Friday, February 13, and the time they sighted—at the end of March —many windmills and sandhills and the village of St. Denis d'Oléron, and knew, heading toward the port of Bordeaux, that the "troublesome" voyage was over at last. Crowds, cannonfire, and torchlit gardens celebrated the Americans' arrival. Still another thirteen-cannon salute signaled their departure the next morning, and after a five-hundred-mile trek through Poitier, Tours, and Amboise, along the River Loire, admiring the fields of grain, flocks of sheep, churches, convents, vineyards, and castles (and despairing of the beggars in certain towns), the party arrived in Paris at nine o'clock Wednesday night, April 8. Early on Thursday, riding out amid the din of the street cries, bells, and clattering carriages, father and son, accompanied in their coach by their fellow passenger, Dr. Nicholas Noël, joined Benjamin Franklin at the Hôtel de Valentinois, in the suburb of Passy, in what John described as a "fine, airy, salubrious situation."[7]

Listening to the stories told by her teatime companions, Diggs and Jay, Abigail was impressed with their understanding of her husband's "rather reluctantly" adapting to French customs. From the start, the farmer, patriot, lawyer, and bibliophile, was torn about life in France. With almost grudging delight, John conceded that France was "one great garden," and admitted that if human nature could be made happy by anything that pleased the eye, taste, or any other sense or passion or fancy, France would be "the region for happiness." He could not help admiring Franklin's splendid establishment, with its view of the Seine and the city beyond, framed with forest greens of the Bois de Bologne. The grandeur of the houses, gardens, libraries, furniture, dress, and entertainment enchanted his eye, but embarrassed his puritan soul. The New Englander was confused.[8]

The habits of homespun and cider, of riding circuit courts and clearing farmland, of ardent prayer in barren pews, were too ingrained in the patriot to license him to enjoy life in and around Paris. In fact, it made him crotchety to think about French mores, especially as they were so conveniently embraced by his colleague, Benjamin

Franklin, with whom he supped on cheese and beer. Franklin's pace was unlike anything known to John. The New Englander, who spoke of sacrificing himself and his family to his country's cause, who pruned his life of all excess, who talked about needing the wisdom of Solomon, the weakness of Moses, the patience of Job, all in one, to cope with his work, was plainly appalled by the pleasure-prone elder statesman.[9]

Unquestionably, John admired Franklin's fine reputation and "great genius" in engineering matters, and thought his discoveries in electricity "very grand." But just as he would not deny him great merit for his role in American affairs, he could never conceal his impatience with those who thought he had foreordained America's fate by the wave of his electric wand. The clamorous display of public reverence for Franklin as an equal of Voltaire, by an evening's audience at the French Academy of Sciences, actually offended him. And if Franklin's relationships with women were too numerous and distracting, the conduct of his household and social life "slack," the management (or lack of management) of his business was unnerving. Before long, John would conclude that Franklin's age and true character made it impossible for him to "search every Thing to the Bottom," that his love of ease and dissipation would "prevent any thorough Reformation of any Thing—and his (*Cunning and*) Silence and Reserve, render it very difficult to do any Thing with him."[10]

The more John was exposed to Franklin, the more frustrated he grew. John preferred to review letters and papers the first thing in the morning; Franklin breakfasted late, and when he finished he met with crowds of visitors—philosophers, academicians, economists, and literary folk, including those who worked on translations of his writings. By the time the visitors left, it was the hour for Franklin to dress for dinner; he dined out every night other than the ones on which he received company, and came home "at all hours," anywhere from nine to midnight. Franklin kept a hornbook in his pocket in which he noted invitations; his associate Arthur Lee said they were the only things about which he was punctual.[11]

At first, John teased Abigail about how he envied Franklin's affectionate relationships with women of all ages who seemed quite ready to "eat him up." Abigail, amused by John's account, wrote back that the recital of Franklin's adventures consoled her in his absence. Pondering the phenomenon of Franklin's amazing appeal, she speculated that his "Mentor like appearance, age and philosophy must certainly lead the polite scientifick Ladies of France to suppose they are embracing the God of Wisdom, in a Humane Form." Abigail also owned that while she never wished the man she loved to be an Angle," she would be as content if those "divine" honors accorded Franklin were omitted from John's life. She had no cause for worry; John was restless about his work. Soon after his arrival in France, the "grave American republican" was once again tormenting himself.[12]

In his diary, on April 21, 1778, just thirteen days after his arrival in Paris, John wrote of encountering a "rope of sand." Almost instantly he was alert to the disputes between the Americans, of the "bitter Animosities between Dr. Deane and Mr. Lee; between Dr. Franklin and Mr. Lee; between Dr. Franklin and Mr. Izzard; between Dr. Bancroft and Mr. Lee and Mr. Izzard; and between Mr. Charmichael and all of them." Shortly, he would not only complain of Franklin's inefficiency—days passed before the statesman signed the documents prepared for him—but of the arbitrary manner in which he had hired his own grandson, William Temple, as his private secretary, without consulting a single soul.[13]

It was one thing, in John's opinion, for all of Europe to regard Franklin as "the most important character in American Affairs"; it was another for John to recognize that the man termed a "magician" was, in fact, a poor executive, party to extravagance and waste. Even Franklin's French was found wanting; he was "wholly inattentive" to grammar and, worse, had an accent that was "very far from exact," in John's opinion.[14]

On May 21, John took steps bluntly—myopically, in hindsight—that would account for the "Revolution" in his life, the new twist to his future. He wrote from Passy to Samuel Adams on a subject that lay "heavily" on his mind, and that he proceeded to detail with total lack of restraint. The expense of the commissioners was vast, in his opinion. Three could not manage at less than three to four thousand pounds sterling a year, and one of them spent from five to six thousand. The system was all wrong, he said. Instead of three, one public minister, at a single expenditure, would be quite sufficient for all the business.[15]

Obviously, John did not have his own expenses in mind. He did not keep a carriage, instead using Dr. Franklin's when it was free. He did not pay a separate house rent and boasted that "few Men in this World are capable of living at a less Expence" than he was. Others, such as Deane, seemed to maintain several establishments, both in

Passy and in Paris, and two sets of carriages, horses, and servants.[16]

The "Revolution" took effect—as far as John was concerned, "toll" was the word—the following September 14; Franklin was elected the sole minister to France. New instructions, drawn up on October 26, dissolving the Franklin-Lee-Adams commission, would be delivered by the Marquis de Lafayette, who sailed for France in mid-February. That John was already aware of the impending change was apparent from a letter he wrote to Abigail on November 27; he mentioned "Hints" received regarding some new congressional regulations, and the possibility of his being sent to the Viennese court.[17]

John was obviously dismayed at the choice. To be kept abroad, to be idle, or even to travel to countries where he would not be formally received, was the most painful situation he could imagine. He was at a loss as to whether he ought to head for home immediately, or stay and write to Congress for permission to leave. He assured Abigail that he would not take any step that would offend Congress or the people. On the other hand, he could not eat "pensions and sine-cures," he said: "they would stick in my Throat."[18]

Unfortunately, since Abigail had last heard from John the past August, she was unaware of his predicament, however self-engineered. For the first time in their fourteen years of marriage, her confidence in their relationship sagged, deeper with each passing day devoid of the letters that were, she said, "my food by day and my rest by night." If her letters were of so little importance and not worth noticing with his own hand, she suggested to John that he might be so kind as to direct them to his secretary. Yet her heart denied the justice of her accusation, at the same time that her soul, she admitted, was wounded at the separation, and her fortitude dissolved in "Frailty and weakness." In searing loneliness she sought her husband's understanding:

> all all conspire to cast a Gloom over my solitary hours, and bereave
> me of all domestick felicity. In vain do I strive to [throw off] in the
> company of my Friends some of the anxiety of my Heart, it
> increases in proportion to my endeavours to conceal it; the only
> alleiviation I know of would be a frequent intercourse by Letters
> unrestrained by the apprehension of their becomeing food for our
> Enemies. The affection I feel for my Friend is of the tenderest
> kind, matured by years, . . . by choise and approved by Heaven.
> Angels can witness to its purity, what care I then for the Ridicule

of Britains should this testimony of it fall into their Hands, nor can I endure that so much caution and circumspection on your part should deprive me of the only consolor of your absence—a consolation that our Enemies enjoy in a much higher degree than I do, Many of them having received 3 or 4 Letters from their Friend[s] in England to one that I have received from France.[19]

On December 2, a moody John wrote a fairly soothing answer to Abigail, considering others to come. He was "astonished" she had not heard from him more often, claiming to have written fifty letters to her. But he also said that it was impossible for him to write as much as he had in America. "What could one write?" It wasn't safe, he insisted, to put down on paper anything that one was not willing to see in the newspapers of the world. He also didn't know which vessels were trustworthy, and pointed out that he was five hundred miles from Bordeaux, and not much less distant from Nantes. He also made it thoroughly clear that

> The Joy which the Receipt of these Packets afforded me, was damped, by the disagreable Articles of Intelligence, but still more so by the Symptoms of Grief and Complaint, which appeared in the Letters. For Heavens Sake, my dear dont indulge a Thought that it is possible for me to neglect, or forget all that is dear to me in this World.[20]

The next day, December 3, with the arrival of Abigail's letters of September 29 and October 10, his tone was far less conciliatory. Her letters, in fact, gave him more concern than he could express: "I will not say a Fit of the Spleen," but something close to it. He had so much ceremony to submit to, so much company to see, so many visits to make and receive, it was impossible for him to write as often as he was inclined to. Besides, he was tortured by still another rumor that "a certain fine gentleman will join another fine Gentleman, and these some other fine gentlemen, to obtain some Arrangement that shall dishonnor me."[21]

Had it been another time, almost any other in his life, John could not have failed to be seduced by Abigail's candor and tenderness. She tried to explain that for fourteen years past, though they had been separated, she had never spent an entire winter alone; some part of the dismal season had been mitigated and "softened by the Social converse and participation of the Friend of my youth." Now she admitted that things large and small, even a Scottish song, moved her to tears and set her wondering:

> *And shall I see his face again?*
> *And shall I hear him speak?*

The paragraph had ended in a prayer: "Gracious Heaven hear and answer my daily petition, by banishing all my Grief."[22]

But John was unable to rally. He was openly embarrassed, impatient, and even angered. In a "State of total Suspence and Uncertainty," awaiting word of his fate, he did not know whether to acknowledge Abigail's letter with pain or pleasure. As he wrote on December 18:

> this is the third letter I have recd. in this complaining style. the former two I have not answer'd.—I had Endeavour'd to answer them.—I have wrote several answers, but upon a review, they appear'd to be such I could not send. One was angry, another was full of Greif, and the third with Melancholy, so that I burnt them all.—if you write me in this style I shall leave of writing intirely, it kills me. Can Professions of Esteem be Wanting from me to you? Can Protestation of affection be necessary? can tokens of Remembrance be desir'd? The very idea of this sickens me. Am I not wretched Enough, in this Banishment, without this. What Course shall I take to convince you that my Heart is warm?[23]

On Sunday, two days after Christmas, Abigail was alone with Charles and Tommy, surrounded by mountains of snow that made her think she was in Greenland. Twenty hours of howling winds only accentuated her despair:

> How lonely are my days? How solitary are my Nights? . . . How insupportable the Idea that 3,000 leigues, and the vast ocean now devide us—but devide only our persons for the Heart of my Friend is in the Bosom of his partner. More than half a score years has so rivetted it there, that the Fabrick which contains it must crumble into Dust, e'er the particles can be seperated.[24]

Within a week, her sentiment turned to sarcasm.

> Surely I have been the most unfortunate person in the world, to *loose, every Letter* you have wrote me since your absence, and to receive only a few lines at various times wrote in the greatest haste, containing only the state of your Health, perhaps making mention of your Son and Servant and then concluding abruptly *yours*.

Furthermore, he would see that she intended to repay him in kind:

I determine very soon to coppy and adopt the *very concise* method of my Friend—and as I wish to do every thing agreable to him, send him Billits containing not more than a dozen lines at the utmost Especially as paper has grown so dear. . . .[25]

The angry tone of Abigail's letter must have provoked her alarmed husband to share his tribulations with their son. Johnny now entered the fray, quite fearlessly for an eleven-year-old. He wrote on February 20, 1779:

I last night had the honour of reading a letter from you to my Pappa dated Jany. 4th. in which you complain much of my Pappa's not writing. He cannot write but very little because he has so many other things to think of, but he can not let slip one opportunity without writing a few lines and when you receive them you complain as bad or worse than if he had not wrote at all and it really hurts him to receive such letters.[26]

The son was pitifully protective of the father, who considered himself treated roughly by the world, and especially by the person he counted on most, Abigail. There was not time for descriptions of churches, plays, parties; it was more useful to conjugate two or three French verbs in all their moods and tenses. "Let me alone, and have my own Way," John begged. "For mercy Sake dont exact of me that I should be a Boy, till I am Seventy Years of Age." The kind of correspondence Abigail sought would do for gentlemen and ladies under twenty, and might possibly be pardonable till twenty-five, provided all was peace and prosperity. But old men, he said, borne down with years and cares, could no more amuse themselves with such things than with "Toys, Marbles and Whirligigs." If he had ever had wit, it was all "evaporated"; if he ever had any imagination, it was all "quenched."[27]

John was horrified at the thought that Abigail's effusive letters would be intercepted. He worried about what security he had against their appearance in newspapers, and reminded her that while some of her letters would do honor to the most virtuous and accomplished Roman matron, others would make them both "very ridiculous": "Pray consider your Age, and the Gravity of your Character, the Mother of Six Children—one of them grown up, who ought never to be out of your sight, nor ever to have an Example of Indiscretion set before her." Admitting that he had grown more "austere, rigid, and miserable than ever before," he thought he had seen more occasion, perhaps, for doing so. In any case, he pleaded, "For Gods sake never reproach me again with not writing or with Writing Scrips. Your Wounds are too deep."[28]

The sum of their winter correspondence convinced John that either some "infernal" had whispered insinuations in Abigail's ear, or that she had forgotten the "unalterable" tenderness of his heart. In any case, her sorrowful and sentimental excursions concluded abruptly with news that darkened melancholy into apprehension. On January 4, 1779, Abigail turned to her friend James Lovell for help.[29]

Abigail had just learned, by "some late intelligence," of the "New arrangement" of the commissioners. Begging Lovell's pardon for distracting him from the weighty concerns of state, her query was this: "Where is my Friend to be placed?" She hoped not at a great distance. In their eleven-month separation she had received five letters only, the last dated August, she informed Lovell. Furthermore, she was aware of the roles each was called to play: John was meant to serve wherever he was needed; she, as with all members of her sex, was to submit with patience. Yet she would remind Lovell that this was a lesson she had mastered completely, having been "so often call'd to the Exercise of it."[30]

Lovell's reply was typical: flirtatious, outrageous, and consoling. He did not hesitate, in any of his correspondence with the "lovely" Portia, to amuse himself by hinting at his own attachments to her, to exploit her privacy (including the possibility of her being pregnant) through the most convoluted innuendo:

> You say 'tis near 11 months since he left Braintree. I find myself
> relieved by that period from a certain anxiety, which was founded
> on my tenderness towards your dear Sex that Mr. A's *rigid patriotism*
> had overcome. He used, in that Spirit, to contemplate with
> pleasure, a circumstance in you, the like of which in Mrs. Lovell
> aggravated my absence from home, exceedingly. In spight
> therefore of his past reproofs to me, I will take pleasure in your
> *Escape.* [31]

Lovell eventually did get down to the business of tempering Abigail's doubts about John—admitting, however, that there was a "strange Delay and something of Mystery in the Propositions that have been lately made here respecting our foreign Affairs." Though he was not entitled to write as confidentially to her about the "mighty

Congress as Mr. A. used to," he added that he had not yet perceived anything that would "affect Mr. A. in a disagreeable Manner."[32]

To understand just what agonies John endured abroad, his crisis of self-confidence and even of purpose, Lovell and Abigail would have had to be with him in the latter days of February 1779. The finality of Congress's choice of Franklin left him in deep depression. He felt ignored, unappreciated. He, John Adams, was simply a man that nobody had ever heard of before, and therefore a man of no consequence. He was inclined to think that all parties—in France and England, both Whigs and Tories, friends of Franklin, Deane, and Lee —differing in many other things, agreed on one: he was not "the famous Adams." Both French and English newspapers hardly fortified his confidence. It was Samuel Adams they touted as *"le fameux Adams"* in contrast to himself, dismissed as a "perfect Cypher, a Man who did not understand a Word of French—awkward in his Figure —awkward in his Dress—No Abilities—a perfect Bigot—and fanatic."[33]

On February 28, John wrote of his fate as a sullen youth. He had quite forgotten, or so it seemed, that he had been responsible for turning the key and opening the door of the political abyss into which he had now plunged.

> The Scaffold is cutt away, and I am left kicking and sprawling in the Mire, I think. It is hardly a state of Disgrace that I am in but rather of total Neglect and Contempt. The humane People about me, feel for my situation they say: But I feel for my Countrys situation. If I had deserved such Treatment, I should have deserved to be told so at least, and then I should have known my Duty.[34]

John had written Congress, he told Abigail, of his intention to return home; unless he received orders that he could execute with honor and some advantage to the public, she might expect to see him in June or July. She might also prepare herself to move to Boston, into the old house, where he would draw writs and deeds, harangue juries, and be happy. On March 3, John took leave of the French ministry at Versailles; on March 8, he and Johnny left Passy for Nantes; not until June 17 were they to embark for America.[35]

John's main regret at leaving France, he said, was that he had finally "happily succeeded, tres heureusement reussi in learning French";

he could speak it fluently, understand it perfectly. His son Johnny suffered no misgivings whatsoever. A conscientious youth who had boarded at school in Passy at Le Coeur, he considered the "Charming prospect" of returning home to his Grandpappa, Grandmamma, and uncles a "feast" to his mind. The joy of being reunited with his mother, sister, and brothers, he said, would be greater than all the pain he had suffered when he had left them. He consoled himself that the pleasure of telling the tale of his travels would somehow compensate for the "toils and dangers" he had endured.[36]

As of June 8, Abigail had still not received a "syllable" from either husband or son for the past six months; justifiably, she complained that she was at the mercy of every hint and rumor. She was "not in a very good humor," she explained to Lovell; she was struggling to suppress all disagreeable thoughts about public slight and indignity until she could talk to Sam Adams and know the truth. Later in the month she learned of the possibility of John's return, with or without leave from Congress, news that was contradicted shortly. Mercy Warren wrote to tell Abigail (according to her husband's information) that there was "No Expectation" in Congress of John's return, that a large majority of Congress "highly Esteem him," and wished him to continue in Europe. Further, if Congress should be in a position to do so, he was the man best qualified to negotiate peace, and he would be "in Employ" at some European court in a short time. All in all, Mercy predicted "some New appointment will be Necessary before Long."[37]

On July 30, a bewildered Abigail wrote directly to Samuel Adams to learn precisely what Congress proposed to do with her "absent Friend." The fact that Lee had been appointed to Spain, while John was left in limbo, as far as she knew, gave her some "disagreeable sensations." Abigail added almost gratuitously that her husband had found nothing "to disgust, disturb or any ways discontent" him with the French nation, but that all the evils he experienced were caused by the Americans. Sam Adams's reply the following day presented "most friendly Regards" and shared word he had received that John had intended to embark for America the past March 6, and should be arriving shortly to tell her about "the States of our Affairs here." By dramatic coincidence, John's boat lay, at this moment, one hundred miles east of Cape Cod.[38]

The *Sensible,* carrying father and son, as well as the artful new

French minister to the United States, the Chevalier Anne César de La Luzerne, sailed into Boston Harbor on August 3. Soon Abigail was to learn that the "call so honorable" had taught her husband many lessons about the subtleties of the "scenes" he had passed through. Yet John was realistic: "I am more and more convinced every day of the Innocence, the Virtue and absolute Necessity of Art and Design. —I have arrived almost at 44 without any." The urgency with which the undiplomatic diplomat would be called to put into practice the lessons he had theoretically mastered would come as a breathtaking surprise, more swiftly than either John or Abigail could have imagined in either the best or worst of their dreams about their future.[39]

EIGHT

This Cruel State
of Separation

John was home just a scant four months when he once
again faced the "melancholy tryal" of leaving his family. This
time, after her husband's second departure for France, it was as
though the previous separation served as a rehearsal for the tears,
loneliness, fears, bitterness, and pride of the next years of Abigail's
life. The letter that would tilt their lives still another time, and in still
another direction, dated October 20, 1779, was signed and sealed by
the President of Congress, Samuel Huntington. It informed John of
his nomination as Minister Plenipotentiary to "confer, treat, agree
and conclude" with representatives of His Most Christian Majesty,
George III, in the negotiations of a peace founded on "solid and
equitable Principles, as reasonably to promise a Permanency of the
Blessings of Tranquillity."[1]

Abigail recognized the invitation to serve as an "honour." It was
only after she said good-bye, on that forlorn Saturday, November 13,
that she took full measure of the void left by John, who boarded the
Sensible, this time, not only with Johnny, but with his son Charles,
John Thaxter, a servant named Joseph Stevens, and a gift of cranberries, along with the myriad supplies. Left behind with Tommy and
Nabby, in the house she found more tomblike than ever, Abigail
began to lose her appetite and her sleep. How to justify her splin-
tered family and the fleeting wedding anniversaries that were drifting
by with alarming regularity in stony separation were numbing questions that preempted all other thoughts.[2]

A sense of loss pervades Abigail's correspondence during this second major separation from John. Increasingly reflective, her hand trembled as she wrote of the "hours days and weeks" when she deliberately chose not to "paint" all her feelings to her friend for fear that she would make him unhappy. Or told him how she wandered from room to room, pitying herself for feeling deserted, unprotected, unassisted, uncounseled. In time she began to think there was a "moral evil" in their separation. When they had pledged themselves to each other, hadn't the holy ceremony closed with the words "What God has joined Let no Man put assunder"? She wondered now whether theirs was a voluntary separation; she concluded with uncharacteristic asperity, "I feel that it is not."[3]

When she rode out the swells of self-pity, as she did repeatedly, Abigail fought for logic that would bring her some peace of mind. In times of greater equanimity she spoke of experience teaching her "patient acquiescence," though it did not lessen her anxiety or affection. But compared to Mrs. Francis Dana, whose husband was traveling with the Adams party, and who was irreconcilable over her separation, Abigail could indeed pat herself on the back as a "mere philosopher" who was *"inured,* but not hardned to the painfull portion."[4]

In a sense, Abigail's endless quest for justification and understanding of her loss—there could never be another "season" in their lives that the family would enjoy together in quite the same way, she said wistfully—might have been due to the need to quench subconscious feelings of guilt at parting with Johnny, who was twelve, and nine-year-old Charles. To both she expressed tender concern for their personal welfare and safety. About their roles and current mission she wrote with the sentiments of a patriot and the goals of, at best, a judicious, inspired parent, and, at worst, a fatally ambitious one.[5]

Neither of the children had wished to leave home. If Abigail thought Johnny's reluctance stemmed from proper deliberation, however, or that he was capable of judging what was most for his own benefit, she assured him that she would not have urged him to leave when he was so "averse." As for Charles, his tears, she admitted, melted her heart a thousand times. But, she insisted, in his case, being the "sweet" favorite of the neighbors, bound to a "golden destiny," it was well that he had gone. Both boys were at an age, in her opinion, when a mother's care was less important; with attention and diligence they

would best learn to discharge their duties to their "Great Preserver,"
to society in general, to their country, their parents, and themselves,
under their father's eye.[6]

Having submerged all qualms and private needs to her tolerable
satisfaction, Abigail was quite prepared to chart her childrens' lives,
Johnny's in particular. Were he beside her, she wrote, she would
remind him of the sacrifices of ease, pleasure, wealth—of life itself—
to be made in their country's defense. She would also assure him that
he had the character of a hero and statesman, that "Nature [had] not
been deficient" with him. Her only worry was that he learn to curb
his impetuous temper: "He that is slow to anger is better than the
Mighty, and he that ruleth his Spirit than he that taketh a city," she
cautioned him.[7]

Abigail's concerns for Charles were perhaps more fundamentally
rooted. This engaging child was to have an opportunity to see a
foreign country, learn a foreign language that might be serviceable
to him, and form, at this early period, friends who would do honor
to him in the future. But he must also, she insisted, pay attention to
his books, and to every branch of knowledge, every opportunity for
improvement, to which he was exposed. She hoped that his ambition
would lead him to master all he undertook, that he would not be
content to lag behind others. He must "strive to excel."[8]

However Abigail lavished her children with worldly hopes of leadership and intellectual aggrandizement, it was religious commitment
that superseded all other considerations. Religion, said Abigail, was
the only sure and permanent foundation of life, the truth she would
"engraven" on the hearts of her children. Distance, time, and undoubtedly *need* conspired in honing the formidable code to which all
her descendants would be bound, in which some would flourish and
others wither. Abigail was addressing Johnny specifically when she
wrote:

> Improve your understanding for acquiring useful knowledge and
> virtue, such as will render you an ornament to society, an Honour
> to your Country and a Blessing to your parents. Great Learning
> and superior abilities, should you ever possess them, will be of
> little value and small Estimation, unless Virtue, Honour, Truth and
> integrety are added to them. Adhere to those religious Sentiments
> and principals which are early instilled into your mind and
> remember that you are accountable to your Maker for all your
> words and actions. Let me injoin it upon you to attend constantly

and steadfastly to the precepts and instructions of your Father as you value the happiness of your Mother and your own welfare.

There was more. There would be no compromise.

I had much rather you should have found your Grave in the ocean you have crossd or any untimely death crop you in your Infant years, rather than see you an immoral profligate or a Graceless child.[9]

By January 1780, Abigail was surfeited with the horrors of the long winter and mountains of snow of a kind not seen in sixty years; one passed by her house on foot, or not at all; sliding was the way to cross the frozen bay. Though it was a hard winter, it was not without high points.[10]

It was the winter of the convention for forming the Massachusetts Constitution, which John had worked on, the winter she must have learned of John Paul Jones's expropriation of the Countess of Selkirk's silver—"knight errant" Abigail called him—the winter when one could buy Tory estates at a bargain, the winter when Lovell's behavior was a diversion: "For a Senator too!" Abigail protested faintly.[11]

Lovell, whom Abigail first met at the home of Richard and Mary Cranch, was obviously intrigued and touched, in his own arch, irreverent way, by her earnest devotion to her husband. In fact, he said that it was by giving her heart to *such* a man that "most of all makes me yours." From the start of their mail-pouch flirtation, Lovell talked about Abigail's virtue, sense, and beauty, teased her about her anxiety for John, named her the "most lovely of the loveliest Sex," and signed another letter with a "sound and affectionate Heart." When he offered to take care of her financial problems, to exchange paper for hard money, when he supplied her with weekly numbers of the *Journal of Congress,* she openly expressed the appreciation of a "greatly obliged Friend," acknowledging her gratitude for the letters that were "a fund of entertainment" and eased her fears.[12]

For Lovell's "exuberances," Abigail maintained a different posture; she scolded openly, though with affection. When he asked questions such as, "How *do* you do, Lovely Portia, these very cold Days, Mistake me not willfully: I said *Days*," she was apt to answer by calling him a "very dangerous Man," also a "most ingenious and agreeable flatterer." His defense was majestic:

Must I suppress Opinion, Sentiment and just Encomium upon the Gracefulness of a lovely suffering Wife or Mother? It seems I must or be taxed as a flatterer. Immured for many Months in a Prison, and, upon escape from thence, confined in a narrow Circle, with He-Creatures, drudging, plodding Politicians, for an equally tedious Period of Time, I did not suspect that my Pen could now run in such a stile of social Intercourse as to provoke a delicate Judge among the Polishers of the Manners of our Race, to call me Adulator.[13]

Lovell's letter of January 6 elicited Abigail's reprimand. It referred to days too short for getting pressing public business off his hands, and nights ten times more ruinous to his health, when he was inside bedcurtains the moment that public duty was discharged. To which Abigail crisply replied that she had charity enough to believe Lovell's associates had been wholly of his own sex for three years past.[14]

One other winter's correspondence allowed for no humor at all. Past experience made Abigail enormously sensitive to how her husband (who had not spared her a detail of his humiliation regarding his first tour of duty in France, nor the "rope of sand" with which he had been so miserably entangled) was treated. Arthur Lee's horrendous allegations against Silas Deane had precipitated the formation, the past spring, on March 24, 1779, of a special committee on foreign affairs to investigate all members of the foreign service, present and past, involved peripherally or immediately.[15]

Deane, the blacksmith's son, Yale graduate and lawyer, would juggle diplomatic triumphs with accusations of embezzlement and double-dealing until his death. His story involves four countries, America, France, England, and Holland, the French playwright and diplomat Pierre Augustin Caron de Beaumarchais, and the American double agent, Edward Bancroft, who was said to transfer correspondence in bottles concealed in the hole of a tree near the Tuileries. Deane, whom the Connecticut Assembly failed to nominate to the Continental Congress for a third time, was sent to Paris in March 1776 on both commercial and diplomatic missions, charged with investing money to acquire supplies needed by the colonies, eight shiploads of which helped contribute to the success of the Saratoga campaign. Deane's other instructions had been to sound out the French foreign office on the question of American Independence and the possibilities of an ambassador to Paris, as well as treaties of alliance and commerce between the countries. By September 1776, Deane was joined in Paris by Arthur Lee and Benjamin Franklin. By June 1778, Deane was on his way home to America to answer to a tribunal, including Samuel Adams, Richard Henry Lee, and Henry Laurens, on charges of corruption initiated by Arthur Lee, Richard's brother.[16]

Deane, Arthur Lee insisted, had been at least as attentive to his own interests as to his country's. He had conspired with Beaumarchais to charge America for supplies the French intended as gifts, and had dabbled in England's funds. At least one reputable gentleman said he would give Mr. Deane fifty thousand pounds sterling for his fortune. As for his association with the double agent Bancroft: Deane had been introduced to him by Benjamin Franklin, who employed his fellow member of the Royal Society—Bancroft was a writer, inventor, and scientist—to spy for him in England.[17]

On April 15, 1780, Congress debated a proposed vote of censure of those actively perpetuating "suspicions and animosities" that might be "highly prejudicial" to the honor and interests of the United States. By April 20, Congress had made the censure official for Franklin, Deane, Arthur and the Virginia merchant William Lee, and Ralph Izard, the British-educated South Carolinian native. John escaped, mercifully, though it was a close call, but Lovell's inferences of an "Accommodation . . . proposed in Whispers" only nudged John to ask for copies of all "Complaints and Evidences" against his conduct as a commissioner. He wished, he explained, to take measures to "justify" himself to Congress, a request that was rejected on the grounds that his "late Appointment" cleared him of involvement in the "animosities." John's friend Elbridge Gerry reassured him that, on the whole, it was his opinion that John's character, in Congress's esteem, was as "high" as any gentleman's in America. John, heartened by his friend's reassurances, was glad to say that he no longer felt like Ariel, "wedged by the Waiste in the middle of a rifted Oak."[18]

On his return to America, Deane, of the opinion he had failed to obtain a satisfactory hearing before Congress, decided to put his case before the public in his address "To the Free and Virtuous Citizens of America," published first in the *Pennsylvania Packet* on December 5, 1778, and then reprinted afterward in other papers and eventually in France. John Adams, unable to maintain a neutral position regarding Deane's ethics, denounced the latter as a "wild boar" to be hunted down for the benefit of all mankind. Deane had responded:

"This man who may have read much," he said, "appeared to have retained nothing except law knowledge and the fierce and haughty manners of the Lacedemonians and the first Romans. These he has adopted as a perfect model to form a modern republican by." Abigail, entirely out of patience with Deane's conduct and the public attention he had "roused," predicted that that "certain gentleman" had "stired up a nest which will sting him till he bleads." To Mercy Warren on January 22, 1779, she wrote: "Tis unhappy that in the Infancy of our republicks such unworthy characters should stain our Anals and Lessen us in the Eyes of foreign powers. Yet this will ever be the case where self Interest is more powerful than publick virtue."[19]

Having survived this unnerving episode with some sense of success, Abigail was dismayed by news from abroad that John, who had already returned there, reaching Paris on February 9, 1780, was still the target of controversy. A group of worthless, ambitious, intriguing Americans, she wrote to Mercy Warren, were circulating reports that John had entertained an illicit correspondence with the British Minister, and had in reality left France for England, rather than America; to no avail could it be pointed out in rebuttal that John had, in fact, embarked for America on the same ship with a French official.[20]

The collective intrigues of the French and the Americans provoked Abigail to wonder whether America, had it been her lot, would have had an easier time contending only with foreign enemies. It was the rancor of internal foes, she was convinced, that made the task of the patriot peculiarly difficult and dangerous. She despaired at the "machinations of envy, the Snares of Treachery, the malice of Dissimulation and the Clandestine Stabs of Calumny." How was John to make his way? "Can the Innocence of the dove or the wisdom of a more subtle animal," she puzzled, "screne him from all these foes?"[21]

As John's champion, protector of his dignity, caretaker of his reputation, shattered by the faintest innuendo of disrespect, Abigail was moved openly to his defense by the announcement in a Philadelphia paper listing two of the newly elected members of the American Philosophical Society, in entirely different styles. The announcement in the *Pennsylvania Packet* referred to "the Honourable John Adams Esq." as a "late Member of Congress;" "His Excellency John Jay Esquire" was mentioned as "Minister of the United States" at the court of Madrid.[22]

This was on January 27, 1780. By March 13, after a period of simmering discontent, Abigail decided to write Elbridge Gerry as "the sincere and constant Friend of one deservedly Dear to me, whose honour and character it is my Duty at all times to support."

> May I ask you Sir, why this distinction? Tho I do not know that you are in any ways connected with the Society, I presume no person will say that the commission with which Mr. A——s is invested, is of less importance than that of Mr. J——ys. I suppose they both bear the same title of Minister plenipotentary. Mr. A——s had acted under a commission from Congress near two years before Mr. J——ys appointment, which if I am not mistaken, both in the Army and Navy gives a pre'eminence of Rank.[23]

To Gerry, Abigail suggested that rank was considered of more importance abroad than in their own young country, and that honorary distinctions ought to be minded. In a twelve-paragraph letter she pointed out that she felt the distinction was aimed not so much at the person as at the state; that there was jealousy of Massachusetts and of every man of any eminence in it. This being so, she asked if it wasn't "particuliarly incumbent" upon the members from Massachusetts carefully to guard the honor of their state and of those who represented it, "which never can be done if such Little Stigmas are sufferd to be fixed upon them." A prophet, she said, was not without honor, save in his own country. Still, John had been embarrassed abroad on his first assignment, and though she was satisfied at its solution, she sought support with "honour and delicacy" for those who chose to serve. She also assured Gerry that her absent Friend never regarded the appendages of rank and precedence any other way but as they affected the public.[24]

By mid-April the correspondence would close with Gerry's healing admission that Abigail's sentiments on a "certain publication" in the Philadelphia paper were indeed "too striking" to escape the notice of Mr. Adams's friends in Philadelphia. Nevertheless, the subject was "delecate in it's Nature," and required "Measures that point not directly at the Object." It was decided, ultimately, that it was best to ignore the oversight, with Gerry promising, with "greatest pleasure", to endeavor to support Adams "as a particular Friend, as well as a valuable Statesman."[25]

After the rigor of the "Canadian Winter" of 1780, Abigail was relieved by quickening signs of spring; the new green warmth promised renewal of her impoverished spirit and weary body. Worry, loneliness, and confinement had drained her so drastically that she wrote now of being "less attached to the world," and speculated about whether she was "better fitted for an other."[26]

Detached though she might seem, Abigail was more involved than she realized. She decided to go ahead and order a "genteel chaise" from Mr. Thomas Bumstead. Seemingly so embarrassed by this indulgence, she referred to it as the "article," the "you know what" that John had, obviously before his departure, "directed" her to make and one he found "horribly dear" when she had. She also had established herself as a knowledgeable trader of small supplies—she was partial to muslin handkerchiefs, bits of ribbon, and silk gloves that were easily contained in small envelopes sent from abroad—in exchange for money, or what she termed family necessities. She was preoccupied with Benedict Arnold's "treachery"; she read and dismissed Lord Chesterfield as "polished," conceding the elegance and grace of his *Letters*. Her sister-in-law was dying, her stepfather-in-law, John Hall, married to John's widowed mother since December 1766, was also hopelessly ill. America's patchy army dismayed her; the prospects of peace, she said, absorbed her soul.[27]

Essentially, however, Abigail was preoccupied with her "statesman," her family abroad, and their whereabouts. Letters filled in the details of their arduous pilgrimage, the thousand-mile trek by mule, calash, and foot, from the northwest tip of the Spanish peninsula, where the leaky *Sensible* had docked in desperation, to their original destination of Paris. July brought news of the events of March. John had been presented to the King, Queen, and royal family of France, but he saw no great prospect of being presented in a similar manner in London; he fancied His Majesty of St. James would not look so placidly upon him as that of Versailles. Whatever doubts he had of a political nature gave way to indulgent praise of Paris. He would fill columns with descriptions of temples and palaces, sculptures, tapestries, porcelains—except, he claimed, if he took the time to do so, he would neglect his duty, which he described with durable eloquence:

> The Science of Government it is my Duty to study, more than all other Sciences: the Art of Legislation and Administration and Negotiation, ought to take Place, indeed to exclude in a manner all other Arts.—I must study Politicks and War that my sons may have liberty to study Mathematicks and Philosophy. My sons ought to

study Mathematicks and Philosophy, Geography, natural History,
Naval Architecture, navigation, Commerce and Agriculture, in
order to give their Children a right to study Painting, Poetry,
Musick, Architecture, Statuary, Tapestry and Porcelaine.[28]

John's rigorous concept of his official role could not have surprised
Abigail, but where it had led him was quite another matter. In mid-
November, dreading the prospect of another "Stern Winter," Abigail
was at work on an extraordinarily ingratiating letter, an artful apology for others less pleasing to her husband. If she had complained
(she was "wholy unconscious" of giving him pain), she assured him
she had done so out of the "ardour of affection" that could not
tolerate neglect, and that no "mediating power" was needed to adjust the difference. "The falling out of Lovers is the renewal of Love,"
she said, urging him to

> Be to my faults a little Blind
> Be to my virtues ever kind. [29]

The puzzling pleasure Abigail found in mulling over what were
admittedly "painfull scenes" was unexpectedly aborted by the arrival
of Edward Davis, Captain of the *Dolphin,* with a letter from John. It
was the only one salvaged from mail that had been thrown overboard
during a chase at sea—and the first word from John in five months.
It was dated September 4, and told her he had been in Amsterdam
for weeks, that he was "much pleased" with Holland, that it was a
"singular Country" unlike any other, and that its "Frugality, Industry, Cleanliness etc." ought to be imitated by their own country. A
subsequent letter, dated September 15, warned her not to expect a
settlement: "You will have no Peace, but what you give yourselves,
by destroying Root and Branch all the British Force in America."
John touched on France as well as England, and on Holland's immense wealth, but did not elaborate, in this letter at least, on his own
situation.[30]

Insidiously, in one instance after another, every project appeared to
John to be a "paradox"; after he had settled in Passy, and boarded
his children at M. Péchigny's school, he sorrowfully concluded that
his mission to France was hopeless. There were those who said America would abandon France, and others who said that France and
Spain would abandon America, and still others who said that Spain

would forsake France *and* America. Even those who foresaw the possibilities of America becoming the greatest manufacturing country of all, and the greatest military and naval power, predicted evil tidings as the result—all would be "terrible," if not the actual ruin of Europe.[31]

The tarnished relationship with France was an especially grievous source of disillusionment to John. In December of 1775 the French had informally assured America of its backing, that it would welcome American ships and seemed already to be thinking in terms of financial aid. Bonded by the threat of their mutual foe, Great Britain, and with Spain's consent, Louis XVI had, by orders signed on May 2, 1776, decisively come to America's help, if not rescue. By stealth and intrigue of highest drama, the supply of 1 million livres worth of munitions administered by the French secret agent de Beaumarchais through a fictious company, Roderigue Hortalez et Cie, and a like amount from Spain's Charles III, would account for eighty percent of America's gunpowder for 1776 and the following year.[32]

The Franco-American Alliance of February 6, 1778, had affirmed the countries' ties—the Treaty of Amity and Commerce granted one another most favored nation status; the Treaty of Alliance was to become effective if and when war broke out between France and Great Britain. Furthermore, the two nations had combined forces in July 1778 to attack the British on American shores. John's doubts about the sincerity of the French had only surfaced during the period when he had replaced Silas Deane as commissioner to live in Paris and negotiate the peace treaty with Great Britain. It was then that he had begun to question not only the honesty, integrity, and efficiency of the Americans, but the loyalty and intent of the French. One could be grateful to the French for their financial aid but quite accurately perceive, as John did now, that the Foreign Minister, de Vergennes, meant "to keep his hand under our chin to prevent us from drowning, but not to lift our heads out of the water."[33]

Given the subtleties and intricacies of the situation in Paris, John was hardly at his best. To be patient, to stand by, to be "so idle and inactive" was not a position at all agreeable to his "genius." He had, therefore, decided to visit Brussels, The Hague, and Amsterdam, to serve his country "by transcribing Intelligence and in every other Way." With Johnny and Charles in tow, he left Paris on July 27, 1780, for what he supposed would be a brief trip—he flattered himself that "something might be done to render us less dependent on France," he had frankly told Vergennes. The brief trip would turn into a year's stay, the beginning of what was possibly the most thoroughly miserable period of his life, personally, and the proudest diplomatically.[34]

By September, before Abigail had even learned of their whereabouts, Johnny and Charles were enrolled at the Latin School in Amsterdam; by December, John Thaxter had taken them to Leyden, where they were to study Latin and Greek and attend lectures at the University. It was cheaper in Leyden, the air purer, and besides, the company and conversation would be better, John wrote to their mother. He did not mention that lack of knowledge of the Dutch language posed a problem for the boys; that misunderstanding was thought by a hurt and grieving father to be the cause of their forced removal from the Latin School in Amsterdam. *"La Desobeissance et L'impertinence de Monsieur votre Fils ainé, qui fait de son mieux pour corrompre son aimable Frere,"* the headmaster had written, *"n'etant plus a soufrir, puis qu'il cherche lui même par sa brutalité, a s'attirer le chatiment qu'il merite, dans l'Esperance de quitter les Ecoles, sous ce pretexte."*[*35]

Obviously unaware of her sons' punishing adjustments, and rising from the ashes of her increasingly anxious solitude, Abigail, as though she were lecturing behind a formal podium, once again clarified her demanding expectations in a letter to Johnny. Writing in January 1781, she reminded her eldest son that he was in a country famous for its industry and frugality, a country that had given birth to many learned and great men such as Erasmus, Grotius, and Boerhaave.

> You must not be a superficial observer, but study Men and
> Manners that you may be Skilfull in both. Tis said of Socrates, that
> the oracle pronounced him the wisest of all Men living because he
> judiciously made choice of Humane Nature for the object of his
> Thoughts. Youth is the proper season for observation and
> attention—a mind unincumberd with cares may seek instruction
> and draw improvement from all the objects which surround it. The
> earlier in life you accustome yourself to consider objects with
> attention, the easier will your progress be, and more sure and
> successfull your enterprizes. What a Harvest of true knowledge and
> learning may you gather from the numberless varied Scenes
> through which you pass if you are not wanting in your own

---

*"The disobedience and impertinence of your older son, who does his best to corrupt his well-behaved brother . . . can no longer be tolerated, as he endeavors by his bad behaviour to bring upon himself the punishment he deserves, in the hope of leaving school, as a result."

assiduity and endeavours. Let your ambition be engaged to become eminent, but above all things support a virtuous character, and remember that "an Honest Man is the Noblest work of God."[36]

About the best thing Abigail could say for the winter of 1781 was that the weather was pleasantly mild. Otherwise, these were stormy times. She lived for letters that did not arrive (it would be nine months this March without a word from either Johnny or Charles), nagged herself over money problems, and could not prevent herself from conjuring up the "Hair Breath Scapes" to which her family must be subjected, recognizing all the while that this tendency to imagine the worst was self-indulgent and "imbecility." By early summer, however, she was alerted by letter to the fact that John was indeed in a precarious situation and that his safety was by no means assured, as far as his reputation was concerned.[37]

The letter of warning, dated June 17, was not even intended for Abigail, but for Sam Adams's wife, Elizabeth Welles Adams. The previous instance of confusion over the two women's mail, a cannister of tea was at stake. This time it was John's future. Abigail claimed that she read the misdirected letter halfway through before she realized it was not hers. "Ought Eve to have laid it by then when so honestly come at?" she asked James Lovell. She had read on, though, knowing well that one did "pay for peeping."[38]

The author of the wayward letter was Alice Lee Shippen, sister of the four Lee brothers of Virginia, one of them being the ornery Arthur, whose reputation was damaged in the tawdry controversy with Silas Deane, during John's first term in Paris. Mrs. Shippen's suspicions of Franklin left nothing to the imagination; implications of damage to John horrified Abigail. Mrs. Shippen wrote, initially about Franklin's plans:

> He has sent his resignation to Congress; this is probably no more than a State Trick to fix him more firm in the Saddle. He says perhaps he is too Old, but he does not perceive any thing like it himself; and then gives a strong Proof of it by recommending his Grandson as the Person who will, in a Year or two, be most fit for our Plenepotentiary. From this recommendation one or the other of these two things is clear, either Mr. F——'s faculties are impair'd, or he thinks ours are. This same Gentleman is now Blackening the Character of Mr. J:A. to Congress more than he did Mr. L——'s, and he has got the french Minister to join him.[39]

With dawning fury, Abigail understood the oblique warnings of Lovell's letters, his capricious hints of strange undercurrents that had surfaced. On June 26 he had spoken of "Proceedings nearly affecting Mr. A's public Character." He thought it proper to tell her, as he did not want her to be uneasy about hints "catched here and there," that a change of circumstances in Europe necessitated changes involving John, according to the majority opinion. Lovell's "poor angry" private opinion was something else: "the real Truth being that our allies are to rule the roost." Lovell enclosed two documents to substantiate his claim, along with his admonition, "Now Woman be secret." One, dating back to January 10, contained Congress's official backing of the Comte de Vergennes's position that John Adams must deal circumspectly, rather than openly, with Great Britain, contrary to John's wish for "a frank and decent Communication" of his mission in Europe.[40]

The second enclosure referred to probably noted that John Adams's instructions of 1779, as sole minister for peace, were changed. Now he was to share his commission with four others, including Jay, Franklin, Laurens, and Jefferson. Collectively they were to undertake nothing in the negotiations for peace or truce without knowledge and concurrence of the ministers of their "generous" ally, the King of France. The shrewd Chevalier de La Luzerne had done his homework in Philadelphia. His lobbying was most effective among those who thought John Adams's interpretation of his orders too high-handed, his stubborn unwillingness to consult the French on his overtures to the British untenable, his "Stiffness and Tenaciousness of Temper" disturbing. John's singular concept of diplomatic conduct even provoked comment from the politically discreet Franklin. "I am persuaded," Franklin said about John, "that he means well for his Country, is always an honest Man, often a wise one, but sometimes, and in some things, absolutely out of his senses."[41]

With sorrow and anger, out of loyalty and love, in a spectacularly forthright series of letters, Abigail now turned to her friends Thaxter, Gerry, Lovell, and Alice Lee Shippen for help. Abigail told of the sacrifice of her best years, her happiness, and her family's unity so that her husband could serve his country. She was sure she was owed an explanation, therefore, for what had transpired. While she did not begrudge the sacrifice of domestic pleasure and independent fortune, she would not tolerate the "slanderous arrow, the calumniating stabs of Malice" that tore an honest character into pieces.[42]

Abigail also made her apologies to Mrs. Shippen. She knew Mrs. Shippen would excuse her unintended indiscretion. But she was wholly ignorant of the nature of the "charades" against her husband, though she now assumed that Benjamin Franklin must have had something to do with her husband's latest embarrassment.

> I can only say that those who have no private Interest to serve, no Friends to advance, no Grandson to plenipotentiarise, no Views incompatable with the welfare of their country, will judge I hope more favourably of a Gentleman whose Heart and Mind are truly republican. . . . It has been the Misfortune of America in the unhappy tradigy in which She has been engaged, that some of her principle characters have disgraced the Scenes. Her Frankling Dean, and Arnold may be ranked with her Hutchinson and Galloway.[43]

It was to Lovell, however, that Abigail made a disarming admission about her relationship with John: "When he is wounded I blead." Her husband was a good man and "would to Heaven" they only had those kind in office. "You know my Friend that he is a man of principal, and that he will not voilate the dictates of his conscience to Ingratiate himself with a minister, or with your more respected Body." It was not complete chance that Abigail was called Portia. Her defense of John was thorough, and yet it did not lack vigorous spontaneity. "The duce take the Enemy for restraining my pen," she said. Franklin, she repeated, must be the culprit. If John was a "Gallant," she would think he had been monopolizing women from the "enchanter." If he was a "Modern Courtier," she would think he had outwitted Franklin in court intrigue. If he was a "selfish avaritious designing deceitfull Villan," she would think he had encroached on the old gentleman's prerogatives. As John was none of these, she could only attribute Franklin's malice against an honest republican to something else.

> Tis fear, fear, that fear which made the first grand deciver start up in his own shape when touchd by Ithuriel['s] Spear. The honest Zeal of a Man who has no Sinnester views to serve, no Friends to advance to places of profit and Emolument, no ambition to make a fortune with the Spoil of his country, or to eat the Bread of Idleness and dissapation—this this man must be crushed, he must be calumniated and abused. It needs great courage Sir to engage in the cause of America, we have not only an open but secret foes to contend with. It comes not unexpected upon me I assure you, he who had unjustly traduced the character of one Man, would not

hesitate to attack every one who should obstruct his views and no Man however honest his views and intentions will be safe whilst this Gentleman holds his office.[44]

Abigail had still not plumbed the depths of her anger, or her curiosity. "I want to ask you a hundred Questions and to have them fully and explicitly answerd. You will send me by the first opportunity the whole of this dark prosess," Abigail virtually ordered Lovell. At last Abigail had taken him precisely at his word. Initially, he had hoped she would command him "freely" in her husband's absence, and she unhesitatingly honored his wish. If her "Friend" was uninformed, she begged Lovell to tell John of Congress's feelings, that he might take proper measures in his defense. Her husband would be devastated, she predicted. "He must and will quit a Situation in which he cannot act with honour." At this time she could see "nothing but dishonour, and disgrace attending his most faithful, and zealous exertions for the welfare of his Country."[45]

Abigail was further incensed by the contents of Lovell's letter of July 13, 1781. His explanation for John's plight was direct. He had obviously discussed the problem with Sam Adams and come to the conclusion that Abigail's "All" was not servile enough to gain the unbounded affection of the foreign court, that Count de Vergennes had sent letters of complaint to "old Franklin," and that the latter had also written "a most unkind and stabbing one hither; which he had no necessity to doing." Lovell added, to Abigail's weary satisfaction, that he could not accuse anyone of lack of esteem for Mr. Adams, but that he saw him "indelicately handled by Means of wrong measures on a general Scale." By August, Lovell assured Abigail that there was no pique or ill will against her Mr. Adams in Congress. What had happened had sprung out of mistaken principles of general policy, and he wished her not to think that there was any idea of criminality in Mr. Adams. "He is much esteemed. But such is the uncouth way of Proceeding here at Times that unintended Chagrin must arise."[46]

Unknown to Abigail, John had returned to Paris that same July. He had received a grudging summons from the Comte de Vergennes to discuss offers of the Russians and Austrians to mediate a peace, John being the only American available with authority to accept such help. By harshly rejecting the Frenchman's proposal, because he suspected that the United States was being compromised in these negotiations,

John did not endear himself further on this mission. "This desireable object [peace] is yet unhappily at a Distance, a long distance I fear," he had concluded.[47]

If, at this hour, John's political life was speculative, his personal life was fragmented. Johnny had already left Amsterdam on July 7 to join Francis Dana, appointed the first American minister to Russia; by August 27 he would be in St. Petersburg, working as Dana's private secretary and French interpreter. Charles, who had been feverishly ill and homesick—his father explained he was a "delightful Child," but had "too exquisite sensibility for Europe"—was to begin, on August 12, his frightening journey home, which would land him at Beverly, Massachusetts, in January of the following year. John himself suffered a violent fever, blaming it on the summer heat, and on the "cold damps and putrid steams" arising from the immense quantities of dead water stagnating in the Dutch canals. He also blamed his anxiety over America's state of affairs in Holland and his excessive fatigue for bringing him as near to death as any man ever approached "without being grasped in his arms." But his broken spirits were shortly mended.[48]

Late in November, John learned of his new responsibilities. His assignment, voted by Congress the past August 16, was to form a treaty of alliance between France, the United Provinces, and the United States, contingent on Dutch recognition of American Independence. By this time Lt. General Charles Cornwallis had surrendered at Yorktown, and John thought himself in a much stronger position to press for permission from the French to work for recognition at The Hague. By December 2, 1781, he could caution Abigail not to distress herself about any malicious attempts to injure him in the estimation of his countrymen. "Let them take their course and go the length of their tether," he insisted now. They could never hurt her husband, whose character was fortified with a shield of "Innocence and honor ten thousandfold stronger than brass or iron. Say as little about it as I do," he pleaded. Reinforced once more with title and position, that of Minister Plenipotentiary to the Netherlands, John promised he would laugh—"laugh before all Posterity"—at those who tried to dishonor him.[49]

As John's future brightened, Abigail's dimmed, her mountainous aspirations paled into sorrowful, self-pitying shadows. In her dearest Friend's two-year absence she could no longer kindle brave words, but talked about the "load" of her heart, and brooded about the "vexations, toils and hazards" of public life. Where should she begin her list of grievances? she asked. First, with the silence between them. She had not received a letter in over a year from either her husband or from John Quincy, her Russian "vissiter"; Charles was still at sea, the welfare of his ship the subject of shattering rumors. Sustaining her end of their correspondence, she wrote John:

> Alass my dear I am much afflicted with a disorder call'd the *Heartach,* nor can any remedy be found in America, it must be collected from Holland, Petersburgh and Bilboa.[50]

Frequently now, Abigail was confined over what she referred to as "slight indispositions" to which she had always been subject, but never severely. Her nervous system, she realized, was "too easily agitated." Money was a continual problem, even more so after she had paid her taxes. She was shocked by how inadequate John's salary really was, infuriated by those around her who, not worth ten Spanish "milled" dollars at the start of the war, indulged now in lavish furniture, equipage, clothing, and even feasting. She pleaded with John on December 9, 1781: "Will you not return e'er the close of another year?" She had plans for them to retire from the "vexations, toils and hazards of publick Life. Didn't he sometimes sigh," she asked, "for such a Seclusion—publick peace and domestick happiness?" For months Abigail continued to plan her purchase of land in Vermont; she referred to it as a "favorite object" without realizing, perhaps, that it was also a symbol of escape from a way of life, "this cruel State of Separation" she could no longer tolerate.[51]

Abigail's dirge intensified with each letter. Eight years, she counted, had already passed since John could call himself an inhabitant of Massachusetts. Her fondest wish was for his return, for reasons specifically known to a feminine heart. She explained:

> the age of romance has long ago past, but the affection of almost Infant years has matured and strengthened untill it has become a vital principle, nor has the world any thing to bestow which could in the smallest degree compensate for the loss. Desire and Sorrow were denounced upon our Sex; as a punishment for the transgression of Eve. I have sometimes thought we are formed to experience more exquisite Sensations than is the Lot of your Sex. More tender and susceptable by Nature of those impression[s] which create happiness or misiry, we Suffer and enjoy in a higher

degree. I never wonderd at the philosopher who thanked the Gods
that he was created a Man rather than a Woman.[52]

Six months later, on June 17, 1782, Abigail received two letters from
Amsterdam that summarily revived her spirits. John was almost
smug: "Your humble Servant has lately grown much into Fashion,"
he had written on March 22. Nobody was nearly as important as
Mynheer Adams, he continued: "Every City, and Province rings with
De Heer Adams etc. etc. etc." Furthermore, he judged he would be
received in "awful Pomp" in a few weeks, a prediction confirmed
shortly, in his letter of March 29, written a day after the states of
Holland and West Friesland resolved to admit him to an audience.[53]

Abigail was exultant. "I will take praise to myself," she responded.
"I feel that it is my due, for having sacrificed so large a portion of my
peace and happiness to promote the welfare of my country which I
hope for many years to come will reap the benefit, tho it is more than
probable unmindful of the hand that blessed them." The patriot once
again rose to the occasion. Ardently though she longed for John's
return, she assured him that she could not feel "the least inclination"
to a peace, but on "the most liberal foundation."[54]

Particularly during the last depressed months, Abigail had given a
great deal of thought to her feelings about "patriotick virtue." At
times, when she might appear wanting in that realm, she assured
John (as though to assure herself), that she urged his return not only
for personal reasons but because she feared for his health and safety
if he remained abroad. Even more important, she believed that the
"wisest and ablest" citizens, such as John himself, were needed to
alleviate the daily suffering at home. Dedicated to the illumination of
whatever discrepancies existed regarding their standards, Abigail
persisted in her analysis of the subject.

> Patriotism in the female Sex is the most disinterested of all virtues.
> Excluded from honours and from offices, we cannot attach
> ourselves to the State or Government from having held a place of
> Eminence. Even in the freest countrys our property is subject to
> the controul and disposal of our partners, to whom the Laws have
> given a sovereign Authority. Deprived of a voice in Legislation,
> obliged to submit to those Laws which are imposed upon us, is it
> not sufficient to make us indifferent to the publick Welfare? Yet all
> History and every age exhibit Instances of patriotick virtue in the

female Sex; which considering our situation equals the most
Heroick of yours.[55]

Happily, Abigail's wish that John's negotiations in Holland be
"blessed" were granted. On March 15, John had bought a house in
The Hague—bordering the Fluwelen Burgwal (the street of the "Velvet Makers")—to serve as the Hotel des États Unis, or, as he called
it, "L'Hotel de nouveau Monde." By April 19 he had reached the
turning point: the States General of the United Netherlands resolved
"that Mr. Adams shall be admitted and acknowledged in Quality of
Envoy of the United States of North America to their High Might-
inesses, as he is admitted and acknowledged by the present." On
June 11 John signed five bonds in the amount of one million guilders
—each bond for a loan by a syndicate of Dutch banking houses, at
5-percent interest—allowing for a 4½-percent commission to the
bankers, repayment to begin in ten years and to be completed in
fifteen. Congress ratified the contract on September 14, 1782. This
was the first of four loans John maneuvered in the Netherlands,
totaling 9 million guilders, or more than $3,500,000. It was the sole
effective support, some would say, to languishing American credit, a
crucial sum that enabled the government of the Confederation to
survive until recognition of Washington's new national government
under the Constitution of 1787.[56]

John was not one to underestimate the success that had hung
"upon a Thread, a Hair, a silken Fibre." He boasted he could not
foresee an opportunity for a century to come that would be "so
critical and of so extensive importance in the political system of
America." He was proud for another reason: without money, without
friends, in the face of mean intrigue, he had carried the cause "by the
still small Voice of Reason, and Perswasion." John had triumphed
against the ceaseless opposition of family connections, court influence, and despotism. But he had also almost ruined his health in the
cause. He was exhausted, feeling a half-century older and feebler
than when he had left Abigail. His mind spun with memories: "What
storms, what Chases, what Leaks, what Mountains and Valleys, what
Fatigues, Dangers, Hair Breadth scapes, what Fevers and Gouts, have
I seen and felt!"[57]

Eventually, John needed to ask himself whether he must stay or go,
remain abroad or return to Braintree. At this opening scene of

"Risque and Trouble," feeling so "wedged" in with public affairs, he was afraid that an offer to resign would occasion "much Puzzle" and be adversely interpreted. British politics were a "Labyrinth," in his opinion. Even John Thaxter observed that the world, in the summer of 1782, was in "all the Anxiety of earnest Expectation, all on Tiptoe. . . ."[58]

Charles James Fox, the British foreign secretary, was eager to grant absolute, unequivocal, and unconditional independence to America, to which the King took absolute exception, whereas John took exception to the King. George, in his opinion, was "an obstinate, miserable man, a monster, another Pharaoh," who, it was predicted, would sacrifice a tottering crown and even forfeit life, to no purpose at all. John sighed as he faced up to the multitude of questions to debate at this juncture in his country's history. If America conducted itself with "Caution, Prudence, Moderation and Firmness," the new country would succeed. But if Congress or its ministers abroad were intimidated by threats, slanders, and insinuations, all would be lost: America would be duped out of the fishery, the Mississippi, and the western lands, as well as the rich forests of Penobscot, where every tree was a prospective ship's mast.[59]

Apart from being uneasy about Congress's "Designs," and about whether or not he was being accurately informed, John was personally unhappy. He despised his state of "horrid Solitude" at The Hague, but remained indecisive about where salvation lay. He was uneasy with Abigail's proposals about Vermont, or even Penn's Hill. Even she questioned her husband's genuine needs, apart from her hopes and his wishes.[60]

Only John could answer Abigail's tumbling questions. Did his heart really pine for domestic tranquility and for the "reciprocation" of happiness he had once known? Was there, on the other hand, "ought in Courts, in Theaters or Assemblies that can fill the void? Will ambition, will fame, will honour do it?" There seemed to be no instant solutions. But there were the facts. She could no longer live in such a lonely state. And she was worried about Nabby, who was too silent, too attentive to her mother (in her mother's opinion), too preoccupied with the separation from her father and brothers.[61]

On August 4, Abigail received a visitor who as much as told her what her next step must be. Doctor Benjamin Waterhouse, who would be appointed professor at the newly founded Harvard Medical School the following year, had befriended John, and was a mentor to both Johnny and Thaxter while in Leyden, was separated from Charles on their voyage and arrived home in June, 1782. He wished "exceedingly" that Abigail join her husband, sure that her presence was necessary to his happiness. One month later, Abigail made a "serious proposal" to John. It was a cold, dry September—the summer drought had shriveled the corn and baked the grass fields to a dull brown. The dismal landscape captured her own mood with desperate truth. She would have been married eighteen years in October; John and she had lived apart now for three years.

> The blossom falls and the fruit withers and decays; but here the similitude fails, for, though lost for the present, the season returns, the tree vegetates anew, and the blossom again puts forth.
> But, alas! with me, those days which are past are gone for ever, and time is hastening on that period when I must fall to rise no more until mortality shall put on immortality, and we shall meet again, pure and disembodied spirits.[62]

Later that November, Abigail wrote again of her abiding hope that God would grant John's return, leaving no doubt of her complete confidence and devotion:

> Give me the man I love; you are neither of an age or temper to be allured by the splendor of a court, or the smiles of princesses. I never suffered an easy sensation on that account. I know I have a right to your whole heart, because my own never knew another lord: and such is my confidence in you, that, if you were not with held by the strongest of all obligations, those of a moral nature, your honor would not suffer you to abuse my confidence.

Abigail also left no doubt about her repeated "proposal" to visit John. She could scarcely bear a refusal, she admitted. Yet she wanted to be asked "up on the best grounds and reasons." If John was in favor of her coming, she would not need to urge him again; if he was against it, she would not embarrass him by making a further request. She had already assured him that she feared neither the enemy nor "old Neptune." What she feared most, and would never accept, was "a half way invitation."[63]

More than two years would storm by between May 1782, when John first expressed his desperate need to be reunited with Abigail, when he said it did not matter on which side of the ocean they met, and her departure on June 20, 1784, for England. These would be years fraught with as many uncertainties as there were possibilities, plans for going or staying wavering with each new aspect of what she referred to as John's "garbled mission." In a way, she seemed to be dancing a minuet of mysterious rhythm: one step forward, two back, three sideways, then sudden, ominous stillness. John's invitations to Abigail pressed, halted, resumed, a composite reflection of America's difficulties in establishing its identity as well as his personal vulnerability.[64]

When solutions eluded John, his mind veered toward explanations and analysis, the probing lawyer asserting himself. He consoled himself by saying that the case of America was a new one, that it had no example in history, that therefore no "reasonings" could be drawn on, no precedents were available for guidance. There was only one way, in his estimation, to negotiate with Englishmen. "That is clearly and decidedly, Firmness, firmness and patience," he recommended to John Jay. He also warned Abigail not to expect peace—not before 1784, anyway. He predicted that the English were not yet sufficiently "humbled," that they would have another campaign unless there was better news for America. Miraculously, there was.[65]

In the autumn of 1782, a year after Cornwallis had sent up a white flag signaling the surrender of his entire force at Yorktown, and the last land battle was fought near Chillcote, Ohio—at a time when Britain and America reminded him of eagle and cat—John could claim fulfillment of all his anxious years of work. That October 17, buoyed by the "full success" of his negotiations with the Dutch, having achieved a loan through the syndicate of Dutch bankers to the Continental Congress, and having signed a treaty of amity and commerce between the two powers, John pressed on to Paris. There he joined Benjamin Franklin and John Jay in negotiating provisional articles of peace between Great Britain and the United States. The signing of the Preliminary Treaty at Versailles on November 30 was celebrated afterwards with luncheon in Passy at Dr. Franklin's.[66]

Just two months later, on Monday, January 20, 1783, a declaration of the cessation of hostilities was agreed on by the Americans and the British. Meetings begun at ten o'clock that morning in the opulent office of the Comte de Vergennes resulted in the historic Peace of Paris, Great Britain's pact with Spain, France, and America promising the longed-for official declaration of the end of hostilities between the old nation and the new. "Thus was this mighty System terminated," John said, "with as little Ceremony, and in as short a Time as a Marriage Settlement."[67]

Never one to thrive in an uncertain political climate, John now found himself immeasurably restless, admitting that the newly forged peace, which put the rest of the world at ease, only increased his own "perplexities and anxiety." The nervous letters that followed echoed his torment. Now he wrote of his intentions to go home with or without the permission of Congress: "Don't think, therefore, of coming to Europe," he warned Abigail. "If you do, we shall cross each other, and I shall arrive in America about the same time that you may arrive in Europe." He also warned her of the hideous solitude among millions that she was sure to experience, pointing out how ardently Mrs. Jay was longing for home. In other words, Abigail was to do nothing but stay in Braintree and wait for her "old friend." Besides, he wished them to live in their own country for another reason. "Upon no consideration whatever, would I have any of my children educated in Europe. In conclusion, I could not consent to it."[68]

Yet, while John yearned for his homeland with all his heart, his intellect craved something different. In reality he craved the chance to stay abroad, nurturing the single hope that he would be needed and wanted by his government for further service, that he would be accorded the one honor that would keep him from returning to his children to live with them in "simplicity, innocence and repose." On February 27, in a letter to Abigail revealing still-tender wounds, John claimed to be adamant about going home unless

> I receive a commission to St. James's. Don't you embark, therefore, until you receive a letter from me desiring you to come. If I should receive such a commission, I will write you immediately by way of France, Holland and England, and shall wish you to come to me on the wings of the wind. But the same influence, French influence I mean, which induced Congress to revoke my commission, will still continue to prevent the revival of it. And I think it likely, too, that English influence will now be added to French, for I don't believe that George wishes to see my face.[69]

John's sense of failure as a diplomat was firmly ingrained. He was almost childlike in knowing the rules, and in being unable to observe them. While grumbling his way through suppers and visits with princesses and their princes, he knew it was much "wholesomer" to act the complaisant, good-humored, contented courtier. But something deep within him imposed limitations; frankly, he admitted his "Courtierism" would never be extensive. Playing his own Hamlet, he recognized the problem: "I must be an independent Man and how to reconcile this to the Character of Courtier is the Question."[70]

His suspicions concerning the French did nothing to help him resolve his problem. French policy was so alarmingly subtle, to his thinking, that one could not be steady enough, patient enough, or determined enough when dealing with it or its perpetrators. In his opinion, Poland, Sweden, Corsica, and Geneva had all been victims, had all suffered the "horrid effects" of the French policy because of their yielding to it, whereas Switzerland, fearless of France, enjoyed her as an ally. If America was supported by a sturdy Congress, it would go clearly to the windward of the French; if Congress wavered, the United States would be stunted in such a way that it would not recover its present momentum in another fifty years, John predicted.[71]

Exhausted, John could not help contrasting his own bleak future and indifferent reputation with that of Benjamin Franklin, whose benign rapport with the detested and damaging Comte de Vergennes infuriated him. Franklin's popularity was due to his being "pliant and submissive," John thought; the result of keeping "Scribblers in his Pay in London to trumpet his fame." Franklin's appointment of his grandson William Temple Franklin as secretary of the commission only fueled his resentment and confirmed his theory that Dr. Franklin and Vergennes meant Billy to be made minister to the French court, and not "improbably" that the elder Franklin would go to London. "Time will shew," John said, inferring that it would decidedly bear out his tormenting prognosis.[72]

Except for their common birthplace being Boston, given their wholly differing moral attitudes, interests, and temperaments, it seemed inevitable that Franklin and Adams would clash over their treatment by and of the French. Franklin had felt obliged to report to Congress on August 9, 1780, that "Mr. Adams has given Offence to the Court here, by some Sentiments and Expressions contained in several of his letters to the Count de Vergennes." Adams, not having proper business elsewhere, seemed to Franklin to have endeavored to "supply" for his own defective negotiations, or those seemingly so to his colleague. Adams, Franklin explained further, felt that America had been too free in expressions of gratitude to France, that she was more obliged to America than America to her. Adams felt America should show "Spirit" in dealing with France.[73]

On the contrary, Franklin thought the court ought to be treated with decency and delicacy, that the King, a young and virtuous Prince, had, he was persuaded, pleasure in reflecting on the generous "Benevolence of the action in assisting an oppressed people" and proposed it "as a part of the glory of his reign." Franklin was persuaded that different conduct was not only "improper and unbecoming, but may be hurtful to us."[74]

Very likely, Adams was keener in comprehending the influential role that de Vergennes meant to play while Franklin was neither "aggressive or suspicious enough" championing the American point of view. Eventually, it was John Jay who would convince Franklin to negotiate peace with Great Britain without consulting de Vergennes. John, admittedly suspicious of court life, where, he told Abigail, he thought "conversation is only to flatter one that he may betray another," was undoubtedly honest but uncomfortably blunt, if not clumsy in his dealings with the French. He was the first of three generations of diplomats who collectively would earn the comment that "Adamses have a genius for saying even a gracious thing in an ungracious way."[75]

Mention of London and service in Great Britain touched every tender nerve of aspiration, dredged up all of his frustrations and his ambitions. He wanted the assignment to Great Britain desperately, and he had virtually applied to Congress for the job, writing to its president early that February. In describing to Elias Boudinot the qualifications he thought necessary for the foreign minister designated to the Court of St. James, he was sketching an exquisitely idealized, though fundamentally accurate portrait of himself:

> in the first place he should have had an education in classical
> learning and in the knowledge of general history ancient and
> modern, and particularly the History of France England Holland
> and America, he should be well versed in the Principles of Ethicks,
> of the Law of Nature and Nations, of Legislation and Government,
> of the civil Roman Law, of the laws of England and the United
> States, of the public Law of Europe, and in the letters, memoirs
> and Histories of those great men who have heretofore shone in the
> Diplomatic order, and conducted the affairs of the nations and the
> world.[76]

John had added that this paragon ought to possess maturity of judgment gained from experience, ought to be active, attentive and industrious, and ought, above all, to possess an upright heart and an independent spirit. He should also "decidedly" be one who made the interest of his country and not the policy of any other nation, or his private ambition or interest or that of his family, friends, and connections, the rule of his conduct. He reminded the president of Congress that in neither America nor Europe had the present revolution been accomplished by elegant bows or by fluency in French.[77]

All that spring of 1783, John balanced despair against pessimism, bitter criticism against blatant hostility. Vergennes was the "vulcan at Versailles" whose chains he would elude. Though they might imprison many, he told himself they would never be strong enough to imprison a giant who would break through them, shatter them "like morsels of glass." He would not be "horse-jockeyed," he insisted. And at least, if he was, de Vergennes and Franklin should not be the jockeys. John grew increasingly dramatic, even paranoid, talking about a wound upon his honor; he would wear no livery with a spot upon it; stains would have to be taken out or he would not wear the coat. In fact, he thought Congress and its ministers had been treated like children, trifled with, imposed upon, deceived. Franklin's reputation had helped lend credibility to Vergennes, and, in truth, John thought he could hope for little success, pitted against them.[78]

John promised his friend General Warren that the moment another person was appointed to Great Britain, he would be going home, leave or no leave. And to Abigail he confided that he was sure "some booby will be sent, in complaissance to two silly courts." Yet he was "soberly" of the opinion that for one or two years to come he could do more good in England for the United States of America than in any other spot upon earth. While he did not go so far as to spell out Franklin as the "booby" he most expected to fill the position he cherished, he could not suppress his abiding revulsion of America's senior statesmen.[79]

A letter written on April 6, 1783, to Arthur Lee embodied the fury that seethed inside John; it overflowed with bitterness.

> I expect soon to see a proposition to name the 18th century the
> Franklininian Age: Le Siecle Franklininien, and I am willing to
> leave the question whether it shall be called Franklininian or
> Frederician, to him and the King of Prussia; tho I think the latter

stands no chance, as a French writer, within a few weeks, says
Franklin will after a few Ages be considered as a God and I take it
Frederich has not enough of the Caesar in him to dispute with a
God.[80]

The English called Franklin the "Founder of the American Empire,"
but John had devised a title he thought more apt: "the Demon of
Discord among American Ministers and the curse and Scourge of
their cause." No one man had, in his opinion, "the least colour" of
a just pretension to the title of founder, not even George Washington. If he did have to name one, however, he would not be ashamed
to say that Mr. Samuel Adams was the man who had acted the "long-
est and most essential part in this Revolution" and, further, he could
say this without fear of being contradicted by Posterity.[81]

It was, of course, not Franklin's politics alone that alienated John.
It was said of Sir Walter Raleigh that his morals were not sufficiently
exact for a great man, and John thought that observation could never
be applied with more propriety than to Dr. Franklin. The latter's
whole life, John thought, considering its vast measure, had been "one
continued insult to good manners and to decency." His referrals of
his bastard son and grandson, with what John called "characteristic
modesty," and his mention of his friend Polly Baker, were outrages
to morality and decorum, not to be forgiven in any other American.
John knew it would be folly to deny that Franklin had a great genius,
or that he had written several things in philosophy and in politics
apparently worth reading; he only meant to make clear that he
thought Franklin's reputation inflated, even grossly exaggerated. It
had become "one of the greatest impostures that ever had been
perpetrated upon mankind since the Days of Mahomet," he told his
friend Warren.[82]

That April, John seemed to grope his way to the pinnacle of uncertainty, to wallow in ambiguity. He was not ambitious, he said, of the
honor of a commission to the Court of St. James. Nor did he entertain
any expectations of a happy life in England. But pride, integrity, and
vanity were involved, he freely admitted. And he truly believed that
Congress could not soon enough send a minister to London to arrange a system of commerce to guard America's interests. He felt
sure that the French were at work in England, and he told Arthur Lee
"we may depend upon it they labor less for our good than their
own."[83]

While he sensed the necessity of a minister, and was sure that he himself could best execute the duties involved, John's private ambitions did not obscure his vision of the grandeur of the future. If the United States could keep united, they would in half a century give "Tone to the World." To his mind, his country was a singular one, a "Temple of Liberty" open to all humanity. He alluded, too, at this time, to the motivating force of his life, surpassing all others, his reverence for his country. "I never had through my whole life any other ambition than to cherish, promote and protect it, and never have any other for myself, nor my children. For this object, however, I have as much as any Conqueror ever had."[84]

For all his lofty purpose, John was still a parent and a husband and, most of all, a vulnerable being. Perplexed, even threatened, he turned to his family with almost childlike simplicity. Parted from them physically, he longed for them spiritually. Needing his independence from them in order to prove his worth, he turned to them when his hopes for fulfillment of his ambitions were most feeble. He was no longer a boy or a young man, and no matter what he wished for his country, he had needs of his own. "My family has become an indispensable necessary of Life to me," he confessed. He was thinking there was no employment however honorable, no course of life however brilliant, that had such a "luster" in his imagination as an absolutely private life. His farm and his family "glitter" before his eyes, every day and night, he told his friend James Warren. "Decide my fate therefore as soon as possible," he begged, "if it is not yet decided."[85]

Taking stock, John concluded that the times had made a strange being of him. He was a domestic animal who was never at home, a bashful creature, a timid man braving the greatest dangers. He was also an "irritable fiery mortal," enduring every provocation, and yet a humble farmer despising pomp, power, and wealth. But whatever else he might be, he consoled himself that there was no conflict in one area, at least. He was "an honest man in all and to the Death."[86]

Midsummer, John returned to the Netherlands to talk and write about America's interests, to confer with patriot friends in the Hague, with merchants and bankers in Amsterdam, to pay respects to the Stadholder. Still, there was no solution to his dilemma, "the most insipid and at the same time disgusting and provoking situation imaginable." He was demoralized; he had decided he would rather be employed in carting street dust and marsh mud, in chopping wood and digging ditches on his farm, than in waiting through the present uncertainty. "Nobody knows that I do anything or have anything to do," he complained to James Warren. He had one consolation, "thank God," he said. "I have planted the American Standard at the Hague. There let it wave and fly in triumph over Sir Joseph Yorke and British pride. I shall look down upon the flagstaff with pleasure from the other world."[87]

John clung to his accomplishments in Holland and as time went on it was apparent that neither the Declaration of American Independence nor the Massachusetts Constitution nor the alliance with France would ever give him more satisfaction than his negotiations with the Dutch, which he would renew triumphantly in 1784, 1787, and 1788. Friendship with Holland erected an eternal barrier against dangers from the house of Bourbon as well as from England, he was certain.[88]

Back in France and in Passy, the morning of September 7, 1783 Benjamin Franklin handed John the Congressional Resolution just arrived the night before. As of the previous May 1 Congress had authorized that a commission be formed by John Adams, Benjamin Franklin and John Jay to enter into a Treaty of Commerce between the United States of America and Great Britain. These somewhat amorphous orders would be more refined only on May 7th and 10 of 1784 when Thomas Jefferson was appointed successor to John Jay as Minister plenipotentiary and joint commissioner in Europe and Jay was elected secretary for foreign affairs. John Adams was to head the new commission of the three plenipotentiaries meant jointly to negotiate with twenty powers—three more to be added that June. Even John's fears about William Temple Franklin were groundless. He was not to be promoted but, instead, replaced as secretary by David Humphries.[89]

About the choice of Thomas Jefferson, John was exceptionally generous. The latter was, after all, an old friend with whom he had often deliberated many knotty problems; of his abilities and steadiness he had always been confident. He thought his fellow laborer in Congress a uniformly wise and prudent man, a steady patriot whose approach to his many "tryals," particularly in the drafting of the Declaration of Independence, and in the formation of the Code of Articles of War and laws for the army, was scarcely equalled either in talent or virtue. John Adams' only reservation about this colleague, at this critical juncture in his life, was his fear that Jefferson's "unquenchable thirst of knowledge may injure his health."[90]

John's September appointment, though somewhat vague as it would turn out, was enough to renew his faith in his pursuit and refurbish his ambition. Now he could issue a wholehearted invitation to Abigail. Possibilities he had explored for hundreds of hours past crystalized now, and his letters to Abigail were full of optimism and purpose. "Will you come to me this fall and go home with me this Spring?" he asked his wife, for the uncountable time. And would she bring Nabby and leave the boys with her brother-in-law, Mr. Shaw, the school master? And would she plan to leave the responsibilities of her household to her father or Uncle Quincy, Uncle Tufts, or Mr. Cranch? John supposed that his letter would reach Abigail in October, and that she would leave for Europe in November or December. He asked that she write to him by every ship to Spain, France, Holland or England, that he might know when to expect her. He also told her that she gave him "more public intelligence than any body." The only hint in Europe of this commission was from her to "Yours, forever."[91]

John's enthusiasm was momentarily deflected by the recurrence of his illness of two years before in Amsterdam. He was feverish, faint and sleepless. But John Thaxter, his former law clerk, friend, secretary, family tutor, nurse, physician and comforter while in the Netherlands together, had sailed for America. John was now dependent on his French servants and Sir James Jay, John Jay's brother. Jay, a physician, advised him to move from the grinding noise of the Place du Carrousel, a thoroughfare wracked with the constant roar of carriages at least twenty-one out of twenty-four hours. Thomas Barclay, the Philadelphia merchant serving as American consul in France, took pity on him and offered his apartments in Auteuil, just four miles from Paris, known as a place of *salubrité* as far back as the twelfth century. By September 22, John's health was improving, thanks to peaceful walks in the garden and restoring rides in an open carriage or even on horseback. His son John Quincy was also a comfort, proving, as his secretary, to write "a good hand very fast."[92]

It had, of course, not only been traffic noise that unnerved John and compounded his illness but the indecision that obscured his future and his severe loneliness and unhappiness without Abigail. The stress too of the financial negotiations on behalf of his country, of the four and six and more month intervals between official communications, let alone letters from home, cost him, he had admitted, "much fatigue and ill health." Self-pity, nearly a disease in itself, had been rampant in John at this time.[93]

But ill as John was he urged Abigail to embark for London, Amsterdam or any port in France. Now all ominous warnings were forgotten. He could only see the positive aspects of her visit. Surely, she would find friends enough, and certainly stimulation enough. Coming to Europe with Nabby, as soon as possible would satisfy their daughter's curiosity and improve her taste. Viewing magnificent scenes, going to plays, seeing splendid buildings, would be of "service" to wife and daughter, apart from making them happy. As for himself, he would now realize the fulfillment of his most ardent wish, he confided to the newly married Charles William Frederic Dumas, unofficial American *chargé d'affaires* at The Hague. "I hope to be married once more myself, in a few months, to a very amiable lady whom I have inhumanly left a widow in America for nine years, with the exception of a few weeks only. Ask Madame Dumas," John continued, "whether she thinks she has Patriotism enough to consent that you should leave her for nine years pro bono publico? If she has she has another good title to the character of an Heroine."[94]

PART
TWO

PART

TWO

NINE

A Mere American

The ship was named the *Active,* all too accurately. It rocked
on the mountainous sea like a giant cradle festooned with billowing white cloth webbed with interminable rope. When the sailors
attributed the violent motion to a "breeze," Abigail could only hope
heaven would defend her from a storm. Just to move a finger made
her dizzy; she could not even bend over to put her shoes on alone.
Crashing bottles, dishes, plates, chairs, and tables only orchestrated
her misery. Sometimes she and the other passengers had to be tied
to their deck chairs or cabin bunks; all too frequently, one of the male
passengers would almost sit in her lap to keep her from falling out
of her chair, while he braced his feet against a table to keep it from
toppling over on her. Other times, when she had to be helped to her
cabin to lie down, "obliged" to hold herself in with all her might, she
was certain that seasickness was the most "disheartening, dispiriting
malady."[1]

Abigail was clearly embarrassed. She would have refused to believe, before embarking on June 20, 1784, that she could lie herself
down at night "in common with half a dozen gentlemen," with only
a curtain between them, having shed as many layers of wool and
calico from her frail frame—though thankfully no more, she said—
as a Yankee bundler. The door of her prison-size, eight-foot-square
stateroom, with its small, solitary window fenced with iron, opened
into the men's cabin, which also happened to serve as dining quarters. It was shut only when it was time to dress or undress; otherwise

she would have suffocated, she was positive, or at least have been poisoned by the foul air that clotted her every breath.[2]

Inevitably, however, Abigail adjusted to the demands of the occasion. Reassured one early morning by the smooth sea and the mild blue sky, she pronounced it time to make a "bustle" over matters, at least in the matter of cleanliness, a virtue both "Cardinel and Deified" in her opinion. If she could not remedy the "odorifferous" cargo of leaking and fermenting oil and potash, she could most definitely see that the filthy passageways were cleansed, so that she wasn't obliged to scrub her shoes every time she traversed them. Her mind made up, she did not waste a moment. Her manservant, John Briesler, luckily recovered from his own bout with nausea, was dispatched to muster as many hands as he could to set to work with scrapers, mops, brushes. In a few hours, and with multiple infusions of vinegar, the boards of the floors were visible; in fact, the job was so well done that Abigail almost thought herself on a different ship.[3]

Next on the agenda was the matter of food, and the cook in particular. Abigail thought him dreadfully disorganized, and his "higgledy-piggledy" manner of presenting dinner intolerable. First came the leg of pork, all bristly, then fifteen minutes elapsed before he produced a pudding, or maybe a pair of roast fowls, and then a piece of beef; when dinner was nearly finished, he was apt to bring on a plate of potatoes. Supervising the cook, Abigail finally taught him how to prepare and present his food decently; on several occasions she concocted puddings on her own that she personally found the only things fit to eat anyway. The cook was not only taught order but cleanliness, the putrid milk pail receiving repeated soapy dousings, though Abigail had already decided that if the passengers did not die immediately of dirt, they would certainly have eaten at least a peck's worth.[4]

All in all, only the hope of ending what Abigail counted as a ten-year separation from her husband—John had set out for Philadelphia in August 1774—could justify this wrenching change in her life. About to turn forty in the autumn, Abigail was sure she would have been otherwise quite content with the "page of the Historian" and never sought this firsthand view of her own. Yet, halfway out to sea, when she had learned to live with the dampness that aggravated her rheumatism and made her head ache until she could hardly read, she began to believe that serenity was not always the most desirable state in life, that perhaps every object was most beautiful in motion: trees agitated by the wind, a fine woman dancing, a ship under sail. Man was made for action, perhaps, and, after all, in an instance of self-discovery, Abigail found herself admitting, "I am quite out of conceit with calms." At eight or nine knots, the ship loping across the ocean at one hundred miles a day, Abigail began truly to appreciate the beauty of the voyage. Bound in her chair, hemming a handkerchief, studying the porpoises and their spiraling gymnastics, she scrutinized the sea with a poet's eyes, finding it "smooth as a Glass, then gently agitated with a light Brieze, then lifting wave upon wave, moving on with rapidity, then rising to the Skyes, as in majestic force to our ship to & fro, alternately riseing & sinking."[5]

Caught by the sea's splendor, as well as revolted by the ship's filth, erosion of privacy, and physical punishment, Abigail was soon intrigued by the challenges of her new life at sea. "Daughter of Eve," James Lovell had teased her, her admitted curiosity irrepressible. The prison had turned into schoolroom, library, theater, and she herself could not help marveling at her resiliency. A fragment from Alexander Pope echoed her determination to make the most of this fresh adventure:

> *Pleasures are ever in our hands and eyes:*
> *And when in act they cease, in prospect rise.*[6]

The kind and ever-watchful captain, Nathaniel Byfield Lyde, though he could not be called a polished gentleman, was certainly a clever one, took an interest in her writing, and brought large sheets of paper to her cabin. In turn, she set out to learn the names of the masts and sails that so preoccupied his attention. Passing his test with a most rewarding accolade, she knew enough to steer the boat herself, the captain had told her. Abigail could also divert herself by reading. *A Political Survey of Britain* by John Campbell spurred her to the huffy conclusion that America equaled, if not surpassed, Britain's advantages. "The one half has not been told" she decided, and she did not forget that two of the most celebrated painters living among the British were Americans named Copley and West. Another book that absorbed her time was William Buchan's *Domestic Medicine.* The author's proposal that a change of ideas was as necessary for health as a change of posture appealed to her as especially pertinent to her remarkable new situation.[7]

When Abigail tired of books, she enjoyed studying her fellow passengers. At a square table in what she called the "great" cabin, she often noticed Colonel Norton, a grave, sedate man, whose literary accomplishments she thought "not very great," playing backgammon with a merchant, Mr. Foster, a great favorite of Nabby's. A Scotsman named Green, Abigail found haughty and imperious; he "plumes himself upon his country," she complained. Edging around gently in her chair on Sunday noon, she saw that Mr. Green was writing, Dr. Clark was eating ham, and Mr. Spead, whose easy and happy "blow high or blow low" humor and wit she thoroughly enjoyed, was reading James Thomson's *Seasons* with his hat on. Almost tipping backwards, she found her maid, Esther, relaxed and knitting, realized Nabby was still asleep in the cabin she shared with a woman coincidentally also named Adams, who was no relation. The atmosphere was certainly relaxed, virtually festive, as she watched the steward bustling about serving wine.[8]

The sense of peace had endured throughout that day. At dusk it looked to Abigail as though thousands and thousands of fireflies bejeweled the ocean, kindled the horizons, and illuminated her most private thoughts in the process. She had agonized about this trip, about the sea, about people she would leave behind, about those she would meet anew. Just the past February, she confided to John her fears about being unequal to the trial, about presenting an awkward figure at court.

> You invite me, you call me to follow you, the most earnest wish of
> my soul is to be with you—but you can scarcely form an idea of the
> conflict of my mind, it appears to me such an enterprize, the ocean
> so formidable, the quitting my habitation and my country, leaving
> my children, my friends with the idea that perhaps I may never see
> them again, without my Husband to console and comfort me. . . .

It was remarkable, now that there was hope of landing at Portsmouth this next Tuesday, that the fear of touching ground was dispelled. In the beginning, she hadn't thought she would survive the thirty days aboard ship; now she felt she could continue for eight or even ten days more. She marveled at how easily one could become reconciled to the most disagreeable situations. Her ability to overcome obstacles surprised even her.[9]

Abigail pulled the thick green woolen cape closer to her slender body as she contemplated the ocean and its "secret world of wonders."

The report of the captain's mate that the ship was within fourteen hundred miles of the British coast reminded her of lines of poetry that described "a sober sense of joy," a "joy prepared to weep." Hers, too, was a joy of many emotions. As "a mere American" she pondered the imminent challenge of court life and its unfamiliar etiquette and how she would fare, given her habits, "taught to say the thing I mean, and to ware my heart in my countenance." But more than her own future, she was concerned for her daughter's. It was because of Nabby that Abigail had grown so fond of the soft-spoken Mr. Foster, who seemed to sense her daughter's needs, soothe her, and entertain her. "Nobody said a word," Abigail wrote Elizabeth Shaw, "nor do I know from any thing but his manner of treating her that he suspected it. . . . She has behaved with a Dignity and Decorum worthy of her."[10]

Abigail was referring to Nabby's role in what her parents called "The Family Affair", which had given greater impetus to their trip abroad than they might have realized. John had recognized immediately on learning of his daughter's romantic involvement that it would require delicate handling, but thought it "may be managed very well. The Lady comes to Europe with you—if the parties preserve their regard until they meet again and continue to behave as they ought they will be still young enough. . . ." The father had not sounded quite so genial when his wife first informed him of Nabby's involvement with the dashing newcomer.[11]

At Christmastime in 1782, Abigail had reported with care that their little circle at home included "another Gentleman" who had opened his office in town, who had earned his welcome by his attractive and appealing personality, despite gossip about his dissipation of much of his fortune. Certainly, from Abigail's vantage point, his behavior was "unexceptionable" since he had taken up residence in town, and in consequence, his business, which was law, had increased. In conclusion, Abigail had said she felt this gentleman would not fail to make a distinguished figure in his profession, if he pursued it steadily. She was not acquainted with any young gentleman whose attainments in literature were equal to his, she had added, or anyone who had more accurate judgment, or more delicate and refined taste. "His days are devoted to his office, his Evenings of late to my fire side."[12]

The tall, darkly handsome, vigorous newcomer with curly hair and a musical voice, the heir to £4,100 and a chaise, a mansion, a ship, and a store, who was the subject of Abigail's admiring scrutiny, was the twenty-five-year-old Royall Tyler, a boarder with the Cranch family. He had entered Harvard at fifteen, and graduated in 1776 as valedictorian of his class; subsequently he had earned a master's degree, read law, and was admitted to the bar in 1779. Abigail, full of praise for Tyler, was beholden, in her scrupulous way, to brush in some less appealing details, though she dealt with them sympathetically.

> Loosing his Father young and having a very pretty patrimony left him, possessing a sprightly fancy, a warm imagination and an agreeable person, he was rather negligent in persueing his business in the way of his profession; and dissipated two or 3 years of his Life and too much of his fortune for him to reflect upon with pleasure; all of which he now laments but cannot recall. . . ."[13]

Royall Tyler had not incurred the village gossip without provocation. Abigail, even if she knew about them, omitted news of the "Great disorders" he was said to have initiated at college, where he was remembered for his drinking, his profanity, his noisy binges, and his shocking response to members of the Harvard faculty who charged him with shattering the glass of some dormitory windows. Though he later apologized, at the time of his reprimand he had said he cared nothing for a little paltry degree that might be bought for twenty shillings at any time. Far graver was another charge, never proven, but never entirely refuted; the volatile yet gifted young man was said to be the father of one Royal Morse, the son of a charwoman at Harvard.[14]

That Nabby knew Tyler's blemished past seems logical, judging from the message of warning she had written to her cousin Elizabeth Cranch in June of 1782, just six months before her own mother was to send news abroad of Nabby's relationship with Tyler. Affection, Nabby assured her cousin, was her inducement for writing. Although she was confident Betsy could protect herself from temptation in any shape, she ought to know that everyone who was formerly acquainted with Tyler told her that he was the essence—the quintessence—of artfulness. Nabby only feared he would ingratiate himself into Betsy's good opinion.

> His character and his conduct are not deserving the least degree of your friendship and I dare say you will discover it soon if you have not at present. I was told the other day that I could not see him and not become acquainted with him. I am determined to avoid the least degree of acquaintance if anything short of affrontery will

answer his whole study, his dissimulation; our sex cannot be too careful of the characters of the acquaintance we form.[15]

Who else but Abigail could have forbidden Nabby to meet Tyler, and who else but this colonial knight, in snowy ruffles, scarlet waistcoat, white vest and knee breeches, could alter her opinion so remarkably? Within six months, Abigail would be hinting not only at a more permanent relationship among all of them, but talking with pride about the increasing "esteem and kindness" in which the town held Tyler. When Tyler began to negotiate for the ample property known as the Vassall-Borland place, with its rolling meadow and mahogany-paneled house that was, ironically, to become the Adams homestead on their return from Europe, and for generations to come, Abigail took this as a concrete move on his part to solidify his relationship in the hope he would not be considered "unworthy a connection in this family."[16]

At sixteen, when the solemn, often inscrutable Nabby captivated Royall Tyler, there were those who thought her a beauty, especially a younger cousin who could never forget Nabby in her riding habit made of blue cotton bound in blue satin. The small matching hat, bravely feathered, and curving over soft, dark curls, had framed a rounded face on which her father's rather puffy features were delicately transposed into an almost cherubic softness. Still, her attraction to Tyler surprised her mother. When people spoke of Nabby, they tended to talk of her "discretion and good sense." Even her mother recognized in her daughter "as much apparent coldness and indifference as ever you saw in one character," acknowledging candidly that Nabby's formidable reserve kept people at a distance. Appearing so unyielding, almost wooden, Abigail spoke of her daughter as not possessing "all" of her mother's sensibilities, a discreet way of saying she thought her daughter quite insensitive. Yet daily, before her stunned and delighted eyes, she noticed that Tyler's attraction was so powerful that he at last succeeded in piercing the waxen exterior; accurately, she could say that his attention "daily becomes more pleasing" to her daughter.[17]

Abigail, investigating her quarry in her typically searching way, but "with decency and without disclosing motives," was delighted to learn that even in his most dissipated state, Tyler always used his mornings for study. If, at Christmastime, he had not quite won

Nabby's hand, he had certainly earned her mother's affection and sympathy. One evening, when he seemed in a state of what could only be described as "misirable doubt" over his status with her daughter, Abigail was compelled to write a note that might clarify his involvement. It seemed only fair to tell him that she might quit America in the spring, that she planned for Nabby to go with her, and that if they did go, she wished to take her daughter with a mind "unattached." Besides, she suggested somewhat bluntly to the would-be suitor, he wasn't established enough to think of a connection with anyone.[18]

The effusive response of the future playwright and judge assured his hoped-for mother-in-law of his "love and respect" and confidence in her.

> . . . . I can safely trust my dearest fondest wishes and persuits in the hands of a Friend that can feel, that knows my situations and her designs. If reason pleads against me, you will do well to hesitate. If friendship and reason unite I shall be happy. Only say I shall be happy when I *deserve;* and it shall be my every exertion to augment my merit, and this you may be assured of, whether I am blessed in my wishes or not. . . .

Abigail's reaction was all Tyler could ask for. To John she wrote that she felt "too powerful a pleador" within her own heart, reminiscent of her own early affections, to forbid Tyler hope.

> I feel a regard for him upon an account you will smile at, I fancy I see in him Sentiments, opinions and actions which endeared to me the best of Friends. Suffer me to draw you from the depths of politicks to endearing family scenes.—I know you cannot fail being peculiarly interested in the present.[19]

John was indeed "peculiarly interested," but not in the way Abigail might have hoped; two days after signing the armistice at Versailles, he adopted a strong position on "The Family Affair." An irate father and thoroughly annoyed husband wrote back to say that the contents of Abigail's letter had awakened all his sensibility. He did not like the subject at all, thought his child too young, and did not, under any circumstances, relish the word "dissipation." Not only did he not know what it meant in this case, but nothing Abigail told him could convince him that there was enough modesty and diffidence in the traits of the suitor to satisfy him *or* their daughter. "My Child is a model as you represent her and as I know her and is not to be the Prize." Furthermore, he did not wish Abigail to criticize their daughter's prudence, and was amazed to hear her refer to Nabby's "want of Sensibility." The more silent she was in company, the better; "I would have this observed as a Rule by the Mother as well as the Daughter," he added.[20]

Royall Tyler had failed on all counts, as far as John was concerned. "Was he a speaker at the Bar?" John asked. If not, he would never be anything, was his tight-lipped conclusion. Besides, John positively forbade any connection between his daughter and any youth upon earth who did not totally eradicate every taste for gaiety and expense. He had never known anyone who had it, and indulged it, that was not made a rascal by it, sooner or later. Unfortunately, he could readily name an example of what he meant by pointing to Tyler's "detestible" brother, arrested for high treason by the London police, and "gallivanting" about in the company of the equally "amphibious" Winslow Warren, son of Mercy and James. Even Tyler's father, though John conceded that he was an honorable man, had not all those "nice" sentiments John preferred. In conclusion, he reminded Abigail that the business of his daughter's courtship was "too serious a subject to equivocate" and, further, that he didn't like this method of "courting" mothers. "There is something "too fantastical and affected" in all this business for me," he said.[21]

At the same time he scolded his wife, John soothed his daughter. He bade his "Image," his "superscription," his "Princess" to take care how she disposed her heart. He also told her that he hoped to come home and help choose a partner for her, or at least give her some good advice. If he was not mistaken about her character, it was not gaiety and superficial accomplishments alone that would make her happy. Rather, "It must be one who can ride 500 miles upon a bolting horse and cross the Gulf Stream with a steady heart. One may dance or sing, play or ride, without being good for much," he reminded her. Then, wistfully, he added that he flattered himself with the hopes of a few years of the society of his daughter, at her father's house.[22]

Despite his strenuous protestations, John took a more pragmatic view of the possibilities of a "connection" between his daughter and Tyler than he revealed to either mother or daughter. Checking on Tyler over the next months, he wrote to various friends for references, and read with studious regard several unsolicited ones. He begged Francis Dana, in St. Petersburg, to tell him in confidence about the character of a Mr. Tyler who had once studied with him, asking about Tyler's moral character, literary talents, and future at the bar, insisting that he not be spared the truth "in the least." He was appreciative of General Joseph Palmer's reassurances of Tyler's behavior since coming to Braintree. Whatever was said about any wild oats Tyler might have scattered before coming to Braintree, Palmer himself could only say that Tyler was "generally respected, & had, I believe, his full share of business."[23]

Once again, however, Tyler showed he had a natural flair for bridging doubts about himself, with father as well as mother. He began the new year of 1784 with a letter to John explaining his silence, and enclosing a reference from Richard Cranch.

> Dear Sir: When a man's views are sweet and his Intentions consistent with Honour and Virtue he seldom affecteth concealing. I will not presume therefore that my attentions to your daughter are unknown to you: If you demand why an affair of so much importance to your Domestic Concerns was not communicated by me sooner—I hope that my youth, the early progress of my professional career, and the continued expectation of your daily return to your Family will be accepted as a sufficient Apology. The increase of the strongest attachments is often imperceptible; while I everyday anticipated your return I heeded not that every day I increased my esteem for her virtues.[24]

Since Abigail was about to leave for Europe, Tyler was writing to John because he felt he could no longer put off seeking his approval of his suit. Though he did not think himself entitled to John's consent to an immediate union, he could not suffer this separation without requesting permission to expect it whenever Nabby returned to her native country. Their mutual esteem, he assured John, "was formed under the Inspection of your lady" and with the knowledge of the worthy family in which he resided. Wisely, Tyler had then obtained a positive testimonial from his landlord of two years, Richard Cranch: "From my acquaintance with him, he appears to me to be possessed of Politeness, Genious, Learning and Virtue; and I think he will make a very respectable Figure in his Profession of the Law. His Business in that Department increases daily."[25]

On January 25, signs of the father's capitulation were clearly recognizable. He must leave all to her judgment, John wrote Abigail. If Nabby wishes to marry, if her object is worthy, if Tyler has sown all his wild oats and will study, John could no longer object. Tyler's flattering references, combined with his purchase of the Vassall-Borland house and land, demanded a new approach. By April 3, John had made peace between Tyler and himself:

> Your connections and Education are too respectable for me to entertain any objections to them: Your Profession is that for which I have the greatest respect and Veneration. The Testimonials I have received of your personal Character and Conduct are such as ought to remove all Scruples upon that head. . . .[26]

As an ultimate sign of peace between them, John offered his true treasure, his books. Graciously, John wrote of his hope that "my Library may be of Use to you, in the Prosecution of your Studies or your Practice, the loan of it is at your Service." As further evidence of his trust, John asked that Tyler take care of his account books and assume responsibility for collecting debts and turning the proceeds over to Dr. Tufts. The ambivalent sequence of his next thoughts spoke of reservation, but also of consent. "But the lady is coming to Europe with her Mother," he added. Neither statement nor question, he said, "It would be inconvenient to you to make a voyage to Europe perhaps." Then, capitulation at last: "You and the young Lady have my Consent to arrange your Plans according to your own Judgments."[27]

Tyler probably received John's letter after Nabby's departure. Even if it had come earlier, it was doubtful that she would have stayed behind; duty, as she told him, motivated her commitment to her parents' plans for her to go abroad. Tyler's reply to his prospective father-in-law was exceedingly wordy, polite, and placating. Marriage, he agreed, was indeed a "Serious Affair," and, he assured John, the "Parties" involved had not proceeded with their plans without "suitable reflections" on its significance to the happiness of their friends and relations, as well as themselves. As a serious, sensible, prospective son-in-law, Tyler also discussed financial entanglements regarding his eighty-three-acre property and his expectation of momentary possession of it. He also acknowledged John's generous invitation to frequent his library with a reverent promise to "endeavour to make that use of it which is becoming a man who wishes to be serviceable to his friends and country." He had ended his letter (he was speaking for Nabby as well, he said) in hopes that their union would afford John and his "Lady" that enviable satisfaction which parents experience when they perceive their children "useful, worthy, respectable and happy." As things were to turn out, Tyler could not have named four more elusive aspects of Nabby's future.[28]

Eventually, it was rather "from necessity than choice" that Nabby decided to leave Tyler to accompany her mother abroad. Abigail understood the sacrifice: "The parting of two persons strongly attached to each other is only to be felt; description fails," she said. When the struggle was resolved, Nabby's self-discipline surprised her mother. She appeared to be calm and cheerful, though the only one who could actually elicit a smile from her, even a sad one, was Mr. Foster, understandably Abigail's favorite shipboard acquaintance. Whether it was her awareness of her daughter's intense inner conflict over her separation, or her own honest affection for the ardent young lawyer with whom she shared great intellectual rapport, or a guilty concern for his thwarted quest, Abigail was moved, one afternoon, though "sincerely" afflicted with seasickness, to write to Royall Tyler. The letter, profusely nostalgic, overflowing with advice, was oddly devoid of any reference to Nabby, except for the oblique mention of Abigail's own ability to "commisirate all your situations."[29]

It was on July 10, twenty days out, with ten more to go, that Abigail wrote to Royall Tyler that she had thought of him "frequently" and traced him in her imagination in one situation and another, following him in the morning sun, during the cool, fragrant, silent hours of the day, even to his professional employment. She spoke of observing his pleasure at his studies of the law, in the company of writers such as Grotius, Pufendorf, and Bacon, and of her admiration for his "close and heady" application to his work, his willingness to try to master the subjects of his study, rather than superficially skimming their surface. She promised him many things: reflection was like a "pale star" that would point to the truth; consideration of what he wished to be would make him what he ought to be; greatness had its seat in the heart but must be elevated by aspiration and by daring, and kindled by energy and force.[30]

Abigail's relationship with Tyler was obviously close; that she cared for him, and about his future, was indisputable. She spoke of his having ambition that should enable him to shine with distinguished brightness as a deep thinker, a close reasoner, an eloquent speaker. But the point she was really trying to get across was that talent, aspiration, and achievement were secondary to strictest honor and integrity. Although Abigail seemed nearly apologetic about her moralizing, she was nevertheless resolute. Tyler might ask why she was compelled to advise one who knew his duty. Her answer was direct: "Who of us my dear Sir practise as well as we know?" She also supposed that nobody took reproof so kindly as one who deserved most to be commended, and that everyone was in want of a friend who dealt plainly and gently with one. Abigail, as the self-designated friend, dealt with Tyler not only plainly and gently but also lengthily. Fame without honor would be ephemeral, "like a feint meter [faint meteor] gliding through the sky shedding only a transient light"; fame acquired with honor was to be compared to "fixed stars" that shine on to endless duration." Abigail's explicit instructions to Tyler reminded him to take care to have sentiments and thoughts worthy of himself, that virtue raises the dignity of man and vice degrades him, that "nothing makes a man truly valuable but his heart, and nothing but that can make him happy, since our happiness depends only on the nature of our inclinations." Trifling passions, she added, made one the sport of vain attachments. "They offer us flowers, but says Montaigne, always mistrust the quenching of your pleasures."[31]

Whether it was the long, solitary hours of ocean gazing that revived specters of Tyler's bygone follies, or merely her instinctive tendency to dwell on the subject of virtue, the sermonlike content of Abigail's lecture to Tyler was modified by the underlying tenderness of her questions. Did he visit their cottage out of habit, though it was deserted, remembering what it once was? And was her place "supplied" by the memory of pleasures from some other scene? Before she put down her pen, she had assured the young man that he had "a share and not a small one" of her affectionate regard.[32]

Early on Sunday, July 18, Abigail counted at least twenty boats with cloud-colored sails, signaling, like flags of welcome, the approach to the English Channel. Captain Lyde announced his hope of landing at Portsmouth within the next day or two, and recommended that passengers pack immediately, during this time of light wind and momentary calm. Methodically, Abigail readied the small trunks the captain referred to as hand luggage, her mind reviewing the events of the preceding month, which had taught her an impressive lesson. If she could not claim to have conquered her fear of the unknown, she could at least be proud that she was as happy as the sea would permit. One's humor made one agreeable or not; men of dark, sour humor had no music in their souls, she thought.[33]

It had, she recognized, taken a great deal of music to drown out the sorrowful memories of her departure from home, from the house of mourning she had left on Friday, June 18. They were no "unmeaning complimenters," but honest yeomanry who lined up from the road to her front door and passed through the sunny parlor, shaking her hand, sharing her tears. Her father's death that past December, her mother-in-law's great age, her love for her sisters and nieces, her devotion to Uncle Tufts, only intensified the pain of leave-taking. That night she wrote last-minute notes and letters; by noon the next day, Sunday, a crowd waved her, Nabby, and the servants, Esther Field and John Briesler, across the gangplank from Rowe's wharf to the *Active,* the ship Abigail had chosen especially because its copper bottom was regarded as a safety feature. Almost immediately, the ship threaded its way out of the thicket of the noisy, busy harbor, and though sick and terrified, Abigail mused about the endless gray distance ahead. The ocean, however else it affected her, awed her. Could she be so near the laws of her forefathers? And was she, "Gracious Heaven, there to meet the Dear long absent partner" of her heart? "How many how various how complicated my Sensations!" Abigail wrote into her shipboard diary that evening. "Be it unto me according to my wishes," she added prayerfully.[34]

One of the onerous realities of leaving home was the knowledge that people would change during her absence, that relationships would be altered by circumstances, if not by age or death. In a few instances they would disintegrate entirely, their traces etched only in memory. Such was the fate of Abigail's evanescent friendship with James Lovell, her enigmatic confidant, protector, and informer. Abigail had been appreciative of his "retailed Politicks"; since his return to Massachusetts she had lost her source of intelligence from Congress. He had been her dispatcher of mail, money, china, glass, and linens. She had always worried that his letters to her would be intercepted, and had warned him that the world would not understand his uniquely familiar writing style. When she had reprimanded him, cautioned him about unfriendly eyes and ears, he had explained that he never meant to hurt her or himself. He insisted he was not a "gallant," but only eager to administer even the smallest degree of satisfaction to a mind very susceptible of anxiety and a little prone, he feared, to see harm where there was none.[35]

But Lovell had come to harm, not because of a letter he had written to Abigail, but because of one to Elbridge Gerry. The discussion that had precipitated this particular letter had centered on rumors of Lovell's suspiciously prolonged absence from his wife in Boston. In his way, inferring rather than explaining his reasons for remaining in Philadelphia, Lovell asked Gerry, "Does my Wife look as if she wanted a toothless grey headed sciatic Husband *near* her? I am more Benefit to her at a Distance than in ♂ as the Almanac has it." The letter, with its unfortunate choice of the male sex symbol, intercepted and reprinted in the British-affiliated newspaper, James Rivington's New York *Royal Gazette,* appalled enemies and friends alike. Lovell's reputation was shattered, even colleagues pronounced him unworthy of his position as a member of Congress, the job, he claimed, that kept him, for financial reasons, from returning to his wife all these years.[36]

Abigail was swift to scold Lovell for "the unbecoming Levity," which he tried to explain away by insisting he had used the provocative hieroglyphic not in any sexual connotation, but as a symbol of the sign of Mars. But Abigail was interested only in the remedy, not the excuse. Only Massachusetts air would exorcise year-old charges of immorality that persisted in Philadelphia, as well as in his home state, that he had violated the most sacred of vows, that a house of ill repute was his residence, and a mistress his "Bosom associate." Though Abigail sailed for England before Lovell's future was settled, she would learn from Richard Cranch's letter to John Adams of her friend's fate. On July 3, 1784, Lovell was appointed naval officer for the Port of Boston. Richard Cranch wrote to John Adams of his hopes that the post would afford Lovell "genteel Living," that his virtues and sufferings in the common cause entitled him to more loyal support. Abigail had never withdrawn hers. This man of "inventive genius," with his fondness for intrigue and his devotion to Abigail, was part of the life she had left behind with finality. Lovell had kept her in the mainstream when she was at her most solitary, and she would always be grateful to him.[37]

On Saturday night, when soft breezes increased into demon gales, and thick fog blocked neighboring land and ships from sight, Abigail brushed away the past to concentrate on her survival. Her fear of crashing into the unknown and unseen was augmented by the sight of the weary captain, who would not leave the deck for food nor sleep. On Tuesday, July 20—in simmering winds and disintegrating fog, past Portsmouth (their original destination), past Dover's heroic stone cliffs, slanting skywards from watery depths—Abigail would own that she had successfully negotiated the final lap of her epic voyage in the fierce embrace of a gentlemen passenger. The couple were buttressed against the rim of the pilot boat, that they might escape the predatory six-foot waves. Some miles later the entire party, reminding Abigail of a parcel of naiads, was disgorged with a roaring thump onto the soaking sands of Deal's inhospitably muddy shore.[38]

Lodgings were available just across the road from the beach; post-chaises would be hired for the next morning at six. Only the seventy miles between Deal and London were left of a journey that had begun in earnest more than two years before. Abigail closed her eyes at the thought of reunion: "Heaven grant it may be a joy, without alloy."[39]

As Happy
as a Lord

~~~~~~

"I am twenty years younger than I was yesterday," John
wrote jubilantly, when he learned of Abigail's safe arrival in
London at eight o'clock on the midsummer evening of Wednesday,
July 21, 1784. Her news made him "the happiest man upon earth";
his only regret was his delay at The Hague. But he was sending her
Johnny, a son who was, "without partiality," as promising and manly
a youth as there was in the whole world—as well as the greatest
traveler of his age—who would help his mother prepare for a visit to
The Hague before the family's departure for France. Johnny was to
buy a coach of four places, as strong and decent a one as could be
had for 150 guineas. This would bring the family to him "conveniently," with the exception, perhaps, of an hour or two of seasickness
between Harwich and Hellevoetsluis. The two children and the maid,
Esther, would ride with Abigail; her manservant, John Briesler, was
to follow on horseback or in the stagecoach. Though every hour they
were parted would seem a day's length, she was not to hurry or tire
herself. John could not advise her about what clothes to bring, except
that she was to buy whatever was needed: "I beg you to do what is
proper, let the expense be what it may."[1]

John Adams was in brilliant spirits. With Abigail by his side, it
would be the first time he looked forward to traveling in Europe.
He thought himself "lucky" that in this fine season they would explore the sights of Utrecht, Breda, Antwerp, and Brussels together,
before settling in Paris, where he felt she would be happier than in

Holland, and would enjoy seeing the city, learning its language. "For my own part, I think myself made for this world," he rhapsodized to his wife.[2]

Word of Jefferson's unexpectedly prompt arrival in Europe, following Abigail's by six days, influenced John to change his mind about meeting his family in The Hague. Jefferson had moved swiftly and courteously, once he had received his assignment. He had journeyed to Boston to tell Abigail of his desire of "lessening some of the difficulties to which she may be exposed," and to inform her of reservations made for both their parties to sail together from New York. As he had arrived in Boston on June 19, too late for Abigail to change her plans to sail the next day, Jefferson could only help by writing John Adams to assure him that his wife "goes on a good ship." With Jefferson in Paris now, John conclusively canceled plans for Abigail's interim visit. "Stay where you are until you see me," he wrote on August first.[3]

It was quiet at Osborne's new family hotel, as quiet as any place in Boston. It wasn't difficult to obey John's wishes; in truth, she was relieved not to expend the time, money, and energy needed to make the trip to The Hague, but to enjoy her present quarters instead. From the terrace she could see the Westminster Bridge in one direction, the Blackfriars in another, with St. Paul's Cathedral asserting itself in the distance. The interior was equally agreeable; she admired the handsome, "genteely furnished" drawing room, of pale green accented with gold and crimson. Considering her staff of cook, chambermaid, and waiter, and despite the expense of three guineas weekly, she easily conceded that "nothing but the dust is wanting to have everything heart can wish."[4]

Traveling from Deal to London—she had wakened at five—Abigail's party encountered a passing chaise whose lone passenger was the victim of a robbery. Soon, the coach in front of hers stopped and there were cries of "Robbery, robbery!" Everyone was alarmed, everyone hid their money. The robber was pursued and captured. He looked about twenty and in despair as he attempted to lift his hat. Abigail thought him pitiful, and his being told that he had but a short time and "then, my lad, you swing" upset her. Though every robber might deserve death, to exult over the wretched was what *our* country is not accustomed to," Abigail reported to Mary Cranch.[5]

Otherwise, Abigail's journey along the smooth, sinuous road to

London was a triumph. Leading in the first of the four post-chaises hired by her and her fellow passengers, she never stopped gazing at the thatched roofs, the cows and sheep that looked larger than any she had ever known, the oxen that seemed smaller, and the absence of fences, except for occasional ones of clipped hedges. From Dover to Canterbury to Rochester, and on to Chatham, past forests and fields of oats, wheat, and beans, the party wound its way over the hilly terrain. When horses and carriages were switched, footmen had eased the way; at dinnertime, when powdered waiters brought eight different dishes besides vegetables, Abigail was positive it was the post-chaises that entitled their party to such respect.[6]

At dusk, the green land tenderly cultivated to the road's edge, as though it were a private garden—or so it seemed to Abigail—gave way at last to stone walks, houses, and squares of park. The city of London surprised her. She thought it both "magnificent and beautiful," the streets much wider, the buildings more symmetrical than she had imagined. With those obliging young men, Charles Storer, a recent graduate of Harvard, and her cousin William Smith to greet her on her one-night stay at Low's Hotel in Covent Garden, and to help her move the next morning to her lodgings at Osborne's, she was content, no mere American but feeling very much the esteemed visitor. Within days, Abigail's acquaintances from Virginia, Maryland, and Connecticut left cards and old Tory friends came to call, John Trumbull was heard from repeatedly, and Dr. John Clark presented himself not only for tea but for breakfast as well. "I can not find myself in a strange land," she said. "I hardly know how to think myself out of my own country. I see so many Americans about me."[7]

As any traveler would, Abigail was bound to make comparisons. She had only to read the *London Chronicle* to refresh her memories (as though she could forget them) of the bitter differences between America and Great Britain. Even Canada, viewing America's growing importance with a "longing eye," was talking about being oppressed by the weight of British "tyrannic jurisprudence," of seriously contemplating a revolt from their present "usurped" master, of determination to add another star to the American constellation. But there was proof, too, in this British newspaper, that certain areas of interest remained fixed: "Teeth, Scurvy in the Gums and Tooth Ach" were mutual enemies on both sides of the Atlantic.[8]

If, however, Abigail had to name one single instance of indelible proof of shared ancestry, common roots, it was John Singleton Copley's exhibit, to which Storer and Smith took her on Saturday, July 14. At Copley's studio she saw the august, full-length portrait of her husband with a map of Europe in his hand, standing before a globe of the world. She pronounced it "a most beautiful painting," before continuing on to a public viewing of a painting of the death of William Pitt, surrounded by his three grieving sons. Almost reluctantly, random thoughts of the past days locked into place for Abigail:

> I saw in this picture, what I have every day noticed since I came here, a strong likeness of some American or other; and I can scarcely persuade myself that I have not seen this person, that, and the other, before, their countenance appear so familiar to me, and so strongly mark our own descent.[9]

Judging London against Boston, weighing people and buildings and food of one city against another, rather impartially, was a preoccupation of Abigail's. She kept repeating, as she went about dining, sightseeing, and dressing for numerous appointments, that she was far better pleased than she had expected to be in London; the sun shone brighter, the fashions were simpler, and the food was less elaborate than she would have believed. "Our country, alas, our country!" she sighed, when she thought of how extravagant some Americans were, compared to the British.[10]

Abigail was in love, she said, with the "London stile" of entertaining. Though one was invited two days beforehand, meals were apt to be simple, having no more than two meat courses. At the home of her old friends, the Atkinsons, she dined on turbot, soup, a roast leg of lamb, and cherry pie, and felt more gratified by the social, friendly style in which she was treated than if a sumptuous feast had been set before her. Another dinner she considered more in the Boston style was composed of salt fish, pea soup, boiled fowl and tongue, roast and fried lamb with pudding, and fruit for dessert. If pressed, Abigail did admit that veal, peas, and cauliflower were her favorite foods.[11]

Abigail's opinion of fashion was somewhat divided; she was to be neither left out nor taken in completely. She was "not a little surprised" to see that dress, except for public occasions, was not very important. The gentlemen looked plain and so did the ladies, though it was true that one still had to wear a hoopskirt and have one's hair dressed, despite the acceptance of a common straw cap with a ribbon, even in company. Muslin was in style, silk was out, except for lutestring with its glossy finish. Determined to adjust her wardrobe to prevailing customs, she shortly found herself captive of the stay maker, mantua maker, hoop maker, the shoemaker, milliner, and hairdresser, all of these being necessary, she ruefully admitted, to transform one into a fashionable lady. But Abigail was amused and aspiring only to a point. She scorned the makeup that half of London used, and she thought the British at their most elegant when they achieved the neatness "which you see in our ladies." On the average, in her opinion, British women tended to be less feminine, less "soft," to have the manners of Amazonians, and to affect masculine attire.[12]

Another affectation that Abigail's candid nature found difficult to tolerate was the calculated way the British paid and received social calls. They left their calling cards without any intention or desire to meet their recipients; to ask if a party was "at home" was automatically to anticipate a negative answer. The party pursued might be flourishing in the next room, obviously at home, but not prepared to receive any company. Because her servant, the utterly provincial Esther, was new to this charade, her answer to another servant's inquiries for Abigail on behalf of her mistress, waiting below in her carriage, was positive: Mrs. Adams was indeed at home. Unfortunately, Abigail knew better and, besides, was exhausted from her morning's outing. To solve the dilemma posed by the well-meaning Esther, Nabby volunteered to finish dressing and hurry out into the corridor to present herself as Mrs. Adams, with neither servant nor mistress the wiser. "You must know," Abigail wrote her sister Elizabeth, "having brought a conscience from America with me, I could not reconcile this to it. . . ."[13]

On Friday, July 30, Abigail, tired out by her visits to the Foundling Hospital and the Magdalen Hospital, and by her long walks in green squares, was determined to stay at home. She had a headache, and Nabby, too, was down with what everyone called the London cold; besides, there had been hints that either her husband or son might arrive. Abigail was writing at her desk, as she did daily to her nieces, her Uncle Tufts, or her sisters. Suddenly a servant rushed into her room, puffing with the wonderful news: "Young Mr. Adams is come." "Where, where is he?" Abigail asked. "In the other house, Madam; he stopped to get his hair dressed," was the reply. Abigail waited. When she saw her son, she was afraid to speak for fear that he might be one of the many strangers she had met in the past months. Then he took the initiative: "O, my mama and my dear sister!" was all that he needed to say to remove all doubt.[14]

Later, Abigail wrote to Mary of her reunion with her son, whom she had only seen in a brief, three-month interval during the past six years and five months. He was now seventeen years old, and, according to Abigail:

> Nothing but the eyes, at first sight, appeared what he once was. His appearance is that of a man, and in his countenance the most perfect good humor; his conversation by no means denies his stature. I think you do not approve the word feelings, but I know not what to substitute in lieu, or even to describe mine. His sister, he says, he should have known in any part of the world. You must supply words where you find them wanting, and imagine what I have left unfinished.

John had gallantly told his wife that the prospect of seeing his family made him feel twenty years younger. Abigail's reaction was the opposite. She felt "exceedingly" matronly with a grown son on one arm, and a daughter on the other. But she was as exuberant as John: "Were I not their Mother, I would say a likelier pair you will seldom see in a Summers day."[15]

One week and a day later, another reunion took place. Nabby returned to her family's apartment at noon to find things mysteriously changed; there were also the additions of an unfamiliar hat, a sword, a cane, and two books. Her own room was rearranged as though someone had been sorting its contents. Almost in one breath, Nabby pummeled Esther with questions about whether her mother had received a letter, and why things were being moved, and who was the owner of the hat, the sword, and cane. Esther's answer was direct: "No, ma'm," she told Nabby, "she has received no letter, but goes tomorrow morning." Suddenly, Nabby understood. Her father had arrived. She did not hesitate for another moment, but flew upstairs, knocked softly at his door, and was received, she would remember, "with all the tenderness of an affectionate parent after so long an absence. Sure I am, I never felt more agitation of spirits in my life; it will not do to describe."[16]

Her father, too, wrote of the dramatic reunion with his family after what he counted to be ten years, except for a few visits:

> On Saturday noon, I had the satisfaction of meeting my friends in perfect health at the Adelphic Buildings in London. I never set my Foot in any other house, till next morning at ten when we all

embarked on board a coach which John [Johnny] had in readiness.[17]

Abigail considered her reunion with her family a prayer answered. The metal of her marriage was shining gold; her husband was "as happy as a lord!" Abigail wrote that "poets and painters wisely draw a veil over those Scenes which surpass the pen of the one and the pencil of the other; we were indeed a very very happy family once more met together after a Separation of four years."[18]

ELEVEN

À la Mode de Paris

Once they changed from horses that refused to budge beyond Westminster Bridge, and had defied the inhospitality of
the England Channel, Abigail began to inhabit a strange new world
of commitments, language, and friendship for which she was quite
unprepared. Beyond Calais, Boulogne, Montreuil, Amiens, and
Chantilly, as Paris loomed, her Braintree world receded. Her memory of Penn's Hill, the white wooden houses and steepled churches,
Uncle Tufts, the many Quincys, the Cranches and Shaws, began to
pale in the exotic Paris air.

The family arrived in Paris on August 13, and four days later they
were settled in the suburb of Auteuil, about four miles from the
Opéra house. The vast stone dwelling with forty beds, described by
John as being centered somewhere between the ghosts of Boileau,
Helvétius and Molière, was ensconced, actually, on the edge of the
Bois de Boulogne, the park he claimed as his own "without any
expense." Passy and Montmarte were silhouetted in the distance;
closer by, turreted chateaux with mansard roofs sat on vast and
rolling lawns like ample, aristocratic dowagers whose portraits were
suitably framed with elaborate cutwork fences. Privacy was preserved
by chestnut-lined driveways that resolved into secretive, ivy-mottled
courtyards.[1]

Abigail instantly recognized that the house was truly "gay and
really beautifull" compared to her lowly cottage, that the superb *allée*
of trees bisecting the ravishing flower beds in back were to her rough

lawn garden at home as silks were to calicoes. But beauty did not make for comfort nor ease. The whole question of trying to staff her French household highlighted the problem of different mores and, even more seriously, inadequate pay. To her own countrymen, her seven servants would be considered extravagant, she knew, unless they understood the whole issue of diplomacy. Quite surprisingly, Abigail's was a thoroughly pragmatic view of diplomacy, which must have evolved instantaneously with exposure to its practice.[2]

Abigail's protectiveness about her country, as well as her private reservations—she often thought the staff was maintained for "plundering" her—provoked sheer outrage. To send a person to Paris in a public character, to be a public jest, was an insult, she argued. Further, for a nation to degrade its own ministers by obliging them to live in "narrow circumstances" was penny wise and pound foolish. Abigail was certain that one entertainment at home fostered more successful negotiations than twenty official meetings. How, then, she asked, was she to accomplish with seven servants what the Spanish ambassador did with one hundred, including fifty in livery, and the English ambassador with fifty, including twenty in livery? Abigail was on a rampage: one foreign ambassador's table settings, she noted, cost more than the American ambassador earned in an entire year. Abigail's solution to financial hardship was to try to imbue her French household with New England order and thrift, an attempt that was rewarded with minuscule victory. The maître d'hôtel agreed to double as footman, on condition that he was given a gentleman's suit of clothing in place of livery.[3]

But, annoyed as she was by what she referred to as servant's "etiquet," Abigail also marveled at its ceremony. If areas of domestic duties had been legalized duchies, they could not have had more rigid boundaries. She employed a gardener, a cook, a coachman for the carriages and houses, and the aforementioned maître d'hôtel, who was in charge of supplies and also, Abigail was sure, of seeing that nobody cheated but himself. The staff also included a *valet de chambre*—their own John Briesler—a *femme de chambre,* who happened to be Abigail's own Esther (and worth a dozen others), and a *coiffeuse* who did some sewing. All these servants to put up with, Abigail complained, and still no washing was done in the house; if the American servants weren't willing to double and treble in their tasks, she was certain she would be "plagued" with half a dozen more.[4]

Having tended turkeys and geese at daybreak in Braintree, having cooked for family and boarders, having spun, sewed, and washed the family's clothing with only occasional assistance, Abigail found almost unforgivable the hairdresser who would not make her bed or sweep out her room, and the cook who would not think of washing a dish. In certain instances, even when the servant's performance was satisfactory, his attitude was a puzzle. Housework was a solemn business, yet the young man in charge of scrubbing floors looked like a "Merry Andrew," dancing as he drove foot brushes over the red tile in the first-floor salon (about one-third larger than the Warren's hall in Milton).[5]

In reality, Abigail had learned about divisions of labor during her brief stay in London. When she had asked her servant to send a barber to her, the servant of whom she had made the request stared at her "queerly." "You mean a hair-dresser, Madame, I believe?" "Ay. I want my hair dressed," Abigail had replied. "Why, barbers, Madame, in this country, do nothing but shave," the servant answered. These "fixed and settled departments" continued to disturb her now that she had crossed the Channel into France, where she found the situation worse, and simply could not adjust to those who would not "lift a pin out of their separate departments." They reminded her, each one, of Swift's high Dutch bride, she said, "who had so much nastiness, and so much pride."[6]

Not only the pressure of supporting servants irked Abigail and John; the cost of furnishing a household was punishing. They had to buy bed linen and table linen, and order silver, china, wineglasses, even decanters. With a guinea not going any further than a copper, they were "mortified" that Congress had cut John's salary by one-fifth, at a time when his family had increased and he was in need of more money, not less. John tried to explain, in letters home, that there was not a man in the world less inclined to pomp or entertainment than himself—it was a relief to be excused from both—but if he knew anything in the world, he knew that it was in the public's best interests to entertain. Nobody, for example, understood economy better than the Dutch nation, yet they were liberal with their own ambassadors.[7]

Unfortunately, it was the smell of filth rather than *muguet* that overwhelmed Abigail's first impression of Paris. It was the "very dirtiest place" she had ever seen, crammed with slovenly shops and narrow streets, filled with building supplies of lumber and stone.

Even in Auteuil, just four miles distant, one could not walk in the streets without wearing boots; mounting her own backstairs, she had to hold up her skirts to avoid soiling their hems, that is, until she set her servants to scrubbing the steps and floors. Although Boston could not boast such elegant buildings, the city was "much superior" to Paris, as London was to Boston.[8]

Yet Paris had its own allure. For one crown apiece, the Adams family (after parking its carriage near the Tuileries), could not only inspect the egg-shaped taffeta balloon with which man was beginning to explore the air, but watch it rise and float over the city. Another intriguing sight, though hardly Nabby's favorite, and for which there was no admission charge, was that of observing the Dauphin in the palace gardens which were open to the public on Sundays. Nabby found the three-year-old child, playing with his shovel under the vigilant eyes of four attendants, "pretty" and "sprightly," but she did make it clear she thought it "ridiculous" that any people should, either from necessity or choice, pay so much homage to a being who might rule them with a scepter of iron. October brought the centennial celebration of the playwright Pierre Corneille. The complex, talented Monsieur de Beaumarchais, the creator of Figaro, was already constantly written about in the newspaper *Mercure de France* regarding his *"nouveau Project de Bienfaissance"* (newest plan of charity). A piece by Handel was *"sans doute un chose curieuse à entendre"* (without doubt a curious thing to hear), of its time, yet also modern, as a music reviewer wrote. A book, regarded as a *"plaisanterie,"* was called *Voyage Autour de la Terre avec Le Globe Aeroflatique (Voyage Around the World in a Hot-Air Balloon)*. Publication of *Nouveau Voyage Sentimental (A Sentimental Journey)* by Laurence Sterne was noted.[9]

Abigail's first destination, once she reached Paris, was the milliner; she needed to replace the four caps, worth at least five guineas, that she had somehow lost on the trip to London. Without her head covered, she could not be seen in public; dignity and modesty were, after all, significant facets of fashion, by her standards. Later, when she sat for Gilbert Stuart, she insisted on covering her head, though the artist tactfully suggested that she do otherwise. This September of 1784, cap in place, children in hand, husband in tow, Abigail descended on Paris and was, almost simultaneously, bemused by its variety, shocked by its contrasts, and eventually entranced by its beauty, customs, and even fashions, which at first had "disgusted" her. Within five months of her arrival, she could boast of knowing that it was a sign of politeness rather than incivility when a man sniffed at a partridge leg to determine whether it was fit for consumption by the ladies. She also claimed she was used to seeing a lady rapturously put her arms around a gentleman and "salute" him first on one cheek, and then on the other. She now considered this a thing of "mere course," and even viewed a touch of rouge rubbed off in the process as an added flourish.[10]

Studying the many beauties as well as some of the "deformities" of the Old World, Abigail began to talk about finding her taste "reconciling itself." At the ballet, for example, she was enchanted, she said, by the dress and beauty of the performers; once they began to dance, however, she felt her delicacy "wounded," and found herself ashamed to look at them. Girls clothed in the thinnest silk and gauze, with short petticoats, "springing two feet from the floor, posing themselves in the air, with their feet flying, and as perfectly showing their garters and drawers," was a sight altogether new to her. And yet, "Shall I speak a truth?" she asked, daring immediately to do so: "Repeatedly seeing these dances has worn off the disgust, which I at first felt, and I see them now with pleasure."[11]

Abigail's appreciation of the arts was expansive enough, at this time, to include French opera, though she thought its robustly gilded and domed building neither so grand nor so beautifully designed as the discreetly columned Comédie Française. She admired the decorative aspects of opera; "And O! the music, vocal and instrumental, it has a soft, persuasive power, and a dying sound," she wrote to her sister. "Think you," Abigail asked Mary, "that this city can fail of becoming a Cythera, and this house the temple of Venus?"[12]

That Abigail was beginning to enjoy herself was of curious concern to her daughter Nabby, the "petite Ange" (so said many French acquaintances), who seemed determined to keep her distance from whatever or whomever she encountered. Almost in spite of herself, her horizons were broadening; as with her mother, she now accepted circumstances that initially had seemed strange to her, though with reservation. "I am accustomed to many things at present, but I am not reconciled to them," she admitted. Two things she took exception to concerned her parents. Europe altered people, Nabby had decided, particularly in the case of her mother, whose head she thought was "more Metamorphosed" than any other aspect of the family, unless it was her own waistline. As for her father, she had not thought it possible, with his firmness and resolution, to be such a perfect convert to everything pertaining to dress and appearance.[13]

Nabby was short-sighted in her evaluation of her parents, particularly her mother. Had she read Abigail's account of Longchamps, her faith would surely have been restored. Abigail reported that she felt foolish as she paraded up one side and down another of a very wide road, for a mile and a half, and then turned around and followed a vast number of carriages. The pace was funereal, and as she found neither utility nor pleasure in the event, she firmly said that she did not expect to "assist" in it again. Abigail was convinced the occasion had been invented to provide some diversion during Lent, a period when the theaters were empty and the churches were filled.[14]

At the start of Abigail's stay in France, not being fluent enough to converse as she would like, she tended to observe rather than participate. She made it clear to all who listened, to all to whom she wrote, that it was too early for her to pass judgment on the French, whose manners were totally different from those of her own country. Despite her lofty intentions, she reached one conclusion, at least, quite swiftly. "If you ask me what is the Business of Life here," she said, "I answer pleasure." From throne to footstool, at least in Abigail's opinion, the French made a science of pleasure; so much so that she wondered how they supported themselves, and was persuaded that the greater part of the population must subsist on bread and water. At least in London, it had seemed to her, though the streets were filled with people, their dress was different. Their appearance indicated to Abigail that they were going about their business—except, of course, on Sundays, when they devoted the day either to church or to a walk. But judging from the gaiety of the peoples' dress and the places they frequented, she concluded that mood and purpose were entirely different in Paris.[15]

Abigail liked to analyze the reasons for people's behavior. Her theory to explain the shocking morals of the French was that theirs was an indulgent religion. Absolutions and dispensations offered by the priests of the Church encouraged pleasure, which, in Abigail's mind, was a word synonymous with promiscuity. She was puzzled by the churches of the French. She admired their architecture, sculpture, and paintings, on the one hand, but found the prodigious masses of gray stone, so often wedged between seven-story houses that screened out the sun, "rather calculated to damp devotion than to excite it."[16]

Abigail admitted that her survey was both limited and transient; when the weather was warmer she hoped to make a more "accurate and critical inspection." She did note, however, in the forbidding gray Church of St. Roch in St. Sulpice, that at any time of day, whenever one entered, one found priests and visitors of all ages on their knees, crossing themselves, murmuring their Pater Nosters and Ave Marias. Then, when her eyes adjusted to the cloudy light, she observed another sort of ceremony, one of individuals opening and closing doors, slipping in and out of "little boxes and closets"— sentry boxes is what she thought they looked like—that edged the floor of the church. Even though she was chilled with cold, she was too curious to leave without inspecting the small grated window that communicated with another closet of the same kind. At the same time that she described the remarkable ceremony of the "closet," she uncovered explanations for the French attitude toward marriage and for their morals in general—or thought she did.

> One of them holds the person who is confessing, and the other the confessor, who places his ear at this window, hears the crime, absolves the transgressor, and very often makes an assignation for a repetition of the same crime, or perhaps a new one. I do not think this a breach of charity; for can we suppose that, of the many thousands whom the religion of the country obliges to celibacy, one quarter part of the number can find its influence sufficiently powerful to conquer these passions which nature has implanted in man, when the gratification of them will cost them only a few livres in confession.[17]

Except for commencement day and election day in Boston, the Sabbath in Paris was incomparable to any American custom. Abigail was in an ideal position to make this pronouncement; her house in Auteuil was just a few rods away from that "Beautiful wood," the Bois de Bologne, where the rites of the Sabbath resounded so evocatively. There was nothing like it even on the Cambridge Commons; people arrived in carts if they did not have a coach, to spend the day singing and dancing. If they did not bring their own picnic, there was cake, fruit, or wine to be bought; they could also purchase ribbons, gauzes, and other such wares from the milliners who set up booths to display their stock. Abigail, though she tended to admire their "appealing stile," was wary of the milliners, and suspected they had "other purposes" in mind than the mere sale of their merchandise.[18]

Just thinking about the milliners, jolly and flirtatious, reminded Abigail of a subject that she confessed made her blush. What was she to think of the manners of a nation that permitted 52,000 females in one city to enroll their names in a notary office for the "most abandoned" purposes, and then allowed thousands of the miserable wretches to die each year of disease and poverty. But if prostitution was unthinkable, so was the way the institution of marriage was manipulated to unite titles and estates, yet foster separate establishments for pleasures and amusements. If she compared French morals to English ones, she wondered which of the two countries would prove the "least pernicious." Women were openly solicited in London, not so in Paris; women on the stage in London were suspect, which was not the case in Paris. Abigail could only conclude that in England vice was like a ferocious beast, seeking whom it may devour; in France it was a subtle poison, secretly penetrating.[19]

If Abigail was critical of the religious life of France, and the odd custom of celebrating Sunday as a "high holiday," as a festival, she was testy, in turn, about the limitations placed by her own country on her own habits of observance. The fact that the American Embassy did not permit chaplains on its premises angered Abigail, who did not consider worshiping at the Dutch ambassador's chapel, in French, a viable alternative. "Do Congress think that their ministers have no need of grace?" she asked. Or was it that religion was not a "necessary article" for them? Soon she would be resigned to acknowledging that Sunday would not feel like Sunday as long as she lived in France.[20]

In many ways, in Paris, or wherever she would journey, Abigail was an archetypal tourist, critical of the new, protective of the familiar. Perhaps it was on one of the days when the Paris sky was bloated with the gray fog she found not "agreeable" to her that she talked of the "cheerful sunshine of America," remembered the "clear blew" sky at home, even longed for an American snowstorm, obviously forgetting the crippling winds and ice that had imprisoned her in the Braintree cottage for weeks on end. At these times she was lost in nostalgia, and found herself sighing ("tho not allowed") for the tea parties she had left behind in America, thinking that if she could only "transplant" her few chosen friends to the village of Auteuil she would find their agreeable conversation a rich repast. Her habits, tastes, and sentiments were too firmly established to be altered by a change of country or climate, she said, and at her age, her greatest enjoyment con-

sisted in the reciprocations of friendship. Recognizing her preferences and her limitations, Abigail found it as difficult to conform to
the French custom of receiving foreigners as she had to the English
system, though for entirely different reasons. Etiquette in France
required strangers to pay the first call, and as Abigail explained to a
friend in Braintree, "You will easily suppose that I have not been so
fond of so awkward a situation as going to visit ladies, merely to make
my dumb compliments, and receive them in return."[21]

For all her considerable reluctance, Abigail's call on the Marquise
de Lafayette was immediately rewarding. It was bound to be so,
because the French noblewoman, the former Marie Adrienne Fran-
çoise de Noailles, was in many ways Abigail's French counterpart.
She was quietly dressed, devoted to her children, direct and open
with people. She was also immediately friendly to Abigail, who had
to wait until the Marquise returned to town in November before
calling on her, John accompanying her on the ride. Abigail's servant
took in her card and returned, as expected, with word that the Marquise was not at home. Just as Abigail's carriage was easing out of the
driveway, the Marquise's servant rushed out of the doorway to call
her back. Almost simultaneously the Marquise herself came out to
greet her personally, Abigail descending from her carriage in turn.
In what Abigail described as "the rapture peculiar to the ladies of this
nation," the pleasant noblewoman pressed the American's hand and
kissed her on both cheeks as though Abigail were a long-absent and
beloved friend.[22]

The Marquise de Lafayette's declared fondness for Americans only
heightened Abigail's admiration for the energetic, friendly young
woman, who preferred to wear chintz during the day and to forgo any
glitter at night. Because of her austere tendencies, Abigail had to
defend the Marquise at dinner the evening she wore a brown silk
dress and petticoat with a double gauze handkerchief around her
shoulders and a white cap on her head threaded with white ribbon.
"The lady's rank sets her above the little formalities of dress," Abigail whispered sternly to the American critic. She restrained herself
from adding that no people were more extravagant than American
women; their fondness for diamond watch chains and girdle buckles
only made her wonder that some of them must be living on twice as
much as any American minister's salary could possibly provide.[23]

As time passed, other Frenchwomen won Abigail's admiration. She
was intrigued by their taste, their musical voices, their intelligence,

their light, airy, genteel manners, cultivated, she knew, only after years of study. For the French, manners were an art form, and Frenchwomen were studious artists. Now a converted admirer of the French, Abigail tried to observe their protocol graciously, with one remarkable exception. It was not accident but a striking difference in attitudes that prevented Abigail from calling on Dr. Franklin's valued friend, the flamboyant Madame Anne Helvétius, also known as Notre Dame d'Auteuil.[24]

Madame Helvétius had once been handsome, Abigail thought, seeing her for the first time. Crowning her frizzled mound of hair was a small straw hat veiled with dirty gauze; more of the filmy muslin swathed her shoulders and her blue silk dress, which looked, to Abigail, as decayed as her beauty. Dr. Franklin had already discussed his taste in women, but still had left Nabby and her mother unprepared for Madame Helvétius. Dr. Franklin liked Englishwomen with the additional graces of Frenchwomen, and this composite was to be found nowhere but in Paris, he assured Nabby. There was no doubt that he preferred Frenchwomen above all others. In Madame Helvétius, he told the Adams women at the beginning of their stay in Paris, they would find a genuine Frenchwoman wholly free from affectation or stiffness of behavior, one of the best women in the world. But nothing Dr. Franklin had said could they relate to this particular woman. The tidy, immaculate Americans, Abigail and her daughter, only hoped they would find other Frenchwomen with manners more consistent with their ideas of decency. Otherwise, Abigail had decided she was sure to become "a mere recluse."[25]

On one of their first visits to Dr. Franklin, they were sitting in his drawing room when Madame Helvétius marched in with what seemed a rather "jaunty" air. Surprised to see other women, she was disappointed not to find Franklin waiting for her. "Ah, *mon Dieu,* where is Franklin?" she asked. Then, lifting up her skirt, she ran out of the room, to return in moments through another door, encountering Franklin appearing through a third. She ran to him, hugged his hand, greeted him with *"Hélas!* Franklin," and two kisses, one for either cheek, followed by a third for his forehead. During dinner, a startled Abigail was uncomfortably aware of the constant movement across the table involving her own husband. With rhythmic continuity, Madame Helvétius, sitting between John and Dr. Franklin, not only locked her hands with the latter but stretched her arms behind the backs of *both* gentlemen's chairs; then, retrieving her arms, she threw both "carelessly" around the Doctor's neck. Abigail would report shortly to friends that she could only think Dr. Franklin could not be adverse to the example of King David: "If embraces will tend to prolong his life and promote the vigour of his circulations he is on a fair way to live the age of an antediluvian."[26]

As the evening passed, the worst of Abigail's suspicions about Madame Helvétius were confirmed. She hoped never to make another acquaintance of this "cast" who, after dinner, hurled herself on a settee, where she showed more than her feet and allowed her little lapdog to curl up beside the Doctor. Next, she kissed the dog, next, the dog wet the floor; next, his mistress wiped the floor with her dress. Abigail was shocked. "This is one of the Doctor's most intimate friends, with whom he dines once every week, and she with him. She is rich, and is my near neighbour; but I have not visited her. Thus you see, my dear," Abigail explained to her niece Lucy Cranch, "that manners differ exceedingly in different countries."[27]

On any given day, Abigail's reactions to the customs of the Old World were as varied as the moody Paris skies, the forbidding pewter grays misting from pale silver to a quiet blue suffused with gentle sunlight. She was scornful and revolted, but, at other times understanding, appreciative, and even amused by the people, sights, and values she was exposed to as a diplomat's wife. Groan and scold as she might about the cost of living, there were certain expenses she knew that she and her family must resign themselves to, and in fact could not avoid. Unlike London, in Paris fashion was the "deity" every one worshiped, from highest to lowest, and there was simply no escaping this fact: dressing one's hair was mandatory and there were no porters or washerwomen who did not have their hair powdered and dressed every day.[28]

Having no choice, the Americans conformed. Johnny had his hair "frizzled," as Abigail termed the unnaturally curly state of her son's dark brown hair; even poor Esther and John, ridiculed by the other servants, submitted, with Esther dissolving in tears for allowing herself to be put in such a foolish position. Thomas Jefferson, who was not one for "show & parade," regarded the idea of dressing his hair as an "affliction," and was tempted to cut it off. As he did not expect to live but a dozen years more, he explained, he was loath to give up one of them to hairdressing. Eventually, all of them were "à la mode de Paris," and not entirely miserable about their situation, either.

Abigail noticed that Esther seemed as "happy as a lark," quite recovered from her initial qualms, going off to the theater to see *Figaro* with another servant, Pauline. "To be out of fashion," Abigail concluded, "was more criminal than to be seen in a state of nature, to which the Parisians were not averse."[29]

Fashion, the idea of dressing according to currently admired standards, was never ignored by Abigail, though she did bring a sensible perspective to the entire pursuit. Even at Braintree, she had exchanged fabrics and patterns with friends and relatives; in Paris, not a spot of rouge, a gauze veil, a jeweled stomacher escaped her vigilant eye. Lengthy reports on fashion, even now, were forwarded by Abigail from Paris, Nabby supplementing them with miniature models made from handkerchiefs. Still, Abigail would only go to certain lengths to be fashionable; by both inclination and purse, she was limited in her pursuit. She found the demands of protocol most trying. Never one to accept dictation with special grace, her resentment over the court requirements for mourning was considerable and shared with her friend Thomas Jefferson. That she outwitted the court in the case of the death of an eight-year-old prince pleased her; she even boasted of her triumph across the seas to Uncle Tufts.[30]

At times of royal deaths, if the court so decreed, special mourning attire was required of all attendants and visitors, including all foreign ministers and their families, for a certain span of time—in this instance, for eleven days. In deference to this rule, both Thomas Jefferson and his compatriot Colonel Humphries spent fifty guineas at the tailor, having appropriately somber clothes cut to their order, since they did not dare to appear disrespectfully dressed on their regular Tuesdays at court. On the given Tuesday, "full trimmed in awful sable," Abigail told Tufts, the two gentlemen called at the house in Auteuil to collect her husband. John, informally dressed, explained at breakfast that he had learned the day before that Court would not be held this Tuesday, and by the next week the mourning period would be over. Abigail, who had already decided not to go out in public in order to avoid the expense of a new black dress—her old one not being the silk for the season—gloated that she "took not a little pleasure in announcing to the visitors what others had felt before them, that their Labour was all in vain."[31]

A Degree
of Tristeness

A North American, Abigail thought, had no right to complain of the rigor of the climate of Paris; this middle of January,
1785, was as mild as a New England May. There were other aspects
of her life that she could not complain about either, though finances
were a continuing problem. Not for a moment were they paid enough
to live in the manner required of people "in the publicke Character
in which they have placed my Friend," Abigail said. On the other
hand, she had the company of her "best Friend," and she had part
of her family with her. She was really so happy in the house in Auteuil
that she almost resented having to leave it for the titled and gilded
dinner parties to which they were habitually invited.[1]

At Christmastime, as he always tended to do, John had taken a long
look back at the outgoing year, and pronounced it one of unquestionable private contentment, at least the past few months, when his
family had been together. There was a pattern now to their days; the
morning of January 4 was typical. Abigail rose in faint daylight; after
the fire was lit and her bedroom cleaned, she knocked on Nabby's
door to awaken her, then at the next door, which was opened by
Johnny, usually with a book in his hand. The four ate breakfast
together, after which John went into the library to read, then write;
Abigail mapped out the day's work for her staff and darned some of
her stockings; Johnny returned to his room to study and translate
Horace and Tacitus; Nabby went to her room to translate the passage
about Telemachus in Homer's *Odyssey*.[2]

The pace changed at noontime. John took his cane and hat and walked his usual four miles, then met back home at two with the ladies, now freshly coiffed. Dining, chatting, and reading aloud— John in one chair, occupied with Plato's *Laws,* Abigail with St. John's letters—made for a short afternoon. Teatime was preceded by Johnny and Nabby's favorite game of romps, the salon on one side of the center hall being ideal for this vigorous pursuit of one another; the glass doors at one end of the room opened into the garden, those at the other end into the courtyard. Tea dishes and cloth afterwards gave way to mathematics books and paper and pencils, and Abigail heard nothing from then until nine o'clock of the rest of her family, except on the subject of theorems, at which John made an ardent and interested teacher. Nine o'clock was a sensible cutoff point, and in order, as Abigail put it, to "relieve their brains," a game of whist prepared everyone for a ten-o'clock curfew. Though this was the schedule for a usual night, there were dozens on which they went out as a family, or on which the children went off to the theater together. Then Abigail would wait up for their return, comforting herself that even on the stormiest nights, the roads from Paris were visible by lamplight. Once she heard the gate bell ring, and Caesar's welcoming bark, she was at peace. She could look out her window to see the carriage turning in the courtyard and reassure herself that the coachman had brought her children safely home.[3]

For all the appearance of serenity, Abigail knew that John was restless, as far as his work was concerned. He stayed for hours at his desk, warning colleagues that their European concerns were "obstructed in everything for want of money," that success with the English—who had some very "wild" ideas about their own political and commercial interests—was "very problematical."[4]

John talked now about being "in the midst of the world in solitude," perhaps because Franklin, ill with a kidney stone, hadn't called at Versailles in a year, and Jefferson had not felt well in weeks. John insisted that he did not mean to "intermeddle," but he needed an ear, someone to listen and understand how important it was for Congress to send a minister to the Court of St. James, or else renounce all thoughts of treating with the English, who were not about to negotiate with the Americans as long as the latter were Paris-based. When John learned, at the end of April, that he had been elected, as of February 24, 1785, the first American minister accredited to the Court of St. James, there was no doubt of his sense of fulfillment. The time had come, "a time foretold by the Prophets, and seers, and Dreamers of Dreams, but never untill very lately steadfastly believed by any to be so near at hand," he wrote Mercy Warren in May.[5]

He sensed the grandeur of the moment, but he also anticipated the pitfalls. When he had a few days to think about his future, he worried that he was more to be pitied than envied. He feared that "groups upon groups" of Tories and refugees in a variety of shapes and shades of colors, as well as members of embassies from other parts of Europe—including impassioned English, Scottish, and Irish—would be watching his every move, most of them "wishing and contriving his fall." This "humble Minister" had no ambition of the sort that achieved popular diplomatic successes. Fortune and figure, birth and grace, titles and ribbons made impressions on courtiers; sacrifice of time, health, and family were the other ingredients of diplomatic success. Everything demanded of him he either despised, or did not possess, or could not give freely. On the whole, whatever there might be "in the feather" of being appointed the first American minister to England, the position, he concluded, was to be dreaded. He did not expect to be cherished or believed in his new post. He was quite willing to settle for a "candid or even a decent" reception in England.[6]

The nine months that Abigail had lived with her husband and two of her children as a family were ending; the reunion that had been so long in coming was as rare as it was fleeting. John's appointment to the Court of St. James opened a new phase in America's quest for recognition; it also signaled the end of Benjamin Franklin's august presence in Europe. On March 7, Congress had given leave to the Doctor to return to America as soon as it was convenient; on March 19, Thomas Jefferson was unanimously elected Franklin's successor at the court of Versailles; Adams and Jefferson were to retain their joint commission to negotiate commercial treaties with European and African nations.[7]

John's appointment not only signaled a new era for American diplomacy but a most immediate wrench within the family. A decision was made that John Quincy Adams must return to America to continue his education; both his father and mother agreed that America was the theater for a young fellow who had ambition to distinguish himself. Arrangements were negotiated with Harvard College's president, Joseph Villard, and John was proud that his son had chosen to go to school in *New* England rather than *old* England. The choice demonstrated the son's respect for a father who was practical enough to know that "young gentlemen of eighteen dont always see through the same medium with old ones of fifty."[8]

To pave the way for his son, who had not been home in seven years, who felt himself a stranger to his American family, who was worried that even his English might sound a little odd, John wrote on Johnny's behalf to Dr. Cotton Mather, to Mercy Warren, and to the Reverend Ezra Stiles. Yet, happy as both parents were to have him going home for his education, parting with their young "Hercules" was a sacrifice. Abigail had grown used to writing her letters sitting in her son's room by his fireside, and to have him copy over her letters, which seemed to improve with the benefit of his penmanship. Abigail admitted that she dared not trust herself to think about his departure: "In proportion as a person becomes necessary to us we feel their loss; and in every way I shall feel his," she recognized fully.[9]

Abigail pleaded with her sister Mary to provide whatever was necessary for her son, and to take care of him in the same way Abigail would of Mary's children "in the like circumstances." That Abigail held very precise, if not autocratic, notions of child-rearing was obvious in her response to her sister Elizabeth's warning of her son Charles's attachment to a young woman: Abigail's sons were to have no passion but for science, and no mistress but literature. Furthermore, no son of hers was to form any sentiments with respect to any female, but those of a general nature, until he was more mature and learned; "so shall discretion preserve them and understanding keep them, if they incline their ears to wisdom and apply their hearts to understanding." She very much feared that Charles, owing to his disposition and sensibility, was more liable to female attachments; her young Hercules sitting beside her in France was much better occupied with his Horace and Tacitus, though she allowed that in time there would be someone "to bring him to the distaff."[10]

For all of Abigail's dedicated thought to Johnny's future, she realized that Europe without him would have "fewer charms." His sister, in fact, the pensive, silent Nabby, did not possibly see how her brother's place "should be supplyd." The loss of her brother's company was another tug at Nabby's security, already tested by her increasingly doubtful relationship with Royall Tyler. One could easily understand why the Marquise de Lafayette, perhaps sensing Nabby's inner conflict, found the young woman to be "grave."[11]

Once Johnny was packed off to America, Abigail concentrated on her move to London. There was some pleasure in contemplating living in a country where she would not be expected to eat and drink so much, where there would be no need for "twisting and twirling" her tongue so much, where she would see more of her American friends. But there were regrets as well. She would certainly miss her garden, the fishpond and fountain just put in order, the arbor of trees arched over sun-dappled walks. She would regret leaving the tulips, the peach and pear blossoms, the grapes, and she reminded herself sharply that she must be sure to send a parcel of flower seeds home.[12]

But Abigail, rarely self-indulgent, refused to wallow in sentiment. She would, indeed, be able to leave her garden behind. She had schooled herself to do so because, she explained to her sister Mary, it contained neither plants of her hand nor children of her care. In truth, she had bought a little bird recently that she felt more attached to than any other object, apart from her own family, animate or inanimate. Probably, without realizing what was happening, Abigail was treating her departure from France as a test of loyalties. She was writing home now about how absolute strangers, visiting at Auteuil, claimed greater attachment to the Adams family than to their most intimate European acquaintances, because of their mutual ties with America.[13]

Rationalize as she might, however, Abigail harbored other regrets about the forthcoming departure for England. She had, despite all the distractions of Paris, remained a true "Daughter of Eve," dependent on the Marquise de Lafayette as she had been on James Lovell, in former days, for information. No one was more current on American intelligence than the Frenchwoman, who corresponded with people in all of the American states, and received newspapers from every quarter; leaving France, Abigail was aware that she might never replace her splendid informant. Abigail would miss the noble couple for another reason. She admired the Marquise de Lafayette for her passionate attachment to her husband ("a French Lady and fond of her Husband!"), and was pleased that she had named a son after George Washington, and a daughter after the American state of Virginia. She also regarded her as a true friend, an accolade never accorded lightly by Abigail, either at home or, especially, abroad.[14]

Mention of Virginia only reminded Abigail of the tall, kind widower Thomas Jefferson, the native of that state who had practically become a member of her family, and whose friendship was prized collectively and individually by all four members of the household at Auteuil. He was like a fond uncle to Johnny; Nabby's heart, sensing his loneliness, had gone out to him and to Martha, his twelve-year-old daughter, who preferred to be called Patsy. The very first month the families were in Paris together, they witnessed, with trepidation, Patsy's induction at the convent, where, moved to tears by the singing and chanting amid the flow of white woolen robes, she was to be educated. As a family, they had shared with Jefferson far more than the official ceremonies and dinners—theater and carnivals as well. These last months, they had tended to dine at Jefferson's on Thursdays, and he with them at Auteuil on Sundays. Within the confines of the Adams family, Thomas Jefferson was pronounced "one of the choice ones of the earth."[15]

On May 20, tearful French domestics waved John, Abigail, Nabby, and the always constant John Briesler, and Esther Field off on the road to Calais. Even Abigail's bird, fluttering frantically in its little cage, held high by the chambermaid, seemed to be wishing its departing mistress a special good-bye, bidding her party special good luck on the six-day journey to London, the beginning of the realization of John's most earnest ambition to bargain as an American at the Court of St. James.[16]

The landscape, as they veered away from the Seine, was a woeful tapestry, due to a burning drought; the grass was all but invisible, the grain pale, the flax quite dead, and at times during the journey, the country seemed to be a heap of ashes. No greens, no vegetables were to be seen from the road; pathetically visible were sheep and cattle stalking the fields like herds of walking skeletons, grazing the grounds in search of rotted roots of grass turned by the plow. John and Abigail enjoyed only one distraction, fittingly provided by their friend Jefferson; his farewell gift was a copy of his own book, privately printed that past May, called *Notes on the State of Virginia.* When he thanked Jefferson later on, John told him that his book was their "Meditation all the Day long," that it would do its author and his country great honor, that the passages on slavery were worth diamonds, that "they will have more effect than Volumes written by mere Philosophers."[17]

In different ways, that early summer of 1785, the three friends recognized loss of some dimension. John thought perhaps it was the melancholy face of nature, or the dull political prospect before him, or his regret at parting with his son, that colored his mood darkly. Or, he speculated, perhaps it was leaving their fine summer situation at Auteuil, and all their friends in and about Paris, that made for such a sorrowful journey. "We have passed through scenes bien plus triste encore," he wrote to Jefferson, as though he meant to comfort and offer hope to all of them.[18]

Jefferson was reticent but still explicit about his friendship with Abigail and John. "The departure of your family has left me in the dumps," he wrote to John. "My afternoons hang heavily on me. I go sometimes to Passy and Mont Parnasse." Jefferson talked now as though he felt that something more than their friendship was at a turning point; he mentioned being ready, at some time, for the "dark and narrow house of Ossian." He also asked in a postscript: "Send me your address au plutot."[19]

Abigail was affectionately forthright in her long, chatty letter; her sensitive appreciation of her husband's true friendship with Jefferson, in light of the bitter twist it would be given in a handful of years, was that much more poignant.

> I think I have somewhere met with the observation that nobody
> ever leaves paris but with a degree of tristeness. I own I was loth
> to leave my garden because I did not expect to find its place
> supplied. I was still more loth on account of the increasing
> pleasure, and intimacy which a longer acquaintance with a
> respected Friend promised, to leave behind me the only person
> with whom my Companion could associate with perfect freedom,
> and unreserve: and whose place he had no reason to expect
> supplied in the Land to which he is destined.[20]

THIRTEEN

In Public Character

The eggshell delicacy of their mission in London did not escape Abigail: "Whilst the Coals are cover'd the blaize will not burst," she wrote to Thomas Jefferson. Ominously, she added, "but the first wind which blows them into action will I expect envelop all in flames." She paused, for it was difficult to concentrate with all the clattering noises of Piccadilly echoing in her suite at the Bath Hotel. Moments later she pointedly observed, "If the actors pass the ordeal without being burnt they may be considered in future of the Asbestos kind."[1]

From May 26, 1785, the Thursday of her arrival in London, until June 6, the date of her letter to Jefferson, Abigail detected hardly a spark—if she discounted a "beginning squib" or two—in the precariously dense atmosphere. Until this time, she and John had absorbed themselves in fulfilling the public duties and private needs of a diplomat's family, critically aware of their vulnerable position and of the awkward sentiments their presence aroused. For the Americans to seek understanding and accommodation, if not precisely friendship, from the British, was to be compared to children expecting a parent's indulgence after a shattering breach of conduct. The parent was formidable in this instance; George III was in his prime.[2]

Throughout the past Saturday, June 4, the citizens of Great Britain had commemorated the King's forty-eighth birthday with poems and hymns, bells and cannons, bonfires and fireworks—the latter tossed into the heavens so that parks, rivers, and towers, from London to

Dublin, burst into light. Nor was that the whole celebration. Noblemen and state ministers and their feathered, flowered, and jeweled
wives, who had jammed the city's hotels for the past ten days (and
increased the price of lodgings "near double," Abigail complained),
drove off at dusk, in the splendid gray carriages crowding beneath
Abigail's window, to greet the King in his palace. His Majesty, said
to be in "charming spirits," was dressed in shades of pale chocolate,
his Queen and children in deep-piled blue and lilac velvets, fretted
with silvery lace. Considering that Abigail admitted to an appetite to
see Europe "in all its forms," once she quieted her fears of facing the
world beyond Braintree, she had reason to be pleased. It was plain
that she could not have made a more successful start at fulfilling her
wish than those first spectacular days when all of London seemed
dedicated to honoring the King.[3]

London, in the summer of 1785, saw the ascent of Britain's first
female aerial traveler: one Mrs. Sage soared skyward in Mr. Vincenzo
Lunardi's balloon, washing down ham and chicken eaten aloft with
glasses of Florence wine. Fascinated as she was by these proceedings,
with which she had already familiarized herself in Paris, Abigail's
attention was mostly earthbound in her attempt to understand a
country for which she harbored such a peculiar assortment of sentiments. Hearing six hundred voices glorifying every hallowed corner
of Westminster Abbey with Handel's *"Hallelujah Chorus"* was an ex-
hilarating and frustrating experience. She struggled to find the words
to describe the impact; the best she could say was that she found
herself "one continued shudder from beginning to end."[4]

Handel was one matter, the ballet was another: she had no trouble
expressing herself specifically on the "gymnastics" at Sadler's Wells.
Though she consoled herself that the petticoatless performers, both
male and female, were well clad underneath with "draws," she regretted the loss of "delicacy, modesty and diffidence" involved in the
entire presentation.[5]

On the one hand, Abigail found herself admiring the English gardens, so ordered and fragrant, proof of what might be "affected by
culture." On the other, committed to an unbiased view, or perhaps
fearful of misplaced loyalty, she dwelt at length on the spectacles of
misery which the old countries, "crowded with inhabitants" and
"loaded with taxes," exhibited. She wrote home about the "variety
of wretchedness," of disease and starvation, of gallows deaths, of
hundreds of starving, homeless children who begged by day and slept

nightly in Hyde Park. There must be some essential defect in the government and morals of a people, she concluded, "when punishments lose their efficacy and crimes abound." And piously she recommended that her niece Betsy Cranch make herself "perfect mistress" of the history of her own country; no one, she thought, could be sufficiently thankful for the blessings they enjoyed, unless they knew the value of them. But overall, gardens and orphans in balance, Abigail's major preoccupation was with the politics of the day. Studiously, though somewhat nervously, she reported that shopkeepers, reflecting their opinion of the British statesman, draped black cloth all over their premises, and nailed up signs reading "No Pitt," "No Shop Tax," "Damn Pitt," and were threatening to attack the House of Commons.[6]

If London, in all its shades and depths, was a curiosity to Abigail and her family, the same was true in reverse. The observers were being observed; official notice of the movements of the Adams family appeared in the *London Chronicle* on Thursday, June 2, and Abigail did not miss a word:

> On Wednesday last arrived from the United States of America, Col. Smith (late Aid de Camp to General Washington during the American war), as Secretary to an Ambassador from that country; and on the day following his Excellency John Adams (with his Lady and daughter) as Plenipotentiary from the United States of America to the Court of Great Britain and we hear he had delivered his credentials to the Marquis of Carmarthen. Yesterday his Excellency John Adams was introduced to his Majesty, and most graciously received.[7]

John had announced his arrival to Francis Godolphin Osborne, the Marquis of Carmarthen, His Majesty's principal Secretary of State for Foreign Affairs, his first evening in London. Seven days later, on June first, Carmarthen guided John to the King's Closet, where he was instructed to offer three "profound" bows, one at the door, one halfway in, and the third directly before the stout, pear-shaped George III. John wished he might have had more time to study the King, with his dimpled chin and fleshy lips, his passion for Handel, for clocks, for books (he had bought £120,000 worth for his library at Buckingham Palace), for Canaletto's drawings of the Grand Canal, for gloriously carved furniture and the most delicate porcelains. Whether George had lost America because he was uninformed, misinformed, or merely insensitive, and whether his eventual madness was correctly diagnosed, would be questions to tantalize John in his old age. But now John had to get on with his long-awaited task.[8]

After a surprisingly gracious bow for a bulky man, John, appearing to stand a little taller before the King, managed to deliver the speech with infinite care, eloquence, and clarity. He had hopes, he told the King, of restoring esteem, confidence, and affection, of reviving "the old good nature and the old Good Humour, between People who tho' separated by the ocean and under different governments have the same language, a similar religion and kindred Blood." George's response to "this audience so extraordinary" was all that John could have wished: "Sir, your words have been so proper, upon this occasion, that I cannot but say I am gratified that you are the man chosen to be the Minister."[9]

Though John was satisfied with his meeting with the King, there were others who felt differently. The *Public Advertiser* on June 6, deemed the idea of an ambassador from America "humiliating."

> Good heavens what a sound! The Gazette surely never announced any thing so extraordinary before. . . . This will be such a phenomenon in the Corps Diplomatique that tis hard to say which can excite indignation most, the insolence of those who appoint the Character, or the meanness of those who receive it. . . .

Insults were dramatically compounded by the same paper that Friday, June 10:

> His Excellency Mr. Adams was, it seems, originally a lawyer, in New England, who, starving there on a meagre practice, took the pious resolution to destroy the law itself, in which he had not found a fortune equal to his merit. Liberty then, or rather the name of Liberty, afforded him the old battered mask for cutting her throat, and exterminating the laws of his country, which, in times of yore, had ever been sacredly held her most faithful guardians.

The "blaize" so shrewdly anticipated by Abigail was stoked by still another voice, this one in the *London Chronicle*, that same weekend:

> It is said that Mr. Adams, the American Ambassador, was so embarrassed at his first audience, as not to pronounce the compliment prescribed by etiquette. The great person before whom he stood, very good-naturedly passed by the omission, and told him that though it could not be a pleasing circumstance to

receive an embassy from those who were once his subjects, yet as the right was insured to them by treaty, he, Mr. Adams, might depend upon being treated with every mark of regard and protection."[10]

From the beginning, Thomas Jefferson confessed to Abigail that he did not envy Mr. Adams's assignment to Great Britain, that it would have "illy" suited Jefferson himself, as he did not love difficulties. He found the London papers teeming not only with news of assassinations, suicides, and thefts, but, what was worse, the blackest slanders. "Indeed, the man must be of rock who can stand all this; to Mr. Adams it will be but one victory the more," he wrote. An introspective Jefferson told Abigail that he was fond of quiet, and willing to do his duty, but that slander made him irritable and could possibly force him to abandon his post. These were weaknesses for which there was some remedy, however. Abigail's counseling might help "preserve" Mr. Adams, Jefferson suggested.[11]

In his own way, with wisdom and charm, Jefferson consoled Abigail. He did not advise any attempt to answer or refute the newspaper allegations, and he joked about their origin. He would not be the last to suggest where the blame lay: it was the quantity of animal food eaten by the English that possibly rendered their character "insusceptible of civilisation." He suspected that it was in their kitchens, and not in their churches, that reformation must be wrought, that missionaries ought to train them not on precepts of religion or philosophy, but cuisine. Having diverted Abigail for a few moments, Jefferson was solemn once again as he alluded to the behavior of an irresponsible press. "But what do the foolish printers of America mean by retailing all this stuff in our papers?" he asked; wasn't it enough "to be slandered by one's enemies without circulating the slanders among his friends also?"[12]

Jefferson's perception of the damaging consequences at home of the newspaper jeers was acute. Friends, relatives, and government officials who read the British newspapers, or reprints of the controversial columns in their own journals, assumed the worst. Abigail, trying to smooth away misunderstandings, assured relatives that the news sharks were uninformed, that the Tory venom was due to envious intolerance of an American minister being treated as envoys of other powers were—with attention, politeness, and civility. But Abigail's bravado was tenuous at best. Intellectually, she understood

Jefferson's advice and respected it, in addition to her sister Elizabeth's recommendations that she rise above the newspaper squibs, conscious of her own integrity, and aware of others' malice, pride, and envy. Exalted stations were a mark for the public eye to shoot at, Elizabeth instructed her, reminding her that according to Joseph Addison, the poet and statesman, "Censure is a tax a man pays the public for being eminent."[13]

All very well, what Jefferson and Elizabeth and Addison said. But Abigail could not be cerebral about a gaping wound. She was furious, and she could not pretend otherwise. "False as hell" was what the press was. She thought again, and corrected herself: "No I mean false as the English." She only wished she could have shouted her pronouncements to the world, but she knew she could really confide to only a trusted few that the "newsliars" knew nothing of the matter between John and the King. Or, for that matter, between John and Queen Charlotte, to whom he had also been presented. He had spoken then "of a rising Empire and an infant Virgin World," of another Europe rising in America. He supposed a philosophical mind like Her Majesty's "could not be more pleased to contemplate this prospect of doubling the human species and augmenting at the same time their prosperity and happiness." The Queen had told him she was glad he was in England, and even asked whether he had found a house.[14]

Abigail was on guard now, hurt, and beginning to talk about people who would "catch at everything," who were given to "misrepresentation." She seemed deliberately to school herself against any deep involvement, and insisted now that there was no fear of her being in love with European manners, or becoming truly attached to England. "The people must love my country and its inhabitants better first," she said; "must discover a more amiable temper towards us." But, for all her reservations, Abigail was committed to some extent. She was, she said, interested in anything that concerned those she loved. She was also a proud woman, almost belligerently protective of her husband, ambitious that he perform well; in all, she was his driven helpmate. Scheduled to be presented, with John and Nabby, at the Queen's circle on Thursday, June 25, Abigail was quite willing to play her role. Very well, then, her hoops and Nabby's would be as wide as any, her feathers as commanding, her ribbons as frivolous. But she would not compromise her own taste. Above all, she vowed to be discreet and neat; in other words, Abigail meant to cope with royal exigencies on her own terms.[15]

"There is no presentation in Europe, in which I should feel so much as in this," Abigail wrote Mary, while waiting for Nabby to finish dressing for the afternoon's "indispensable" ceremony. With her New England frugality, burnished with patriot's pride, Abigail had issued meticulous instructions to the dressmaker about her court dress. She was to be as plain as she could be, while being as elegant as she could be; she would tolerate no foil or tinsel about her. Court dress, after all, could be worn nowhere else, not even to the Queen's weekly receptions, she reasoned, so decency without extravagance would be her aim.[16]

At one o'clock Thursday afternoon, an hour before she was due at court, Abigail was quite content with herself, in her "rigging" of white lutestring; the lustrous silk, overlaid with white crepe, was festooned with lilac-colored ribbons and imitation point lace. Three ruffles (customarily worn by married ladies) ringed the wrists of her sleeves, and her vast hoopskirt, not quite as wide as her three-yard train, was caught up in a ribbon at her left side, out of her way, since, unlike the Queen, she had no one to bear it for her. She thought her jewelry was as discreet as her dress; pearls were visible at her ears and neck, but those tucked in her hair were hidden with a "very dress" lace cap decorated with two white feathers. Brushing away a nonexistent wrinkle in her skirt, Abigail pronounced herself "very tasty." Maternally, she reserved "beautiful" for Nabby, whose white crepe dress was embellished with ribbons and blossoms, her cap not only feathered but flowery as well. Still, reassured as she was by her own appearance and Nabby's, Abigail suffered stage fright. Just before she stepped into her carriage to ride to court—John was to follow with his new aide, the appealing young Colonel William Stephens Smith—she thought how "gladly" she would have welcomed an excuse from ceremony. There being no choice, and the moment of panic having passed, Abigail, once she arrived at the palace, was absorbed absolutely by the proceedings.[17]

Certainly, Abigail missed none of the grandeur, solemnity, or theatrics of the pageant. She was pleased (or was it relieved?) that the Swedish and Polish ministers, as well as the Marquis of Carmarthen and Sir Clement Cotterel Dormer, greeted her cordially. She and Nabby, with the three daughters of the Marquis of Lothian and two brides, were, in a sense, the "soloists" among an audience of two hundred, waiting gravely for the performance to begin. For all her anticipation she was a bit startled when a heavy door opened abruptly and the royal family entered, the King walking to the right, the Queen and the Princesses bearing down on the group gathered at their left. Abigail's instant reaction to the King was to find him "personable," though she did not quite know what to make of his flushed red face with its stark white eyebrows. But whispered greetings began almost immediately, and there was no more time to concentrate on any aspect of the ceremony except to ready herself for the King. The wry humor of her meeting with His Majesty was not lost on Abigail, according to her report:

> Lord Onslow said, "Mrs. Adams"; upon which I drew off my right-hand glove, and his Majesty saluted my left cheek; then asked me if I had taken a walk today. I could have told his Majesty that I had been all the morning preparing to wait upon him; but replied, "No, Sire." "Why, don't you love walking?" says he. I answered, that I was rather indolent in that respect. He then bowed, and passed on.[18]

Abigail's presentation to the Queen was even less satisfactory than her husband's; both of them, she sensed, suffered "disagreeable feelings." The German-born Queen, whose florid complexion was only accentuated by her purple and silver robes, was neither well-shaped nor handsome, in Abigail's opinion. The Princess Royal, Charlotte, and Princess Augusta, dressed in black and silver, garlanded with diamonds, fared better. Grudgingly, Abigail allowed that they were pretty, though hardly beautiful, that they were well shaped, and that their fair complexions betrayed only a "tincture" of the King's countenance. In spite of her reservations, she did admit to thinking the Queen and her daughters held forth with "much affability, and the ease and freedom of old acquaintance."[19]

For the Queen's court, Abigail found few kind words. Their rank and title might compensate for their lack of personal charm, but in general she pronounced them "very plain, ill-shaped, and ugly; but don't you tell anybody I say so," she wrote to Mary. Fine feathers did not necessarily make fine women, and on the whole, Abigail was the smug chauvinist. Many of the English wore vastly richer clothes, but none were neater or more elegant than the Americans—thanks to the taste of her dressmaker, Mrs. John Temple, whose company she valued personally, regretting only that Mr. Temple was so deaf she could not hold much conversation with him. Thinking about her afternoon's venture at court some hours later, Abigail was more piqued than pleased. As an American, she was not one to "tremble" at the name or sight of majesty; nor did she consider the King's bothering to "salute" her as a "dignified honor." In conclusion, she really felt that never in her life was she to find herself in a more "contemptible" situation than when she stood, that afternoon, for four hours, waiting for a gracious smile from His Majesty—hardly a "mighty boon," in her opinion.[20]

The Queen's question about the state of the Adamses' new dwelling in London touched on a project that had engrossed Abigail almost from the hour she set foot in the bustling city. She had taken on the search for housing alone, not wishing to bother John, who was so preoccupied from morning to night with petitions, applications, and letters from Americans in need of help of one sort or another, that Abigail thought a galley slave would have an easier task than her husband did. Her primary search was for something "airy" rather than grand, but she succeeded in achieving both with a house in the northeast corner of Grosvenor Square, in the parish of St. George, Hanover Square.[21]

The gracious, gray stone house on the corner of Duke and Brook Street, which Nabby would describe to her brother Johnny as a "decent" house—a little out of repair but still not one to make him blush with embarrassment—afforded the family a sense of tidy space and privacy. Sixteen could be seated in the dining room with no trouble, but a smaller and cozier room was available for family meals. Upstairs, one could entertain in the drawing room and retire to the smaller parlor, while John had available to him both a room for an office and another for a library. Perhaps John's favorite "room" was the square itself, an elegant green copse with gravel walks, presided over by an equestrian statue of George II, bathed at night in a permanent moonlight of sixty glowing lamps, by Abigail's actual count. For someone who thought a man his age ought to walk at least four or five miles a day, John felt in luck living on the square, especially when he hadn't time to exercise in nearby Hyde Park, or St. James, or Kensington Gardens.[22]

One other remarkable aspect of the house on the northeast corner of Grosvenor Square was its prestigious neighbors or so the upholsterer who was also the undertaker said. But the houses of the Duchess of Bedford, Lord Thurlow, the Marquis of Carmarthen, and Lord North, which framed the square, though duly noted by Abigail, did not especially impress her, or so she insisted. She was too much a republican to be charmed with titles alone—or too much an American, she might have added. "I have not taken a side with Lord North," she assured her family, "but are still opposite to him." She could compliment herself on her "good genius" about her house on Grosvenor Square, not because of its illustrious neighbors, but because of its brilliant location; the air was pure, even though the square was in the great city. Its private park reminded her of the Boston Common, and the bargain rental of £160 a year included the repainting of two rooms at no further cost.[23]

Another reason Abigail seemed to be so pleased with her English residence was—perhaps with Auteuil as precedent—that she was now accustomed to the complexities of a large household. Her New England Esther was designated ladies' maid, her duties including dressing Abigail's and Nabby's hair (a business she was now most proficient at, her mistress said) and caring for linen and sewing. The housemaid was to do beds and clean stairs; two footmen were to ride the back of the carriage and tend the table and the door; maintenance of the carriages and horses was the province of a special coachman. The butler, the indispensable Mr. Spiller—"a very spruce body" as well as a civil, well-bred man—was to keep the weekly accounts and act as a kind of overseer of the wine, table, and sideboard, and the lesser servants. It was all highly departmentalized, and privately Abigail really did not think she was exaggerating when she said that her Mrs. Newcomb had "done" more for the family in Braintree than the whole lot accomplished together in Grosvenor Square.[24]

On the surface, and certainly personally, all went better for the family than it had in years. The house on Grosvenor Square, as Nabby accurately described it, was nothing to be ashamed of—a pleasant place, indeed, to entertain old friends and acquaintances. Yet Abigail persisted in maintaining an arm's-length position; she could not allow herself to grow too attached to her life in England, as friends had promised she would, for reasons almost as involuntary as breathing.[25]

Basically, the English irritated her; they were too full of "narrow" prejudices, too rigid to respond to her dream of a friendly and liberal exchange between the old and the new England. And why, she asked herself over and again, did the British choose to examine every action America took through a magnifying glass, to view every tiny commotion as high-handed, as signs of lack of authority or government? Of course, she knew the answers, but there was little chance for her to relay them to others. In company, when she heard the English criticize her country and make false assumptions about her fellow Americans, Abigail forced herself to remain tightlipped, only because of her razor-sharp sense of protocol. Their slights and their haughty pride tested all her discipline; if remarks were not addressed to her, she explained to a friend, she did not think herself authorized to enter into a political dispute. But as carefully as she might censor her behavior, she could not deny her sentiments. She recognized in herself a deeply ingrained sense of closeness, even fondness, for this maddening England that insistently challenged her family's presence on its territory, and the very existence of her own country across the sea. Abigail understood something else, being a fair woman. She understood the basis for some ill will and harsh words, especially among British merchants who had extended credit to Americans unable to meet their payments. The situation was fragile at best. She thought Britain depended on its friendly union with America; she spoke of the countries not being able to "quit" one another. Abigail was uncomfortable with the unpredictable. She was puzzled, worried, intent on trying to judge just how the pulse of the ministry was beating. She was certain, however, that if the two countries did not have peace between them, the horrible alternative was war.[26]

By June, there were intimations; and by July, sharp clues to British intentions were in the open. On Friday, July 1, the *London Chronicle* removed all doubt about the British position regarding America:

> His Excellency John Adams has pressed the Marquis of Carmarthen to open negotiation for the payment of the Negroes that were taken from the subjects of the American States during the war. The Marquis has refused, declaring that the American States have in no one instance complied with the Definitive Treaty of Peace, and until that shall have been fulfilled, he must decline entering into that or any other negotiations. Mr. Adams has pledged himself to the New England provinces that when he shall have completed the above business he shall obtain the so much coveted intercourse with the British West India islands.[27]

Immediately, Abigail understood the difference between manner and method. The "Civil and polite" reception of the American minister and his family by George III and his ministry, as respectful as any accorded ministers from other powers, in no way insured justice to America in other respects, she wrote Johnny, with justified apprehension. Personally, the family had been shown all the courtesy they had any right to expect; admittedly, Abigail expected quite a bit, as she was proud of her country and in no way ashamed of its "great actions," which had theoretically "dismembered" it from the British Empire. Politically, things were amazingly different. John shared his wife's reservations and wished, almost wistfully, that British conduct toward his country was "of a piece" with that shown to its representative.[28]

Unfortunately, July's unpromising appraisal remained in effect that autumn and winter. If John thought the Marquis of Carmarthen and Mr. Pitt were the most liberal of all the British ministry, he was still unable to say that either gentleman had helped in solving the differences between the countries. The "bones of contention" remained achingly numerous; while the British conceded that the Americans ought to be repaid for their captured slaves, their attitude toward complying with the seventh article of their Definitive Treaty was something else. Withdrawal from certain posts of defense such as Oswego, Niagara and Detroit depended on "certain other matters," a position it only took moments to evaluate. The British meant to occupy American territories as a security for the payment of debts owed them, a supposition entirely substantiated months later when Lord Carmarthen reminded John of the fourth article of the treaty concerning violations by American debtors.[29]

However chastened he may have been by the many problems, John was optimistic about the outcome. Though he frowned on the "immense debt" American merchants owed British manufacturers (one that certainly "sours this people beyond measure"), John thought the British shortsighted, and was astonished at the way they deluded themselves with the "bubble" that Americans were weary of their independence. It was too late for punishment, for imposing heavy duties and clumsy prohibitory acts; to forbid, for example, the export of tools to America could, at most, be regarded as a petty reprimand. Those who foresaw the consequences—and John thought himself an able visionary—recognized British restraint as a spur to Americans, whose chemistry reacted most creatively in adversity. England "will never leave us until they drive us into power and greatness that will finally shake this kingdom," he predicted shrewdly.[30]

John was equally astute in his evaluation of the King who ruled his kingdom so tenuously. There were some who called the King a great "dissembler"—a glib description when contrasted with John's thoughtful perception of George's elusive personality. Strangely, though John was frustrated by negotiations with the British, aware of their limited acceptance of his country, he was still able to muster some fragmentary sympathy for the royal family. By December, when he had had time to study the considerable responsibilities of George and Charlotte, he was able to admire their ability to cope with duties he thought appalling. To say that John was forthright was to be charitable; friends as well as enemies were more likely to characterize his stark honesty and direct manner as blunt and awkward. Minor frivolities were an enigma and a trial for him, and he could only think it "paying very dear" to be a king or a queen, or anyone obligated to spend even one day a year chatting with thousands, let alone hundreds, of people. The idea of finding small talk suitable for each individual both intimidated and alarmed him—it was a task, he said, out of proportion "to all his own forces of Mind or Body."[31]

Perhaps because of their contrasting personalities, and possibly because of the King's fateful influence on his country's destiny, John was fascinated by George, and scrupulous in his observation. No detail was too homely to incorporate in the masterfully idiosyncratic portrait he drew of the ruler in a letter to John Jay. The King, John reported, was a man who favored order and regularity, who was methodical about his personal habits, who was not a bit lazy, who even made his own fire at the palace. John had also learned that the King shaved himself, sometimes wore a scratch wig to the levees, and appeared doomed to oversee the fragmentation of his empire. On December 3, 1785, John wrote:

> The King, I really think is the most accomplished courtier in the Dominions. With all the affability of Charles the Second he has all the Domestic virtues and regularity of conduct of Charles the 1st. He is the greatest talker in the world and has a tenacious memory stored with reserves of small talk concerning all the little things of life, which are inexhaustible—But so much of his time is and has been consumed in this that he is in all the great affairs of society and government as weak as far as I can judge, as we ever understood him to be in America. He is also as obstinate—The unbounded popularity acquired by his appearance of graciousness added to the splendor of his dignity, give him such a continual feast of flattery that he thinks all he does is right and pursues his "own ideas" with a firmness which would become the best system [of] action. He has a pleasure in his own will and way without which he would be miserable which seems to be the true principle upon which he has always chosen and rejected ministers. He has an habitual contempt of patriotism.[32]

If John, despite grievous frustrations, seemed wise and even tolerant about the British monarch, Abigail was unyielding, if unconsciously entertaining. She wished no favors, but she did expect the courtesy and recognition she believed was due her country; she thought herself "complimenting" the power before which she appeared, as much as she was complimented by its notice of her. On further exposure, she recognized that she would never be a court favorite, and as early as September 1785, she decided never to set foot in court except when etiquette required her to submit to the penalty, in her role as a public character. Just to think about the royal family was disturbing; actually to see its collected members was worse. She truly did not think them attractive, and could find no common ground with a Queen "stiff with diamonds." She relented only slightly to allow that the King was a "stout, wellmade man" who would look better if he had not sacrificed so much to Bacchus. She thought his daughter Elizabeth a short, clumsy miss who would not be considered a bit handsome if she was not a princess. On the whole, when pressed to think of something polite to say about the family, she tended to concentrate on their complexions.[33]

Whatever her reservations, London held an obvious advantage for Abigail. She was, at last, plunged into the heart of life, no longer merely a mail-pouch participant. She had always assured John that she was interested in every transaction concerning those she loved. In this allegation Abigail tended to underestimate herself.

More accurately, Abigail took an interest in every transaction in which all humanity was involved; she feasted on the profundities and trivia concerning not only family and country, but coachman and King. Abigail's private conversations as well as her correspondence, during this time, brimmed with opinions on everything and everybody. She pronounced Parisian rouge, even enhanced with a royal blaze of diamonds, no match for the blooming health, sparkling eyes, and modest deportment of the dear girls of her native land. She fretted, as well, that she might be called snobbish by the American refugees, the Tory sympathizers, whom she could not entertain in her official capacity. She thought Sarah Siddons the most glorious actress alive, but was disgusted, even horrified (allowing for an "early predjuce") that her gentle Desdemona should be touched by a sooty Moor, a man of African color. Abigail's further reservations about Shakespeare concerned his language, which was unequaled, in her opinion, for its beauty, but unfortunately also for its harsh, uncouth expressions. She supposed that with some alterations the playwright's work might be made more agreeable for the stage. Apparently, while professing a desire to see "this European world in all its forms," Abigail had in no way abdicated her right to her emphatically defined beliefs.[34]

Of the trio in London, however, Nabby was the surprise. For the first time in letters to Johnny, written in the summer of 1785, she made herself known, disclosing opinions, appetites, and insights that erase the wooden figure glimpsed in previous self-portraits, and through her mother's eyes. Instead, a sensitive, shy, lonely young woman emerges, with unsurpassed family loyalties and unsuspected vision. Her bountiful acceptance of the father she barely knew, the void she felt herself in after Johnny's departure, indicate her deprivation and need in the years of growing up apart from both. Nabby's appreciation of John was singular. She managed to catch him at his best angle; what others viewed as awkward or blunt behavior, she termed candor, openness, integrity—all the cherished qualities she would wish to inherit from her father. It was a case of loyal and mutual admiration. Nabby bloomed in her tentative way; she teasingly referred to herself as "my Ladyship," as the "Honourable Miss Adams you know," while a proud, affectionate father talked about her blend of "drollery and modesty" when others saw acquiescence and even sadness.[35]

Nabby's relationship with Johnny was of another order. He was not only her brother, but her companion and friend. The finality of their separation almost devastated her. Now the arrival of his letters at Grosvenor Square were apt to be the main event of any of her days —tea or chocolate grew cold, bread-and-butter squares turned soggy, as the seemingly diffident sister was magnetized by every word he wrote.[36]

In return, in her room over the breakfast quarters, she pulled up the green velvet–cushioned chair to her desk, rolled back its louvered dome, glanced fleetingly over the rooftops out her window (she counted more than one hundred chimneys one day) and absorbed herself in the writing of one of the dozens of encyclopedic letters to her "dearest of brothers." She wrote with mournful tenderness, without restraint, as she might have to a lover. "Every day, hour, and minute, mon chere frere, pains me more and more," she confided:

> I would walk, my Brother is gone—I would ride, my Brother is gone. I would retire to my chamber alas I meet him there. I would meet him in his apartment, but where is JQA? I would go to my

work and he would read to me, but alas, this is passed, and I am to draw the comparison between Auteuil and Grosvenor Square and sigh and—and wish to recall the former.[37]

Methodically, Nabby went about scheduling her life in her brother's absence. It would obviously have been different had he been with her, or if she had been "blessed" with a sister who might have shared the amusements offered, made the invitations to assemblies and balls more welcome. Since this was not the case, she was convinced that happiness lay in performing secretarial duties for her father and Thomas Jefferson, which included deciphering their special code, and tending to her private correspondence. Johnny's letters, in this period particularly, were especially meaningful to Nabby; they were nearly tangible links meant to reinforce a relationship of fleeting duration and stunted promise.[38]

Nabby wished to make a pact with her brother to ease their separation. She wrote pitiably that they had once been strangers and now were nearly strangers again, with a difference—by "constant and unreserved" communications they would not lose knowledge of each other's sentiments and dispositions. "Tell me all that I am entitled to know of what passes within your own mind and from what sources your derive pleasure and from what you receive pain," she begged Johnny. She seemed to be telling him that having found roots, she could hardly bear to crush them, and that she needed his love and his help, and revered his opinions:

Tell me also all that you wish to, respecting myself or others. Remind me of all my errors, mistakes, and foibles, and convince my judgment. Guide my opinions and may you also approve of all past present and future decisions. . . . If I ever take any important step contrary to your judgment it will be because you aren't present to judge it.[39]

The beauty of their correspondence was that Johnny fulfilled his role with affectionate generosity. Erudite and compassionate, he allowed that it would be a "mortification" to him to hear from Nabby less frequently than she had promised. In return, he vowed to set apart half an hour weekly to write to her. In the brief intimacy of their exchange, the summer and winter of 1785 and 1786, the two roamed through an amazingly broad field of subjects, including talk about flirtations and aspirations, about courts and customs, about women's education and about romance. As might be expected, the letters were as revealing of the brother as the sister.[40]

Johnny's interests, contrary to his mother's opinion, were not confined to Roman and Greek literature. Wonderfully normal for his age, he confessed to finding one young woman, who was staying with Aunt and Uncle Shaw, "uncommonly interesting," elaborating that she was "exceedingly well proportioned, had a fine shape, very fair complexion." In further chitchat, Johnny referred to another subject he thought of interest to Nabby, the education of the young ladies of Boston, but here his enthusiasm waned drastically.[41]

Americans had no theaters and no masquerades, but they did have assemblies and balls, a surfeit of them in Johnny's judgment, and the most "ridiculous" way of spending time that was ever invented. American women went into company too young, and talked nonsense too fluently, while European women seemed to receive an excellent education *before* they were introduced into the world. In particular, the young ladies of Boston offended him because they seemed to find it beneath their dignity to know anything but how to dance and talk scandal—and "for this last particular," he insisted, "they have attained great perfection." In all these sentiments, Johnny assured his sister, he spoke "not the truth only, but all the Truth," and nothing, he warned, was meant for repetition.[42]

Undoubtedly, John Quincy set the tone of their correspondence; certainly, Nabby sustained it. Loving, assertive, even mischievous, she wrote now of American visitors and drunken coachmen, of breakfast at 4:00 P.M. and dinner at 11:00 P.M. ("ridiculous beings these are"), and refused to permit the glorification of European women. Englishwomen were too masculine in their dress, in her opinion, and as far as their talents for conversation were concerned, they seemed to reach the height of sociability when they managed to say "yes" and "no." Nabby, in droll spirits, did not hesitate to tease Johnny about an old flirtation. Careful to avoid names, she merely asked in sisterly fashion: "Does not your heart go pit a pit, now bounce, as if it would break your rib?"[43]

When Nabby was serious, which was most of the time, she wrote as intelligent but largely unschooled young women had written to their formally educated brothers for generations. She was candid about encouraging Johnny's criticism, about needing his approval; she wished to know whether her letters were "too particular," whether her brother found himself "informed" by her scribbling, and was pleased by it. The unique aspect of the correspondence was its complete contradiction of the uninspiring impression Nabby made on others, as well as herself, convinced as she was that she lacked willpower and tended to be dutiful and joyless. For the most ephemeral of moments, the girl who claimed she was not fond of "very laughing characters," who denied any pretense to soaring imagination, revealed aspirations and curiosity that would be tragically aborted. "Above all things," she confided to her brother, she aspired to join a party of travelers in a trip around the world.

> I cant see why People who have the inclination and ability, which to be sure is the most essential of the two, should not gratify themselves by indulging it and seeing as many and various parts of the world as it should lead them to if they are possessed of proper principles. To explore would not injure them but make them wiser and better and happier.[44]

Though she had appeared to frown rather than laugh, to reject rather than accept, Nabby was fully aware of the opportunity her new life abroad had afforded her. "Pray dont you feel a great deal wiser than if you had never been outside the limits of the State of Massachusetts Bay?" she asked her brother.[45]

Something else charmed her about her travels. She understood and rather enjoyed her elevated prestige, and relished the news that her friends at home were impressed with her visits to the Tower of London, to St. Paul's Cathedral, to George III's court. Their country had a "wonderful likeing," she told her brother, for those who could say they had been "here and there." As Nabby seemed to enjoy sharing her adventures "here and there," she recorded her days on an almost hourly basis, from breakfast to teatime, from theater to ballroom, from millinery to mantua-maker. A spontaneous reporter, she described the Prince of Wales as very fat and supposed his careless, lounging air was what was generally referred to as ease and politeness; the Princess Royal, though the handsomest member of the family, shared with the rest an expression of "great vacancy." The Queen, she went on, was a "haughty Proud imperious dame" whose countenance was "hard and unfeeling as if carved out of an oak knoll." And "Thank Heaven" she did not feel dependent on the Queen's frowns and smiles.[46]

No doubt, Nabby was in high gear now, every syllable her mother's daughter. Her pen flourished with confidence, bristled with opinion. She exercised restraint on only one subject and one person: her references to her father's secretary were so circumspect that initially it was impossible for her brother to surmise Colonel William Stephens Smith's precise relationship with his sister. But if Johnny was oblivious of this newcomer's role, his mother was not. Her awareness of his possible position in her family was mounting. So was her appreciation of the change he had wrought in their lives, and in Nabby's particularly. Abigail's mood these days depended, more than she admitted, on Nabby's, and there seemed to be no question that Nabby was happy for the first time in more months than her mother cared to count. Here it was September—they had known the colonel since June—and their lives were brighter for his presence, a fact that Nabby acknowledged most directly.

Shyly, Nabby told John Quincy of her father's delight in Colonel Smith, of his pleasure with his "Principles and Sentiments as they respect his appointment with him." Next she related an outrageously flattering incident that could not help but endear the colonel to her. One afternoon he had switched carriages, jumping from his into hers, waving instructions to his companion of seconds ago to proceed on his own to call on Mr. Adams. "Perhaps you will say the Colonel sacrificed politeness to gallantry," a radiant Nabby suggested to her brother, obviously forgoing such a reservation. More definitively, she wrote: "Mamma I suppose will tell you in what relation this Gentleman is Considered in this family—and you my Brother know that your approbation is dear to me."[47]

Approbation was the key word now. If approval was important to Nabby, it was even more so to Abigail. If there was one potential flaw in the romance between the colonel and her daughter, it was the possibility that those who were aware of Nabby's commitment to Royall Tyler would consider her hasty, careless, or frivolous—or all three—in her new bond with William Smith. But these would be people, Abigail reasoned, who did not know that Nabby had ended her relationship with Tyler months earlier, to the relief of her parents, whose doubts Mary Cranch cultivated relentlessly. Though Cotton Tufts's reports were more objective, they too did nothing to dispel accumulating evidence against Tyler. Between both aunts, Uncle Tufts, various cousins on one side of the ocean, and Nabby and Abigail on the other, a dozen quills were at work scratching out messages across two continents that doomed one romance as it prepared for another. In retrospect, the turn of Nabby's affairs was hardly surprising. Rather, it seemed predestined, the way having been studiously prepared before she had even sailed out of Boston Harbor little more than a year before.[48]

FOURTEEN

Circumstances and Connections Respectable

When, on August 2, 1784, Abigail arrived in London with
Nabby to wait for John, she wrote a letter to her sister Mary that
invited intrigue:

> If at any time you wish to communicate to me, anything that no
> other person ought to see, let it be always inclosed in an other
> letter with such a mark upon the outside as this

What might be embarrassing ought to be private, Abigail thought.
Though the sisters might try to hide their brother's existence from
the outside world, to one another they worried over his relentlessly
bad news. Alarmed by his intemperance and his debts, they feared,
only too prophetically, that the "drama was not fully played out." It
almost seemed as if they were preparing for his predicament of the
next years—to hear him charged with counterfeiting, to wait in suspense to learn that he had been found guilty of passing notes others
had fabricated, but not actually of forgery. The neat little symbol in
the corner of the letter would act as their flag to signal news they
would want to slip into a pocket, news they did not wish to share with
others.[1]

But news of their brother, their "unhappy connection," was not the
only secret between Mary and Abigail. There was also "the family
affair" to deal with, and Mary Cranch might easily have availed herself of the secret cipher to help channel her insistent flow of opinions
regarding Nabby's romance with Royall Tyler, which had taken a

curiously optimistic turn just a few months before Nabby boarded the *Active*. With Nabby and Abigail gone, Tyler, as a boarder with the Cranch family in Germantown, might have been safer in a lion's cage. Though his life was not actually threatened, his future as he had conceived it—meaning marriage to Nabby—was under siege. His recollection of their tearful farewell, of "throwing" himself into a chair despondently after Nabby's departure, was translated as a scene of foolish hysteria by Mary and her daughters. Their version was that Tyler had sobbed irrationally about not seeing Nabby again, that he had bawled "like a great boy who had misbehaved and was obliged to go to school without his dinner." The cousins' imitations of Tyler's hysteria made John Quincy laugh as they had never seen him before, or so they claimed. What motivated the Cranch family's malicious behavior is difficult to ascertain, but there is no doubt that while many kept Tyler under scrutiny, Mary would have had him in chains. Possibly she could not forgive him his "wild oats" days; perhaps she was disappointed that he preferred Nabby to her own eligible daughters. Whatever the reasons, her boarder did not have an easy time. Mary, especially, was insatiably curious about how he spent his time and his money, even when and how often he wrote letters; no detail was too petty for her shrewish pen.[2]

Mary had assured Abigail that her letters would not be of politics, that she knew her sister expected subjects in which her "heart" was interested. She met her promise exhaustively. Initially, for Mary, considering the rest of her "reports," Tyler received passable grades. To Abigail, while she was in Auteuil, Mary wrote: "His business I think increases and as far as I can judge he attends it with steadiness. He has his share at this court." By January 4, 1785, she had, however, sounded the alarm. Captain Lyde was to sail the next Sunday, she wrote Abigail, yet

> Mr. T would not write till the court which began to sit this week was over so that unless he writes in Boston which I should think he may he will not write by this vessel. I dont know how it is with you but I had rather have a Letter by every vessel than a volume at a time and that but seldom. I wish you could see him when he is writing shut up in his chamber for a week together with about forty books round him. I told him one day [a] Letter . . . from the Heart *in season* was worth all of them. I asked him what example he could make for his neglect. He said he should make none. I confess I felt too much [to] answer him.[3]

An ignored Mary Cranch was indeed a most vengeful Mary Cranch. Tyler was far too independent, his habits too unconventional and too whimsical for her approval. Besides, he was rudely impervious to her suggestions, a factor that could only orchestrate her main theme, his unsuitability for marriage to Nabby. Of course, she had more to say, she assured Abigail, but would wait for another vessel. What she omitted, her sister Elizabeth Shaw supplied, though in somewhat more sympathetic tones, based, of course, on the assumption that Tyler was the villain of this on-going drama. Mrs. Shaw lamented that "infelicity" must be Nabby's present portion, advised her sister of the necessity of "Candor, & impartiality" because it was not sufficient to hear only one side, and assured her that "Time was the helper," and that her own prudent goodness of heart would direct her in the "critical, delicate" part she had to act.[4]

Abigail was quite aware of the delicate course on which she was uncomfortably embarked, and confided her misgivings to Uncle Tufts. Her impression of the romance was not a satisfactory one, either, though her view of it differed from her sisters'. Nabby was disturbingly quiet, and, to a degree, her mother understood her moods. Every thoughtful young person who was about to "connect" herself for life had to think through the decision. Still, Nabby showed none of the joy Abigail remembered of her own young life, and she did not need to tell her uncle that her own marriage had been of the happiest kind. Most of all, she very much wanted this same happiness for Nabby. While Abigail had, at the beginning of the year, addressed Tyler as "the person to whom care & protection I shall one day resign a beloved and only daughter," she found herself doubting her own words. Troubled, she confided as much: "This Sir is between ourselves."[5]

Another letter from Mary, that June, did nothing to soothe Abigail. Mary's saga of Tyler's eccentric handling of a packet of mail from Nabby that he was meant to distribute among friends and relatives continued in obsessive detail. Letters that had arrived in the fall he gave out in the spring; letters received in April he hadn't delivered until that June. Mary even suspected that Tyler kept some of them for himself, and said she thought about asking her niece not to enclose letters meant for the family along with those to her fiancé. Mary had more to say and only wished her sister could be reached more easily so that she might not feel so inhibited about the information she felt bound to send her. By no means a skimping intelligence agent (though a self-appointed one), Mary made an offer: "If there is any thing which you may wish to be informed of which I have not told you ask me and I will endeavour to satisfy you." Burdensome as her household duties were, demanding of her time as the periodic examinations of Abigail's woolens were (to keep the moths from devouring them), Mary was happy, she told her sister, to be helpful to her in every way.[6]

By July the matter had reached a critical stage. To answer Abigail's inquiries about Tyler, to reply to her hopes that he was "very busy and to great purpose," Mary could only say, "I hope so too." She knew very little about him these days. He was seldom in Braintree, and even then "very little" at home. She did know that he had attended the courts in Boston the last winter and that summer, and that he would not be home until the sessions were over. Obviously, "Certain parts" of her letter were bound to cause Abigail and Nabby anxiety, Mary surmised correctly. They also effected a decision that had been in the offing for months now.[7]

It was at morning chocolate with her mother that Nabby finally unwound her knot of troubles. Abigail would repeat her daughter's words to her sisters; they would haunt her the rest of her life. "Do you not think a gentleman of my acquaintance a man of honour?" Nabby asked. "Yes, a man of strict honour," Abigail answered, adding, "I wish I would say that of all your acquaintances." There was no mistaking Abigail's meaning. "But a breach of honour in one party would not justify a want of it in the other," Nabby said. Abigail took only a moment to decide that this was the time to speak up. "If you are conscious of any want of honour in the part of the gentleman, I and every friend you have in the world would rejoice if you could liberate yourself."[8]

Nabby's reaction was instantaneous. She picked up her skirts, ran out of the room, and bounded up the staircase and into her own room. Two hours later she sent down to her mother copies of two letters from Royall Tyler (she had received four in the past fourteen months—the last, a short one written in December), and her own personal note. She wanted her mother to know how concerned she was about her father's thoughts, and wondered whether he was one of the "friends" who wished for her liberation from her engagement. She dreaded his displeasure, and promised never in the future to take a step he had not approved. She also thanked heaven that her mind was not in so weak a state as to feel a "partiality" that was not returned. No state of mind was so painful as that which allowed fear, suspicion, doubt, dread, and apprehension. "I have too long known them all," a stoic Nabby confided to her mother.[9]

Abigail did not waste a moment that evening. Nabby had given her permission to "communicate" her thoughts to her father, if her mother thought it proper. Abigail obviously thought it exceedingly proper, and within moments, father and daughter were in one of the most personal conversations of their entire relationship, the father awkward and sorrowful over his daughter's sad bewilderment, almost apologetic. Tyler was a stranger, and John explained that though he had not given his consent as freely as he wished, his sympathy for their affection for one another reflected his own romantic attitude toward marriage. Now, if her feelings were different, her plans changed, he hoped she had arrived at her decision with mature deliberation, because it was a serious one. If she had reason to question Tyler's honor, or if she supposed Tyler was capable of telling her he had written when he had not, then Nabby's father assured her he would rather follow her to her grave than see her united with Tyler. As a result of this talk, Abigail was able to write on August 11 to warn John Quincy of surprising news to come. She assumed he would approve of Nabby's wise conduct and admire her firmness of mind and her prudence, which did her honor. "Be silent!" the mother pleaded. "We are all rejoiced because it came of her own accord free and unsolicited from her and was the result I believe of many months anxiety as you were witness."[10]

Neglect was presumed the primary reason for the demise of Nabby's romance. By the same yardstick, it was impossible for a young woman in Nabby's ambivalent state not to be exhilarated by the attentive Colonel Smith's affectionate interest. Abigail would later confide to John Quincy that they were not long at Grosvenor Square before she saw that "the gentleman who made a part of the family" was happier reading to the ladies and walking, riding, and going to the theater with them, than in any other company or amusement. So much so that she felt anxious about his being a "stranger" to Nabby's situation; yet she felt awkward about saying anything to him, not sure the colonel was aware of his own feelings. Finally she could not restrain herself another moment, and was convinced it was her duty to speak

up, to "hint" to the colonel about Nabby's "being under engagements in America."[11]

Though Abigail introduced the subject "carelessly," she was proud
that not a syllable of her message was lost in transmission. As a result,
the colonel decided it would be best for him to go away on business,
from which he would not return until December. He also assured
Abigail that in the future his attentions would only be "general," and
asked her to excuse him if, on some occasions, he appeared negligent. Abigail commended his resolution, struggling successfully, she
thought, against confiding to him that she hoped the estrangement
would be a temporary one.[12]

Abigail made an odd-looking Cupid—her slender, erect figure and
thoughtful eyes were less than cherubic—but her aim was neat, her
targets readier than she imagined. On the colonel's return, he dined
with the Adams family, but retired immediately, skipping the fireside
conversations of previous months. After several weeks of what Abigail would later describe as "perfect distance," the situation changed
abruptly. After theater one evening the colonel asked for a moment's
audience. "As the connection which appeared an insurmountable
obstacle to the accomplishment of the wishes nearest his Heart, existed no longer—and from the opinion he had of the Lady" he had
assembled his credentials and asked that Abigail read them and then
bring them to John, who was already upstairs in bed.[13]

Abigail read with pleasure, but without surprise, of the thirty-year-
old colonel's commissions, of testimony to his brave conduct during
his seven years in the army. She had liked the colonel immediately.
The tall soldier with a "good" figure and a ruddy complexion, a
graduate of Princeton University, class of 1774, the son of a New
York merchant, appeared to be a "modest worthy man," she wrote
Thomas Jefferson, and she had known all along that their family
would have "much pleasure" in connection with him. What she did
not know was that the colonel, too, was on the rebound, from a Miss
Read, with whom he might once have been happy, though of course
not now, in view of his new ties. "You need not fear I'll make another
slip with her," he reassured his dear friend the Prussian general and
fellow soldier, Baron Friedrich von Steuben.[14]

From all appearances and actions, Colonel Smith was charming and
modest; it was only in his confidences to von Steuben that he appeared another man, this one ambitious, striving, impecunious, flirta-

tious. "I put up at the Pall Mall near the Palace of St. James, thinking it best to strike at the highest peg at once," he had written. He had been pleased with his reception by the Adams family, though hardly mesmerized by them initially. "Mrs. A——is a very sensible and discerning woman, and Miss is an amiable and sensible girl"; at court they had "behaved to a charm." A short while later, in a letter to Rufus King, he was more enthusiastic: "Mr. A. full answers yours and Mr. Jays account of him, & the ladies of his family do honour to this country. As for the young lady—she is more than painters can express, or youthful poets fancy when they love." And though it was treason to say so in this hemisphere, and being absolutely impartial, he had to assert that they were "fully equal" to any attending the Queen's reception.[15]

Charmed as he now seemed by the Adams family, he was still captive of a most elemental problem. "I should have no objections to an enlargement of salary for reasons obvious as follows," he mentioned to King. He planned to live with Mr. Adams's family, though he had no right to expect this. He was worried that Mr. Adams would find his own allowance short, no matter how economical he was, for his station was remarkably expensive and required a "tolerable" supply of money to maintain standards he had set for his family and his country. As for himself, Smith wrote: "I mean with Apulius to choose my allowance as I would my coat rather neat and fit than too long or too full, for what ever exceeds convenience and moderation turns more to burthen than to use." But without facing the reality of his expectations or his position, Colonel Smith's "burthen" was a considerable one. He had entered, in his own words, on "a very extensive and Gay theatre, the acts many, the Plott immense. I move with great caution lest I should stumble—I must confess I do not find that intoxication which I was led to expect," he concluded critically.[16]

Surprisingly, for one so thorough and astute as Abigail, her correspondence reveals not a trace of doubt about the colonel's integrity. She seemed to accept him off the battlefield in gleaming uniform; his own pleasant, competent, interested personality, bolstered by official commendation, was enough to justify her approval as well as John's. Yet a casual acquaintance, a passing visitor, Matthew Ridley, caught the colonel in an entirely different light and reported his impressions of him and the entire Adams ménage to Catherine W. Livingston with blunt yet skilled strokes. The family was well, Abigail appeared "a very good woman and one I am much pleased with," but he had reservations about the newcomer. "Colonel Smith is entirely in the gay Circle —he keeps his chariot—will a Secretary's Appointment afford this?" Ridley asked, without needing to hear the answer. "I know the Ambassador complains that he cannot make his appointment do and I sincerely believe him. I am convinced it is impossible it should."[17]

Perhaps the parents, ingrained skeptics of all luxury or frivolity, were blinded by their delight in Nabby's new mood, grateful for her shy smiles. It would seem as though they had lost their way in an unaccustomed climate, their judgment dulled by their gratitude. Nabby joined conversations now, and no longer sat around in defeated silence, writing in her small notebook, copying lines from Shakespeare that left no question but that Royall Tyler had sorely wounded her:

> *I am sorry I must never trust thee more*
> *But count the world a stranger for thy sake*
> *The private wound is deepest, oh time most accurs'd.*
> *'mongst all foes, that a friend should be the worst.* [18]

In December of 1785, Nabby recorded her change of heart in her journal. The tone was tentative, but the careful, girlish script was deliberate: "Events have taken place respecting myself, in which, perhaps, my future happiness may be interested. To that Being, under whose guidance I would fain believe all our actions to be, I must submit and leave the events."[19]

The news at which Abigail had hinted for months was considered official when she wrote to Mary on February 26: "Your niece is engaged to a gentleman worthy of her; one, whom you will be proud to own as a nephew." Abigail was so pleased by the "Circumstances and Connections respectable" that she could not pass a higher "encomium" upon the prospective son-in-law than to say that he often reminded her of her dear brother Richard Cranch. The colonel appeared to be a gentleman in every thought, word, and action, "domestic in his attachments fond in his affections, quick as lightning in his feelings, but softened in an instant; his character is that of a dutiful son, and most affectionate brother."[20]

And that was not all. As though the display were incomplete, Abigail had further medals to show. The colonel was also a hero of sorts, having trod the "uncultivated wilds" through Indian country, having received ample testimony from Generals John Sullivan and George

Washington, having been appointed by the latter and by Congress to inspect the evacuation of New York, and afterwards commissioned as Secretary of the Legation to the Court of St. James. He was a man of such stellar attributes that Abigail could not help but conclude that as an officer his character was "highly meritorious; as a citizen he appears all that ought to be." Colonel Smith was a man who loved his country, and was willing to devote his talents to its service. With his "high" sense of honor and his independent spirit, founded on religion and morality, Abigail was proud to say there was every reason to believe that her son-in-law's character would bear the "strictest scrutiny."[21]

Abigail shared her confidences with Uncle Tufts as well as with her sisters. The patient, kindly man had reassured Abigail of his appreciation of their difficult position regarding Royall Tyler. The faithful friend had read the anxious sentiments of a parent with sympathy, and wished he could have given Abigail fresh information that would put her mind at ease. He had hoped time would remove doubts. He scarcely knew what to say except that the subject was so delicate he wished her to burn his letter as soon as she had read it.[22]

Mary Cranch was guilty of no such thoughtful subterfuge; to her, Colonel Smith's entrance into their lives was a brilliant personal victory, a vindication of all her dedicated effort. At last she could unburden herself of all that was on her mind about what a time the dear girl must have had ever since she had been in Europe, how she wished now to congratulate her dear niece for acting with a spirit worthy of her parents, how she feared making mischief, yet fretted over whether she had done her duty toward her. Further, what a relief it was that they would have more tranquil moments now than they had enjoyed for these past three years. Quite willing, however, to postpone these tranquil moments for a little bit later, Mary went on to ask whether Abigail had received her letter describing Tyler's habit of detaining mail, and to fill her sister in on his activities, about which she had to make a grudging confession: "I know no more about his business than you do."[23]

Only temporarily out of touch with Tyler, Mary was to note in the following months that since his "dismissal," Tyler seemed gayer than ever, that he showed Nabby's letters around, that he had built a windmill to power his chocolate mill and bolting mill. Also, he indulged in ballooning, had put his sleigh into elegant repair, was assisting in a course of lectures on natural philosophy, planned to change his lodging, and had hired a Negro woman and also a boy to take care of his stock, which consisted of three horses, a yoke of oxen, and a cow (this last from a neighbor). Just in case Mary had left a crevice of doubt as to her opinion of Nabby's former suitor, she added that it was the belief of their relatives that Tyler was a man of no abilities with no profession, and that Nabby had bettered herself.[24]

Mary, who could be not only ugly but clumsy about her likes and dislikes, was, not surprisingly, very strongly suspected by Tyler of meddling and influencing Nabby's decision. She protested her innocence of the "fibs" and "foul play" that Tyler complained about, even talked about being "thankful" that she had been so "cautious" in what she had said about him. Just how influential she was in coloring Nabby's opinion is difficult to appraise. Yet there is firm evidence that her campaign against Tyler was long-standing. Even before Nabby had put one foot aboard the *Active,* Mary had managed to alienate her niece, an admission she found it impossible to make until Tyler had departed from both their lives. Then she wrote to her sister Abigail:

> Could I be with her I would convince her how tenderly I love her. I would if possible regain those affections which I lost by endeavouring to preserve her from being miserable. I thought I did right. She mistook my motive or she would have thought so too. I shall leave it to her reason and good sense to determine whether I do not deserve a higher place in her affections. . . .[25]

By the third week of April 1786, Abigail had faced the reality of the impending marriage. The zealous soldier, Abigail complained cheerfully, would hardly give her time to tell her friends that such an event was likely to take place. She claimed that she had no idea why he was in a hurry, though sympathy generously tempered her anxiety. Any time now, John might be reassigned, and it would be consoling to have Nabby happily settled with her colonel. But conscientious, prudent woman that she was, she worried about the finances involved, knew the young couple would find marriage "very chargeable," and was under no illusions about either of their fortunes. Keeping house was easier in America, and required half the salary one needed in London, where, as a public character, one was expected to be surrounded by servants, whom she considered the "greatest moths" she could conceive of. In spite of all caution, one ran into debt easily.[26]

But there were other problems she faced in parting with Nabby. Perhaps Thomas Jefferson's presence in London, at John's urgent invitation that he help negotiate with the Portuguese and Tripolitan ambassadors, had revived a barely quiescent sense of distance from friends and family. When Jefferson and Adams left London on April 4 to tour England's gardens together, Abigail was reminded of the pain of past partings and of the privileged time together these past months; this six-day sojourn marked her first separation from John in almost two years. Abigail felt threatened now. She wished she might keep Nabby and the colonel with her if she did go home, which she believed was the best place for all of them. She admitted she could not refrain from imposing her puritan values—which dictated that learning, personal merit, and virtue were "the only distinctions worth making"—on London's fashionable world, or on those who styled themselves the "polite people," any more than she could have installed a picket fence around Buckingham Palace. But she *could* nurture her own preferences for herself and for Nabby.[27]

Money, values, and even personal deprivation paled next to the subject of romance. She had compassion for the colonel, and knew her husband would understand why the young folks wished to rush into marriage; because of what a "dance" he had had, she thought he would consent immediately. With happy resignation, Abigail realized there was little to justify postponement. Judging from her own lot—so many circumstances at "first sitting out" had surprised her and required an adjustment—she did not think it worthwhile now to object to Nabby's present connection. Though it would be very hard to part with her daughter, Abigail rationalized that at least she had the consolation of being able to say, "I have not an anxiety with respect to the man."[28]

On May 25, Abigail told Mary that it was not unlikely that when she wrote again she might "add another nephew to the list of your relatives." The couple had rented a furnished house, and had need of linens, china, and glassware, which Abigail was busily assembling. When they learned that the Bishop of St. Asaph was going to the country, a date was finally settled. Dispensations from church ceremonies were usually granted only to members of Parliament and the nobility, but special attention was given to the colonel's request; twenty-four hours later, because they were foreigners and in consideration of Mr. Adams's station, the couple had their license. The young couple, as timid as partridges in Abigail's opinion, were terribly afraid of a bustle, and said they wished as few people at their wedding as decency permitted. They did, however, invite John Singleton Copley and his wife and daughter, "worthy good people" with "delicate manners," without elaborating on the fact that a wedding was to take place when the bishop arrived.[29]

Nabby had done pretty well, her mother thought, repeating after the bishop "I, Abigail, take thee, William," an embarrassing phrase for one accustomed to acknowledgment of intention with a silent curtsy. But, generally speaking, the ceremony performed on Sunday, June 12, was satisfactory; the bishop, a surprisingly sensitive and liberal man, made some omissions in the traditional ceremony, for which the Adams family thanked him "in our Hearts." Once the marriage was official, Abigail was especially reassured when the kindly bishop took the trouble to say that he had never performed a wedding ceremony with more pleasure, and added, from the knowledge he had of the parties involved, that he had never known a couple with a better prospect of happiness.[30]

The wedding that united Nabby and her colonel also signaled the breaking up of her parents' household. The separation was as difficult for daughter as for mother; though the Smiths actually moved into their house on Wimpole Street on July 1, they returned home to Grosvenor Square for dinner each day. But the house seemed empty now, and Abigail, who could not help thinking that time had flown strangely fast this past year, yearned for the countryside; she was feeling like a shut-in in a noisy, smoky town. It was not so much that she was confined physically as spiritually; she was sequestered in the house on Grosvenor Square with the realities of separation from all but John. She now appreciated for the first time that a person might be alone in a crowd. And she no longer wondered, as she used to, how people who had no children substituted cats, dogs, and birds, as well as friends.[31]

John was tremendously sympathetic; the pleasure of having his wife *and* his daughter by his side had spoiled him. He dreaded Nabby's leaving. She and her husband had been gone exactly twenty-four hours when he changed his morning schedule. Usually, it had been the pattern for John to work in his library after breakfast, for Abigail to retire to her bedroom, and for the two to meet again at one o'clock in the afternoon. But not this morning. It was barely eleven o'clock when Abigail heard her door soundly thumped, and opened it to find her husband with hat and cane in hand. "Well, I have been to see them," he said. "Could you not have stayed in the house until the usual hour of departure?" Abigail asked. "No, I could not. I wanted to go before Breakfast." And he had, though one o'clock in the afternoon was the usual time for his daily walk.[32]

Despite florid self-congratulations and her family's enthusiasm for Nabby's "connection," Abigail could not exorcise the past. The night before the wedding, she dreamed of Royall Tyler; it was as though some evil spirit had sent him to visit her. Overwhelmed by guilt, she tossed in her bed, the tangled deeds and misdeeds of the past year parading through her mind until her head ached with confusion. On the one hand, she was sure that Royall's failure to write to her daughter in no way indicated his lack of affection for her. But on the other, he had been warned—she herself had heard Nabby say it repeatedly —that she would "erase" from her heart and mind every sentiment of affection, however strong, if she was conscious that it was not returned, for she was incapable of loving a man who did not love her. Abigail almost admired Tyler's eccentricities; she understood that he was an original, but she also understood her daughter's needs. At her most conciliatory, she worried about Tyler being "mortified" by Nabby's rejection of him, sympathized "not a little" with his loss of all hope of a connection he had obviously cherished, and wished him every possible happiness.[33]

Having thought all the good and charitable things she could about the man who had nearly been her son-in-law, she was unable, however, to negate her doubts or her bitterness, which verged on fury. While Abigail talked about respecting Tyler's abilities and his amiable qualities, she also mentioned that he was as unstable as water, that he lacked the foremost of virtues, sincerity. Memories brimmed, and she recalled how she had found herself "trembling," before coming to England, for the fate of her only daughter, and hoping that the separation would be therapeutic, that it would help "fully develop and try characters" that were obviously in need of ripening. Tyler's abilities, specifically applied, might have won him respect, but bound as he was to "triffel" with a thousand themes, his waxen wings would melt, she predicted, and he would fall "headlong" to the ground. But it wasn't just her own reservations and Mary's vicious denunciations that convinced her that Tyler, with his "certain habits," would be happier if connected with another family than theirs; it was Uncle Tufts who had confirmed all her doubts.[34]

Being a punctilious businessman and a courteous gentleman, Tufts had thought it best to settle Tyler's involvement with the family's business, now that he was no longer to be part of it. But that was easier said than done. No matter how many letters he wrote, or how many times he journeyed to Braintree, he could never get the young lawyer to give him a proper accounting of what moneys he had collected, what papers he had on file. Tufts, who eventually spoke of "not a little rejoicing" that Tyler and Nabby had broken off their correspondence, was truly puzzled and tried to understand Tyler's irresponsible behavior. Was it Tyler's resentment at doing business with a former near-relative, or was it his "moveable spirit" caught from his windmill project, that accounted for his oddly elusive attitude? Whatever it was, Tufts had grown impatient. "I shall not long be interested to feed hallucinations," he told Abigail. On July 6, Tufts thought he might have to resort to the law to retrieve the Adamses' papers and money, and he asked that Abigail consult with John as to whether he thought it proper to "specially order" the delivery of all books and papers into his hands—"such an order to be used as prudence may direct," he added. Before he had a chance to receive an answer, Tufts was able to report with relief, in August, that Tyler had "voluntarily" turned in the material sought, offering some vague excuse about the scarcity of current coin impeding the collection of moneys owed.[35]

At her angriest, Abigail would call Tyler a "hyena," indignant that she and Nabby should be dupes of his "cant & grimace." She would have liked to obliterate the suffering he had caused them; she hoped she would never again hear from him or about him. She was, of course, forgetting about her sister Mary, who refused to give up her vigil. Tyler had moved out of the Cranches' household around May, on the worst of terms. Except for breakfast and dinner on Sundays, he came and went as he wished, mostly before the family rose, and after they went to bed. Mary said she did not like this kind of boarding, and thought it would be better for him to lodge where he dined. Besides, she wanted his room for her nephews. As though complying with her thoughts, and without a word, he appeared that July, took some of his clothes, and was no longer, from that time on, to be seen, even at the meeting house. Thus far his mill and farm had been maintained, as had his office, and he appeared to be having his house repaired.[36]

By September, news of Tyler altered drastically. "He looked I cannot tell you how," Mary reported of her recent encounter with him. "He did not rise from his seat, perhaps he could not." He had gone off as quickly as he could, and he had not spoken to her. She learned that he had not only returned the necessary papers to Tufts, but also the gifts of a miniature and a morocco pocketbook, at Nabby's request; her stiff little note to him also mentioned her hopes of his being "well satisfied with the affair as is. . . ." Mary had learned still more: that Tyler owed his laborers, that his farm was mortgaged and that it was predicted he would not be able to hold on to it for long at the rate he was going. Most of Mary's information was secondhand because Tyler, after visiting his mother in Jamaica Plains over that summer, returned to Boston, still restless and visibly unsettled, to board with the Palmer family, his warmest and now seemingly his only friends. Palmer (whose daughter Mary, though eighteen years Tyler's junior, would eventually marry him), seemed alone in his loyalty to Tyler. Maintaining that he was entirely ignorant of the cause of Nabby's conduct, he even wrote to ask her the reasons for her change of heart. Palmer insisted that Tyler was as worthy a young fellow as any who had ever lived, that he was attentive to his business, but that he had many enemies who had been libeling him.[37]

Ultimately, Royall Tyler was to elude the eyes of Germantown and Braintree by circuitous and surprising routes. He was disturbed by rumors that a group of farmers, angered by depressed economic conditions in western Massachusetts, planned to attack the federal arsenal at Springfield. He decided to join up with General Benjamin Lincoln, the leader of the state troops, as his aide-de-camp, and was able to successfully squash the rebellion led by Daniel Shays, who eventually retreated into deep Berkshire snows, and further to Vermont. Then, as though to prove that a man who enjoyed tilting at windmills and riding balloons had other appetites as well, Tyler went on to New York where his play, *The Contrast,* premiered five weeks later, on April 6, 1787, an intriguing accomplishment on several levels.[38]

The Contrast was to be regarded as the first American play to be produced commercially. It would also be interpreted as Tyler's comment on his flawed romance with Nabby Adams. As Abigail speculated to Mary in a letter that July, the writer was indeed drawing a contrast between his own character and another gentleman's, whose name wasn't difficult to guess at in any disguise. The subject was that of broken engagements and the contrast between a colonel—a gen-

tleman who has read Chesterfield and received the polish of Europe
—and an unpolished, untraveled American named Billy Dimple, a
"good natured, decent-dressing young fellow, with a little dash of the
coxcomb."[39]

Tyler's play was thought by some to be the first American comedy.
It also had to be judged as a private satire, if not revenge, on Nabby
Adams and close relations. There were parts for all of them in his
play. Aside from the polished and unpolished males in leading roles,
there was a "grave" heroine named Maria, who was willing to die to
make her father happy, who spoke dramatically of those who had
never lived with their parents and did not know what influence "a
father's frowns have upon a daughter's heart." Another bit of Maria's
dialogue sounded as though it had been transported from a corner
of the library at Grosvenor Square. Of whom could she have been
speaking when she said, "His late conduct towards me has turned my
coolness into contempt. He behaves as if he meant to insult and
disgust me; whilst my father, in the last conversation on the subject
of our marriage, spoke of it as a matter which laid near his heart, and
in which he would not bear contradiction"?[40]

Nor did Tyler forget to write about New England gentlemen who
have such a "laudable curiosity of seeing the bottom of everything,"
about a deacon's daughter with twenty acres of land ("somewhat
rocky though"), a Bible, and a cow. Did he have Abigail or Mary
Cranch or even Nabby in mind when he wrote about women who look
as if they didn't know a journal from a ledger, but when their own
interest was concerned "they know what's what, mind the main
chance with the best of men"? Which of the three inspired one
character to cry out against a woman who had kept him from speaking
his mind all his life, who threatened to "henpeck" him even though
she was dead? And who provided the model for the female who kept
saying, "My will is yours . . . my will is yours . . . but took special care
to have her own way, though, for all that?"[41]

Increasingly as she strove, however lamely, to put Tyler at a distance
and to face candidly the emptiness of her household since Nabby's
marriage, Abigail thought more of home and found less that was
worthwhile about life in London. Not that she didn't admire the
French ambassador, who filled his house each Sunday with hundreds
of people, and served them oranges and sweetmeats and coffee,
blending the magnificence and splendor of France with the neatness
and elegance of England. Not that she didn't appreciate the gossip

(and pass it on) about the Prince of Wales, rumored to be married to Maria Anne Fitzherbert, of an "ancient and respectable family," who was said to be expecting a child in the course of that summer. But Abigail did not think of this sort of exposure as being in society, or the polite life, as she conceived of it. Its impersonality was distasteful to her, except for one aspect: one could leave these parties without disturbing a soul; since one was never introduced, even when one saw the same person three nights in a row, one could never be rude.[42]

Abigail made it a rule now, whenever a vessel arrived from Boston, to send a card to its captain, whom she usually found very intelligent, she said, to come for dinner in Grosvenor Square. In this way she could question him about new houses, bridges, trade, whether Boston was growing more frugal or more luxurious, even how the trees were flourishing in the Boston Common. It was a "feast" to her when she could sit and talk about her country and learn about its husbandry, fishery, its trade, which she realized was "in a cloud" that she hoped would be dispelled in time. Even a feast had drawbacks. "I do not believe that ever any people made a greater show with less capital than my dear mistaken countrymen. Our Countrymen owe millions here, hard to believe, but "alass it is a miserable truth."[43]

Abigail admitted she was weary, as she repeatedly dwelt on the "useless insipid life" she led, compared with her time in Braintree. However melancholy she might be, Abigail did not lose her sense of humor. Though the bride, Nabby, was as slender as a greyhound, half her size when she had left America, the same could not be said for her mother. She wished she could send to Mary or Mrs. Shaw a little of what Shylock was so determined to take from poor Antonio.[44]

And John had kept pace. If one horse had to carry both of them, she should pity the beast. True, her weight was increased, her hair was dressed and powdered and suffered more "torture" than in America, and she was two years older—these were changes, she admitted. But they were the only ones. Her clothing was the same; she wore the same calicoes, chintzes, and muslins, wound with double-gauze handkerchiefs, as she had by her Braintree fireside. And more important, "the Heart and mind are the same," she assured her sisters, as was her regard for her family. She ought to be home with them, with her "lads," she ought to be seeing her friends "in a social way, loveing them and being beloved by them." In this tentative mood, the latest letter from her friend Thomas Jefferson was especially welcome.[45]

FIFTEEN

One of the Choice Ones of the Earth

In her first sprawling letter to Thomas Jefferson, in Paris, written almost immediately on her return to London, Abigail cheerfully explained her reasons for "freely scribling." Their obviously comfortable, trusting, uniquely familial relationship was one that Abigail was not about to abandon. Rather, she harbored a "little vanity" in the hope of sustaining it: "Having heard you upon some occasions express a desire to hear from your Friends, even the Minutia respecting their Situation, I have ventured to class myself in that number and to subscribe myself, Sir, your Friend and Humble Servant." Jefferson's reply on June 21, 1785, was handsome. Having "duly" received the honor of her letter, he thanked her for her "condescension" in having taken the first step in a correspondence he had "so much desired."[1]

Their exchange of thirty-five letters (of which Abigail wrote twenty), spanning thirty-two months, is remarkable in all ways: in its affectionate intimacy, in its preposterously bitter ending, as well as in its infinite variety. They gossiped: Jefferson pronounced Cardinal de Rohan a "debauchee, and a booby"; Abigail suggested, with feline flair, that Madame Helvétius must be "melancholy" now that Franklin, "as she used to call him," was gone. They consoled each other on the vagaries of "hireling scribblers." They consulted on whether to charge house rent to the government"; Mr. Franklin had always done so and if Mr. Adams did, Mr. Jefferson would follow (experience having taught him, he said, that "my expenses will otherwise

exceed my allowance"). They passed cultural notes—Abigail referring to Jefferson's "favorite passion," Handel—and fashion notes,
Jefferson wondering, now that the French Queen had vowed to wear
none but French gauze, what might happen to the English looms.
They shopped for one another attentively, at all times conspiring on
ways to avoid customs duties. An American might bring in the Irish
linen shirts Abigail ordered for him, Mr. Jefferson suggested, when
he crossed the Channel; someone could tuck her small orders of lace
and ribbons in his pocket, Abigail proposed.[2]

In the ensuing months, Abigail was able to send Jefferson a five-
yard-long tablecloth with twenty napkins (the usual size was 4 3/4
yards with eighteen napkins) at seven pounds, and two pairs of nut-
crackers, among other collectibles; Colonel Smith, whom he'd gotten
to know during his stay in London, tended to bulkier errands concerning a harpsichord, a letter press, and a horse's harness. Jefferson
responded to Abigail's favors with generosity and flattery. Requests
for yards of cambric and four pairs of shoes (one of "blew" satin)
were graciously filled. Concerning the choice of biscuit figurines, he
was painstaking and gallant. Three of her choice, Minerva, Diana,
and Apollo, were readily available, but the fourth would have to be
entirely of his choosing. He had settled on Mars, after much searching, he explained, declining the offer of a fine Venus on the grounds
that two figurines at one table, at the same time, would be "out of
taste."[3]

Abigail was apologetic about having Jefferson run errands for her;
he, in turn, insisted it was the other way around. John had advanced
the sum (roughly thirty-two pounds) that both men agreed was
needed to secure Jean Antoine Houdon, who was bound for America,
to do a sculpture of George Washington. Jefferson, therefore, insisted he was "considerably" in debt to both Adamses, but especially
to Abigail. Certainly he would not entertain her contention that her
trivial requests were "a little like putting Hercules to the distaff."
Rather, he insisted, he gave Abigail so much trouble that unless she
found some means of employing him for herself in return, she would
leave him with an "unpleasant load" on his mind. This was hardly a
serious threat, considering how copiously Jefferson poured his opinions on page after page, making the ground for their discussion only
that much greener.[4]

If Jefferson's distaste for the British was adamant, Abigail's was
hardly less so. But even her admission that London's superb hackney
coaches were superior to Paris was going too far; her "boast" Jeffer-

son considered a "flout." He wrote back shortly that he would not give up "the polite, self-denying, feeling, hospitable, good-humoured people" of France, though their carriages might be "rather indifferent" for ten such races of "rich, proud, hectoring, swearing squibbling, carnivorous animals" as that with which Abigail resided. Steadfast in his protection of the French, he claimed that with a better religion and a better form of government, their country would be most enviable. Whatever their failings, he painted a joyous picture of the people he did "love" with all his heart—one he would alter with darker colors before too long.

> Here we have singing, dancing, laugh, and merriment. No assassinations, no treasons, rebellions nor other dark deeds. When our king goes out, they fall down and kiss the earth where he has trodden; and then they go to kissing one another. And this is the truest wisdom. They have as much happiness in one year as an Englishman in ten. The presence of the queen's sister enlivens the court. Still more the birth of the princess. There are some little bickerings between the king and his parliament, but they end with a sic volo, sic jubeo ("as I wish, so I rejoice").[5]

As Abigail concurred eagerly that the English suffered from a great want of many French commodities, such as good sense, good nature, political wisdom, and benevolence, Jefferson's facetious remarks about King George III could not have fallen on more responsive ears. He wrote Abigail, in late summer of 1786, about news of an attempted assassination of "your King," who was, in his opinion, truly the "American Messias, the most precious life that ever God gave, and may god continue it." A startled Abigail read on, as Jefferson explained:

> Twenty long years has he been labouring to drive us to our good, and he labours and will labour still for it if he can be spared. We shall have need of him for twenty more. The Prince of Wales on the throne, Lansdowne and Fox in the ministry, we are undone! We become chained by our habits to the tails of those who hate and despise us. I repeat it then that my anxieties are all alive for the health and long life of the King. He has not a friend on earth who would lament his loss so much and so long as I should.[6]

While the tone of their letters was generally bright—even sunny—on more than one occasion it slipped to a melancholy gray, especially on Abigail's part. Her discontent had little to do with the physical aspect of England—only a mile into the countryside one could have as fine weather and clear sky as any to be found in America, and be easily rid of the city's smoke and fog. Rather, it was the attitude and values that troubled her; "if the manners of the people were as pure as their Air," no one would have reason for discontent. But such was not the case, and her dissatisfaction was only heightened by John's frustrations and his observation of conscious guilt and shame in the faces of the noblemen, who seemed to make the most awkward conversation with him.[7]

Already, in February of 1786, Abigail had expressed the hope of returning to "the purer and honester manners" of her native land, "where domestic happiness reigns unrivalled, and virtue and honor go hand in hand." She hoped to make their "escape" in one more season, complained of being in "the situation of Sterne's starling," the caged bird of *Sentimental Journey.* Nabby's marriage, pleased as she was about it, left her more introspective than ever, and lonelier. Nothing seemed to go right; even a barrel of cranberries had arrived that fall in poor condition. Her generally irritable state was aggravated by the general mourning in court that November for the late princess Amelia; if all the faces there were not black, all the bodies appeared so, in Abigail's opinion. Nor was she about to fill Mary's request for some dark brown silk. Dark colors were for women with dark pasts or peevish dispositions, Abigail wrote back. Besides, she added, dark clothes did not suit dark complexions.[8]

At her most homesick, Abigail spoke of her gratitude for Elizabeth's account of the song of her children's bird. "Do you know," she asked Elizabeth, "that European birds have not half the melody of ours? Nor is their fruit half so sweet, nor their flowers half so fragrant, nor their manners half so pure, nor their people half so virtuous." Wryly conscious of her partiality, Abigail had the wit to warn Mrs. Shaw, "But keep this to yourself, or I shall be thought more than half deficient in understanding and taste."[9]

Some might have attributed Abigail's gloomy spirits to the sameness of her surroundings, but such was not the case. She had traveled into the country in July with John and the Smiths; in August she joined John on a business trip to Holland concerning America's commercial treaty with Prussia and the need for a Prussian minister's signature (the nearest such minister residing at The Hague). John and Abigail left London on August 3, and made a 120-mile crossing in about eighteen or twenty hours, by way of Harwich, Hellevoetsluis, and Rotterdam. Rather pleased by their mission, Abigail wrote home about "one of those theatres, upon which my partner and fellow-traveller had exhibited some of his most important actions, and rendered to his country lasting blessing."[10]

On the whole, the trip was a success. Profoundly moved, John believed that the constitutional reforms wrought by the Dutch patriots were the first evidence that the American Revolution had made its mark on Europe. However, while the neat, cordial people, with their hospitable greetings, including bells and a military guard, were thoroughly appreciated, Abigail was not intrigued by the scenery. The silence and dead calm were monotonous, wanting in "dear variety." One saw meadows, trees, canals; then one saw canals, trees, meadows. At one point Abigail thought she would have welcomed an English robber, and would have heard with pleasure the drumming of carriage wheels along the way. Her greatest mistake, she said, was taking along Plutarch's *Lives.* Between reading about the cruelty, devastation, and horror of the Roman emperors and visiting the dark and dreary Dutch churches, she claimed she was haunted every night with troublesome ghosts, and vowed the next time to bring *Don Quixote* as her companion.[11]

Of her next tour, in January 1787, Abigail could hardly complain of want of variety. After she had spent a fortnight in "amusement and dissipation" at Bath, "that seat of fashionable resort," frequented by William Pitt, Hester Thrale Piozzi, Samuel Johnson, Edmund Burke, and Sarah Siddons, she had returned, she assured Richard Cranch, "with double pleasure" to her own fireside, adding virtuously that this was "where only, thank Heaven, my substantial happiness subsists." She admitted that she sometimes liked to mix in the "gay world and view the manners as they rise," but she was grateful not to be entirely absorbed by it. Revealingly, she understood that her early education had given her "not an habitual taste for what is termed fashionable life."[12]

Abigail's party in Bath included twelve Americans, a Venetian nobleman called Count Zenobia, and an entourage of domestics. Architecturally, Bath was a picture, and hardly an Ionic column escaped her vigilant eye, let alone a crescent, parade, square, or circus chiseled into the sweeping valley crowned with stubby hills. "Noble" and "magnificent" were Abigail's words for the precise beauty of Bath. But Bath was more than architecture; it was a resort for the infirm (its waters were said to cure leprosy) and for the "gay, the indolent, the curious, the gambler, the fortune-hunter," and even for those, like the thoughtless girl from the country, who went "out of wantonness."[13]

Abigail was obviously dazzled by the sights, the decoration and dress, the balls and concerts, plays and private parties that Bath offered. She was also uncomfortable; in contrast with Holland, she now encountered too much variety. She felt threatened, her values challenged. In Bath, a "glittering star" was all that mattered; character was unimportant. Defensively, she said she thought a place ought to be select, to consist of persons respectable for morals and understanding. Her exposure provoked a "train of moral reflections":

> What is the chief end of man? is a subject well worth the investigation of every rational being. What, indeed is life, or its enjoyments, without settled principle, laudable purposes, mental exertions, and internal comfort, that sunshine of the soul; and how are these to be acquired in a hurry and tumult of the world?

Instead of exciting a "gayety of disposition," Abigail took refuge in the depths of her New England soul. She vowed never to visit Bath again.[14]

Interestingly, despite her driving chauvinism about her native country in almost all its aspects—from terrain to dress to entertainments to birdsong to people and politics—Abigail was not unaware that America was in trouble, at least in the Massachusetts area. On the contrary, she wrote on January 20, 1787, referring to Daniel Shays and his followers, that the "riots and dissensions" in her state were a matter of "very serious concern." But it was gratifying that a book that Captain Cushing was carrying home with him would show that John had worked hard to strengthen and support their government and to help people understand the dangerous consequences of unbalanced power. If only people would read and listen, Abigail urged, they had the "means of being the first and the happiest people upon the globe."[15]

She was referring to the first volume of *Defense of the Constitutions of Government of the United States,* just published in London. John had been moved to write these "hasty speculations" for many reasons. "To defend the separation of the legislative, executive, judicial powers from each other, and the division of the legislative into three branches, from the attacks of county committees, riotous assemblies, and uninformed philosophers and statesmen, will be the burden of my song," he explained. Such a distribution of power was "the unum necessarium of liberty, safety, and good order," and therefore, John promised, "no pains taken to preserve it will be thrown away." The essay, the first of three, seemed especially urgent at this time because of the "commotions" in New England and John's fear that it was "much easier to pull down a government in such a conjuncture of affairs . . . than to build up, at such a season as the present."[16]

Eventually, Abigail would have the satisfaction of knowing that John's *Defense* had reached America and some of its intended audience at the time of "great crisis." Richard Henry Lee would write the following September (1787), that the book had probably had its "proper influence in forming the federal government." Meanwhile, Abigail brooded about the "Tumults," and had not, since the start of their correspondence, spared Jefferson any of its threats. In her opinion, men without conscience or principles were leading a deluded multitude to an "allarming" height. Pretending to harbor grievances that had no substance except in their imaginations, these ignorant, restless desperadoes cried out for a paper currency, for equal distribution of property, for annihilation of all debts, for the abolition of the state Senate as a useless branch of government, and the Court of Common Pleas as unnecessary.[17]

The list would give Jefferson an idea of the "materials" of which the rebellion was composed, and the necessity of the wisest and most vigorous measures to suppress it. Instead of the laudable spirit of which Abigail knew Jefferson approved, which made people watchful over their liberties and alert to their defense, those "mobbish" insurgents, she feared, were for "sapping the foundation, and distroying the whole fabrick at once."[18]

Perhaps because Jefferson immediately responded to Abigail's fears with soothing assurances that he was not alarmed at the "humor" shown by their country, and that, on the contrary, he liked to see a people "awake and alert," Abigail modified her position. Attempting to deal judiciously with what she could not stomach, namely disloyalty of any stripe, she conceded that the rebels, who were certainly a minority, though a troublesome one, might prove "sallutary" to the state at large. They might lead to correction of the causes of the "commotions"—the luxury and extravagance that pervaded all orders of their countrymen and women. These made vanity "a more powerful principle than patriotism."[19]

Jefferson only reinforced Abigail's most recent position a few weeks later. On February 22, 1787, he wrote:

> The spirit of resistance to government is so valuable on certain
> occasions, that I wish it to be always kept alive. It will often be
> exercised when wrong, but better so than not to be exercised at all.
> I like a little rebellion now and then. It is like a storm in the
> Atmosphere.

Once again, Jefferson had had the final word. His political differences with Abigail, and, for that matter, with John seemed a matter of nuances. Expressed so openly and genuinely, they could hardly be considered harbingers of a less fortuitous relationship, unless one construed a few falling leaves as proof of a rotting tree.[20]

Although their correspondence maintained a dependable rhythm, at least in its early period, a three-month hiatus occurred during the autumn of 1786. Jefferson might have waited even longer to resume it, considering that an injured wrist left him with obstinate swelling, but for urgent news that depended on Abigail's cooperation. When friends informed him that his little daughter would be sailing for England in May, he had taken the liberty of writing back that Abigail would keep her under her wing until he could send for her. About his daughter Mary, who was called Polly, he continued:

> She is about 8 years, and will be in the care of her nurse, a black
> woman, to whom she is confided with safety. I knew your goodness
> too well to scruple the giving this direction before I had asked your
> permission. I beg you to accept assurances of the constant esteem
> with which I have the honor to be Dear Madam your most
> obedient and most humble servant.[21]

Abigail's reply, on January 29, was entirely reassuring. She suggested the use of British oil on his sprained wrist and was sending a servant in search of some, presumably to forward to him. As for his daughter, she would be "punctually" attended to, with all that was in Abigail's power.[22]

That same month, Abigail could talk of expectations of still another visitor. Mrs. Smith (as Nabby was now dignified in letters home) was expecting a baby. This meant that Abigail would turn "Grandame" in the spring, and there were some days, she allowed, when she did not feel so ancient as that event would make her. Certainly she did not take the news lightly, convinced as she was that "a thousand new cares and anxieties as well as pleasures attend new relatives." In preparation, there was a nurse to be looked for and clothes to be made, and often she and Mrs. Smith, "looking as sober as a Deaconness," spent afternoons together edging fine white linens and muslins with delicate laces.[23]

Abigail, however, had no intention of waiting the winter out, for either the Smiths' infant or her friend Jefferson's small daughter. The course of philosophical lectures she had subscribed to took up much of her time and she was "loth to lose any of them" as she might never again find "so good an opportunity," she wrote Mrs. Cranch. Her health, unfortunately, very much circumscribed her aspirations. Her inability to go out to dinner, the theater, or the Court of St. James was a trivial matter; to be deprived of seven of the twelve lectures she counted on was, she feared, a permanent loss. The five lectures she managed to attend, on electricity, magnetism, hydrostatics, optics, and pneumatics, she considered "connected with and . . . subservient to the accommodation of common life." She was thrilled by the "assemblage of Ideas entirely new": "It was like going into a Beautifull Country, which I never saw before, a Country which our American Females are not permitted to visit or inspect." She wrote wistfully about the lectures she had missed, and how they would have afforded her "much matter for future recollection and amusement."[24]

Exposure and frustration made Abigail analytical about her own lot. She decided she would not choose to quarrel with the assertion that the study of "Household Good, as Milton terms it," was no doubt the "peculiar" province of the female character. Yet surely, as rational beings, women had to have an alternative, a way that their minds might "with propriety receive the highest possible cultivation." The advantages of learning were quite specific, according to Abigail's reckoning. Mary Cranch was her immediate audience; yet Abigail reached out, at the same moment, to argue on behalf of the world of women:

Knowledge would teach our sex candour, and those who aim at the attainment of it, in order to render themselves more amiable and usefull in the world, would derive a double advantage from it, for in proportion as the mind is informed, the countenance would be

improved and the face ennobled as the Heart is elevated, for
wisdom, says Soloman, maketh the face to shine.

Counting on Solomon to reinforce still another argument, Abigail
pointed out that even the "Luxurious Eastern Sage" did not think
that a woman who spoke with wisdom was "inconsistent" with one
who tended to her household, or less inclined, for having gone beyond the limits of her room and kitchen, "to superintend the domestick economy of her family."[25]

Remarkably, Abigail's impassioned arguments on behalf of women
having learning opportunities did not exclude an awareness of the
price. And there was a price, for she believed sincerely that it was
most dangerous for a female to be distinguished for any qualification
beyond the rest of her sex. Whatever her deportment, she was sure
to encourage "the jealousy of the men and the envy of the women."
Abigail's solution was succinct: the remedy lay in "increasing the
number of accomplished women, a monopoly of any kind," she concluded, "is always envidious."[26]

On June 26, 1787, almost five months after the date of Jefferson's
note regarding his daughter, a party of three presented themselves
on Abigail's doorstep; Captain Ramsey delivering a clinging, miserably tearful Polly, accompanied by a young mulatto named Sally Hemings. Minutes later, Abigail wrote to advise Jefferson to collect his
child in person as her adjustment was painful. Also, the "old Nurse"
that Jefferson had counted on to care for her, Betty Hemings, had
been replaced by her daughter Sally, who appeared to be fifteen or
sixteen years old, though she was in reality only fourteen. In the
captain's opinion, Sally would be of "little Service." On further acquaintance, the sister of James Hemings, Jefferson's young servant in
Paris, did not inspire greater confidence, but rather deepening concern. Abigail thought of her as wanting "more care than the child,"
of being "wholly incapable" of looking properly after Polly, "without
some superior to direct her."[27]

At first, Abigail despaired of making a conquest of Polly. After five
weeks at sea, in the company of only men, except for Sally, she was
as "rough as a little sailor" and almost inseparable from the captain.
When Abigail tried to comfort Polly and to distract her with promises
of a visit to Sadler's Wells, and the glories of the amusement park's
dancing, music, and trained animals, she met with sobbing rejection,

Polly insisting that she would rather have Captain Ramsey's company for "one moment, than all the fun in the World."[28]

Abigail persisted, however. She ordered new clothes for Polly, and Sally as well, believing the ones they wore only "proper for the sea." She collected a library for the child, who delighted in reading aloud to her hostess. She also listened with earnest sympathy to Polly's pitiful story. The little girl, who was five when her mother died, nearly four months after giving birth to another daughter, Lucy, also dead, had lived most recently with her Aunt Eppes in Philadelphia, whom she loved. Their parting was hard enough without the two cousins, who had helped her board ship at Norfolk, having disappeared while she slept. To Abigail's mind, this had understandably left her hostile and suspicious.[29]

On July 1, Jefferson wrote that he could not come for his little daughter, though he had wished to do so. But he had just returned from his journey, useless in terms of healing, though not in terms of his study of the difference between the quality of rice of the Carolinas and that of Piedmont, so plentiful in Marseilles. He would be sending a French-speaking servant, Petit, in his place. As the departure neared, Abigail was tormented, "almost in a Frenzy," fearing the burden of still another adjustment for Polly.[30]

Both wept as Polly stepped into her carriage; the child's promise of a return visit eased the break. Abigail was captivated by Polly's maturity, intelligence, womanly behavior, and beauty, and saddened that "such fine spirits must be spent in the wall of a convent."[31]

Even John was won over completely: "In my Life I never saw a more charming Child," he wrote Jefferson. Abigail was touching in her claim to Jefferson that she had turned into so "successful a rival" to Captain Ramsey, as far as Polly's affections were concerned. Unpredictably, the bond that had been forged so resolutely, in such a short time, between woman and child, would soon be the single lasting link between Abigail and Jefferson.[32]

One of the reasons Abigail "consented" to part with Polly so soon was her plan for a journey into Devonshire County, recommended by Dr. John Jeffries, for reasons of health. She had been ill through much of the mild, early-blooming spring with a chronic disorder "long accumulating," which she blamed on the bilious state of her blood, on the dampness, and on the long wait between meals, of which there were only two a day. Her condition provoked an intermittent fever that not only kept her from her studies, but also drained her of the energy needed for looking after her newborn grandson, William Steuben Smith. Euphorically, she had announced the infant's arrival the previous April 26, 1787:

> I am a grandmamma. A grand—oh no! That would be confessing myself old which would be quite unfashionable and vulgar. But true it is. I have a fine grandson since three weeks ago today. I regret a little that it was not a daughter for then I would have claimed the little for the great one.

Abigail's regret about her own incapacity was mollified a good deal by Nabby's attitude; the young mother's instant devotion and competence ("who could have thought it?") was as surprising as it was pleasing.[33]

Three months later, on July 20, when Abigail set out on her medically advised tour, she was fortified by a substantial party that included infant, mother, and nurse (the colonel was on a mission to the Queen of Portugal), Esther Field, not yet married to John Briesler, their coachman, a postilion, and Edward Farmer, a footman. The six-hundred-mile, month-long itinerary would include visits with relatives (or, more accurately, relatives of relatives—Richard Cranch's nephew John, for one), and to ancestral places such as Weymouth, which was a pleasingly familiar town, a small seaport surrounded by hilly countryside, comparable to its American namesake.[34]

Whatever Abigail lacked in physical strength, she did not suffer diminished powers of observation. Her journal and letters reveal the full flavor of her reportorial gifts—and also her rabid nationalism, which blinded her to the fact that she was sounding very much like the "mob" at home she so deplored. Three years after her arrival in England, the "mere American" apologized for nothing, much less her impassioned criticism. In a country as fertile as the Garden of Eden, it seemed an outrage to her that the landed property vested in lordships, and controlled entirely by the rich, left the peasantry "but slaves to the Lord, notwithstanding the mighty boast they make of liberty." It was intolerable to her that money earned by the sweat of the peasant's brow must go to feed the pampered lord and fatten the greedy bishop, while the poor, in their sunless, crumbling cottages, slept on rags and ate all too little.[35]

Abigail's idealistic view of America persisted; it still seemed beyond her ken that there could be a body of poor in Massachusetts deprived enough to fight for the right to keep their farms and to stay out of debtor's prison. Having such a determined sense of justice, Abigail had to be totally ignorant of the truth when she railed on to Mrs. Cranch about how the United States had such "little cause of complaint," not just by comparison with despotic monarchies, but with England, the so-called "land of freedom!"

> The ease with which honest industry may acquire property in America, the equal distribution of justice to the poor as well as the rich, and the personal liberty they enjoy, all, all call upon them to support their government and laws, to respect their rulers, and gratefully acknowledge their superior blessings. . . . [36]

Perhaps the most comfortable part of the journey was spent with John Cranch, visiting various branches of his family such as Mr. Burnell, the shoemaker, and Mr. Tratham, the grocer. They were serious, industrious, good people, "more like our New England people," she claimed. Uneasy about British distinctions between tradesmen and gentry, Abigail was for the "middle ranks of society," where virtue and morality could be found. Furthermore, she said, in regard to education and manners, American farmers, tradesmen, merchants, and members of the "learned professions" were certainly equal to the English gentry.[37]

Fortunately, Abigail's report on her tour was not entirely negative. She recorded the high spots with care and unstinting appreciation. Her visit to Blenheim Palace inspired her admiration, for both aesthetic and political reasons, because of its beauty and because the British had thought to reward the Duke of Marlborough, victor at the battle of Blenheim, so magnificently. A tidy figure in summer cottons, shawl, and cap, Abigail must have brought her notebook with her, for not a bush or a blade of grass, a marble bust, a bridge, a lake, a valley, a painting, or a piece of patterned damask eludes her record. Upon consulting the gardener of twenty-five years, she learned that his staff of sixty-three cared for the eleven miles of park and the four miles of gardens. Possibly only a farmer's wife could appreciate the grass that was mowed and swept every other day to a "looking-glass" smoothness.[38]

Once indoors, prompted by an attendant who had "by heart the whole history of all that is to be seen," she noted fastidiously the measurements of Blenheim (348 feet from wing to wing), and counted the library (184 feet long, with 24,000 volumes under gilt-wire latticework) as being sublime in scale, "the most costly, as well as beautiful place" she had ever seen. A life-size statue of Queen Anne, dressed in damask-patterned marble, presided at one end; the inscription at its base was duly noted:

> To the memory of Queen Anne, under whose auspices John, Duke of Marlborough, conquered, and to whose munificence, he and his posterity with gratitude owe the possession of Blenheim, in A.D. 1746.[39]

Abigail was most moved, however, by another inscription. It honored John, Duke of Marlborough, and was carved into the 130-foot column fronting the palace, which supported his statue:

> . . . In a long series of uninterrupted triumphs
> Broke the power of France
> When raised the highest, and when exerted the most;
> Rescued the empire from desolation,
> Asserted and confirmed the liberties of Europe.

A rueful Abigail wrote in summary: "Thus is the gratitude of the nation expressed, and thus do the heirs of Marlborough triumph." She could not help but compare John's tenuous situation with the permanence of the recognition accorded the English hero. Lately, and increasingly, John had complained of spending "thirty years a rolling like a stone," never three years in one place, and the uncertainty of his fate and his reception at home—whether he would "sit down" in a private life as a farmer, or go to Congress, or "God knows what."[40]

Far from planning on any monument to be built in John's honor, Abigail was grateful to learn, after she had returned from her tour in the fall of 1787, that final arrangements had been made for the purchase of the handsome house formerly owned by Royall Tyler, which had reverted to the possession of Leonard Vassall-Borland, a grandson of the West Indian sugar planter whose property encompassed eighty-three acres of fields, pastures, salt marsh, and woodland. Cotton Tufts and Thomas Welsh concluded negotiations on September 26 for the sum of six hundred pounds and, that same day, Tufts wrote to John regarding the adjoining fifty-six acres selling for twenty-five dollars an acre. John's reply echoed a devoted theme:

> My view is to lay fast hold of the Town of Braintree and embrace it with both my arms and all my might, there to live—there to die—

there to lay my bones—and there to plant one of my sons, in the Profession of the Law and the practice of Agriculture, like his father.[41]

In reality, Abigail had been thinking in practical terms about returning home since the past spring, when she had written Mrs. Cranch about "trimming" her cottage, and requested the dimensions concerning a "floor cloth" for the little parlor in Braintree. Her plans were obviously propelled by the knowledge that in preparation for the expiration of his commission on February 24, 1788, John had written last January to Secretary Jay, requesting formal recall, not only from the British court, but from his mission to the Netherlands, and from his joint mission with Mr. Jefferson to the Barbary powers. He was, he explained, determined to come home, and wished to embark in early spring. On October 5, 1787, Congress voted that the Honorable John Adams be permitted, as per his request, to return to America. They also accorded him the only monument he and Abigail might have hoped for, that "the thanks of Congress be presented to him for the patriotism, perseverance, integrity and diligence with which he had ably and faithfully served his Country." What Congress did not think to do was to enclose actual letters of recall, thereby posing problems of protocol, especially as far as the Dutch government was concerned. This meant that John might not return to America without a final visit to Holland to take his leave personally.[42]

Wherever Abigail turned now, in the fall and winter of 1787 and 1788, she was increasingly ill at ease. She could not abide the "studied civility and disguised coldness" covering the malignant hearts of St. James. John brought her no reassurance; a basic factor in his determination to return home was his belief that Congress could not renew his commission with "honour and dignity" when Britain failed to send a minister in return. And, he complained, as it seemed that England had wholly forgotten that such a place as America ever existed, he thought it almost beneath their dignity to take pains to refresh British memory.[43]

Looking beyond England afforded only further worry. "To what do all political notions tend which are agitating France Holland and Germany?" Abigail asked of Thomas Jefferson. "Will Liberty finally gain the assendency, or arbitrary power strike her dead?" she wondered. Jefferson's reply was stirring, but not comforting. In Paris, he said, "great events" were in preparation that would change the face of Europe. Provincial assemblies were already at work shrinking the powers of the Crown.[44]

All tongues in Paris (and throughout France) had been let loose; it seemed to Jefferson as though none in London had spoken more freely or more universally against the government. A new France was in the making:

> Caricatures, placards, bon mots, have been indulged in by all ranks of people, and I know of no well attested instance of a single punishment. For some time mobs of 10; 20; 30,000 people collected daily, surrounded the parliament house, huzzaed the members, even entered the doors and examined into their conduct, took the horses out of the carriages of those who did well, and drew them home.

As for the royal family, Jefferson reported that the Queen, going to the theater at Versailles, was greeted with a "general hiss"; the King, long in the habit of drowning his cares in wine, "plunges deeper and deeper; the queen cries but sins on." With the added threats of England arming, and the King of Prussia's invasion of Holland, Jefferson posed an inconvenient question. "May not the scene which is preparing render it necessary," he asked, "for Mr. Adams to defer the return to his own country?"[45]

The question was academic. On December 5, Abigail wrote a short letter to him, asking if he would permit Petit to purchase ten ells of double Florence of any fashionable color, except orange. She noted that the Massachusetts convention would be considering the ratification of the United States Constitution the second Wednesday in January 1788. She also added that Mr. Adams's resignation had been accepted and that they would quit England as soon in the spring as they could go in safety.[46]

Repeatedly, as Abigail planned for her return to America, she spoke of changes she would find, as though to prepare herself for the worst, as well as for the simply different. It was natural to wonder about the impact of the new Constitution: "There are things in it which stagger all my dispositions to subscribe to what such an assembly has proposed," Jefferson had written. John, too, expressed reservations about the remarkable document. He wished, for instance, for a Declaration of Rights "with all my Heart; though I am Sensible of the Difficulty of framing one, in which all States can agree." A more complete separation of the executive branch from the legislative would be "more safe for all," he said. The press, he added somewhat enigmatically, he wished "better secured," by which he may have meant better regulated. But a man in his position, after a ten-year absence from his country, ought to be "modest" about his judgments, he said, and he concluded that he would vote for the Constitution as proposed and promote a convention "after some time," to amend it.[47]

Abigail was also concerned about John Quincy's problem, which Mrs. Cranch had brought to her attention. What some would eventually judge a nervous breakdown, she treated as a simple case of severe fatigue. She feared a little, she answered her sister, that her eldest son would be "so much of a bookworm and scholar that he will grow negligent of those attentions which are due to the world."[48]

Abigail would not only have her own children to settle with, but the additional responsibility of her brother's wife and children. William Smith had died in the winter of 1787, and in spite of his acknowledged "follies," Abigail could not help but be sympathetic to his distressed family. Mention of her brother's name invariably provoked a tortured exploration of his life, from which she and her sisters kept, by plan, a guilty distance. The roundabout references to the "gentleman," the "unhappy connection," the "poor man," and total avoidance of his given name, afforded a protective code. Yet there were lapses from such determined objectivity and anonymity, in which Abigail roamed her memories trying to understand her brother's "strange" disposition, his implausible mixture of "benevolence and kindness without judgement, good sense without prudence and learning without conduct." His wife hadn't helped either. Catherine Louisa was a sentimental, excessively ambitious woman who read too many romances, and who tried to live out her fantasies. There would be no stopping her if she could move herself and her children into the enchanted castles she built, Abigail supposed.[49]

It was one matter to speculate on the damage done to her brother by his wife, but another to analyze her parents' role in his failure. Yet she could not help acknowledging in retrospect that some "very capital mistakes" had been made in his education, though they were unintended, of course. Abigail, whenever she thought in this vein, was quick to apologize to her parents' memory. Perhaps the prospect of taking care of her own sons once again aroused dormant worries. There were no grounds, thus far, for coupling her son Charles's name with that of her brother, no intimations that their fates might be similar. On at least one occasion, however, she did, perhaps subconsciously, follow the one name with the other. She did speak of her hopes that Charles's conduct would never "pain" his friends. And she did speculate about children having little knowledge of the solicitude and anxiety of a parent, and recall her father's deathbed prayers for his son's reformation and salvation. One cheering note in her momentary gloom was her plan for her niece Louisa, her brother's daughter, whom she truly loved, to come to live with her in Braintree.[50]

On February 20, 1788, John was to have his final audience with George III. On Friday, nine days later, John planned to make "that most horrid passage" to pay his respects at The Hague, Abigail informed Jefferson. Though an inconvenient and unpropitious journey—time was "short and pressing," and the counterrevolution had catapulted his friends from office—John had no choice. Congress, Abigail explained, was to blame; without a proper letter of recall, John could not risk any offense that might affect credit arrangements adversely. Then, on what seems to have been her own initiative, judging from the previous correspondence between the two men, in which Jefferson had sought John's counseling on the subject of Dutch credit, Abigail followed with a remarkably ambiguous thought, as though plucked from midair. In one breath she allowed that John would be "delighted" to meet Jefferson at The Hague, but held out little hope of his doing so, as time was "pressing"; then again, she suggested, her letter might reach Jefferson early enough to allow the "possibility" of his joining John.[51]

On March 11, John complained to Abigail that he would have been in London at the hour he was writing, if she had not laid a "Plott" that brought him to Amsterdam. Because of her letter, Jefferson had come "post" to meet him; their mission would be to put money matters on a surer footing. Money borrowed from the Dutch would sustain the United States through a "trying interval," Jefferson insisted; it would help them to pay their debts and avoid bankruptcy for the next two years, until the new government could accumulate a treasury through taxation. "I was very much averse to this, but he would take no denial," John wrote. At Jefferson's urging, John arranged for America's fourth and final loan of one million guilders, at five percent interest, to be redeemed in fifteen years. Balefully, John continued, "I thought myself dead, and that it was well over with me as a public man"; now he had begun to think that he should be forced "after my decease, to open an additional loan."[52]

Due to negotiations, John was not sure when he would be able to leave—either on Saturday or the following Wednesday, March 19. The delay was extremely painful, he assured Abigail, telling her that "you must blame yourself for it altogether." In consequence, should she meet southwesters on the coast of America, and have her voyage prolonged three weeks, he cautioned her to "remember it is all your own intrigue which has forced me to open this loan. I suppose," he concluded, "you will boast of it as a great public service."[53]

In spite of the last-minute tensions, and in the midst of the "bustle and fatigue of packing, the parade and ceremony of taking leave at Court, and else where," the three friends left no doubt of the "unchangeable esteem and respect" in which they held one another. When Jefferson wrote Abigail that "young poets complain often that life is fleeting and transient," it was inconceivable, at that time, that he might be writing an epitaph to their friendship. On the contrary, he would feel "bewidowed" without them; their presence on his side of the Atlantic had given him "confidence" that he could turn to them in difficult times. A lonely Jefferson confided to Abigail: "Insulated and friendless on this side the globe, with such an ocean between me and every thing to which I am attached the days will seem long which are to be counted over before I too am to rejoin my native country." It would lighten his days, Jefferson continued, if Abigail would honor him with her correspondence. He also thought she would have much to tell him, and he little that would interest her. Perhaps, he allowed, she could make him useful in the "execution" of her European commissions.[54]

Abigail was ardent in her appreciation of Jefferson's affectionate words. She thanked him for "all his kindness and Friendship" toward herself and her family, "from the commencement" of their acquaintance. The offer he made of correspondence, she told him, was "much too flattering, not to be gratefully accepted." Furthermore, she requested him to "say every thing that is affectionate for me" to his daughters, meanwhile assuring him that she was "With the Greatest respect Esteem and regard" his "Friend and Humble Servant."[55]

On the first of May, with England out of sight, and weeks of sailing ahead, Abigail took stock, as she tended to when she had the luxury of objectivity. She felt confined, and found the ship tedious, as before, but her troubles were nothing, she reminded herself, compared to those of her pregnant maid, Esther, who required "as much care as a young turkey" and was "very near her Time." The desperate situation demanded all her faith: "I think that God will suit the wind to the shorn Lamb," she wrote in her diary, "that we may be carried through our difficulties better than any apprehensions. Abigail's worst fears were realized. On May 28, Esther was delivered of a daughter, "a poor little starvling" who was either born dead or died a short while later. Abigail, somewhat in shock, dressed the dead baby, which she referred to as "the little animal," for its burial. The day after, in a state of immense relief, she decided they had all gotten through "this business" much better than she had feared, and now their only concern was for a "good wind." She also hoped and prayed she would never have to go to sea again. This was her "absolute" wish. She was exhausted and out of patience. She had seen enough of the world. From this point on, she ended her diary, she would "be content to learn what is further to be known from the page of History."[56]

PART THREE

SIXTEEN

In a Flurry
with Politics

Truly, every mark of respect was paid to "His Excellency John Adams, Esq. late Ambassador from the United States of America, to the Court of Great Britain—with his Lady," on their arrival home the lightly windy morning of June 17, 1788. The next day, one could read all about the festive event in the *Massachusetts Centinel:* about the cannon fired at the lighthouse signal, about the thousands who cheered (three huzzahs worth), about the Secretary of State, who boarded the state barge to congratulate His Excellency, and to invite him, in the name of the Governor, into the waiting carriage at pier's edge. Then, as church bells began their jaunty, day-long song of welcome, the party rode off to the Governor's residence, where the ambassador was congratulated on the eminent services rendered his country "in a manner becoming freemen, federalists, and men alive to the sensations of gratitude."[1]

Within twenty-four hours, John rushed on to Braintree while Abigail remained at the Governor's house another day, until John Quincy could call for her and bring her to Peter Boylston Adams's house. There the family gathered for a week before actually settling in their new dwelling, bought long-distance through Dr. Tufts's attentive negotiations. Abigail and John now owned the gracious house that Royall Tyler had lived in and Richard Cranch had aspired to, and even without subsequent and commodious additions, the place was an affluent-looking one, in comparison with their "Humble Cottage," the family home they had formerly occupied. Yet Abigail was noticeably miserable; even Mrs. Smith commented that she could see through her letters that her mother's spirits were "hurried" and her mind was in "continual agitation." Nabby warned her mother, "You must overcome this, or you will certainly be sick."[2]

There were many reasons for Abigail's "bewildered" state. She was home almost one month before she could write, her hand was so swollen (probably due to arthritis). She was also extremely irritated by the "shocking" state of the house, which was only half-repaired; she had little patience for the "swarm" of carpenters, masons, and farmers buzzing about as she tried to place her furniture, much of it damaged aboard ship, or too cumbersome to move about in the first place. She did not mean to seem humorous when she said that she looked forward to embracing both Mrs. Smith and the colonel, but alerted one to "wear no feathers" and the other to come without heels on his shoes, or he would not be able to walk upright.[3]

Of the two of them, John was initially in better spirits. He harbored no illusions about their new home. He described it rather modestly: "It is but the farm of a patriot," he wrote to a friend living in England. The view, however, was another story: standing in two or three spots, one could see "some of the most beautiful prospects in the world." And though he was critically concerned about his future, he was convinced that he was "much better accommodated" in America, that his compensation for loss of access to London bookshops and to his few friends abroad was handsome. Reunion with his three sons was a moving experience. With regret he spoke of time sacrificed to public service that he might have shared with his children.[4]

John could boast now of two sons at Harvard and a third, John Quincy, clerking for the eminent lawyer Theophilus Parsons, in Newburyport. They were "regular" in their manners and studies, and were admired in "all quarters" for their good character. The three pleased him enormously: John Quincy, with his "decided" proofs of great talent; Charles, the most winning, the "most of a gentleman of all"; and Thomas, as fine a youth as either of the others, if a "spice" of fun in his personality did not lead him astray. The single omission in John's review of his children was a conscious one. Mrs. Smith's present state was nebulous; she wrote to her parents from Jamaica, Long Island, of living in the country in a "land of strangers," of visiting New York only occasionally, of not being disposed to acquire new friendships or acquaintances, of having as much "society" as she could wish in her own family. She failed to mention her husband's plans, a void in her letters that made her parents extremely uneasy. By November, John had written his daughter that his anxiety for her prevailed on him to make a "great sacrifice," to consent to her mother's visiting her on Long Island.[5]

The exchange of letters, starting in July 1788, that culminated in Abigail's troubled journey to her daughter was marked with tender concern on all sides. Gingerly, John approached Nabby, hopeful that his anxiety for the couple's welfare had not "betrayed" him into "any improper expressions, or unbecoming curiosity." He wished, however, to be informed, "as fully as may be with propriety," of Colonel Smith's views regarding his future. In the very next sentence, however, the initiative was reversed; the father passionately informed the daughter of his views of her husband's career. John spoke with deep love, and from tortured experience, as he explained how he would rather see his son-in-law at the bar than in public service; the bar was the most "independent place on earth," while a "seeker of public employments" was, to his thinking, "one of the most unhappy of all men." Without realizing its inverted relevance to his own career, he pleaded the course he so admired; one that eluded him throughout his public life: "I had rather dig my subsistence out of the earth with my own hands, than be dependent on any favour, public or private; and this has been the invariable maxim of my whole life." John spoke sensitively of Smith's merit, and the public employment he was entitled to, but also of his being a man of "too much spirit as well as honour" to solicit, if it entailed the smallest degree of "meanness," for any office. For these reasons, John reiterated the desirability of independence; the colonel must have a "resource," of which none was better than the bar.[6]

The sad honesty of Nabby's response, her appreciation of her father's concern, which, despite all his attempts at delicacy, was blatantly forthright, told much about their relationship. The two had grown close in their time abroad; Mrs. Smith, as her father's confidante, was able to give as well as to take advice.[7]

"Thank you, sir, for your solicitude," Nabby replied on July 27. She, too, confessed an attachment to the law, and thought its study the "most conducive to the expansion of the mind of any of the learned professions." Also, she was well aware that the most eminent men on the continent were lawyers; she hoped that one day all her brothers would pursue the law, and that her son might sometime be his grandfather's pupil. It was at this point, however, that the note of optimism faded. Though her husband had not yet settled on his future career, the law was not a practical consideration for the colonel, to Mrs. Smith's way of thinking. So many were already established that there was little encouragement for someone "lost in public view" to enter into its practice. She allowed that a "few combining accidental circumstances" might bring a man, "without any extraordinary exertions on his own part," to public attention, but that in her own experience, such cases were rare.[8]

Her father's prospects were another tale. In his letters to his daughter, John spoke not only of his son-in-law's future, but of the perils of his own. Mrs. Smith, vigorously ambitious and affectionately supportive in answer, insisted that in contrast to her husband's predicament, it would not take long to renew "remembrances" of her father's reputation. And, yes, John's suggestion that he might return to the bar seemed plausible, presuming, of course, that the lesser parts of the practice would be left to young practitioners. Mrs. Smith had higher aspirations for her father. Though he might grumble that public judgment and public voice bestowed on others every public office he might accept or consider an honor, she was not taken in. Though he might grieve, "in strict confidence," that he hadn't more of the "esteem, admiration, or respect of his country," Nabby's belief in her father was consummate:

> It is my opinion that you will either be elected to the second place
> upon the continent, or first in your own State. The general voice
> has assigned the presidentship to General Washington, and it has
> been the opinion of many persons whom I have heard mention the
> subject, that the vice-presidentship would be at your option. I
> confess I wish it, and that you may accept it.[9]

In a sense, Nabby's vision was clearer than her parents'. John, as ever, was torn between public and private life; his habit of self-analysis was almost as intense and merciless as in his youth. Only the multiplicity of years benefited him with a more incisive view of alternatives. "We are all in a flurry with politics," he wrote to Abigail on December 2, 1788, during her visit to the Smiths, and none were more so than he himself. What share he was to have in the new government was the salient question, and he was at a loss to guess the answer. In a suspended state, he brooded all that autumn on the matter: on September 12, Congress had designated January 7, 1789, as the day for appointing presidential electors, and on February 4 as the day for casting ballots. For a man in the habit of balancing every-thing, as John claimed he did, he faced up to the choice between two related "articles": public and private life, vanity and comfort. "I have the alternative in my power," he assured Abigail. "If they mortify my vanity, they give me comfort. They cannot deprive me of comfort without gratifying my vanity."[10]

To the best of his ability, John strained for objectivity during this trying time. As a "traveller," an outsider in any country, he was determined not to fault anything—his carping these days concerned his own failings, mostly—for to do so would betray a "littleness" of mind. In his attempt to balance things and to locate his own niche in a dazzling landscape, however, it was impossible for him to abstain from making judgments.[11]

As he looked around, he thought America's increased population was "wonderful," the plenitude of provisions of all kinds "amazing" and cheap in proportion to their abundance and the scarcity of money. Agriculture, the fisheries, manufactures, and commerce were "well," exceeding his expectations. He was less complimentary about politics: the "old, stanch, firm patriots" who had conducted the Rev-olution were being displaced by "pilots more selfish and much less skilful." Four months later this criticism would be forgotten, John's self-debate quieted. On April 6, 1789, the Senate, with nine of its twenty-two members present, witnessed the counting of sixty-nine ballots unanimously electing George Washington as President, and thirty-four electing John Adams Vice-President. Six months later, Thomas Jefferson would be appointed Secretary of State; Henry Knox, Secretary of War; Alexander Hamilton, Secretary of the Trea-sury; Samuel Osgood, Postmaster General of the month-old national Post Office Department; and John Jay, Chief Justice of the Supreme Court.[12]

Abigail's approval of the new government fairly beamed from the pages of her letter to Mrs. Cranch. In spite of her acute awareness of her "delicate situation," by virtue of her husband's high office, she was undaunted. Her excuse for commenting on political affairs was disarmingly straightforward: "Perhaps, there is no person who feels more interested in them." She proceeded also because her pleasure was irrepressible, as she congratulated her country on recent judicial appointments "in which an assemblage of the greatest talents and abilities are united which any country can boast of; gentlemen in whom the public have great confidence, and who will prove durable pillars in support of our government." It was as though all problems were solved, or capable of solution with a little forbearance, by virtue of the new government:

> Thus have we the fairest prospect of sitting down under our own vine in peace, provided the restless spirit of certain characters, who foam and fret, is permitted only its hour upon the stage, and then shall no more be heard of, nor permitted to sow the seeds of discord among the real defenders of the faith.[13]

Abigail began the vice-presidential years with unprecedented optimism; she had never been in more buoyant spirits in her entire life. As New York was the capital of the new nation, she set out to join John in his new post on June 19, 1789, a year and a day after her return from England. Her present voyage, via Providence and Newport, where she boarded the Hancock packet, commanded by a trustworthy Captain Brown, was again, in a sense, as tumultuous as her first had been. Five days of winds and thunderstorms and sickness landed her in New York safely, but in wry despair that her vow to stay away from the sea had been "kept as my former ones have been." But any resemblance to her first voyage was purely physical. The once "mere American" had bloomed into a commanding presence who would expect deference from others. She traveled with her niece Louisa, her brother William's daughter, as companion, and with two maids, and felt the "want" of Mrs. Briesler as her hairdresser.[14]

Whatever initial reservations Abigail had regarding her journey—making it, affording it, arranging it—had been dispelled by John's loving letter. He, too, was in great spirits. He insisted that she come, and overwhelmed her with ways to arrange her life so that she might leave home in easy mind. She could leave Thomas at college, but bring Charles; she could bring John Briesler (who would join them on July 4); she could let their brother plow and plant as he wished, as much as he wished, sharing half the butter and cheese with his family. As for money—she was to borrow from some friend. And if she could not borrow enough, she must sell horses, oxen, sheep, cows, or whatever she could, at any rate, rather than stay home. Anything went, anything was possible; John was prepared for the ultimate sacrifice: "If no one will take the place, leave it to the birds of the air and beasts of the field, but at all events break up that establishment and that household. . . ." John had taken a house a mile outside of the town of New York, where there was room of all sorts, though no furniture, and he was waiting for her "tenderly." Abigail's vivid, elated letters, written over the next few months, attest to her belief that she had chosen the right and only course, and she was almost apologetic, as well as apprehensive, about her thriving state.[15]

Richmond Hill caught Abigail's fancy immediately. The tall, tiered, columned house, with its eleven-foot ceilings, its gardens, and its majestic view of the Hudson and the farms of New Jersey beyond, now covered with a golden harvest, was precisely in keeping with the houses Abigail had lived in and visited abroad. A winding, tree-lined road led to the house. On one side the fields were green, the pastures full of cattle; on the other, the city rose in the distance. The large flower garden in the back was enclosed with a hawthorn hedge; its adjacent grove of pines and oaks was happily "fit for contemplation." There was order to Richmond Hill, and there was wilderness, as well. Partridges, woodcocks, and pigeons were plentiful, and birds of great variety, to Abigail's delight, serenaded her morning and night.[16]

Not only was the prospect all around "Beautiful" (a word Abigail used repeatedly) in the "highest degree," but all was "sublime" and "delicious," except perhaps for the local hams, which she pronounced "miserable." And for once the house was, though not in good repair, in decent order, with not only John, but the Smiths and their one-year-old son John, ready to greet her. With beds and a few other minor details to attend to, Abigail was almost instantly ready to assume a responsible social life, as rigorous and organized as any she had known (and criticized) abroad. As there were no public walks, no public amusements, and one dinner for every six given in Boston, the system of rotating receptions or levees assumed emphatic significance. Once Martha Washington settled on Fridays at eight o'clock, the pattern was set. Abigail then chose to receive on Mondays, her rooms lighted and put in order for those who cared to come to make their bow and curtsy, to take coffee and tea, to chat for half an hour or longer. The same "ceremony" was performed on Tuesdays at Mrs. John Temple's house—"Lady" Temple, as Abigail insisted on calling the former Elizabeth Bowdoin* ; Wednesday was Mrs. Knox's turn, and Thursday, Mrs. Jay's.[17]

Abigail managed her Monday evenings, as well as her weekly din-

---

*After November 11, 1786, John Temple, a native of Massachusetts, claimed succession to the baronetcy of Stowe in Buckinghamshire, England, and the couple called themselves "Sir" John and "Lady" Temple.

ners for twenty-four that were certain to include government officials, with an uncertain staff that did not fare well in comparison with its London counterpart. In the best of domestic times she could claim a "pretty good Housekeeper, a tolerable footman, a middling cook, an indifferent steward and a vixen of a House maid." She fretted about help who drank; she was "sincerely" sick of the Negroes she encountered, and could no more do without Mr. Briesler, she said, "than a coach would go without wheels or Horse to draw it."[18]

Not only had Abigail to cope with problems of help in running her home, but also of health; housing a family of eighteen under her roof meant nursing the two Smith children through a round of whooping cough, and Charles, Louisa, and the maid Polly through bouts of dysentery, apart from overcoming her own chronic frailties. But even as the fall colors mellowed, and she realized that Richmond Hill would be bleak in November and inaccessible in severe winter, and that it would take forty or fifty cords of wood to keep six fireplaces warming (at seven dollars a cord for walnut, five dollars for oak), the house did not lose its appeal. It was "more to my mind than any place I ever lived in," Abigail wrote Mrs. Cranch.[19]

"The Beautiful prospect" before her, wherever she looked, from whatever vantage point, was inspiration for Abigail; for the only time in her life, by her own admission, she could not spare a moment's mourning for having left Braintree behind. She was in brilliant spirits; the season was plentiful and she urged her loved ones to "rejoice and be glad." So unusual was her state of mind that she had barely settled at Richmond Hill when she began to worry about being "too happy in the situation of it to have it lasting." She felt humbled by her own good fortune, guilty that she could not share her noble house, views, and garden with sisters, nieces, and friends. Though her own strain of self-analysis was neither as virulent as John's nor as capriciously indulgent, it was persistent. This and her fierce Puritan birthright transcended all as Abigail wrote to Mrs. Cranch on July 12, 1789, requesting a favor of her "near and intimate Friends":

> It is to desire them to watch over my conduct and if at any time
> they perceive any alteration in me with respect to them, arising
> as they may suppose from my situation in Life, I beg they would
> with the utmost freedom acquaint me with it. I do not feel within
> myself the least disposition of the kind, but I know mankind are

prone to deceive themselves, and some are disposed to misconstrue the conduct of those whom they conceive placed above them.[20]

The truth was, of course, that Abigail's "situation in Life" had measurably altered her manner and expectations. Her fears were as readily borne out as they were understandable. Only to study her references to herself as her "Ladyship," to friends such as "Lady" Temple, and especially to the Washingtons illuminates her own new, sharply defined sense of social position and expectations of homage. Abigail was pleased to claim to live "upon terms of much Friendship" with the President and his wife. She wrote about both of them with sensitivity and affection, but also with a more formal dimension, that of deference. Inadvertently, Abigail treated the Washingtons as uncrowned royalty, as "court" subjects, eligible successors to the monarchical figures of her recent past.[21]

The day after Abigail's arrival at Richmond Hill, she took Nabby with her to pay her respects to Martha Washington. She could not have been more pleased to be received with "great ease & politeness," and reported as much about the President's wife to Mrs. Cranch:

> She is plain in her dress, but that plainness is the best of every article. She is in mourning. Her Hair is white, her Teeth beautifull, her person rather short than otherways, hardly so large as my Ladyship, and if I was to speak sincerly, I think she is a much better figure. Her manners are modest and unassuming, dignified and femenine, not the Tincture of ha'ture about her. *His Majesty* was ill & confined to his Room. I had not the pleasure of a presentation to him, but the satisfaction of hearing that he regreted it equally with myself.[22]

Martha Washington was three months younger than her husband, and twelve years older than Abigail. She had aged gracefully since the time of John Wollaston's portrait of a young woman with a round, pleasant face, calm eyes, a restful mouth, and a good figure. Perhaps, because most of her correspondence was destroyed, she has been (except for her wealth) underrated by history. It has even been suggested that she was incapable of writing her own condolence notes at her husband's death. The content of one of her rare surviving letters dramatically explains her appeal for Abigail. Her sentiments, in fact, echo Abigail's; they also underline their mutual sense of sacrifice.[23]

Martha Washington was eloquent about her goals and her wishes for herself and her family; her "first and dearest wish" was to grow old with her husband "in solitude and tranquillity," to be with her grandchildren and her "domestic connexions." There was something "not quite as it ought to have been" that she, "who had much rather be at home, should occupy a place, with which a great many younger and gayer women would be extremely pleased." Yet she could not blame her husband for acting according to his ideas of duty in obeying the voice of his country. But unlike Abigail, Martha Washington was not an introspective woman, nor had she suffered such intense loneliness or financial harassment. Her solution to her state was less tortured and more direct; no parson's daughter, she looked to herself rather than to the heavens for her answers. She was determined to be cheerful and happy whatever her situation; she believed "the greater part of our happiness or misery depends on our dispositions, and not on our circumstances. We carry the needs of the one or the other about with us in our minds wherever we go." Given this sort of wise companionship, it was no wonder that Abigail thought of Mrs. Washington as a "most friendly good Lady, always pleasant and easy." She also commented on Mrs. Washington's lack of affectation as well as her being "one of those unassuming characters which create Love & Esteem." Furthermore, she was "quite a Grandmamma."[24]

George Washington was equally impressive. Abigail found the "August President" a "singular example of modesty and diffidence." The exemplary soldier, the self-educated surveyor, the blue-eyed, sinewy, superlative horseman who loved to dance, was recovering from a fever when Abigail paid her second visit to Mrs. Washington. The President was unable to sit up; Abigail was therefore invited to meet him in his own room.

> He was laying upon a settee and half raising himself up, begged me to excuse his receiving me in that posture, congratulated me upon my arrival in New York and asked me how I could Relish the simple manners of America after having been accustomed to those of Europe. I replied to him that where I found simple manners I esteemed them, but that I thought we approached much nearer to the Luxury and manners of Europe according to our ability, than most persons were sensible of and that we had our full share of taste and fondness for them.[25]

The next day, Washington, accompanied by Martha, showed admirable ingenuity; he rode out to return Abigail's call (at her invitation) by placing his bed in his carriage, drawn by six horses and attended by four servants. With all her "feelings and Sensations" of respect, admiration, and affection, Abigail found herself, she told Mrs. Cranch, "much more deeply impressed than I ever did before their Majesties of Britain."[26]

The style in which the Washingtons chose to celebrate the new year of 1790 again earned Abigail's unqualified approval, even in comparison with palace festivities. To Abigail's delight, their drawing room "was as much crowded as a Birth Night at St. James, and with company as Brilliantly drest, diamonds & great hoops excepted." Abigail, as always, stood at Mrs. Washington's right hand, though sometimes, "through want of knowing what is right," others usurped her position. This was when Washington unfailingly came to Abigail's rescue, a gesture so meaningful it was scrupulously called to Mrs. Cranch's attention: "On such an occasion the President never fails of seeing that it is relinquished for me, and having removed Ladies several times, they have now learned to rise & give it me, but this between our selves, as *all distinction* you know is unpopular."[27]

In truth, Abigail exulted in Washington's admirable grace, his having "so happy a faculty of appearing to accommodate & yet carrying his point." So much so, in fact, that she truly believed that if Washington was "not really one of the best intentioned men in the world he might be a very dangerous one." Abigail's concept of Washington went far beyond niceties. Above all, Washington was a figure of grandeur, "peculiarly fit" for his exalted station. No other man, she claimed adamantly, could "rule over this great people and consolidate them into one mighty Empire but He who is set over us." Having virtually crowned Washington head of state by her unequivocal confidence—"He is polite with dignity, affable without familiarity, distant without Haughtyness, Grave without Austerity, Modest, wise & Good"—she was dismayed by his bout of illness in May 1790.[28]

During the several days that Washington lay perilously ill with influenza, which was epidemic at that time, Abigail confronted the possibility of his death. Shocked into the realization that John would be Washington's successor, she admitted to fears of "a thousand things" that she prayed she would never be called to experience. She dreaded the thought of Washington's death for a reason that few people would believe, and only those who knew her best, she said.

"Most assuredly" she did not wish for the highest post; Washington alone was the key to the future: "It appears to me that the union of the states, and consequently the permanancy of the Government depend under Providence upon his Life. At this early day when neither our Finances are arranged nor our Government sufficiently cemented to promise duration, His death would I fear have had most disasterous concequences." On May 30, Abigail wrote with extreme relief to inform Mrs. Cranch that, "thanks to Providence," Washington was again restored to health. Fortunately, thoughts of what she might have been "called to" had therefore been of only momentary concern.[29]

Abigail's mood of flourishing contentment with her lot as the Vice-President's wife was sustained throughout the winter of 1790. Not that she wasn't painfully aware of its fragile composition. She might be moving at any time, since Philadelphia had been chosen as the next capital. She suffered over the Cranches' needy state and lent them money. She was anxious about Sister Shaw's pregnancy, and said overtly that she thought it a "foolish Business to begin after so many years, a second crop." Of the "great national objects" coming before Congress, none was of greater magnitude, in her opinion, than the national debt. This was a subject of such vast weight, she claimed, that it required the wisest heads and "honestest" hearts to "adjust" it with any degree of satisfaction. "I hope to see an adoption of all the State Debts, and ways and means devised to pay them," she wrote Uncle Tufts. "Whether there will be sufficient courage in the Legislature to take so decisive a step," only time would tell. Repeatedly, however, she expressed the opinion that this issue was for her "one of the main pillars upon which the duration of the government rests."[30]

Problems of finance, of government and its "Herculean Labour," challenged Abigail's practical wisdom and intelligence. Opinions flowered judiciously, remarkably so, for one so passionately enthralled by every nuance in the growth of her developing country. "What one member esteems the pillar, the bulwark of the constitution an other considers as the ruin of his state," she conceded readily. Her magnanimous perspective, however long-ranging, blurred pathetically the more closely she, John, or their family were involved. Just as she appreciated the extraordinary efforts of others to evolve fresh sets of laws and patterns of protocol, so she sincerely expected reciprocal understanding of her own role and, more crucially, John's. To be rewarded instead with derision was incomprehensible to her; to be abused by the press about their judgment and conduct was intolerable. Fragile egos were wounded; all too quickly, Abigail was on the defensive, tormented, and made to sound petty.[31]

She had managed to "smile," or so she claimed, when the "Boston puffs" criticized the "dissipations" of New York, meaning the official entertainments. The newspaper editors had gone about absolving the President of responsibility for or participation in these affairs, implying, to Abigail, that the Adamses were the catalysts for these infamous indulgences. Abigail felt aggrieved. She objecting to reading that the President was "perfectly averse to all marks of distinction" when anyone could see that on special occasions he wore his regimental uniform adorned with an eagle "most richly set" with diamonds sparkling from his buttonhole. Abigail certainly did not call this being averse to distinction. Not that she begrudged the President these luxuries—his coach and six horses, his ten thousand dollars worth of furnishings, his diamonds. In fact, she was quite positive that "he ought to have still more state, & [that] time will convince our Country of the necessity, of it." What irked Abigail was the editors' inconsistency; for the past year she had noticed they were as "liberal" as one could hope to the President; their attitude toward the Vice-President, however, was entirely another matter.[32]

Abigail thought she knew the reason. Twice John had cast the tie-breaking vote, with the Senate divided nine to nine, in favor of the President having the exclusive power to remove his appointees from office. This vote aroused suspicion and criticism and was misconstrued as a vote of power into his own hands, or as having such potential in time. Unfair treatment, Abigail protested. "All was silence" when John had voted to reduce the duty on molasses, but everyone had chosen to pounce on him because of his controversial position on this other issue. Furthermore, even darker motives were attributed to John's insistence on bolstering presidential powers; it was another manifestation of his monarchist tendencies, his critics whined.[33]

In many ways, John had plummeted into this morass by his own ardent pursuits. Some might find the study of government "dry," he said, but for him, "no romance is more entertaining." John was tantalized by the possibilities of the "experiment" of the Constitution of the United States, of the "fresh essay at imperium in imperio."[34]

A lifelong student of other theories, John had defined his own in his *Thoughts,* and refined them in his *Defense:* a government ought to be "well ordered, mixed, and counterpoised" in order to achieve a "balance between the legislative and executive powers," or (in what seemed a harmless analogy) a balance between "aristocratical and democratical interests." Busy as he was in the year 1790, John was once again at his desk, still burnishing his theory that *balance* was the mainstay of government. Beginning in April 1790, and continuing for twelve months, the *Gazette of the United States* would publish thirty installments of John's *Discourses on Davila.* By exploring the Italian-born historian Enrico Caterino Davila's *History of the French Civil Wars,* translated into English in 1647, it was his intention to relate the lessons of that convulsive period to the present. Balance was the mainstay of government and was urgently needed to remedy the sorrows of bloodied, revolutionary France.[35]

Unlike John's other works, *Discourses* confused rather than clarified. He had long cautioned against the fraudulent use of words such as *monarchy,* and had openly written of the problematic nature of equality and natural aristocracy. But words like *monarchy, aristocracy,* and *hereditary,* tumbling about the pages of this exhaustive effort to synthesize his own theories, repulsed many. All too quickly he would be forced to justify their use, to assure the skeptical that mention of these concepts did not equate with espousal of them, that he was a "moral and irreconcilable enemy to monarchy." What John was trying to communicate was a deeply held belief that a balanced government was best able to fill its eventual goal: the happiness of society. This type of government, in its highest expression, was most sublimely one of "laws and not men."[36]

Eventually, John would regard the *Discourses* as a "dull, heavy volume" that did not add to his popularity—a breathtaking understatement, considering the criticism it sparked, and the tormenting test of friendship it provoked almost immediately on publication. Fortunately, Abigail, for the time being, chose to think of John's critics as unknown, somewhat distant beings, "uneasy wrestless spirits" to be found in all quarters of the world, rather than nesting on their very doorstep.[37]

One of the "uneasy spirits" haunting both Abigail and John was a man named Edward Church, brother of the infamous Benjamin Church, physician, poet, and traitor. Abigail thought the *Massachusetts*

Centinel had gone too far in displaying favoritism when it had printed, this past August, Church's scathing poem, refused initially by New York printers and signed "A Republican." Neither John nor Abigail could understand the attack; vaguely, they were given to believe that Church was retaliating for an unanswered letter, for an unacknowledged blow. In any case, the author's aim was deadly:

> *Resign your awkward pomp, parade and pride,*
> *And lay that useless* etiquette *aside;*
> *Th' unthinking laugh, but all the thinking hate*
> *Such vile, abortive mimickry of State. . . .*
>
> Ye Wou'd Be Titled! *whom, in evil hour—*
> *The rash, unthinking people cloth'd with pow'r,*
> *Who, drunk, with pride, of foreign baubles dream,*
> *And rave of a COLUMBIAN DIADEM—*
> *Be prudent, modest, mod'rate, grateful, wise,*
> *Nor on your Country's ruin strive to rise,*
> *Lest great COLUMBIA's AWFUL GOD shou'd frown,*
> *And to your native dunghills hurl you down.*

Church continued, ignoring the Adams name, but pouncing on his title:

> *Resist the VICE—and that contagious pride*
> *To that o'erweening VICE—so near ally'd. . . .*
> *With unlick'd Lordlings sully not your fame,*
> *Nor daub our PATRIOT with a LACKER'D name.*

And finally the ultimate blow was dealt:

> *O WASHINGTON! thy Country's hope and trust!*
> *Alas! perhaps her last, as thou wert first;*
> *Successors we can find—but tell us where*
> *Of ALL thy virtues we shall find THE HEIR?*[38]

   Church had also written about "idle lackeys" sauntering at the door, and about "floods of wine." Abigail tried at first to meet adversity with dignity, but in private she despaired: "The Vice President ten times to one goes to Senate in a one Horse chaise, and Levee's we have had none," she wrote to Mrs. Cranch. "The Pressident only, has his powderd Lackies waiting at the door. So that under a Hipocritical mask [Church] attacks one & hold[s] the other impiously up

& stiles him a Saviour & God. How inconsistant, railing at Titles & giving those which belong to the Deity." Weary and resigned, Abigail added, "Thus it is to be seated high. I pray Heaven to give me a conscience void of offence, and then the curse causeless shall not come."[39]

With March's piercing winds tamed, Abigail was able, the first week in April, to tend to her garden and to extol the early-spring attributes of Richmond Hill. The Smiths, who had been living with her that winter, were planning, on the first of May, to go into housekeeping on their own once more. Their temporary absence at this moment reminded Abigail of how lost she would be without them, especially the children. Though partial to William, whose "mild and sweet temper" she mentioned frequently, she loved John, born in 1788, and named for Grandfather John Adams, as well. Both were sources of amusement and diversion, and she consoled herself that they would spend at least half their time with her in the future, even when they lived under separate roofs. Abigail was an abundantly affectionate grandmother who considered the youngsters almost as "near" to her heart as her own children. She was also a traditionally possessive grandmother; without a qualm she boasted to Mrs. Cranch that William had come from his Grandmamma Smith's "an almost ruined child, but I have brought him to be a fine Boy now."[40]

By the end of the month, however, Abigail's somber preoccupation with her depleted household was abruptly diverted by rampaging illness. An unseasonable April snow, more than had fallen the entire winter, and consequent cold, wet weather turned her house into what she accurately described as a "mere Hospital." Colonel Smith suffered one of his severe bilious attacks; Charles and several of the servants were felled by violent fevers; the housekeeper lay helpless with St. Anthony's disease, a wretched inflammation of the skin. Four weeks later, influenza had invaded the household, prostrating all but John, with Abigail suffering what she called a "double share." Now the housekeeper would be leaving, infirm and also at odds with another quarrelsome servant, and Abigail was pressed to rearrange her staff. She needed someone who understood pastry, someone to supervise the cooking and make tea for public evenings, someone to clean and to iron; Abigail wrote to Boston for help with her search. More than once she was reminded what a prize her English servants were; if she did not have Briesler to help her now, she thought she might be tempted to give up public life.[41]

As always, the economics of supporting her household compounded Abigail's other problems. Word that her tenants in Braintree might be leaving made her wish she could substitute cash for land, or that her property was as "moveable an article as a carriage" which she could bring to New York. In this city she would have no difficulty renting one house for four hundred dollars, a price she could hardly eke out for their five houses and farmland combined, in Braintree. By mid-June she was thoroughly distracted, torn with the cares of Braintree and the confusion of rumors of a southbound capital. Perhaps she was "too short sighted, or too much blinded," or too fatigued, or too impecunious, but she could honestly see no real advantage to leaving Richmond Hill and what she thought a "very delightfull situation," unless, of course, the powers involved could make a permanent choice. Mention had been made of Baltimore as a possible capital, a city where one would not be comfortable, she had heard. Furthermore, if she could see that the public would benefit from the move, she would, she promised, "submit with more satisfaction." But to know that "sowerd" members of Congress wasted time in every session disputing the subject was, at the least, "a very unpleasant thing."[42]

On July 16, 1790, Philadelphia was named the capital of the United States until 1800, at which time a federal city was to be founded on the Potomac River. The machinations behind this plan troubled Abigail, aware as she was of the purported bargain made between Virginia and New England. Hamilton's plan for federal assumption of state debts was supported by Jefferson and Virginia; in turn, New Englanders, encouraged by Hamilton, would vote for the Potomac capital. Still, Abigail saw no "essential benefit" for the public in the new location; personally, she was terrified of the prospect of "violent Heats."[43]

On August 29, Abigail called on Martha Washington, who would be leaving for Mount Vernon the next day. Abigail gravely expressed her cordial wish that they would be parted for only a short time; having lived close to Martha "in habits of intimacy and friendship," Abigail believed that no lady could be "more deservedly beloved and esteemed" than the President's good wife. She wrote of other neighbors with equal generosity and charm. Though she had once blamed her "bad" writing on the lack of new subjects or objects, and fretted that if she did meet up with a "curious" character she would be reticent about mentioning the same, she need not have apologized. She rallied admirably when it came to telling Mrs. Cranch of her association with the Upper Creek Indians:

> I have nothing new to entertain you with unless it is my
> Neighbours the Creek savages who visit us daily. They are lodgd at
> an Inn at a little distance from us. They are very fond of visiting us
> as we entertain them kindly, and they behave with much civility.
> Yesterday they signed the Treaty, and last Night they had a great
> Bondfire dancing round it like so many spirits hooping, singing,
> yelling, and expressing their pleasure and satisfaction in the true
> savage stile. These are the first savages I ever saw. Mico Maco, one
> of their kings dinned her yesterday and after dinner he confered a
> Name upon me, the meaning of which I do not know: Mammea.
> He took me by the Hand, bowd his Head and bent his knee, calling
> me Mammea, Mammea. They are very fine looking Men, placid
> countenances & fine shape.[44]

In the fall of 1790, as she faced the inevitability of moving to Philadelphia, Abigail increasingly acknowledged her fears in the same breath as she tried to temper them. "No one is without their difficulties, whether in High, or low Life"—this she positively knew. And in a certain way, one's troubles were private matters: "Every person knows best where their own shoe pinches." But she could no longer contain her sighs; "low spirited and heartless," Abigail was on the edge of grief. Did they not pity her? she asked her sisters and her dear Dr. Tufts. Here she was again, as in Europe, boxing and casing her possessions, spending money she could not afford. Here she was, once more facing the prospect of having to move in new circles, form new acquaintances, make and receive a hundred ceremonious visits, not one out of ten of which would give her any pleasure or satisfaction. Moreover, and most relevant to her sense of deprivation, was her irretrievable loss of Mrs. Smith, who had given birth to a third son, Thomas Hollis, on August 8, and William and John, to whom she was openly "much attached." Even so, she could not express everything that burdened her heart; there were "many other things I have upon my mind and spirits which I cannot communicate by letter," she told Mrs. Cranch. One week later she was less reticent, though she still omitted reference to the colonel. She wrote on October 10: "My separation from Mrs. Smith is painful to me on many accounts. There is at present no prospect of their going with us, and if their prospects here were as fair as they ought to be, I should be less solicitious for them."[45]

Inevitably, financial matters were an additional gnawing issue. Abigail faced soaring expenses with exasperation; it would cost $160 to ship their belongings, and $400 for a house located two miles out of the city of Philadelphia that had "not a garden spot upon it." And if Philadelphia real estate tried her patience, her Braintree rentals drove her that October to rare, if not singular, criticism of her husband:

> I have the vanity however to think that if Dr. Tufts and my
> Ladyship had been left to the sole management of our affairs, they
> would have been upon a more profitable footing. In the first place
> I never desired so much Land unless we could have lived upon it.
> The money paid for useless land I would have purchase[d] publick
> securities with. The interest of which, poorly as it is funded, would
> have been less troublesome to take charge of then Land and much
> more productive. But in these Ideas I have always been so
> unfortunate as to differ from my partner, who thinks he never
> saved any thing but what he vested in Land.[46]

The squall was over as suddenly as it had begun—a lone, bitter signal of Abigail's inner turbulence. A sense of isolation prevailed; she mourned what she termed her "destiny," to have her family scattered, scarcely to be able to keep one member nearby. Outwardly, she tended the necessary chores, arranging to have her furniture on shipboard by October 20, to have St. Germain pears and the best russet apples sent from Braintree to Philadelphia, to spend the first stage of her journey to the nation's newest capital in New York with the Smiths. She even took time to recommend the use of flannels next to the skin to ward off colds suffered by her sickly brother-in-law, Richard Cranch, and his wife. "Make little waist-coats & put them on the first comeing of cold weather," she said; had she as much spare room in her stays as Mrs. Cranch did, Abigail assured her sister, "I would not be without them." Abigail herself was taken ill while visiting Mrs. Smith; delirious with fever, she was confined to her room till early November. In her threadbare state of mind and health, the trek from New York to Philadelphia hovered ominously. As though she anticipated the trials of the next episode of her life, Abigail referred to the journey before her being "like a mountain & three ferries to cross."[47]

SEVENTEEN

A Prospect
of Calamities

Filled with misgivings over her move to Philadelphia, Abigail nevertheless claimed to be neither "disappointed nor dis-
comfited" on her arrival during the second week in November 1790.
Her desertion of the drafty, unfinished house, still occupied by tardy
painters, to spend that dismal Friday evening at the City Tavern,
belied her equivocation. The next morning, however, Abigail took
possession of the Bush Hill with a vengeance, and within twenty-four
hours a seemingly infinite accumulation of boxes, barrels, chairs,
tables, and trunks were partially ordered, once-sullen fireplaces radiated light and warmth, and beds stood sturdy and hospitable.
Within a week Abigail would nurse Thomas, downed with rheumatism on Sunday, administer an emetic to Louisa on Monday, and tend
Mrs. Briesler for one of her chronic stomach pains on Tuesday; "to
complete the whole," on Thursday a violent, feverish pleurisy
gripped another member of the household. Conscientiously uphold-
ing her social duties, however, Abigail managed to receive callers in
her own chamber, the only "decent" one, from 11:00 A.M. until 3:00
P.M., stormy days excepted.[1]

Whatever the difficulties she encountered in the arduous process
of settling her family, friends assured Abigail that others were even
less fortunate. Mrs. Washington's house, for example, was not likely
to be ready before the new year ("And, when all is done, it will not
be Broadway"); the boat carrying Mrs. Knox's furniture had not been
heard from. But news of others' trials did not alleviate Abigail's own.

Her best trunk of clothes was damaged during its leaky voyage, which meant several of her dresses were spoiled, including a favorite black satin and another that Mrs. Smith had worked on most diligently. It was all "the blessed effects of tumbling about the world," Abigail said, in a lame attempt to put events in perspective.[2]

Comparisons were inevitable. The Schuylkill River, from where she viewed it, bore no more resemblance to the Hudson, she said, than she to Hercules. Furthermore, while Richmond Hill had been "sublime," its architecture "Grand," its tree-shaded entrance "perfectly Romantick," Bush Hill could boast not a bush, a shrub, nor barely a tree; the British had left the property naked but for the pine grove in back, where a row of statuary guarded a graveled walk. Nevertheless, Abigail allowed that it was "a very beautiful place" in its own way, poised elegantly in a meadow in which a shepherd pastured his sheep.[3]

Quickly settled, Abigail was to make another surprising concession. She soon discovered to her unreserved delight that the women of Philadelphia were well educated, well bred, and well dressed, and that she was received in their "brilliant" drawing rooms with every "mark of politeness and civility." So much so that she soon worried she would spend a "very dissipated winter" if she accepted one half of the invitations she received. Furthermore, she pronounced the dancing in Philadelphia "very good," was only faintly patronizing about the theater being equal to "most" outside of France—"very neat, and prettily fitted up"—and said that the actors "did their best" in *The School for Scandal.* She also enjoyed "Ministers of State" and their "Madams," as she insisted on calling the wives, as "company of the best kind." Her weekday plans included going to dance at Mr. Chew's on Tuesday and to "sup" at Mr. Clymer's on Friday. "So you see I am likely to be amused," she wrote Mrs. Smith on January 8, 1791.[4]

Two months later, Abigail's timorously rising expectations were blunted by the most extreme cold she had experienced since her return from England. As for the broad plane of blinding snow—it "puts out my eyes," she complained. Her evaluation of life in Philadelphia, though still flattering, was a good deal more realistic. She had come to think of the surrounding countryside as too level for her style; its uniformity "wearies the eye, and confines the imagination," she told Mrs. Shaw. She also tended to think of herself as a kind of prisoner, more than ever before in her life. Though the house was only two miles from the city, after each rain she had to "wallow" through "mortar," horses sinking to their knees, three-quarters of the way to Philadelphia, before reaching any paved road. Sheer cold made the prospect of travel even less pleasant; holes and roughness along the way were equally harrowing. Yet there were compensations. Philadelphia was as verdant in March as Massachusetts in May, the house was airy and comfortable, and there was so much more "society" in Philadelphia than in New York, even if she could not always participate, that Abigail had to admit she was "much better pleased and satisfied" than she had expected to be.[5]

She was also pleased on another count: she was planning her return to Braintree in May, roads permitting, where she hoped to stay for five months. She apologized to Dr. Tufts, "Friend, Guardian and parent," for troubling him with arrangements, but his "many kind offices, and long habit of doing good," had led her and the whole family to look to him for advice and assistance. Would he ready the house with candles, soap, flour, sugar, tea, coffee, chocolate, and cider? She would need a half-dozen barrels of the last. Not anxious to stock any "superfluous" articles, she did order two kitchen tables, one six feet long and four feet wide, as well as a couple of washtubs. Then there was the garden to think of; arrangements must be made to have it manured and turned. And, as always, no letter to Tufts was complete without some comment of a political nature.[6]

The present session of Congress, Abigail wrote the doctor on March 11, 1791, was "marked with great dispatch of Business, much good humour, & the varying in Sentiment upon some very important Subjects." She enclosed a copy of the bill, signed February 25, chartering the Bank of the United States. Opposed by many Southern members of Congress on the grounds that it was financially hazardous as well as unconstitutional—Congress hadn't the power to incorporate a bank—Abigail assured Tufts that it was thought in Philadelphia, "by those who are esteemed the best judges," that the bill would not have any of "those concequences" that some of its detractors imagined. Though she worried about this divided stand and speculated that if she lived ten years longer she would see "a division of the Southern & Northern States, unless more candour & less intrigue" should prevail, she was optimistic on the whole:

The Accession of the State of Vermont during this Session to the Union, and the Uninimnity [unanimity] with which they were

Abigail Smith Adams at twenty-two, two years after her marriage to John Adams on October 25, 1764, wrote: "My Good Man is so very fat . . . and I am lean as a rale [rail]." Pastel by Benjamin Blyth. *Courtesy: Massachusetts Historical Society.*

...hard Cranch married Abigail's elder ...er, Mary. Abigail said he had a ...ave, Yet chearful Countenance." ...stration from Daniel Munro ...son's *Chappel of Ease. Courtesy: ...sachusetts Historical Society.*

The Reverend William Smith graduated from Harvard in 1725 and served for fifty years as the minister of the First or North Parish of Weymouth. From *Chappel of Ease. Courtesy: Massachusetts Historical Society.*

Abigail Smith Adams's birthplace, the parsonage in Weymouth, Massachusetts, bought for £45 in 1738, was also the setting for John Adams's courtship of Abigail. The ink and watercolor drawing is unsigned. *Courtesy: Massachusetts Historical Society.*

Right: The Boston Commons in 176 scene of the "merry-andrew Tricks" British soldiers who already camped and drilled there. Engraving by Sid Smith, 1770, after a watercolor by Christian Remick in 1768.
Courtesy: The New York Public Library, Asto Lenox and Tilden Foundations.

John Adams in 1766, age thirty-one, described by Abigail, because of his travels in the practice of law, as "such an Itinerant . . . that I have little of his company." Pastel by Benjamin Blyth.
Courtesy: Massachusetts Historical Society.

John Adams's birthplace, right, in Braintree, Massachusetts, later called
Quincy, in 1735. After marriage, John and Abigail moved to the house
on the left, John Quincy's birthplace. Painting by Frankenstein. *Courtesy:*
U.S. Department of the Interior, National Park Service, Adams National Historic Site,
Quincy, Massachusetts.

Martha Washington in 1790. Abigail thought her "plain in dress, but that plainness is the best of every article." Portrait by Edward Savage. *Courtesy: U.S. Department of the Interior, National Park Service, Adams National Historic Site, Quincy, Massachusetts.*

George Washington, Abigail said, wa a "singular example of modesty and diffidence." Painting by Edward Savage, 1790. *Courtesy: U.S. Department of the Interior, National Park Service, Adams National Historic Site, Quincy, Massachusetts.*

Abigail Adams saw "George Town and Federal City or city of Washington" on Sunday, November 16, 1800. She left in mid-February, when John was voted out of office. Drawing by G. Beck, engraving, T. Cartwright, 1801. *Courtesy: The New York Public Library, Astor, Lenox and Tilden Foundations.*

ft: Marie Antoinette being led to
·r execution on October 16, 1793.
nis event greatly distressed Abigail:
Not content with loading her with
nominy, they blacken her memory.
." Engraving by A. Caron, 1800.
urtesy: The New York Public Library,
tor, Lenox and Tilden Foundations.

ouisa Catherine Adams in London
nen her husband served as minister
the Court of St. James in May 1815.
inted by Charles Robert Leslie, who
ouisa felt made "Portraits [which
·re] . . . most striking Likenesses."
urtesy: Diplomatic Reception Rooms, U.S.
partment of State.

John Quincy Adams considered sitting for his portrait by Charles Robert Leslie as having "undergone the operation." He was recalled from England by President Monroe to become secretary of state. *Courtesy: Diplomatic Reception Rooms, U.S. Department of State.*

A preliminary sketch of Abigail Adams by Gilbert Stuart. Abigail's first sitting took place in 1800; on its completion, December 1816, Abigail said the portrait looked "no more like [her] than any other person." *Courtesy: Massachusetts Historical Society.*

received is a most happy and important event in our Annals and will add weight to the Northern Scale. Kentucky is also agreed to be received but her Government is not yet organized. Thus Sir one pillar rises after another and adds strength I hope to the Union.[7]

It was hardly news to Abigail that "No station in life was ever designed by Providence to be free from trouble and anxiety," and neither the blessings of three sons having graduated from Harvard "with so much reputation," nor the pleasures of Philadelphia numbed the pain of family problems. Thomas's rheumatic condition was a nagging preoccupation for her, every damp day a warning of his future, a reminder of his past. Abigail did not think he looked well or would fare well in Philadelphia's summer heat. Further, the urgent question of how he was to earn his living compounded his difficulties. He definitely preferred merchandizing, but since he lacked capital, it seemed that law was the logical alternative—one, however, that Abigail realized would be a "force" to his inclinations.[8]

An alternative to either merchandising or law was banking, and Abigail considered a possibility that Thomas might go to Holland to work with the banking house of the Willinks, with whom his father had negotiated a loan for the United States. This appeared, in some ways, to be the most satisfactory solution, considering Thomas's interests. Still, Abigail told John Quincy, she hesitated to give advice. It wasn't that she doubted that Thomas would be "steady industerous and indefatiable" in his pursuits, but that, with less than whole-hearted commitment, the possibility of failure was greater, and the adviser was therefore more liable to bear the blame for an unfortunate outcome.[9]

Ostensibly wary, professing neutrality, yet blithely ignoring her own presentiment on the subject, Abigail was, in fact, hardly cowed by the hazards of taking a position on this or almost any issue. Only the approach was problematical. "I have sometimes found great address necessary to carry a point," she confided to John Quincy, "and much prudent caution to effect my scheme." Very likely, Abigail was unaware that she had just described with critical accuracy her pivotal involvement in all her children's lives.[10]

On July 15, 1790, John Quincy was "regularly admitted and sworn to the office of an attorney," ending a peripatetic apprenticeship to Theophilus Parsons of Newburyport, begun after his graduation from Harvard College in 1787. The prospects of his practicing law, an overcrowded profession in Massachusetts, presented a "dismal proposition" for this impecunious young man. On the morning of August 9, John Quincy established his office in the front room of the family house on Court Street in Boston, wishing all the while that he had been bred a farmer, a merchant, or "any thing" by which he could earn his bread.[11]

At a comparable age, his father had despaired over his expectations for "Happiness, and a solid undisturbed Contentment amidst all the Disorders, and the continual Rotations of worldly Affairs." The son, heir to the father's ambitions and frustrations, searched for less cosmic answers. In a sense, his parents were his universe: their standards of morality, education, and purpose embraced him, goading, inhibiting, and luring him. He was full of gratitude for the "innumerable favours" he had received from the "best of Parents," but, by his own bitter admission, gratitude was the only return he could make for all their trouble and expense, their labors and cares on his behalf.[12]

Repeatedly, in the letters he wrote during this precarious period of his life, John Quincy was "all too apprehensive" that he might never cease to be "burthensome" to his parents and hoped that "application, honour and integrity," combined with whatever faculties he possessed, would make him worthy of their sacrifice and demonstrate that their labors had not been in vain. Increasingly obsessed by his perceived shortcomings, he wrote that his only reason for remaining in Boston was that he knew of no more advantageous situation, and therefore, if "Fortune should be disposed" to befriend him, "she will have a larger scope here, than she could have in the woods." On another occasion he repeated the major theme of his despair: "At my time of life it is a grievous mortification to be dependant for a subsistence even though it be upon a Parent."[13]

Both of "the best of Parents" sought to help their troubled son. John's "Solemn advise" was improbably intellectual; he suggested that John Quincy could best help himself by "Mastering the Roman learning." Beginning with Livy, father advised son to "take your Book, your Dictionary, your Grammer, your Sheet of Paper and Pen and put down in Writing every Word with its meaning as you find it in Ainsworth. You will find it the most delightful Employment you ever engaged in." John added kindly: "Above all Things Keep up your Spirit and take Care of your Health." He also hinted that he would give John Quincy the "Whole" management of his estate if he would take it, but wondered if such a responsibility might interrupt his studies too much.[14]

Abigail's solution was more pragmatic; brisk, motherly admonitions were her medicine. She congratulated John on being "so well accomodated," on having a good office and library, and on boarding with an agreeable family, her cousins, Dr. and Mrs. Thomas Welsh. Furthermore, she promised, "You will get Business in time and when you feel disposed to find fault with your Stars, bethink yourself how preferable your Situation to that of many others." Though she understood that "a style of dependence must never be urksome to a generous mind," she stressed that there was no "kind" parent who would not "freely" contribute to the support and assistance of a child "in proportion to their ability," provided that dependence was not the result of "idleness or dissapation."[15]

But John Quincy remained unpersuaded by his mother's beseechings, punishingly aware of his own inadequacies. He reminded his mother that while he was grateful for her concern, appreciation was currency of negligible value, "Thanks being however the exchequer of the poor."[16]

As late as August 20, 1790, Abigail appears to have been oblivious of the fact that her son's loss of "sprightliness and vivacity" was rooted in romantic as well as economic deprivation, the one undoubtedly inseparable from the other. John Quincy was in love—seriously enough, apparently, to be considering marriage to Mary Frazier, whom he had met in Newburyport. His law-school classmate and "steady friend," James Bridges, knew of his "attachment," as did his sister and confidante, Mrs. Smith, as well his Cranch cousins. According to his brother Charles's account to their sister of *"the* Lady" who had the honor to inspire John Quincy with a favorable opinion of the fair sex, "nothing so like perfection in Human shape, appeared since the World began."[17]

Initially, John Quincy's conduct of his romance must have been awkwardly discreet, if not desperately secretive, as Bridges eventually explained, "This I used to impute to the want of passion on your side —which you would by no means allow, you may remember." John Quincy was far more open with his sister about his feelings for Mary Frazier—worrisomely so, judging from Nabby's reaction. She hoped he would "excuse" her if she did not believe his "confession of the existance of an attachment to which reason and Providence would oppose their influence." Her mother's daughter, certainly, Mrs. Smith refused to think that her brother had "given his mind up uninfluenced by reason and Prudence." Nor could she advise him to become, at this stage, "speedily engaged in an attachment upon which must devolve your future happiness, prosperity, and success."[18]

If it was not too late, Mrs. Smith would favor his "first settling in business and taking time to form a more extensive acquaintance with the World." Though already "sensible" that his "knowledge of Mankind is more enlarged and Extensive than perhaps any young Man of your age Possesses," as one who felt interested in his prosperity and welfare, she thought it was possible that he might yet be deficient in practical knowledge. Speaking from daunting experience, Mrs. Smith contended that "when the Heart is so deeply interested it sometimes blinds the eyes of reason, and judgement." However protective she felt, Mrs. Smith was also yielding. If John Quincy's mind was "already engaged," she would not hesitate, she said, to believe that the "object" was in every respect worthy of his partiality.[19]

Thomas was the first to tell his mother of John Quincy's love, and this news was confirmed by both of her sisters. Elizabeth Shaw rather coyly commented that Abigail's eldest son had been "vastly attentive to the Ladies of late—& that *one happy fair*" was distinguished. "Aye my Sister," she inquired, "what will you say, should *your Hercules* be conquered" by a young woman passing through the "dangerous age of Sixteen." Certainly, in her opinion, the "celebrated beauty had everything to gain from her relationship with a "faithful Friend" who could point out the path of duty, sustain her emotionally, "make the fair field of Science, & Literature still more pleasing." Mary Cranch chimed in at this particular stage of her nephew's romance to reassure Abigail that she could trust in her son's prudence, and note that Mary Frazier "is young but has had a very good education."[20]

Elizabeth Shaw's speculation about Abigail's reaction to the conquest of John Quincy was soon resolved. Abigail was firm in her position. Little of her advice to her son was surprising in light of a recent exchange. John Quincy had taunted her, fully aware of the type of young woman who would have met with his mother's approval. Not without affection, he had commented on the engagement of one presumably affluent Nancy Quincy, a distant cousin, to the Reverend Asa Packard. How this step must have "blasted" his mother's "darling project" for his own advancement, "even before the bud," he had written. He had continued that he hoped his mother would not think the worse of him if he assured her that he never would be indebted to his wife for his property. Though he had once seriously thought that he should "easily be enabled to make matrimony an instrument" of his advancement or his ambition, such, he concluded almost wistfully, "really" was not so.[21]

Abigail's position regarding John Quincy's romantic prospects was admittedly influenced by the interminable vicissitudes of her daughter's fortune, and she did not hesitate to say so. Mrs. Smith had just given birth to her third child, and it was Abigail's hope, confided to John Quincy, that his sister would not add to her stock further until her future brightened. Recognition of the Smiths' bleak prospects resulted in "one piece of advice" gravely imparted: "Never form connextions untill you see a prospect of supporting a Family, never take a woman from an eligible situation and place her below it. Remember that marriage is chargeable, also that misfortunes surround even the finest prospects."[22]

As for John Quincy's current relationship, Abigail was willing to make some concessions, if he would bear in mind that it was best to make himself "easy and keep free from entanglements." She allowed that some good might come of her son's love affair:

> So far it will serve to make you attentive to your person, for you are a little inclined to be negligent, as far it may be of service to you, besides it may keep your Head from rambling after other objects, but if it makes you anxious & uneasy and when you are reading, Slides in between your subject and you then you have cause to be allarmed, so take heed.

And then, with all the maternal inspiration at her command, she assured her son:

> I do not doubt you will do very well only have patience, and I will prophesy for you, that you will be able by the close of one year to pay your own Board, and if you do that tis as much as you ought to expect, and if you do not why dont worry your face into wrinkles about it. We will help you all we can, and when you are better off than those who assist you, you shall help them again if they want it, so make yourself easy. . . .[23]

The resolution of John Quincy's romance was more logically advised than accomplished. He, above all, had the clearest insight into his confused state. His mind teemed with questions; the "suspense" about his own prospects depressed his spirits, admittedly "not naturally very lively." The "impression of fear is strong, and that of hope but weakly supported," he told his mother. And, he might have added, confusion reigned. Nevertheless, late in August he informed Abigail that "some apprehension" on his account might be safely quieted. "You may rest assured, my dear Madam, that I am as resolutely determined never to connect a woman to desperate Fortune, as I am never to be indebted to a woman for wealth. The same Spirit," he presumed, "will operate equally to prevent either of these cases." He further guaranteed that he would never request his mother's consent to any "connection" of his until he was able "to support that connection with honour and Independence."[24]

John Quincy's determination, though it was everything his mother could hope for, was closer to a hope than to the truth about his circumstances. Only recently, John Quincy had written his concerned friend, James Bridges, *"You* may know (though it is known to very few) that all my hopes of future happiness in this life centre in the possession of that girl." The bewildered Bridges responded to his "dear Adams" that he had "scarce ever been more surprised" than by his friend's disclosure of the nature of his connection with "Miss F." Bridges's respect for his friend's sense of purpose led him to assume that John Quincy's fate was "fixed with respect to the important article of matrimony." Indeed, Bridges added, "the solemnity of the style would not admit suspicion that you were trifling with my curiosity."[25]

Abigail was ill the entire month of October, suffering from recurring fever and tremors that left her sleepless. Her fragile health was further undermined by her concern for Mrs. Smith's baby, a victim of smallpox. John Quincy's recent letter, a detailed lament of his inadequacies—"alone in the world, without a soul to share the few joys I have, or to participate in my anxieties and suspense"—which he realized "must be as disagreeable to my friends who read, as it is to me who write"—did not improve his mother's spirits. He was feeling not only lonely but unsuccessful. He was deeply disappointed with his maiden address before the jury in the Court of Common Pleas. Lack of time and experience, and the diffidence he had always felt about his own talent at "extemporary speechifying," had robbed him of proper presence of mind; worse, it had drained him of all self-esteem.[26]

Besides John Quincy's ravaged mental state, Abigail was also anxious about persistent reports of his attachment to a young lady. Whether or not such rumors had a basis in fact, their very existence was worrisome. Abigail reminded her son that such "Common

Fame" might injure the future prospects of the lady in question, and his own were not such "as can warrent you in entering into any engagements." Once again, she warned that a "too early marriage will involve you in troubles that may render you & yours unhappy the remainder of your life." Then, as though anticipating yet another vain promise, Abigail was pleasant if blunt: "You will say that you have no idea of connecting yourself at present & I believe you." But if this was the case, "Why gain the affections of a woman, why give her cause to think you attached to her?" Didn't he realize that the cruelest situation for a young lady was to feel herself attached to a gentleman when he can "testify" it in no other way than through his actions? "I mean when his situation will not permit him to do otherwise," she clarified.[27]

Abigail shrewdly echoed her husband's suggestion about seeking their son's help in making the farm more productive. Having thus assuaged his pride, she offered him title to some modest rental fees and arranged to supply him with hay and wood. To her immense relief, John Quincy responded by apologizing for having been a "child to complain," and vowed that as long as it was convenient for his parents to favor him with a "continuance of their support," he would remain in Boston anticipating "some favourable chance." He made her "very easy" upon the subject and she trusted he would be convinced that all her anxiety was for his benefit, and that his happiness would ultimately be the result of "wisely adopted" resolution.[28]

John Quincy sought to appease his mother on another troubling subject. He insisted that there would "never more" be any cause on his part for further reports of his attachment to a "young Lady," as they were "henceforth" separated—she in Newburyport, he in Boston, forty miles apart. Distance, Abigail was assured, would allow "no further opportunities to indulge a weakness" which she might perhaps censure, though she would excuse it, he concluded defensively, if she knew the "object." For Abigail's part, anxious to be done with this worrisome episode, she promised John Quincy that he would "hear no more from me upon that topick." One of the many good rules and maxims learned from her "worthy Grandmother" was to reprimand "with justice, with dignity," but never to lessen her authority by reproaches. "The concecuence was that Love towards her and respect for her opinion prevented a repition [repetition] of the offense."[29]

John Quincy visited his parents in Philadelphia in the winter of

1791, in hopes that a change of air, exercise, and the "novelty" of Philadelphia might have a favorable effect on his health and attitude. Furthermore, in spite of all his disclaimers, he hoped to "converse, with more freedom than I can write," on the subject of the presumably renounced Mary Frazier. Abigail's reasoned arguments about age and financial position were convincing, presumably, for by springtime John Quincy was in wholehearted pursuit of other priorities. Amid diverse stories persisting of a break between the two young people, inaccurately supposed "groundless" by Bridges, John Quincy informed his brother Thomas of his momentous decision. "I must bid a long and lasting farewell to the juvenile Misses. It is to the severer toils of the Historic Matron that I must henceforth direct all the attention that I can allow to that lovely company," he wrote on April 2, 1791. Signing himself "Publicola," he had decided to follow his inclination to record his political views for newspaper publication. Behind this decision lay a desire to defend his father's ideas, dubbed "political heresies" by Thomas Jefferson. Pledging "devotions to the eyeless dame who holds the balance and the sword," he asked his brother Thomas to bring along in his trunk—if he had room—a set of the past sessions' laws and journals of both Houses, and to fill in for him missing numbers, specifically enumerated, of the *Gazette of the United States.* [30]

John Quincy's newly determined course was bolstered later that same month by news that his mother had spoken to his father, and together they had agreed that he should be given an annual allowance of twenty-five pounds quarterly, under Dr. Tufts's aegis, the first payment to commence in July. June brought further means of support. He became an attorney for his father, empowered "to ask, demand, sue for, and recover and receive" all rents and arrears of rent due now or in the future. His father's show of faith was precisely noted, not once but twice, on this document: "Power, from my father," was inscribed horizontally across the top, and proudly repeated in the top corner, in two determined vertical lines: "Powers from my father to let his house." [31]

If Bridges's appraisal of Mary Frazier was accurate, John Quincy had been persuaded by family and circumstances to make the propitious choice. When he supposed that John Quincy was about to marry "Miss. F.," Bridges apologized for doing "injustice to your Goddess, by supposing her heart to be cold and unfeeling." Wretched that his critique might disrupt their friendship, he sought to qualify his remarks. After all, he supposed, his acquaintance with Miss Frazier was too general to give him opportunities "of sifting the qualities of heart which might therefore have contained the seeds of the most engaging sympathy." Still endeavoring to strike a more positive note, Bridges clumsily proceeded with his tangled analysis, writing optimistically in one sentence about "seeds" that lay "dormant," and in the next sentence about seeds that never shoot forth "where the chilling damps of vanity reside." Considering how young and beautiful she was, " 'tis no discredit to her to imagine her under the baneful influence of that Passion," Bridges reasoned.[32]

By the fall of 1791, John Quincy, seemingly free of Mary Frazier, had found new confidence, and said as much to Thomas. He was "growing much stronger," and even allowed that he had acquitted himself in court "more to my satisfaction than I ever had ever done before." He was still disturbed by having to subsist upon paternal bounty, but had achieved some perspective on his situation. At least he would endeavor to deserve this support, and, in the long winter ahead, intended to pursue with "much ardour the studies connected with his profession and with science in general."[33]

This marked change was duly noted and sensitively appraised by his "steadfast friend and earnest well-wisher," Bridges. He was sure that "Dear *Publicola*" must have struggled with his conscience before he "clasped his sickle to reap in the field of politics." Furthermore, Bridges bade "adieu" for both of them to "Private life [and] domestic tranquillity, with all their blissfull appendages." On January 23, 1792, Bridges would congratulate John Quincy on his appointment "to be one of a very respectable committee to instruct and reform the politics of the town of Boston." He evaluated his friend's new responsibility, with calculated accuracy, as "more an auspicious omen of futurity" than having "any present intrinsic value discoverable. . . ."[34]

Abigail was justified, at least to her own satisfaction, in her hopes that "Patience and Time" (she failed to mention money) would smooth the rites of John Quincy's passage to maturity. So much of what she had tried to teach him, she had learned at her daughter's expense. In the same breath that she could wholeheartedly "prophesy" her son's well-being, she despaired of any prospect that "bids fair" for the support of Mrs. Smith and her family. The "poor Girl" was called "to quite a different trial" from any in her mother's experience, and Abigail's sense of inadequacy was magnified by physical separation. The colonel, compulsively entrepreneurial and lacking in scruples, a speculator in land on a monumental scale, had left his wife alone with three children, the youngest, Thomas Hollis Smith, just four months old. The colonel had resigned his appointment by Washington, September 1789, as marshal of the District of New York, and departed for England on December 8, just before Christmas—an awkward time, in Abigail's opinion. His going was a mysterious puzzle, sudden and unexpected, initiated for the purpose of collecting debts owed his father's estate, and also of "assisting" his family—or so she had been told. A letter Smith wrote from London on June 22, 1792, reveals his calamitous financial status. Regretful of the "inexpressible pain" that he had caused a colleague who endorsed notes on his behalf, Smith told him that his own return to the United States depended "entirely" on him. "I cannot leave this until I see my bills paid."[35]

While Abigail assumed intermittent care of her grandchildren, what really disturbed her was her inability to afford to send for the whole family, as she had managed to do in the past. "It is vain to say what we ought to have been able to do. I feel what I cannot do," Abigail wrote Mrs. Cranch. Though the colonel's family was very kind, a father's house was the "desirable" place for her daughter. Thanks to Mrs. Smith's weekly letters, her mother's worries were confirmed and even exacerbated.[36]

In return, Abigail's letters to her despondent daughter, a young woman never in the best of times known for "vivacity and sprightlyness," were, during the colonel's absence, openly and stridently supportive. Filled with a kind of stern compassion, they did not absolutely mute Abigail's tenderness, or veil her frantic concerns. "We know not what we can do or bear, till called to the trial," the mother advised; she also observed that the equanimity of Nabby's disposition would lead her to a "patient submission to the allotments of Providence."[37]

Abigail tried to amuse her daughter; Mrs. Smith's son Johnny was an "enlivener" of her household, spending an hour at a time chasing his grandfather about the room with a willow stick. Conversely, and to his entertainment as well as the "derangement" of the carpet, "grandpapa" was inveigled into the after-dinner sport of driving Johnny, enthroned in a chair, about the room for half an hour. She also tried to instruct, telling Mrs. Smith that the children's education would occupy much of her time; and, she added, "you will always

keep in mind the great importance of first principles, and the necessity of instilling the precepts of morality very early into their minds."
To this end, Abigail recommended *Divine and Moral Songs for Children*
by Isaac Watts, which stressed the role of the Supreme Being as
creator, benefactor, and preserver, teaching brotherly love, sisterly
affection, filial respect, and reverence. She frankly hoped these would
mitigate her grandson's addiction to a hundred little stories such as
"Jack and Jill" and "Little Jack Horner" with "neither a rule of life,
nor a sentiment worth retaining." As a memory exercise and practice
in speaking, the latter might be useful, "but in no other way," she
stated firmly.[38]

She was equally adamant about the limitations of the social life of
a married woman living alone—precisely her daughter's position;
Mrs. Smith was "perfectly right" in refusing to go out in public
during Colonel Smith's absence. Under her parent's wing, her situation would be different, with no notice taken of her comings and
goings. As she lived now, however, she could not be too circumspect
—the eyes of the world always focused on those whose situation
might possibly be subject to censure. Even the friendly attentions of
one's acquaintances were liable to be misconstrued. Abigail anxiously reiterated that she did not offer her opinion through any apprehension of Mrs. Smith's "erring," but only as "approving" her
determination.[39]

As weeks passed without news from the colonel, Abigail was made
desperately aware of Mrs. Smith's deepening depression. In her loving efforts to rouse her daughter, Abigail probed her own life for
common truths:

> Why do you say that you feel alone on the world? I used to think
> that I felt so too; but, when I lost my mother, and afterwards my
> father, *that* "alone" appeared to me in a much more formidable
> light. It was like cutting away the main pillars of a building; and,
> though no friend can supply the absence of a good husband, yet,
> whilst our parents live, we cannot feel unprotected. To them we
> can apply for advice and direction, sure that it will be given with
> affection and tenderness.[40]

Given Mrs. Smith's bleak situation, the news of the President's
appointment of the colonel in March 1791 as supervisor of New York
State was, understandably, viewed as a miraculous rainbow on an
obscure horizon. Both parents—John was no less wary or solicitous

than Abigail—grasped its significance, and the hope it held. Within thirty-six hours each wrote to the colonel, still abroad, expected home by May, who had very much hoped that the President would provide for their son-in-law, their letters remarkably alike, at once circuitous and direct. John prefaced his message of March 14 with news of the addition of Vermont and Kentucky to the nation, and the rapid rise of stocks and credit. He then continued:

> I took my pen, however, merely to mention your appointment to the office of Supervisor for the State of New-York, which will necessarily require your personal presence before the first of July. This place, I presume, is well worth your acceptance, as it will be a decent and comfortable provision for yourself and family, while it will be an honourable and useful employment. I am therefore anxious that you should have the earliest notice of it, and return without loss of time.[41]

Abigail's letter elaborated only slightly on John's. She wrote on March 16, partly, she said, to inform the colonel that his son was in perfect health, and full of "mirth and glee," as fine a boy as he could wish, and partly to congratulate him on his appointment; Mrs. Smith would be forwarding the official document. There was no mistaking her sense of urgency, however:

> You will see by the bill the necessity there is of your returning with all possible dispatch. The Secretary of the Treasury told Mr. Adams that he would write to you, and it is probable that he will by this opportunity. He informed Mr. Adams, that it was the President's intention to unite the office of Supervisor and Inspector for the State of New-York, and not to divide the state, as he will be obliged to do, in some states where there are many ports of entry, consequently the salary will be something handsome, and well worth your acceptance, though the duties of the office will be proportionably arduous. I thought it would be of importance to you to get sight of the bill as soon as possible.[42]

Though the problem of the Smiths was solved, temporarily at least, Abigail and John faced a far from serene summer at home in Braintree. When Abigail's "enjoyments" were "damped, curtailed or molested," she was apt to blame "folly" in herself or others, "or the hand of Providence." In one instance, however, the source of unhappiness was far less abstract. Thomas Paine, that "Star of Disaster," was all too clearly accountable for the heartrending collapse of the already eroded friendship of the Adamses with Thomas Jefferson.[43]

In May 1791, Paine's latest work was available in Philadelphia. Called *The Rights of Man,* published first in London that February, the searing document was dedicated to George Washington "in defence of those Principles of Freedom" the President had "so eminently" established. The two-part work was a rebuttal of Edmund Burke's scathing *Reflections on the Revolution in France, and on the Proceedings of Certain Societies in London Relative to that Event.* Paine pronounced the English Constitution the bulwark of reactionary government, insisting that there "never did, there never will, and there never can, exist a Parliament, or any description of men, or any generation of men, in any country, possessed of the right or the power of binding and controlling posterity to the end of time, or of commanding for ever how the world shall be governed, or who shall govern it." Furthermore, he wrote, all such clauses, acts, or declarations by which the makers of them attempted to do what they had neither the right nor the power to do, nor the power to execute, were, in themselves, "null and void." As far as Paine was concerned, "the vanity and presumption of government beyond the grave" was "the most ridiculous and insolent of all tyrannies."[44]

Paine's wishful annihilation of the assumptions of the English Parliament of 1688, and of the English Constitution that John believed was the only workable form of government, was difficult enough to stomach; but to have Thomas Jefferson in the adversary's corner was a bitter blow. With stunned disbelief John Adams read Jefferson's endorsement incorporated at the start of Paine's document: "I am extremely pleased to find it [*Rights of Man*] will be reprinted, and that something is at length to be publicly said against the *political heresies* which have sprung up among us. I have no doubt our citizens will *rally* a second time round the standard Common Sense."[45]

Neither John nor Abigail failed to understand Jefferson's reference to "heresies." These were the serialized installments of John's own *Discourses on Davila,* which he stopped writing because of "the rage and fury" of readers. The "political heresies" for which Jefferson and Paine attacked John involved his condoning government "beyond the grave." John's approval of the monarchical rule of Great Britain was construed by Paine to be a shameless endorsement of the tyranny and arrogance inextricably linked with a monarchy. In fact, the usurpation of government by personality was the single element in the

history of politics most feared by John. It was with profound unease
that he, with Abigail, watched the French Revolution nurture lawless-
ness and repression, discarding all tenets of balance and discipline.[46]

"Student of Government" was a "title" John claimed during his days
at Harvard, as a young man with a sense of mission concerning
political ideas. As such, he keenly appreciated his unique position as
one of the few members of the human race to enjoy the opportunity
to select and elect their government in form and purpose. Neither
naïve nor inexperienced in matters of political innovation, John was
now made to seem foolish, pompous, and almost treasonous in the
unpopularity of his support for Great Britain's government. However, in his opinion, the British political system provided a government that was "well-ordered, mixed and counterpoised" to a degree
surpassed only in the fledgling United States. Unfortunately, this
remarkably dispassionate analysis of government was offset by the
complex, diffuse manner in which it was registered in *Discourses on
Davila.* John's classical education made him abhore the revolutionary
French concept of freedom—a submission to "Control by the uncon-
trolled"—and at the same time provided the tools to analyze and
comprehend the philosophical and political ramifications of the British Constitution.[47]

Popular support of France, and the fluency of Jefferson and Paine
as rhetoricians, made Adams's published articles an obvious and
vulnerable target for misinterpretation. He had perhaps expressed
himself most clearly and simply on the subject of his beliefs in a letter
to the Marquis de Lafayette nine years before, on May 21, 1782:

> I have the honor and consolation to be a republican on principle;
> that is to say, I esteem that form of government the best of which
> human nature is capable. Almost everything that is estimable in
> civil life has originated under such governments. Two republican
> powers, Athens and Rome, have done more honour to our species
> than all the rest of it.

As one who tried always to achieve the balance he preached, he had
added, "I am not, however, an enthusiast who wishes to overturn
empires and monarchies for the sake of introducing republican forms
of government, and therefore, I am no King-killer, King-hater, or
King-despiser."[48]

Abigail, though her tone was less frenetic, held similar opinions on the French and their "moral earthquake." "The Devouring capacity of the Galick nation increases with their power and ability of ratification," she wrote to Cotton Tufts. The "Beneficial effects" of three branches "in lieu of one" were exemplified, she said, in the governing of Pennsylvania. In contrast with Abigail's homely but forthright chronicle of political philosophy, John's habit of analysis of all facets of a question seemed always to lead him into convoluted and pretentious forms of expression. His letter to Lafayette continued:

> If the common people are advised to aim at collecting the whole sovereignty in a single national assembly, as they are by the Duke de la Rochefoucault and the Marquis of Condorcet; or at the abolition of the regal executive authority; or at a division of the executive power, as they are by a posthumous publication of the Abbé de Mably, they will fail of their desired liberty, as certainly as emulation and rivalry are founded in human nature, and inseparable from civil affairs. . . .

Still hammering away on the dangers of the single assembly, he continued:

> It is not to flatter the passions of the people, to be sure, nor is it the way to obtain a present enthusiastic popularity, to tell them that in a single assembly they will act as arbitrarily and tyrannically as any despot, but it is a sacred truth, and as demonstrable as any proposition whatever, that a sovereignty in a single assembly must necessarily and will certainly be exercised by a majority, as tyranically as any sovereignty was ever exercised by kings or nobles. And if a balance of passions and interests is not scientifically concerted, the present struggle in Europe will be little beneficial to mankind, and produce nothing but another thousand years of feudal fanaticism, under new and strange names.[49]

Immediately on publication of the first installment of the *Discourses,* John knew he was in trouble. He defended himself to his friend Dr. Benjamin Rush with exacting argument, denying his attachment to monarchy, or that he had changed his principles since 1776. On April 18, 1790, he wrote:

> I am a mortal and irreconcilable enemy to monarchy. I am no friend to hereditary limited monarchy in America. This I know can never be admitted without an hereditary Senate to control it, and a hereditary nobility or Senate in America I know to be unattainable and impracticable. I should scarcely be for it, if it were.[50]

He had written in January 1776, recommending a legislature in three independent branches. To such a legislature, he assured Rush, he was "still attached." Once more he explained himself:

> I am for a balance between the legislative and executive powers, and I am for enabling the executive to be at all times capable of maintaining the balance between the Senate and House, or in other words, between the aristocratical and democratical interests. Yet I am for having all three branches elected at stated periods, and these elections, I hope, will continue until the people shall be convinced that fortune, providence, or chance, call it which you will, is better than election.[51]

John was feeling "ill-used"; he begged Rush for help: "Do not, therefore, my friend, misunderstand me and misrepresent me to posterity." He also felt quite alone. Though he had "acted in public with immense multitudes," he had "few friends," and those few were "certainly not interested ones." He was mistaken, luckily. He was befriended by the writer who called himself "Publicola," and who attacked Jefferson's inscription in Paine's *Rights of Man* with caustic precision. Many, including Jefferson, who sent a copy on to Paine, assumed that Publicola was John Adams's pseudonym. Publicola, however, was none other than John Quincy Adams, whose lengthy, lawyerly reply, in a series published in the *Columbian Centinel,* beginning June 8, 1791, might be considered official notice that Jefferson's seemingly imperishable relationship with the Adams family was forever frayed.[52]

With shrewd deliberation, Publicola pleaded his case. The late revolution in France, an event "so astonishing and unexpected in its nature, and so important in its consequences," had arrested the "peculiar" attention of the whole civilized world, including philosophers and politicians who speculated on what foundation this newly acquired liberty would be rooted in. Two among these were Edmund Burke and Thomas Paine, whose separate publications, "founded upon very different principles," were received with "the greatest avidity." Publicola termed Burke's work "one continued invective upon almost all the proceedings of the National Assembly since the Revolution, a severe and indiscriminating censure upon almost all their transactions." Paine fared no better. Publicola considered his applause of everything the French wrought as "undistinguishing" as Mr. Burke's censure.[53]

At no point in his implacable denunciation did Publicola mention Jefferson by name. But there was no mistaking the identity of the "very respectable gentleman" to whom Publicola addressed himself:

I confess, Sir I am somewhat at a loss to determine what this very respectable gentleman means by *political heresies.* Does he consider this pamphlet of Mr. Paine's as the canonical book of political scripture? As containing the true doctrine of popular infallibility, from which it would be heretical to depart in one single point? . . . compel all countrymen to cry out, "There is but one Goddess of Liberty, and Common Sense is her prophet."[54]

Publicola's remarks were reprinted in New York and Philadelphia, and eventually in London, Edinburgh, and Dublin. They added "fuel to the funeral pile of liberty," in Jefferson's opinion. The Adamses, on the other hand, believed Jefferson's support of Paine bordered too closely on social disintegration, as favoring "a mere popular tyranny." Though the signs were not clear, crossroads were reached; from that time on, "general types" known as conservatives and democrats would marshal the people of the United States "in opposition to each other, when not affected by disturbing influences from without." But this last conclusion was hindsight on John Quincy's part; for the moment, raw personal wounds required immediate attention. Their perpetrator, Thomas Jefferson, after weeks of deliberation, offered medicine that, in many ways, was more irritating than soothing.[55]

Jefferson took up his pen a dozen times, and laid it down as many again, "suspended between opposing considerations." He was determined finally, on July 17, 1791, to write "from a conviction that truth, between candid minds," could never do harm. And also that the "friendship and confidence" that had so long existed between them "required" his explanation. To begin with, it was James Madison who had lent him Paine's pamphlet. When he had finished reading it, he was to send it to a Mr. Jonathan B. Smith, whose brother meant to reprint it. Continuing his explanation, Jefferson said that he thought it proper, as a stranger, to enclose a note, and "accordingly" he had done just that. Because he wanted "to take off a little of the dryness of the note," he added that he was glad the pamphlet was to be reprinted, that something was "to be publicly said against the political heresies which had sprung up among" them. Subsequently, he had been "thunderstruck" upon seeing his note reprinted at the beginning of the pamphlet, and had hoped it would not attract notice.[56]

Unfortunately, this was not to be; the writer named Publicola had come forth, attacking not only the author and principles of the pamphlet, but Jefferson himself as its sponsor. Champions of Paine's *Rights of Man* surmised that Publicola was none other than John Adams, and "thus were our names thrown on the public stage as public antagonists," Jefferson concluded. "That you and I differ in our ideas of the best form of government is well known to us both; but we have differed as friends should do, respecting the purity of each other's motives, and confining our differences of opinion to private conversation."[57]

Sadly, for someone who pledged privacy and protested as much "in the presence of the almighty," Jefferson had not kept his word; he had analyzed his differences with John in discussions with a number of others. On May 8, 1791, he had written to Washington, mentioning Adams's "apostacy to hereditary monarchy and ability." On May 9, 1791, he had confided to James Madison that he had had Adams in mind when he mentioned "political heresies." As late as July 3, to his son-in-law, Thomas Mann Randolph, he had elaborated on the problem of his so-called "note" of endorsement and how he "knew immediately that it would give displeasure to some gentlemen just by the chair of government who were in sentiment with Burke and as much opposed to the sentiments of Paine." Even as he avowed his silence, he was full of detailed explanation:

> I could not disavow my note, because I had written it. I could not disavow my approbation of the pamphlet, because I was fully in sentiment with it, and it would have been trifling to have disavowed merely the publication of the note approving at the same time of the pamphlet. I determined, therefore, to be utterly silent except so far as verbal explanations could be made.[58]

John answered Jefferson the day after he received his letter. On July 29, 1791, at great length, Adams gave Jefferson "full Credit" for his "relation" of the manner in which his note was written and prefixed to the Philadelphia edition of Paine's pamphlet. However, the person who had committed the breach of his confidence, by making it public, "whatever were his intentions," had sown the seeds of more evils than he could ever atone for. The pamphlet, with

Jefferson's name affixed to so "striking" a recommendation of it, had done the damage. Industriously propagated in New York and Boston, reprinted in many newspapers, the pamphlet was "generally considered" as a direct and open personal attack on John. Thanks to the pamphlet and its renown, his writings were deliberately misinterpreted. Thanks to Jefferson, John was held up to the ridicule of the world for his "meanness," for wishing to subjugate the people to a few nobles, for favoring the introduction of hereditary monarchy and aristocracy in America. Further, old friends and colleagues snubbed him now; even Sam Adams, in his role as Lieutenant Governor of Massachusetts, warned the public against hereditary powers, as if the danger of their enforcement were imminent.[59]

John rose swiftly to his own defense, pleading with Jefferson for a fair assessment:

> If you suppose that I have or ever had a design or desire, of attempting to introduce a Government of Kings, Lords and Commons, or in other Words an hereditary Executive, or an hereditary Senate, either into the Government of the United States or that of any Individual State, in this Country, you are wholly mistaken. There is not such a Thought expressed or intimated in any public writing or private Letter of mine, and I may safely challenge all Mankind to produce such a passage and quote the Chapter and Verse.

He believed that he asked no more of his friend than he ought, considering their relationship: "If you have ever put such a Construction on any Thing of mine, I beg you would mention it to me, and I will undertake to convince you, that it has no such meaning."[60]

John knew the worth and the drawbacks of his "unpolished writings." On the positive side, he could claim that they had helped to crush the "late Insurgents," participants of Shays's Rebellion in Massachusetts, to form the new state constitutions of Pennsylvania, Georgia, and South Carolina, and to inspire the assent of all states to the new national Constitution. Proud as this record might be, the negative aspects were almost shattering. He had paid dearly, and would continue to do so, for his honest contention of the unpopular truth that God and nature had created inequalities that no human legislator could ever eradicate. He had had the daring to question, in effect, the qualities of equality, to search out whether citizens of a republic were equal as to "age, sex, size, strength, stature, activity, courage, hardiness, industry, patience, ingenuity, wealth, knowledge, fame, wit, temperance, constancy, and wisdom," and to conclude that the "answer of all mankind must be in the negative."[61]

There was no question in John's mind that his writings had cost him readers and believers, though he might not have understood the reasons for the unpopularity of his gnawing analyses and painstaking (and sometimes repetitive) exhumation of political ideologies. But an agonizing sense of failed justice, whatever the explanations, permeated a ringing passage of his letter to Jefferson:

> Of the few who have taken the pains to read them, some have
> misunderstood them and others have willfully misrepresented them,
> and these misunderstandings and misrepresentations have been
> made the pretence for overwhelming me with floods and
> Whirlwinds of tempestuous Abuse, unexampled in the History of
> this Country.[62]

The conclusion of this remarkable letter to Jefferson contained John's warm pledge that their fifteen years of friendship "without the smallest interruption" and "without the slightest Suspicion" until Jefferson's endorsement of the Paine pamphlet was still "very dear" to his heart. There was no office John would not resign rather than give a "just" occasion to one friend to forsake him. And, he added, he had no doubt that Jefferson's motives for writing him "were the most pure and the most friendly." Nor had he any suspicion that Jefferson would not receive his explanation "in the same candid Light."[63]

Jefferson responded at length on August 30, happy to find that John saw the "true point of view" of the way he had been drawn into the "scene." He embroidered further on his explanation and on how John's antagonists, "very criminally," in his opinion, had presumed him to be Publicola, and on that presumption had "hazarded" a personal attack on him. No person saw this "unjustifiable assault" with "more uneasiness" than he himself. Magnanimously affirming his clear conscience, he continued:

> You will perceive from all this, my dear Sir, that my note
> contributed nothing to the production of these disagreeable pieces.
> As long as Paine's pamphlet stood on its own feet, and on my
> note, it was unnoticed. As soon as Publicola attacked Paine, swarms
> appeared in his defence. To Publicola then and not in the least

degree to my note, this whole contest is to be ascribed and all its consequences.[64]

It was Jefferson's hope that he had proved himself as innocent "in effect" as he was in intention. And with the business and its effects now over, it was Jefferson's hope that their friendship would never be "suffered to be committed," whatever use others might think proper to make of their names. Jefferson concluded his letter by asking that John present "Mrs. Adams with all the affections I feel for her," a gesture totally lost on Abigail. Her silent condemnation would be revoked only momentarily, and in tragedy, thirteen years later, long after she had stopped believing that there could be "any event in this life which could call forth, feelings of mutual sympathy" between herself and Jefferson.[65]

Though hardly a premeditated plan, her visit in October of 1791 would be Abigail's last to Philadelphia for five years. It was not so much that the capital was less sparkling, but that she was increasingly weary. The "Bustle of Removal" from Bush Hill to a house in the heart of town, the revamping of her staff, and the scheduling of receptions and dinners left her with only a few hours to herself. A "happy" day was the rare one in which she had no engagements; a frequent ambition, about which she confessed she no longer suffered any "reflections," was to live in retirement.[66]

Abigail's serious complaints about her health began in mid-December and, by April, had increased to the point where she worried about how she would manage the journey home at all. Her body was worn with rheumatic pains and fevers that, at times, left her wrists lame and her eyes so sensitive that she could not read, write, or sew by candlelight, let alone leave her bed. Faithfully nursed by one or more of her nieces, Louisa most frequently, she was only weaker for the bloodlettings and emetics she was subjected to in the name of a cure. She also recognized that a "critical period" in midlife augmented her problems. Further, even she, who was always first to regret any "increase" in her figure, was concerned now about her immense loss of weight.[67]

Another loss, however, was far more hurtful. In one of her rare instances of self-pity, Abigail admitted that February's news of Colonel Smith's intention of carrying off his entire family to England for two years was "a heavy stroke" to her. She felt deprived of the tender care of an only daughter. Rather pathetically, Abigail tried to present the positive side of this wrenching news. The colonel, she wrote Mrs. Cranch, had made "a very advantageous contract with some Gentlemen," which she could not wish him to decline as he was going "upon sure footing."[68]

It was, however, extremely doubtful that Abigail knew the details of the colonel's livelihood. Smith, whose apparent appetite for acquiring a great fortune could never be satiated in the government post he had held for less than a year, was involved in buying and selling immense land grants in New York State, recently released by treaty with the Indians. At one point he was said to have bought five townships; it would be the eastern portion of the Van Zandt farm, in New York City, including twenty-three acres between the East River and the Boston Post Road that he would own and forfeit. Presently one of his clients was reputed to be the English peer Lord Pulteney, and another the King of Hanover. At the time of the Smith's actual leavetaking, scheduled for the end of March, Abigail mentioned again how "hard" it was to part with her only daughter, and how the thought of their separation "depressed" her spirits "very much" during her sickness, however keenly she realized "we must all have our trials, some of one kind & some of an other."[69]

Abigail's inability to accompany John back to Philadelphia in the fall of 1792, because of her failing health, was considered a temporary measure. Recognition of the more permanent arrangement came two years later, when John finally packed up all the furniture left behind in Philadelphia. His acknowledgment of Abigail's "distress and distraction" over its condition on arrival ("very strongly described") was countered with his promise, sincerely but rashly made, that "whatever crashes have happened shall be the last from removals."[70]

Actually, John's role as a "commuter" was not an unfamiliar one. At least in broad outlines, and with some improvements, it echoed earlier times. John went to work in Philadelphia, remaining for two months or six months, however long Congress sat, or as long as he felt obligated to stay. But Abigail was alone for shorter periods than before, and the mails were also remarkably steady. Expert in her role, she was to cope with the farm and her aged mother-in-law, to supervise a building program she had secretly initiated with Dr. Tufts's assistance, and, perhaps most significant of all, to hear John out and see him through this period of waiting on his ultimate destiny. He counted on Abigail's "delicious" letters, receiving at least one a week, valuing each one's importance: "To a heart that loves praise so well, and receives so little of it, your letter is like laudanum," which someone had told him was "the Divinity itself."[71]

As self-centered as John might seem, he never failed to praise Abigail's contributions and her handling of her many duties, and to acknowledge gallantly that others were not unaware of her capabilities. Clearly, Abigail bolstered not only his ego but his purse; with regard to their farm, John said he was "charmed" with her "bravery and activity." Because she was "so valorous and noble" a farmer, he was "little anxious" about their agricultural endeavors. The decisions were hers to make, though he could not resist slipping in advice to manure their barley field and "harrow it well." And with affectionate recognition of her independent spirit he called her a "Disciple of Wolstoncraft!" and was proud to repeat a friend's recommendation that Mrs. Adams be made "Autocratix" of the United States. "This, however, must be secret," he added solemnly, "because it is a sort of treason."[72]

Beyond affection, admiration, and respect, it was trust, above all, that was the crowning and eternal glory of their relationship. "What I write to you must be in sacred confidence and strict discretion," John confided in Abigail. As before, he concealed little from her, epic or petty, in wisdom or outrage. She responded just as intimately and movingly and, on occasions when she felt protective of him (disappointed in friendship, robbed of recognition), with like volatility.[73]

As of January 1793, when their correspondence was resumed after a hiatus of nearly ten years, the specter of France—revulsion at its "King-Killing," fear of its "fire, impetuosity and vehemence," conviction that "anarchy, chaos, murder, atheism, blasphemy" were not liberty—haunted their thoughts and crowded their pages to one another. The personality of the French Republic's minister, Edmond Charles Edouard Genêt, only intensified their dismay. Citizen Genêt, with his brazen recruitment of Americans to help despoil Spanish and British territories and vessels, was thought to be "enamoured to distraction with republican liberty," both "very crude and inaccurate in his ideas of a republic, and "totally uniformed" of the operations of the human heart. His Jacobin successor, Joseph

Fauchet, seemed "not quite so unreserved" but nevertheless appeared to be in "great distress." According to his brother-in-law, Louis Marie, Viscount de Noailles, who visited John, the Marquis de Lafayette was alive but in poor health, and Abigail's "old friend," the Marquise, was buried in obscurity in France. Horrified by Marie Antoinette's demise, Abigail was inclined to wish, she said, that every arm extended against the "unhappy" country of France be withdrawn so that the country might be left alone to form the constitution of its choice. Whether this was to be republican or monarchical was inconsequential, in her opinion, provided it was a regular government "of some form or other which may secure the faith of treaties, and due subordination to the laws."[74]

At a time of "wild projections and notions" in their own republic, "discussions" between Abigail and John ranged from the purpose of taxes to the practicality of a banking system to the scourge of a two-party political system, a concept encouraged by those hated "hell-hounds" of rival newspapers who promoted Federalist versus Anti-Federalist views. And speaking of the press, Abigail was outraged at its treatment of Washington. "Take his character all together," Abigail said, "and we shall not look upon his like again."[75]

If the press could mistreat Washington, who was not used to such "threshing," and whose skin was "thinner" than John's, Abigail could only wonder what was to be expected of his successor. John, too, was in a mood for speculation, but his concern was more immediate. The question of whether he would be elected to serve a second term as Vice-President led him back to his ancient dilemma: the choice between public and private life, if indeed he would have a choice, and the choice "between great cares and small cares." As before, his correspondence with Abigail was the forum for exhaustive exploration. He had looked into himself, he told her, and seen "no meanness nor dishonesty there" and "no timidity." Still, he saw "weakness enough."[76]

The veteran political figure was, in many ways, the youthful, yearning bridegroom, though there were indications of significant and revealing changes. John had mellowed; he was also more realistic. At times he wished himself a "private man," yet, on a little further thought, he knew privacy was not the answer. Life on his "sweet little farm" would not "relieve" him; his thoughts would be "at the

Hague and at New York," he admitted, not without apology, "if I was at Quincy."[77]*

As elections loomed, John was his usual self, the master experimentalist, probing formulas of success and, more often, failure. Always confident of Abigail's discretion ("A woman *can* be silent, when she will"), and allowing that he was most "impatient and distressed" when his mind was in suspense, he plunged forth on his miserable analyses of his prospects.[78]

On the one hand, he warned Abigail on January 9, 1793, when he had heard that the votes from Kentucky were said to be all for Thomas Jefferson, that it would be best to prepare their minds and, as well as they could, their circumstances, to get out of "this miserable scramble." He complained that his country had, "in its wisdom," elected him to "the most insignificant office that ever the invention of man contrived or his imagination conceived." Then again, once he won his second term—he was reelected with seventy-seven votes— he still found no peace, but speculated even more frantically about whether Patrick Henry, Thomas Jefferson, John Jay, or he himself would be voted into the top two offices once Washington announced his retirement. Furthermore, he hated the politics of election and regretted fervently that the Constitution had helped to "create, excite and support perpetual parties in the States, mixing and crossing alternately with parties in the Federal government." That their country would be "deformed with divisions, contests, dissensions and civil wars as well as others" was one of his sharp grievances.[79]

A letter to Abigail written three years later, on January 7, 1796, when he realized Washington's retirement was at hand, showed John to be as tormented as ever about his future. Though the words of his self-debate were slightly changed, the content was all too familiar. He was not able to see what "duty" would demand of him, yet he did admit that Washington's future plans were of "very serious" concern to him. Launched on murky waters, John spoke again of how it was "no light thing" to think about retirement; of how his country, his children, and his own character had claims that forbade him to serve the public in disgrace. For the first time John seemed to be openly examining the possibility that he might serve his country in the top post and, typically, he explored the negative possibilities first. If he had reason to think either "want of abilities or of public confidence"

*Braintree was renamed Quincy in 1791.

would follow him in a "high station," he ought to decline. That being the case, however, he could not serve under another. Undoubtedly, thinking he might end up subordinate to Jefferson, he said it would be a "dangerous crisis in public affairs if the President and Vice-President should be in opposite boxes."[80]

As usual, John warned Abigail that these "lucubrations" must be confined to her own bosom. As the weeks wore on, he wavered first one way and then another, alternately yearning for the presidency and backing away from it, pleased to be regarded as "heir apparent," and suffering over the probability of having to make a voluntary retreat to spend the rest of his days "in a very humble style." If Jefferson and Jay were to be President and Vice-President, as was not improbable in his judgment in mid-February, he promised Abigail he would retire "without noise, or cries, or tears." And even if either one was elected President and he Vice-President, he would take the same course, and retire "without murmur and complaint to his farm forever."[81]

As election day drew closer, John was nearly pathetic in his dilemma. "I am weary of the game," he wrote Abigail on February 10, 1796, "yet I don't know how I could live out of it." He assured her that he didn't enjoy "slight, neglect, contempt, disgrace, nor insult more than others," yet he was begging to fulfill a mission and he was sincere in his belief that he had "firmness of mind enough" to bear high office "like a man, a hero, and a philosopher." He might groan like Achilles, he warned Abigail, and "roll from side to side abed sometimes, at the ignorance, folly, injustice and ingratitude of the world," but there would be compensations. Savoring these, John admitted the possibility of his being elected President, and Jefferson or Jay Vice-President, for four years or even, "by reason of strength and fortitude," for eight years. He seemed suddenly cheered by this last thought and remembered to urge Abigail to "be of good courage therefore, and tremble not." He saw nothing to "appal" him, and he felt "no ill forebodings or faint misgivings," or "smallest dread" of private or public life. If private life was to be his portion, his farm and his pen would "employ" him the rest of his days. If public life was to be his fate, he had already hinted to Abigail at a new era in their relationship: "I should be resigned, and become more easy and cheerful, and enjoy myself and my friend better than ever I did."[82]

EIGHTEEN

Splendid Misery

Abigail was frankly threatened by John's "elevated station." The presidency encompassed so many dangers and difficulties that it appeared to her "as a slippery precipice, surrounded
on all sides by rocks, shoals and quicksands," she wrote Elbridge
Gerry on December 31, 1796. If a man such as Washington, in the
"full tide" of favor and affection, tasted the bitter cup of calumny and
abuse, she could not help worrying incessantly about his successor's
expectations. The bitter cup, she said, was an "imported cup, a foreign mixture, a poison so subtle as to have infected even native
Americans."[1]

Weeks before, on December 5, John, the Federalist candidate, had
won seventy-one votes in the presidential election. He had edged out
Jefferson, the Democratic-Republican candidate, by three votes, and
Thomas Pinckney and Aaron Burr by somewhat more comfortable
margins: fifty-nine votes were cast for the former, thirty for the latter.
The hazards implicit in John's minuscule lead did not escape Abigail.
"President by three votes," some would call him shortly. When she
concluded that in no one but Washington could there "again" be
united "such an assemblage of fortunate circumstances to combine
all hearts in her favor," she was more prescient than even she herself
might have imagined.[2]

In many ways Washington, in his prime, symbolized an innocent
and already bygone America. The "Assemblage of fortunate circumstances" had altered; it would seem a simpler matter to battle for

independence than to manage its victory. The description of Washington's administration as "perplexed" and of his measures as "impeded" also applied, in Abigail's mind, to the latest phase of her country's development. Its infancy had involved matters of moral decision and physical peril; its adolescence was arousing unnerving strife in all directions in the realignment of objectives, values, and friendships. When she spoke of being sensitive ("perhaps too keenly") to the "abuse of party," she referred to a new phenomenon, the crystallization of the two-party system in America. Henceforth, there would be not only Federalists but Republicans, opposing champions of centralized versus decentralized government. The ramifications of the close election and the polarized parties, as well as the persistent enthusiasm of so many Americans for the French Revolution, posed burdensome problems for Abigail and John. None was more provocative, perhaps, than the unnerving fact that Jefferson, once their most esteemed friend, was now their most threatening rival. The press seemed to revel in the situation, undermining John's confidence almost at the instant he took office.[3]

John referred to them as "insidious compliments." These were the insults showered on him, principally, at this time, by the publisher of the *Aurora*, Benjamin Franklin Bache. John was accused of having "immortalized" himself as an advocate for hereditary government; Jefferson was held up as a "true republican." It was implied that John would somehow perpetuate Washington's appointment on May 30, 1794, of John Quincy Adams as Minister to the Netherlands, leading to an Adams line of "seigneurs or lords" of America. By contrast, Jefferson, with daughters only, would have no successors.[4]

Jefferson himself was concerned by the damage the press perpetrated during the election period. On December 28, 1796, in a post-election letter, he wrote to John Adams:

the public and the public papers have been much occupied lately in placing us in a point of opposition to each other. I trust with confidence that less of it has been felt by ourselves personally. In the retired canton where I am, I learn little of what is passing: pamphlets I see never; papers but a few; and the fewer the happier.

Jefferson also took the trouble to warn Adams that he might be "cheated" of his succession by a trick "worthy of the subtlety" of his "arch-friend." Jefferson was referring to Alexander Hamilton, who, he said, was able to make Adams's real friends "tools" to defeat their and his best wishes. He also remarked that since the day the Treaty of Paris was signed, America's outlook had never been so grim. "I devoutely wish you may be able to shun for us this war by which our agriculture, commerce and credit will be destroyed."[5]

But all of this was not his real concern, Jefferson maintained. Blithely he protested that he left to others "the sublime delights of riding in the storm, better pleased with sound sleep and a warm berth below, the society of neighbors, friends and fellow laborers of the earth, than of spies and sycophants." Furthermore, no one, he predicted, would congratulate John with "purer disinterestedness" than himself. "I have no ambition to govern men. It is a painful and thankless office." Jefferson had ended his letter with high hopes that the newly elected President's administration might be filled with glory and happiness for himself and "advantage" to others. This, he continued, "is the sincere wish of one who tho', in the course of our voyage thro' life, various little incidents have happened or been contrived to separate us, retains still for you the solid esteem of the moments when we were working for our independence, and sentiments of respect and affectionate attachment."[6]

It was a pleasant letter, under the circumstances, and probably would have been appreciated by John. The latter never received it, however, owing to Jefferson's punishing ambivalence about his old friend and recent rival. Instead of sending the letter directly to John, he enclosed it with another he wrote four days later, on January 1, 1797. In this letter to James Madison, Jefferson wrote about the new election at length, discussing how its outcome had never been "a matter of doubt," how no arguments were wanting to reconcile him to relinquishing the first office, or "acquiescence under the second." In fact, with regard to the presidency, he thought it was "impossible that a more solid unwillingness settled on full calculation, could have existed in any man's mind, short of the degree of absolute refusal," than his own. He had, however, no feelings that would "revolt at a secondary position." Being Adams's junior in years, in Congress, in diplomatic service, and in civil government, he assured Madison that pride did not enter into this "estimate."[7]

It was in the last part that Jefferson explained his reasons for the enclosure of his letter to John. He wished Madison "to possess the actual state of dispositions" between himself and John. More important, he asked that Madison return the letter "if anything should render the delivery of it ineligible" in his opinion. And for someone who protested his innocence of all political machinations, Jefferson was amazingly current. Under certain circumstances, he suggested to Madison, concessions to Adams might be appropriate:

> If Mr. Adams can be induced to administer the government on its true principles, and to relinquish his bias to an English constitution, it is to be considered whether it would not be on the whole for the public good to come to a good understanding with him as to his future elections. He is perhaps the only sure barrier against Hamilton's getting in. . . .[8]

In contrast with Jefferson's disingenuous behavior over their eroded friendship, both Abigail and John discussed the dismaying breach with honorable sincerity. How this awkward state would affect their relationships in neighboring and highest government offices was explored for months after the election with various friends. Of several, including Tristam Dalton, John's Harvard classmate, a United States Senator, and General Henry Knox, it was Elbridge Gerry who assumed the role of confidant and arbitrator, who made prolonged attempts to explain the one to the other in his letters to Jefferson, Abigail, and John. The respectful replies of the Adamses to this venerable friend amply reveal the acute sensitivity of the problem he so sincerely meant to solve. Abigail was candid but affectionate about Jefferson in her letter to Gerry of December 31, 1796:

> I fully agree with you in sentiment as it respects the election of Mr. Jefferson. I have long known him, and entertain for him a personal friendship, and tho I cannot accord with him in some of his politicks, I do not believe him culpable to the extent he has been represented. Placed at the head of the Senate, I trust his conduct will be wise and prudent, and hope it will be a means of softening the animosity of party and of cementing and strengthening the bond of union.

As ever, Abigail did not evade a major point:

> There never was any publick or private animosity between Mr. Adams and Mr. Jefferson. Upon the subject of Pain's *Rights of Man* there was a disagreement in sentiment. Mr. Jefferson "does not look quite thro the deeds of men." Time has fully disclosed whose opinion was well founded.[9]

In general, John, too, discussed Jefferson with genuine regard, an almost contrived sense of optimism, and, given the record, eminent vulnerability. His reserves of bitterness were deep, however, and in rare moments he acknowledged their existence. Had Jay or some others in question been elected in his place, he would not have been "alarmed" for the public, though his vanity might have been "less modified" by such an event. But to see such a character as Jefferson, or such an unknown being as Pinckney, brought over his head and "trampling on the Bellies of hundreds of other men infinitely his superior in Talents, Services" filled him with apprehensions for the safety of all. He was convinced that if such a "project" had succeeded earlier, the Constitution could not have lasted four years, at which time the people of America would have been "set afloat and landed the Lord knows where."[10]

Despite this devastating confidence to General Knox at the end of March 1797, John was in a conciliatory frame of mind, judging from his other correspondence. He seemed to be counting on his "high" friendship with Jefferson to ward off the realities of recent truancies, though Jefferson's "entanglements with characters and politics" were admittedly a source of "inquietude and anxiety" and thought "pernicious." He was hopeful, however, that Jefferson's advancement to the vice-presidency, and his situation in the Senate, "an excellent School," would "correct" him and "keep him steady," despite the flattery of the too many French surrounding him. John optimistically summed up his position on Jefferson to Gerry on February 20, 1797:

> The cause of the irritation upon his nerves which broke out in
> some disagreeable appearances a few years ago is now removed.
> . . . I expect from his ancient friendship, his good sense and
> general good dispositions, a decorum of conduct at least if not as
> cordial and uniform a support as I have given to my predecessor,
> which is and shall be the pride and boast of my life. . . .[11]

Jefferson's response to Gerry's "dispositions" on the subject of John Adams was expectedly cordial, dissimulating, and ruinously prophetic. Knowing Adams's worth "as intimately and esteeming it as much as any one," Jefferson discounted all inferences of ambition or jealousy on his own part. As far as he was concerned, he assured Gerry, the second office of the government was "honourable and easy," the first but "a splendid misery": "You express apprehensions that stratagems will be used, to produce a misunderstanding between the President and myself. Though not a word having this tendency has ever been hazarded to me by any one, yet I consider as a certainty that nothing will be left untried to alienate him from me."[12]

In the course of his protracted letter to Gerry, Jefferson ignored the possibility that his recent correspondence with Madison, among others, might well have "hazarded" the "misunderstanding" between him and John Adams, and would encroach further. He also seemed to ignore a letter the past April that indeed proved him a master of the "stratagems" of alienation. To Philip Mazzei, his former neighbor, he had written:

> In place of that noble love of liberty and republican government which carried us triumphantly through the war, an Anglican monarchical aristocratical party has sprung up, whose avowed object is to draw over us the substance, as they have already done the forms, of the British government. The main body of our citizens, however, remain true to their republican principles; the whole landed interest is republican, and so is a great mass of talents. Against us are the Executive, the Judiciary, two out of three branches of the Legislature, all the officers of the government, all who want to be officers, all timid men who prefer the calm of despotism to the boisterous sea of liberty, British merchants and Americans trading on British capital, speculators and holders in the banks and public funds, a contrivance invented for the purposes of corruption, and for assimilating us in all things to the rotten as well as the sound parts of the British model.[13]

"It would give you a fever," Jefferson had continued, to name the "apostates" who had gone over to these "heresies," the "men who were Samsons in the field and Solomons in the council, but who have had their heads shorn by the harlot England." Though Jefferson avoided mention of John Adams, he achieved the effect of having spelled out his former friend's name in capital letters. Yet he seemed forgetful of the existence of this or any other negative expression, and a year later failed, in his letter to Gerry, to assume any responsibility for promoting the "tendency" toward the "misunderstanding" between himself and the President. On the contrary, it was more convenient for Jefferson to blame the "machinations" of the Hamiltonians who surrounded Adams, and who were "only a little less hostile" to the President than to himself. Unfortunately, at this time,

Jefferson's point was shrewdly made; Hamilton was a far more immediate threat to Adams than he himself.[14]

Inferences of intrigue on the part of Alexander Hamilton and his
followers were not, of course, news to Gerry, who had loyally reported the "active agent" to Abigail. Hamilton's mysterious allegiances during the presidential elections had raised grave doubts. As
John was a wholehearted admirer of Hamilton's newly conceived
banking system, the latter's support of Thomas Pinckney as the Federalists' candidate for President was indeed a puzzle. Surprisingly,
John adopted a seemingly benign attitude, choosing to speculate that
Hamilton had thought to vanquish Jefferson rather than him in his
support of Pinckney, or that he had favored closer connections with
Britain than he thought John "disposed" to foster.[15]

Abigail, however, took a very different tack regarding Hamilton's
defection. His political connivances made the presidency the "slippery precipice" Abigail had feared even before John's election. Now,
uninhibited by sentiment, as in Jefferson's case, she lashed out in fury
at this faithless colleague. Speculating on Pinckney's attraction for
Hamilton, she wrote to Gerry on December 31, 1796:

> There are some characters more subtle than others, more easily
> wrought upon, more accomodating, more complying. Such a
> person might be considered as the ostensible engine which a
> Master Hand could work. To what other motive can be ascribed
> the Machiavelian policy of placing at the head of the Government a
> gentleman not particularly distinguished for any important services
> to his country, and scarcely heard of beyond the State which gave
> him birth until sent upon a publick embassy.[16]

Given Abigail's anxieties about the hazards of office, age, and her
poor health, which was only accentuated by Philadelphia's seasonal
heat and disease, retirement to Braintree seemed more "eligible" to
her on the eve of the presidency. She harbored no illusions whatsoever about the "elevated seat" to be occupied by her husband; she
judged it as a "mark at which envy, pride and malevolence will shoot
their envenomed arrows." Regardless, she did not permit alternate
choices. While her "desire and wish to shine in public Life" was
"wholly extinguished," she confided to Gerry, she personally considered herself "as the small dust of the balance; when compared to the
interests of a nation. To preserve peace, to support order, and con-

tinue to the country that system of government under which it has become prosperous and happy" was life's purpose. "The sacrifice of an individual life," on the contrary, was important only to its near connections, and "ought not to be taken into consideration."[17]

The ultimate extent of Abigail's commitments was expressed in a magnificent letter to John, when they had been separated for three months. A beaming sun, streaming across her writing table, gave "honors" to this day on which he was to declare himself in the Senate as head of the nation. She wrote on February 8, 1797:

> My thoughts and my meditations are with you, though personally
> absent; and my petitions to Heaven are, that "the things which
> made for peace may not be hidden from your eyes." My feelings
> are not those of pride or ostentation, upon the occasion. They are
> solemnized by a sense of the obligations, the important trusts, and
> numerous duties connected with it. That you may be enabled to
> discharge them with honor to yourself, with justice and impartiality
> to your country, and with satisfaction to this great people, shall be
> the daily prayer of your A.A.[18]

On the following day, February 9, the official announcement of his election having been made, John sent off a brief note to Abigail: "The die is cast," he wrote, "and you must prepare yourself for honorable trials." He also said they must wait to know whether Congress would do anything about helping them to furnish their house. If it didn't, he would have no house before the next fall, and then "a very moderate one, with very moderate furniture." By March 5, the housing question was answered; they would occupy the Washingtons' dwelling. John also confided that he had never had a more trying day than the previous one, his inaugural day, March 4.[19]

John did not sleep well the night before; in fact, he thought he might faint during the delivery of his inaugural address. But he did get through it and reported that there was scarcely a dry eye at the ceremony in the House of Representatives in Philadelphia, except, perhaps, in the case of Washington, who looked as "serene and unclouded as the day." It was John's impression that he even seemed to enjoy "some sort of triumph" over him, as though saying to his successor, "I am fairly out and you fairly in! See which of us will be happiest."[20]

John's inaugural speech commemorated the justice of the country's Revolutionary War. He also spoke of the future, of an "inflexible determination to maintain peace and inviolable faith with all nations," and to maintain "neutrality and impartiality" among the belligerent powers of Europe. He mentioned his "attachment" to the Constitution of the United States and a "conscientious determination to support it, until it shall be altered by the judgments and the wishes of the people." He also spoke of an "equal and impartial regard to the rights, interests, honor, and happiness of all the States of the Union, without preference or regard to a northern, or southern, eastern or western position." He expressed "personal esteem" for the French nation and a "sincere desire to preserve the friendship" that had done so much for the "honor and interest" of both nations. Not least, he spoke of a citizen, without mentioning President Washington by name, whose actions, regulated by "prudence, justice, temperance, and fortitude," had led a people to "independence and peace, to increasing wealth and unexampled prosperity."[21]

"All agree that, taken altogether," John wrote to Abigail, his inaugural day was "the sublimest thing ever exhibited in America." Four days later, however, he was far from exultant. According to a general report, there was more weeping at his inaugural address than ever seen "at the representation of any tragedy." But whether it was from grief or joy was the question on his mind. Whether it was due to the loss of their beloved President, or the accession of an unbeloved one, or to the pleasure of exchanging Presidents peaceably, or to the novelty of the thing, he just could not say. One thing he knew: he was too sensitive to act well in such an "exhibition." Perhaps there was little danger of his having another such scene to "feel or behold," he speculated. Two or three people did venture to whisper in his ear that his speech had made an agreeable impression. Now, however, as of March 17, the world was "as silent as the grave."[22]

John, disturbed by the sudden "stillness and silence," turned to Abigail, as always. There was a desperate tone to his letters. The President's house was not ready; he was constantly busy at business mostly new to him; the weather was bad; the news wasn't pleasant; he had a "great" cold. He was cryptic about his meeting with the Vice-President, saying only, "He is as he was."[23]

From what John could see and hear and read, the Federalists were afraid to approve of anybody but Washington, and the Jacobin papers damned with faint praise and undermined with "misrepresentation and insinuation." John sounded naïve, bewildered, almost inadequate, even sullen. The future was suddenly dark and secretive and ominous. He foresaw a "scene of ambition" beyond all his former "suspicions or imaginations" and a government, therefore, about to turn "topsy-turvy." He made doomful predictions about the next election. Anglophiles would back Jay or Hamilton, and Francophiles would support Jefferson, "and all the corruption of Poland would be introduced" unless the American spirit rose and said, "We will have neither John Bull nor Louis Baboon." Even now, so transparently threatened by Jefferson, he told Abigail that if the Federalists took to "playing pranks," he would resign office to let his former friend lead the people "to peace, wealth and power if he will." However prepared John thought himself, he was unprepared: "Jealousies and rivalries, have been my theme, and checks and balances as their antidotes till I am ashamed to repeat the words: but they never stared me in the face in such horrid forms as at present."[24]

In this downcast state, John yearned for Abigail's "invaluable" company and support, as ardently as he had in his youth when an ocean sprawled between them, and he mentioned this in every letter. He appreciated that Abigail was home nursing his mortally ill mother, but he was impatient. "I must go to you or you must come to me. I cannot live without you till October," he wrote on March 13, 1797. One month later, not knowing his mother was dead as of April 21, and that Abigail would come, John pleaded again for attention: "It seems to me that the mother and the daughter ought to think a little of the president as well as the husband. His cares! his anxieties! his health? Don't laugh. His comfort; that his head may be clear and his heart firm, ought to be thought on more than the husband."[25]

Abigail wrote to John on April 26, a day before her departure, saying that her "agitated" mind wanted repose. She had buried their aged parent and a niece. She was free to come to him; she no longer suffered "apprehensions" that either of her charges would be lost without her care. Echoing bygone times, she reassured John: "I want no courting to come. I am ready and willing to follow my husband wherever he chooses."[26]

At noon on Thursday, May 4, Abigail reached the Smiths' residence in Eastchester, that family having returned from England after less than a year's stay. Mrs. Smith, the mother now of a two-year-old redheaded daughter, Caroline Amelia, born 1795, appeared to be in good health, though "fleshy" and morbidly silent, her heart apparently "too full" to discuss her plight. The colonel was absent, visiting properties elsewhere. Just what properties these were, or their status,

Abigail was too polite to question. But she was dismally aware that her daughter's fortunes had once again plummeted. It was astonishing to think that just a few years ago, on their return from England, Abigail's principal worry, thoroughly articulated by John, was how to curb the colonel's flamboyant display of wealth. Given to riding about in a coach-and-four, full of "monarchical trumpery," disdainful of government "favors" (meaning appointments), the colonel soon was the recipient of explicit advice from his father-in-law. "Tell not of your prosperity, because it will make two men mad to one glad," John had warned, "nor of your adversity, for it will make two men glad to one sad."[27]

The colonel's excessive appetites betrayed "weakness" and "too little knowledge of the world; too little penetration; too little discretion," John complained to Abigail. Yet there was a strain in this obviously flawed character that appealed to the critical father-in-law, who admitted as much. "I wish, however, that my boys had a little more of his activity," John said. They were overprotective parents, he implied, suggesting to Abigail that he might soon treat his sons as the pigeons treat their squabs: "Push them off the limb, and make them put out their wings or fall."[28]

All this was a sampling of what had gone before; present circumstances "depresst" Abigail's already "too low" spirits and robbed her appetite. If the mother could not find the words appropriate for discussion with her daughter, she could confide unsparingly in her sisters. Mrs. Smith was the blameless victim of "folly and madness of speculation and extravagance," who had been educated in different "habits" from those her husband would accustom her to. Yet now, alone with her children, she was paying dearly for the life of dissipation she had never enjoyed. A ray of hope was provided by the boys, but certainly the grandmother was not free of worries on their behalf. As though the atmosphere at the Smiths' was contaminated, Abigail wished her grandsons might be sent away to live with her sister Elizabeth, widowed and now remarried in 1795 to the Reverend Stephen Peabody of Atkinson, New Hampshire. Abigail was certain the influences in that household would be more wholesome. In this helpless and hopeless frame of mind, Abigail continued on to New York. There she was somewhat cheered at seeing her son Charles, his baby, and his wife, Sarah, a younger sister of Colonel Smith's whom she found surprisingly "discreet" and "quite different from many of the Family."[29]

On Wednesday morning, May 10, Abigail concluded her two-week journey from Braintree. Her party of thirteen, including the Briesler family—Mr. Briesler she continued to find indispensable to the "Wheels" of the President's family—was met by John about twenty-five miles outside of Philadelphia. Abigail promptly left her carriage for his, stopped for dinner in Bristol, then suffered a hazardous road the rest of the way, furrowed to a depth of two feet by torrential rains. At sunset the Adamses reached the ample brick mansion on the corner of Sixth and Market streets, recently vacated by the Washingtons.[30]

Worn emotionally and physically, Abigail spent two days in bed recovering from her travels. But shortly she was caught up in events, and plotted her days in timetable order within the third week of her arrival. She rose at 5:00 A.M., ate breakfast at eight, tended to family arrangements until eleven, then dressed for the day. She received callers, an average of sixty a day, from noon until two or three, dined, then paid her own calls, or simply drove out for pleasure, until seven. She was also committed to dinners of almost forty guests with some regularity (though she complained that her drawing room was not yet furnished), including the Cabinet of five, thirty-two senators, and the Vice-President. Finding suitable domestics was still a problem, though Briesler, to Abigail's relief, did the hiring and dismissing among a "very sad set of creatures." At the end of May, despite her complex responsibilities, Abigail would claim she felt "less anxiety" about the ceremonial part of her duties, though she certainly did not minimize them. She was reminded that Uncle Tufts's wife had once "stiled" her niece's situation as a state of "splendid misery"—unknowingly echoing Jefferson's description to Elbridge Gerry of the presidency—and thought this description "not far from Truth." On the whole, though reasonably settled, Abigail was considerably less charmed with Philadelphia this time around. Mostly, it was changed because speculation in property, politics, and religion had gone far, in her judgment, in "depraving" the morals of the higher classes. There was a tawdry aspect to Philadelphia; in her less charitable moments she pronounced the city as "vile and debauched as the city of London."[31]

Generally it was Abigail's custom, once the details of her household were neatly drawn, to look to a broader canvas. Even John commented on her "admirable faculty" of employing her mind, and on her studious addiction to "scribbling" letters to one member or another of her family, which would become the vivid and nearly weekly bulletins of his presidential years. With dauntless freedom, Abigail reported now about friends and, even more often, about foes —brilliant testimonies of her political curiosity and monolithic loyalty to her husband, which would not tolerate a ripple, let alone a gust of criticism. Her weather eye covered the French and the English, all nationalities of ships at sea, Indians at war, predators on Louisiana and other controversial territories, members of the Cabinet and Congress, and, precisely two months after the inauguration, the press, who had pained her before, but never with such nightmarish brutality.

The President was well aware that his entrance into office was marked by a misunderstanding with France, and he had written as much to John Quincy in March. At noon on May 16, he met with both houses at the first session of the Fifth Congress to explore a peaceful resolution of this grievous "misunderstanding." The facts were not promising. Angry members of the French Directory, lashing back at Jay's Treaty, at what they believed to be America's overly conciliatory settlement with Great Britain, not only refused to recognize America's minister to France, Washington's appointee, Charles Cotesworth Pinckney, but annulled the treaty of amity and commerce written into the Franco-American Alliance of 1778. Detaining hundreds of vessels previously granted freedom of the seas, capturing and plundering them, was indeed, at the least, conducive to misunderstanding, and, more realistically, to declaration of war. The President, however, was committed to the policy of neutrality he had helped Washington to nurture; salvation, to his mind, lay in negotiations rather than warfare. "Thrown on perilous Times," John proposed to send a commission to negotiate the alarming breach.[32]

Not surprisingly, Abigail believed John's proposal admirable, and was dismayed by those who thought otherwise. As a result, however, and as he had predicted, John was quickly acquitted of the "crime" of praise from the likes of the *Chronicle, Argus,* and *Aurora.* The Francophile press turned with sickening swiftness on the President who had committed the "unpardonable sin" of proclaiming that America was "just and impartial to foreign Nations." Though the Senate had backed the President, and despite ample evidence, including Pinckney's dispatches, of what Abigail considered the "unbecomeing and indignant conduct of France towards the United States," she was shocked to find there were factions so protective of French interests as to be willing to risk the lives and futures of Americans. An unquestionable leader in this divisive pursuit was Benjamin Franklin Bache, founder of the seven-year-old newspaper the *Aurora,* whom Abigail accused of opening the "batterys of abuse and scurility" for which John would serve as the unhappy and constant target.[33]

Her early and enduring fears were rudely affirmed. A press that had vilified the beloved President Washington could certainly be expected to turn on his successor. Just the past March 6, the *Aurora* carried an article applauding the end of Washington's service to his country. America's first President, it read, had "carried his designs against the public liberty so far as to have put in jeopardy its very existence." As a result, Bache, its publisher, was beaten by an angry reader, despite his disclaimer that one Dr. Michael Leib had printed the insult during his absence. Rather than being resolved, Abigail's fury was only heightened.[34]

She had been over this territory before, exploring at length, especially with her son Thomas, the principles that enabled a man, "not insensible to due praise," whatever criticism he might be subjected to, to concentrate on the "real good" of his fellow citizens. Of course, she had concluded, a man who attained eminence of "any kind, and by whatever means, even the most honorable," would be exposed to envy and jealousy. Steeling herself against Bache and his compatriots, Abigail dismissed their insults. "I can read them all with a true Phylosiphical contempt," she wrote Mrs. Cranch that June. Further, she would have liked them to know the President's true opinion of them: "Their praise for a few weeks mortified him, much more, than all their impudent abuse does." Shakespeare's *Julius Caesar* was her model:

> There is no terror, Cassius, *in your threats;*
> *For I am arm'd so strong in honesty*
> *That they pass by me as the Idle wind,*
> *Which I respect not.* [35]

For all of Abigail's studious rationalizations, she was, understandably, supremely miserable over the "low Billingsgate," the scathing language hawked at John's every move, and his family's as well. Determination was not enough to make her invincible. She studied the newspapers out of habit, and what she read crippled her composure and undermined her sense of security over what were to be catastrophic consequences.[36]

It was at the beginning of May 1797, while Congress deliberated America's course regarding the French, that the twenty-eight-year-old editor Benjamin Franklin Bache, nicknamed "Lightning-Rod Junior," with his illustrious grandfather in mind, went into full battle with President Adams. Filling columns of the *Aurora* with Anti-Federalist, anti-Adams propaganda, mimicking and mauling, Bache ignited such intense hatred on Abigail's part that he might have been shooting bullets instead of words.[37]

A President who considered France's refusal to receive the American minister as the "denial of a right" must be in his dotage, Bache suggested. Also, any advocate of Jay's Treaty must be "as foolish as the napping old negro woman," and furthermore, Jay had been sent to the Court of St. James "to throw himself on the magnanimity of the British Kings." Without hesitation, Bache went on to clarify—in five columns, in one instance— his belief that America had therefore given improper advantages to the enemy and violated its faith with the French, who justifiably declared all "common intercourse at an end." Was this the "denial of a right" on the part of the French Republic? Bache asked. Such "round assertions" might answer Mr. Adams's purposes to a degree, he concluded, but their influence must be "very limited and of transitory duration," for "they cannot deceive long."[38]

Needless to say, Abigail found Bache incorrigible and his insults insufferable. He insisted that the President held out the idea of negotiation only to "deceive" the American people, that his protestations were so much "Presidential War Whoop" in which his peace initiatives masked preparations for war. Adams could talk all he wished of foreign influence, but what a pity, said Bache, that he was not as free from British influence as from French. The President did not mention a word about British depredations, Bache challenged, "and yet Mr. A. is not under foreign influence!!!" Bache posed a question to his readers, simultaneously providing a taunting answer: "Does Mr. A suppose that 'the most enlightened nation upon earth' is to be gulled by such bare faced artifice?" If he can believe this, he must suppose himself the President of a nation of *Ourang Outangs* instead of men." Unsatiated, Bache would call Adams a "hypocrite for the purposes of the basest deception," and remind him, at still another time, that "His Serene highness" was "the President by three votes" and never the choice of Pennsylvania.[39]

May 31, 1797, was the official date of President Adams's appointment of a commission to heal America's crippled relations and to secure a treaty of commerce and amity with France. As Abigail predicted, the designation of the three envoys extraordinary, including Charles Cotesworth Pinckney of South Carolina, as with every other governmental measure, was indeed "censured by those who made a point of abusing every thing." On the whole, Abigail was comfortable with the appointees. John Marshall, the lawyer from Virginia, she judged a "very fair and Honorable man, and truly American," who would meet with no objection—unless it was that he was not Frenchman enough for those who preferred to send Jefferson or Madison, among others of similar sentiments. When Francis Dana turned down the appointment on grounds of health, Abigail recognized that his substitute, Elbridge Gerry, was controversial. Not a sound Republican and "at least an unsound Federalist," or so it was said, he could count opponents on both sides. But Abigail was firm. She had great confidence that John would not have nominated Gerry if he did not believe him to be an honest man and a friend to his country who could be neither "deceived nor warped."[40]

As Abigail assumed, the newspapers did not hesitate to "abuse" John's appointment. Nearly daily, Bache proclaimed that "if ever a man playd the hipocrite for the purposes of the basest deception the President by three votes is the man." Bache's assaults, however, were neither unexpected or unique. Abigail was also infuriated by the "misrepresentations" of Peter Porcupine, the pen name of the English-born William Cobbett, who advertised at the beginning of the year, in the pages of the *Aurora,* the provocative premise of his new publication, *Porcupine's Gazette & Daily Advertiser.* It was Porcupine's contention that newspapers had done Americans "more real injury than all its open enemies," and that they misled the people at home and misrepresented them abroad. Furthermore, these "vehicles of sedition and discord" had encouraged the Western territories to rebel, had given rise to the depredations of Britain "by exciting the people to such acts of violence against that nation, as left her no room to doubt that we were determined on war." At the conclusion of his editorial, Porcupine, aptly named, bristled for the kill. He mentioned the existence of a party in America "who favour monarchy and aristocracy," and, without naming John Adams, though the implication was obvious, wondered whether its members ought not to be considered "traitors."[41]

By June, Abigail saw the task of the President as "very arduous, very perplexing and very hazardous." He needed a rest, and respite from Philadelphia's heat. She too needed a change; she longed for her rosebush, her clover field, the "retirement" of Quincy, and a chance to talk to her sisters and friends. If she appeared homesick in her letters, it was because she was worn with criticism, shrill with anger. Attacks based on political differences were difficult enough to weather, but those that pierced the family domain, such as Bache's criticism of John Quincy's recent nomination as minister plenipotentiary to the court of Berlin, drew blood.[42]

Abigail was extraordinarily sensitive on the subject of family appointments, singularly so in the case of John Quincy. She and John took great pride in the letter George Washington wrote at the end of his term in office regarding their son. If his wishes were of any avail, it was the departing President's "strong hope" that his successor would not withhold "merited promotion" from Mr. John Quincy Adams because he was his son. Washington had elaborated this point on February 20, 1797: "Without intending to compliment the father or the mother, or to censure any others, I give it as my decided opinion that Mr. Adams is the most valuable public character we have abroad, and that he will prove himself to be the ablest of all our diplomatic corps. . . ."[43]

John Quincy himself plainly and firmly expressed his private feelings on several occasions when he discussed his career with his mother. After he had been notified of his transfer from The Hague to Portugal, his letter to Abigail of November 14, 1796, bordered on the sarcastic:

> The appointment to the mission of Portugal I find from your letter was, as I had before concluded, unknown to my father. I have already written you upon the subject, and I hope, my ever dear and honored mother, that you are fully convinced from my letters which you have before this received, that upon the contingency of my father's being placed in the first magistracy, I shall never give him any trouble by solicitation for office of any kind. Your late letters have repeated so many times that I shall in that case have nothing to *expect*, that I am afraid you have imagined it possible that I might form expectations from such an event. . . . I had hoped that *my mother* knew me better that she did do me the justice to believe that I have not been so totally regardless or forgetful of the principles which education had instilled, nor so totally destitute

of a *personal* sense of delicacy, as to be susceptible of a wish tending in that direction.[44]

It was no wonder that Abigail, knowing the background of her son's appointment, and his own sensitivity about his position, was crushed by the "misrepresentations" of the press. She sensed the "spirit of envy and Jealousy operating," and accused Bache, who was "never at a loss for a lye," of getting his news "wholesale." There was a perfectly plausible reason for John Quincy's seemingly abrupt change of missions from Lisbon to Berlin. In the President's judgment, the north of Europe was "more interesting" than the south "at present," the neutral powers of Denmark, Sweden, and Prussia being more naturally allied to American interests. John Quincy, therefore, with his "talents, Sagacity and Industry," might be more profitably engaged in collecting and transmitting intelligence of the "views and designs" of those courts and nations. The role of the King of Prussia in future relations with France and England was crucial; the emperors of Russia and Germany were "important luminaries for the political telescope." In short, as the President explained to his son, "the future system of Europe and how we can preserve friendship with them all, and be most useful to them all," was the sum of his latest assignment. To have so purposeful a mission undermined was an outrage, and Abigail confided as much to Mrs. Cranch. "But Malevelence is unbounded," she concluded at the end of this sorry tale, without realizing the ugly dimensions of her complaint until not quite a week later.[45]

Abigail sat down to read the July 7 edition of Boston's *Independence Chronicle & Universal Advertiser* and rose in fury and disbelief. Incredibly, the "impudent" Bache's *Aurora* had been surpassed in its insulting practices. Judging from the day's contents, the editor of the *Chronicle* achieved "more of the true spirit of Satin" than even Bache by combining the poisonous "billingsgate of all the Jacobin papers" with "Lies, falshoods, calimny and bitterness of his own." How could she judge otherwise? For what other purpose could he print a paragraph about how the President was to receive $114,000 for his four-year term? As everyone knew, the salary was the same "Nominal" sum granted to President Washington, without half the value. Furthermore, the money was no more the President's than the money voted to rig one of the frigates being built at that moment. Every dollar was at the country's disposal, to be accurately accounted for.[46]

Compounding the insult, the *Chronicle* attacked John Quincy, claiming that the twenty-three-year-old son of the President was receiving a salary of ten thousand dollars a year, as though it were a personal grant from his father. Actually, John Quincy was ten days short of turning thirty, and salaries such as his were settled by law. Furthermore, a resident minister received $4,500 yearly, and a minister plenipotentiary, $9,000. John Quincy's fault lay in his being the President's son rather than in his being singled out for a larger salary. Abigail wished that she could somehow get the papers to print the truth; she thought the "mischief" due to lack of inquiry into facts. But she despaired of being able to rectify matters, and repeated her now practiced vow that her family "addhere" to duty and keep themselves "unprejuced" [unprejudiced] as the best means of survival.[47]

With little or no respite from the press, however, Abigail was increasingly embittered. Never one to nurture her grudges in secret, she confided to her cousin, the merchant William Smith, her solution for dealing with that "contemptible Hireling" Bache and his associates. It was her recommendation that the "triumvirate" of printers in Boston, New York, and Philadelphia "richly" deserved that "French Freedom and *Liberty*" exercised against the eighteen or twenty printers in France. Not one to turn the other cheek gracefully, Abigail could not let Bache's reference to John and herself as "Darby and Joan" slide by without comment. One line of Henry Woodfall's ballad about "The Happy Old Couple" surfaced: "When Darby's pipe's out, Joan won't smoke a whiff more"; for the rest, Abigail sought Mrs. Cranch's research. Fully attuned to the ridicule intended, Abigail seized the chance to repay Benjamin Franklin's grandson by commenting on a void in his existence. Abigail considered Bache's "polite allusion," in contrast with Franklin's dubious marital status, "highly honorary to the domestic and conjugal Character of the President who has never given His Children or Grandchildren cause to Blush for any illegitimate offspring."[48]

Abigail was relieved to survive the celebrations of the Fourth of July more easily than she had anticipated. Fortunately, the weather was cooler than its usual "Bake House" temperature, but, in general, she thought the day a "tedious" one. Washington had set the style that she was obliged to continue—a costly one, involving the expenditure of five hundred dollars to provide the two hundred pounds of cake and two quarter casks of wine, besides spirits, that were consumed.

Counting the governor, the military, and all of Congress, the guest list averaged 150 people, and Abigail, who dreaded the day, admitted to moments when she thought "President Washington to blame for introducing the custom, if he could have avoided it."[49]

Once this celebration was out of the way, Abigail focused on Quincy. She worried about the President's health and thought it "absolutely necessary" that he return home. Her need was equal to his; she cherished, as always, every mention of her garden, particularly her rosebush, and yearned to "enhale one & taste the other." She sent instructions ahead for preparation: she wished to have her house whitewashed, and she required more female help, particularly a cook; she hoped some black woman in Boston would undertake the job for two months. Mattresses needed to be put on featherbeds; extra beds needed to go into the new "out Chamber" for the male servants. Wine could be drawn from casks in the cellar; punch was to be made by the gallon, with brandy added. Also, a quarter-cask of Madeira wine must be purchased for immediate use, along with quantities of flour, loaf sugar, brown sugar, coffee, Hyson and Souchong teas, crackers, and dozens of lemons. She did not forget to request oats, without which the coachman and horses would be "undone."[50]

Plans for home always reminded Abigail of her children. She had arranged, in fact, to have Mrs. Smith and the infant Caroline stay with her in Quincy. At first thought, her association of Mrs. Smith's family with those of John Greenleaf, Robert Morris, and their partner, John Nicholson, seemed remote, as her son-in-law, the colonel, was not connected with their case. As the bankruptcy proceedings involving the three men unfolded, however, it was apparent that Abigail's almost fanatical preoccupation with its sordid details had a drab logic of its own.[51]

Because of the collapse of the North American Land Company and its grand-scale speculations in Northwestern real estate, both Greenleaf and Morris would be locked in debtors' prison, the latter for more than three years, before the Federal Bankruptcy Act of 1800 effected his release. And for Abigail, in the aftermath, to visit Morris's wife, Maria, the sister of William White, Pennsylvania's first Protestant Episcopal bishop, was a wrenching experience. The companion of her youth, in Abigail's memory "gay and blithe as a bird, blooming as a rose in June," had faded to a pale, dejected figure, the image of that of her own daughter, the colonel's wife. Abigail searched Maria Morris's situation for intimations of Mrs. Smith's fate, and made no secret of her profound worry for the one with whom she was "more closely connected." With "one bubble bursting after an other," Abigail pondered a lesson lost on both the Morris and Smith families. They ought to have been taught, she said, that all speculative wealth had a "shallow foundation."[52]

Gray melancholy ignited to white fury when Abigail turned to the subject of William Blount, senator from Tennessee, and his "diabolical plot." A letter from the senator to the Cherokee Nation had been intercepted and forwarded to the President, who, in turn, sent it on to the Senate. Its contents, disclosed to the public on July 6, 1797, told of Blount's attempts to enlist the Creeks and Cherokees to help the British gain the Spanish territories of West Florida. "When shall we cease to have Judases?" Abigail worried, considering the incident an insult not only to her country but to her husband in particular, providing "a glorious kettle for the Jacobines to swim in." Though she was comforted to learn that the British had not accepted Blount's services, she wished only the worst of punishments for this disgraceful public servant who had been arrested for debt on four different occasions. The Senate would expel Blount, she predicted, and she was positive it was the responsibility of the House to impeach him.[53]

"We are in perils by Land, and we are in perils by sea, and in perils from false Breathren," Abigail concluded after the exposure of Blount's treachery. Nor was she alone in her fears; they were seriously confirmed by Oliver Wolcott, the Secretary of the Treasury. Knowing of the Adamses' plans to return to Quincy that summer, Wolcott was said to be "anxious" about the President going so far from the seat of government "at so critical period." Abigail must have given Wolcott's thoughts—which, in hindsight, might have been interpreted as a warning—at least passing weight, as she did mention them in a letter to Mrs. Cranch. But the next sentence, written as though to soothe Wolcott's fears or perhaps her own, assured her sister that her husband would never leave his ministers if he thought his presence necessary. Her fatigue—she wrote with desperation of her need to escape the heat and the oncoming "sickly season," and of her chronic "Complaints of the Bowels"—undoubtedly blurred her judgment.[54]

In truth, she could hardly wait to leave Philadelphia to forget the prospects of "an Indian war on all sides," of the threats of "quarrel with Spain," of, all in all, "so many affairs so very critical" occurring daily. She spoke longingly of her need for a sea breeze and for the comforts of family friendship. Her scathing impatience with Congress was recorded for the benefit of William Smith weeks before. On June 10 she had written:

> We hope that Congress will be *warmed* out of the city by the middle of July. I *believe* they will rise before, not by accomplishing the business but by not doing it, this dead weight of Pennsilvanna consisting of members who are always opposed to every riming proposition, more Jacobins than any other city, who all wish to see our Government prostrate, and a proportionable part of timid men who fear offending the terrible nation. All these causes have their influence upon a proportion of those members who wish for an excuse to rise without doing anything more than negotiate. . . .

Plainly, Abigail felt shortchanged and knew the reasons why:

> We want more men of *deeds,* and fewer of words—a speech which space take[s] up ten collums of a newspaper and part of an additional supplement must contain very weighty and important matter indeed to induce people to hear it patiently, or read it afterward.

But on July 19, she wrote Smith in an entirely different vein:

> You must not think me too variable when I inform you that the wind has changed to the Northward, and that if no western or southern gale assails us we propose sitting our Faces towards you on the beginning of next week. . . .[55]

The main event of the summer of 1797 was, in family terms, the news of John Quincy's marriage to Louisa Catherine Johnson in London on Thursday, July 26. The President supposed the "match" had grown out of a spark kindled at Nantes in 1779—a faint one indeed, as Louisa had been four years old at the time—when he and the twelve-year-old John Quincy had visited the Johnsons on their return to America. Louisa was the second oldest among seven daughters and one son of the prosperous Joshua Johnson, whose brother Thomas was governor of his birthplace, Maryland. Johnson, originally employed in London as factor of an Annapolis shipping firm, had waited out the Revolution in Nantes. Then, at Washington's appointment on August 7, 1790, he served as American consul in London, until the year of Louisa Catherine's marriage.[56]

The consul's ample house, staffed with eleven servants and located near the Tower of London, was not only convenient but inviting. John Quincy found his way there on his return from Holland, the morning of November 11, 1795. He was twenty-eight years old on his reintroduction to the Johnson family. Louisa Catherine was twenty, with dark cascading curls, angelic cheeks, and pleading eyes. Her grandson Henry likened her to a Romney portrait as a bride, and to a figure of delicate Sèvres porcelain in old age. The news of the romance came as a surprise to Abigail, still worrying over the an-guished tone of her son's most recent letter. Owing to the usual two- to three-month delay between the mailing and delivery of letters, her calming words were no sooner dispatched than she received the next installment from her son insinuating a special interest in an "amiable young lady."[57]

Until now, John Quincy, serving his country abroad, had viewed himself as a "banished man condemned in foreign climes to roam." His brother Charles mourned with great sensitivity that his brother's "virtue and genius and talent" seemed "doomed" to vegetate in foreign soil. To remove a twenty-eight-year-old American from his country to be "in a measure" forgotten by his fellow men, to deprive him of "that domestic happiness" for which youth "so ardently sigh[s]," was a cruelty for which the honor of the appointment could scarcely compensate. The comparison was indeed dramatic. Charles was settled in a mutually devoted, loving marriage, able to support his wife with a "charming prospect" of putting something by in his youth for "the wintry blasts" of age; by contrast, John Quincy was far away, "unconnected with the woman he most admired, supported on a bare maintenance." John Quincy would forgive him, he hoped, "if I exhibit a wish too ardent for your concern."[58]

It was Charles's marriage to the "choice of his heart" that had "awakened the dormant feelings of your soul," Abigail assured John Quincy, "and uncovered the fire which smothered, gleamd up again, upon the recollection of the sacrifice you had made." His reaction was "natural," she said, and despite his remorse that "stern pru-dence" had quenched the "unwilling flame"—undoubtedly a refer-ence to Mary Frazier—all was not lost. There was still time, despite his conviction that "sincere friendships" were more generally found at an early age, when the heart was "tender soft and unsuspicious . . . before Ambition and avarice freeze up the generous current of the Soul." He was not to despair, therefore, of one day feeling a similar regard for a "kindred soul" yet in reserve for him. Meanwhile, she clearly was hoping that he would remain single; his destiny was to be considered. That "particular providence" which presided over all creatures had some demands upon him, and called him to exercise those talents entrusted to him. These could better be performed in a single state than a married one.[59]

Abigail again referred obliquely to Mary Frazier as she continued, reminding her son that a "connection" at that earlier period of his life would have "embarrassed you, and greatly frustrated your future usefulness." It was her advice to "let the consciousness of having acted right console you." Conceding that she might be encouraging false hope, she believed the "object of his regard would never connect herself while he remain single." Then again, Abigail speculated, this "object" might not appear to him in a few years with all those "outward attractions" that the bloom of eighteen years had given her. Still, Abigail remained even-handed, musing that "Time will dim the Lusture of the Eye, and wither the bloom of the face, tho it may perfect and mature those mental attractions which yeald a more permanent and solid satisfaction, when the ardour of passion setles into the more lasting union of Friendship."[60]

It was in May that his parents realized John Quincy was not quite the pitiable fellow they fretted about. Beginning with letters dated from February 20, 1796, he hinted repeatedly at his new situation. During the mild winter "beyond all example" he could hardly "snatch" so much as a quarter of an hour to write even a short letter. Perhaps he might give the reason for this at a future time, "or perhaps you may guess at it without being told." Another letter mentioned Louisa Catherine Johnson as having chosen, with her mother, cloaks for Abigail and Cousin Louisa. He said the Copley family was well, but "perhaps you will hear of another family that has been still more attractive to me; but of this I may write more on a future occasion." Still another time he said he considered the birth of a son to his cousin as a "sort of reflection upon me; for a good example always contains a censure upon a bad practice." In exhilarated spirits he had begun, he informed his mother, "to think very seriously of the duty incumbent upon all good citizens to have a family. . . ." If she thought this was the language of a convert, he invited her to inquire "how he became so," though he thought he was not yet prepared to answer that.[61]

Reactions of both parents to John Quincy's inferences were equivocal, to say the least. His father wrote back that his son's last letter to his mother had caused him to "suspect" that "some family—or other afforded the means of making your winter in London tolerable at least." The same letter caused his mother to surmise that her son was not so proficient in the maxims of Horace and Pope as he flattered himself. "Some fair one has shown you its sophistry, and taught you to admire. Youth and beauty have penetrated through your fancied apathy and you find yourself warmed by one and invigorated by another, as you tell me that the enthusiasm of youth has subsided." Still unwilling to relinquish her vision of John Quincy as a patriot and a public man—a public trust, in a sense—Abigail hoped "for the love I bear my Country that the Syren is at least half Blood." And at the bottom of the letter she added a forlorn parenthetical sentence, alluding most likely to Mary Frazier: "(Marie—has she no claims)?"[62]

There was no question that Abigail was uneasy about John Quincy's foreign "connection." Though she had not heard so much as a "lisp" from anyone but himself, she wrote John Quincy that she was persuaded it was one of the Misses Johnson who had become his "flame." "Have I guest right?" she asked. "Whom you call yours shall be mine also," she offered cordially. He had sufficient years to judge for himself, only, she added, "Weight well. Consider maturely of the most important actions of your Life." Some weeks later, when she presumed that John Quincy had returned to The Hague, she wrote Thomas that she wished his brother might not have "staid too long in England for the peace of his mind and the tranquility of his Heart," as, from some hints in his last letter, she inferred that Cupid has "new bent his Bow, nor misd his aim." She also said she hoped "however my dear Thomas" that he would be "proof" against Cupid's shafts until he returned to his native land, and there "chuse a wife whose habits tastes & sentiments are calculated for the meridian of your Country."[63]

As soon as he became aware of his mother's reservations, John Quincy sought to ease them as thoughtfully as he knew how. A solicitous and sensitive son, he wrote with amazing candor, considering the complexity of his position:

> Your apprehensions as to the Tastes & sentiments of my friend;
> your fears that they may be Anti American or liable to contrast too
> strong an attachment to the tinsel of courts was perfectly natural,

and all your observations on the subject were received by me with gratitude, as I know them to proceed from serious concern and the purest parental affection. I should be a bold man indeed to affirm that there is no ground for them; that the Lady is Superior to such attractions and despises such splendour.—But she has goodness of heart & gentleness of disposition as well as spirit and discretion and with those qualities I shall venture upon the chances of success, and hope you will find her [to] prove such a daughter as you would wish for your son.[64]

John Quincy, when abruptly called back to The Hague in June 1796, had asked Louisa Catherine to accept his portrait, as a "token of affection [that] will cease only with the last pulse of the heart of him whose image it is." He hoped it would often meet her eye with half the delight he derived from looking at a corresponding pledge, her miniature. "Albeit unused to the melting mood, I found the separation not a little painful," he confided to his mother, to whom he painstakingly unburdened the logistics of his immediate future.[65]

This was to be, first of all, a temporary situation. The reason was plain. Though older with this second love, John Quincy was no wealthier and could not support a family on the salary he received. And while the "matrimonial propensity" was "irresistible" to him, he had "very reluctantly," owing to the *"Grace of consideration,"* concluded that he might not yet take upon himself the encumbrance of a family. Despite postponement, John Quincy left his mother in no doubt that his affections "have taken their direction, and if those with which they have been returned can stand the test of an absence which must be of indefinite duration, you may consider my choice as irrevocably fixed."[66]

In his own thoughts, John Quincy's plans were firm. He proposed to complete the three years he had originally planned to devote to his present mission. Meanwhile, he intended to explore opportunities that would afford him the means to support a wife. He knew that he could always return to the bar, but felt keenly that these years abroad, years of "total abandonment" of both the practice and study of the law, had deprived him of whatever fitness he had for a profession that, in truth, held little appeal for him in the first place. In his search for a profitable future, he allowed that he might be induced to settle in one of the Southern states. John Quincy hesitated as he wrote these last words. Going south would take him a great distance from home, his beloved "native spot," and "more especially from you," he told his mother. He also admitted that it must seem like ingratitude or want of public spirit for him to be thinking along these new lines.[67]

John Quincy had anticipated a difficult "test of absence" in his relationship with Louisa Catherine. The hazards of separation, however, were as nothing in the face of the trauma caused by the extraordinary event of the collapse of Joshua Johnson's finances. In less than a year, John Quincy, the debonair bridegroom-to-be, the yearning family man, the aspiring private entrepreneur, vanished as abruptly as he had materialized, a charming but illusory figure destroyed along with his father-in-law's fortune. The effects of these catastrophic circumstances on Louisa Catherine, and John Quincy's increasing sensitivity to his patriotic duties, polarized the couple. Indeed, to Louisa's despair, John Quincy seemed to change into a moralizing monument to public service, whose boasted philosophy—his "unlimited attachment and devotion to his country—was a "dreadful" thing. His bookishness was "obnoxious," his affection questionable. To John Quincy, Louisa betrayed for the first time "repellent spirit" of bitterness and wounding sarcasm. Perhaps, unwittingly, the two were revealing the elements of personality that would undermine their future happiness.[68]

Had Louisa's adored father not met with such a debacle, the "test of absence" would not have exposed such frailties. Certainly there would have been little cause for the pressure exerted by daughter and father to expedite a wedding at The Hague. Joshua Johnson's determined letters of November 29 and December 16, 1796, left no doubt as to his desire for a speedy marriage. A troubled and embarrassed John Quincy replied on January 9, 1797, "I regret sincerely the impossibility which will prevent me from concurring in a measure so conformable to my wishes." In his present situation, "so unsettled and precarious," he regarded the assumption of a family and its necessary appendages as an act of folly that would subject him to *"dependance,"* a state to which it was his "settled Resolution" never to submit. His "removal" from his post was the only circumstance that could possibly justify his indulgence of his inclinations, and that seemed a questionable event at this time. He added apologetically, "It is an awkward task to unfold the state of ones personal concerns to any Man," and the next day he wrote to Louisa Catherine advising resignation and acquiescence during the separation they were "doomed" to suffer. Though their marriage seemed more remote, he said, it was not less secure. She ought to consider "untoward Events as a test of character, and that a large portion of all human merit consists in suffering with dignity and composure, without weakness or unavailing regret."[69]

John Quincy was not insensitive to Louisa's unhappy position; he could not "give pain without sharing it" himself. Nevertheless, he seemed to dwell on the more hurtful aspects of the matter. "You will perhaps enquire why I return to a subject which I know must be disagreeable," he wrote, when he had already explained his position. Perhaps he felt a continuing need to clarify matters, or excuse what he must have regarded as unseemly, aggressive behavior on the part of the Johnsons. After studying both the father's and daughter's letters in sequence and contrast, John Quincy "concluded," he wrote Louisa, that she had made the proposal, and that her father's anxiety "to promote the object of our wishes and his affection for you prevailed upon him to determine upon this Step." He betrayed his susceptibility to social rigors by adding that an abrupt wedding at The Hague would have been "consistant neither with your dignity, nor my delicacy."[70]

The series of Louisa Catherine's letters that follows expresses, not surprisingly, the humiliation, stress, and anguish of an exceedingly mercurial, vulnerable young woman scorned. First she blamed herself—"It is my too great anxiety to see you that has created this impression and distrust"—and claimed that "love too warmly expressed, too candidly avowed," had precipitated her anguished embarrassment. Then she scolded: his very "decisive" letters, especially one of December 20, had "astonished and mortified" her—so much so that she could scarcely believe he could recall to whom he was writing. With some sarcasm she swept away the "unnecessary apprehensions" he had "indulged" in, that she might go to Holland. She would clear up his misunderstanding. Her father had informed her that the calamitous state of his affairs might necessitate the family's departure for America; consequently he had suggested—"if it would tend in any way to alleviate my distress"—the possibility of a meeting in Holland. Louisa had "fondly and foolishly" imagined that such an opportunity would be welcomed in mutual joy. Furthermore, there were ways John Quincy might have softened his rejection—but never mind:

> I go to America, you to your embassy, where I ardently pray the greater disposer of events, to grant that peace to *your* bosom which

mine has, and will lay a stranger to untill that period arrives which will prove, that *I* am as incapable of betraying affection or slighting engagements as of breaking a determination decidedly adopted. In this sentiment I am proud to acknowledge myself as firm as you.[71]

Louisa reproved John Quincy's behavior—"harshness, so evidently displayed"—and then, in a mercurial, abrupt change of tone, continued almost cheerfully. Her letter in no way signified a change in her affection:

No my best friend rather esteem it a proof of the sincerity of my attachment, rest assured that the woman who is capable of calmly submitting to receive such a letter without asserting very sufficient spirit to answer it, *is not, cannot* be worthy of your esteem.

She never doubted John Quincy's affection, after all. Nor could she have supposed for "one moment" that he was capable of betraying affection or slighting their engagement. Further, she did have a mature understanding of his nature; she reminded him that she knew him too well to doubt that he would ever vary from a purpose "deliberately formed decidedly adopted."[72]

Louisa Catherine had perhaps touched on the essential characteristic of the young John Quincy: he was a man in transition, sorting through his relationships with his family, country, and beloved. On January 18, 1797, he wrote his mother that he was still awaiting orders to proceed to Lisbon, to fulfill the duties of this last May's appointment as minister plenipotentiary to Portugal. In an apologetic mood, John Quincy reexamined his reasons for wishing to quit his diplomatic career and to settle in a Southern state, both suggestions having met with parental disapproval. His station at The Hague, though comfortable for a single person, would not support a family. Therefore, he thought it was "certainly" preferable to try to earn his way by private efforts than to "chill in the torpid and comfortless solitude of a celibacy without prospect of its termination."[73]

Also, addressing another parental issue, John Quincy did not think himself indispensable to the public good. The affairs of his country would not suffer "in the smallest degree" by his retirement, and many able and willing young men might substitute for him "with perfect ease." Furthermore, when he originally proposed his plan, he had no right to expect that President Washington would encourage an extended diplomatic career, and under the next President—his father—he was "certain and determined never to be the subject of an appointment." Then again, if his father was not made President, he was "strongly suspicious" that he should not hastily receive one. However, all these reservations had evaporated with his appointment to Portugal. With new obligations to continue in public service, his views of a private settlement were "no longer the same."[74]

John Quincy now broached to his mother the subject of his domestic arrangements, allowing that he did not know whether he would find it in his power to make final plans. It was his intention, when he received orders, to go through London and marry his "companion" there, but—and his sigh was almost audible—he said that "various accidents may take place to make this design impracticable." "If so," he concluded, "I shall submit to the gloomy prospect of a solitary life during my future mission like that which I am leading in the present; or even much worse, unless I can prevail upon my brother to continue with me a year or two longer in case he should not be stationed here at the time of my departure."[75]

Should the *"Spirit of Party* intrude itself into the chair of the Union," his father knew as well as he did what he should have to expect, for no other reason than their relation to one another. But this possibility did not represent a catastrophe. He had never been anxious for promotion, he assured his mother, nor, he trusted, would he ever be. This was "far from being a pungent Passion" in his heart. Furthermore, his strong conviction of the "vanity of all human greatness," coupled with "a sense of Independence and delicacy," would always deter him from a "very fervent wish for anything that it is in the power of man to confer or deny."[76]

Finally, on July 6, 1797, John Quincy received orders to leave for Lisbon. He wrote to his mother of finding himself for the third time "launched upon an unknown Ocean, without Plot or compass," and of plans to go to London, but to stay no longer than "absolutely necessary." On July 18, while in London, he received a new set of letters from both the Secretary of State and the new President—his father—directing him to wait for a commission, and instructions to the court of Berlin. Eight days later, he was married to Louisa Catherine in the church of the parish of All Hallows Barking. Abigail learned of the wedding on November 2, in Quincy, while reading the newspaper. The lapse of information was a matter of distance, not lack of affection or courtesy.[77]

The couple had written to "dear and honoured parents" a combined letter dated July 28, which had not yet been received. "I have now the happiness of presenting to you another daughter," John Quincy wrote,

> worthy as I fully believe of adding one to the number of those who already endear that relation to you. The day before yesterday united us for life. My recommendation of her to your kindness and affection I know will be unnecessary. My sentiment of her merit, will not at this moment especially boast its *impartiality,* but if there be as I believe an inseparable chain of connection which binds together all the domestic virtues, I have the strongest pledge that she, who has in an amiable and respectable family, adorned the characters of a daughter and Sister, will prove an equal ornament to that of a wife. . . .

Louisa Catherine added her own postscript:

> The day before yesterday by uniting me to your beloved Son, has given me a claim to solicit your parental affection, a claim I already feel will inspire me with veneration to pursue the path of rectitude, and render me as deserving of your esteem and tenderness, as those who stand in the same relation my pride would be severely wounded to yield the palm in the fulfillment of my duties either as wife or daughter. To be respected as these characters, and to meet the approbation of my Husband and family, is the greatest wish of my Heart. Stimulated by these motives, (your affecion the Reward) will prove a sufficient incitement never to sully the title of subscribing myself your Dutiful Daughter. . . .[78]

Both inscriptions are poignant in view of ensuing difficulties. Louisa Catherine, especially, would torment herself for the rest of her years over the innocence of her words and her role. With hindsight, John Quincy said that although he had "indeed long observed" his father-in-law's distress and that of his family, he had never anticipated its direct impact on his marriage. The new bridegroom's most immediate problem was the defense of Mr. Johnson against his creditors, but in a sense it was Louisa Catherine who was the episode's most serious casualty. Her idol—her father—had toppled; her security was forever undermined, and the loss of her small personal fortune was forever mourned. Across the years, "beggar as I am" was her echoing phrase; with no private means she dismissed herself as a figure of "contempt." Repeatedly she explained her father's bankruptcy as one of those "unforeseen misfortunes, so cruelly taught to our Mercantile Community." Throughout her adult life, the failure of a very small payment, she claimed, "threw a shade over our brightest prospects, and gave a colour of imprudence to a marriage, formed under the brightest and most promising auspices." Her father's misfortune

> gave a colouring to my future days, which could never be eradicated. It overtook *me* in the *zenith* of my happiness, at that peculiar period of life which marks a future destiny; and that colouring appeared to stamp my character, with a base deception which my Soul utterly scorned, and no evidence could ever be brought forward in my favour afterwards, to prove the perfect innocence of my conduct. The loss of Fortune so small as the best to which all knew I could have pretended to was scarcely a consideration—but the apparent dishonour of palming myself upon a family under such circumstances, was a baseness from which my spirit was revolved, and it has and still does make the wretchedness of my life. It has turned every sweet into gall.[79]

It is essential to realize that this devastating appraisal of the effect of her father's loss of fortune was written in 1840, in her journal, tellingly called *The Adventures of a Nobody*. She was sixty-five years old then and savaged by chronic illness and the deaths of unborn children as well as those of an infant son, a treasured namesake and only daughter, and a grown son. By her own admission her temper was so "harrassed, so imbued with strange and singular opinions" that she was "utterly and entirely incapable [of] repose and contentment." She felt that she had been a torment to herself, and a still greater one to her husband, who "bore with her with the patience of Socrates," she said, but "who like Socrates glides smoothly on in the course which he has laid out for himself."[80]

Abigail, aware of John Quincy's marriage, oblivious of any hint of catastrophe, cordially and fittingly requested that her nephew William Cranch call on the Johnson family, who had embarked early in September for Maryland.

> I have not yet heard of their arrival which gives me no small anxiety. I pray you to give me earliest intelligence of them, and I request you to visit them and present my congratulations to them on their arrival and to inform Mrs. Johnson that Mrs. Adams was well on the 19th of September and sustaind the painful separation from all her family with a becoming fortitude.[81]

Meanwhile, Thomas Adams, one of the three witnesses to the wedding, other than the bride's immediate family, had written home to tell his mother of his newly acquired "amiable and accomplished sister." John Quincy was "very happy," Thomas said, and doubtless would remain so, as the young lady had "much sweetness of temper" and, in his estimation, seemed to "love as she ought." Thomas also spoke highly of the Johnson family, who were returning to Washington, where they owned property. He elaborated still further on his affectionate portrait of Louisa Catherine that September 10. His remarks, given his customary reticence, were especially meaningful to his mother: "She is indeed a most lovely woman, and in my opinion worthy in every respect of the Man for whom she has with so much apparent Cheerfulness renounced father and Mother kindred and Country to unite her destinies with his." "This is a great deal for Thomas to say," Abigail reported to Mrs. Cranch. Meanwhile, she wrote abroad for a miniature of her new daughter-in-law and a lock of her hair.[82]

Considering that Abigail, by her own ready admission, would rather prepare "to come Home than to go from it," her return to Philadelphia in November was marked by some pleasant surprises. She found her house in perfect order, and her staff of old hands, responsibly managed by Briesler, unscathed by the summer's epidemic of yellow fever. In fact, she said she could not wish to be better off than she was, respecting her domestic help, which, admittedly, greatly enhanced the comfort of life. But she would wish, had she a choice, for another set of circumstances where Mrs. Smith was concerned. There was little that was redeeming about the situation in Eastchester, from her firsthand observation.[83]

Mrs. Smith had lived on a farm for eighteen months, twenty miles from New York City, awaiting the return of her bankrupt husband, who seemed periodically to seek refuge from his creditors. Her life was so solitary—locating a newspaper was almost impossible—that, as far as Abigail was concerned, her daughter might have been living outside of America. Abigail hoped that Mrs. Smith and Caroline might spend the winter with her in Philadelphia, but she was decidedly wary of how to approach her troubled daughter. What she could and could not say to Mrs. Smith, she bared with characteristic candor to her sister Mrs. Cranch. The continuing dialogue was reminiscent of an earlier period in all their lives. Though Abigail did not go to the trouble of setting up a system of marking envelopes in the interests of privacy, she did mention, on a number of occasions, John's concessions. After she had "scolded so hard," he pledged not to open any further letters from Mrs. Cranch and would be satisfied, he promised, with whatever parts Abigail was willing to communicate to him.[84]

Whether Abigail wished to spare her husband her own anguish over their daughter's delicate situation and what looked like total abandonment, or whether she feared he might disapprove of Mrs. Cranch's and her own so-called solutions, was not entirely clear. The former was as resourceful as ever, and her advice appeared to be a continuation of the past summer's conversations and observations. Mrs. Cranch might even have suggested divorce, judging from the content of Abigail's answer of mid-November:

> I have contemplated the plan you mention. It may be put into
> effect if future circumstances require it. At present, it would be
> expensive and lonely, and not less subject to unpleasant feelings
> than being here on a visit, which is all that at present is expected,
> nor will she be obliged to appear on my publick Evenings, unless it
> is her choice.[85]

At her bleakest moments, as the winter wore on, Abigail did not believe that the colonel would return. Her negative outlook was understandable. Months of failed promises and dead ends had undermined her faith. She had been present when Mrs. Smith received word from the colonel's brother that a letter with money enclosed awaited her. The two women's journey to New York proved to be a fruitless search for the would-be messenger. In spite of all her doubts, however, Abigail was relieved by the colonel's return the week of February 17. Though she did not suppose he could satisfy his creditors, she had feared that her daughter would "lose" herself, if left alone any longer. It was almost as though Mrs. Smith hinted at suicide, talking as she did of existence being a "burden to her." Abigail was still wary of the colonel's "vissions, of Ideal Schemes etc.," and believed that at most her son-in-law might "settle" so as to be able to do business in the future. But, on the whole, the colonel's return released Mrs. Smith from "that worst of States," which, in Abigail's thoughts, was "a constant anxious expectation, and antic-ipation."[86]

However much Abigail was consumed with family, extending to nieces and nephews—she offered one member a set of law books, another a remedy for a lung ailment ("I have a great opinion of cabbage leaves"), another a fashionable "drapery dress" ("too youthful for me")—her eye on the outside world stayed keen and steadfast and guarded. News from abroad that the Holy Roman Emperor of Austria, Francis II, had made peace with the Directory of France ("to call it a Republick would be a subversion of terms") was an event "big with consequences" to Abigail's mind. But then, every tremor regarding the French aroused her suspicious interest. That Bonaparte's troops had invaded Switzerland—their capture of Basle in December was vivid in her mind, and Berne would be taken in March—only substantiated her conviction that "tyrants stick at nothing." And though she tended to discredit rumors of a threatened invasion of England, she did not doubt that the French might be "mad enough" to make the attempt. The news out of France that was of most vital concern to her, however, was that regarding her fellow Americans. France's dealings or lack of them, with the American envoys, and the deadening silence concerning their peace mission, aroused what she referred to with deliberately measured understatement as "unpleasant sensations."[87]

One aspect of the relationship absolutely escaped her. She was "at a loss" as to how people who fought against England's "usurpation" of America could "crouch so tamely" to France, a much more dangerous and daring nation. She plainly feared the French, and accused them of aiming not only at American independence and liberty but at "total annihilation" of the Christian religion. The French laws were those of the loathsome Athenian legislator Draco, whose punishments were said to be written in blood. The French were "Robbers, Murderers, Scoffers, backbiters"; in short, in Abigail's opinion, there was no crime, "however black or Horrid," that was unfamiliar to them.[88]

The deeper, in fact, Abigail concentrated on the French and their influence in America, the more discernible was the hysteria that permeated her thoughts: "America must be punished, punished for having amongst her legislatures Men who sanction these crimes, who justify France in all her measures, and who would rejoice to see fire, sword and Massacre carried into the Island of Great Britain untill she became as miserable, as France is wretched." The news confirming her grievous suspicions—word from John Marshall via Ambassador William Vans Murray that neither he nor his colleagues had been recognized by the French—pitched Abigail into near despair. She feared for her nation, for her husband's political party. Her volatile state was dramatized in prayer. She wrote Mrs. Cranch on January 20, 1798:

> O My Native State, wash ye, make yourselves clean from these
> abominations. You are Guilty of sending three such Men,
> V[arnu]m, F[reema]n, S[kinn]er. Not a single state but what has
> some, Connecticut excepted, the many of them would not go all
> lengths. Virginia has but two Federilists, North Carolina but one.
> Can we expect such measures to be adopted as the safety and
> security of the Country require? Every Man who sees the danger
> may toil & toil; like Sussaphass [Sisyphus], (I believe the Name is
> misspelt) the weight recoils.

Furthermore, Abigail was sure that the envoys did not write for fear
of interception, and she understood they were not permitted to associate with any French citizens. In short, she concluded that they were
"in a mere Bastile," and that their return was expected daily.[89]

In a sense, Abigail's outpourings were measures of her frustration.
She had no recourse, no way of defending her husband's views to the
world at large. Periodically she would refute bruising attacks by requesting members of her family to place in a sympathetic newspaper
a letter or essay of rebuttal that one or another of them had written.
Essentially, however, she was a warrior without arms or armor, a
Federalist without office, a writer without a journal, a lecturer without
a platform or audience. That "The Spots of the Leopard" were
"constantly visible" was both redeeming and punishing. She took
notice of each public happening but, also, in her wounded state,
assessed its impact on the President's image with an extraordinary
bias that often distorted its significance.[90]

Such was certainly the case in Abigail's relationship with the Phila-
delphians. Their intended celebration of George Washington's birthday was a cruel blow. Needing to "vent" her indignation on paper,
she pleaded with Mrs. Cranch not to expose "it, nor me." She feared
"It will be call'd pride, it will be calld mortification." She despised
both, caring nothing for herself, "but as it respects the Character I
hold—I will not knowingly degrade it," she explained on February
15, 1798:

> These Philadelphians are a strange set of people, making
> pretentions to give Laws of politeness and propriety to the union.
> They have the least feeling of real genuine politeness of any people
> with whom I am acquainted. As an instance of it, they are about to
> celebrate, not the Birth day of the first Majestrate of the union as
> such, but of General Washingtons Birth day, and have had the
> politeness to send invitations to the President, Lady and family to

attend it. The President of the United States to attend the celebration of the birth day in his publick Character of a private Citizen! For in no other light can General Washington be now considerd, how ever Good, how ever great his Character, which no person more respects than his Successor. But how could the President appear at their Ball and assembly, but in a secondary Character, when invited there, to be held up in that light by all foreign Nations. But these people look not beyond their own important selves. I do not know when my feelings of contempt have been more calld forth, in answer to the invitation.[91]

The President took the earliest opportunity to decline his invitation. Abigail commented that if the Virginians pleased to do so, it was "natural & proper" for them to celebrate the day, and so might others who "chuse." But it was the propriety of doing so "in the Capital in the *Metropolis* of America as these Proud Phylidelphians have publickly named it, and inviting the Head of the Nation to come and do it too," that was, in her view, "ludicrous beyond compare." Somehow the President's reply had found its way into the *Aurora,* achieving results not intended by its editor, but polarizing its readers instead.[92]

"Every one was inquiring the why? & the Wherefore?" Abigail reported to Mrs. Cranch weeks later. Many who had subscribed to the ball did not attend, once they learned of the President's position on the invitation. Even the Vice-President was said to be "shocked" with the "impropriety" of the proceedings, though he lent his name to them. Abigail seemed pleased, if surprised, at Jefferson's position, unaware of his comment to Bostonian Harrison Gray Otis, a member of the House of Representatives, that "The late birth-night certainly has sewn tares among the exclusive federalists." Refusing to believe rumors that Jefferson had been the "first mover" in implementing the birthday celebration—"give the devil his due, but lay no more than he deserves to his Charge," was her philosophy—she also found some consolation in the fact that among the 150 in attendance, only fifteen were women, and these so "mortified" that their presence went unannounced in their newspapers.[93]

Six days after the celebration of February 22, Abigail was able to achieve some detachment, some face-saving reason for having been so acutely insulted. It was as though national rather than private esteem had been at stake in the commemoration of Washington's birthday. She told Mrs. Cranch, "I hope in time they will learn how to appreciate themselves as a Nation. They have had, & now have a Head, who will not knowingly Prostrate their dignity & character, neither to foreign Nations, nor the American People."[94]

Abigail was up with the rising sun on the morning of March 27. "Visions" occasioned by "reflections" made sleep impossible. It was a critical time at home and abroad, and she agonized over John's dilemma as President, *"knowing what he thinks ought to be done,"* yet faced with the eternal puzzle of his administration, the uncertainty of whether the people were "sufficiently determined" to second the government. Dispatches from abroad, dating to January 9, had arrived and were completely pessimistic, reinforcing Abigail's fears of an America driven to war with France and bound to defend herself.[95]

The dispatches posed another problem. Their message must remain private, contrary to clamoring opinion, or endanger the lives of the envoys, who were still in Paris. Support of the President's views came from an unexpected source. Of all people, the journalist Peter Porcupine, "a strange mixture," defended John Adams against accusations that he was deliberately provoking war. Distinctly, Porcupine was all for rousing those who, in Abigail's words, were "for going shares with France submitting intirely to her will," those quietly disposed to receive "every lash she pleased to inflict." In contrast with Bache, Peter Porcupine was saying that all men now agreed that Congress ought to do something, and immediately. If they did not, the journalist warned against the "odium" attached to indecisive measures. Furthermore, everyone knew that the "Snail like mode of proceeding which we have long beheld is not the fault of the President."[96]

It was no wonder that Abigail embraced this remarkably friendly opinion and allowed that she had a "great curiosity to see the Creature" who was the only "thorn" in Bache's side. She was plainly puzzled by this man who called himself Peter Porcupine, who could write "very handsomely," and also "descend & be as low, and vulgar as a fish woman." And she could not understand why there weren't others who did not sense the country's precarious position. She was eloquent in her frustration, and wrote to Mrs. Cranch on March 27, 1798:

> Union is what we want, but that will not be easily obtaind. It is
> difficult to make the people see their danger, untill it is at their

doors, or rouse untill their country is invaded. The Senate are strong. They are much more united in their measures than the House. There is an attempt in this city to get a petition signed to congress declaring their determination not to go to war with France, and they hope to sit this measure in opperation through the different States. Is it possible that any person can suppose this Country wish for war by which nothing is to be obtaind, much to be expended and hazarded, in preference to Peace?

As Abigail continued her explanation, her exasperation was almost audible:

> *But in self defence* we may be involved in war; and for that we ought to be prepared, and that is what the President means. What benifit can war be to him? He has no ambition for military Glory. He cannot add by war, to his peace, comfort or happiness. It must accumulate upon him an additional load of care, toil, trouble, malice, hatred, and I dare say Revenge. But for all this he will not sacrifice the honor and independance of his Country to any Nation, and if in support of that, we are involved in war, we must & we ought to meet it, with firmness, with Resolution & with union of Sentiment.[97]

These were the days when Abigail thought "All Good people" ought to pray "Heartily" for the President and for the country. The minister, Samuel Blair, Jr., prayed "that he may hear a voice saying unto him this is the path, go thou in it."[98]

NINETEEN

Enough of Public and Private Anxiety

As silently as she could, on Wednesday night, April 26, 1798, Abigail slipped into the New Theatre on Chestnut Street in Philadelphia. Avoiding the President's box—she was attempting to be "perfectly in cogg [incognito]"—she sat instead with friends, including the Secretary of the Senate, Samuel Allyn Otis, and Representative Daniel Buck and their wives. It was only the second time she had ventured out to the theater this season, frankly motivated, in this instance, by "Great curiosity" about the special song implanted between a three-act play called *The Italian Monk,* a monologue on Sir John Falstaff, and a two-act opera called *Rosina.* The special song, "Hail Columbia," coupled Judge Joseph Hopkinson's impressive, recent lyrics (just about forty-eight hours old) with Philip Phyle's stately music, already familiar as "The President's March" of Washington's term, and was indeed timely:

> *Firm, united let us be,*
> *Rallying round our liberty,*
> *As a band of brothers joined*
> *Peace and safety we shall find.* [1]

The rousing reception of the song gave Abigail a headache, but one she bore with joy. The song signified political redemption, at last, for John. Until now, Abigail had complained, French tunes "usurped an uncontrould sway." Only recent cries of "perfidy" from the American envoys in France, and charges ranging from discourtesy to dishonesty, had drastically altered sentiments. One heartening example of the new American atavism afforded Abigail particular satisfaction. On recent evenings, she had been told, the first popular song of the French Revolution, the vibrant "Ça ira," favorite also of the Federalist Francophiles, had been shouted down by cries for the native "Yankee Doodle Dandy" and for "The President's March." Now Abigail could hear for herself, with the greatest satisfaction, Hopkinson's healing and binding words that transformed the march into a national song.[2]

The theater was full, the audience irrepressible. At curtain time, its members joined the British singer and actor Gilbert Fox on the fourth round of "Hail Columbia," clapping thunderously throughout the last chorus, rising and giving voice to cheers that might have been heard, Abigail supposed, a mile away. She was exultant, supremely gratified that the new national song reinforced the President's message to Congress. At last, after groping through months of tangled rumors, John was able to expose the bizarre facts of the imperiled relationship between America and France. She welcomed respite from intense anxiety for all involved, on all counts. Her own personal involvement was no secret. How could anyone be an indifferent spectator, Abigail asked her nephew, William Shaw, "in Times so critical, so allarming and so big with Concequences as the present?"[3]

If John Adams had appointed a diarist for his administration, he could not have hoped to find one more observant, informed, and literate, albeit partisan, than his own wife. Frustrated by peripatetic reports from France, exasperated by the Federalist press, the faction in favour of war, whose "wicked and base, violent & calumniating abuse" could only be quenched, in her opinion, by the passage of a sedition act, Abigail sought justice at her writing table. If she was denied the larger audience she might like to proselytize in her husband's and her nation's cause, she could at least set the record straight for the devoted few. As though it were a scheduled assignment, she reported to her family almost every morning, during the spring of 1798, the suspenseful antics of what would be known as the XYZ Affair, and its role in America's "Quasi-war" with France. A remarkably thorough journalist, she supplemented her observations with copies of official papers. Also an inventive and persistent publicist, she suggested to her correspondents that certain documents be forwarded to friendly newspapers, as opposed to the Federalist press. Keenly aware of her absorption in current issues, she was known to apologize for having "wearied" her readers with politics. And then,

as though freed of further restraint or inhibition, she plunged on-
ward with her searching examination of the proliferating drama.[4]

The American commissioners had reached Paris on October 4 and
conferred with three agents of the Minister of Foreign Relations,
Charles-Maurice de Talleyrand-Périgord, on October 18. These
were the Messrs. Jean Conrad Hottinguer, Lucien Hauteval, and a
Mr. Bellamy, the X, Y, and Z of dispatches that reached President
Adams on March 4, relating the French price for peace—a $10 mil-
lion loan plus a fee (actually a bribe) of $240,000. On March 19, an
angered President informed Congress of the mission's failure to
reach terms "compatible with the safety, honor, or the essential interests of the nation." The President's next problem, whether to agree
to Congress's request to make the dispatches public, was of intense
interest to Abigail. It was "a painful thing," she told Mrs. Cranch on
March 20, that the President could not share the dispatches with the
public. However, considering the "critical state of things," the safety
of the envoys, whose precise whereabouts were unknown, was of
primary concern. Besides, they would cease to be useful abroad "if
their communications are all to be communicated." She also recalled
that under the old Congress, dispatches were never made public.[5]

On April 3, 1798, as a result of the previous day's resolution by the
House of Representatives, John Adams forwarded the controversial
dispatches to Congress with the request that they might be "considered in confidence." On April 5, the House voted to print twelve
hundred copies. Abigail had anticipated this turn of events. She was
also personally offended, supposing that the real reason for calling
in the dispatches was doubt of the President's word. Angered, she
wrote to Mrs. Cranch:

> The publick exegiency of our Country, and the real in some, and
> the Pretended unbelief of others, produced a torpor, and an
> indicision which call'd for Conviction and proof as strong as holy
> writ, that all, and more than was exprest, in the Presidents last
> message, was necessary to be done to put our Country on its gaurd
> and to inspire them with a determined resolution to preserve their
> Rights, their freedom and independence, all of which are attack'd
> by the most base, profligate and abandoned Culprits which were
> ever permitted to scourge the Nations of the Earth. . . .[6]

For someone who admitted that she had not seen the dispatches,
Abigail seemed to have absorbed their every word, as related to her
by informants she vaguely referred to as "Members," presumably of

Congress. Her direst suspicions that "Talleyrand & the Directory would have been bought" were now confirmed. Her interpretation of their machinations was starkly personal. The French, as far as she was concerned, pressed corruptive measures on the President's representatives in order to prove the President "deficient in knowledge, a false man."[7]

Abigail was equally emotional about the effects of the dispatches on the Jacobins in the Senate and the House. They were "struck dumb, and opend not their mouths, not having their cue, not having received their lessons from those emissaries which Talleyrand made no secret of telling our Envoys are spread all over our Country; and from whence they drew their information." Not for a moment did Abigail doubt that Talleyrand was "too scrupelous to take a *fee.*" She warned Mrs. Cranch: "We are ensnared. We shall be destroyd unless that snare is broken, and that speedily."[8]

In early April it was warm enough to pick salad from the garden; by July, Philadelphia was again a "baking-oven" threatened with yellow fever. A graph of the weather, as the heat thickened from spring to summer, would accurately chart Abigail's intensifying concern for the fate of her country. She was dismayed by a generally apathetic population, by the "imps" (Bache being a primary one) and their deliberate misinterpretation of events. She distrusted the French and the other foreigners who were "shifting" ground now that the envoys' story was unraveling. As far as she could judge, those aliens would return to their wicked ways as soon as their plans were "concerted and matured," to sow their "seeds of vice, irreligion, corruption, and sedition."[9]

Altogether, it was a "very dark day," and it was with a sense of resignation that Abigail met the question of whether the outcome of the envoys' "Goblin Story" portended war or peace for America. On April 11, 1798, she wrote to her daughter:

> You ask me, if we shall have war? I answer, that we already have war; the French have been at war with us for these many months: but your question is, I presume, will America declare war against France? Which is what I cannot say. I hope we shall have spirit and energy sufficient to arm, and defend ourselves; and that obliges us to declare war, the sooner the better; for at present we suffer the miseries and misfortunes attendant upon war, on one side only, having done all that honour, justice, patience, and forbearance can possibly demand, or humanity require; we must submit our cause

to Heaven, and use the means which Providence has put into our power for our defence.[10]

Once again, in her analysis of the "great evils" her country suffered, Abigail regretted America's "blind attachment" to France, whose whole system of revolution had become, in her opinion, "the tyranny and oppression of every kingdom, and country, which they have conquered, or fraternized as they term it. . . ." Success had deafened France, as far as she was concerned, "to every principle both of law and equity"; with withering disdain she referred to the members of the Directory as the "five Kings of France."[11]

In all the darkness, however, there was one bright aspect, the valued reward that public opinion was changing with miraculous speed. Abigail was heartened by the augmenting support, by "addresses" on the President's behalf. Merchants, mayors, and aldermen, from Boston to New York to Baltimore, filled meeting houses and churches now to pay official thanks to the President for his "firm and steady conduct" on behalf of their interests. On May 9, nearly eleven hundred young men gathered at Philadelphia's Merchant's Coffee House and marched two by two, sporting black cockades instead of those striped in France's colors. They observed, much to the chagrin of the Jacobins, the President's officially declared "Day of Public Humiliation, Fasting and Prayer, throughout the United States." People were now saying that if Jefferson had been their President, and Madison and Burr their negotiators, they would all have been sold to the French.[12]

As Abigail addressed the situation as a whole, while still basically disapproving of the publication of the envoys' dispatches, she was somewhat relieved that at least the truth would be known: that the "unjust aspersions" cast upon the President concerning his wish for war were groundless; and that the efforts of the French emissaries "sowing and spreading their Sedition" in hopes that the President might resign in favor of "the Man of the People" were in vain. The latter, Thomas Jefferson, who had so hurtfully numbered Adams among the "apostates," would be quieted at last. Also, James Madison could no longer talk, as he had before the disclosure of the dispatches, about being saved from the "rash measures of our hotheaded Executive," or accuse the President, the "perfect Quixote as a statesman," of taking as much pains to get into war as Washington had taken to keep out of it. All the "jacobinical abuses, and foul aspersions," Abigail proudly assured her daughter, gave her no other pain "than what arises from the injury done to the people by mislead-ing and disceiving them."[13]

In May, though Abigail longed for the time when she might "sit" her face northward, she remained in Philadelphia, enthralled by the predicament of the American envoys to France. As the weeks evapo-rated, however, and when rumors persisted that the envoys had left Paris for London months before, she grew impatient and skeptical. She did not understand their prolonged and seemingly fruitless jour-ney. A letter she read on May 16 in the *Columbian Centinel,* whose author purported to have more recent news than even the govern-ment about the envoys, was a further irritant to her. The author, Sylvanus Bourne, made two startling claims. First, he insisted that from now on, the French, having released the ship *America,* out of New York, captured by a French cruiser and docked in Amsterdam, would do everything to support and protect further dealings with the United States. Bourne's second piece of news concerned Gerry, who was said to have conferred, along with his two colleagues, on three occasions with the French Minister for Foreign Affairs, and that negotiations appeared to be "in good train."[14]

Though she was not prepared to deny what might be fact, Abigail considered both propositions possibly the worst news she could hear. Geared for combat now, champion of the bill empowering the Presi-dent to raise voluntary corps in case of need, she preferred to dismiss the Bourne letter in the belief that the French "serpents" were toying with America. Their actions were calculated, she insisted, to "deceive and amuse," the more effectually to "devour" the Americans. Only when she heard of an order to stop all depredations on America's commerce, and to restore what had been stolen, would she believe the French considered America's friendship of "some use and value." Meanwhile, she hoped that whatever concessions the French were making, if legitimate, would not dampen the "ardour of Patriotism" just "rousing from its stupor." The best negotiators Abigail could conceive of were those who pledged their lives and fortunes. "Our preliminaries," she told Mrs. Cranch in the third week of May, are "fortifications, Armed vessels and voluntary Corps."[15]

Her jingoistic mood was neither spontaneous nor confined, but was slow-simmering, and born of deeply embedded distrust. Abigail was convinced that if the progress of Jacobinism was to be arrested at all, combat was the means. Like a disease requiring the most radical treatment, Jacobinism would not be remedied on peaceable terms, she cautioned her nephew William Shaw. Further, if there was a nation on earth capable of going to the necessary lengths to make the proper sacrifices, it must be a nation already possessed of substantial liberty, one that knew how to distinguish this prize from the sort of liberty France was trying to propagate throughout the world. If ever there was a call to arms, it was Abigail's:

> Rely upon it my Dear Nephew and impress upon the minds of your young Friends, that France has setled her plan of Subjugating America: her system is fully known. She will aim at getting possession of Louisiana and the Florides and of Cannady from thence. She can pour in her Armies upon us, she can as she has done, Arm the Slave against his master, and continue by her Agents and emissaries, whom with truth & reason she bosts of having thickly scattered through our Country, Saving her principles, her depravity of manners, her Atheism in every part of the United States, by these means she will seduce the minds & sap the foundation of our Strongest pillars, Religion & Government.[16]

She did not think of herself as proposing "visionary" ideas of future events. Events had already progressed to a most alarming point. As far as she was concerned, it was every individual's duty "to rise, and unite 'to stop the progress' to arrest the poison" before it contaminated their vitals. Her next words would echo for generations: "Let not the Question be asked What can I do? but what may I do?" Abigail might have been shouting from a hilltop, instead of recruiting all of America in a lone letter to Shaw. "Let every citizen become a soldier," she begged, "and determine as formerly on Liberty or Death! let them seek the blessing of the most High, and acknowledge God in all their ways," she prayed.[17]

As summer approached, Abigail grew increasingly impatient. Anxious for action, and eager to return to Quincy, she notified Mrs. Cranch of her intentions to send her trunk by ship to Boston. But when she and the President would follow was another proposition. As far as she knew, the envoys were still in Paris and she was discouraged with the entire situation. "They know not how they have tyed the Hands here," she said. But all was not entirely at a standstill. She believed that her sister would learn with pleasure that a bill calling off all intercourse with France had been passed in the Senate by eighteen votes to four, and also that the treaty with France would no longer be binding. As for the Directory's complaints about the President's speeches, Abigail supposed the "Poor wretches" wanted the President to "cringe," which was hardly his response. "He is made of oak instead of the willow," Abigail assured Mrs. Cranch. "He may be torn up by the Roots, or break, but he will never bend."[18]

A June day and the delivery of a letter from Ambassador William Vans Murray, dated April 12, produced some startling clues to the envoys' suspense story. The message that France was prepared to treat with Mr. Gerry "alone" was the essence of Murray's news. Furthermore, the other two envoys would be "ordered away." Abigail could barely believe what she read. Was it possible, could it be believed, that Talleyrand had deluded and fascinated Gerry to such an extent that the latter should "dare" to take on such a responsibility? She could not credit this situation, she told Mrs. Cranch, and yet she recognized that Gerry's sin was "obstinacy, and mistaken policy."[19]

The President was "distrest." He had counted on Gerry, who had surprised him by acting on his own judgment "against his counsellors." Abigail, too, was upset. Yet she remained loyal to Gerry, though pessimistic about his course of action. "Gerry means the Good of his Country, he means the Peace of it, but he should consider, it must not be purchased by national disgrace & dishonor. If he stays behind he is a ruined man, in the estimation of his countrymen. This is all between ourselves," she cautioned Mrs. Cranch. "You will be particularly reserved upon the subject." Abigail explained this request further by adding that she did not want to hurt Mrs. Gerry's feelings, or be guilty of judging "hardly" an old and steady friend.[20]

Talleyrand's decision to negotiate with Gerry, apart from her personal misgivings, seemed only to accentuate Abigail's near terror of the French nation. She rose to the pinnacle of indignation in her letter to Mercy Warren on June 17:

> You and I, my Dear Madam, have trod together, through one
> Gloomy Scene, of War, havock and desolation; and we have seen
> our Country rise superiour to oppression, and despotism and take
> its Rank among the Nations, presenting at this period, the *only*
> *spectacle,* of a Free Republic, which has not been Revolutionized, by
> the Gormandizing and insatiable third of that power, which like the
> Grave, crys Give, Give, whilst the departed wealth, opulence and

liberty of Batavia, the Cruelly oppress'd Geneva, Genoa, all Itally, and the partitiond and Barterd Venice, with the Barbarously Sacrificed Switzerland, and Bern cry to us with an awefull warning voice, to behold their Fate, and secure ourselves by a direct opposite conduct to that which has proved fatal to them.[21]

Abigail's fear of Bonaparte's troops was only heightened by the recent tragedy of Switzerland. Their "insolent proposition & threat" to the so-called neutral power, the seizure of Basle and Berne in the past months, proved to Abigail that "tyrants stick at nothing." Europe was turning into a burial ground, a place of torment and martyrdom—a fate, she told Mrs. Warren, that she wished their own country might be spared: "I would hope that the destroying Angel may not be commissioned to visit us in wrath, but that he may visit us on an errand of love, to warn us against those contaminating principles and abominations, which have made all Europe one Golgotha."[22]

By June 18, Abigail had received word about two of the envoys who had left Paris. Marshall had returned to New York after a fifty-three-day voyage from Bordeaux, and Pinckney was said to be in the south of France, where his daughter might be treated for a condition "supposed" to be consumption. Only Gerry remained behind in Paris. He felt gravely threatened by Talleyrand's mention of powerful French factions in the United States. Sensing the possibility of a war, he seemed to think it wisest to continue negotiations with the French minister. "A very wrong step," Abigail said. "It is an insult upon our Government," she wrote William Smith on June 26, "to chuse out whom Talleyrand pleased to treat with." Her rampant disapproval was only exacerbated as the correspondence between Talleyrand and the envoys seeped into America and was published "exultantly" by Bache. It was some relief to Abigail that dispatches came to the government's attention by other means. At least these would counteract the villainy intended by Talleyrand, and convince "the most unbelieving" of the close connection between the "Infernals of France & those in our own Bosoms." Once again, she was in despair over the press. In any other country, she said, "Bache & all his papers would have been seized," but Congress's "dilly dallying" about passing a bill enabling the President to snap up suspicious persons and their papers prevented such action. At least she could take some satisfaction that Talleyrand's machinations would alter abruptly once he learned that the cry of the majority of Americans, attributed to Charles Pinckney, was "Millions for defence but not a sixpence for tribute." And if "money tribute must be the terms," then Abigail resolved that "the Cannons mouth must answer the Demand." Given the present situation, she was certain that she "would not be in Mr. Gerry's coat." On June 25, she wrote: "I expect Congress will declare war before they Rise."[23]

The first days of July were hot beyond anything Abigail could remember. The city was sickly and foul-smelling, and Abigail did not think she could last in Philadelphia another week. It was hopeless, she said, for her to attempt dinners, and she canceled further drawing rooms. As it was, she could hardly manage to rise out of her chair without dropping back into it seconds later. Even writing was a chore. It was not only the suffocating heat, but the flies. She could barely get two words on paper before she had to put down her pen to brush away the insects swarming about her face and desk. Fortunately, the rooms in her house were large, with lofty ceilings; also, she found that cold baths afforded some consolation for the lack of air.[24]

Despite intense discomfort, however, and complaints of ninety-degree temperatures in the shade, Abigail kept her vigil. She forwarded dispatches, dutifully noting bills and acts regarding the organization and staff of the army and navy and the new Marine Corps, appropriations for distribution of arms, and presidential authorization to issue letters of reprisal against France. On July 2, the President nominated George Washington as commander-in-chief of the army about to be raised. If it were in his power to nominate him for President, John Adams wrote his respected predecessor on July 7, he would have "less hesitation and more pleasure."[25]

Abigail understood completely the role Washington must fill. His country called, and "No Man can do so much for it in that Line," she said. His appointment would unite all parties in the country, give "weight, force and energy to the People," and "dismay our Enemies." She hoped and trusted that the general would not refuse an appointment made, it was true, without his knowledge or consent. She considered the move one of those "strokes" required by the "Prospect and Exigency of the times."[26]

On the morning of July 11, James McHenry, Timothy Pickering's successor as Secretary of War, returned from Mount Vernon with Washington's acceptance. Nominations for officers were sent to the

Senate that same day. Washington would remain at Mount Vernon, Abigail supposed, contrary to rumors, until war was declared. This decisive step was not one that Congress, at present, was prepared to take—a remiss position, as far as Abigail was concerned. They only would be responsible if "unpleasant consequences ensue."[27]

For months Abigail had talked of the probability of war, but then, abruptly, at the end of July, she began to allow for the possibility of peace. Though she referred, somewhat archly, to Gerry's homecoming ("if not detained"), and wondered, given his behavior, whether he was "in *the free* use of his understanding," rumors of his successful negotiations—however unreliable, considering their source—spurred fresh appraisals. Furthermore, latest accounts from Europe, according to the despised Bache, predicted that French armies had reached their zenith, their numerous possessions giving them "employment enough" without their searching for other conquests.[28]

Such reports made a decided impact on Abigail's judgment. She seemed convinced now, as she was about to leave for Quincy, that the French would never attempt more than a "partial" invasion of America, if any at all. Still, hers was a much-qualified optimism. She remained, at heart, as distrustful as ever of the French. It was because of that nation that America had felt "no small share of the baleful influence of the Age of Reason." Again, it was that nation which she regarded as the "chief engine" in destroying and undermining religion throughout Europe.[29]

On the whole, Abigail felt threatened by the French, particularly by their emissaries in America, and the suspected connections between these "Infernals of France & those in our own Bosoms." Instinct, rumor, and fact nurtured a numbing fear of unknown forces, documents, plots to undermine her country. "We cannot depend upon any thing, as we know not what a day will bring forth," she wrote William Smith. With such uncertainty, she took the position that a state of military preparation would bring security, but that weakness and disunion would invite the French to destroy America. Furthermore, it was her passionate conviction that the only way to gain ascendancy over the intrigues and machinations of the Jacobins was to insist on the return of their various emissaries to their native countries.[30]

If Abigail left for Quincy with one burning issue unquenched, she took some comfort in the settlement of another. This was in regard to what she considered sedition against the President's administration that bordered on treason. In some respects, in her own mind, disloyalty to the President and to the country were indivisible. Buffeted by the press in earlier days, she could not, any more than before, turn her cheek or put down her pen, or cease reading the very writers she so loathed and feared. If she had meant to plead her case at trial, she would not have had to supply evidence beyond the newspapers of the day, and her own letters, to confirm the damage suffered on personal and political levels. The press called John "His Serene Highness"; Abigail was facetiously referred to as the "excellente wife of the excellent President." To read only the Federalist newspapers was to be assured that the country was "under the Sway of the Great Mogul or a Delia Lama." The signature "Hem! Hem!" was signed to a squib taunting John over the ball that honored Washington instead of himself.[31]

More punishing, however, was the press's treatment of the President's position on France. Abigail minced no words about her interpretation of the intent and effect of those "imps" and "contemptable Hirelings." Nothing less than "destruction" was the price she predicted America would surely pay for those who would deliberately "deceive and misrepresent the views and designs of the French."[32]

She was not alone, however, in longing for some sort of penalty to be exacted from those she considered enemies of America and of the President. Alexander Hamilton was also asking why "renegade aliens connected with some of these presses" weren't sent away. And Harrison Otis had informed Congress on June 16 of his "humble opinion" that there was greater danger to America from French infiltration than from any other source. In his opinion, it was "owing to this cause that all the Republics in Europe have been laid prostrate in the dust."[33]

The evolution of the Alien and Sedition Acts of 1798, suggested perhaps by the current British legislation, fascinated Abigail, affording her mixed moments of satisfaction and doubt. She gladly welcomed a solution to a problem that had grieved her for years. Laws "competant enough to punish the stirer up of sedition, the writer and Printer of base and unfounded calumny," she told Mrs. Cranch on May 26, "would contribute as much to the Peace and harmony of our Country as any measure." The passage of what she referred to as the "Alien Bill" was the fulfillment of her hopes—that is, she added, if it passed without being "curtailed & clipt" until it was made nearly useless.[34]

The Alien and Sedition Acts were actually four separate acts passed in different stages; they were embraced by Abigail, word for word. The first of the four, the Naturalization Act, passed on June 18, 1798, "to establish an uniform rule of naturalization," decreed that no alien could become a United States citizen unless he had declared his intention at least five years before his admission, and maintained an American residence for fourteen years.[35]

The Alien Act followed the Naturalization Act, and was passed June 25, 1798. Now it was lawful for the President of the United States "to *order* all such *aliens* as he shall judge dangerous to the peace and safety of the United States, or shall have reasonable grounds to suspect are concerned in any treasonable or secret machinations against the government thereof, to depart out of the territory of the United States, within such time as shall be expressed in such order. . . ."[36]

The Alien Enemies Act of July 6 addressed itself to times of declared war between the United States and any foreign nation or government, or of invasion or "predatory incursion." In such circumstances, the act read, "all natives, citizens, denizens, or subjects of the hostile nation or government, being males of the age of fourteen years and upwards, who shall be within the United States, and not actually naturalized, shall be liable to be apprehended, restrained, secured and removed, as alien enemies."[37]

It was Section 2 of the fourth act, the Sedition Act, however, that addressed itself to Abigail's most searing complaints. She objected very much to the "dilly-dallying" preceding its passage on July 14, for here, at last, she was provided with a legal weapon against the press. It was as though the act designated for the "punishment of certain crimes against the United States" was written to her order; it seemed merely to rephrase in cooler terms her most spleenful wishes for retaliation against Jacobin journalists. Accordingly, a fine not exceeding two thousand dollars, and imprisonment not exceeding two years (Abigail might indeed have wished for more on both counts), were to be imposed

> "if any person shall write, print, utter, or publish, or shall cause or
> procure to be written, printed, uttered or published, or shall
> knowingly and willingly assist or aid in writing, printing, uttering or
> publishing any false, scandalous and malicious writing or writings
> against the government of the United States, or either house of the
> Congress of the United States, or the President of the United
> States, with intent to defame the said Congress, or the said

President, or to bring them or either of them, into contempt or disrepute; . . . or abet any hostile designs of any foreign nation against the United States. . . .[38]

At the time of the passage of the Sedition Act, the significance of Section 4 might have seemed obscure and even unimportant. The single sentence, however, stating that this act "shall continue to be in force until March 3, 1801, and no longer," told volumes about the gathering explosion in certain quarters over the validity, as well as the constitutionality, of the act, which Abigail believed sincerely, and somewhat naïvely, to be the cure-all for at least one stunning set of problems.[39]

Perhaps it was John Quincy Adams who most succinctly described the effect of the Sedition Act when he compared it to "the falling of a spark into a powder magazine." He would study that most provocative legislation of his father's administration intently and always see it as nothing less than a sweeping conflagration. In the end he recognized it as an "ineffectual attempt to extinguish the fire of defamation" that had, instead, "operated like oil upon the flames." All the same he was its defender, if not its champion. Thirty-eight years after the Sedition Act was introduced, and years after its repeal, John Quincy tried to explain that given the relative situation of the United States and France at that time, such measures of defense against French secret emissaries were more necessary than they would have been in an avowed and open war. Though his mother might readily have espoused her son's theory, others expressed immediate and drastic disagreement of varying intensity.[40]

Jefferson, for one, felt more remote than ever from Adams's philosophy of government. He took pains to dramatize his critically divergent views by drafting what would be called the Kentucky Resolutions, the first part of which was passed in the legislature of that state on November 16, 1798, and the second part a year later, on November 22, 1799. Their thesis was bolstered by James Madison's so-called Virginia Resolutions, passed on December 24, 1798. Taken together, the resolutions protested, inherently, a central government usurping the powers of individual states. Jefferson's document resolved that "whensoever the general government assumes undelegated powers, its acts are unauthoritative, void, and of no force." Madison declared that in case of a "deliberate, palpable and dangerous" exercise of powers not granted by the Constitution, the states had the right and the duty to interpose their power. The following January, Jefferson summed up his opposition to the Alien and Sedition Acts with crystalline clarity. He stood, he wrote Elbridge Gerry, "for freedom of the press, and against all violations of the Constitution to silence by force and not by reason the complaints or criticisms, just or unjust, of our citizens against the conduct of their agents."[41]

The Alien and Sedition Acts made for vibrant exchanges between Adams and Jefferson, even in their retirement. "I know not why you are not as responsible for it as I am," Adams wrote in 1813, pointing out that Jefferson's name was "subscribed" to the acts as Vice-President, just as his was as President. "Neither of Us were concerned in the formation of it. We were then at War with France: French Spies then swarmed in our Cities and in the Country. Some of them were, intollerably, turbulent, impudent and seditious. To check these," Adams concluded, "was the design of this law." Furthermore, he asked, "Was there ever a government, which had not Authority to defend itself against spies in its own Bosom? Spies of an Ennemy at War?" In still another letter the same year, he argued that if there were no "Checks and Balances" to be resorted to in the "Laws of the Land," and no reparations to be made to the injured, would not man become the judge and avenger of his own wrongs?[42]

Throughout the interminable postmortems on the Alien and Sedition Acts, Abigail would remain steadfast as well as puzzled. In the fleeting resumption of her correspondence with Jefferson in 1804, she took vehement exception to the latter's pardon of James Thomson Callender, the Scottish-born journalist fined and imprisoned under the Sedition Law for his anti-Federalist activities. With habitual candor, Abigail would "freely disclose" what had "severed the bonds of former Friendship," and place Jefferson "in a light very different" from that in which she had once viewed him. On July 1 of that year, she wrote:

> One of the first acts of your administration was to liberate a wretch who was suffering the just punishment of the Law due to his crimes for writing and publishing the basest libel, the lowest and vilest Slander, which malace could invent, or calumny exhibit against the Character and reputation of your predecessor, of him for whom you profest the highest esteem and Friendship, and whom you certainly know incapable of such complicated baseness.[43]

Abigail was extraordinarily explicit in her conviction that Jefferson's judgment was flawed. That his behavior had undermined her husband's authority and, in fact, insulted his record was equally plain in her analysis:

> The remission of Callenders fine was a public approbation of his conduct. Is not the last restraint of vice, a sense of shame, rendered abortive, if abandoned Characters do not excite abhorrence. If the chief Magistrate of a Nation, whose elevated Station places him in a conspicuous light, and renders his every action a concern of general importance, permits his public conduct to be influenced by private resentment, and so far forgets what is due to his Character as to give countanance to a base Calumniater, is he not answerable for the influence which his example has upon the manners and morals of the community?[44]

Abigail's return to Quincy in July 1798 was preceded by her usual requests for assistance from Mrs. Cranch and Dr. Tufts, beginning in February this time, with her housekeeping chores. Otherwise, she feared, without help things would not be done "to my mind." In thought, if not in deed, the distance between Philadelphia and Quincy vanished as her eyes invaded every corner of her house and property. The kitchen and stairs must be painted a "plain" yellow ("unless the floor was too thin"), smoke ought to be cleaned off the "chimny peice" in the parlor, a supply of charcoal was needed, the time for laying a wall in the garden was after the frost was out of the ground. When there was time enough for the paint to dry, without persons treading on it, was the best time to paint. Therefore, it was best done early, and with boiled oil added. She cautioned both her sister and her uncle that they must not put "too many Irons at once in the fire," and then proceeded to plan for some radical alterations to the house and outbuildings.[45]

Because they were "so confined" in Quincy after the larger and grander houses of the past years, and because of the more extensive staff they now maintained, Abigail embarked on an extensive building program with unique provisions. The President was not to learn about her plans until they were accomplished and the house was "snug." Also, she meant to bear the expenses out of her own monthly allowance. She explained her actions to her own satisfaction, at least. "I know the President will be glad when it is done," she told Mrs.

Cranch, "but he can never bear to trouble himself about any thing of the kind, he has no taste for it, and he has too many publick cares to think of his own affairs."[46]

Abigail was both sensitive and fastidious in her concern for the "Book Room," as she called the library she was renovating, which would be John's sanctuary. Two east chambers were to be combined into one and the roof was to be raised, in order to achieve a room she hoped would be large enough and "pleasent." When the room was done, she asked that Mr. Cranch put the books in order. She could not be specific or adamant enough when she talked about order. Ultimately, William Shaw was the recipient of uncompromising directions about the library: "Every Letter & paper are placed in Alphabetical order in desks & places designed for them, and every different department relative to War office, Marine office, Secretary & Treasury office distinct," she advised, "so that no trouble occurs in searching for papers."[47]

When her return became an immediate prospect late in July, Abigail's extensive shopping list to Mrs. Cranch included requests for Hyson tea, brown sugar, coffee, spices, a gallon of brandy, and, since she now had four menservants, some bedsteads with sacking bottoms. Also some sheeting and toweling to be bought specifically, with receipts saved, "for the use of the Household of the President of the U.S." She enclosed a bill worth one hundred dollars and added that she needed spoons, kitchen knives and forks, yellow dishes and plates, half a dozen one-pound "spermiciti" candles, and a flask of sweet oil.[48]

For the first time, however, though Abigail's preparations for her homecoming were as thoughtful as ever, her anticipation was dampened by the recent deaths of some friends, the ill fortunes of others, and the "dark & thick cloud" conceivably ready to "Burst" on her country. Her path to Massachusetts, she said, was "spread with sorrow, and covered with mourning." Seemingly unable to rally, she wrote frequently now of "ligaments" giving way one after the other, of the voice she heard warning her that "this Lifes a dream, an empty Show." Being Abigail, she was not unmindful of her blessings, but she was also vastly mindful of her "Frail tenure" on earth. "The dark side of the picture is a deep shade," she concluded, unaware, until she was actually back in Quincy at the end of July, that her mental depression foreshadowed a physical collapse. Once home, almost upon the hour of her arrival, Abigail was confined to her bed. The

President, admitting to "indifferent" health himself, reported to John Quincy in Berlin, as of October 16, that his mother's "complication" of disorders included chronic diarrhea, an intermittent fever, and a diabetic condition. John had already confided his sorrowing concern for Abigail to George Washington: "Her destiny is still very precarious and mine in consequence of it."[49]

TWENTY

Evils of a
Serious Nature

John returned to Philadelphia alone in November of 1798.

The thought of Abigail, "wrecked and exhausted," making the journey with him—and he had no doubt of her willingness to do so—frightened him, and he said as much. He wrote back from Philadelphia assuring her that her company was "much desired" by everybody, and by none so much as he. But the thought of her attempting the journey "terrifies me," he added, "lest it should prove fatal to a life that is dear to me beyond all expression."[1]

By the end of December, Abigail had reluctantly given up all thoughts of leaving Quincy. Though she felt better than she had for the four previous months, she recognized herself as "tender, and impared" by constant confinement. The weather, too, had offered her little choice. The roads were blocked by snow; it would take oxen and shovels to open the way and even then, Abigail feared, two sleighs could not pass without one plunging to the side. She was defeated by the severe wind as well, and the intense cold that froze and even broke bottled supplies stored in her cellar, despite their being packed in seaweed and burning coals.[2]

She was, of course, not happy with her decision. She shadowed John's footsteps incessantly in her imagination, her feelings of loneliness ("not a creature from Boston had looked in on her") fused with a sense of guilt. She thought of herself as having "quitted" a place, namely Philadelphia, that it was her duty to occupy, of having deserted a "post" that required her attendance.[3]

John was patient, solicitous, and tender in response to Abigail's agonized letters. Repeatedly he reassured her that if it were not for his fear that the journey over the horrid roads in the cold and damp weather would put an end to her, her coming to Philadelphia would be of "inexpressible" satisfaction to him. He tried to convince her, as well, that her low spirits were the effects of long and exhausting illness. They were also the "evils of a serious nature," and he bade her to banish, as much as possible, all gloomy thoughts and avoid everything that might endanger a return of her old disorders.[4]

To help Abigail to reconcile herself to her fate, he had a great mind, he said, to give her a sampling of his, which was composed of little or no company, a daily "peck of troubles in a large bundle" of often "illegible" papers, and idle, empty ceremony; all of these were contributory factors to his sinking health. "You and I," he concluded sadly, "seem to have arrived prematurely at the age when there is no pleasure."[5]

Abigail understood John's message fully. She had long preached survival methods to others. One must call reason and philosophy to one's aid, she would say, to prevent "untoward occurrences of Life" from depressing one. Miraculously, she was personally almost always able to tap a third resource that remained undiminished in adversity, whether at the heights of snow or the depths of loneliness. This was her boundless curiosity about all phenomena of life, which was nurtured during periods of isolation by her flourishing correspondence. Hers was almost a sensual appreciation of the letters that very nearly transformed sheets of paper into physical incarnations of those she would have sought out to speak with and to touch. Furthermore, she encouraged intimacy that bordered on conspiracy: "You may write to me in a confidence which you know you may not talk in," she assured her nephew William Shaw, employed now as the President's secretary. How was he liking Philadelphia and its inhabitants, and how was he succeeding at the public dinners? she thirsted to know.[6]

By the same token, Abigail was truly responsive; she was of the confessional school herself, giving as well as receiving. At rare times when she did not feel up to writing, for one reason or another (flies buzzing about, her eyesight, illness), she was quick to explain her deficiency. In this particularly troubled winter of 1798, frail of mind and body, she apologized for, in essence, failing to keep her bargain with William, piteously volunteering that her "Imagination has full scope in the wide field of conjecture." Her powers of concentration seemed to fail her; her mind flew from "one object to another, fixing sometimes upon one, and sometimes upon the other." She was "puzzled" and "perplexed" and cried out for "more light" on the objects of her consuming concern, for which she so earnestly sought plausible resolutions.[7]

One object of Abigail's concern, among many, was the state of her family, perhaps especially that of the Smiths. Their prospects were pathetically limited now. The past July, at the time of Washington's appointment as commanding general, the Secretary of War had carried to Mount Vernon a list of officers for Washington's "Selection and Approbation & arrangement," as Abigail explained to her cousin William Smith. As a result, Colonel Smith had been named adjutant general, and the President had forwarded the nomination of his son-in-law to the Senate. Hours later, three members of the Senate paid an evening call on the President to request the withdrawal of Smith's nomination on the grounds of his being a speculator, and that he was bankrupt and anti-Federalist. The President's defense was immediate and resourceful. He accentuated the positive aspects —the colonel's bravery as an officer, the likelihood that others to be appointed were also speculators, the unlikelihood that the colonel's prospective position would entail financial responsibilities, the implausibility of his being anti-Federalist, in view of his recent nomination by George Washington.[8]

When, on July 19, 1798, the Senate confirmed all nominations except the colonel's, Abigail was angry and suspicious. The first to acknowledge her son-in-law's "folly and indiscretion," which had earned him vast unpopularity, she was a steadfast admirer of his soldiering. A man of as much military skill and knowledge as any on Washington's list had been discarded, in her opinion, and she suspected as the reason the manipulative influence of that extraordinary trio of Cabinet members, Oliver Wolcott, Timothy Pickering, and James McHenry, though she did not mention them by name.[9]

"It was the last day of the session & their were many Secrut Springs at work," she wrote her cousin William on July 23. Some were the "tools" of others, she speculated, and some were glad to retaliate for their disappointment in their commander-in-chief, and some were glad to do anything they thought would wound the President. And some, she did allow, had acted on principle, though judging from their choices, they made no improvement on the colonel, in his mother-in-law's eyes. She worried about the colonel, who would have served with "Zeal Bravery and Skill," being wounded and hurt far more by this rebuff than any he had received before. He had not solicited the appointment, but he had said he was ready and willing to serve his country if he was called into service. Pensively, she speculated that the result would have been different if there had been more time.[10]

On December 19, the President discussed still another opportunity with the colonel in a remarkable letter that left little question of the dilemma both faced at this moment. Notice was on its way to the colonel from the Secretary of War, informing him that some officers had proposed that either he or a Mr. Hammond be made a lieutenant colonel commandant, the higher offices all being filled. "This event has embarrassed me," John told his son-in-law. "I know not what to do. I know not whether the Senate will not negative the nomination if I make it, nor whether you will accept the appointment if they should advise and consent to it."[11]

The President was blunt, out of apprehension rather than cruelty. He wrote harshly, as though compelled to remind the colonel that his future was at a standstill unless he mended his ways. The doubts he had confided to other members of his family were in the open now. He must be "explicit," he insisted, and he was. It was with "inexpressible grief" that he observed Smith's "pride and ostentation," which excited so much envy and resentment among his neighbors that if they had to "alledge" against him any instance of dishonorable and dishonest conduct, they would not only do so, but neither forget nor forgive these allegations, factual or not. Those whose vanity, the President continued, caused humiliation in others, could depend on meeting their revenge, which was precisely what was happening now. Furthermore, he was convinced by prevailing reports that if he was to nominate Smith to anything more than a regiment, he had no doubt that the nomination would be voted down by the Senate.[12]

There was nearly an element of self-pity in the President's concern for the colonel—provoked by desperation, perhaps. "It is a great misfortune to the public," John wrote, "that the office I hold should be disgraced by a nomination of my son-in-law which the Senate of the U.S. think themselves obliged to negative. If the disgrace should be repeated, it will be a serious thing to the public as well as to me and you and our children." Having unburdened himself without inhibition, the President relented. He asked that the colonel inform him immediately whether he wished him to make the nomination, and whether he would accept it "if made and consented to." His signature was that of an "affectionate" father-in-law.[13]

Two days later, on December 21, the President informed his son Charles that another had been recommended in the colonel's place, one Samuel B. Malcolm, who was favored over the colonel by the "worthy man and great magistrate" Governor Jay. This new loss would be even a greater misfortune for the colonel, the President predicted, than the loss of all his property. There was some family ill will that he never understood but that was obviously "fatal" enough to Smith.[14]

Spring brought no respite. In May the President wrote the colonel of reports of the latter's "improper speculations in the neighborhood of Detroit," of "Indian pretensions" fomented by him and his associates. John was infuriated. "If you desire the command of Detroit," he wrote the colonel, "you might sollicit it of the Secretary at War, the commander in Chief of the army or Major General Hamilton. I will not interfere with the discipline and order of the army because you are my son-in-law."[15]

Abigail was aware of some of the colonel's difficulties immediately, but became aware of others only later. In either case, she was always apprehensive about their effect on Mrs. Smith and the children. Especially concerned about her grandsons in Mrs. Peabody's care, she speculated candidly about their future struggle to make their way in the world, "without the gifts of fortune, dependent only upon their own industry and talents." She wished this idea "imprest" upon their minds, she instructed her sister. The most she could hope for was that her grandsons might be educated, and that they might not make the "worse members of society, provided they do not inherit too great a share of pride," which she wished to see "suppresst, should it discover itself."[16]

Her sighing doubts gave way when she wrote, in various rearrangements of the same thoughts: "I make it my rule, not to repine—if all is not according to my wishes. I still have more than my desserts." Then, refusing to be vanquished, she recruited help for Mrs. Smith to the best of her ability. Repeatedly, she asked members of the family to write to her troubled daughter. "Now and then tell her what is passing," she bade William Shaw, for example, advising him that his cousin would "take it very kindly" if he would do so.[17]

But the plight of the Smiths was only one "object" among many that made Christmas of 1798 a trial for Abigail. Thomas was expected

home momentarily. Having dutifully accompanied his elder brother
to Berlin, he had begged for a replacement so that he might return
home. Just when and on what vessel he would arrive were questions
for Abigail to agonize over. She half expected him with Captain
Jenkins's but did not find him on the passenger list. Nervously she
gauged the "thick" weather and the velocity of the winds, and worried now whether Thomas might instead be aboard the *Barbara.* The
ship, rumored to be foundering at Salem, was one she seemed not
to trust—just its name undermined her confidence, she implied, perhaps because it sounded frivolous to her. Lonely, sickly, Abigail
could find no solace, even when her thoughts turned to her other
sons.[18]

She was relieved, of course, by John Quincy's assurance that he and
his wife were in good health after a period of illness she only learned
about four months later. But she was preoccupied this Christmas with
grave news of John Quincy's disastrous financial setbacks, suffered at
the hands of the trusted family friend and recent bankrupt, Dr.
Thomas Welsh, and compounded by the ill luck and poor judgment
of his own brother Charles. She was bewildered; the situation was
"unaccountable." Though the facts were vague, the message was
plain. John Quincy's savings of four thousand dollars, invested in real
estate at the discretion of Charles as well as Welsh, were "sunk";
fortunately, the power to draw on two thousand more had not been
exercised. As details of the transaction sharpened, Abigail was more
troubled than ever.[19]

From Charles himself, wretched with worry and guilt ("my sleep
has been disturbed and my waking hours embittered"), Abigail
learned of his own share in the mismanagement of his brother's
funds. Charles, never known to have "the power of resistance," in his
mother's estimation, in an effort to bolster Colonel Smith's limp
fortune, had exchanged John Quincy's mortgage for a note from
Justus Bush Smith, the colonel's brother, a prosperous landowner.
As land values had declined abysmally, there was every reason to
believe Justus Smith's note was worthless and that therefore John
Quincy's investment was a hollow one. Abigail, solicitous of all concerned, including the bankrupt Dr. Welsh, suffered most of all, understandably, on John Quincy's account. Hoping to transfer his
financial affairs into Dr. Tufts's safekeeping as quickly as possible,
she enlisted her cousin William's help in clarifying their content,
explaining, just after Christmas, on December 28, that she could not

bear it that the "poor fellow should be plundered by every one, in whom he has placed confidence."[20]

While it was certain at this particular moment that John Quincy was the victim of this sorry set of circumstances, time would prove his brother Charles to be the true sacrificial figure. Essentially of frailer fiber than his siblings, weaned too early, perhaps, from the family circle, he was a lawyer, first in Alexander Hamilton's office, then with Federalist congressman John Laurance, speculator in New York State properties. The realities of failure pervaded his very being. The following autumn, on a visit to Eastchester, Abigail would visit with Charles and his wife, and cherish the "sprightly Eyes" of his two daughters, Susan and Abbe (Susanna Boylston and Abigail Louisa), three years and one year old, and their fine complexions. The sight of them, however, elicited little joy, and she spared neither herself nor Mrs. Cranch the tragic realities of the situation. Charles's plight was a heartbreaking repetition of their own brother's, a trial of the "worst kind," Abigail recognized from harsh experience. "Any calamity inflicted by the hand of Providence, it would become me in silence to submit to," she wrote her sister, "but when I behold misiry and distress, disgrace and poverty, brought upon a Family by intemperence, my heart bleads at every pore." Charles was an alcoholic, and the family would in the next year become increasingly resigned to the catastrophic end "which seems so inevitably to await us," as Thomas would write his father.[21]

As she surveyed the landscape that was her family's life, increasingly menaced by darkening shadows, she fought for some balance. "Who of us pass through the world with our path strewed with flowers, without encountering the thorns?" she consoled herself. "In what ever state we are," she reasoned, "we shall find a mixture of good and evil, and we must learn to receive these vicissitudes of life, so as not to be unduly exalted by the one, or depressed by the other."[22]

Her own complaints of sleepless nights—she got no more than one night's rest out of five or six these days—reflected, of course, her inner state of turmoil. During this tedious period of halting recuperation and formidable solitude, the problems of her family's distance and disarray were equaled if not surpassed by her country's restive challenge to war with France. Abigail was all but consumed by these "untoward occurrences," as she referred to them, but not quite. With her ingrained genius for survival, preaching "reason" and "philosophy" to herself as she always would to others, she knew her needs and fulfilled them as best she could. If she could not, for example, indulge herself in what was practically her favorite amusement, talking politics around the evening fire—or anywhere, in fact—she settled for the next best amusement, writing about it.[23]

Fortunately, she was comfortable with her nephew William Shaw; she both trusted and admired her sister Elizabeth's son. Her letters to him, written during the waning days of 1798 and the ensuing months, were to be a meticulous seismographic record of every tremor and volcanic force that jolted the already severely fissured presidential administration. She explained the tone of one "rather censorious" letter with considerable charm: "As women are *not masons,* or *bound* to keep secrets, they are entitled to a greater lattitude of speech than Men."[24]

As firm as her word, her criticism was unsparing and wide-ranging. The press remained an enduring source of irritation. She would hope that Peter Porcupine would have less "Billingsgate" when Congress sat, and that the son of John Fenno, Boston-born founder of the *Gazette of the United States,* would maintain the "purity" of tone established by the father. David C. Claypool's paper, the *American Daily Advertiser,* was only interesting while Congress sat, because he recorded the debates earlier than the rest. Despite his death from yellow fever on September 10, 1798, Bache was, as always, Abigail's leading target. "Ye yet speaketh," she noted caustically; the party that had supported the loathsome editor still stood by the press devoted to his cause, so that the *Aurora* could hardly be counted as an Adams sympathizer.[25]

Whether their influence was foreign or domestic or both, it was imperative, in her opinion, that decorum be maintained by the press. And it would be; the "rascalls" would certainly yield to the law, if there were not such a "milk and water" Attorney General in office, she insisted. Then again, the way things were going with Kentucky and its mother state, Virginia, and their disaffected attitude toward the Alien and Sedition Laws, Abigail wondered if the government would have to pay out the tribute due to Talleyrand before the two states would be quiet.[26]

The question of those who were disloyal to the President's views on the subject of France was explored in detail, with the guilty "Brainless" ones brashly named. William Findley of Pennsylvania, Anthony New, Matthew Clay, and John Clopton of Virginia were members of the House of Representatives who "ought never to be admitted to the table of the President again." There were still others, and surely, if she was in Philadelphia, "not a wretch of them all should come." She could not mention the President's opponents without thinking about Jefferson. "Why then should the Matzzie Letter writer be invited?" she asked William. She had to guess at the answer, she said, but she supposed that he would be invited as Vice-President—as an officer of the government, she added as an afterthought.[27]

Abigail would flatly comment on the reelection to Congress of Matthew Lyon, who had spat in the eyes of Connecticut Representative Roger Griswold, as "mortifying" proof that "something was rotten in the State of Denmark." Lyon, called "ignoramous" by the Federalist press, was not a "Noble British Lyon" but "the beastly transported Lyon," Abigail had said of the Vermont representative, who was born in County Wicklow, Ireland. On the very day of her writing to Mary Cranch, Lyon had to defend himself with fire tongs from Griswold's beating cane. Abigail also briskly disputed the value of Dr. George Logan's self-appointed mission to France, the Philadelphia Quaker's personal interview with Talleyrand, and his subsequent report to the President of the French foreign minister's conciliatory views. Her disapproval of Jefferson almost always kindled some provocative soul-searching.[28]

She was unquestionably preoccupied, at the start of 1799, with those who opposed the President, with "a low groveling faction" that continued to exist, encouraged by the "Ambitious and designing views of some disappointed and unprincipled Men." Yet she did not include Jefferson among the latter, though she did indicate her unease concerning his role. "The absence of the VP at this time," she wrote William, "when a Spirit of resistance to Government appears in the State to which he belongs, and the State immediately descended from it, has an unfavourable aspect . . . and subjects him to suspicions which whether well or ill founded, injure him in the minds of all Good Federalists." There was never any doubt, now or later, that Jefferson's position was difficult for Abigail to understand.[29]

In subsequent discussion of her "relative attachment" to most of the Federalists of the Senate and House, she referred obliquely to a "Friend," once esteemed and loved, who could only have been Jefferson, whom she had "too much reason to fear . . . an apostate." His change, she told William Shaw, on January 25, 1799, was a "painfull reflection as it respects my self, but more so, as it affects my Country."[30]

As passionately as Abigail wished "all party bickerings and personal resentments would yeald to the great and momentous national interests," she faced bitter denial on both counts. The battle for power had begun; opinion on whether to go to war with France was fragmented not only without, but, more significantly, within the Federalist party, even at the highest levels of the President's administration. As Wolcott, Pickering, and McHenry remained loyal to Hamilton, their colleague of the Washington administration who was committed to war with France, John never could claim their loyalty, and only, in fact, incurred their active deception.[31]

But there was no question at this time that the country was preparing to defend itself in case of war. During the past months, from March 27 through July 16, 1798, Congress had approved twenty acts in the cause of national defense. A Navy Department was established on April 30; treaties with France were repealed on July 7. Three frigates were to be completed and an additional twelve armed vessels built; the President was authorized, to provide, "if the same shall appear to him necessary," small ships not exceeding ten in number. U.S. merchant vessels would now be armed; French vessels of war and privateers could be seized without a formal declaration of war. A provisional army of ten thousand men was to be raised. The choice of Alexander Hamilton as the army's second-in-command under Washington would be accurately measured by John Quincy as the "forerunner of greater defeats" for his father.[32]

Washington had recommended Hamilton, Pinckney, and Knox for the three major-generalships. But Hamilton had already solicited Washington for "a station . . . *proportion to the sacrifice*" he would make. This clearly meant he must be made second-in-command, with the title of inspector general. "The public must judge for itself as to whom it will employ," he wrote on June 2, "but every individual must judge for himself as to the terms on which he will serve and consequently must estimate himself his own pretentions."[33]

Hamilton's lobbying was effective; Knox, who had outranked Hamilton in the old war, refused his commission. The President, home in Quincy with Abigail, seemed stunned by the turn of events. And though he reprimanded his Secretary of War, James McHenry, for his part in the intrigue, he was hardly a match for the formidably ambitious Hamilton. The latter was blatant: "If the Chief is too desultory, his Ministers ought to be more united and steady," was Hamilton's theme. His own policy would include maintenance of a regular army and navy; he talked about "looking" to possession of Louisiana and Florida, of sending an army to Mexico, of intentions "to squint at South America." Hamilton was an expansionist; the President, in his single-track fashion, was intent, despite warlike preparations, on working toward a peaceful settlement with France. At a time when Abigail felt the country threatened "from within & from without" news of Elbridge Gerry's long-impending return to Boston on October 1 was full of promise.[34]

Sick as she was, Abigail could not resist taking a "peep" at Gerry's papers, now in the President's hands. She read them carefully and was greatly relieved by their content. Later, in January, before their publication, when there was talk of Gerry's impeachment, she no longer worried about her old friend. The truth about the papers was a happy one. Gerry would not "sink" in the estimation of his countrymen. However much they all condemned his separation from his colleagues, his remaining alone afterward, his appearing to be more "yealding than the Honor of his country required," and "tedious" in his communications, his honesty and integrity were unquestionable.[35]

Gerry brought to the President welcome news of Talleyrand's wish to negotiate with America in order to avoid war. His story, combined with official and unofficial correspondence—the body of material that would eventually reach the public domain—marked the beginning of the end of two years of monumentally complex international negotiations. The French, after baiting the Americans on their initial peace mission in the fall of 1797, had crucially reversed their course. They had had little choice. The Directory had merely meant to express displeasure with America's ratification of Jay's Treaty by authorizing spoliations on American commerce, rather than initiating war. Talleyrand's intelligence warned him of overconfidence in France's popularity with America; some of the most fervent American opponents of the treaty with England had lost sympathy for the French since the disclosure of the highly undiplomatic treatment recently accorded America's representatives. Talleyrand's information was as accurate as it was dismaying. A statesman of thorough habits, he had turned in dissatisfaction from Joseph-Philippe Létombe to Victor-Marie Du

Pont, from whom he would receive the *report précis* he so urgently needed in order to deal seriously with America.[36]

Du Pont, who had left his post at the Charleston, South Carolina, consulate in May 1798, to succeed Létombe as consul general of the French Republic at Philadelphia, was refused recognition—"exequatur" was the official word—by the President. But on May 31 he did have a fruitful meeting with Thomas Jefferson as well as others, who collectively elaborated on the grave situation between France and America. Three days after his arrival in France, Du Pont was writing, on July 6, 1798, of the many in America whose hope for a peaceful solution lay with Talleyrand and *"dans la sagesse, la dignité, la puissance, la modération du Directoire."* Otherwise, Jefferson warned, France would push America over to England's side.[37]

Talleyrand, who was already convinced that an Anglo-Federalist trap must be avoided—rumors were rampant that the British minister proposed to lend the United States a naval force to combat France, in return for recruiting Americans for the Royal Navy—now viewed the situation as urgent. Undoubtedly responding to the measures the President had chosen to "formulate" in the two legislative chambers, Talleyrand, in a letter of July 16, put some crucial questions to Du Pont. What precisely were the actions of the French cruisers along the coast and in the Antilles that were causing such an uproar? What were the procedures of the colonial tribunals and consuls regarding prisoners? How were arrests made? How were neutrals treated? Americans?[38]

Du Pont, who was to settle in America in 1800, responded exactingly. His letter of July 21 ran to forty-one paragraphs, tabulating in relentless detail American complaints. He was also emphatic in his belief that previous reports by him and his colleagues on the reckless behavior of the French in American waters had been either lost or overlooked. Otherwise, it appeared to him that the Directory, without precedent and contrary to the principles of justice necessary to and evident in any healthy political system, had ignored its country's excessive acts of violence, spoliation, and piracy against America's commerce. In fact, far from being stopped, corruption was encouraged, as men with the title of consul were almost always, in the Spanish colonies at least, captains' agents and gunrunners. At the conclusion of his fervent report, Du Pont restated his belief in the gravity of differences between the two countries that might result in consequences *"fatale."* He also reaffirmed his confidence in Talleyrand. The reputation of the *"Citoyen Ministre,"* and his personal acquaintance with the United States, would put him in the best position to judge the situation, and arrive at a decision *"le plus favorable aux intérêts et à la gloire de la nation."*[39]

Fortunately, Du Pont had not underestimated Talleyrand. There was no mistaking this time that not only had Talleyrand read Du Pont's account, but so had members of the Directory. An order went out that depredations on American commerce were to end on July 31, 1798.[40]

Elbridge Gerry's story concerning the "softening" on the part of the French Directory, and Talleyrand's wish to negotiate with America, was further substantiated in the fall of 1798 by a report from William Vans Murray, friend of John Quincy, seven years his elder and his replacement as the United States minister in Holland. Both the Gerry and Murray reports undoubtedly influenced the President's determination to avoid war with France. On December 8, a little over a week after his arrival in Philadelphia from Quincy, he spoke at the opening of Congress. To the dismay of the Cabinet members, he had altered their draft of his speech. He had tossed out their uncompromising words asserting that sending another minister to make a new attempt at peace would be "an act of humiliation," and requiring France, "if she be indeed desirous of accommodation," to initiate the requisite steps. On the contrary, the President, though resolute, was also yielding:

> The United States will steadily observe the maxims by which they have hitherto been governed. They will respect the sacred rights of embassy. And with a sincere disposition on the part of France to desist from hostility, to make reparation for the injuries heretofore inflicted on our commerce, and to do justice in future, there will be no obstacle to the restoration of a friendly course.

The President made a genuine peace offering, as he continued:

> In making to you this declaration, I give a pledge to France and to the world that the executive authority of this country still adheres to the humane and pacific policy which has invariably governed its proceedings, in conformity with the wishes of the other branches of the government, and of the people of the United States.

There was, however, no mistaking his commitment to protect his country:

But considering the later manifestations of her policy towards
foreign nations, I deem it a duly deliberately and solemnly to
declare my opinion, that, whether we negotiate with her [France]
or not, vigorous preparation for war will be alike indispensable.
These alone will give us an equal treaty and insure its
observance."[41]

Abigail weighed every single syllable of the address. She sounded
defensive when she reported to William, on December 20, that the
President's speech had been "firm, very cool & moderate" even
"mild" compared to what had been expected. "It is what it ought to
be; not a personal feeling in it," she told him, "but as connected with
the honour and dignity of the nation."[42]

One month later, on January 21, 1799, the Directory's answer
(through Dutch mediation) reached the President. Its members
maintained that France's wish for reconciliation was already known
in Philadelphia. If the United States insisted on misconstruing
France's motives, then responsibility for the consequences was
theirs. Ten days later, Murray exercised decisive influence. His letter
to the President summarized his talks with the French agent, Louis
André Pichon, at The Hague, and included Talleyrand's assurance
that a new American envoy to France would be "received as the
representative of a great, free, powerful, and independent nation."[43]

The President deliberated his next step, but not for long. In the
face of anticipated opposition from his Cabinet, he made his decision
alone, "in his own secret heart," John Quincy would say. That February 18, he sent a message to the Senate nominating William Vans
Murray, the Marylander who had served in Congress from 1791 to
1797, presently at The Hague, as minister to France. Reaction, especially among those who professed ignorance of the latest exchanges
between France and America, included "surprise, indignation, grief,
and disgust." The Federalist Theodore Sedgwick echoed many others who stridently disapproved of sending a new mission to France
and, not knowing much about Murray, decided that he was unworthy
of the responsibilities involved: "Had the foulest heart and the ablest
head in the world been permitted to select the most embarrassing
and ruinous measures, perhaps it would have been precisely the one,
which has been adopted."[44]

The President was extremely wary about the success of his suggested appointment. He wrote Abigail on February 22, 1799:

> Since my nomination of Murray I have been advised by some to name my son John and Mr. King, with Mr. Murray. But I answer that the nomination of either Mr. King or Mr. Adams would probably defeat the whole measures. Rivalries have been irritated to madness, and federalists have merited the Sedition Law, and Cobbett the Alien Bill.

However provoked he was, he assured Abigail he would not take revenge: "I do not remember that I was ever vindictive in my life, though I have often been very wroth. I am not very angry now, nor much vexed or fretted. The mission came across the views of many, and stirred the passions of more. This I knew was unavoidable." How difficult he felt his position to be, however, was indicated by his mention to Abigail, at this point, of future plans: "I have no idea that I shall be chosen President a second time; though this is not to be talked of. The business of the office is so oppressive that I shall hardly support it two years longer."[45]

Two days after Murray's nomination, five senators called to dissuade the President from his plans. Or, as an alternative to a single minister, they suggested sending three, the public having been told that "in a Multitude of counsellors there is safety." Abigail did not take to these suggestions readily. The very day she learned of them, on March 4, she wrote to William:

> I cannot but own that this intelligence has given me much pain and anxiety; and I shall not feel less, untill I hear from you. I should regret indeed if a Majority of the Senate should become the Dupes of intrigue be it as it will. Each have exercised the powers given them by the constitution—and time will discover, who is right & who is wrong.[46]

On March 9, Abigail assured William she was "better humourd" than when she had last written. However, she was "very wroth with a certain set of people who profess to be federalists just as long as the measures of the government forward and promote their interests but lose all confidence and exclaim against them when ever their views are opposed." Her outburst was precipitated by charges that the President would not be advised, that he "would act of his own Head," that he was "determined to support Gerry in opposition to all his Friends." Gerry's entire mission to France, despite his reports, was suspect to Pickering and his followers, who threatened him with severely censorious measures. As with Gerry, William Vans Murray was another fixed target of this faction.[47]

There did seem to be no letup. Critics insisted the President must "tread back" the steps he had taken, as the Senate would never advise and consent to the nomination of Mr. Murray, who was neither a man of experience nor of talents. Absurdity added to incredulity: "Then comes the New Nomination, aya the Senate advised to that in order to defeat the measure." Three would go, three chosen by the President in a conciliatory move. Abigail wondered at the extraordinary additions to Murray. Oliver Ellsworth, Chief Justice of the Supreme Court, was in ill health, though she conceded he was a kind man, and Patrick Henry was so old that he would not go, she correctly predicted, the latter replaced by William R. Davie, governor of North Carolina.[48]

Abigail insulted was irrepressible. "But are not the Senate pointed out by the constitution as the advisers of the President?" she mimicked, obviously repeating a particularly irritating question and answering it in the affirmative, with mock deference. "Are there any others whom he is obliged to consult?" was another repetitious question. The popular answer that "Washington always did consult with others" was a flawed one in Abigail's judgment; for in doing so, she would point out, he had paid a large price, criticized by many for being "led" by Hamilton. "And why was not the Secretary of State consulted?" she continued. "Aya theres the rub." The answer was obvious, as Pickering had done his utmost to negate the President's actions. In sum, such had been the "zeal without knowledge of some of our hot Heads," Abigail said, though she noticed, with relief, certain "cooling down" on their part.[49]

In April the President returned to Quincy, earlier and in better health than Abigail had anticipated, considering his "close application" to his business for four months in a row. Her bitterness toward the past winter's proceedings, presumably nurtured by the President's confidences, was magnified. "He has sustained the whole force of an unpopular measure which he knew would excite the passions of many; thwart the views of some, and shower down upon his Head a torrent of invective," she wrote Elizabeth Peabody on April 7.[50]

Abigail blamed "ignorance malevolence and jealousy," touching on the fact that the information on which the President had based his decision to reopen negotiations with France was largely unknown. "Yet thinking as he did, the measure necessary," she continued, "and upon grounds which it was not proper to devulge, if to our own Country, not to others, and if to one, it would necessarily go to others —he took the Step and braved the effort." The reaction had, in some instances, approximated his expectations; in others it had been something of a shock to him, and therefore to Abigail. "He has been abused and calumniated by his enemies," she said, but "that was to be looked for." Matters were different, however, in "the House of his Friends, by those calling themselves friends of their country—They have joind loudest with clamour. . . ." It was Abigail's claim, though, that the President was not dismayed, that "time and circumstances will prove who has been right."[51]

If anything, however, the clamor was to be augmented, rather than lessened, by the President's departure from Philadelphia. Six months, the President would discover upon his return to Trenton* on the advice of his old and trusted friend Benjamin Stoddert, Secretary of the Navy, was an ideal amount of time to set his political house in disarray, to guarantee his political doom. The President had taken his example from Washington, who had retreated to Mount Vernon for long periods of time while in office. But John Adams's own position was not comparable. He commanded neither the loyalty nor the respect of Washington's appointees, and although he knew their differences with him, he seemed to have no conception of the significance of those differences. Concern for Abigail, fatigue, and naïveté would be given as explanations for his attitudes. John Quincy worried about his father's "unguarded letters"; in his definitive judgment, "too much trust in the honesty of others was the source of the mistakes which did the most to injure his reputation in his lifetime." Historians would cast him as a master of issues not men.[52]

Left on their own, certain members of the President's Cabinet did all they could to postpone accommodation with France, hopeful, in the end, that the mission so contrary to their ambitious war policy would be suspended. Though Abigail's retrospective commentary on the French-American negotiations, written the following December, mirrors only a partial view of the complexities of the "most noted event" of her husband's administration, the distortions are immediately evident. Three months before the three American envoys presented their credentials at the Tuileries on March 8, 1800, and nine months before the signing of the peace treaty at Mortefontaine, Sep-

*The temporary home of the government, owing to the epidemic of yellow fever in Philadelphia.

tember 30–October 1, when the Directory was overthrown and Bonaparte became the self-appointed First Consul, and Talleyrand the
foreign minister of the Consulate, Abigail wrote of the drama to Mrs.
Cranch. Of "the wisest, the most resolute and disinterested action"
of her husband's life, she reported on December 30, 1799:

> I think every days experience must convince the people of the
> propriety of sending the Envoys at the time they went. After the
> President had received the Letter from Tallyrand containing the
> assureances from the Directory which he requir'd, he would not
> allow it, to be made a question whether they should proceed tho
> he knew certain persons set their faces against it as far as they
> dared. Gen'll. Hamilton made no secret of his opinion. He made
> the P[residen]t a visit at Trenton, and was perfectly sanguine in the
> opinion that the Stateholder would be reinstated before Christmass
> and Louis the 18th upon the Throne of France. I should as soon
> expect, replied the P[resident], that the sun, moon & stars will fall
> from their orbits. . . ."[53]

Were the governments to change, however, the President speculated that there was nothing wrong with the envoys' being in France.
Finally, he had answered Hamilton by asking a question:

> if France is disposed to accomodate our differences, will she be less
> so under a Royall than a Directorial Government? Have not the
> Directory Humbled themselves to us more than to any Nation or
> Power in contest with her? If she proves faithless, if she will not
> receive our Envoys, does the disgrace fall upon her, or upon us?

The President, according to Abigail's account, had concluded that
America would be no worse off than it was at present, and that the
people of the country would be "satisfyed" that every honorable
method had been tried to accommodate the differences.[54]

One month later, when it was definite that the American envoys
would have to deal with Bonaparte, Abigail was more irreverent than
awed at the prospect. Some called him "King," she noted, but in her
opinion, his head was in more danger in Paris than in Egypt. She even
questioned just how long he would be able to call it his own. She did,
however, allow that he was "an adventurous Man," and though one
did not know what he stood for, or what his views were, she did not
sound so much impatient as curious. "Times must develope them,"
she said, and, furthermore, "astonishment with respect to [the
French] has long ceased, and wonder is baffled."[55]

TWENTY-ONE

At Least Fall
with Ease

A curious warning preceded Abigail's November arrival in Philadelphia. The coming winter, John had written her on October 25, 1799, the "red letter day" of their thirty-fifth anniversary, would be the last they would ever spend in Philadelphia. She would be wise to leave early in April, and not come south again for a year and a half at least. An election was approaching, he said, that would set them at liberty from their "uncomfortable journeys," and he would never have her think of "going to Georgetown upon uncertainties, or rather upon the certainty of leaving it on the fourth of March, with five hundred fifty or six hundred miles to ride through the mud."[1]

Despite John's pessimism, which could only have been deepened by the heartbreak of Charles's impending death and the bleak certainty of Colonel Smith's future, Abigail was swiftly entrenched in her role of President's wife. It was a tribute to her stolid sense of duty, her pride, her vanity, her constant moralizing ("No cup so bitter, but what some cordial drops are mingled by a kind Providence," and "Gloom is no part of my Religion"), that she was almost immediately on arrival able to plan drawing rooms, receive and visit, even note in scathing detail whose bodices were too revealing (and "litterally look like Nursing Mothers"), whose cheeks were "Rouged up to the Ears." Her own interest in fashion, however, was far from casual. Just how fastidious she was—and Mrs. Smith as well—was revealed in her requests of Mrs. Cranch.[2]

Would her "dear Sister," Abigail wrote on December 4, look in her clothes trunk in her Quincy garret for her white lutestring dress and silver-trimmed coat, which she regretted having overlooked?—also for the silk-embroidered muslin dress belonging to Mrs. Smith, who, with Caroline, was spending the winter with her parents. Meanwhile, the colonel, head of a regiment at Washington's recommendation, was settled at his camp in Plainfield, New Jersey. Abigail wished for some red broadcloth as well, since cloaks of this material were "all the mode," especially when trimmed with white fur, and "much more rational" than wearing only a shawl in winter. And though she appreciated the practicality of muslin ("new every time it is clean & new trimmed"), she preferred the use of silks and thought at her age she was privileged "to sit a fashion."[3]

As exhaustively as Abigail was preoccupied by social and domestic concerns (she turned to New England on behalf of her larder as well as her wardrobe, sending for twenty bushels of white potatoes and half a dozen barrels of cider), her correspondence flourished. The trick, she found, was to rise one hour earlier than her family to go into the President's room and write as quickly and fully as she could manage in this rare time of privacy. The hushed room, with its three tall southerly windows and the eastern one that caught the earliest sunbeams, seemed not only to invite but to foster Abigail's fluent, frank, and often impassioned observations on the current scene. She pronounced the political sky of Pennsylvania "more dark and gloomy than the natural Horizon," and, still at dagger's point with the majority of the press, she was ever vulnerable to the "curiosities" produced by its "Tools." Allowing that she would rejoice in being a false "prophetise," she predicted that the state would weep "tears of Blood" over its "unbounded" reception of foreigners.[4]

In an equivocal mood, tainted with defeat these days, Abigail portrayed a President abused by strangers and supposed friends, and complained of the "uphill machine" that was her nation's government, failed by "American Ambition, delusion and frenzy" and by "underminers" serving local and personal views and interests at the expense of the greater cause. As for the "Mad democratic Stile" and the "impudence" of the British-born, Oxford-educated Thomas Cooper, who blasted the President for his "seizure" of power to make treaties and to enact laws against foreigners, she could only "presume," she told Mrs. Cranch, that he subjected himself to the penalty of the Sedition Act.[5]

The claws of partisan politics were also visible to Abigail in that winter's irksome tale of Jonathan Robbins, the wretched seaman accused of piracy and murder aboard HMS *Hermione*. He claimed to be an American born in Danbury, Connecticut, and therefore impervious to British punishment. In truth, Robbins was an Irishman named Thomas Nash, whose surrender to British authority by the President's decree, defended by Chief Justice John Marshall before the House of Representatives, was governed by the terms of Jay's Treaty. Abigail deplored the time wasted on this "trifling business" inflated unfairly by the "noise" and "clamour" of the Jacobins, who deliberately fostered the suggestion of presidential injustice to a deserving American, who threw "obstacles in the way of every measure useful and benificial to the public." And sensitive to private as well as party forms of sabotage ("the time for intrigue is approaching"), Abigail wrote her chilling indictment of Timothy Pickering on December 11, 1799, five months and one day before his dismissal.

> There is a man in the cabinet, whose manners are forbiding, whose temper is sour and whose resentments are implacable, who neverless would like to dictate every Measure. He has to deal with *one,* who knows full well their respective departments—and who chuses to feel quite independant, and to act so too, but for this He is abused. But I am mistaken if this dictator does not get himself ensnared in his own toil. He would not now remain in office, if the President possesst such kind of resentments as I hear from various quarters, he permits himself to utter—From this fountain have flowed all the unpopularity of the Mission to France, which some of the federilists have been so deluded as to swallow large draughts off.[6]

However persuasive, vivid, or prescient Abigail's observations were, it was probably her response to George Washington's death on Saturday, December 14, that demonstrated most uniquely her unsurpassed talents as commentator on the passing scene. On Christmas Day she reported that all classes were plunged into "universal melancholy" because of the former President's death. And yet her drawing room, two days later, drew its largest crowd ever, upwards of a hundred ladies whose grief, she noted wryly, "did not deprive them of taste in ornamenting their white dresses." But if the black fans, flowers, plumes, and swags of ribbon commemorated the death of the beloved statesman with a touch more elegance than was seemly under the circumstances, Abigail was understanding. As she expected this to be the last winter in Philadelphia that would afford them the opportunity to wear "gay attire," the ladies, she said sympathetically, "intended shining."[7]

Initially, Abigail's own tribute to Washington was luminous with appreciative insights, though characteristically not without critical edge. The whole was formally conceived as though meant to be addressed to the nation at large, instead of an audience of one, Mrs. Cranch:

> This Event so important to our Country at this period, will be
> universally deplored. No Man ever lived, more deservedly beloved
> and Respected. The praise and I may say addulation which
> followed his administration for several years, never made him
> forget that he was a Man, subject to the weakness and frailty
> attached to humane Nature. He never grew giddy, but ever
> mantaind a modest diffidence of his own talents, and if that was an
> error, it was of the amiable and engageing kind, tho it might lead
> sometimes to a want of decisions in some great Emergencys.

Having hinted at Washington's possible flaws with masterful subtlety, Abigail was perhaps somewhat less delicate in calling attention, at long last, to her husband's attributes. She continued:

> If we look through the whole tennor of his Life, History will not
> produce to us a Parrallel. Heaven has seen fit to take him from us.
> Our Mourning is sincere, in the midst of which, we ought not to
> lose sight of the Blessings we have enjoy'd and still partake of, that
> he was spaired to us, untill he saw a successor filling his place,
> persueing the same system which he had adopted, and that in times
> which have been equally dangerous and Critical. It becomes not me
> to say more upon this Head.[8]

Undoubtedly genuine in her professed appreciation of "the Man who united all Hearts," Abigail wearied of a mourning period that was too long and fawning. In the words of one writer she admired, "Our Washington's Character was whiter than it was brilliant," yet the brilliance had "drugged" all beholders. By the end of the year, Abigail was convinced that "sufficient" had been done to express grateful feelings of a people toward the "Character of even a Washington." Her worst fears that things had gone "too far" were surpassed when she read the eulogy delivered in Newburyport's First

Presbyterian Meeting House, referring to the "saviour" of the country, who, "having reached the summit of human perfection," had "quitted the region of human glory."[9]

Abigail had even less tolerance for the "Mad Rant of Bombast" heard by parishioners in Charlestown and reprinted in the *Boston Centinel.* In twelve pages and twenty-three paragraphs, Rosewell Messinger assured readers that while the sun of the firmament was not darkened, the foundations of the earth did not tremble, the rocks did not fall to dust or mountains melt away, nonetheless the veil of liberty's temple was "rent in twain" with the retirement through the portals of everlasting fame of their "spotless high-priest." The most trying passage for Abigail must have been one suggesting that grief must pierce the center of Adams's heart now that the "prophet" with whom he walked had departed, and offering the hope that God would make him "Columbia's second Savior."[10]

By January 28, 1800, Abigail was clearly out of patience:

> To no one Man in America, belongs the Epithet of *Saviour* of his Country That Washingtons Character, when we take into view, his Education, the place of his Birth, and the various scenes in which he was call'd to act, exhibits a most uncommon assemblage of Modesty, Moderation, Magninimity, fortititud, perseverence and disinterestedness, will be most readily allowed. . . .

However, Americans needed to be reminded of the simple fact that in her estimation, "at no time, did the fate of America rest upon the Breath of even a Washington, and those who assert these things, are Ignorant of the spirit of their countrymen, and whilst they strive to exalt one character, degrade that of their Country."[11]

After six weeks had been devoted to honoring George Washington —more time than was accorded kings or princesses, to her knowledge—Abigail came to terms with how his memory might best be honored: "Wise and judicious observations upon his Character are those only which will out live the badges of mourning. Simple Truth is his best his greatest Eulogy. She alone can render his Fame immortal."[12]

More than the melting snows or the flowing rivers, it was the weeping willow that Abigail hailed as the "first harbinger" of spring. Usually, the sight of the hopeful yellows and promising greens renewed her spirits. But this time they saddened her, and each time she rode by them she was reminded of the final farewell she must say to this city of bricks and crowds and ceremony that she had learned to live with in comfort. The idea of leaving a place for the last time made her pensive. "It is like burying a Friend," she said. But leave-taking was always difficult, especially when the alternative seemed particularly unsuitable. The city of Washington, from all she could tell, was "ill calculated for the residence of such a Body as Congress"; the houses, she had heard, were "so distant, the streets so miry, and the markets so ill supplied."[13]

By March, Abigail's sense of displacement was dramatized by political deliberations that sapped her of optimism and cramped her perspective. She was disdainful of congressional debates prolonged for electioneering purposes. If, for example, Virginia's "Little Johnny" Randolph lived to be the age of an antediluvian, his services would never be worth the cost of his lingering "magpye" chatter on the merits of disbanding what he insulted as a "mercenary" army, an army of "ragamuffins." This tiresomely zealous congressman, who looked no more than a lad of seventeen or eighteen, was like the fly on the wheel in the Aesop fable, as far as Abigail was concerned, calling attention to the dust he had raised. She was even more discouraged by the "contrived business" of the anti-Federalists and wondered just how long the "Ghost of Nash" would be allowed to haunt Congress. Brooding over the handling of the Nash-Robbins case, which she did repeatedly, she was more and more convinced of the shameful way the Jacobins wasted every "subterfuge, mean art & declamation" on the subject, and "not from a Love of Justice, or apprehension that a fellow creature was unjustly punished, but merely to hold out to their party that the President had Encroached upon the Judiciary, and assumed an influence which was unconstitutional."[14]

Abigail knew the truth to be different, and that the President had acted "in strict conformity" with Jay's Treaty. She was shattered that her husband should suffer such political turbulence, let alone such virulent criticism, especially when the nation he governed enjoyed as much peace, quiet, security, and happiness as any people could boast. Abigail's recommendation for a solution to the insulting dilemmas of political life indeed verified her admission that her mind was not in a cheerful state, or a particularly hardy one. Her talk of limiting elections was pitiful testimony to the crushing pressure that was the eternal price to be paid by those who occupied high office. Sadly, though momentarily, the democratic way had failed her. It was her suggestion to Mrs. Cranch that "one or two more Elections will be quite sufficient I believe to convince this people that no engine can be more fatally employd than frequent popular Elections, to corrupt and destroy the morals of the people. . . ."[15]

On May 2, Abigail held her last drawing room in Philadelphia. The same day, her trunks were loaded, along with newly carved marble hearths and special jams, on a boat bound for Boston. Though she was extremely busy winding up her affairs in Philadelphia, planning, supervising, and even staffing her ambitiously expanded house in Quincy from afar, political questions of the day had never received her closer scrutiny. "As present appearances indicate," this would be the last time she would live or visit in Philadelphia. Latest reports were extremely sobering, and obviously anxiety-provoking, she told Mrs. Cranch:

> That New York would be the balance in the skaill, scaill, (is it right now? it does not look so), New York by an effort to bring into their assembly anti-federal Men, will make also an antifederal ticket for President; and this will give all the power sought by that Party, which at the sacrifice of all that Good men hold dear and sacred, they are determined upon.[16]

Abigail bitterly doled out blame for the President's unfairly compromised position to Cooper and Randolph, and to William Edward Livingston, the representative from New York who had introduced a resolution calling for examination of the presidential papers pertaining to Jay's Treaty with England. The "host" of James Thomson Callender's lies about the President, circulated in *The Prospect Before Us,* wrought irrevocable damage, according to Abigail. The Scottish "wretch" warned readers about taking their chances "between Adams, war, and beggary, and Jefferson, peace and competency." He also made savage references to the President as "that strange compound of ignorance and ferocity, of deceit and weakness," and, worse, insisted "the people of the United States have a million good reasons for wishing to see a peacable, a constitutional, and a speedy termination of the reign of Mr. Adams."[17]

Unfortunately, Abigail did not have to look to the likes of Callender for sources of defection. Her cryptic paragraph to her cousin William Smith only hinted at the insidious turmoil within the President's Cabinet. On May 16 she wrote: "You will learn that great Changes have taken place in the Cabinet—some will mourn, some will rejoice, Some will blame others will confuse, all this was foreseen." This was not quite true. Neither Abigail nor John indicated any knowledge of Hamilton's hope that Adams would be succeeded by Washington; his conspiracy had been foiled only by the latter's death. Nor was it probable that either realistically suspected the breadth of the network of opponents rallied by Hamilton—or their treacherous capabilities. Yet a day of reckoning did inevitably arrive. The President's explosive condemnation of his Secretary of War, whose deference to Hamilton insulted his own judgment, precipitated McHenry's offer to resign, which was readily accepted on May 5, effective three weeks later. Emboldened by this first step in fortifying his staff, the President's next move was the dismissal of Pickering. Proud of their replacements—John Marshall of Virginia as Secretary of State, Samuel Dexter of Massachusetts as Secretary of War—the President had no knowledge, apparently, that in his retention of Oliver Wolcott as Secretary of the Treasury, his political life was still terminally threatened.[18]

Before Congress adjourned on May 13, each party held a caucus of congressmen to select its candidates for President and Vice-President. The Federalists nominated President Adams and Charles Cotesworth Pinckney, and the Republicans nominated Jefferson and Aaron Burr. There was nothing about the "Election Storm" that promised Abigail the sun she craved. Gloom hung "heavey" at her heart. As one who "must" share all the malice and reproach accorded her "better half," knowing how sincerely his measures were meant to promote the best interests of his country, she was openly dismayed by the "tongues of falshood." Surely, she thought, she suffered enough anxiety to humble a prouder heart than hers.[19]

Summer in Quincy by no means brought the tranquillity Abigail sought. She was troubled by news from Berlin, five months past, that Louisa Catherine had suffered her fourth miscarriage. She fretted about Thomas and whether this "good, amiable, and virtuous" son would succeed in business. But most of all, she concerned herself with events as they affected the President, none more provocative than the trials held in Philadelphia the summer of 1800. They were conducted by Judge Samuel Chase, a native of Maryland, signer of the Declaration of Independence, and appointee of George Washington to the Supreme Court on January 26, 1796, and were thought to make a mockery of the First Amendment.[20]

Congressman Matthew Lyon of Vermont was sentenced to jail for four months and fined because he had protested Adams's "unbounded thirst for ridiculous pomp, foolish adulation and selfish avarice." Thomas Cooper was convicted of tending to incite "insurrection against the government" because he had attacked Adams for enlarging the army and navy and because, in Chase's words, he had "intended to mislead the ignorant and inflame their minds against the President and influence their votes in the next election." Though William Duane (successor to Benjamin Franklin Bache, who had died before coming to trial) managed, by legal machinations, to keep out of jail for his anti-Federalist attacks, he would eventually be indicted the following October.[21]

However much Abigail thought she was prepared for the worst—she had predicted an entire year of abuse and scandal, "enough to ruin & corrupt the minds and morals of the best people in the world"—she was continually unnerved by the severity of the diverse attacks on the President. There were Hamiltonian factions everywhere striving for the election of Pinckney over Adams, spurred by their leader's vow to do anything, at all costs, even at the price of electing Jefferson, to prevent Adams's reelection. The Hamiltonians' complaints were numerous: both the President's mission to France and the treaty with Great Britain diminished the military and, therefore, Hamilton's ambitions to command a grand army; the Alien and Sedition Acts had been controversial from the start; the President's handling of the Robbins-Nash trial was unacceptable; his secrecy and independence were intolerable.[22]

The President's decision in May 1800 to pardon John Fries, the Pennsylvanian charged with treason and sentenced to death for inciting hundreds of men to rebel against a federal property tax instituted two summers before in preparation for war with France, would prove unpopular with members of both parties. The death penalty was shocking punishment, in the President's opinion; it required "the closest attention of my best understanding, and will prove a severe trial to my heart," he had written Colonel Pickering during the latter's last days in office.[23]

Pickering, too, declared the idea of taking a man's life "painful," but felt a "calm and solid satisfaction," he said, "that an opportunity is now presented, in executing the just sentence of the law." Wolcott backed Pickering: the execution would "inspire the well-disposed with confidence in the government, and the malevolent with terror"; the execution would "be enough to show the power of the laws to punish." To Pickering and Wolcott, and to Judge Chase, who confirmed the death sentence on retrial, the President submitted a series of questions on May 20 in an attempt to weigh other opinions before arriving at his own decision to free Fries. "It highly concerns the people of the United States, and especially the federal government," he had said, "that, in the whole progress and ultimate conclusion of this affair, neither humanity be unnecessarily afflicted, nor public justice be essentially violated, nor the public safety endangered." Federalists called his act of pardon a "fatal concession to his enemies." His enemies, however, viewed his reversal of their considered opinion as still another insult, another example of his intolerable independence, another proof that his reelection was undesirable.[24]

The word was out—confidentially, of course—that "Mr. Adams must be sacrificed." Hamilton charged himself with compiling the evidence, freely given by such persons as the recently unemployed Wolcott, who believed "it would be a disgrace to the federal party, to permit the re-election of Mr. Adams." Hamilton could count on Wolcott's cooperation "in every reasonable measure" for effecting the election of Pinckney in place of Adams.[25]

By the end of October, with the subversive assistance of Wolcott and others, Hamilton's paper, "The Public Conduct and Character of John Adams Esq., President of the United States," was complete. Though meant for Federalist consumption, it was, thanks to Aaron Burr's mysterious interception during its printing stage, destined for a far wider audience than originally anticipated. Avidly dispersed by the opposition press, Hamilton's document was considered by the despised editor Willian Duane as having done "more mischief to the parties concerned than all the labors of the *Aurora.*"[26]

Perhaps the strangest aspect of what John Quincy would call the "strange history" of Hamilton's paper was its author's failure to realize that the product of such warped logic would destroy not only Adams but Pinckney and the Federalist cause at large. Hamilton, leaving no insult to the imagination, stated with breathtaking boldness that though he did not deny Adams's "patriotism, integrity, and, even talents of a certain kind," he would be deficient in candor if he concealed his conviction that the President did "not possess the talents adapted to the Administration of Government," and that there were "great and intrinsic defects in his character, which unfit him for the office of Chief Magistrate. . . ."[27]

Hamilton had reached his conclusion, he assured his readers, after

"careful observations" of Adams several communications, of his conduct of foreign affairs and so-called diplomatic negotiations, and of
his "serious errors" of administration. After intense scrutiny, Hamilton had concluded that Adams was "a man of an imagination sub-
limated and eccentric; propitious neither to the regular display of
sound judgment, nor to steady perseverance in a systematic plan of
conduct. . . ." Hamilton had begun, in fact, he wrote, "to perceive
what has been since too manifest, that to this defect are added the
unfortunate foibles of a vanity without bounds, and a jealousy capable of discoloring every object."[28]

In sustaining his assault, Hamilton had turned his quill into an all
but lethal weapon. Mr. Adams was responsible for "undermining"
the government; there was "real cause to apprehend" that it might
"totter, if not fall, under his future auspices." And yet, most grudgingly, having vented all his prejudices and insults, Hamilton granted
that he resolved not to advise withholding a single vote from the
President. It was even apparent to him, he added, that the majority
of Federalists, "for want of sufficient knowledge of facts, are not
convinced of the expediency of relinquishing him." And finally, after
dismembering his target, Hamilton perversely stopped short of burying him. "Reluctantly," Hamilton decided he would not oppose
Adams's reelection, despite his "unqualified conviction of his unfitness for the station contemplated. . . ." Party loyalty had apparently
won the day. He would not entirely abandon the President because
of the "great importance of cultivating harmony among the support-
ers of the Government on whose firm union hereafter will probably
depend the preservation of order, tranquillity, liberty, property; the
security of every social and domestic blessing."[29]

The President's immediate reaction to Hamilton's cruel paper was
remarkably magnanimous, at least outside the family realm. He
would wait nine years before answering Hamilton in a series of eighteen letters published in the *Boston Patriot.* More vengeful with age,
or perhaps freer to speak his mind, he would, still later, refer to
Hamilton as "a bastard Bratt of a Scotch Pedlar." But for the time
being he was almost generous. "I am not his enemy, and never was,"
the President had written to a friend on December 3, 1800. "I have
not adored him, like his idolaters, and have had great cause to disapprove of some of his politics. He has talents, if he would correct
himself, which might be useful." The President insisted he would
dread neither Hamilton's "menaces" nor his pamphlets, and observed that Washington had been similarly threatened. He had

nevertheless reached a conclusion regarding Hamilton: "There is more burnish . . . on the outside, than sterling silver in the substance."[30]

As a result of Hamilton's attack, Abigail was, not unexpectedly, even more defensive of her husband. She wrote again of the President's "pure views and intentions," of his walking "steadfastly on, tho the shafts and arrows of disappointed ambition are hurled at him from every quarter." She wrote Mrs. Cranch that she could not speak for the President regarding "the little Gen'll," as she referred to Hamilton, "because no one else knows all the circumstances, or can deny what he has published for facts; many of which are as grose lies as Duane has told in the *Aurora*. . . ." Someday soon, she promised her sister, the two of them would laugh at the folly and pity the weakness, vanity, and ambitious views of Hamilton, and there would be a time, she hoped, when Hamilton might appear "still more odious than he now does." For now, however, Abigail was resigned to the fact that the damage was done. The voice was unanimous in all quarters: "It is Hamilton has done his own business."[31]

Repeatedly of late, Abigail mentioned "trials of various kinds" that seemed reserved for her grey hairs and declining years, and talked of how she counted on a "strong imagination" as a refuge from sorrow, as a "kindly solace for a feeling heart." In the case of her son Charles, it almost seemed as though his death was to be her refuge from sorrow over his life. Passing through New York on her way from Quincy to Philadelphia the second week in November, Abigail had realized that Charles was dying. She had visited him at the home of a friend, where his wife, Sally, was tending him. Bloated with disease, sometimes deranged, her son was mortally ill, beyond hope of recovery, the doctor said, and she knew then that she had seen him for the last time.[32]

Three weeks later, on November 30, Charles, an alcoholic wreck, was dead of complications of liver and lung disease and dropsy. "Weep with me," Abigail beseeched Mrs. Cranch, "over the Grave of a poor unhappy child who cannot now add an other pang to those which have peirced my Heart for several years past. . . ." Sorrowful as she was, Abigail faced the truth of Charles's last years. She was consoled by knowing that the once "darling" of his Father's heart was "beloved, in spite of his errors"; people spoke in grief and sorrow of his "habits." Grasping for straws of comfort, Abigail noted that

Charles, even near death, had not looked like an intemperate man. Though bloated, he was not red.[33]

It was just as they were about to sit down to supper that the grandsons, William and John Smith, who were boarding with Aunt Elizabeth Peabody, in Haverhill, heard Jefferson announced as successor to their grandfather. As a result, neither could swallow a bit of food; their aunt scarcely managed better. Both of the colonel's sons recognized their economic dependence on their grandfather; it was John who wondered, now that their benefactor was jobless, who would carry them through college.[34]

The monetary issue was also John Quincy's urgent concern, but for entirely different reasons. Even though his father had managed his properties prudently, he had hardly grown rich in public service. He wrote to Thomas from Berlin on December 20, 1800, authorizing "all and every part" of his own property to be placed under his brother's management, "whether of principle or interest," as subject to his father's disposal. "You will not mention to him that I have given you this instruction," John Quincy had added, "for I wish not to make a show of offering service where it is not wanted. . . ."[35]

Abigail's own reaction to having her husband voted out of office was complicated and difficult, no matter to what degree she had prepared herself for the outcome. Despite "Peace with France,—a Revenue increased beyond any former years—our prospects brightening on every side," her husband was rejected. "What must be the thoughts and the reflections of those, who, calling themselves Federalists, have placed their country in a situation full of dangers and perils; who have wantonly thrown away the blessings Heaven seemed to have in reserve for them?" she wondered. She blamed New York as the source of the defection, and specifically the intrigues of two men. In her opinion, Hamilton had sowed the seeds of discontent and division among the Federalists, and Burr had seized the lucky moment of mounting into power on Jefferson's shoulders.[36]

According to Abigail's analysis, South Carolina's abandonment was also fundamental to the Federalists' loss to the Jacobins. Spring's "advance skirmishes" had failed, despite Hamilton's encouragement, to persuade Pinckney's state to elect its native son. When votes were counted, Pinckney had won sixty-four, one less than Adams, and far from the hoped-for mandate that would have elected him President. With seventy-three votes counted equally for Jefferson and for Burr,

Abigail was reminded of an "old and just" proverb: "Never halloo until you are out of the woods." The Federalists had been gulled by Southern promises that had "no more faith, when made to Northern men," she said wistfully, "than lover's vows."[37]

In dealing with the consequences of the election in her private life, Abigail was sensible and even gracious. She confided to her son Thomas that for herself and for the family she had few regrets: "At my age, and with my bodily infirmities I shall be happier at Quincy. Neither my habits, nor my education or inclinations, have led me to an expensive style of living, so that on that score I have little to mourn over. If I did not rise with dignity, I can at least fall with ease, which is the more difficult task." She was, however, concerned about her husband, and told Thomas her reasons: "I wish your father's circumstances were not so limited and circumscribed, as they must be, because he cannot indulge himself in those improvements upon his farm, which his inclination leads him to, and which would serve to amuse him, and contribute to his health."[38]

As absorbed as she was by personal and immediate concerns, however, even in defeat she remained the eloquent patriot above all:

> I feel not any resentment against those who are coming into
> power, and only wish the future administration of the government
> may be as productive of the peace, happiness, and prosperity of the
> nation, as the two former ones have been. I leave to time the
> unfolding of a drama. I leave to posterity to reflect upon the times
> past; and I leave them characters to contemplate.

Her own intentions were clear; she expected to return to Quincy as "conveniently" as she could. As it was John's thought that they retire together, "and not one before the other," it was mid-February before she headed north.[39]

The day after he arrived in Washington, November 2, John had issued an invitation to Abigail: "The building is in a state to be habitable, and now we wish for your company." He was obviously moved by the potential, if not the immediate, physical splendor and political significance of what he referred to as the President's House: "I pray heaven to bestow the best of blessings on this house, and on all that shall hereafter inhabit it. May none but honest and wise men ever rule under this roof!" He would not attempt a description of the house, however, telling Abigail, "You will form the best idea of it from inspection."[40]

The wise husband was not to be disappointed. Abigail left

Philadelphia for the "unseen abode" with a party of nine borne by ten horses, and arrived at her destination on Sunday, November 16. Woods were all that Abigail saw from Baltimore to Washington, except for one windowless cottage. It was, indeed, coming into "a new country," negotiating through the ten-mile clearing of trees and tree stumps, circled by wilderness, however romantic.[41]

Within the city ("which is only so in name"), she seemed rather surprised to find that enough buildings had been built to accommodate Congress, but, as they were scattered rather than close by, she saw "no great comfort" for their inhabitants. She could not, however, once ensconced in the President's House, deny the fascination of her view of the Potomac River and its thriving traffic. Nor could she fail to be somewhat awed by the "grand and superb scale" of the "great castle," her temporary home, or be dismayed that there was not a sign of a fenced yard without, and not a single completed apartment within; the main staircase, furthermore, would not be up that winter. Necessities were to be tended first. Twelve fireplaces must be lighted to alleviate the chilling dampness; there was no place to hang the laundry for the time being but in "the great unfinished audience Room"; replacements were needed for broken or stolen china and looking glasses only tall enough for dwarfs, she insisted, before she established the drawing rooms the ladies clamored for.[42]

A demanding perfectionist as usual, when it came to organizing her household, Abigail was hardly satisfied by either the number or the abilities of her servants. Even though she said thirteen white servants were worth twenty blacks (it would take thirty to manage house, garden, and stables when complete), she was not impressed. She was quick to criticize the former for their general lack of diligence, enterprise and energy, as she was the latter for listlessness, indolence, and "apparent want of capacity for business." As always, it was Briesler who seemed to pave the way to somewhat gracious living; in this instance, he located nine cords of wood, two hundred bushels of coal, and the bells that were so essential for communication in the vast and understaffed household.[43]

As much as Abigail complained about housekeeping and social obligations—it was a day's work to market and to return calls, especially to those who lived in Georgetown, the dirtiest hole she had ever seen to trade or live in, and an absolute quagmire after a rain—she was in an adventurous spirit. She was proud of her ability to content herself almost anywhere for three months, and she was entirely ap-

preciative of her neighbors' cordial attention, manifested by Major
Custis's welcoming note, Mrs. Lewis's haunch of venison, and re-
gards with "love" and an invitation to Mount Vernon from Mrs.
Washington.[44]

The city of Washington and the President's House were, after all,
Abigail understood full well, not built for immediate gratification,
but "for the ages." As critical as she appeared, she meant to hurt no
one. She specifically asked that her comments not be repeated. "You
must keep all this to yourself," she told Mrs. Smith. Instead, she
would have her daughter, when asked how her mother liked Washington, say that the "situation is beautiful, which is true." And even
now she found the crimson-draped upstairs oval room "handsome,"
and thought that when it was completed, it would be "beautiful."
Essentially, her complaints about her living situation, taken as a
whole, came down to this very matter of the finished and the unfinished. The meticulous housewife who made an art of supplying,
staffing, and even building her home sincerely believed things would
have proceeded more efficiently in Washington in other hands—
Northern hands, specifically. "If the twelve years, in which this place
has been considered as the future seat of government, had been
improved, as they would have been if in New England, very many of
the present inconveniences would have been removed," she had
assured Mrs. Smith.[45]

Abigail suffered from feverish chills, rheumatism, and depression,
and yet she could barely tear herself away from Washington before
February 13, "the great important day" when it was expected that the
future President ("future Ruler," she called him) would be known.
Though she recognized present politics as a "mere turn penny," and
professed to leave speculation to others more closely involved, she
was as deeply absorbed as ever in the personalities who governed her
nation's affairs. She turned over and over in her mind the merits and
demerits of Jefferson and Burr, the principals in the drama of the
"present Crisis." She was hardly clear in her own mind as to how she
hoped the House of Representatives would enforce their responsibility to differentiate between the candidates initially tied by equal
votes for the President's office.[46]

"Long acquaintance, private friendship, and the full belief that the
private Character of one" was "much purer than the other" inclined
her toward Jefferson. Also, his age and experience seemed to give
him prior right. And yet she was too much of a conservative to be

comfortable with this choice, with the "visionary system of Government" that would undoubtedly be adopted under Jefferson. Worrying about the resulting "Evils" that would affect the country, she was sometimes inclined toward Aaron Burr, the more "bold, daring and decisive Character" who would support, she believed, the present system for a longer time. Shakespeare's *King John* seemed to exemplify what she was talking about:

> *A Sceptre, snatch'd with an unruly hand*
> *Must be as boistrously maintain'd as gain'd;*
> *And he that stands upon a slipp'ry place*
> *Makes nice of no vile hold to stay him up.* [47]

There were other differences between the candidates that disquieted her. Neither one met Abigail's standards on the question of religion. Jefferson made "no pretentions to the belief of an all wise and supreme Governour of the World." He was not, therefore, in Abigail's opinion, a believer in the Christian system. And though she would not accuse him of being an atheist, she rather thought he believed religion was only useful for political purposes. As for outward forms, she had once heard him dismiss them as "mere Mummery." Burr, on the other hand, was hardly a desirable alternative. Though he might be more of a believer, Abigail was convinced, because of his practices, that he had more to answer for.[48]

Members of the House of Representatives began to cast their votes on February 11 and were finished six days later, on the thirty-sixth ballot, when Jefferson won the backing of ten states, one more than was essential to his election. But Abigail had not been able to wait for the final count. She was persuaded to leave before the roads were even more tortuous, and by Friday, February 13, she had safely reached Baltimore, in spite of her niece's pleas to turn back. Abigail seemed in fine humor, and nearly smug as she reported to William Shaw that in answer to her companion's nervous queries about how she could travel such "horrid" roads through such "shocking wilderness" without some gentleman with her, other than the coachman, she had laughed, scolded, and "bragged" that she was too independent to want a gentleman always at her side. Though she allowed it would have been "very agreable" to have one along, she explained that she was "accustomed to get through many a trying scene and combat many difficulties alone."[49]

John was to follow Abigail, he promised; he would begin his five-hundred-mile trip home on March 4, as soon as he had done with unfinished business. Meanwhile, he was burdened with preparations for his leave-taking, with nominations of judges and consuls and other officers. March 3 found him signing commissions of his new appointees under the Judiciary Act passed on February 13. By appointing John Marshall as Chief Justice of the Supreme Court, and others whom Jefferson deemed his "most ardent political enemies," John committed, at least in his successor's opinion, the most provocative, perverse act of all his term in office. It was the "one act" of his life, "and one only," that Jefferson would claim as a source of "personal displeasure," as "personally unkind." It was "but common justice," Jefferson would explain, to leave a successor free to make his own choices.[50]

Unquestionably, John had concerned himself profoundly with the realities of "total relinquishment" of public life. For all his yearning for Penn's Hill, for his trees and flowers and fences and rocks, he was enormously apprehensive when they were almost at his fingertips. What should he do with himself? he wondered, posing the question repeatedly to many of his friends. "Something I must do or ennui will rain upon me in bucketts," he had confided to Cotton Tufts the past December. Would books and farms answer his needs? Or foddering his cattle morning and evening? Or a walk every noon to Penn's Hill? Perhaps, if he had enough money, he might work at his farming, but clearly he did not. Nor was the bar available. He claimed to have forgotten all his law and lost his organs of speech, and besides, he had given all his law books away. Suffused with worry, he was preparing for the worst, fearing that he would suffer another trial when he came to exchange the routine of domestic life, without much exercise, for a life of distant voyages in which he had been engaged for forty-two years.[51]

John came home to the stillness of Quincy and his shrunken realm on March 23 to find one hundred loads of seaweed in his yard, to be used as fertilizer. With a certain bitterness he was reminded of another wayfarer. "I thought I had made a good exchange," he wrote to Samuel Dexter, "if Ulysses is an orthodox authority in this case, which I do not believe, of honors and virtues for manure."[52]

For months it was not only John but Abigail who worried about adjustment to rural life. Elaborating on concerns already mentioned to her son Thomas, she talked to others about John's being too old to have further opportunities to labor in the bustling world, and said his "small means" did not promise a great deal. And though she dwelt on the "fervent Wish" that she and John be allowed to lead "peaceable and quiet Lives" from now on, she too did not find it easy to relinquish power. As she explained to Elizabeth: "As one of the principle pleasures of my Life has been to do good according to my ability with the means indulged me; my sole regret, as it personally respects myself is, that those means will in future be so greatly curtailed, and limited. . . ."[53]

Just as she had trusted that the "wish and the will" to help others would not forsake her in private life, so Abigail trusted she would behave with grace in other trying circumstances. She had no "disposition" to seclude herself from society just because she had met with unkind or ungrateful returns from some of its members. She vowed to have the discipline not to become "querilious" with the world, "not to molest or disturb the administration of the new government" —provided it did not adopt measures "ruinous" to her country. With inspired vision she wished "for the preservation of the Government, and a wise administration of it. In the best situation, with the wisest head and firmest Heart, it will be surrounded with perplexities, dangers and troubles, that are little conceived of by those into whose Hands it is like to fall."[54]

Certainly there was no reason to question Abigail's idealized dream of her future role. But as clover is to the bee, so politics was to Abigail. In May, settled in Quincy, possibly inspired by such an abundance of flowers and greenery, she was her own vigorously opinionated self. Her view of the United States, as of spring 1801, was guarded: "If we do not look down and pitty Things, we have equal reason to commisirate an infatuated deluded multitude who are hastning upon themselves more missery than they have enjoyed of tranquility & happiness for twelve years past." And her prediction for the future was indeed pessimistic: "Measures are in agitiation which will darken our Hemisphere, and overspread the whole Horizon; and the multitude are driving, not knowing the Destruction which must overwhelm us in one common calamity."[55]

More cheerful, another day, Abigail thanked Colonel Smith for his present of raspberry bushes and a pot of strawberry vines. She also asked that he give a message to his wife: "Tell her I have commenced my operation of dairywoman; and she might see me, at five o'clock in the morning skimming my milk."[56]

PART
FOUR

TWENTY-TWO

Faithful
Are the Wounds

Abigail "trembled" for their safety, and now, "God be praised," John Quincy, Louisa, and their five-month-old infant, George Washington, had docked in Philadelphia on September 4, 1801, after a fifty-eight-day passage from Hamburg. Naval officers carried this welcome news to the Adamses' Quincy door on September 12, and John responded with instant hospitality. Accountable for John Quincy's return—to save him possible embarrassment with the incumbent administration, he had instructed John Marshall to prepare letters for his recall from Prussia the previous February—the father wrote that he could "hardly wait" to see him and his family. Further, he hoped John Quincy would consider his parents' house as his home, for himself, his "lady," his son, and for their servants and domestics. With somewhat oracular cadence, he had added, "We can accommodate you all as well as Destiny intends that you and I ought to be accommodated, at least until you have Time to deliberate your future arrangements."[1]

Eleven days later, Abigail sent her special "Welcome, welcome" to her "Dear Son" after a seven-year absence. She was concerned about the effect the sudden change would have on him and his family, and about their exposure to the prevalent fever. Implicit in her abiding solicitude for her son was concern for her daughter-in-law Louisa. She now knew a great deal about Louisa and feared for her. Louisa's difficult confinement the past April had made Abigail anxious for her son "in all respects." She thought of him as "burdened" by his "poor weake and feeble wife and Boy" and confided as much to Thomas, especially now that she anticipated "how many cares of Body and mind" John Quincy would encounter "to Begin anew the World in a profession he never loved, in a place which promised him no great harvest, where there are so many reapers."[2]

Abigail was plain-spoken on all counts. "Mrs. Adams is going to a place, different from all she has ever yet visited, and amongst a people where it is impossible for her to be too guarded," she wrote on September 23. Furthermore, "every syllable she utters" would be received with "carping malice; such is the spirit of the party." Abigail's concise explanation was penetrating, nevertheless. Louisa's family "have been very basely traduced—There are persons no doubt hurrying after Mr. Johnson's office." Abigail referred to Louisa's family, living in pressed circumstances in Washington, her father "very very much broke in spirits," supporting his family as Superintendant of Stamps, a position he owed to John's presidential largesse.[3]

Abigail hoped that Mr. Johnson would retain his post in the new administration, but meanwhile it was not only Louisa but John who must keep vigilant. "You too my son must look for your share of calumny and arm yourself against it by patience temperance and moderation, and," she concluded, "by applying yourself solely to your own private affairs." Not only personal but political tides surged against this vaunted son. His mother despaired over the humiliating prospect of a mind "so richly stored" for employments of the highest kind, obliged to go to the "drugery" of law. That the "post of *honour*" during the ruling administration was a private station was hardly consonant with her ideals of patriotic service. Despite bitterness toward those who had thwarted her husband's career, she recalled with pride the "refined sense of duty" that had led to John's sacrifice (and therefore hers), in the "great interest of the public."[4]

On their arrival in Philadelphia the couple had separated, John Quincy to go to Quincy and, as he explained to his parents, Louisa and the baby to spend a few weeks in Washington with her family. In both cases the reunions proved difficult. John Quincy's "inexpressible delight" at "finding" his parents once more was severely diminished by the feeble state of his mother's health. Louisa felt the "great emotional strain" of her family meeting almost too much for all of them. That her "very much altered" papa seemed quite enchanted with George, and would seldom let him out of his hands, was somewhat consoling.[5]

During their brief separation, John Quincy assured Louisa on several occasions that both his mother and father would receive her in Quincy with "most cordial affection." He also urged her to bring her sister Caroline with her to pass the winter, as his parents would be happy to see the latter as well. Further, until they were settled, Louisa's stay in Quincy would contribute, he said, "to make this spot more the abode of happiness." In this series of tender letters to his "best beloved," John Quincy wished to be remembered "most kindly" and "affectionately" to her parents, sent "ten thousand kisses to George," and guaranteed his wife that he was her own "to the last gasp." Expectations heightened, John Quincy was not alone in his appreciation of Louisa. Thomas, charmed by her, wrote to tell his mother she would be "pleased with the sprightliness and vivacity" of John Quincy's wife; "when she is in only tolerable health, her spirits are abundant."[6]

Unfortunately, Louisa was not in "tolerable health." She suffered a fever, fatigue, cramps in her hands, and "unusual agitation of my spirits," undoubtedly aggravated by this intimate encounter with her compromised family. Furthermore, her troubled papa "had so set his heart upon receiving you," Louisa wrote John Quincy, that he would not let her go to Quincy until her husband came to fetch her. In response, John "resolved to indulge my own inclinations," to please his father-in-law and, more important, to assuage his apprehensive wife. In late autumn he journeyed to Washington to bring his "dearest Louisa" home to Quincy, where she remained until their move to Boston, the week before Christmas 1801.[7]

Louisa suffered an alarming cough and pain in her chest, and was confined to the house during her entire visit. She remained ill, despite being bled and blistered. Dismayed by her daughter-in-law's pitiful state, the "frame . . . so slender" and "constitution so delicate," Abigail harbored "mean fears" that Louisa "will be of short duration." Her fears for Louisa, however, were subordinate to those for John Quincy. Abigail had reached the anguished conclusion that her son's constant state of anxiety on his wife's behalf added "a weight to his brow" which years alone could not have effected "in double the space."[8]

Both Abigail and Louisa left separate versions behind of those perilous weeks in Quincy. Abigail's are recorded in her immediate correspondence. Louisa's corrosive first impressions are summarized beginning July 1, 1840, when, it is essential to remember, she set out at sixty-five to recollect them in *Adventures of a Nobody. Adventures,*

Louisa's third autobiographical sketch, both substantiates and contradicts her earlier *Record of a Life; or, My Story,* begun July 23, 1825. Louisa, then fifty, claimed "no pretentions to be a writer and no desire to appear anything more than a mere commonplace person with a good memory and just observation."[9]

Before reading Louisa's *Adventures,* it is also imperative to recall the author's emotional composition at this period in her life. In later years, "lagging hours" hung on her "with a tedious weight," producing "too vivid and too painful contemplation of the past." Louisa was pathetically aware of a "constitutional irritability" that was "trying to her friends and painful to myself," and "disagreeable" to all who lived with her. Few, Louisa supposed, "laboured harder" than she to "correct their faults so keenly" that she might not "burthen" those whose happiness she most desired. *Adventures,* she granted, was written with the "sincere consciousness" of her "defects."[10]

Memories, once unlocked, were haunting and insidious. Louisa illuminated her introduction to Quincy in-laws, relatives, and neighbors and their customs of worship, dining, and dress with brilliance, but also with relentless self-pity that bordered on madness. Always, she returned to her financial plight. She had no private expenses because she had no means and therefore no responsibility; thus, she asked, "Could it be surprising" that she was "gazed at with surprise, if not contempt?"[11]

It took Louisa very little time to decide that the qualifications necessary to an "accomplished Quincy lady," were in "direct opposition" to the life she had led in London and at court in Berlin. Her "dreadful ignorance excited no sympathy," and though Abigail gave her instructions and advice, Louisa did not "readily" learn. Worse, her strength failed her and, concluding that she was inadequate, even useless, she became "cold and reserved, and seldom spoke at all which was deemed pride."[12]

If time did not bemuse Louisa's memories, it is certain that her chaotic emotions fazed the entire family. On her first day in Quincy, Abigail's niece, her deceased brother's daughter Louisa Smith, would not eat her dinner and ran sobbing from the table. She was thought to be jealous "to excess" of the Adamses' show of "too much distinction" to their daughter-in-law, according to the latter's interpretation of this unseemly occurrence. Furthermore, Abigail's attempts to treat John Quincy's wife in the "kindest manner," with special dishes and delicate preserves, were miserably rejected. Though she said she was "very grateful," the special effort only made Louisa feel even more alien, stamping her with "unfitness," as if she were "aparté" in the family. In perhaps the only cheerful passage of her lament, Louisa does record that the "old gentleman" took a "fancy" to her, and that "he was the only one" to do so, thereby initiating a rare relationship with John, her admirer to the end.[13]

When Louisa looked beyond her in-laws' house, she found even less to admire. Her caricature of Quincy is a classic. Hindsight found her caustic in her "impressions" of Quincy:

> Had I stepped into Noah's Ark I do not think I could have been more utterly astonished. Dr. Tufts, Deacon French! Mr. Cranch! Old Uncle Peter! Capt. Beale!!! It was lucky for me that I was so much depressed, and so ill, or I should certainly have given mortal offence. Even the Church, its forms, the snuffling through the nose, the Singers, the dressing and the dinner hours, were all novelties to me; and the ceremonious partys, the manners, and the hours of meeting 1/2 past four were equally astonishing to me.[14]

Beyond Quincy there was the experience of Boston. Though the latter might be considered the land of learning, never would Louisa consider it the land of wit. There was something, in her opinion, *"lourd et pesant"* in that scientific atmosphere that destroyed all sympathy for *"les folies brilliantes"* that gave "a playful varnish to the sombre colourings of real Life." Quincy and Boston were too demanding. They disallowed fantasy, which was perhaps the essence of Louisa's being. Even at fifty, Louisa owned she would "willingly deceive myself with the idea that the world is young and innocent."[15]

Louisa seems to have deceived herself concerning some of the most significant periods and relationships of her life. In her bewildered search for comprehension of her "faults" of character, truths wavered according to vantage point. At one time in her life she looked back on an idyllic infancy and youth "fraught with Bliss in the bosom of strong and unchanging Parental affection." At another, recalling the difficult move from French to English schools in 1783, which had coincided with an attack of pleurisy, she conjured up a "serious, melancholy, and almost gloomy" ten-year-old whose mother always talked of her "awkwardness." In this version of her youth, she became the "object of ridicule" among her classmates because she did not speak English. She had, in self-defense, developed a "hautiness and pride of character" that proved impossible for her to sublimate. As a result she was known as "Miss Proud."[16]

This suffering Louisa also reminisced about her attraction to Roman Catholicism, her abhorrence of the mechanical drudgery of music and everything in the shape of work, her fondness for dancing and singing. She established the fact of her sisters' fine health, and how little they felt the sensitivity that proved "allways" so great an obstacle to her own happiness.[17]

Like the pendulum of a clock, Louisa swung from one mood to another. She spoke of her "visionary education" and at another time regretted that many of the "modern studies" were not thought "requisite" to women because they had a "tendency to render them masculine." Although in certain instances it is impossible to choose fact over fiction, in other cases, tangible evidence belies Louisa's interpretations. To be dismissed is Louisa's claim of learning "too quickly" that because of her father's misfortunes, and despite John Quincy's utmost exertions, she was "sunk" in the latter's estimation "without a hope of ever recovering the standing that was irreparably lost." Evidence to the contrary, on October 8, 1801, and in countless other instances, proves that John Quincy was a "devoted friend and husband" and father who wrote of his longing to kiss his infant's "slavering lips!" As for those of the mother, he had continued, "I say nothing—let her consult my heart in her own and all that pen can write or language express will shrink to nothing." He would "creep or wade or swim," go to Washington by stage or land or water, in order to "fly to the arms of my best beloved under her paternal roof."[18]

Louisa's version of Abigail's relationship with Catherine Johnson gives more cause to doubt Louisa's veracity. Her mother, she claimed, was "excessively disliked" by Abigail, possibly because of Mrs. Johnson's "too earnest" entreaties on behalf of her husband. As a result, Louisa guiltily supposed that the President, in appointing her father to office, had "indulged the kindly feelings of his heart contrary to the interests of his future prospects," thereby laying the foundation for his future loss. "My own sense of the injury to himself was as strong as that of Mrs. Adams," she concluded.[19]

Contrary to Louisa's impression, her mother enjoyed a cordial relationship with Abigail, with whom she maintained a politically sophisticated correspondence until her death. Abigail had gone out of her way, upon the Johnsons' return to the States, to invite Mrs.

Johnson and her son Thomas to visit the first week in April 1800. Only passingly acquainted with Mrs. Johnson before John Quincy's marriage, she said, she felt "a much greater and more powerful attraction" to know her more than casually since the families were "united by marriage." She had found Mrs. Johnson, Abigail told her sister Mary, "more than an agreeable person," in fact, "a sensible well bred woman with polite and affable manners." She also wrote John Quincy on April 27, to ask that he "tell your Louisa, I have had the pleasure of her Mother's and Brother's company for the past three weeks, that her mamma looks youthful, for a grandmamma," and how the women sat together and talked of their children "with all the delight of fond parents." Abigail proved herself a "sympathizing Friend" at Mr. Johnson's death in May of 1802. In her kindly condolence note she spoke of the injustice inflicted on Joshua Johnson and his family and hoped the widow might "Bind up her bleeding heart, and heal her wounded mind."[20]

Louisa's latter-day memories of Abigail, so coldly critical in some cases, may blur but can never negate the earlier years when she addressed a lifetime of letters to a "Dear Mother" from an "Affectionate Daughter." Abigail responded in kind. Louisa always acknowledged her own inadequacy in the face of Abigail's worthy strengths. She considered herself neither as patriotic nor as religious nor as gifted a writer. She sometimes implied indirectly that Abigail was too possessive of her grandchildren. Yet these women had a compelling bond. When Louisa was lonely, ill, and mourning the death of her infant daughter in St. Petersburg, she was "solicitious" to return home for many reasons. Among these was her need for her mother-in-law. She was quite sure that in "Mrs. Adams I should have found a comforter a friend who would pity sufferings which *she* would have understood."[21]

Christmastime 1802 was a time to focus on Thomas's "entanglement." Persistent queries from friends about a Miss Ann Harrod, called Nancy, whom Thomas had known for years, launched Abigail into a grave discussion of marriage.[22]

Her theme was unsurprisingly constant. How could she not approve of the institution, when her own marriage was her *raison d'être*? She had read somewhere that "Celibacy is existance thrown away, and every unmarried day is a blank in life," and quoted as much to

Thomas. Nevertheless, she did not recommend early marriages, or ones the participants could not afford.[23]

Finances were fundamental to Abigail's philosophy. In principle, when she despaired that the world was unkind to her children in its "gifts of fortune," she consoled herself that their "virtue honour and integrity" were "riches of more value than silver and gold!" In practice, however, one could not pay bills with character alone, and Abigail's reservations about her sons' marriages, in all three cases, always stemmed from this most practical issue, though she argued on broader concerns. There were many ramifications to marriage. "So important an event as a connection for life" introduced into a family "a near relative with all those claims which bind society together," claims having to do with honor, peace of mind, domestic comfort, and happiness. Abigail was somewhat defensive when she wrote Thomas on December 13, 1802, that "I have not in any instance opposed my will to the inclination of my children. I have only advised them not to hazard their happiness or that of others, by connecting themselves before they saw the path plain before them."[24]

In her blunt evaluation of his brothers' marriages, Abigail left Thomas no doubt that their paths were navigable but not ideal. "None of them had disgraced themselves or family by dissolute or unprincipled connection," she said, nor "have any of them advanced themselves in the world by their marriages, or confered any honour, or brought any Emolument into their family by them." In conclusion, Abigail told Thomas, "You therefore stand upon a ground of equality with them." Having said her piece, Abigail relented. If Thomas's "attachment" was of "so constant so persevering a nature as to be fixed upon Miss Har[r]od," she assured her son that she had "not the smallest objection" against the young lady. "Nay," the more she thought of this "very amiable girl," the more she was convinced that Miss Harrod was "calculated" to make Thomas as good a wife as anyone with whom she was acquainted. "Nor," she assured Thomas, would she be "ashamed to place her" beside either of her daughters.[25]

The questions of Thomas's life at this time had to do with occupational opportunity as well as marriage. His parents were both anxious and sympathetic. Abigail offered him a small allowance, some "pin money," and asked that he "say no more," except to write to her. Thomas's relationship with his mother was a close one. He was often her confidant, and sometimes she worried that she was thought to "deprecate" him in favor of John Quincy. On the contrary, Thomas was her "good and amiable," always "dutiful and affectionate child." He was younger, however, and hadn't been placed in "such conspicuous stations," she would explain, and therefore could not be "supposed to have the knowledge and experience of his Brother."[26]

Thomas's abhorrence for law was fully understood by Abigail. In her support of her son, Abigail intimated one of her rare differences of opinion with John. She knew "very well," she told Thomas, that "it has been in compliance with the wishes of your father that all my sons studied Law—but it was contrary to my judgement, and I know it was so to your inclination." As a lawyer, Thomas complained, he did not earn as much as a clerk, and certainly could not think of supporting a wife.[27]

It was not for lack of enterprise that Thomas had remained in law. The previous winter he had grasped at John Quincy's invitation to move to New York State, to make their home on lands they would take in settlement for the discharge of Justus Smith's notes. "It is the most promising spot on the continent for enterprize and industry," John Quincy had written Thomas. "What say you to joining me in the plan, and going with me?" The lands promised "Independence, thrift and sport," and represented John Quincy's last attempt to control his own destiny. "Why should we wither away our best days, and sneak through life," he asked, "pinch'd by penury over the black letter for the sake of a few luxurious indulgences in a large town?"[28]

Thomas was thirty at this amorphous period of his life. He was a ready convert to his brother's invitation. He was prepared "only at a shortwarning" to embrace with "zeal, ardor, any practicable enterprize which may justify a renunciation of my present ill-requited labors in an ungracious profession." Thomas, who was said to be a "handsome man, of fine manners and address, and of an agreeable vein of conversation," was also a modest man. He had reached the amiable conclusion at this juncture in his life that "head-work is bad business, and I never was fond of it." His capital, he thought, was chiefly "in my hands and feet."[29]

John Quincy's invitation proved fruitless, but Thomas left the law for publishing, attempting to revive a failed journal called *Portfolio*, to which his father and elder brother contributed. In two years' time, Thomas was again at loose ends, out of patience with everyone, including himself. Thomas prospered in an atmosphere of affection, optimism, and approval. He was therefore emotionally unable to tolerate John Quincy's propensity to "doubtful speculation." Would John Quincy "leave off *croaking*?" he asked. Thomas appreciated the value of "anticipating . . . evils and dangers, the more surely to avoid them." However, from a "constitutional infirmity of mind," he was "stimulated most to action, not by adversity or the apprehension of it, but by the hope of reward," he explained to his brother. "You must sometimes at least give us cheering and comfort, if you wish to see us smiling."[30]

The year 1803 was decisive for this vulnerable young man. In December, reluctant but respectful of John Quincy's advice, Thomas returned to Quincy vowing to make a "show" of his profession, which haunted him "like a spectre." He hoped to find the solitude of Quincy "in some measure supportable." He vowed that he would "not be idle," but read, study, "buckle to with some earnestness." He would do his utmost "to keep off the *Blue Devils*," those savage attacks of depression that overwhelmed him periodically. It was "great comfort" to him, this December of 1803, to find his mother "wonderfully recovered" from her fall down an entire flight of stairs the past June, and "as active and busy as ever about her family."[31]

However severe or "croaking" John Quincy appeared to Thomas at stressful times, he was a patient, perceptive, and loving brother. He instructed his mother as to the terms on which she was to receive Thomas back in Quincy, and in so doing, he probably aired some of his own idealized preferences. Abigail, John Quincy advised her, was to leave Thomas "entirely and in the most unqualified manner to his own choice and humour." In fact, he wished "that no *advice*" be given on his brother's "mode of life and his pursuits." John Quincy was "fully confident," he continued, "that the most effectual means" of reconciling Thomas "both to his removal and to his future residence at home will be to leave him in the complete satisfaction with his own *independence*; that sentiment so natural and so powerful upon every mind, and which is of peculiar weight upon his."[32]

Perhaps more sensitive to Thomas's perplexities than John Quincy might credit her, Abigail had already attempted to ease them in her own way. If she could not solve his career problems, she would at least smooth his romance, or attempt to do so. To this end she had deliberately sought out, almost a year before Thomas's return to Quincy, the company of a "very charming young lady" for a week's visit. "Can you guess who?" she had asked Thomas, rather coyly. She explained further that she had "had a Mind" that his father should see Nancy Harrod and was pleased to report that he had liked her "very well." Her own enthusiasm was dulled, however, by what must have seemed to Thomas almost hopeless equivocation. Abigail again pronounced Nancy a "serious solid sensible amiable woman" qualified to make a good wife. "You will never meet with any obsticle from me," she added, "when you can see your way clear to support a family."[33]

Practical considerations did not, however, interfere with Abigail's truly affectionate relationship with Nancy. The latter was to become a favorite in the "social circle" clustered at the Quincy fireside, where discussions of poets and profundities flourished. Abigail shared with Nancy her admiration, for instance, of Robert Burns, "poor fellow," who had felt "povertys cold wind and crushing rain beat, keen and heavy on him." Abigail claimed Burns as a "sympathizer" with her own philosophy. His "vivid Immagination, his delicate sensibility, his strong and ungovernable passions, his high sense of honour and pride of independence," she concluded, made him "ill calculated to bear the insolence of office, or the proud man's contumely." Here, undoubtedly with John in mind, Abigail digressed into speculation about "whether the fine and delicate sensibilities of the soul are a real blessing." She knew the cost only too well:

> They so often are wounded by the insensible by the unfeeling beings which surround them of which much the larger portion of mankind are composed. That like the rose of Cowper they are shaken by the rude blast—or witherd by cold neglect, instead of having the fear of sorrow wiped away by the sympathizing hand of congenial tenderness.

But she also valued them, and would not, in fact, tolerate the alternative:

> Yet who that possesses them would be willing to exchange them for a cold hearted apathy, and a stoical indifference. A fine tuned instrument is soonest put out of order, yet what lover of musick would wish to possess in preference an ordinary-instrument?[34]

On February 19, 1805, Abigail wrote Nancy that the time was not distant "which will give me a legal right to call you mine." Meanwhile, she assured Nancy of "both love, and esteem," and added an endearing postscript. Miss Juno, the companionable Newfoundland puppy, "wags her kind remembrance," feeling the loss of "one kind benefactor." One month later, before her marriage to Thomas, Abigail suggested that Nancy, if she could "wave all difficulties," come to live with her in Quincy and, in so doing, feel as though she had "only exchanged one parents House for another." It was her "sincere and ardent wish," Abigail assured her prospective daughter-in-law, "that we may prove mutual comforts and blessings to each other."[35]

Nancy and Thomas and their eventual offspring were far from the only family members Abigail invited to live with her and John. At times the so-called "tranquil shades of Quincy" teemed with children, grandchildren, and servants, a force of twenty-one by actual count. Louisa Smith was a permanent member of the household. Sally Adams and her daughters were always welcome. Abigail considered her widowed daughter-in-law "a valuable woman," deserving of a "better lot" than she had met with, and therefore she was "desirous of showing her every kind attention" in her power. With grandchildren "driving around" enough to "craze" and concern one, her namesake Abigail, called Abbe, "wild as a bird," little John "pale as a corps," it wasn't any wonder that Abigail found it necessary to apologize for having "avoided" writing, except to sisters and children, for the past two years.[36]

Her official excuse was offered on political grounds. Private letters were often intercepted and therefore, "the most innocent expressions so warped and twisted—so ungenerously mangled as to be made to speak a language wholy foreign to the Heart and to the Sentiments of the writer." In truth, however, Abigail's writing was circumscribed for personal reasons, as well, having to do with health, mood, pressures of duties, and sheer lack of space.[37]

Sometimes, Abigail allowed, she was in such a turmoil that she did not feel "retired or quiet enough" to sit down with her pen. She would begin a sentence, be interrupted, return to it again, and decide that what she had written was of "no value." Forenoon was best for thinking and seeing, she had concluded, but not for privacy, especially during the winter.[38]

The parlor belonged to John Adams in the forenoon, and was where he read and wrote. John, who had earlier complained that there was nothing but the plow between himself and the grave, who had wished he might have been a "shoemaker rather than an American Statesman," was enjoying life. He might talk about being "buried and forgotten at Mount Wollaston," but he was happier in retirement, to his overwhelming amazement, than in all the years before his presidency. John had taken immediate "shelter," as predicted, not only in the labors of agriculture, but in the "amusement of letters." He began his autobiography in October 1802, supposing that some of his posterity might "probably" wish to see in his own handwriting "a proof of the falsehood of that Mass of odious Abuse of my Character, with which News Papers, private Letters and public Pamphlets and Histories have been disgraced for thirty years." Not only in memoirs, but in correspondence, he reviewed, affirmed, and defended his role in building his nation, exchanging hundreds of letters with colleagues, friends, and family until his death. John was encouraged in his endeavors, and his position in the parlor was uncontested. "It is proper he should have it to himself," Abigail decreed.[39]

As her own chamber afforded her no serenity—her grandchildren played there, her daughters-in-law congregated and wrote there—Abigail, who loved to be by herself when she wrote, could only snatch a few moments at a time to maintain her own correspondence, while Juno lay at her feet and snored. Though her eyes suffered, and though she did not write as prolifically as usual during this period, her scope had not diminished, nor was her pen less pointed. She took strong issue with both national and international figures. Aaron Burr's "duplicity" was a disturbing phenomenon. "Are all means lawful," she asked Thomas, "to accomplish the views of Ambition? So thought MacBeth, and so acts Bonaparte," she would conclude.[40]

Her "obituary" on behalf of Alexander Hamilton, confided to Hannah Cushing on September 1, 1804, was honestly put, almost tinged with generosity, considering his destructive role, as she viewed it, in her husband's career:

Altho I do not wear crape I rejoice not in the face [fate] of a man who possest talents and was capable of rendering himself highly serviceable to the country—he had merited their praise and their gratitude—God only knows whether it was in Mercy or in judgement that he is taken away, but I believe the sun will rise as bright and benign and diffuse its Blessing as equally now as before. I believe the seasons will perform their annual round tho Hamilton sleeps in the grave and that should occasion call for Heroes and Statesmen and patriots, we shall find them springing into Life and activity as we have before.

In regard to her country's present situation, Abigail foresaw more danger from the divisions and parties into which it was split, and the "innovations" made in the Constitution, "than from the Death of any one man however Brilliant his tallents or distinguished his abilities." She fervently hoped that her country would not be "intirely shorn of its beauty" because one star had fallen. "Surely," she insisted, "we must have had small pretentions if shrowded with Darkness visible, and coverd over with gloom and despair We sink under the weighty fall of one man." Probing her judgment about Hamilton, "willing to allow him all he deserved," she concluded:

> If there was much to praise—there was much to pardon and forgive. Why then idolize a man, who showd on many occasions that he was a frail, weak man subdued by his passions, against his solemn vows and obligations that he was a vain ambitious man aspiring to govern when it was his duty to submit that he daringly insulted the Authority whose Station he knew forbid him to reply or retaliate. . . .[41]

On the subject of John Quincy and his election to the United States Senate on February 3, 1803, to serve beginning March 4, Abigail was far more than a keenly opinionated spectator of the passing political scene. In some ways, she began to relive the vicissitudes of her husband's career; she was proud of her son but wary of his future. John Quincy understood that his election would "probably affect very materially" my future situation in life. And Abigail was just as positive that her son had begun another ascent, steeper and more treacherous, though possibly more rewarding, than any of his earlier years.[42]

In Washington, on October 21, at 11:00 A.M., John Quincy took his seat in the Senate. Only ten days later he sharply disagreed with his colleagues over a resolution to wear black crepe to honor three illustrious patriots. His argument was firm. He considered the proposal "improper in itself, tending to unsuitable discussions of character, and to an employment of the Senate's time in debates altogether foreign to the subjects which properly belong to them." The matter of the black crepe presaged larger issues on which John Quincy would take an independent stand, proving himself accountable only to his own intelligence and conscience, as when he opposed his party in his votes for the Louisiana Purchase and for the Embargo Act of 1807.[43]

By late December of 1803, John Quincy was already worried about the consequences of his conflicting positions. In a country so "given up" to party that "not to follow blindfold the one or the other is an inexpiable offence," he knew he was in trouble. Between both parties he already saw the impossibility of pursuing the dictates of his own conscience "without sacrificing every prospect, not merely of advancement, but even of retaining that character and reputation" he had enjoyed. Yet his choice was made. If he could not hope "to give satisfaction to my country," he was "at least determined to have the approbation of my own reflections."[44]

Abigail, following his career rumor by rumor, syllable by syllable, was acutely aware of John Quincy's problem. "No Man in Congress," she wrote him on January 10, 1804, was "so delicately situated." Taking his family connections into consideration, he must expect that "a jealousy will be ever awake" in both parties. Whatever the hazards, she was imperturbable: "I wish not to see you a cypher, nor is it possible you can be one." Furthermore, her support was his armor. She was "always" satisfied with his vote, she wrote John Quincy, "because I know that it will proceed from a sense of what you consider right, and proper devested of party spirit." She acknowledged, however, that he had "indeed" embarked on a tempestuous life and must prepare for the storms.[45]

Abigail might have been John Quincy's devout admirer, but she was not a blind one. She took him to task literally, exhaustively articulating her criticisms of his personality, conduct, diet, health, and appearance. She was concerned about his "stiffness," his "reserve and a coldness of address upon entering company," allowing that this characteristic might be due to his having lived abroad "during critical periods." She reminded him to be "guarded in words and looks so that nothing improper escaped his lips." She warned him that his proclivity toward pen and books would only "further his difficulties" in health matters. John Quincy suffered from rheumatism, loss of weight, and an insistent cough, and it bothered Abigail when friends described him as looking "pale, thin and slender." Straight as she was on matters of religion, morals, and ethics, she was not above compromise on the subject of dress. To John Quincy she repeated what she'd read in a play that won her wholehearted approval: "A good coat is tantamount to a good character and if the

world be a stage it's as necessary to dress as to act your part well."
He might have been a schoolboy instead of a senator when his
mother preached to him:

> Now I hope you never appear in the Senate with a Beard two days
> old, or otherways make, what is called a shabby appearance.
> Seriously I think a mans usefulness in society depends upon his
> personal apperance. I do not wish a Senator to dress like a Beau
> but I want him to conform so far to the fashion, as not to incur the
> Character of Singularity—nor give occasion to the World to ask
> what kind of Mother he had? or to charge upon a Wife negligence
> and inattention when she is guiltless.[46]

At one point, Abigail enlisted Louisa's assistance in remedying
John Quincy's problems, virtually dictating her recommended solutions. "I wish you would not let him go to Congress without a
cracker in his jacket," she wrote, advising that "the space between
Breakfast and dinner is so long that his stomach gets bled with
flatulencies and his food when he takes it neither digests or
nourishes him." Another time, should her son's cough persist, Abigail advised Louisa to "put a Blister between his shoulders—coughs
are dangerous if of long continuance." In her effort to have Louisa
"unite" with her in the cause of John Quincy's diet and appearance,
Abigail tried tactfully to make her point without undermining her
son's gift or character.

> Whilst the sublimity of his genius intitles him to admiration the cut
> of his coat, the strangeness of his wigs, or colour of his neckcloth
> are the subjects of reprehension. It is vain to talk of being above
> these little decorums—if we live in the world and mean to serve
> ourselves and it, we must conform to its customs, its habits and in
> some measure its fashion.[47]

In her zeal to promote a more attractive John Quincy, Abigail
might appear to have been superficial if not presumptuous. But her
letters reveal perceptive and profound reasons for the "anxious
hours" she spent on her son's behalf. She was a firm believer that
"when a man enjoys Health, good spirits are a natural attendant, and
he is more disposed to attend to his personal appearance." She
confided her secret fears to Hannah Quincy that John Quincy's self-
neglect signaled deeper problems. "There are some Maladies so
deep rooted, that the most delicate hand dare not probe." An attempt might reveal "an incurable wound." In Abigail's most candid

judgment, she was "certain" that a "depression of spirits" was the chief cause of her son's "low state of Health."[48]

After summering at home, John Quincy and Louisa returned to Washington in November of 1805, leaving their children, George and John (the latter born July 4, 1803), in Abigail's charge. Louisa felt "hourly" the loss of her children, and "suffer'd" constant anxiety at not hearing from them, she wrote from Washington. Having been "compelled" to leave them behind, she could not "command" her feelings and must trust to her mother-in-law's kindness, she wrote Abigail, to hear about them frequently.[49]

Abigail responded in affectionate detail. John, her favorite, stayed with her; George boarded with the Cranch family. She painted an enticing portrait of John for his parents. His face was as round as an apple, as rosy as a carnation, his eyes as brilliant and sparkling as diamonds. His preoccupation with opening and closing the shutters of her chamber seemed to delight rather than annoy her. John met weekly with George, whose "remarkable appetite" Abigail thought worth mentioning.[50]

Something, however, about the word *compelled* in Louisa's letters jarred Abigail's sensibilities. She would tolerate sentiment but not what she judged to be self-pity. Her stern admonitions may have been more damaging to Louisa than either woman realized at that time. Abigail assured Louisa that her children were fine, "better off than they would have been in any boarding house in Washington where they might have been confined in some degree or mixed with improper persons." On January 16, 1806, she wrote:

> There cannot be anything more disagreeable than transporting
> young children twice a year, either by water, or in crowded stages
> at such a distance, and however reluctant you might feel, at being
> separated from them, I should suppose that your own judgement
> experience and good sense would have convinced you of the
> propriety of the measure without compulsion. I have experienced
> separations of all kinds from children equally dear to me and know
> how great the sacrifice and how painful the task—but I considered
> it the duty of a parent to consult the interest and benefit of their
> children.

A month later, Abigail verged on the unkind when she wrote: "Whilst as a Mother you must be anxious to hear frequently from your Children, You will still bear in Mind that they are Mortal, and that no solicitude or care can at all times shield them from the common lot of mortals."[51]

Perhaps she was not so absolute as she seemed to Louisa. A curious sentence crops up in a letter that she wrote to Hannah Quincy. She mentioned that she found John "lively and sensible," affording her much amusement. She added, "I hope I shall not have any cause to regret that I undertook the care of him." The latter thought strikes a doomful note, all too prescient, had Abigail substituted George's name for John's and lived to know his tragedy.[52]

Of all of Abigail's intriguing though restricted correspondence during the early years of retirement to Quincy, by far the most extraordinary was her exchange with Thomas Jefferson. When Jefferson's daughter Mary, known as Polly, died on April 17, 1804, John Quincy did not exaggerate in reporting that his mother "was a good deal affected at seeing the account of it" in the newspapers. Polly was twenty-five years old, married to Congressman John Wayles Eppes and a recent mother at her death, but Abigail's "attachment" of her London years to the small, tearful, lonely, nine-year-old visitor "to a strange land amongst strangers" was indestructible. From the moment she learned of the tragedy, Abigail had wanted to write to Jefferson, and fought her more immediate feelings of resentment of this long-ago friend. Even at the depths of their relationship, however, Abigail always tried to understand Jefferson and, perhaps unwittingly, forgive him. She said as much to her son Thomas; she "could not believe all Jefferson's better intentions are swallowed up by those who hold a rod over him." She continued: "There is a little corner of my heart where he once sat, as a friend whom I esteemed and loved for his real or imagined benevolent propensities—from whence I find it hard wholly to discard him—notwithstanding I pitty his weakness and abhor those principles which govern his administration."[53]

Pity overwhelmed all other emotions as Abigail struggled with the compassionate letter she could not suppress. She initiated the exchange of seven letters with Thomas Jefferson over a five-month period predicated on far more than sympathy. Affectionate respect and valued friendship were revealed as acute considerations in the care and time expended by both in their explanations to one another, alternately judging and judged, accusing and defending. On May 20, 1804, Abigail confided her dilemma to Jefferson:

Had you been no other than the private inhabitant of Monticello, I should e'er this time have addrest you, with that sympathy, which a recent event has awakend in my Bosom. But reasons of various kinds withheld my pen, untill the powerfull feelings of my heart, have burst through the restraint, and called upon me to shed the tear of sorrow over the departed remains, of your beloved and deserving daughter, an event I most sincerely mourn.[54]

Abigail's recollection of her bosom wet with the tears of the clinging child who had met such an untimely death awakened memories of another loss of which she rarely spoke. It had been some time since she conceived of "any event in this Life" that might, at least on her part, evoke feelings of mutual sympathy. Now, she wrote Jefferson, they had the loss of a child in common, and she knew all about "those chords which bind the filial to the parental Bosom," and "when snaped assunder, how agonizing the pangs of separation." Mutual wounds drew mutual sympathies. "I have tasted the bitter cup, and bow with reverence and humility," Abigail said, "before the great dispenser of it, without whose permission, and over-ruling providence, not a sparrow falls to the ground."[55]

Jefferson had forwarded Abigail's letter of condolence to his widowed son-in-law, who fully appreciated Abigail's extraordinary gesture. "If I am to judge of its excellence from the sensibility excited by its perusal it contains the generous effusions of an excellent heart," John Eppes replied on June 14, 1804. "The successful rival of her husband in public estimation could not under any circumstances excite sympathy in the breast of any ordinary female." Therefore, Eppes concluded, "a sound heart and a sound understanding could only under such circumstances have produced such a letter." Eppes then advised Jefferson that in expressing toward Abigail "the Sentiments of your heart you will of course know no limit but the extent of your feeling." On the other hand, under "existing circumstances," how prudent it might be to indulge in the expression of any private feeling toward John Adams was "extremely doubtful." Eppes was convinced that "the thread of friendship between you is on his part broken never more to be united." Furthermore, "The mind capable of receiving . . . a successful rival with his honours blooming round his brow is not to be found in the man who bore implacable hatred to the living Franklin, who has not withdrawn that hatred even from his ashes."[56]

Jefferson had not waited for Eppes's response, however. The latter could have had no notion of the earlier ties of Jefferson to Abigail and all her family. In Jefferson's piteous state ("Having lost even half of all I had," his "evening prospects" now hung on the "slender thread of a single life," his remaining daughter), he greeted Abigail's overture with fervent appreciation. He should "ever remember" her kindnesses to Mary with gratitude and friendship, knowing full well the "indelible impression" she had made on his dead daughter. At the same time, he was thankful for the occasion "furnished" him of expressing his regret "that circumstances should have arisen which have seemed to draw a line of separation between us."[57]

Reaching out now to reconstruct a happier past, Jefferson assured Abigail that the friendship with which she "honoured" him had "ever been valued, and fully reciprocated." Though past events might be trying to some minds, he never believed hers to be "of that kind, nor felt that my own was." Without shading the truth of their presently tarnished relationship, Jefferson was gallant. "Neither my estimate of your character, nor the esteem founded in that," he assured Abigail, "have ever been lessened for a single moment, although doubts whether it would be acceptable may have forbidden manifestations of it."[58]

The olive branch was now offered Abigail with whole heart. Jefferson gave notice that he intended to open himself to her "without reserve," to take advantage of an opportunity he had "long wished" was his. Though he had no idea how he would be received, he felt relief "from being unbosomed." When he was assured by return mail of Abigail's mutual feelings, he apologized for "this transition from a subject of domestic affliction," and launched into political events and their "unfortunate bearings" on private friendships. "The injury these have sustained has been a heavy price for what has never given me equal pleasure."[59]

The thrust of Jefferson's grievance against her husband was quickly put to Abigail. "I did consider his last appointments to office as personally unkind." By naming some of his "most ardent political enemies," John had seen to it that Jefferson must forfeit "faithful cooperation" with his own views, or be put to the "odium" of appointing replacements friendlier to his policies. If his respect for her husband did not permit him to ascribe the whole blame to the influence of others, Jefferson told Abigail, "it left something for friendship to forgive."[60]

Abigail, of course, flew to John's defense. Here was Portia revived, only this time her argument was lame and flawed. She could muster reasonableness, proceed with deliberation, but in this almost singular instance, facts rendered her case faulty, and also puzzling. It is unlikely that Abigail meant deliberately to deceive Jefferson; it is also unlikely that she could have so miserably confused dates pertaining to her husband's last appointments in office.

Writing to Jefferson on July 1, 1804, she was certain that John's act was not intended to give "any personal pain or offence." She thought it was her duty, however, to explain, so far as she then knew them, her husband's "views and designs." Patiently she continued: "The constitution empowers the president to fill up offices as they become vacant. It was in the exercise of this power that appointments were made, and Characters selected whom Mr. Adams considerd, as men faithfull to the constitution and where he personally knew them, such as were capable of fullfilling their duty to their country." Furthermore, Abigail reasoned, John had followed the example of President Washington, who had left no vacant offices to be filled by his successor.[61]

Abigail continued to placate Jefferson on this sensitive subject. "No offence was given by it, and no personal unkindness thought of. But the different political opinions which have so unhappily divided our Country, must have given rise to the Idea," she supposed, "that personal unkindness was intended." It was in the next sentence that she committed her basic error:

> You will please to recollect Sir, that at the time these appointments were made, there was not any certainty that the presidency would devolve upon you, which is an other circumstance to prove that personal unkindness was not meant. No person was ever selected by him from such a motive—and so far was Mr. Adams from indulging such a sentiment, that he had no Idea of the intollerance of party spirit at that time. . . .[62]

In fact, Thomas Jefferson was elected president on February 17, 1801; John's appointments were made in March. It was another fact that John Adams was excruciatingly aware of "the intollerance of party spirit." While Jefferson and Abigail would tend, in this brief exchange, to reexamine their differences, the issue of the appointments died here. Jefferson, discreetly silent on the matter, offered no rebuttal. Now it was Abigail's turn to "freely disclose" what had "severed the bonds of former Friendship" and placed Jefferson in a light "very different" from that in which she had once viewed him.

This was the liberation from jail and the reimbursement of the fine of the "wretch" James Callender, imprisoned initially for his crimes of writing and publishing "the basest libel, the lowest and vilest Slander, which malice could invent, or calumny exhibit" against the character and reputation of her husband. The act of overruling her husband's decree Abigail regarded as a "public approbation" of Callender's conduct and therefore as a "personal injury" to herself. "This was the Sword," Abigail explained to Jefferson, "that cut assunder the Gordian knot, which could not be untied by all the efforts of party Spirit, by rivalship by Jealousy or any other malignant fiend."[63]

As though to bolster her argument, Abigail went on to mention how Callender had proven an enemy not only to her husband, but also to Jefferson. She made her point about Callender without specifying the latter's breathtaking reference, in July 1802, in the *Richmond Recorder*, to Jefferson's "concubine," his slave Sally, and the latter's child, whose features bore a "striking though sable resemblance to those of the president himself." Abigail rested her case: "The serpent you cherished and warmed, bit the hand that nourished him, and gave you sufficient Specimens of his talents, his gratitude his justice, and his truth."[64]

Though the subject of Callender was explosively provocative, it proved to be the catalyst of a sweeping discussion on the entire issue of political loyalties. Abigail argued for respect "which is a necessary bond in the social union, which gives efficacy to laws, and teaches the subject to obey the Majestrate, and the child to submit to the parent." How, then, could such "vipers" as Callender be "let lose upon Society," thereby leveling "all distinction between virtue and vice"?[65]

In response, Jefferson stood up to Abigail. Patiently and at length, he explained his position. He had discharged every person prosecuted and punished under the Sedition Law, because he considered "that law to be a nullity as absolute and as palpable as if Congress had ordered us to fall down and worship a golden image." Furthermore, he had freed all charged under the "pretended Sedition law" without asking "what the offenders had done, or against whom they had offended." As a result, there were those who accused him of acting "to protect, encourage and reward slander." But there were other motives, he suggested, such as "those which inspire ordinary charities to objects of distress, meritorious or not, or," he continued, "the obligations of an oath to protect the constitution, violated by an unauthorized act of Congress."[66]

Though Abigail made some concessions to Jefferson's arguments, she hardly capitulated. Jefferson's motives for liberating Callender wore a "different aspect" from her original impression, or that of others she had heard speak on this subject. With regard to his explanation of the act under which Callender had been punished, however, Abigail allowed that "different persons entertain different opinions respecting it." It lay not with her, she said "to decide upon its validity"; that, she presumed, "devolved upon the supreem Judges of the Nation." Still, she would argue:

> I have understood that the power which makes a Law, is alone competent to the repeal. If a Chief Majestrate can by his will annul a Law, where is the difference between a republican, and a despotic Government? That some restraint should be laid upon the asassin, who stabs reputation, all civilized Nations have assented to. . . . No political Character has been secure from its attacks, no reputation so fair, as not to be wounded by it, untill truth and falsehood lie in one undistinguished heap.[67]

Clinging to the Federalists' notion, derived from English common law, that the First Amendment did not deprive Congress of power to influence speech and press, Abigail feared the worst without definition. "If there are no checks to be resorted to in the Laws of the Land, and no reperation to be made to the injured, will not Man become the judge and avenger of his own wrongs, and as in the late instance [alluding to the duel between Hamilton and Burr] the sword and pistol decide the contest?"[68]

Abigail and Jefferson exchanged two more letters at this time, three months before his reelection in December as President, with George Clinton voted Vice-President. Jefferson's last, written September 11, 1804, alluded to Abigail's mention of the "one other act" of his administration that she considered as personally unkind. This was Jefferson's dismissal of John Quincy from his appointment, made by a local judge, as commissioner of bankruptcy. This action, taken shortly after Jefferson became President, looked "so particularly pointed" that even some of Jefferson's friends had commented on it.[69]

Jefferson now seemed to sense a permanent barrier that all his goodwill could not penetrate. "Perhaps indeed I may have already trespassed too far on your attention," he replied. But he still cared about establishing rapport with Abigail. "With those who wish to think amiss of me, I have learnt to be perfectly indifferent," he explained, "but where I know a mind to be ingenuous, and to need only truth to set it to rights, I cannot be as passive."[70]

On his honor, he continued, this was his "first knolege" of John Quincy's replacement. The position had not been official, and the commissioners were not permanent officers, but chosen occasionally, as cases arose, their nominations confined "exclusively to federalists." Dissatisfied with this system, or lack of one, the legislature had voted that the President be responsible for the appointments. The object of the new law was to "correct, not confirm, what was deemed the partiality of the judges." Jefferson, attempting to achieve political balance, had thought to "put in a proportion of federalists equal," he believed, "to the proportion they bear in numbers through the union generally." Had he known of John Quincy's involvement, he assured Abigail, "it would have been a real pleasure to me to have preferred him to some who were named in Boston in what were deemed the same line of politics."[71]

Abigail's reply was delayed by three weeks of illness. On October 25 she was at last back at her desk, acknowledging that she had "little thought" of entering a correspondence on "political topicks" when she had first written to him. She did not regret having done so, however, as it had led to "some elucidations and brought on some explanations, which place in a more favourable light occurrences which had wounded" her. "Having once entertained for you a respect and esteem, founded upon the Character of an affectionate parent, a kind Master, a candid and benevolent Friend," Abigail told Jefferson, she could not "suffer different political opinions to obliterate them from my mind."[72]

In summary of the result of their discussions, Abigail delivered varying evaluations. She could not consider Jefferson's sprawling explanation of his role in John Quincy's dismissal in any other light "than what the Gentlemen of the Law would term a quible—as such I pass it." She also reminded Jefferson of his assurance, on his last visit with her in Washington, that "nothing" would give him "more pleasure" than to serve her or her family. "I will do you the justice to say at this hour that I believe what you then said, you then meant."[73]

Nor did Jefferson win her over in his argument that the right to control the freedom of the press was the states' rather than the nation's. Abigail could not agree "that the constitution ever meant to withhold from the National Government the power of self defence, or that it could be considerd an infringement of the Liberty of the press, to punish the licentiousness of it." Furthermore, she would question whether in his ardent zeal to "rectify the mistakes and abuses" of the former administrations, he was not led "into measures still more fatal to the constitution, and more derogatory to your honour, and independence of Character?" Abigail had, of course, known the answer to her question all along: "Pardon me Sir if I say, that I fear you are."[74]

For all her convictions, Abigail did allow that time and posterity would judge, with "more candour and impartiality" than the conflicting parties of their day, what measures best promoted the happiness of the people. Meanwhile, despite nostalgic affection and respect for one another, it was apparent that more than "mere differences" blocked a continuing relationship. "Faithful are the wounds of a Friend," Abigail told Jefferson. She bore him no malice, cherished no enmity, would not retaliate if she could. Rather, in the true spirit of Christian charity, "I would forgive, as I hope to be forgiven." And now she would not further intrude upon his time, but close their correspondence with her sincere wishes that Jefferson might be directed to that path "which may terminate in the prosperity and happiness of the people . . . by administring the Government with a just and impartial hand." In his doing so, no one would "more rejoice" than herself.[75]

Weeks later, on the evening of November 18, 1804, Abigail asked John to read the copies she kept of her correspondence with Jefferson. The next morning he had completed the whole of them. Noting this event in a footnote, he wrote, "I have no remarks to make upon it at this time and in this place."[76]

Six years later, on January 16, 1811, Jefferson sent his copies of his correspondence with Abigail to Dr. Benjamin Rush, explaining that "yielding to an intimation in her last letter, I ceased from further explanation." Owing to Rush's persistent efforts at mediation, Jefferson and Adams revived their correspondence; Jefferson's next brief and poignant exchange with Abigail was again to be initiated by personal tragedy.[77]

TWENTY-THREE

Rather Too Much
than Too Little

Warning of Colonel Smith's "don Quixot expedition" came to Abigail indirectly. John Quincy reported to his mother that the colonel, in his letter of November 28, 1805, was soliciting his "friendly attention and Civilities" on behalf of his "very intimate friend General Miranda." Abigail sensed danger immediately. She was convinced that Francisco de Miranda was one of Talleyrand's agents, "and as such," she cautioned John Quincy, "every movement should be carefully watched as we shall hear more of that man. He is capable of tumbling the waters and fishing in them too."[1]

Abigail's interpretation of Miranda's powers was prophetic, though she probably did not envision how directly they would assault her immediate family. Shortly, Colonel Smith stood accused of "High Misdemeanor," or "providing means for a military expedition against a nation with which the United States is at peace." The colonel, in his efforts to further Miranda's dream of liberating South America, particularly his native Venezuela, from Spanish rule, recruited soldiers to sail southward on February 2, 1806, aboard the *Leander*, a merchant vessel chartered from a Mr. Samuel Ogden, in the company of several other vessels.[2]

The colonel had made one other provision for which his family, rather than his government, held him liable, and caused his father-in-law to wonder whether he was "mad." He had secretly encouraged his son, William Steuben, to leave Columbia College to enlist in Miranda's cause. Soon, at Puerto Cabello, two schooners were unexpectedly lost to the Spanish, and William, among other Americans, was rumored, falsely, as it turned out, to be imprisoned in Caracas, threatened with a sentence of death unless his father would disclose to the Spanish minister, Don Carlos Martinez de Yrugo, everything he knew of Miranda's plans. The colonel refused, but William, after harrowing delays, found his way home. Meanwhile, that May, Mrs. Smith joined her husband at a small house within prison limits, where the couple anxiously awaited the colonel's trial in the circuit court in New York that began on July 14, 1806.[3]

One of the perplexities of "the mysterious project and expedition of Miranda" was to judge the truth of the American government's involvement, along with Colonel Smith's, in this catastrophic venture. The colonel swore in an affidavit that the Miranda expedition "was set on foot with the knowledge and approbation of the President," but claimed that the latter had prevented the Secretary of State, James Madison, from testifying to that effect. The colonel, a broken, pathetic figure, superseded by a Mr. P. A. Schenke as surveyor of the port, the post he naïvely hoped might at least have gone to his brother Justus rather than to a stranger, knew his enemies had been "long struggling" to remove him from office. Only he had "never supposed the President of the United States and Mr. Madison capable of uniting with them in his destruction."[4]

The extent of Jefferson's implication in the affair was difficult to fathom. Miranda, the colonel claimed, had told him that "certain propositions" had been made to the President and the Secretary of State, but that the degree of assent, acquiescence, or negation that they gave was "altogether" unknown to him. But this much the colonel did know: he, who was "trembling alive" for his country, "tottering on the confines of perditions, had been made a sacrifical figure," cast away in order to "tranquillize the Minister of an Usurper, a Military Despot, trampling on the liberties of his country." The colonel, the irrepressible, frustrated warrior, disassociated himself from the speculative aspects of Miranda's expedition. His effort, he protested, had been made in a far nobler and immediate cause. He did not mention Napoleon, but predicted the worst in his name: "Millions may be lavished to tranquilize a Tyrant for a moment, but his insatiable appetite will never be gratified, untill the whole resources of our Country are subjected to his will." Then he would finally prove to America what he had already proved to Europe, the colonel said, "that he knows no rights but his own, nor no rule of Justice, but his pride and ambition."[5]

John Quincy, to whom the colonel had turned as though to a sympathetic juror, studied the colonel's letters and was, indeed, compassionate, though realistic. From a legal point of view, John Quincy was convinced that "the knowledge or even the encouragement and approbation of the President and Secretary of State to the original prospect will be of no avail on the question of the legality of the enterprize." He also concluded that the "gloomy cast" of the colonel's future, and that of his family, was "only the natural consequence of the principles and practices which have for many years been in unceasing operation." Nevertheless, he believed that Jefferson's removal of the colonel from his office was sufficient punishment, seemingly implying that the trial imposed excessive hardship on his beleaguered brother-in-law.[6]

Jefferson was no favorite of John Quincy, or of Louisa. Both frequented the President's house, and both reacted adversely, in private. Louisa, in retrospect, called everything about Jefferson "aristocratic except his person which was ungainly ugly and common." She would remember his manner as "awkward, and excessively inelegant," and judge his "peering restlessness" as a sign of his fear "of being scanned more closely by his visitors, than was altogether agreeable to his self-complacency." John Quincy's impressions of Jefferson, though less scornful than his wife's, betray impatience, disbelief, and disrespect.[7]

Pride where his father was concerned, and a sense of protectiveness of him as well, had dampened John Quincy's nostalgic memories of his walks and talks with Jefferson in Paris. He made a promise to himself that he "certainly never should solicit Mr. Jefferson for any place whatever." He was also less than admiring of the "waxing and waning opinions of this Gentleman concerning the French Revolution," and scorned Jefferson's "itch for telling prodigies." The latter's contention that he had learned to speak Spanish in nineteen days at sea was crisply dismissed in a single sentence: "But Mr. Jefferson tells large stories." Given John Quincy's disaffection with Jefferson, it was no wonder that his sympathies lay with Colonel Smith regarding his involvement with General Miranda. "As far as relates to Colonel Smith the President, I should think has already done enough," John Quincy wrote Louisa. "He has ruined him as completely as his heart could wish—more is unnecessary."[8]

In May, Abigail's sister Elizabeth Peabody had written to her to say that the accounts in the newspapers regarding the *Leander* and the colonel gave "all much pain, and regret." Whether Miranda's motives were "any better [than] those of Cortez, or the first Mexican Adventurers," she could not pretend to say. What she could express was her regret that, at the President's and her sister's stage of life, any of their dear children should be "involved and tormented with Evils." She would have hoped their virtues "should have prevented & secured" their elders from such stress. In August, Elizabeth wrote again to say that she was glad Colonel Smith had been honorably acquitted, though she was fearful that his wife must have gone through "many distressing scenes."[9]

Unfortunately, even as late as December, Mrs. Smith's position was still "more necesitous" than originally realized. Rumors abounded now that Colonel Smith had gone west and was somehow involved with Aaron Burr's purportedly treasonous plot to separate the Western states from the United States. With the colonel away, Mrs. Smith's family was affectionately solicitous of her needs. John Quincy, for example, offered, with Louisa's wholehearted approval, to care for young John Smith, just graduating from Harvard and in need of support in his study of law during the ensuing three years. John Quincy was also his mother's intermediary in this situation. Abigail was confident of her daughter's "prudence and her desire to economize," and that she would make a little go far. Still, Abigail asked that John Quincy, on his visit to his sister, inform himself of her needs "as fully as you can," without wounding her feelings any more than such an inquiry necessarily must. Her next request was that John Quincy converse "freely and fully" with his sister to prevail with her to break up housekeeping and come to Quincy for the summer. Abigail wished she might have said more, but, in an effort to be discreet, she acknowledged that there were many things not "proper" to write. "There are delicacies to be observed towards those who are in distress."[10]

Though she did not mention the possibility of the colonel's association with Aaron Burr, she did say that the latter had led President Jefferson's administration into an inextricable "labyrinth." She was sympathetic and even understanding, though somewhat enigmatic as she continued: Mr. Jefferson was so much blamed for countenancing de Miranda's "wild enterprise that I cannot but suspect he has committed himself equally by crying the wolfs the wolfs, when no harm was intended."[11]

In early March 1807, Abigail had barely recovered from a rheumatic attack ("my head still feels cracked,—shattered I am sure it is—")

when she received a letter from Mercy Warren. The letter, a reminder of "ancient friendship," made Abigail intensely reflective. Frail physically, she sounded, for the first time, defeated by passing events. She seemed to assume that Mercy felt similarly. "So rapid have been the changes," she told Mercy, "that the mind, tho fleet in its progress, has been outstriped by them and we are left like statues at what we cannot comprehend."[12]

However, in spite of protestations to the contrary, Abigail traversed the realm of current affairs and personalities as nimbly as of old. Having done with Napoleon and Burr, in particular, Abigail's conclusion to her letter was superbly cordial: "We shall always be happy to hear of the welfare of friends whom we have loved from our early years. . . ." Also, she had derived, she said, "sincere and durable gratification" from their communication.[13]

Only four months later, all had changed, Abigail's sentiments having been bitterly altered by Mercy's "misrepresentations" of John's role in her *History of the Rise, Progress and Termination of the American Revolution, Interspersed with Biographical, Political and Moral Observations.* Mercy's *History* was published in 1805, and why it took John until July 11, 1807, to state his objections remains a puzzle. Perhaps his increasing need to be read to, due to failing eyesight, delayed his completion of Mercy's three-volume work. Or possibly a sense that his critique might impair their friendship caused him to hesitate. Nevertheless, as of July 1807, John had read "much, if not all" of Mercy's *History.* He was not about to write a review of it, but, as there were "several mistakes" relating to him personally, he proposed at his "leisure" to point out some of them to Mercy in the "spirit of friendship," so that she might have an opportunity "in the same spirit to correct them for any future edition of the work. . . ."[14]

John, cut to the quick, took issue with Mercy passage by passage, all three volumes worth, initiating an exchange of ten long, involved letters of accusation and reproach that mounted to screaming pitch before they were done. John meant to answer "insinuations rather than charges," but whatever he might call them, he ardently refuted Mercy's claims that "Mr. Adams' passions and prejudices were some times too strong for his sagacity and judgment," that "nothing was done" when Mr. Adams was sent to England, and that ("in the most exceptionable passage" yet found) "unfortunately for himself and his country," Mr. Adams became "so enamoured with the British Constitution and the Government, manners and laws of the nation, that a partiality for monarchy appeared, which was inconsistent with his former professions of republicanism."[15]

Furthermore, among what John considered her many injustices and inaccuracies, Mercy claimed that John had resided in England for four or five years when actually it had been less than three, the dates being August 1785 to April 19, 1788. But this, John conceded, was "an erratum of little consequence." The same could not be said of the passage on page 392 of the third volume that an almost apoplectic John proceeded to quote. In this passage Mercy claimed that "after Mr. Adams's return from England he was implicated by a large portion of his countrymen, as having relinquished the Republican System and forgotten the Principles of the American Revolution, which he had advocated for near twenty years."[16]

John acknowledged that "a man never looks so silly as when he is talking or writing concerning himself." However, he had no choice; her "severity" he told Mercy, "had reduced him to the necessity of pouring out all myself." What, indeed, was he to conclude from her history? Was he to suppose that General Warren and his lady were the "first propagators of the stories which were spread through the Union before the election of Mr. Jefferson, and which were fully believed by the ignorant German boors in Pennsylvania and by many of the ignorant voters in all the Southern States . . . that John Adams had married his daughter in England to the Prince of Wales, and his son John Quincy Adams to the Princess Royal of England, and had entered into a treaty with King George to make his son-in-law King of North America?" Or was he to attribute to the Warren family the "honor" that was done him in the backwoods of Pennsylvania and Kentucky "of being hanged in effigy by the side of Mr. Jay with a purse of English guineas in my hand?"[17]

Painstakingly, John enumerated further "demonstrations" of Mercy's friendship. He bridled at her contention that he was "ridiculed by the fashionable and polite society of France" as being "deficient in the *je ne sais quoi* so necessary to polished society." He posed a question to her: "Franklin, Jay, Laurens, Jefferson, Monroe, Livingston, Morris and Armstrong, I suppose, were not deficient in this *je ne sais quoi*? Now in full stride, John cited numerous other examples of Mercy's friendship, of her "disposition to wink him out of sight, to represent him in an odious light, to lessen and degrade him below his station." In essence, Mercy had denied John recognition of his contribution to his country in terms of years and substance, and, in doing so, had wounded him to the core of his being.[18]

In response, Mercy was intransigent. She was "so much at a loss" for the meaning of very many of Mr. Adams's paragraphs and the "rambling manner in which your angry and undigested letters are written," she told him, that she "scarcely" knew where to begin her remarks. But begin she did, by saying: "Had not Mr. Adams been suffering under suspicions that his fame had not been sufficiently attended to, or that his character was not invulnerable he would not have put such a perverse construction on every passage where he is named in a work in which the author aimed to do him complete justice. . . ." The exchange was finished on August 27, when Mercy turned accuser: "There is a meanness as well as malignancy in striving to blast a work that many of the best judges of literary merit . . . have spoken of [as] very flattering to the author." In conclusion, Mercy told John that his late letters "cap the climax of rancor and decency and vulgarism. Yet, as an old friend, I pity you, as a Historian I forgive you."[19]

Mercy, less self-righteous than she appeared, fretted, nevertheless, about her injured relationship with John. She proceeded to turn his correspondence over to an "astonished" Elbridge Gerry, the successful arbiter of later years, who was already a skilled diplomat. Able to pass judgment only after seeing the letters, he advised that "very angry, vindictive, and indecent phraseology" warranted "but one dignified line of conduct on the part of a lady, and that is silence." Mercy followed Gerry's advice only halfway. At almost the end of the year, on December 28, she referred indirectly to her differences with John. She was of the opinion, she wrote Abigail, that "no variation of sentiment with regard to subjects which make up the great Bustle of the world" ought to affect "the hearts of true friendship." Furthermore, she believed that it was possible to denounce one another's politics, "yet love you as ever," and hold fast to esteem and affection. "Men nor women were not made to think alike—it cannot be."[20]

For Abigail, the friendship was in ruins, although she was wrenched by the course she chose. When Mercy's husband died the following year, at the age of eighty-four, Abigail expressed her belief that "former friendship" demanded a "sympathizing letter" from her. However, she recognized Mercy and John's fundamentally opposing political beliefs, and was sadly resigned to the fact that the "Bitterness of Party spirit had severed [them]." After the injustice to

John's character, and the chance given Mercy to acknowledge her errors, "which she wholly omitted to do," Abigail felt she had no alternative. "I thought a letter of the kind would appear insincere," she wrote to her daughter on December 8, 1808, "and altho I feel for her bereavement and know how heavily she must feel it, I have declined writing to her."[21]

Frequently, when friends thought her overburdened with care, Abigail would tell them that she would "rather have too much than too little," that "life stagnates without action." She understood her needs; it all came down to the fact that she could never bear "merely to vegetate." Treated with calomel and opium pills and a gruel-and-water diet to alleviate her rheumatic pains and frequent fevers, it was so common for her to be "indisposed" for weeks at a time that she dismissed these confinements as "a matter of course." Undaunted, she refused to concede that "age is dark and unlovely," and deliberately sought the "rich mental feast," to be found in the story, for example, of a young American who had accompanied her father to the Scottish Highlands, told in *Letters from the Mountains* by Mrs. Anne Grant. Such a story made her forget "that the roses had fled from my cheeks, and the lustre departed from my eyes."[22]

Weather was definitely a factor in Abigail's outlook. Just as snow did not "suit" her constitution, spring, on the other hand, symbolized the "renovating season," bringing her "innocent pleasure" in the charms of the first asparagus, the first "daffies," the newly leafed gooseberry bushes. When she reported the production of eighty tons of English hay, she sounded rashly boastful. Enthusiasm being, to her mind, "the wine of life," if all else, including books and the bounties of the earth, failed to sustain her interest, politics alone might have provided the magical elixir that "cheers and supports the mind." It was inconceivable to her, aged as she felt herself to be, that she or anyone else might willingly stand remote from current events. She summarily dismissed her daughter's claim to a hatred of politics. "When your native country is so seriously threatened," she told Mrs. Smith, "you cannot be a descendant from the spirit of '76 to be totally indifferent to what is passing."[23]

What was passing, the effects of the Embargo Act imposed by Jefferson on December 22, was of keen interest to Abigail, not only as a patriot but as a concerned parent. Regardless of John Quincy's personal reservations about Jefferson, he had publicly backed the

President's policy regarding the Embargo Act, to harsh accusations of desertion from his own party. In fact, his sense of duty had led him to support the administration and therefore to find himself in opposition to the Federalists "in general." In his forlorn position—he had no communication with Jefferson other than in the "regular order of business in Senate," and yet was severely estranged from his own party—John Quincy viewed his political prospects as "declining," and his term of service "near its close."[24]

From the beginning, Abigail and John had agreed with their son's position. "Under the decrees of France and Great Britain, dooming to capture and confiscation all our ships and cargoes trading with either of those powers, we had no alternative but this or taking our side at once in the war," John comforted his "Great and Good Son" at this critical moment. All three had studied the tumultuous events leading to the passage of the Embargo Act, which was meant to end British impressment of American seamen. All three were infuriated when, on the previous June 22, 1807, the British frigate *Leopard* had fired on the American *Chesapeake,* claiming four men aboard to be British deserters. The Americans' denial was answered with earsplitting broadsides that killed three and wounded eighteen, in the process of capturing the alleged British deserters, who, in reality, included one American Negro, an Indian, and a native of Maryland.[25]

On July 2, Abigail, John, and John Quincy were exposed to another display of British belligerence. In response to Jefferson's decree that British warships leave United States territorial waters, the British had only more aggressively pursued impressment of British subjects from neutral vessels. The Nonimportation Bill of December 14, proving ineffectual, had then given way to the Embargo Act, put into law on December 22, under which United States vessels were forbidden to leave for foreign ports; those heading for American ports, bound for coastal trade, were required to post a bond double the value of the craft and the cargo in order to guarantee that the goods would again land at an American port; and foreign vessels were forbidden to carry goods out of American ports. Now all would be chaos. Trading became a matter of smuggling, and shortly it was apparent that the embargo was more damaging than healing, the opposition strongest in New York and New England. The legality of the act was questioned; Timothy Pickering proposed a New England convention for the purpose of nullifying it. On March 1, 1809, President James Madison, having little choice, would repeal the Embargo Act. On

March 15, trade would be reopened and Madison authorized to proclaim resumption of trade with France or Great Britain, should either power, or both, cease violation of Americans' rights.[26]

Even at its inception, when John Quincy had considered the Embargo Act as the "last anchor of our peace," and predicted that the "little finger of war will be heavier than the loins of Embargo," he had fully understood that his own party would punish him for his theoretical disloyalty. His situation was "critical" and his future in doubt. So patent was his party's hostility that Louisa wrote Abigail at the start of 1808 that their situation that winter was "not very pleasant" because it was "universally" believed that John Quincy had in fact changed his party. As a result, Louisa reported, the Federalists were "extremely bitter," and yet John Quincy's talents were of "too much real importance for them to venture publicly to throw him off," though "in private they circulate reports very much to his disadvantage."[27]

Both parents, knowing how much John Quincy risked now that he seemed to have lost all party support, were more intensely loyal than ever. His father, his consummate admirer, praised his son for having "too honest a heart, too independent a mind and too brilliant talents to be sincerely and confidentially trusted by any man who is under the dominion of party maxims, or party feelings." His mother, ever his implacable advocate, reminded John Quincy of the example set by the Roman Fabius, who had exposed himself to universal censure and reproach for making the cause of his state and its preservation his foremost concern. "This love of the public good was the soul of his actions," Abigail informed John Quincy, "and inspired him with that inflexible firmness and constancy for the service of his Country . . . whatever injury he received from it." Fabius, then, she said, was a "Character worthy of imitation—deserving of just applause." Furthermore, she continued, although John Quincy might differ from some of his nearest and best friends in his judgments and opinions on important subjects, she would "much sooner suspect the soundness of their judgments than the purity and uprightness of your intentions." And finally and most urgently, it was "the sincere wish and fervent prayer" of his affectionate mother that "so long as you live, may you hold fast your integrity."[28]

When John Quincy chose to support Madison instead of Federalist Charles Pinckney, as the next presidential candidate, he incurred further abuse from members of his own party, and applause from his mother. Abigail had come to believe "Mr. Madison the fittest and one of the most sensible and candid of Virginians, a moral man unexceptionable in private life." Practicing what she had preached to her son, she chose an independent course. In her country's present state, she judged that "union is essentially necessary to our very existence." As the Federalists amounted to very little on the political scale, and had "not the least" possibility of success, she concluded that "the best and least exceptionable on the other side is a desirable object."[29]

Spring of 1808 was mild, but that was the best one could say. The embargo had taken its toll. "Commerce is dead and agriculture is chief mourner," Abigail reported to Mrs. Smith, now reunited with her husband and living in the Chenango Valley, in New York. "Not a ray of light breaks through the Gloom," she added. Information had arrived that Napoleon was "hunting" for ways to tighten restrictions on commerce and oblige Americans "if possible" to take a part for or against him. Abigail also noted that "another unhappy affair" had taken place in the East Indies between the British and the Americans on the issue of impressment, and had resulted in bloodshed. She feared there might be a war, what with the British, so "very insolent and haughty," exercising their power "without much regard to right." But she took consolation in the belief that "all events are under the controul of a Supreme Being who will order and direct them. I trust for our best good: and may it please him to avert from us the horrors of war."[30]

John Quincy's term as senator was to expire on March 4, 1809, but he was denied the opportunity to run again. James Lloyd was named in his stead, nine months ahead of the normal date of election, and on June 8, John Quincy sent a letter of resignation to the two Houses of Congress, "consistent," Abigail thought, "with his principles." Her indictment of the Federalist party was complete. The party had behaved in a most "ungenerous" fashion—one that no honest man could justify. Her son had been "vilified abused and calumniated" because he would have an opinion of his own. As the Federalists had abandoned him, the Republicans had courted him, behaving toward him "with more candour and liberality than they usually practice." Certainly, John Quincy had been wounded in the "House of his Friends, yet his elevation of mind," Abigail consoled herself, "will enable him to bear with mildness and patience the jealousy of his equals which upon this occasion has been very conspicuous."[31]

By the end of August, Abigail was worn with the "vexatious top-icks" of politics, but could not turn her back on them. It seemed to her that "party spirit distorts every effort for the public good into a conspiracy to overturn the constitution; and native Americans united with foreigners to degrade the hand which gave them birth and humiliate themselves to become tributary vassals. . . ." For all her anguish, she was probably the proudest mother on American turf. John Quincy dwelt in a superior realm. From her beatific vantage point, Abigail viewed John Quincy as a "man who loves his country better than gold; and who dared to strip the mask from the face of deformity—and hold up to public view the true and real picture—I consider it a family trophy—as a coat of arms and pride myself more in being the Mother of such a son, than in all the honours and titles which monarch could bestow."[32]

A year of being "teazed" by rumors—Federalists were betting that Mr. Madison would offer John Quincy a foreign embassy post pro-vided that he joined the President's party—concluded with John Quincy's appointment, three months after his nomination, as minis-ter plenipotentiary of the United States at the court of His Imperial Majesty the Emperor of All the Russias on June 29, 1809. The ap-pointment was meaningful to John Quincy for immensely disparate reasons, positive and troublesome: he was proud to be chosen; he regarded the post as one "of great Trust and importance"; and, blessedly, it was "totally unsolicited." He accepted the post with the "vague hope" of rendering to his country "some important service," and, in turn, it was his "desire to justify the confidence" shown him by Mr. Madison. It was, after all, the "duty of a citizen to obey the call of his country," but John Quincy was frank about an underlying cause for his "satisfaction." This was the opportunity "of being removed, at least for a time, and with honor," from "most virulent and unrelenting persecution."[33]

On the other hand, John Quincy had reason to pause at this junc-ture in his forty-three-year-old life. His was a heightened awareness of the "deep sense of the stormy and dangerous" elements of this new phase of his career. Also, his personal motives for staying at home were, in his own words, "of the strongest kind"; the infancy of his children and the age of his parents were causes of immediate concern. In his mother's case, he had to deal with the upsetting facts of her distressed health. By her own admission, Abigail had not felt so ill in the past five years. In February 1809 she suffered an extreme and dangerous case of dysentery and later struggled with what she termed "St. Anthony disease," which caused her face to swell and inflamed her eyes until she was nearly blind. Her description of her plight to Elizabeth Peabody conveys Abigail's fortitude and wit, but also her enveloping depression, which she longed to overcome. St. Anthony "must be a very bigoted saint, a favorer of the Inquisition, and a tyrant," to punish her so severely that she had come near losing her senses. "If such are the penances of saints," she told Mrs. Peabody, "I hope to hold no further intercourse with them." She would have liked, that June of 1809, to take a little journey, and thought that one would be of service to her, but found, she said, that "as years and infirmities increase, my courage and enterprise diminish."[34]

At noon on Saturday, August 5, 1809, all members of the party bound for St. Petersburg gathered at the corner of Boylston and Nassau streets in Boston. Those who ascended the waiting carriages that would trundle them over the Charles River bridge to Mr. William Gray's wharf in Charlestown, where they would board his ship *Horace,* included John Quincy, Louisa, and their youngest child, Charles Francis; Louisa's sister, Caroline Johnson; John Quincy's nephew and private secretary, William Steuben Smith; a chambermaid, Martha Godfrey; and a black manservant named Nelson.

On August 6, the morning was cool and foggy, land had evaporated from the horizon, all the women were seasick, and John Quincy confided to his diary that while separation from his family and friends had always been painful, it had never hurt to the degree he felt now. He had left behind two children and parents he was in "hopes" of meeting again. His father and mother, he wrote, were also "deeply affected" by his departure. His mother's letter, received just before sailing, was unforgettable and "would have melted the heart of a Stoic," he said. "My dear Children," Abigail had written, "I would not come to Town to day because I knew I should only add to yours and my own agony. My Heart is with you. My prayers and blessing attend you. The Dear Children you have left, will be dearer to me for the absence of their parents."[35]

Both John and Abigail had, admittedly, looked to John Quincy as the "prop and support" of their advanced and declining years. His "judgment his prudence his integrity his filial tenderness and affection his social converse and information" had made his society "peculiarly" dear to his parents as the world receded from them "with its pleasures and amusements." Each day they had valued these qualities increasingly; they were John and Abigail's "Solace and Delight." Indeed, Abigail had suggested to Mrs. Peabody that a man of John Quincy's worth "ought not to be permitted to leave the Country—a Country which wants such supports."[36]

Illness had perhaps made Abigail extremely vulnerable, mainly because she did not really believe she would see her son again. Parting with him "was like taking our last leave of him," she wrote to her sister Elizabeth on August 27. "We can barely stretch out our hands to the Anchor of hope with the prospect of living to see his return even should providence spair his Life. We know and feel," she continued, "that we are cut off from that society which was our delight; from that fillial attention which smoothed the rugged road of life, and supported our declining years."[37]

She had not grown so infirm, however, that she had lost her vision of John Quincy's proud destiny. As though raising her head higher, sitting firmer in her chair, she assured her sister that John Quincy had received "an appointment which did honour both to the giver and receiver," and that he conceived it his "duty not to decline the service of his country from whatever party calld." John Quincy had "embraced the whole," and his mother was convinced that as the "interest and welfare" of his country was his "object—without consideration of party distinctions—his soul feels no contraction."[38]

On Thanksgiving Day, Thursday, November 30, 1809, Abigail was unable to attend church owing to a troublesome eye. But she did go to dinner with a thankful heart, she hoped. She could not help noticing, however, and even counted exactly the empty places at her festive table. She consoled herself that the "young shoots and branches remained," two from each family, the "promising successors of their dear parents." She wished that they would enjoy their plum puddings, and that she might keep secret her "anxious solicitude . . . respecting some of their absent parents."[39]

TWENTY-FOUR

The Young
Shoots and Branches

"As long as I live," Abigail had vowed, "I shall feel interested in all the interest and concerns of every Branch of my
family." The branches swayed wide now, and though she acknowledged Mrs. Smith's claim on her "as the first," distance complicated
her concern for John Quincy and his family.[1]

They had reached St. Petersburg safely on October 23, 1809, after
seventy-nine days aboard the *Horace*, though she did not learn this
welcome news until weeks later, and probably first in a newspaper.[2]

Abigail traced the *Horace*'s adventurous route past Newfoundland,
past Norway, past Denmark, almost as busily as the ship's Captain
Beckford. She followed the party farther, from Kronstadt into St.
Petersburg, and had she known about them, she would have kept
them company in the "five indifferent chambers" engaged by John
Quincy at the Hotel de Londres. The winter's cold cramped her
hands, making it impossible for a time to write, and to keep herself
from "quite congealing to a statue," she kept close to her Quincy
fireside, anxiously committing to memory the *Travelling Sketches* of an
Englishman named Robert Ker Porter, who had spent the years 1805
to 1808 in Sweden and Russia.[3]

It was, of course, Porter's impressions of Russia, both verbal and
visual, that riveted her attention. Already quite a student of Russian
history, familiar with the lives of Peter the Great and the Empress
Catherine, she found Porter's impressions, in the harsh February of
1810, with the Boston harbor frozen completely as far as the Light-

house, painfully relevant. If she thought Boston's climate almost unendurable, if the "genial influence of the sun" was almost as life-sustaining as her very ability to breathe, she could not help but "shudder" for her children in icy St. Petersburg, where, she learned, birds dropped from the trees, dead and stiff, where water thrown into the air reached the ground frozen, where the sun rose at fifteen minutes after nine in the morning, and set at forty-five minutes after two in the afternoon.[4]

How Louisa would survive the rigorous Russian winter, and how John Quincy's eyes would endure the hurtful glare of the snow, posed dreadful problems to Abigail. In her need for solace she sought the companionship of the one person besides John who cared as she did about the Russian "branch" of her family: Louisa's mother.[5]

Catherine Johnson and Abigail had a world in common. As they shared children, grandchildren, and a taste for politics (Mrs. Johnson's appetite was almost as insatiable as Abigail's), the two women turned gratefully to one another to exchange family news from loved ones in Russia, as well as information, theories, or merely enticing gossip about the current scene in Washington—Mrs. Johnson's home—and abroad. The breadth, candor, and commitment of their correspondence are reminiscent of the earlier exchange between Abigail and Mercy Warren. As she had with Mercy, Abigail acknowledged Catherine Johnson as her peer, and was quick to tell her that, "tho retired from the world," she liked to know what was passing—expecially if she could obtain it "from one who is so capable of describing Life & manners." She paid Mrs. Johnson a dubious though well-meaning compliment when she spoke "sincerely" of her love for Mrs. Johnson's daughter Caroline, called Kitty, now in Russia with her sister Louisa. Kitty's improved mind and sprightly wit, the "easy affability of her manners," indicated, Abigail told Mrs. Johnson, that "she had stronger marks of her descent from you than any of your other daughters."[6]

Though increasing bouts of illness wearied, saddened, and even frightened her, Abigail's mind remained youthfully vigorous, her opinions as partisan and passionate as ever. Conviction rang through the multitudinous pages of her letters—admittedly her lifeline out of Quincy—leaving not a flicker of doubt about her positions on the President and his Cabinet, on Napoleon, on the press. She was in fighting form, at least intellectually, and the spectrum of her interests was nearly infinite. In Catherine Johnson she found an ideal audience and collaborator.[7]

At Abigail's initiation, they discussed the "very unpleasant occurrences" at the seat of government, particularly the "disunion" in the Cabinet caused by President Madison's attempt to appoint Albert Gallatin as Secretary of State. All of Abigail's chauvinistic leanings surfaced now. The Swiss-born statesman was capable enough, but Abigail thought the public voice (her own included, of course), favored a "Native American" in that role; Gallatin was, therefore, best off in his present office, that of Secretary of the Treasury.[8]

As always, Napoleon was a subject for prolific speculation. "Pray is the report in the public papers true," Abigail asked Mrs. Johnson, regarding Napoleon? Had the Emperor adopted the son of Jérôme Bonaparte and made him a prince of the realm? "We all know what a facility he has had of making Kings and Queens spring up like mushrooms," and as a result, she concluded, "we are very apt to think our American Blood as pure as any that flows in the veins of any of his Dukes & Dutchesses," some of which may have "creapt through Scandles ever since the flood." Soon she would despise Napoleon's "indiscriminate plunder" of American commerce and predict that his action was not "very like" to promote his influence or interest in America, insisting that "power without right will never do."[9]

Nor had Abigail made peace with the "venal hirelings" of the press. Russia was at war with Britain and in alliance with France, and Abigail took particular exception to the British newspapers' description of John Quincy as a meddler, and as the bearer of dispatches to Bonaparte. The American Federalist-sympathizing papers copied the British, clearly intending, in Abigail's opinion, to pass their allegation "where it will" for the truth, in order to undermine her son and "render the Mission to Russia as unpopular as possible." Some of the newer writers even exceeded the originals, Cobbett and Callender, for example, in their willingness to "do the dirty work of their employers," Abigail told Mrs. Johnson. If she had to point to factions dedicated to discrediting John Quincy's mission, she would immediately name the British partisans in America.[10]

And once on the subject of the British, her old animosities were revived sometimes in unexpected ways. In the spring of 1810, she went to the trouble of describing her garden in affectionate detail, as she viewed it from her living-room window. She mentioned the full bloom of the trees, the "rich luxurience of the grass plotts," the early flowering of the cowslips, daffodils, and columbine. One other early flower, however, had not yet found "assylum" in her garden. This was the Crown Imperial, excluded because it bore "too monarchial a title to find admittance in the catalogue of an Humble citizen" such as she. The flowers she chose to plant would "gracefully return the labour and toil bestowed upon their cultivation." Furthermore, envy would not nip their buds, or calumny destroy their fruits, or ingratitude "tarnish their colors." "You see," Abigail had the grace to observe to Mrs. Johnson, concluding this horticultural digression, "I cannot wean myself from the subject of politicks."[11]

The correspondence between Abigail and Mrs. Johnson took on a more urgent tone when it included news from Russia. Abigail steeled herself against disappointment—she knew that the River Neva, for instance, was generally frozen over until May and that therefore she could not hope for word from John Quincy or Louisa until springtime. Nevertheless, she found the four- to sixth-month intervals between letters extremely worrying. It was, as it happened, in exchange of their meager information that Abigail learned from Mrs. Johnson of Louisa's difficulties, of the "perplexity of your situation," as she wrote to her daughter-in-law on May 15, 1810. Louisa was finding her life "uniformly dull," and was missing the comforts of home in America. Her impatience with her situation was "excessively difficult to controul, and utterly impossible entirely to command." It would require, by her own forlorn admission, more philosophy than she "ever shall boast," to meet with her current challenges. Besides, shocked by the morals and manners of the Russians, and "so conscious" that she could not "in any degree" acclimate herself, Louisa foresaw nothing ahead but "perpetual mortifications."[12]

It soon became evident that another factor was most powerful of all in ruining all hopes for even a reasonable adjustment—money. John Quincy wrote about the expense as well as the difficulty of forming a suitable domestic establishment for an American minister. His stress only heightened Louisa's sensitivity on the subject of finance. Acutely conscious of "having not a sixpense in the world," Louisa wrote Abigail that every bill she was forced to bring to her husband made ruin "stare him in the face." John Quincy tolerated this problem very patiently, but Louisa could not. It had "ever" been her maxim, she told Abigail, knowing she had married penniless, "to make my expences as light as possible." And, she added, she was "under the necessity," presumably due to straitened finances, of relinquishing society in Russia altogether. Submerged in self-pity, Louisa had gone on to write Mrs. Cranch, with whom her two sons George and John boarded, on the subject of her impoverishment. Never until now, she said, had she "so sensibly" felt the loss of the little property she had once been taught to expect. Otherwise, had her situation been different, she could have offered some trifling gifts of affection to her "darling Boys which though they are in themselves nothing, contribute greatly to endear an absent friend." Alas, fortune proved unkind, and she had only to depend on Mrs. Cranch's goodness to let her sons know of their mother's affection.[13]

Louisa could not have found a more empathic audience than Abigail. She understood precisely the hurdles her daughter-in-law faced and was achingly, if not angrily, familiar with the deprivations enforced by the meager American ambassadorial salaries—and in fact with government salaries overall. To meet European standards in terms of dress, servants, and liveries (especially the latter) challenged an American's pocketbook as well as his pride, and she said as much, voluminously.[14]

Since Abigail had lived abroad in this "connection," Louisa's lament over rents, over the entire wretched spectrum of official finance, and, as a specific example, over the fact that a plain leghorn hat with a simple ribbon cost four and a half guineas evoked bitter agreement. In her elder years, Abigail increasingly resented the strict economy enforced on her by the fact that John had "neither riches or affluence to bestow on his posterity." She wished that her "rich flourishing country," who owed their fisheries and great landed possessions to her husband's "exertions and firmness," would, at the least, "blush at their ingratitude." She took sly revenge in availing herself of John's free mailing privileges, the only way, to her mind, that her country did reward its servants. Therefore, she openly and frequently urged her friends to write to her by way of her husband, so that they might avoid payment of postage.[15]

The outcry of criticism of the "magnificence" of the Madison White House was still another proof of her country's miserly attitude in the face of European regard for opulent appearances. If it had been her decision to make, she would aim for a presidential salary of $100,000 and, moreover, for a twelve-year term. Her experience abroad had led her to believe that the social standards of monarchical countries had to be met before meaningful diplomacy could be conducted.[16]

When, however, the moment came for Abigail to discuss personal finances, her general indignation subsided. On January 21, 1811, she wrote to Louisa: "The subject which preys upon your mind, and which you have repeatedly mentioned, is surely no fault of yours. It was well known to Mr. Adams before he was connected with you and can never be a complaint against you." Nor, Abigail continued, had any of his "connections" reminded her of her financial position, or lack of one. Nor could it "by any means" lessen her influence with him. Further, his honor and his reputation must be as dear to her as though she possessed "ever so large a fortune." In fact, Abigail said, "I should esteem it a misfortune for you to have carried him a fortune unless he had possest sufficient to have balanced it—believe me my dear," she had concluded, "altho you might have felt more independent; you would not have been happier." In light of Louisa's cruel references to her mother-in-law in future years, Abigail's sensitive and kindly consolation is poignant in its inability to salvage an overwhelming situation.[17]

In a further effort to cheer her daughter-in-law, Abigail wrote affectionately and intimately of Louisa's children, John and George. John looked "daily" more like his mother; George, on the other hand, resembled his father in many respects. He even partook of "a little too much positiveness," an error that Abigail assured Louisa she had tried to correct in his father in early life. But "the Boy inherits it, by regular descent as his Father did before him," and in Abigail's opinion, "Age, a knowledge of the world, and experience will correct it, and molify it into firmness," she promised. But her best advice to Louisa was to remember that " 'Hope Springs Eternal in the Human Breast'; the hope of returning to your family and friends—Let that cheer your drooping Spirits and invigorate."[18]

Convinced that John Quincy's position in Russia was not "by any means an Eligible one," Abigail took measure of her private feeling that she and John had just "minutes" to live, and John's trembling hold on a teacup, or even a knife, warned her of the "final separation." Abigail's proposal to Louisa on May 15, 1810, seemed the logical solution to an altogether troubling situation: "You must extricate yourself by a return to America." What alternative was there, "what shall I say that Country deserves," she asked, "which will not support its own dignity, a country rich in resources, and increasing wealth? yet it will have no mercy as respects pecuniary affairs." As a result of her lengthy confrontation with the problem posed, Abigail had reached the conclusion that "to give the same sallery to every foreign minister, is like a Tailors making a coat, and requiring it to fit all sizes."[19]

By mid-July, slightly mellowed though no less determined, Abigail spoke of hopes that John Quincy might leave Russia "consistant" with the President's views and the benefit of his country, or that the entire issue might be resolved by a vote of greater financial compensation from Congress. Two weeks later, persuaded that "when the means are so inadequate to the end, it requires great skill and judgement to shape the course," Abigail set out to effect her courageous theory. The remarkable content of her letter of August 1, 1810, to President James Madison is best reflected in his answer to Abigail. On August 15, Madison wrote:

> I have received your letter of the 1st instant. Altho I have not learned that Mr. Adams has yet signified to the Department of State his wish to return from the Mission to St. Petersburg, it is sufficiently ascertained by your communication, as well as satisfactorily explained by the considerations suggested. I have accordingly desired the Secretary of State to let him understand that as it was not the purpose of the Executive to subject him to the personal sacrifices which he finds unavoidable, he will not, in retiring from them, impair the sentiments which led to his appointment. . . . Be pleased, Madam, to accept my acknowledgements for the gratifying expressions with which you favour us, and be assured of my high esteem and very respectful consideration.[20]

In light of her definitive move, Abigail's subsequent communication with Catherine Johnson is puzzling. She was, she wrote in mid-September, "gratified, at the marked and particular attention" that the Russian imperial family had shown to their children. The Czar had indeed honored Louisa and her sister in the eyes of all his court, and those of the whole diplomatic body, by choosing to dance with them at the opening of a ball. She appraised the Czar's action as not only conferring personal distinction, but publicly manifesting "his Friendly Disposition" to the United States. "You know Madam," Abigail continued, "what weight and influence these apparently trifling circumstances (as some consider them) have in the Courts of princes." As nearly garrulous as Abigail was up to this point, she dissembled when commenting on the most meaningful issue of this letter. "If he has written to be recalled as you have heard," she told John Quincy's mother-in-law, "he has not informed me of it," although, she admitted, she had expected that he would do so "upon account of the expence of liveing, to which his sallery is by no means adequate." However, judging from some of his letters, she added, "I think it may be in his power, most essentially to serve his Country if he remains another year." Possibly she was being practical, believing it would take just about that span of time before John Quincy might tactfully extricate himself from his duties in St. Petersburg. But there was no suggestion of political pragmatism when Abigail wrote of her hopes to Mrs. Peabody in late November that the Adamses' residence in Russia "will not be of long continuence."[21]

On October 10, as testament to Abigail's persuasion and Madison's consideration, the President wrote to inform His Imperial Majesty that John Quincy, "influenced by private consideration of an urgent value, having desired to return to America, we have yielded to his request." Five days later, on October 15, 1810, the Secretary of State sent this choicely worded message to John Quincy:

> It having been intimated to the President, by a person particularly
> attentive to your interest that your return from the Mission to St.
> Petersburg has become necessary to avoid the ruinous experiences
> to which it subjects you, I am directed to signify to you, that
> however acceptable your continuance there would be, he cannot
> under such circumstances refuse his acquiescence in your wish, nor
> will he allow your return to impair the sentiments which had led to
> your nomination. . . .[22]

The following day, President Madison wrote on his own, affirming his "unabated friendship" for John Quincy while reassuring him, in regard to the letter received from his "highly respectable mother," that, as it was not the intention of the Executive to expose him to "unreasonable sacrifices," it could not withhold permission to retire from them. Accordingly, John Quincy would be receiving a letter of leave and a blank commission giving him the care of America's affairs in Russia until a successor might be appointed. Having completed his official obligations, Madison took on another, far more personal tone, revealing his canny perception of uniquely motherly ways or, perhaps, of Abigail's persuasive convictions.[23]

As Madison had received no direct communication from John Quincy, it was his hope, he said frankly, that the "peculiar urgency manifested in the letter of Mrs. Adams, was rather hers, than yours, or that you have found the means of reconciling yourself to a continuance in your Station." Besides having confidence in the value of John Quincy's services, "which led to the call upon them," there were "considerations" bearing against a sudden return from a short mission. Among them, Madison indicated, was the difficulty of suppressing "unfavorable conjectures" in the mind of the Czar as to its cause, as well as the danger of a protracted intermission, if not an entire discontinuance, of United States representation in St. Petersburg. For this reason it was particularly expedient, in case he made immediate use of the official documents sent him, that he spare America pains by guarding against "misconstruction" of his departure, and prepare the Russian government for any delay in filling the vacancy, "which may be unavoidable not withstanding the purpose of preventing it."[24]

This last paragraph proved compelling in a way even Abigail could understand, damaging as it was to her private wishes. While Madison would not disguise his wish that John Quincy's continuation of his valuable services might be found "not inconsistent" with his other undeniable duties, he could not, on the other hand, demand unreasonable sacrifices. Reason was accommodating, however, and the President was "entirely persuaded" that John Quincy's patriotism "will cheerfully make the sacrifice."[25]

The weight of the snow in the "baldpated" winter of 1811 smashed three chimneys and crushed the new shed Abigail had built for vegetables. It was impossible to move about Quincy, and dangerous in Boston. As much as Abigail dreaded the winter, it was the climate of the times that she found far more "difficult." President Madison had issued a proclamation the past October 27, announcing the United States' possession of West Florida from the Mississippi to the Perdido, and authorizing its military occupation as part of the Orleans Territory. On January 15, 1811, Congress assembled in secret session and adopted a resolution authorizing extension of United States rule over East Florida as well, in the event that a foreign power took steps to occupy it.[26]

Another controversial issue, apart from the question of the Floridas, was the renewal of the Bank Charter, due to expire March 4, and denounced by "Old Republicans" as the last relic of Federalist power. Another "great" subject before Congress was the question of the British impressment of American seamen and the resulting proposal of the Nonintercourse Bill against Great Britain. This was indeed "a difficult time," and John seemed to elaborate on Abigail's sighing assessment, predicting changes and revolutions "such as eye hath not seen nor ear heard; changes in forms of government, changes in religion, changes in ecclesiastical establishments, changes in armies and navies, changes in alliances and foreign relations, changes in commerce." On the whole, Abigail and John agreed that the acquisition of the Floridas was for the best; if not for the purchase of Louisiana, the United States could never have commanded the navigation of the Mississippi, without which the Western regions would surely have revolted against the Union. Not surprisingly, Abigail favored a systematic view of government and its laws, supportive and respectful of "rulers." If some laws were not "so judicious or well calculated to promote the order of society as they might be," she was for letting people petition for redress, not for their rising up in rebellion.[27]

Concentrating now on her "flying reports," as Abigail called them ("sketch" was another term she used), to Russia, to Washington, to her daughter's home in the Chenango Valley, to neighboring Boston, she balanced her extensive political analyses with accounts of "trivial circumstances of a domestick kind." She apologized for her homely gossip about the newly married, born, and ill, explaining that, as she mixed "so little with the gay world," she had little that was amusing to pass on. She made still other apologies about her decaying health and faculties; the pain of aging riddled her correspondence with sorrowful regret over dimming eyesight, dwindling mobility, and eroding memory, not nearly so "tenacious" as in her youth. Yet, despite the indisputable fact of these ravages, aspects of Abigail's being remained powerfully whole. Her dedication to particular truths about religion, parental commitment, handwriting, and even punctuation not only remained inviolate but increased in intensity. As though she were confirming her professed interest in all members of her family—"the young shoots and branches" and twigs alike—Abigail shared her judgments with ardent disregard of age or sex.[28]

It was on Sundays, Abigail wrote Caroline Smith, probably her favorite grandchild, that she was especially in her grandmother's thoughts. If Caroline could not attend public worship, Abigail suggested that she nevertheless spend her Sabbaths in a useful manner. In Abigail's opinion, every moment should be devoted to some useful purpose, that the moments might be asked as they passed "what report they bore to Heaven." The more one cultivated and improved some intellectual powers, "the more capable we should be of enjoyment in a higher and more perfect state of existence; the nearer we should be allied to angels."[29]

Abigail's advice to George, the more "easily managed" of the two brothers—John, she thought, had not yet "Got the Mastery of his fire"—was much along the same lines, and as rigorous. She hoped he would "daily acknowledge" that almighty power to whom he was indebted for every moment of his existence and to whom he was "accountable" for his time and the improvement of his talents. And, echoing the long-ago advice to her cousin Isaac Smith, Jr., Abigail eagerly sought to teach her grandson the value of youth, how it was not to be wasted, that "it is a treasure, you can possess but once." Now, at her elderly stage, Abigail thought there would be no price "too great to give," if she could possess the retentive powers of youth. The true value of these, she confided wistfully to George, she had not "rightly estimated, but by their loss."[30]

Abigail's esteem for polished penmanship and for a literate writing style was certainly heightened by her own deprivation; young women of her era had received no such instruction, and she lamented this her entire life. She could not, therefore, stress seriously enough, to each and every one of her grandsons, the importance of developing "an easy correct stile—it is necessary . . . as a scholar and gentlemen and a professional man." Abigail pointed out that Addison's papers in *The Spectator* were esteemed by the learned as a model of letter-writing, adding that unless one studied one's own language "correctly," one could never write it "elegantly." Furthermore, she cautioned against abbreviation of words, insisting that "twas" would never do for *was,* or "twould" for *would.* [31]

After scrutinizing John's handwriting, Abigail pronounced it more "legible" than before, assuring him, however, that "there is room enough yet for you to improve." In fact, she would be "glad" to see her grandson proving "better, and better every day. This is your duty, this is what you live for," she insisted. As though to conclude her thesis, Abigail reminded John that his father "is at great expence for your Education, and he expects you will not be wanting in diligence and application."[32]

Impartial as she was about sharing her thoughts, Abigail moved easily between the generations. It was inevitable that she turn from her grandsons to their father, and the advice she delivered to John Quincy undoubtedly reflected her sense of what her own children had missed during their separation from their father. Both John and

George were now boarding with Mrs. Peabody in Atkinson, New Hampshire, and Abigail was determined to remind John Quincy of his unalterable duties to his sons at "this critical period of their lives." The boys were maturing now, "coming into life," Abigail wrote, "and it is of great and important concern to them to be trained up under the eye, care and admonition of their father, to imbibe his sentiments, to catch the fire of his patriotism, and to drink from the fountain of knowledge which he has acquired in the various and important occupations in which he has been engaged." Directly put, John Quincy's supervision would be "most valuable" to his sons, "as it would give them a taste for and a Love of Literature, which they cannot be expected to attain in so high a degree as they would under your Eye." Also contained in every letter was the message, implicit or stated openly, that however valuable their son might be to others, to his parents and all his family John Quincy's presence was invaluable.[33]

When Abigail learned of the death in Washington of one of Louisa's sisters, she sought to "lead" her daughter-in-law to the only source of consolation "from whence you can draw comfort to sooth and calm your agitated Bosom." Abigail was uneasy, considering Louisa's admitted want of absolute faith. Groping for the answer, Abigail found herself hoping fervently that "some light might spring up" unforeseen, but effective in rescuing Louisa from her "difficulties."[34]

The light, when it finally shone "in the midst of surrounding darkness," was indeed something about which to cheer. Its source was the appointment of John Quincy as associate justice of the Supreme Court of the United States. Abigail was exultant; the words sang on her page. "An appointment so honorably made, so unanimously concurred in, and so universally approved," she informed Louisa on March 4, 1811, "cannot fail to excite in his Breast the most pleasant sensations." As though Louisa might need further convincing, Abigail copied an extract of a letter published in the newspaper the *Patriot.* With exquisite pride she savored the enobling words she might easily have written herself concerning the Honorable John Quincy's nomination and the newspaper's conviction that he "will no doubt be approved":

When the Bench of Justice shall be irradiated by worth, and
tallents so transendently great, as those of Mr. Adams, when virtue
and patriotism so rare and so distinguished shall become . . . the
administrator of our Laws the Nation will indeed be blessed, if his

influence may have the weight which will be due to it, in the supreme court of his Country.[35]

Abigail wrote with monumental enthusiasm to both John Quincy and Louisa that March 4. His father had already sent word that she was confident would be given "due respect," and while Abigail promised her son not to impose her judgment "as a Law upon him," she did bid that he "forsake not the Law of thy Mother." The general consent both in the Senate and by all political parties "must weigh in your mind powerfully," she continued. Furthermore, that none of his friends had solicited the appointment, or found it necessary to "encumber" the President with letters of recommendation, was proof of his popularity.[36]

There was no stemming Abigail's conviction that her son had at last found his niche. That he had done so she considered a providential "call" as much as a presidential act, one he could not refuse. Again, with the bounding energy of a young Portia, she argued her case as though her beloved son's survival, as well as his family's, depended on his acquiescence. In the first place, she held the judgeship in "higher affirmation" than that of the presidency—though both were grounded on the same principles of "immutable justice and integrity"—because the duties were less arduous, the responsibilities of a different kind. Another attraction of the office was its permanence, which would "in great measure" set John Quincy free from divisive party spirit. It seemed also that, with the family united in Washington, John Quincy might better superintend his children's education. And, of course, in view of his parents' tenuous health, his presence, Abigail assured him, would "prolong and heighten the few remaining pleasures & comforts which remain to advanced Age." John was seventy-six, Abigail sixty-seven; firmly, though with "the tenderest Solicitude" for his happiness, Abigail concluded her case: "I will take it for granted that after mature reflection you will resign yourself to the call of your Country, and hold the office of Justice with an honest heart, and a steady hand."[37]

She was in high spirits when she informed friends that early March of John Quincy's appointment "so unsolicited, made so cordially and unanimously confirmed, and so universally approved," adding, in her letter to Mrs. Johnson, that she would "permit" no doubt as to his return. As the days passed, she grew more eager about the merit of the appointment, and therefore more restive. By the end of the month she was wondering whether there would be any impropriety on Mrs. Johnson's part in inquiring of either the Secretary of State or of the Navy if any vessel had been ordered to bring Mr. Adams home from St. Petersburg. By the end of April, Abigail wrote John Quincy that she hoped he would be coming to the "paternal mansion" on his return. She "dwelt with Delight" on this prospect, she continued, but her joy was tempered by "knowing how easily and how suddenly all may be blasted."[38]

Unfortunately, Abigail's acknowledgment of fate's vagaries proved prophetic. John Quincy was "staggered" by his new commission, suffering as he did from a long-standing sense of his own ineptness in judicial tribunals. He was mindful, however, of how his decision would affect his parents. Despite his personal wish for more southern climes and his ardent inclination to be restored to the bosom of his country, his family, and his "darling boys," the thought of returning home caused him "extreme perplexity of mind, and a conflict of emotions." Fortunately, in a sense, "the blessing of Providence" resolved his dilemma. His wife was pregnant. On June 11, 1811, he wrote that "a duty of still more commanding nature" required him to decline acceptance. Later, on August 12, he told his mother that the birth of his daughter Louisa ought to convince her that "the climate of St. Petersburg is not too cold to produce an American." When he had explained his situation "sufficiently" to President Madison and his father, he turned his attention once again to his mother. He now told Abigail that the office represented "everything" that might have made his family comfortable: a settled station, useful and honorable occupation, security to support a family, the happiness of being home with his parents and *all* of his children. "All this," he said, "I have irrevocably put away from me."[39]

On June 30, John Quincy wrote to Abigail to assure her that he understood her efforts to remove him from St. Petersburg. "I know," he said, "that your letter to the President was written from the tenderest and most affectionate concern for myself and my family." He also acknowledged that his and Louisa's letters to her, on their arrival in Russia, had fully justified her alarm. "Happily," he now assured her, he had adjusted, and had managed to buckle down his expenses to the "very edges" of his means.[40]

By the end of July, Abigail knew the finality of John Quincy's plans. The news, she admitted, cast "a great damp" upon her spirits. In a state of moody resignation she spoke of presuming that it was for the best. Eventually, she was able to concede that "one judge is perhaps as much as falls to the share of one family" She referred to her son Thomas Boylston, newly appointed chief judge of the County of Norfolk, Massachusetts, including the counties, she noted respectfully, of Plymouth, Barnstable, and Bristol.[41]

Her almost obsessive anxiety on John Quincy's account was undoubtedly augmented by other family problems. The Cranches lingered in illness, and Colonel Smith's note of June 29 informed his mother-in-law that John and Caroline were accompanying their mother to Quincy so that she might consult about the unpleasant symptoms of an "approaching cancer." By November, Abigail's "Chapter of Melancholys" was filled with "such impressive scenes" that would not "soon or ever," she was positive, be eradicated from her mind. The very least of the challenges that made the year 1811 "one of the most trying" of her lifetime was having to nurse her husband after he had struck his leg on a sharp stick and cut it, on going outdoors to view a comet.[42]

Catherine Johnson, Louisa's mother and Abigail's "esteemed friend and correspondent," whose loss would be "long regretted," died on September 29 of a fever that swept Washington, indiscriminately attacking the young, the middle-aged, and the elderly. With the death of Mary Cranch on October 11, one day after Mr. Cranch's demise, Abigail wrote to her surviving sister that the "three fold cord is broken." By November, observing her daughter's struggle through the horrible aftermath of radical surgery, Abigail felt her mind "wrought up to a pitch beyond what it would bear." So lacerated by repeated strokes of woe that she could mingle "tear for tear" with all those bereaved, Abigail reviewed in exhaustive detail the ramifications of Mrs. Smith's disease, as though, by facing its horror, she might challenge its threat.[43]

Abigail had not seen Mrs. Smith for three and a half years. Despite the hot and dusty six-day journey in an open carriage, her daughter looked well upon arriving in Quincy, although the appearance of the supposed tumor was "allarming." She sent her daughter to see doctors in Boston on July 10, with prayers that her ailment would not end in "one of the most to be dreaded of all complaints."[44]

Initially, the guarded diagnosis rendered by Doctors Holbrook and Welsh was not entirely pessimistic. The lump in her breast was movable and therefore more easily cured. The doctors saw no need for "outward application," and considered Mrs. Smith's general state of health "so good as not to threaten any present danger." On the other hand, they admitted that they could not say her condition would not "terminate" in cancer. Meanwhile, they prescribed hemlock pills.[45]

Colonel Smith's reaction to Abigail's scrupulously phrased report was one of blustery indignation. With unexpected thoroughness, he had explored the disease, the prognosis, and the treatment and dismissed the diagnosis as contradictory and dissembling. He hammered at phrases repeated by Abigail: "present danger" . . . *"may* terminate in cancer" . . . "live many years in present state" . . . "no applications" . . . "hemlock pills," and brashly concluded: "point, no point." Having vented his fear and frustration, the colonel relented —he would apologize later that he was "ignorant" of the case and agree that it was best to follow the doctors—more kindly concluding his letter with the wish to move the family to Quincy so that his wife might be with her mother. He would find a furnished house or a "Genteel apartment." He was done with public life, and sought only retirement, which he could find in Quincy as well as on the banks of the Chenango.[46]

Further consultations took place the end of August. Dr. Tufts recognized Mrs. Smith's lump as a tumor, advised against hemlock pills, also against anything "to worry or irritate the part." At the end of September, Mrs. Smith received decisive advice from Dr. Benjamin Rush, to whom she had written about her own case after reading his treatise on the subject. Again, Abigail rushed the news to the colonel. "If the operation is necessary as the Dr. states it to be, and as I fear it is, the sooner it is done the better provided Mrs. Smith can bring her mind, as I hope she will consent to it." Dr. Warren of Boston, considered the "first surgeon," would perform the operation and, no doubt, call in skillful assistants. It was her hope, Abigail continued, that Mrs. Smith would "write her mind" to the colonel, and that if she consented, he would be with her through the "painful tryal."[47]

Mrs. Smith was conscious during the twenty-five minutes of surgery that took place on October 8, 1811, performed by Dr. Warren and his son, attended by Doctors Welsh and Holbrook. One month later she was still unable to use her hand, to feed or dress herself, though she could totter from one room to the next, and sit up most of the day. The operation proved almost as traumatic for the mother as for the daughter. Abigail's grief flooded the pages of her letter to John Quincy, to whom she pronounced herself tried in the "furnace of affliction." Rather than fill her pages with "Dirges," however, she would "sing of mercies as well as judgment," and would find consolation "in that religion that teaches us submission and resignation."[48]

Despite brave pronouncements and intentions, however, Abigail could find little peace, and seemed stunned by the implications of her daughter's dangerous operation. She spoke of Mrs. Smith as a "Heroine," and admitted that her own mind was at times "lost to itself" over the "Amputation" of her daughter's breast. By the end of December, when Mrs. Smith was able to leave the house for the first time in three months, Abigail was slightly cheered. She thought now that she had better cause to believe in Mrs. Smith's prospects of "perfect recovery." Though her daughter's arm still required the support of a sling, Abigail clung to a positive view of the situation. After all that Mrs. Smith had endured, "what a blessing it was," she said, "to have extirpated so terrible an enemy."[49]

John Adams, who resumed correspondence with Thomas Jefferson on January 1, 1812, after an eleven-year hiatus, was concerned not only for his daughter but for the fate of his son-in-law. In his initial letter of the reconciliation—effected by Dr. Rush's resolute urging of both men—John noted that his daughter, having "successfully" gone through a "perilous and painful Operation," was detained in Quincy, kept from her husband and family at Chenango, "where one of the most gallant and skilful Officers of our Revolution is probably destined to spend the rest of his days, not in the Field of Glory, but in the hard Labours of Husbandry."[50]

At the start of 1812, Abigail wrote of an inflammation of her eyes and lungs that left her virtually speechless. To someone as self-admittedly "sociable" as herself, this was a "great deprivation." Still, she could write to John Quincy, and her "sketch" of current affairs, he said, was always of "double and treble interest." Abigail wrote to St. Petersburg and Gothenburg (John Quincy was shortly called to Ghent, where he helped in negotiations with the British) by way of France, England, and Denmark, always mindful of possible interception, and of the eight-month intervals before letters would reach their destination. In April, ill as she was, dosed with opium and calomel pills and saline mixtures, she alerted John Quincy to congressional plans to commence an embargo of sixty days. The bill had already passed the House, and all was "hurry and dispatch" to get every vessel to sea. They were "fast approaching a crisis," and what would happen was "only known to that Being who governs the destiny of

Nations." War with England, as much as it was to be "deplored," now appeared "inevitable" unless that nation desisted from "unjust pretensions and her injurious conduct." "I think we may say we are more sinned against, than sinning," she wrote John Quincy, observing that England's injustice toward America had exhausted all peace measures.[51]

The United States declared war against Great Britain on June 19, 1812. Six weeks later Abigail personally plunged into a skirmish of sorts, writing to the Secretary of State on behalf of her son-in-law, Colonel Smith. His recent appearance at Quincy—he had come with two of his sisters, Nancy and Abbe, just two weeks ago to collect his wife—was an obsessive reminder of a disappointed life. John deeply regretted that "such Talents, such Tacticks, such discipline and such experience should perish and be lost" because the colonel was not a "sagacious Politician," and had been led astray by Burr, Miranda, and many others. While the father-in-law positively declared the colonel "fitter for the command of the North Western Army, and fitter for Secretary of War," than at least four other current generals, he was resigned to the fact that "his Pride, his Marriage with my Daughter, and the Collissions of Factions have rendered his Appointment impossible."[52]

Abigail agreed wholly with John in his opinion of the colonel, both the good and the bad. Yet constitutionally, or so it seemed, she could not abandon all hope for her son-in-law's future, and that of Mrs. Smith and their children. It was on August 5 that Abigail addressed Secretary of State James Monroe on a subject of "much delicacy," avoiding any mention of the colonel's name. She presumed that she need not list the latter's former services, or the loss of property his family had sustained, or the wounds he had received in the service, or those qualities that "so well" fit him for military command. "It is impossible that all these should not have come into remembrance" when the new army was being organized, she said. Therefore, she wondered, would the "unfortunate affair," during which the colonel had been "deluded" by Miranda into believing his venture was countenanced by the government, exclude him from further service? These, she admitted, were circumstances "most sincerely regretted" by Mr. Adams and herself at the time, "altho we knew that the motive was a mistaken, and misguided zeal to liberate an oppressed people." Now, in the same spirit, Abigail assured Monroe, the colonel was "zealous to support the laws and government of his country as in former days he was to maintain its independence." Furthermore, she added, raising a compelling issue, she had heard from a friend that if the colonel could be "honorably called he should live ten years the longer for it." And finally, if there were "difficulties" with her application on the colonel's behalf, "in the mind of the President," she promised she would "submit in silence."[53]

When, on September 6, Abigail had received no response from the President, she consoled the colonel that it was "often observed that the spectator sees more of the game than the others." The colonel responded by admiring "the style and dignity of her communication to the Secretary of State," and though he believed it was too late, he appreciated her interest. If his proferred services had been accepted with alacrity, he could have rendered "material" service; now, however, he was having second thoughts about going to "an ill-arranged camp."[54]

Vain as these efforts were, Abigail's affectionate appreciation of her son-in-law would some years later be confirmed and seconded by others in electing him a representative to Congress. On Monday, January 25, 1813, the colonel wrote his mother-in-law that the votes of the people "so flatteringly expressed, brushes off from my shirt the gall of bitterness, which the past administration had very unjustly soiled it with, and has burst asunder the bonds of iniquity, which the present one had shackled me with." The powers of government had "pointed at, and exerted against" him, and he had "sustained the attack with a becoming fortitude." The "steady friends of liberty and their country have poured balm into my wounds. They are healed," he assured Abigail. "I can never forget the insult. I may forgive the injury."[55]

Abigail turned sixty-eight on November 22, 1812. She considered it "one of the marvels of the age" that she had got rid of her "croaking" cough, that John was in sound health, and that both of them, as she reported to Caroline, were "as tranquil as that bald old fellow, called Time, will let us be." On the average day, Abigail rose at six and, in imitation of His British Majesty, she said, kindled her own fire. She then called from the stairwell to rouse the servants, and returned to her room to dress. If no one stirred, she called again, raising her voice to a slightly higher pitch, testy about the "blockheads" who required a second nudge. By eight o'clock the fires were lighted, the breakfast prepared. For the next hour, deliveries of coal, cheese, turnips, and sundries were made. On one occasion the arrival of a herd of pigs resulted in the purchase of a spotted swine. Due to the constant flow of callers, Abigail had difficulty finishing her breakfast on certain mornings and vowed repeatedly, if unsuccessfully, "never to be incommoded with trifles."[56]

Weather permitting (it was pleasant this November), Abigail made calls at noon, returned to dine at three; John sometimes played whist with a friend at five. At nine in the evening, Abigail was often "engaged" in writing her letters, and eleven was her usual bedtime. If mail arrived—especially a packet from Russia—the schedule was promptly abandoned. "Avaunt, all cares," Abigail would say; to learn that all members of her family were in good health she counted an enormous "blessing."[57]

Milestones in her life, especially this birthday, found Abigail appraising "this long period of my sojourn," recalling what she had done for herself or others that might be remembered with pleasure or approbation. She regretted her "many, very many follies and errors of judgment," and took comfort in the truth that "vile passions" had never had control over her; she bore no enmity toward any human being. She hoped for God's forgiveness for her errors; she believed devoutly that "purity, benevolence, obedience, submission and humility" were virtues that, if faithfully practiced, would find their reward. With amiable logic she concluded: "I am one of those who are willing to rejoice always. My disposition and habits are not of the gloomy kind. I believe that to enjoy is to obey."[58]

Two months later, Abigail's conscientious optimism was severely disrupted. John Quincy's letter of September 21, which reached her only on January 15, 1813, informed his "dearly beloved Mother" that it was now his turn, as it had been hers the past two years, to bear the unwelcome task of communicating tidings of affliction. His infant daughter, one year and one month old, who had looked like Grandmama Adams ("very handsome, with the finest pair of black eyes you ever saw"), had died. He had mourned the loss of his brother's infant, and now he grieved for his own. He had hoped the baby Louisa would contribute much to the happiness of all their lives, as she had to the "charm" of his.[59]

Abigail wept, then regained her composure and rode out a few days later in a snowstorm to Atkinson, to comfort George and John. Both boys had spoken often of their sister. Her death was a grim if useful lesson, and Abigail reminded them "that no Age, is exempt from the decree of mortality . . . that the blooming youth is as liable to be cut off as the full grown Man or Infant Bud." At this sensitive period, Abigail's remarkable combination of resignation and resilience was fully in evidence in her letter of condolence to Louisa. In her fervent effort to prove to her daughter-in-law that one might survive such an appalling tragedy—that, in fact, one had an obligation to do no less—Abigail shared her long-sublimated grief over the loss of her own infant, Susanna. She wrote on January 30, 1813:

> For ourselves only we can mourn, and how selfish is that served? Early in Life I was called to taste the bitter cup. Forty years has not obliterated from my mind the anguish of my soul upon the occasion. I have since that day sustained more weighty afflictions, but it has pleased Heaven to support me through them and to permit me to live to advanced Age. Let us with gratitude bless our preserver that we have yet so many blessings left us. Such I hope will prove to you, and to their Father [of] your surviving children who most earnestly long for your return to your native country, that they may embrace you and their Brother of whom all the Americans who have seen him speak highly.[60]

One month later, she urged John Quincy not to let "gloom and melancholy take root in your mind." While she understood that his "wounded heart must have time to recover from the stroke" he had suffered, she would remind him of the duties that "you are called upon to discharge," to which he must devote his "mind and attention." As a diversionary measure, or perhaps as a practical reminder that politics was one of his "duties," Abigail enclosed a newspaper clipping dated February 11, 1813, noting the election of President James Madison with 128 ballots, and of Vice-President Elbridge Gerry with 131 ballots.[61]

John Adams expressed his condolences in far more abbreviated terms than Abigail's, yet his terse note was revealing and compassionate. "The loss of your Child has deeply affected me," John wrote on March 1. "I sympathize with you and my daughter under this Severe affliction. But you are perfectly acquainted with all the Consolations of Phylosophy and Religion. I feel to this moment a Similar Loss, and another of a deeper die."[62]

It was clear, as the months slipped by, that Louisa could not now or ever share the absolute faith of her husband's parents, especially

Abigail's outright declaration that her "confidence in the supreme maker will remain unshaken." It was not that Louisa was godless, but rather that her belief was of a more tenuous nature. The "gleam" of comfort that Louisa found in religion and "in God who gives us strength to bear up against the afflictions which assail us in our passage, through this vale of tears" was only just that, haltingly supportive, but hardly all-embracing.[63]

Seven months after the event, on April 4, 1813, Louisa struggled, as though her baby had died only that morning, "to controul the pangs of my bursting heart," pleading that she not be "condemned for a grief which is beyond my reason to subdue." Her heart was "almost broken," her health "gone," her peace of mind, she feared, "forever destroy'd." It was her desperate hope that she might find "Release" from the suffering that made her existence "a calamity to all who surround her." Louisa's pervasive sense of loss was compounded by guilt. Her sister-in-law, Mrs. Thomas Boylston Adams, had "at least" the happiness of knowing that accidental circumstances hadn't caused her child's death, in contrast to her own plight. Louisa blamed herself, and a fall she had taken while cradling her baby in her arms, rather than a combination of fever, dysentery, and possibly erysipelas, for precipitating what she supposed was a fatal injury.[64]

Her anxious tale did not end here. Louisa thought Abigail ought to know that John Quincy's health was a source of "perpetual anxiety" for her, and that she believed it was "absolutely essential" for him to leave for a milder climate. She thought it her "duty" also to tell Abigail not only that was John Quincy's breast "attacked" (she did not specify how), but that he was in the hands of a "very careless Physician" who, though a man of "great abilities," paid little attention to patients unless their symptoms were critical. She was "in terrors," therefore, about what another winter might produce, and was confident that given a few months in less extreme weather, he might be "rapidly restored." With unabated melancholy, Louisa confessed herself unable to write to her sons in America; she had set her heart on seeing them this coming summer. Should she "never more have this greatest blessing," she hoped Abigail would assure them of her tender affection and prayers for their "future happiness prosperity and welfare" in whatever station they would fill, as well as her hopes that they might prove "an honour to the name they bear."[65]

Almost simultaneously in April, when Louisa had written her ago-

nized letter, and months before its arrival, Abigail had taken a positive step toward remedying this sorrowful situation. Her course was
influenced by John Quincy's recent and numerous references to his
desire to return home to see his children and his parents and to the
raw fact that he and Louisa were "literally and really sick of the
climate" in Russia.[66]

Abigail's letter of April 3, 1813, politely but pointedly reprimanded Secretary of State Monroe for not returning or even acknowledging an earlier letter, one of John Quincy's, that she had
forwarded to him in late February. She presumed that "in the multiplicity of Business, it has been forgotten," but she had not forgotten
her original intent—to inform Monroe of John Quincy's wish to
return to America. Pressing her petition now, she said that she was
"anxious to learn if there is a probability of Mr. Adams's return the
ensuing season, and whether any method may be devised for him and
his Family to get back to America with safety during the War."
Monroe, she wrote further, could not wonder at her solicitude on this
subject when he took into consideration her age and that of her
husband. Also, he ought to bear in mind the time her son had been
absent in the service: "I will not say of an ungrateful Country, because I hold it to be the Duty of every good citizen to serve his
Country, not withstanding he may receive from her, ill usage, and
contumely."[67]

Though Monroe's separate letters of April 10 to John and Abigail
failed to promise John Quincy's immediate return, they were nevertheless gratefully received. It was "impossible" to say when their son
would leave for home because John Quincy was involved in the
negotiations between America and Great Britain, to be mediated by
the Czar of Russia in St. Petersburg. "His service in that negotiation
is consider'd of high importance to his country," Monroe assured
Abigail, "and it is hoped that it will not interfere in any respect with
his views, or with those of yourself or his father in regard to him."
Furthermore, Monroe allowed, whenever their son "resolves to return home, every facility which the government can allow, will be
extended to him."[68]

Monroe had offered even more details to John about his son's
future. After conferring with President Madison, the Secretary of
State was authorized to say that in case of peace with Great Britain,
the mission to London would be offered to John Quincy. The latter's
conduct had "obtained" the "approbation" of the President to work

on both the peace and commercial treaties, and it was of "great importance" that his country have his services.[69]

The tone of Abigail's next letter to Monroe was palpably warmer. The Secretary's intelligence "excites many reflections," she answered on April 20. As she evaluated John Quincy's honored future, Abigail's own past loomed intensely. She knew precisely where her duty lay. She had been "early instructed," she confided to Monroe, "to relinquish all personal considerations and enjoyments to the calls of my country." She had learned long ago to be a patriot first, having "submitted" to years of responsibility for a young family, to years of separation from her "protector, the friend of my youth, my companion and the husband of my choice."[70]

Separation from John Quincy was not a new or recent phenomenon, either, but toward the close of her life Abigail confessed that she bore his distance with "still greater and increased reluctance." Now, facing the possibility of an indefinite time before they might meet again, she was both candid and eloquent in her acceptance of her son's new role in history. Though she had "daily hoped" John Quincy would return as he had wished to do, that he had been useful to his country, that he merited and had received the confidence of the President, she told Monroe, "is no small satisfaction to me." Therefore, she "fully and willingly" relinquished her son to his country on "an occasion so highly important and so pregnant with consequences to this nation . . . fervently praying that he may be an instrument in the hand of providence to restore peace upon a just and honorable basis between the contending nations."[71]

Abigail's communication to John Quincy was even more enthusiastic. "It had been my constant and daily petition to heaven for you: that you might be made an instrument in the hand of providence of much good to your native Lands," she wrote on April 23. "Should my petition be answered by accomplishing an honourable peace for your Country," she assured her son, "I should say with Simeon mine Eyes have seen thy Salvation." To God and my Country I resign you —relinquishing all personal considerations." She did add, even so, that she still hoped for the pleasure of seeing him and his family "the ensuing season." She suggested that however much attention she gave to his two children in America, she could not—no one could— "supply" their father's place. "Should you come nearer to us and peace be restored," she promised, "I should not object to their being sent to you."[72]

Abigail had not forgotten Louisa nor her problems, but at this triumphant moment she optimistically sent love to her "dear daughter," with the hope that more prosperous days were in reserve for her and her children. "I never was of a Desponding nature—what ever may be the allotments of providence for me or mine," she assured her son. "My confidence in the supreme maker will remain unshaken and my belief that all partial evil will terminate in universal good is firm, altho we cannot perceive how or when. The History of Joseph and his Brethren," she suggested, "is a lesson full of instruction."[73]

The summer of 1813, though free of contagious disease and promising of a fine harvest, ultimately proved to be a labyrinth of tragedy. On June 1, the *Chesapeake* was captured by the British frigate *Shannon*, and Abigail regretted the fate of the "brave but too daring" captain, James Lawrence, and the loss of more than a third of the crew. By July 24, Abigail learned that the enemy had entered the mouth of the Potomac with five ships and one armed brig, that an attack was expected hourly, and that women and children were flying in all directions in great confusion.[74]

For Abigail, however, the most painful event of the summer was the most private, and not unexpected. Just the past May, Colonel Smith's sister Nancy had informed Abigail that Mrs. Smith's purported rheumatic pains were now acknowledged as a cancer that was wasting her entire body. Now, in July, Abigail recognized the fatal truth of the colonel's guarded message about his wife's wish to spend her "state of convalescence" rather within "the vortex of your kindness and assiduities than elsewhere." He added that he would attend the congressional session at Mrs. Smith's urging, but hasten to Quincy immediately thereafter.[75]

Mrs. Smith, accompanied by Caroline, John, and her sister-in-law Nancy, arrived by carriage and was carried into her parents' house on the July 26. Three weeks later her father abruptly concluded a letter he was writing to Thomas Jefferson. He could not proceed with his philosophical ramblings. He wrote instead: "Your Friend, my only Daughter, expired, Yesterday Morning in the Arms of Her Husband her Son, her Daughter, her Father and Mother, her Husbands two Sisters and two of her Nieces, in the 49th. Year of her Age, 46 of which She was the healthiest and firmest of Us all: Since which, She has been a monument to Suffering and to Patience."[76]

Abigail, too, wrote Jefferson of her "irreparable" loss. Just one month before Mrs. Smith's death, and eighteen months and some thirty letters after the gentlemen had renewed their friendship, Abigail added this postscript to one of John's letters to Jefferson:

> I have been looking for some time for a space in my good
> Husbands Letters to add the regards of an old Friend, which are
> still cherished and preserved through all the changes and
> vicissitudes which have taken place since we first became
> acquainted, and will I trust remain as long as
>
> A Adams.

On August 22, Jefferson's cordial, nostalgic letter allowed that "a kind note at the foot of Mr. Adams's letter of July 15th" had reminded him of the "duty of saluting" Abigail "with friendship and respect; a duty long suspended by the unremitting labors of public agreement," which ought to have been "sooner revived." Touching on the use and passage of time, depleted health, and the "comfortable cares" of grandchildren, he then inquired after Abigail directly and personally. "I will now take time to ask you how you do, how you have done," he wrote, "and to express the interest I take in whatever affects your happiness."[77]

At the end of September, Abigail requited Jefferson's interest with tragic dignity. She wrote him of her "great affliction for the loss of my dear and only daughter, Mrs. Smith," knowing that he too had been "called to separations of a similar kind." Having unburdened herself of the details of her daughter's illness and death, Abigail seemed to feel she owed her correspondent an explanation. "You called upon me to talk of myself, and I have obeyed the summons from the assurance you gave me, that you took an interest in what ever affected my happiness." As though he might visualize her wretched state, she added a fragment of a poem:

> *Greif has changed me since you saw me last,*
> *And careful hours, with times deformed hand*
> *Hath written strange defections o'er my face.*

Her final words left no doubt of lasting friendship: "But altho, time has changed the outward form and political 'Back wounding calumny' for a period interrupted the Friendly intercourse and harmony which subsisted, it is again renewed, purified from the dross."[78]

Though Jefferson's correspondence with Adams flourished, there would be only a few more exchanges between him and Abigail. As was his way, he dwelt briefly on the subject of Mrs. Smith's death, though with obvious feeling. "On the subject of the Postscript of yours of Aug. 16 and of Mrs. Adams's letter, I am silent," he wrote to John on October 12–13, 1813: "I know the depth of the affliction it has caused, and can sympathise with it the more sensibly, inasmuch as there is no degree of affliction, produced by the loss of those dear to us, which experience has not taught me to estimate." In other times of tragedy he had found "time and silence the only medicine, and these but assuage, they never can suppress, the deep-drawn sigh which recollection for ever brings up, until recollection and life are extinguished together."[79]

Jefferson's wisdom was incontestable: time, faith, and silence were indeed universal healers. But there was another powerful element in Abigail's salvation, according to her nephew William Cranch. Speaking of his aunt's "wonted elasticity" of mind, he assured her that "great trials are reserved for strong minds."[80]

TWENTY-FIVE

The Close
of the Drama

Abigail rose from her writing table to retrieve a piece of paper from another part of her room. On the way she caught her image in her "faithful" mirror. She used the word *faithful* as a synonym for *accurate*. Though she did not like the "pale meagre vissage" that "started up to her view," what she described to Elizabeth Peabody as a "striking emblem of yellow autumn and the falling leaf," she admitted that she had known the "same serious truth" about her appearance for some time now.[1]

Old friends did not recognize her; she agonized for them and for herself as they searched her withered face for some familiar clues to earlier impressions. When John was able, at last, to bring home the portraits Gilbert Stuart had initiated twenty years before, Abigail regarded John's as a "Speaking likeness," but hers, "alas," was recognizable only to those who had known her twenty years ago, and never now to her grandchildren.[2]

In the winter of 1814, when her house was like a "hospital of invalids," herself among them, Abigail suffered a violent cough and rampaging rheumatism—she wrote with her middle finger bound—that all but imprisoned her in her upstairs chamber. John fell ill in February, more critically than in several decades, due to a cold caught when he walked in the snow during a venture into Boston. "Great care is necessary for us both to prop up our feeble fabric," Abigail conceded to Mrs. Peabody.[3]

Her hair was "frosted," her eyesight failing, her memory like a "sieve." As the world seemed to be "receding" from her, she foraged with greater anxiety for the "mental food" essential to her "support," by which she meant her "survival." Try as she did to retain what she read, she was often left only with an "impression" that she likened to a "press copy—faint, difficult to retrace," and that sometimes eluded her entirely. John shared this "calamity" of mental and physical debility, though Abigail thought his powers of retainment much better than hers. Sometimes, depending on circumstances, she sounded as though she would accommodate herself to the prerequisites of age with amiable grace, expressing the hope that she might not be found wanting in "patience and submission, humility and gratitude," in retirement from active scenes. As there was an order to nature, as there was a morning and a noon, there must be an evening, she supposed, when the "lengthening shadows admonish us of approaching night—and reconcile us to our Destiny."[4]

At other times, however, Abigail was less reflective, less conciliatory, more eager than ever to strike a bargain with "Time." Her outer appearance, she insisted, distorted her true image, a far more glorious one than her humiliating mirror reflected. The mirror's image was superficial, recording decay rather than virtues of the heart and "the faith of Hope that invigorates the Soul." The mirror showed the "witherd" exterior but did not substantiate her belief that "as we approximate nearer and nearer to the source of excellence we may find our graces increasing with added years untill we Bloom with celestial lusture Brighter & Brighter."[5]

Of considerable significance was the fact of Abigail's endurance, her amazing recuperative powers, mightily reinforced by her abiding faith. She marveled at her very existence, at being permitted "a longer sojourn" than she had ever expected, and this thought inspired her conviction that she was meant by some great design "to fulfill some duty, to report of some mission or commission, to relieve some wants, to correct some errors, to sooth some anguish," and, if she could, to "dispell gloom" among her friends. Suffering from rheumatism, scarcely able to walk, and having to rub her side and hip with camphorated spirits and tincture of flies, Abigail insisted that she was nevertheless quite prepared to serve in any capacity, august or humble. "At the age of seventy," she told Harriet Welsh, "I feel more interest in all thats done beneath the circuit of the sun than some others do at—What shall I say 35 or 40? Yet such people say they feel as keenly and as sensibly as others? Who can think it?" she asked. Obviously, she could not. "Well everyone to their fancy," she allowed.[6]

Faithful to her vision, Abigail proceeded to fulfull the obligations, as she now conceived them, of her prolonged destiny. She reported, corrected, supported, soothed, as need arose, especially regarding Mr. Madison and the war, her granddaughters' marriages, the deaths of friends, the burning of her nation's capital. As a devoted admirer of President Madison, believing him to be "what Pope call'd the noblest work of God—an honest Man," she was dismayed that the Peabody household seemed "to have imbibed an undue prejudice against the chief majestrate from the papers stiled Federal." "Justice" was all that their government sought, yet they were "maligned abused and ill treated by their own nation, and falsly accused" of waging war for the sake of ambition and conquest. "You good folks," Abigail reminded Mrs. Peabody, "hear and read one side only—remember truth and justice have two ears."[7]

The Peabodys, as opposed to Abigail, sided with the many New Englanders who railed against the administration's "restrictive system," the burdensome taxes, and the embargo. "Now I will tell you wherein we differ," Abigail wrote Mrs. Peabody on May 12, 1814. She had not liked embargoes and restrictive systems "any more than you," she assured her sister, but believed the government had resorted to them "with the purist and best intentions." Her sister could rest assured that Mr. Madison would no more sacrifice the interest or independence of the nation than would any of his predecessors, no more than John Quincy "who would sooner lay down his life." Correcting and soothing and, in a sense, informing all at once, Abigail wished Mrs. Peabody to understand that Mr. Madison was no more hostile to commerce than General Washington had been, that he had had embargoes in his time, "tho," she allowed, "not of so long duration."[8]

Abigail advised from experience, furthermore, that it was "impossible" to judge the difficulties that arose on all sides to "obstruct the best intentions, and wisest plans which are suggested by the rulers of a nation." Many of these "obsticals which are every where springing up" could not be known to the people at large, and therefore it was "much easier to blame to find fault, and to complain, than to find remedies for the evils." After assuring Mrs. Peabody that she could "instance" many cases that had occurred during the administrations of previous Presidents, Abigail concluded with only a tinge of embarrassment that there was "no knowing" where she should stop, once she touched "the chapter of politicks," and that she could preach on the subject . . . "as long as many long-winded gentlemen—and perhaps with as much effect."[9]

Even Colonel Smith complimented his mother-in-law on her "affectionate and correct Counsel" to his daughter, Caroline, in regard to her forthcoming marriage to her brother John's friend John P. De Windt. Abigail's thoughts on marriage, aired on the eve of her fiftieth wedding anniversary, her "golden jubilee," were honest, even intimate. She had had "few rubs" of a matrimonial nature, but she had had "some" in her long life. And there were times when she "insisted upon my own way, and my own opinion, and sometimes yealded silently!" Yet, after half a century, she could say "my first choice would be the same," if she had the youth and opportunity once again to make it. But her specific advice was to "look out well," for, "the die once cast, there is no retreat until death."[10]

In Caroline's case, though marriage meant separation from the "prop" of her age, her "Solace," her "comfort," Abigail was relieved "to see and know that she was happily settled in life," for to have left Caroline "destitute of a protector" would only have increased her anxiety. She recognized that her beloved Caroline was neither beautiful nor wealthy; nevertheless, she considered her granddaughter "a jewel of no small value," and vowed she would be "very scrupelous for her."[11]

Because she believed much of happiness in life depended on "connexions," Abigail justified her need to know more about De Windt than the facts of his being an only son, having an independent fortune, being discreet and regular in his habits, and not "in the least given to the expence of fashionable pleasure." After prodding the colonel for details, Abigail was pleased to learn that the mother of this "solid sensible young gentleman" was fifty years of age and had been a widow for ten of them, that the family estate at Fishkill, New York, was "handsome," and that every inquiry made about him was "satisfactory." While she admired the fact that De Windt had asked the colonel for Caroline's hand, taking care to have "as few repellents as possible," she insisted to the colonel that she maintained "the supremacy of the Ladies in this matter." The father, after all, might give his consent when the "Lady might be otherways engaged," or choose to reject the suitor. On the whole, although she approved of the outcome in Caroline's instance, she "rebelld" against the system, she confided to Harriet Welsh, "as encroaching upon the sovereign heights of the Ladies."[12]

Caroline was married in Quincy on Sunday evening, September 11, 1814. Abigail, though feeble after a ten-day illness, had "rallied all my resolution and fortitude" to provide the cake (already at hand) and a cold supper of ham, chickens, pies, puddings, custards, whips, cheesecakes, and melons for twenty-six, including Dr. Welsh and Harriet. The couple left on Monday by stage, accompanied by the colonel and a servant, meeting up with their carriage-and-four in Boston. De Windt always kept such a conveyance, and although this method of transportation was considered "making a Dash," and provoked gossip in Quincy about the bridegroom being "dissapated," the truth of the matter was "far from this," Abigail assured Mrs. Peabody. Betraying her deeply embedded disapproval of Colonel Smith, despite her true affection for this errant son-in-law, Abigail continued: "There is not anything in his manners the least ostentatious or concequential. His habits and taste are quite the reverse, and very different from part of the stock from which she is descended, altho she has not a spice of it in her own composition."[13]

The specter of the colonel's frailties was raised once more, this time in connection with the marriage of Abigail Louisa Adams, the daughter of Abigail and John's dead son, Charles. Unlike Caroline, Abbe was beautiful, like a "half blown rose," Also, unlike her cousin, she was naturally pensive—a trait instilled in her, her grandmother supposed, by her religious sentiments, with which Abigail differed sharply. "Negation of every amusement," she insisted, was not part of her own religion, for, as she interpreted the Scriptures, "there is a time to dance and to sing." Nevertheless, despite edgy but affectionate disapproval of this granddaughter, Abigail was as zealous about Abbe's prospects as she had been about Caroline's.[14]

The fact that Abbe was only sixteen years of age was an additional cause for Abigail's and John's concern. "I have always been an advocate for early marriages," John wrote to his daughter-in-law Sally Adams, Abbe's mother, on October 26, 1814, "when circumstances of character, fortune could apologize for them." But sixteen was a very early age to assume the care of "so important an establishment as that of a family." The grandparents left no doubt as to the requisites of their seal of approval of this marriage. They wished to know "the young gentleman's age, his profession, whether farmer, merchant, lawyer, physician or divine; the residence and condition of his family; his own means of subsistence etc etc," John concluded, "for I am as little an advocate for enthusiasm in love as I am in politicks or religion."[15]

Fortunately for all, Mr. Alexander Johnson of Utica, New York, the prospective groom, was the son of a "most respectable and worthy merchant," and there was reason to be satisfied with the connection "on all counts." Mr. Johnson was "well bred, self possessed, affable, conversable," and he had an independent income. Also, there was nothing in his personality or background that "savors in the least," Abigail told Mrs. Peabody, "of conceit, foppery or arrogance."[16]

Though Abigail was appreciative of the "faithful and constant" attention of Louisa, her brother's child, and of the "sprightly vivacity" of Susan, her son's child, neither compensated for the irreparable void that Caroline's departure had made in the Adams household. If Caroline found as many "joyful faces" to receive her as she had left "sorrowful hearts" behind her, she would have no reason to complain as her grandmother did now. It was, however, the permanence of their separation that saddened Abigail, a reminder of other separations of even more awesome finality. One of the penalties of a long life was loneliness; the death of her friend Mercy Warren acutely accentuated Abigail's solitude.[17]

It was her habit now, writing to Caroline, to confide in her at length and in depth, observing how her "pen runs on," because she tended to forget "all time" in writing to her. Abigail was comforted that Caroline had visited Mrs. Warren, and predicted that her granddaughter's memories of her would always be pleasant. "Seldom does old age wear so pleasing, so instructive an aspect," she told Caroline.[18]

Mercy Warren turned eighty-seven on October 6, 1814; her death twelve days later, on October 18, her son wrote Abigail, had made "another inroad in their friendship." The son referred kindly to Abigail's "constant, ardent, almost sisterly affection" for his mother. Regarding the more painful aspects of their friendship, of the previous "inroad" on it, he remained silent. Their rapprochement after the schism created by Mercy's *History*, in which John thought he had been demeaned by being given too shallow a niche in the grand monument that was his country, was due, most of all, to mutual ties that transcended the presumptions and vanities of both principals.[19]

Though the friendship had been resumed only after the affectionate mediation of Elbridge Gerry, Benjamin Waterhouse, and perhaps

Abigail most of all, the framework had never completely disintegrated. When their mutual friend, Waterhouse, conveyed Mercy's conciliatory regards to John, the latter's reply was affable, though he remained sorely wounded. "I should have no scruples to return her love," John replied, "for it is very certain I can never cease to love her, let her treat me with ever so much Injustice or Cruelty." Despite genuine anguish, as it had been with Jefferson, so it was to be with Mercy: John had "long since found by Experience," he told Waterhouse, "that when I have once conceived a real Friendship for another, I can never lose it all."[20]

Though her own efforts to mend the breach between John and Mercy initially seemed somewhat stilted, Abigail proved herself a judicious and effective arbiter. On her return from a visit with Mercy at Plymouth, she wrote on August 9, 1812, that after reviewing the subjects of controversy between the "two ancient Friends," she must candidly tell Mercy that she judged "both in the wrong." It was her theory, however, that if "unavoidable circumstances" had not obstructed personal intercourse, "neither party would so have judged, or so have written." Abigail further assured her friend that no personal animosity existed in the "Breast of the person who considered himself as injured," although, she admitted, he did harbor a reservation. This was the "regret," she continued, "that his principles and actions should thus be transmitted to posterity by the eloquent pen of Mrs. Warren, whose sentiments and opinions so cordially harmonized with his own in former days." Her own delicate situation had prevented the expression of her sentiments, she concluded, until she had found that her silence might be "misconstructed."[21]

Mercy's response was exuberant: "Blessed are the Peace-makers!" In that "glorious band of righteous" she classed her friend Mrs. Adams. She also politely reminded Abigail of John's promise to forward from his letterbook a number of letters both "wounding and grievous" to his aged friend, "beyond what either he or Abigail may imagine." On December 17, 1812, it was clear that Mercy's cheer was premature. Elbridge Gerry reported to Mercy that Mrs. Adams appeared "a little uneasy" at his expression of pleasure over the possible termination of differences. "Should there be any future prospect of restoring mutual friendship to my respected, my highly respected friends; I shall pursue the object with unremitted endeavours," he promised Mercy.[22]

In subsequent correspondence, Abigail and John were uniquely in contradiction with one another, regarding Mercy Warren. On December 30, 1812, Abigail "could not suffer the year to close," she wrote Mrs. Warren, "without noticeing your repeated favours and thanking you for them. So long as we inhabit this earth and possess any of our faculties," she continued, "we must and do feel for our posterity for our Friends and our country." It was a long letter, touching on the personalities, events, and problems that had led them "so near the close of the drama." It reaffirmed Abigail's belief in the need for the war, and conveyed her resignation to the likelihood that neither of them should live to see its end. In conclusion, Abigail forwarded to her "Dear Friend" a token of love and friendship, a lock of her own hair, combined with one of John's, "at his request," placed in a handkerchief, in a pin set with a pearl, with the promise, health permitting, to pay a visit to her in the spring. Abigail meant to reciprocate, by this memento, for a ring of similar content that Mercy had sent earlier along with the "assurance that we can never forget former amities," that "the age of us all now reminds us that we have more to think of than the partial interruptions of sublimary friendships."[23]

John, however, was not to be entirely placated by the contents of lockets or rings. Months after the women's effusive exchange, he was checking on historical versions of America's earliest naval transactions. He had thought it "natural" to begin with Mrs. Warren, and after reading her account, he was dismayed at how she had "carelessly and confusedly hurried over" what he believed to be "one of the boldest, most dangerous and most important measures and Epochas in the History of the New World, the commencement of a new maritime and Naval military Power." Had Mrs. Warren never read the "Law of Massachusetts. Nor the Journal of Congress? One would think that this momentous Business was all performed by a few rash Individuals and private Adventurers. History," John had concluded, writing to Elbridge Gerry on April 17, 1813, "is not the Province of the Ladies." With obviously pained effort, John sought to balance his critique, saying "These three Volumes nevertheless contain many Facts, worthy of Preservation." On the other hand, "Little Passions and Prejudices, want of Information, false Information, want of Experience, erroneous Judgment, and frequent Partiality, are among the Faults."[24]

Though Mercy undoubtedly was never able to reconcile John to her historical interpretations, she, being the "ingenious Lady" he deemed her, was able to recreate at least the aura of their formerly affectionate relationship with considerable elegance. Having heard that his health was declining, for example, she was "quickened" to answer this letter, inviting him to ride out for a visit: "What think you, Sir," she asked, the summer of 1814, "of a little jaunt to Plymouth in company with Mrs. Adams and my sweet Caroline?" And though she did not label it an official apology, she most certainly extended a peace offering of sorts when she wrote: "The years admonish that the harbingers of dissolution are drawing near after three score and ten," yet she most sincerely hoped that the life of a gentleman "who acted so great a part in a revolution that astonished the world and lived to set his seal to an honorable peace after a desolating war" might be spared to see peace restored to the United States, "notwithstanding the severe threats of our old inveterate enemy."[25]

Mercy's victory was considerable. John could not accept her "polite" invitation to Plymouth because threescore and nineteen years had reduced him to the "situation, the temper and humor" of the man who, the British historian Clarendon had said, "would not have slept out of his own bed for any office the King could have given him." But he could visit in spirit and by pen and feel free to speculate on the character and conduct of New England (Would Mercy have thought that in the short span of forty years, New York would rival and even exceed Plymouth, Duxbury, and Boston in "Patriotism, Fortitude and Courage?") and predict that the war between their country and Great Britain, if sustained, would soon "rekindle the flames in Europe." He could also sign the letter "Old Friend John Adams," and did so. At her death, then, Mercy, John, and Abigail were reunited. It was Abigail, however, who paid singular tribute to the "venerable friend" of "more than fifty summers ripening," telling Caroline on October 23, 1814, that she could "with truth say" that "take her all in all, we shall not look upon her like again."[26]

As "deprest" as Abigail was, owing to the deaths of "Early Friends," to her collapsing health, to her country's "calamities," a letter from John Quincy, now in Ghent, gave a "new spring" to her spirits and she felt, she said, greater "warmth" in the atmosphere for his being so much nearer to her. She could not "endure" the thought of John Quincy's returning to the cold of Russia, much as she esteemed and respected its sovereign, and she frankly wished for his release from his mission so that she might once more "behold" him on his return home.[27]

Abigail was bursting with questions, but she did not dare ask any of John Quincy, knowing that every syllable was "watched for and multiplyd and missaplied." This autumn of 1814 was a time of "anxious expectation" for their country, when, she wrote John Quincy, "every Breize that blows comes fraught with tydings." New York was "all alive" now, taking every measure for its defense. Boston, just waking from its lethargy, was like a "sleeping Lyon," which, when chased, will at last "manifest" its strength.[28]

The "chase" was spurred by the British destruction of Washington on the morning of August 25. Abigail groped for language vivid enough to express her fury over this "Humiliating and disgracefull Catastrophy," and her disdain for the apathy that had blinded her government to a sense of its dangerous and defenseless situation. It was one thing to be afflicted by events beyond one's control—to these she would "bow with submission to the Sovereign will"—but when calamities accrued through lack of foresight and energy, through the "incapacity of those who govern and direct the counsels of the nation," there was reason to complain.[29]

According to Abigail's analysis, the "whole force" of Great Britain, including fourteen thousand veterans of the Duke of Wellington's Peninsular campaign, liberated by the routing of Napoleon Bonaparte the past April, was now "leveld" against every vulnerable quarter of America on the seacoast and in the cities, including Chesapeake Bay, New Orleans, and Lake Champlain. Entirely "sensible" that destruction of the capital by these "modern Goths and Vandals" was "intended to disgrace us in the eyes of all nations and posterity," Abigail was determined to minimize their success. Her son must know, she wrote, that Washington was a city "in name in embrio— a wilderness city, thinly inhabited, without a back country to supply a Militia and inhabited by slaves who were as much feared by the inhabitants as the enemy who attacked them."[30]

Abigail had elaborated on the subject of Washington to Mrs. Peabody. "The Capital," which "softer ages might have made . . . a city," was, after all, the foster child of General Washington, intended to perpetuate his name, fame, and achievements, and projected to cost more than a million dollars. "Such was the Capital invaded by six thousand regular troops and a large British Squadron," actually "a Giant to contend with a pigmy." Regretfully, Abigail concluded that America had become a divided house, and that nothing but union and decision could save its citizens from becoming "hewers" of wood and "drawers" of water for their British taskmasters.[31]

Weeks later, on October 18, 1814, Abigail reported to John Quincy that the defense of Boston was satisfactory, that she was not "at ease" about Baltimore, that her grandson John Smith was an orderly sergeant of a company called the Iron Greys (formed of the "best blood and families of New York"), and that she thought the British defeat at Lake Champlain and Plattsburg was "marvelous in our Eyes." Perhaps it was best, after all, she speculated, "that Great Britain should show herself thus haughtily, overbearing and insolent to unite all parties in execrating her government and holding her in as much abhorence as the Exiled Tyrant of Elba."[32]

On the thirteenth of February, 1815, bells of the Old South and Federal Street churches rang so suddenly that Bostonians within hearing distance thought they must signal a fire. Then they heard people crying "Peace!" and saw them shaking hands and congratulating one another; other men and women just ran about wildly. Printers, working a small press, struck off the handbills pronouncing peace and showered them on the crowd, while rockets thrown from the State House roof lighted the sky and bonfires blazed on neighboring hills. Bakers, hatters, and papermakers wove back and forth from State Street to the South End, then to the North; three sleds full of sailors, drawn by fifteen horses apiece, were preceded by a military company. Until official intelligence arrived, however, Boston would postpone an oratorio, an illumination, and a public ball, planned in public celebration of the momentous event.[33]

Understandably, Abigail's spirits were in a "whirl" as she savored the news of the total defeat of the British forces at New Orleans. This "late glorious victory" had closed the war with a "lustre" upon the American army that time, she predicted, would not efface. The peace, though she regarded it as a "blessing," left many "difficult points" unsettled, and therefore she welcomed John Quincy's letter of December 24, 1814, the date of the signing of the treaty of peace between America and Great Britain.[34]

Abigail had studied John Quincy's healing words gratefully and decided they must reach a larger audience. Therefore, on March 5, 1815, she seated herself by the fireside, adjusted the green eyeshade that soothed her precarious vision, gathered sheets of paper and a pen, and proceeded to copy the entire contents of John Quincy's letter. The conditions of the peace, John Quincy had written from Ghent, were not those that might have been the most desirable, but those that the "situation of the parties at and during negotiation made attainable." Though decisions on key issues such as impressment, indemnities, and military control of the Great Lakes lay in abeyance, John Quincy was at ease with the compromise. Abigail took heart, and hoped Harriet Welsh would, and others beyond, with her son's assurance that "we have abandoned no essential right, and if we have left everything open for future controversey, we have at least secured to our Country the power, at her own option to extinguish the war." Abigail had forwarded this particular letter to Harriet with specific instructions. She relied on her friend to see to its publication, and she asked that John Quincy's evaluation of the circumstances of the peace be attributed anonymously "from one of the ministers to his friend."[35]

Abigail was aware, when she wrote to Harriet Welsh, that John Quincy would join his wife in Paris to wait for further orders from the President. She learned the nature of these orders on March 7 with his nomination as ambassador to England. Understandably, she thought it "a singular circumstance in our Family History, that both Father & Son should make peace with the same nation at the distance of 30 years." On March 8, 1815, she wrote to John Quincy: "You are now my son, to appear as your Father did before you, the first minister after peace. You have the advantage of knowing the Country to which you go and the nation is to receive you. May you find both honor and honesty. You will have some knotty affairs to discuss, and adjust, in all of which, I wish you success." Meanwhile, Abigail assumed that during his stay in Paris, John Quincy would "certainly" pay his respects to Louis XVIII, and revisit the spots of his youth. As for England's Queen Charlotte, just five months younger than she, Abigail would not, even for her crown, she said, "be obliged to exhibit her person at court, so old and decayed."[36]

On May 5, 1815, Harriet Welsh flew to Abigail's door "like a winged mercury," with a letter, at last, from John Quincy. The first to come her way since December, it was "a sunshine," she said, "breaking through the clouds" to brighten the gloom of the past month. Abigail had cried till her eyes were swollen when her sister Mrs. Peabody died suddenly in her sleep at three o'clock in the morning of April 10, and then, eight days later, when her grandsons George and John sailed on Sunday, April 18, aboard the *New Packet* bound for England, like Odysseus's son Telemachus, she thought, "in search of their father."[37]

Abigail thought of her sister's death as a "loud call" to live in habitual preparation for her own departure. Her age and her infirm health gave her little reason "to boast of tomorrow" and therefore to hope to see her grandchildren again. And yet, with almost miraculous recuperative powers, she managed to recharge her own spirits by practicing what she preached to others. "Cultivate a cheerfulness of mind which doeth good like a medicine," she would urge seemingly vanquished friends, begging them not to permit "rubs and stings of outrageous fortune" to deprive them of their serenity. Furthermore, seasons in human life differed; some called for mourning, others for rejoicing. Mid-June 1815 found Abigail once again viewing her life and times with optimism.[38]

Now Abigail spoke of being "delighted" by prospects on land and sea, by "thriving" industry, by borders "at peace," by waters "covered" with ships. And, as one who was "ever curious," she was full of "wonder and astonishment" at the "novel scene" in France, at Napoleon Bonaparte's return from exile in Elba to force King Louis XVIII's abdication, so that he might reign as Emperor. Always a riveting figure to her, Abigail called Napoleon the "8th wonder of the world," and as long as no blood was spilled and he ruled "peaceably," she was willing that he "enjoy his power, and authority."[39]

In August, when a defeated Bonaparte was rumored to be seeking asylum in America, Abigail deliberated the consequences. Bonaparte was "quite done over, teeth and claws all drawn," she assumed, and therefore she did not believe "he would eat us all up." On the contrary, she wrote Harriet Welsh, she thought it "a novel winding up" if, after so many battles, and "so many hair breadth scapes," the beleaguered warrior should lay his bones in America, the "only free country now in Being." Concentrating on the larger picture now, Abigail wondered what the allied powers would do about "poor suffering France." Would they put the Bourbons on the throne again? Would France be quiet then? "Only from necessity—yet they must be reinstated," she concluded.[40]

With the end of the war in America, Abigail admitted ruefully that "that fruitful subject" which had always given her something to write about had also ended. As she was "not living in the world," in either the political or the social sense, and had "retired from all the gay scenes of it," she was "reduced," she claimed, to the state of Madame Sévigné, to writing about herself and her family. Because she thought news of family "occupations, occurrences, situations" made for the most interesting letters of all, or so she presently claimed, she offered "no apologies therefore" to her correspondents.[41]

John, frail as he was, enjoyed his books, his pen, and the company of those who shared his literary interests. Abigail's situation was identical. Both of them challenged Quincy's limitations with brilliant success. Though her eyes might "complain," making it necessary at times for her to sit in darkness, shading them, she could never stop putting them to work. "Participation," after all, was "the root of pleasure in reading a fine passage," and to share it with someone only heightened its enjoyment. Abigail was in perfect agreement with Laurence Sterne, who had said he would have a companion "if it was only to say how the shadows lengthen as the sun darkens." Solitude was a "cold, unsocial feeling," and Abigail was frank about searching out companionship, about wanting a "talk" with a friend, as she wrote one morning to Harriet Welsh.[42]

In the course of her remaining correspondence, Abigail enjoyed "talks" with many people on many subjects. She was strikingly candid, for example, on the subject of religion. "There is not any reasoning which can convince me, contrary to my senses," she told John Quincy, "that three, is one, and one three." Though she allowed that "we are permitted to see but through a glass darkly," her conclusion was incontrovertible. "I acknowledge myself a unitarian—Believing that the Father alone, is the supreme God, and that Jesus Christ, derived his Being, and all his powers and honours from the Father." At one point she had observed, to her sorrow, "a narrow selfish exclusive system gaining ground, instead of that Liberal spirit of Christianity recommended by St Paul." It was to Louisa that she wrote on January 3, 1818, "True religion is from the Heart, between Man and his creator, and not the imposition of Man or Creeds and tests."[43]

Another subject she explored in depth and with conviction was that of modern writers and their works. She found in Byron a "wild exentric imagination—some touching and pathetic strokes of nature and genius," but concluded he was a "gloomy malicious envious and unprincipled man, neither capable of love or friendship," that his genius was "abortive and misapplied." Swift received even less flattering notices. Abigail could never love Swift. He had none of the milk of human kindness in his nature.[44]

Furthermore, Walter Scott's recent biography of Swift put him in such a "cruel and Barberous light" in respect to his treatment of three ladies, that her dislike had "arisen to detestation and abhorence of his character." As to Scott's verse—it reminded her, though she liked to read it, of silver and gold lace, the lamé trimming on women's dresses, "more ornamental than solid." By comparison, Milton, Pope, and Thompson were "sterling Bullion and have never been rivaled by any of their successors."[45]

With Louisa in London, Abigail found herself reliving her own past with extraordinary intensity. She rose before daylight to write by the rays of the early-morning sun, though she could not "make returns with equal interest." Louisa had "performed" her journey from St. Petersburg, she wrote Abigail, with "as little uneasiness and as few misfortunes as could possibly have been anticipated," and she had, as a result, "really acquired the reputation of a heroine at a very cheap rate." Once settled in the London suburb of Ealing, Louisa wrote of Spain's attempts to "shake off aggression," of France's "gloom" as the Bourbons carried with them "destruction in all its varied forms," of England's "poorly conducted drawing rooms." She lapsed only occasionally into melancholy references to her father's vanished fortune and to her dead infant, and, on the whole, Abigail sensed that Louisa's mind was more at ease than it had been in "that cold dark region of Russia." She also gratefully acknowledged that her daughter-in-law was a "very good correspondent," making no secret of her bitter satisfaction at the astonishing similarity between Louisa's critique of British society at present and her own, thirty years earlier.[46]

The two women, a continent apart, had in fact achieved a remarkable degree of friendship. As a result of their letter-writing they acknowledged openly and generously a sincere appreciation of one another's gifts. Louisa marveled at Abigail's talent for endowing even "trifles" with interest; the "Easy course" of her thoughts seemed to the younger woman "to flow upon the paper like an unruffled stream, clear and smooth." By contrast, Louisa regretted that she could never "mould" her own thoughts to her will, that her style was "always loose, unconnected and irregular," and that she frequently found it "impossible to express a single idea."[47]

Abigail, sincerely pleased by Louisa's "flattering and complimentary" appreciation, knew not, she said, "how to replie to it." Somewhat apologetically, she launched into a discourse on her underprivileged education, how neither grammar nor spelling had been a consideration for women in her youth, and how she had lamented this "deficiency" throughout her life. If, as Louisa said, she wrote with care, it was from habit. She made no pretensions to style and trusted to the candor of her correspondence "to receive the matter, as flowing from the heart; without regarding the elegance of diction." Nor would she permit Louisa to "deprecate her own letters. "Your stile," Abigail assured her daughter-in-law, "is much more correct and elegant than mine, and your letters are much approved and admired."[48]

Louisa, who became a frequent and valued correspondent of John's after Abigail's death, would later translate French literature into English (*La Morte de Socrate,* by Lamartine), and write poetry of a dark hue, such as "To the Raven" ("Ill boding would'st thou seem to say/That Lifes a dream?/That time unheeded flits away/like younder stream?"). Louisa had earlier expressed how much Abigail's "approbation" meant to her, that it afforded her "the greatest pleasure" and did, indeed, "excite encouragement." John, complimented her as well, telling her how her journals had "the form and impression of the age." When Louisa's grandson Henry Adams read her papers, he pronounced them "Good, too—some of them." It was this grandson who found Louisa "an exotic, like her Sèvres china," who declared her "Louis Seize, like the furniture." As both china and furniture had belonged to Abigail and John, Louisa, in regard to her writing as well, owed something to the earlier generation.[49]

Swept back in time, now that Louisa was in London, Abigail could not refrain from passing on the latter's report that all was "ceremony," all was "show," all was "stile," and that the United States did not furnish its foreign ministers with enough salary to make them "conversant" with the nobility, "except in Business."[50]

Ten months later the picture was radically altered, and Louisa, never so healthy since her marriage, and fearful of growing fat, would tell Abigail of being "plunged into the great world" until three or four in the morning, of waltzing with the Duke of Wellington, of counting the Duchess of Cumberland among the number of her "fashionable" acquaintances." For the present, however, Abigail, spurred by Louisa's litany of deprivations, speculated about the King and Queen, about court dress and manners.[51]

Thirty-year-old memories were precipitated by vivid and painful realities. Remembering that George III had always treated her "both politely and respectfully," she was sorry for the "poor old King," for his "derangement." The Queen, she speculated, "must have grown pretty old, and the few personal graces she ever had, time must have diminished." Then again, on thinking of what sort of a figure she herself would make, if obliged to hold a drawing room, she concluded that "constitutions in England wear better than in our climate." Abigail, who had always taken notice of fashion, as much out of pride as preference, now combed English periodicals for details, acknowledging to Louisa that she had some curiosity to know "whether the old fashion of large hoops still prevails; and how the head is decorated." In her day, she recalled, capes and feathers were worn, and those so high as to make it difficult to sit in a carriage. If these still prevailed, she supposed "they must make an awkward appearance." For all her disdain of the English, their customs and royalty, Abigail expressed fawning delight at the thought of her family being invited to two royal marriages. "Your attendance in your Diplomatic Character at the Celebrations, *will make an Epocha in the History of our Family,* if it should be written," she would tell Louisa on September 30.[52]

On the morning of January 18, 1816, Abigail, describing herself as attacked by a "dangerous complaint," chose to write her will. She wrote carefully, considerately, and, she hoped, impartially. She gave one farm property, a bequest from her uncle Norton Quincy, to her son John Quincy Adams; she gave the half she owned of the property left to her by her father to her son Thomas Boylston Adams; she considered both of equal value, worth about $2,200 apiece. She directed that her stock, amounting to four thousand dollars, "perhaps more," be disposed of and divided in varying proportions among her grandchildren, daughters-in-law, sister-in-law, and nieces, along with specified pieces of jewelry, dresses, and coats of silks, satins, and lace, and "bodily Linnen." She parceled out one share apiece in the Haverhill Bridge among granddaughters, as well as her gold necklace and "drops" of her earrings; one share apiece in the Weymouth Bridge went to each of her sons. She gave Rebecca Dexter, wife of Richard Dexter, in token of her faithful nursing in various sicknesses thirty dollars; Esther Briesler received twenty dollars and a red silk dress. She hoped that "no unkind or hard thought will be entertaind" because she had given more to Louisa, her brother's child and her devoted companion. "Her case is peculiar,"

Abigail stated, "having no relative upon her Mothers Side but a Sister —I commend her to the kindness of my children."[53]

Six weeks after writing her will, Abigail was surprised and grateful to be alive, though so "feeble" that she was convinced she would "never be good for much again." Theoretically, she had been cured by quantities of bark wine and the solicitous care around the clock of Louisa and Susan and others. Abigail harbored another theory about her recovery. She was convinced, as she wrote to John Quincy, that the desire to see her dear children once more was "one of the strongest ligaments which has bound me to earth."[54]

In times of abiding loneliness and stress, Abigail, who seldom thought twice about her dreams, tended to elaborate on them. On one occasion, during a seemingly interminable separation, she had mentioned dreaming of seeing her daughter. Another time some weeks before John took his oath as President, she wrote graphically of dreaming of large black bulls, twenty-four-pound leaden missiles, flying in the air, all "directed" at her. Now she dreamed of her grandson John running into her arms on his return from Europe. Having survived such a threatening illness, she now assumed that there were "yet further duties for me to perform or further trials for me to endure," and in either situation, she concluded, "I trust the ruler of the skies." Her most recent dream affirmed her faithful hope that she would live to see John Quincy and his family once more.[55]

On June 7, 1816, Harriet Welsh invited Abigail to come to have strawberries fresh from the vine. On June 10, Abigail visited Boston for the first time in a year. She was rapidly (and surprisingly) gaining strength, but she was correct. There were further trials to endure. Colonel Smith had been reelected to office on the Democratic ticket, but his opponent, Westel Willoughby, had challenged him on his small majority. As a result of the decision reached by a committee headed by his old adversary Timothy Pickering, Smith relinquished his seat on December 13, 1815.[56]

Six months later, on June 16, 1816, the colonel was dead of a liver ailment and gout. To witness the deaths of persons younger than she, Abigail considered "one of the afflictions of a long life." She had not thought she would survive the colonel, and she mourned, as did John, this "good hearted, unfortunate gentleman." John, in fact, claimed that "the viccissitudes of human life have not been more exemplified in the biography of Napoleon, than in that of Colonel Smith." Abigail wrote Louisa that she considered the colonel "a

Brave Officer, but through Life an unfortunate man, with a Noble and generous spirit, a tender heart, and kind affections." Meaning "no ill and not suspecting it in others," he "too often became the prey of the artfull and the designing."[57]

In early July, John happily issued a report on his wife's health. John Quincy, he wrote, would be "overjoyed" to see how his mother had recovered "her former alacrity, spirit, wit," and how he himself took "great delight in riding out with her every fair day." The fact that Abigail was restored to her "characteristic vivacity, Activity, Witt Sense and Benevolence" presented a problem, however, to her loving but anxious husband. At this time of her life and his, when he foresaw "but a few minutes before both of us must depart," Abigail's "incontrollable attachment to the superintendence of every part of her household" made him "tremble." He despaired over her rushing activity, her conviction that "she must take upon herself the Duties of her Grandaughter Neice, Maids Husband and all. She must allways be writing to You and all her Grandchildren," John observed, an activity he apparently judged to be as dangerous to his wife's health as her domestic exertions. "I must say she must," he added, "because she will."[58]

Abigail and John lived the last moments of their lives with humor, intelligence, and courage, above all. John, in genial spirits, referring to himself as "Mr. Old Folks," wrote exultantly of being invited into all societies and how he was "much caressed" by so many. Abigail was amused and delighted as well by their popularity. "Your father and I have lived to an Age, to be sought for as Curiositys," she wrote John Quincy on August 27, 1816. Accordingly, they had not received so much company in years. Mixing now with what John called "all the aristocracy," the "bonton" of Quincy, Abigail reported four parties in a row, asking Harriet Welsh, "Will you be allarmed to hear that the President & Lady have and are to attend them all?"[59]

Further capitalizing on her prized momentum, Abigail even journeyed into Boston. While John visited the governor, Abigail was determined to watch the troops from her carriage as they carried on their "evolutions." When Commodore Bainbridge and his officers insisted on improving her view by detaching her horses and lifting her high in her carriage, the gentlemen demonstrated, to her delight and satisfaction, she would report to friends, that "gallantry still exists." Also, with the drive and concern of former years, Abigail sought to further the career of her granddaughter Susan's young suitor. Abigail thought the "tall" and "well made" Charles Thomas Clarke a "modest, solid sensible gentleman" with a "good face." She not only investigated his family background, but also wrote to U.S. Attorney General Richard Rush (the son of Benjamin Rush) on November 20, 1816, expressing the hope that President Monroe might intercede on the young man's behalf, her theory being that a transfer from an inactive ship to one in the Mediterranean would facilitate his promotion.[60]

There was, indeed, a sense of energy rather than resignation about Abigail's approach to her waning life. Time, whatever measure was left to her, afforded challenges which she accepted, almost welcomed, with anxious appetite. It was as though she meant to profit from past errors, to make amends for having "spent in vain" so much "valuable Time" when she might instead have "done more service in the world, and acquired more substantial knowledge." Brushing aside her wistful regrets, Abigail admitted to succeeding "pretty well" in reading, in French, the essayist Jean-François de La Harpe's correspondence with the Czar of Russia and Count Schavaloni. On the whole a confirmed optimist, she vowed to look ahead and never behind.[61]

Abigail was "sick of that conversation which spends itself in railing at the times we live in," she wrote John Quincy on November 5, 1816. She was, in fact, "apt to think they are not made better by these complaints" and, on occasion, "to know they are made worse, by those very persons who are loudest to complain of them." If living in the past was one of the habits of age, Abigail pronounced it "high time" for every man who grows old to guard against doing so, for, in her opinion, "there is no occasion to invite more peevish companions for the last hours of Life than time and decrepitude will bring in their train."[62]

As Abigail now evaluated her "journey," she admitted to having met up with her share of the "too selfish—too ambitious too uncharitable, the malicious and the envious." But, on the other hand, "these vices were counterbalanced by opposing virtues" and, she reasoned, "this is a very good world." She added that she had always considered a "laughing philosophy much wiser than a sniveling one—as he who enjoys must be happier than he who suffers." She was "determined," therefore, she promised John Quincy, "to be pleased with the world, and wish well to all its inhabitants."[63]

On November 20, 1816, when newspapers reported John Quincy's recall to America to serve as Secretary of State under President Monroe, Abigail's prevailing belief that her life had been "lengthened out" for a reason was resoundingly confirmed. "I should rejoice in any honorable circumstance that would bring you, to your native Country," she wrote immediately to John Quincy. Four months later, on March 12, 1817, Abigail's message conveyed greater urgency: "The voice of the nation calls you home. The government calls you home—and your parents unite in the call. To this summons you must not, you cannot refuse your assent." Nor would he, she presumed, "have a disposition to regret so honorable an appointment—by so unanimous a vote."[64]

Abigail beamed with pride. John Quincy's nomination had been confirmed by one dissenting vote only; no one since George Washington had been chosen for public office with "more universal approbation." In fact, her son's appointment "was more agreeable to her," she claimed, "than if he had been elected President." She did not fail to recognize that, in part, her motives for wanting her son home were "selfish and personal." At the same time, she and John truly believed that John Quincy, now fifty years old, must return, or "renounce" the idea forever.[65]

Though supremely dedicated to John Quincy's homecoming, she was nevertheless wary that his path was somewhat problematic. Her principal source of "uneasiness" was the rumor that Henry Clay was "openly unfriendly" to her son, and consequently had refused a Cabinet appointment. Abigail knew that John Quincy and Clay had differed, during negotiations at Ghent, on the importance of such issues as the fisheries and the navigation of the Mississippi, yet, even allowing that these issues might generate animosity, she could not conceal her disappointment that Mr. Clay was not "a more liberal minded man." A veteran of the vagaries of political life, her experiences enforced perhaps by the situation with Clay, Abigail felt compelled to remind John Quincy that he must never be "so dazzled by the brightness or glare of high station as to forget that a Breathe can create, and a Breathe destroy." In still another effort to prepare him for his return, she warned him that he "could not fail to be shocked at the changes." He would find the old mansion "like its owners, gone to decay—when I look in the glass I see that I am not what I was, scarcely know a feature on my face—but not the less ready or willing to welcome you and yours, and to accomodate you, untill like a bird of passage, you again take your flight."[66]

On the evening of August 9, 1817, Abigail learned from her "watchful centinel Harriet" that the ship *Washington* had docked in New York. In response to this "grateful intelligence," she wrote to John Quincy the next day to say that she and John were waiting to welcome "one and all" to the "old Habitation, altered only by the deprivations of Time, like its ancient inhabitants. Come then all of you," she urged, "we will make you as comfortable as a cup of cold water, tempered with love and warm affection can render you." In turn, Louisa notified her mother-in-law of her family's imminent departure for Quincy on August 15, warning her that changes were not a one-sided matter. Her family "too were much altered" since last they all had met. Furthermore, she had lost all her good looks and all her flesh on the voyage, she claimed, "owing to a bad miscarriage at Sea added to the usual inconveniences attending the passage."[67]

At 10:00 A.M. on August 18, Louisa Smith announced a carriage in sight descending the hill. When it arrived moments later, Abigail was already at the door. Young John, just as she dreamed he would, was the first to run to Abigail, flinging his arms around her neck. George, calling out to his grandmother, "Oh! Grand! Oh! Grand!" followed immediately. Only Charles hung back, half frightened, though respectful. Time would pass, he was to admit in his memoirs, before he understood his brothers' sensitivity to their grandmother's rebukes, or "fully shared" their "affection and reverence" for her.[68]

Contrary to Louisa's admonition, Abigail found her daughter-in-law looking "better and younger—all sunburnt and brown." Within a week she had persuaded Louisa to take a short holiday in Boston, to leave her to tidy up the house, now covered, from parlor to her own bedroom, with trunks, books, and papers. Many of the last, Abigail noted, were inscribed in her daughter-in-law's handwriting: Louisa was now acting as her husband's private secretary, owing to his weak eyesight and trembling hands. And, as Abigail had anticipated, John Quincy and Louisa, "like Birds of passage," departed for Washington one month after coming to Quincy, leaving their three sons behind. George was at school in Cambridge, John and Charles in Boston, and Abigail appeared as responsive as ever to their moral, intellectual, and physical needs, as she assessed them.[69]

Shortly, Abigail would be describing John as a "fine boy" provided his spirits did not "run away with his Judgement," and Charles as a "thinking Boy, much slower, but not less sure in the end." She advised her nephew William Shaw, whose help she had enlisted on her grandsons' behalf, of the "great importance that they should be kept Steady," explaining that, as they had been out of school for three months, it would be hard to return, "especially amongst all strangers." Besides, the books differed from those they were used to studying. With seemingly unabated energy, Abigail, far from delegating responsibility, also wrote her grandsons directly to advise them to be "strict" about observing rules concerning their studies, that "diligence and punctuality" would not fail to make them esteemed by preceptors and schoolmates. To remedy their depleted wardrobes, Abigail engaged Mrs. Sampson to sew them new pantaloons.[70]

The fall of 1817 was cold and dry. Abigail suffered chills and "violent" pains in her hands, yet she persisted in her successful attempts to "rouse" herself. Her grandsons came to Quincy on Saturdays; George often read to his grandfather. The De Windts, including Caroline's mother-in-law and servants, paid a lengthy visit. On the whole, Abigail was content. Having kindled her own fire at six in the morning, she wrote Harriet Welsh, rather gloating that her friend must be "fast asleep" at that hour; she had "much to brag of at 73." Though she could not see "to thread her needle, nor sew quick nor go here and there as she could in days past," she was in better health than in other periods, "in general good spirits, always endeavoring to look on the bright side without gloomy anticipations." She allowed, however, that some things took place that she could wish "otherways."[71]

One situation that she certainly wished to be altered was the miserable plight of her grandson William Smith, who was, according to Louisa, living in the "cheapest" of boardinghouses, his wife, Louisa's sister, pregnant. The entire set of circumstances conjured up unhappy memories for Abigail, and fears, which she expressed to Louisa, that William, whose monetary inheritance could probably not equal the colonel's debts, was "as deficient in judgment as his father was." Still, Abigail was able to end this letter, written December 12, 1817, on a positive note. Though she had wished for their parents' presence to complete the "festival," she had passed a "Pleasant Thanksgiving Day" with nine of her grandchildren.[72]

January 7, 1818, was as mild as a September day, yet Abigail lay ill, dosing herself with barley water. Confinement was always difficult for her, as much if not more in old age than when she was younger. As she explained to a friend who might think her "impudent" for venturing into Boston if the weather was the least bit unfavorable, or permitting John to do so, "there is such a thing as staying at home until it becomes wearisome to us. Change of pace or dear variety compose part of our happiness."[73]

These days it was her daughter-in-law Louisa who once again rescued Abigail from monotony, who provided her with "a rich entertainment." Louisa's letters transported Abigail from her Quincy fireplace to the heart of Washington, plunged her into the center of Monroe's administration. As they had during Louisa's stay in London, they made Abigail a "sharer" in her daughter-in-law's life, exposing a grateful mother-in-law to more information "in this way" than she could glean in a whole session of Congress. Only in her correspondence with her children did Louisa intimate her more problematic nature, her need for "timely reflection," her tendency to "fret under disappointments" where her family was involved. Apart from these letters, Louisa, addicted, by her own admission, to "larking the follies" of her neighbors, "highly entertained" Abigail, who pressed for their continuation, though she might only be able to offer a "meagre dish" in return. But Abigail had underestimated the results. Louisa's Washington soon became Abigail's, and in the process of feasting on the present, she provided her daughter-in-law with a vast banquet of the past, seasoned in her own provocative way.[74]

Abigail had met President Monroe in July, when, on his tour of the Northeast states, he had called on her and John in Quincy. She admired him, and had presented him with two roses, one red and one white ("York and Lancaster United"), and commented on his "agreeable affability and unassuming manners." Louisa, too, used the word "affability" in connection with Monroe. She mentioned his six footmen in livery, two head servants out of livery, his elegant furniture. She also described Mrs. Monroe's white figured-silk dress with a profusion of point lace, her white hat and feathers, her "high polished and easy manners" that did "honor to her station." But tastes differ, Louisa had added, and "dear Dolly was much more popular."[75]

Years fell away as Abigail responded on the subject of the Monroe White House. She was as objective as she could be, having been recently attacked for behaving "coldly" in her own drawing rooms. But ancient bitterness surfaced, as she asked, "What would have been said in her day if so much style, pomp and etiquette had been assumed?" Of course, she knew the answer: "The Cry of Monarchy monarchy would have resounded from Georgia to Maine." She did not, however, condemn this new system, though she would not have "ventured" upon such steps. She thought, however, there was no other way than the Monroes' to bring order out of confusion after Jefferson's and Madison's "medley of Liberty and equality."[76]

As Abigail now had a captive audience, Louisa's references to most any subject, such as protocol, etiquette, or finances, stirred fluent memories and evoked impassioned advice. Louisa must remember that she had "a very circumspect and critical part to act," that her "every step" would be "more critically scrutinized" than in any previous situation, that "an Heir apparent is always envyed." Louisa must spare herself with entertainments, must "return the civility" but not "sacrifice too much to it; the sallary of a Secretary of State did not justify the expense." Louisa must be aware, owing to demeaning official salaries ("not one of all the Presidents who have held office —have not carried poverty home with them"), that Abigail had had to make her own pastry and bake without an oven, as no such conveniences were available, or affordable, in the "great house" in which she had lived in Philadelphia. Consequently, should houses be built for heads of government departments, Louisa must urge the formation of a committee of ladies to "superintend" them, and the architect Charles Bulfinch to plan them. Bulfinch, architect of Boston's State House and, after Benjamin Latrobe, of the nation's capitol, might not design these according to the prevailing "National Stile," Abigail did allow. But he would, she assured Louisa, bear in mind practical considerations such as family conveniences, insulation against the cold, and the limitations of five-thousand-dollar salaries in regard to servants.[77]

She advised the formation of still another "council of the Ladies" to "set in concert" how they must deal with the matter of rank between senatorial and secretarial wives, Mrs. Monroe's own practice to be taken into consideration, of course. And, while on the subject of protocol, Abigail would propose, she told Louisa, the creation of a new office, that of a Minister of Ceremonies, similar to the British Garter King of Arms. For "with all our boasted simplicity," Abigail insisted, "there is not upon the Globe a prouder people; or one more tenacious of Rank and titles from the Subaltern, to the president of the United States, without the honesty to acknowledge it."[78]

Returning to the subject of finances still another time, Abigail was unusually succinct. She would not recommend parsimony, but would, on the other hand, avoid extravagance. And finally, she hoped Louisa did not think she had taken "improper Liberty" with her. The "ground which I have travelled, is new to you," she explained, and "to find it safe is an arduous task."[79]

The first sign of a green pea shooting through the earth was proof that spring, after weeks of chilling rain, had arrived the third week of May 1818. Sprouting plum blossoms were another sign, but Abigail was too preoccupied to enjoy this favorite season fully, in view of news she had just learned: Louisa, in writing to Harriet Welsh, had indicated that she did not feel up to visiting Quincy. Abigail now set herself the task of appealing that unhappy decision, pathetically admitting that "I cannot bear the idea." Both would need respite, John Quincy especially, after five or six months of strenuous labor. Her son was already said to have "the Character of the most industerous man in Washington," and Abigail reminded Louisa that "a string too long stretched will Break." Then again, what stronger motive could John Quincy have for visiting than the prospect of seeing his children and parents? "How few times more" would he see the latter?[80]

Abigail rephrased her message a number of times, writing her son directly only at the end of the congressional session, "unwilling to add" before then, she said, to his "incumberances." Desperate in her desire to see him once more, she described the plight of age in pitiful detail. With each passing hour she felt less able to read, to write, even to breathe. "Every day steals something from us," she said, reminding her of her inability to sustain her faculties against the "depradations of time"; a body without mind, she observed, agreeing with Mr. Jefferson, was "one of the most humiliating Spectacles" of all. "Come thou and see us, while something of that remains," she begged her son.[81]

At the beginning of August, Abigail still hoped for visitors from Washington. Despite profound anxiety over her eroding abilities, and concern that their age "with hasty steps" was pushing them off the stage, she and John courageously stayed their dwindling course. They gathered daily in the parlor overlooking the garden, where John, no longer able to guide his pen, now dictated his letters; Abigail, seated on the sofa in rustling silks, sorted baskets of fresh laundry, wrote letters, and read—specifically, this August, the life of Andrew Jackson. The general who had first earned her admiration during his daring victory at New Orleans appeared to her now "as suave as Bonaparte without his unbridled Ambition."[82]

A most welcome letter from Louisa informing Abigail that she and John Quincy were leaving on August 25 almost coincided with the couple's arrival one week later in Quincy. They had returned once again to Washington when John Quincy received warning that his mother was ill. Benjamin Waterhouse had visited Abigail on October 20, and "fear," he said, had induced him to write the next day that Abigail was suffering from typhus fever and had the "free use" of Madeira wine to "compensate" for her natural vigor.[83]

It was Louisa who wrote to her father-in-law immediately. She explained that John Quincy was "totally incapacitated" by the tragic news and unable to write to his father, revealing, meanwhile, her own tangled emotions. She would "readily" set out for Boston "if in any shape" she could offer assistance. On the other hand, knowing that Abigail was surrounded by "the most tender and watchfull friends," she would "only add one to the many who are desirous of proving their attachment." Then again, if she did go to Quincy she would have the satisfaction of knowing that she had exerted herself in every way "to restore one on whose existence so much of the happiness of the family depended. . . ."[84]

On Thursday, October 22, Harriet Welsh, Lucy Greenleaf, and Mrs. Dexter took turns sitting at Abigail's bedside. That night, Dr. Holbrook seemed more encouraging. Abigail, aware of how weak she was, remained alert the next day. On October 26, Harriet Welsh wrote for the third time to Louisa that "we have still hopes," as Abigail was holding her own. Finally, with Abigail "seemingly conscious until her last breath," according to Thomas, the "apaling event" took place on Wednesday, October 28, when she died around 1:00 P.M. She was buried on Saturday, November 1; John insisted on walking to the meeting house in the procession, faltering only at the end, in the unseasonable heat.[85]

Thomas Jefferson read in the newspaper of the death of his "old and steady Friend"—for that was the way Abigail had signed her last letter to him—John's warning of October 20 having already instilled in him an "ominous foreboding" of "the fatal event." On November 13, 1818, Jefferson wrote his bereaved friend: "Tried myself in the school of affliction, by the loss of every form of connection which can rive the human heart, I know well, and feel what you have lost, what you have suffered, are suffering, and have yet to endure." The same trials had taught him, as he had said before, that "for ills so immeasurable, time and silence are the only medicines." He would not, therefore, "by useless condolances, open afresh the sluices of your grief, altho' mingling sincerely my tears with yours, will I say a word more, where words are vain. . . ."[86]

It was four years after Abigail's death that John captured, with quill and ink, the definitive portrait of her valuable life. Reading the *Life and Letters* of Rachel Wriothesley, Lady Russell, took him back forty years, he told his granddaughter Caroline, to the time in 1775 when he had sent them to his young wife that she might "contemplate herself." At that time John thought it extremely probable "from the daring and dangerous career I was determined to run" that Abigail would one day find herself in the same situation as Lady Russell, that is, with her husband without a head. Much as he admired the Englishwoman, he admired his own "Lady" far more. In loving tribute he wrote: "This Lady was more beautiful than Lady Russell, had a brighter genius, more information, a more refined taste, and at least her equal in the virtues of the heart."

John also spoke of Abigail's "equal fortitude and firmness of character, equal resignation to the will of Heaven," of her being "equal in all the virtues and graces of the christian life." Again, like Lady Russell, Abigail had "never by word or look" discouraged John from "running all hazards for the salvation" of his country's liberties. And perhaps most crucial to the spirit of their lives, Abigail had been willing to share with him, and had encouraged their children to share with both of them "in all the dangerous consequences we had to hazard" which, at times, must have seemed infinite.[87]

Acknowledgments

The path to Abigail Adams starts at the Massachusetts Historical Society. When I took my first step toward her biography,
the late Lyman H. Butterfield was Editor of The Adams Papers and
held forth at The Society in a top-floor sanctuary whose bay windows
overlooked Boylston Street and the Fenway. As I was a journalist
rather than a correctly laureled scholar, and he was more an admirer
of Abigail's daughter-in-law, Louisa Catherine, I shall never fail to
appreciate his guarded objectivity about my quest. A slight man with
puzzled eyes and a distant cordiality, he seemed to be testing my
powers of endurance even more than intellect as he explained the
tangled scope of the Adams family, its accomplishments, trials, idi-
osyncracies. He spoke with such commanding fluency and affection,
however, that Abigail (pronounced by him as Abigull) and John appeared to join us around his desk and, as daylight vanished, this
spellbound visitor thought it might soon be time for all four of us to
adjourn for tea. Perhaps inadvertently but surely irrevocably, Lyman
Butterfield's inspired affinity for the Adams family proved totally
contagious.

Mrs. Wilhelmina S. Harris, Superintendant of the Adams National
Historic Site, worked as secretary to Mr. and Mrs. Brooks Adams, the
last of that name to live in the family home. I doubt that anyone will
ever know a more enthusiastic champion and concerned guardian of
the family history and heritage. Walking about the Adamses' house
with her, or sitting around the white kitchen table as she vividly

recounts Adams lore, her voice hushed as she imparts some especially personal detail, one senses, as with Lyman Butterfield, that Abigail and John are alive and flourishing, only momentarily gone to another part of the house Mrs. Harris protects, or out for a carriage ride.

My research both began and ended in the Society's library, its formidable resources hospitably offered to me by the present director, Louis Tucker. His staff, including Peter Drummey and Ross Urquhart, are responsible for innumerable answers regarding citations and for providing illustrations. Celeste Walker, the Adams Papers Assistant Editor, has responded generously and patiently to questions ranging from the species of a puppy named Juno (a Newfoundland), to the date of the death of Abigail's mother-in-law.

I am beholden to my agent, Jane Cushman, for her editorial wisdom; I also thank her for her appreciation of Abigail and John as I do, most profoundly, my editor, Tom Dunne. At St. Martin's, Amelie Littell has been a significant participant from start to finish; David Smith has been a searching and improving copy editor; and Edmée Reit has been zealous in her care of the index. *Abigail Adams* is the better (and more accurate) for having been read by Dr. John E. Crowley, Assistant Professor of History, Dalhousie University in Nova Scotia. As for the typing, Dorothy Ryer, with the help of Johanna Krogstadt, observed the eighteenth-century spellings and random capitalization with accuracy and aplomb.

At the last, the source notes for *Abigail Adams* seemed to take on a vast dimension of their own, and I am indebted to Anne Emmanuelle Birn for her rigorous pursuit of them, and to Lalita Kolenz and Ivana Mestrovic. I am convinced that the whole of the book finally coming together between covers is due to the lawyerly skills, discipline, and dedication of my daughter-in-law, Anna Hayes Levin.

Others who befriended *Abigail Adams* include Christopher Angell; James Oliver Brown; Anne Burnier in Paris; Sally Coolidge; Rachel Dach at the Pennsylvania Historical Society; Barbara Dubivsky; Eleanor Elliott (a relentless prodder); Admiral Harry Hull and his son Kimball, whose wife and mother respectively is a descendant and namesake of Louisa Catherine Adams; James H. Hutson, Chief at The Library of Congress; my nephew William Schwalbe (a thoughtful critic); my brother Douglas Schwalbe; and Roger Starr. I wish I could personally thank all the unknown researchers at the New York Public Library who have so kindly answered at least a hundred questions on writing the bibliography for *Abigail Adams.*

And, finally, there is the rest of my family to thank. The writing of *Abigail Adams* was a family project, a cottage industry from start to finish, from Xeroxing to filing and editing. The foundation of my private library for research purposes is based on Xeroxed editions of the long out-of-print but essential works reposing in many university libraries. Their acquisitions are due to the diligence of my daughters, Emme and Kate, my daughter-in-law Anna, my sons, Peter and John. My son-in-law, Dr. Jonathan Deland, has acted as a special consultant on Abigail Adams's diseases.

Kate was in grade school when I began *Abigail,* and a favorite filer. Most recently she has proved a thoughtful, witty, and decisive editor. Further, there is not one word of this book that my husband, Wilbur Arthur Levin, has not read at least three times. A stern grammarian, a rigorous statistician and patient philosopher, he has proven himself to be, in Abigail's words, "Dearest Friend" to me and, therefore, to *Abigail Adams.*

Notes

As early volumes carrying Abigail Adams's correspondence
are out of print and microfilmed copies not readily available, I
have thought it most useful to readers to cite the published rather
than unpublished sources whenever possible. Throughout, for example, in cases of repetitive material, that is, when I have read a letter
in an early volume, then on microfilm, then among volumes published by The Adams Papers, I have cited the latter in an attempt to
make Abigail and her world most accessible to readers. The following
abbreviations refer to persons most frequently mentioned below in
the Notes for *Abigail Adams*.

AA	Abigail Adams
JA	John Adams
AAS	Abigail Adams Smith ("Nabby")
WSS	William Stephens Smith (Colonel)
JQA	John Quincy Adams
LCA	Louisa Catherine Adams
CA	Charles Adams
TBA	Thomas Boylston Adams
MC	Mary Cranch
RC	Richard Cranch
ESP	Elisabeth Shaw Peabody
CT	Cotton Tufts
TJ	Thomas Jefferson

MW   Mercy Warren
JW   James Warren

All sources are cited fully at their introduction in each of the chapter notes, then shortened on repetition within each chapter. Most frequently cited sources, whose complete citations can be found in the Bibliography, have been abbreviated as follows:

AFC   *Adams Family Correspondence*

Bancroft, *History*   George Bancroft, *History of the United States of America*

DAJA   *Diary and Autobiography of John Adams*

Earliest Diary   *The Earliest Diary of John Adams*

Familiar Letters   *Familiar Letters of John Adams and his Wife Abigail, during the Revolution*

Frothingham, *Joseph Warren*   Richard Frothingham, *Life and Times of Joseph Warren*

JA Works   *The Works of John Adams*

JQA Diary   *The Diary of John Quincy Adams*

JQA Memoirs   *Memoirs of John Quincy Adams*

Letters of JA   *Letters of John Adams Addressed to his Wife*

Life of JA   John Quincy Adams and Charles Francis Adams, *The Life of John Adams*

New Letters   *New Letters of Abigail Adams*

Roof, Col. Smith   Katharine Metcalf Roof, *Colonel William Smith and Lady*

Schouler	James Schouler, *History of the United States of America*
Selected Writings of JA and JQA	*Selected Writings of John and John Quincy Adams*
Three Episodes	Charles Francis Adams, *Three Episodes of Massachusetts History*
Writings of Thomas Jefferson	*The Life and Selected Writings of Thomas Jefferson*

Preface

1. AA to JA, December 9, 1781, *Adams Family Correspondence*, ed. L. H. Butterfield, 4 vols. (Cambridge: Harvard University Press, The Belknap Press, 1963–73), 4:258.

2. *The New York Times*, June 28, 1960, p. 24.

3. Ibid.

4. Phyllis Lee Levin, *Great Historic Houses of America* (New York: Coward-McCann, 1970), p. 26.

Abigail Adams, *Letters of Mrs. Adams*, 3rd ed. in 2 vols. (Boston: Charles C. Little and James Brown, 1841).

5. AA to Francis Adrian Vander Kemp, February 3, 1814, pp. 274–5, ibid.

6. *The Works of John Adams*, ed. Charles Francis Adams, 10 vols. (Boston: Little, Brown & Co., 1850–56), 10:359.

Henry Adams is most acclaimed for his two works, *The Education of Henry Adams* (Boston: the Massachusetts Historical Society, 1918; Sentry ed., Boston: Houghton Mifflin Company, 1961) and *Mt. Saint Michel and Chartres* (Boston and New York: Houghton Mifflin Company, 1913).

7. JA to AA, August 10, 1776, *AFC*, 2:83. (Original in JA Letterbook, Reel 90, Adams Papers, the Massachusetts Historical Society, Boston reads "My best, my dearest, my worthyiest, my wisest friend in this world. . . .")

JA to Mary Palmer, July 5, 1776, *AFC*, 2:34.

8. The mansion in London is located at 9 Grosvenor Square, presently the property of the Japanese. In Paris, the Adamses rented a house from the Comte de Rouault. The house, now known as the Hotel des demoiselles de Verrieres, may still be seen at 45 rue d'Auteuil in the 16th Arrondissement. It is now owned by La Compagnie franaise Pétrole and is used as the office of the president of Total CFP. Neither house is open to the public.

9. E. B. White, *Essays of E. B. White* (New York: Harper & Row, 1977), p. 237.

10. *The New York Times*, July 24, 1983, sec. 2, p. 1.

The Gilbert Stuart portrait, with her husband John's, hangs in the National Gallery of Art in Washington, D.C. Stuart recorded the payment of a $100 deposit "Received of Mrs. Adams" on May 20, 1800. Andrew Oliver, *Portraits of John and Abigail Adams* (Cambridge: Harvard University Press, The Belknap Press, 1967), p. 132. The Adamses then waited impatiently for the portrait to be finished. In December 1804, John Quincy Adams wrote to his mother: "Stuart is nowhere, and perhaps if I had the right to call on him for the picture he might be induced to finish it, under the apprehension that it would be liable to injure his reputation by its being exhibited in the owner's possession in its unfinished state— At any rate, it is so excellent a likeness, that being the only one extant of you, I am very anxious to have it in our own power to whoever of us it may rightfully belong." JQA to AA, December 19, 1804, Reel 404, Adams

Papers. When the portrait was finally comp-leted fifteen years later, Abigail wrote: It is "no more like me than that of any other per-son. . . . It has however a strong resemblance of you." AA to JQA, June 8, 1815, Oliver, *Portraits*, p. 137.

Webster's New World Dictionary, 2nd coll. ed.

11. AA to MW, December 1777, Reel 348, Adams Papers. The entire quotation reads:

"Our Country is as it were a Secondary God, and the first and greatest parent. It is to be preferred to wives, children, friends and all things the Gods only excepted."

12. AA to MC, January 31, 1767, *AFC* 1:60; AA to JA, September 14 [i.e.13], 1767, *AFC*, 1:62; AA to JA, December 27, 1778, *AFC* 3:139; JA to AA, July 1, 1774, *AFC*, 1:19.

1. In Youth the Mind Is Like a Tender Twig

1. *The Boston Weekly News-Letter*, January 5, 1744.

2. ESP to AA, April 5, 1778, *Adams Family Correspondence*, ed. L. H. Butterfield, 4 vols. (Cambridge: Harvard University Press, The Belknap Press, 1963–73), 3:4.

3. The dramatic contrasts of weather, which apply to Weymouth as well as Quincy, are recorded by Charles Francis Adams in his *An Autobiography* (New York: Houghton Mifflin Co., 1916), p. 6, and in Henry Adams's *The Education of Henry Adams* (Boston: the Mas-sachusetts Historical Society, 1918; Sentry ed., Boston: Houghton Mifflin Company, 1961), pp. 8–9. Among Abigail Adams's mul-titudinous references, including mention of daffodils as "daffies," see her letter to Abigail Adams Smith, May 8, 1808, De Windt Collec-tion, the Massachusetts Historical Society, Boston.

4. No definite record exists regarding Abi-gail's height. Wilhelmina S. Harris, Superin-tendent of the Adams National Historic Site, has written on November 4, 1981: "As you requested, we had our museum aide measure Abigail's gown [carefully preserved under glass in a bureau drawer at the Site]. She found it to be from shoulder to hem 51 1/2 inches. Adding head, shoulders, neck and feet to the amber satin dress, Abigail wore for the Gilbert Stuart portrait, she would seem to have stood about 5 feet 7 inches tall."

Francis Adrian Van der Kemp to AA, No-vember 5, 1813, Reel 416, Adams Papers, the Massachusetts Historical Society, Boston.

LCA to George Washington Adams, June 14, 1812, Reel 413, Adams Papers. The baby "looks like Grandmama Adams . . . the finest pair of black eyes you ever saw."

JA to AA, November 4, 1775, *Letters of John*

Adams Addressed to his Wife, ed. Charles Francis Adams, 2 vols. (Boston: Freeman and Bolles, 1841), 1:76.

AA to Isaac Smith, Jr., February 7, 1762, Smith-Carter Collection, the Massachusetts Historical Society, Boston.

AA to Hannah Lincoln, October 5, 1761, Abigail Adams, *Letters of Mrs. Adams*, 3rd ed. in 2 vols. (Boston: Charles C. Little and James Brown, 1841), 1:3–4.

5. AA to Hannah Lincoln, October 5, 1761, *Letters of Mrs. Adams*, 1:5.

6. AA to Isaac Smith, Jr., March 16, 1763, *AFC*, 1:4.

AA to John Thaxter, February 15, 1778, *AFC*, 2:391.

7. The Mary Phillips School, for example, located near Christ Church in Boston, charged three shillings weekly for instruction in this craft, advertising in *The Boston Gazette*, April 7, 1766.

AA to ESP, February 26, 1811, Shaw Family Papers, Library of Congress, Washington, D.C.

AA to Isaac Smith, Jr., March 16, 1763, *AFC*, 1:4.

AFC, 1:53, n. 1.

Sibley's Harvard Graduates, 17 vols. to date (Boston: the Massachusetts Historical Soci-ety, 1873–), 11:370–6.

8. Charles Francis Adams, *Three Episodes of Massachusetts History* (Boston and New York: Houghton Mifflin and Co., 1892), pp. 700, 704, 708–9.

9. *Sibley's Harvard Graduates*, 7:588–91.

The Oath of a Free Man was "I doe sol-emnly bind my self in the sight of God that when I shall be called to give my voyce touch-ing any such matter of this State, in which Freemen are to deal, I will give my vote and suffrage as I shall judge in mine own conscience may best conduct and tend to the publike weal of the body, with respect of persons, or favour of any man." (Cambridge, Massachusetts: Stephen Daye, 1638).

10. AA to Caroline Smith, February 2, 1809, Abigail Adams Smith, *Journal and Correspondence of Miss Adams*, ed. Caroline Smith De Windt, 2 vols. (New York and London: Wiley and Putnam, 1841), 1:216.

December 25, 1765, *Diary and Autobiography of John Adams*, ed. L. H. Butterfield, 4 vols. (Cambridge: Harvard University Press, Atheneum, 1964), 1:274.

Three Episodes, pp. 704–5.

AA to MC, September 11, 1785, The Abigail Adams Letters, American Antiquarian Society, Worcester, Massachusetts.

AA to JA, October 25, 1775, *AFC*, 1:313. See also obituary of Elizabeth Quincy Smith, *AFC*, 1:273.

AA to Isaac Smith, Jr., March 16, 1763, *AFC*, 1:4.

11. See Eunice Paine to Robert Treat Paine, February 21, 1749, Robert Treat Paine Papers, the Massachusetts Historical Society: "I shall think myself obliged to you for every help to me in my search after this knowledg which has a Lasting Seat in the Soul. . . ."

AA to Isaac Smith, Jr., February 7, 1762, Smith Carter Collection.

12. AA to Hannah Lincoln, October 5, 1761, *Letters of Mrs. Adams*, 1:6.

13. *The Earliest Diary of John Adams*, ed. L. H. Butterfield (Cambridge: Harvard University Press, The Belknap Press, 1966), p. 12.

Summer 1759, *DAJA*, 1:108.

Sibley's Harvard Graduates, 7:588–91. *Sibley's* refers to Parson Smith having slaves, giving a woman named Phoebe her freedom. If she chose to remain with one of his daughters he added one hundred pounds to that daughter's inheritance "for her trouble."

14. *DAJA*, 1:109.

ESP to AA, March 27, 1784, Shaw Family Papers.

15. RC and JA to Mary Smith, December 30, 1761, *AFC*, 1:1.

JA to Benjamin Waterhouse, March 25, 1817, Worthington Chauncey Ford, ed., *Statesman and Friend* (Boston: Little, Brown, and Company, 1927), p. 131.

16. JA to Skelton Jones, March 11, 1809, *The Works of John Adams*, ed. Charles Francis Adams, 10 vols. (Boston: Little, Brown & Co., 1850–56), 9:610–13.

JA to AA, successive letters, including October 4, 1762, and August 1763, *AFC*, 1:2, 8.

17. December 26, 1765, *DAJA*, 1:274.

John Adams's father died on May 25, 1761, leaving one-third of his estate to his wife. John Adams's slightly smaller share of the remaining two-thirds divided among the three brothers was due to his having received a "Libberal Education." Wills and Deeds, Reel 607, Adams Papers. See also *DAJA*, 3:277.

18. Joseph Gardner Bartlett, *Henry Adams of Somersetshire, England and Braintree, Mass.* (New York, privately printed, 1927), pp. 93–5.

Samuel Bates, ed., *Records of the Town of Braintree* (Randolph, Massachusetts: D. H. Huxford, 1886), pp. 39, 46, 83, 87, 90, 99, n. 17.

JA to [?], February [?], 1799, JA Letterbook, Reel 95, Adams Papers.

John Adams's Book: Being Notes on a Record of the Births, Marriages and Deaths of Three Generations of the Adams Family, 1734–1807, ed. Henry Adams II (Boston: Boston Atheneum, 1934), pp. 1, 3.

19. *DAJA*, 1:65–66.

20. Ibid., 1:95, 99.

21. JA to Nathan Webb, October 12, 1755, JA Letterbook, Reel 118, Adams Papers.

DAJA, 1:54, 271.

The description of Otis is based on his portrait in William Tudor, *The Life of James Otis of Massachusetts* (Boston: Wells & Lilly, 1823).

22. JA to AA, July 3, 1776, *AFC*, 2:28.

23. *DAJA*, 3:260.

January 1761, *DAJA*, 1:195.

24. At that time there was controversy over the choice of having smallpox in the "natural" way, as opposed to the "artificial" way, by inoculation. A census after the epidemic of 1764 proved to the dubious that in 4,977 cases of inoculation only 46 had died. Of the 619 who endured smallpox without inoculation, 124 had died. Zabdiel Boylston, John Adams's great-uncle, experimented with inoculation against smallpox on June 26, 1721, on his own child and two servants. He published an "Historical Account of the Small Pox inoculation in New England upon all

sorts of persons, whites, Blacks, and of all Ages and Constitutions" including some "Short directions to the unexperienced in this Method of Practice," in London in 1730, dedicated to the Princess of Wales. It was only after Edward Jenner's discovery of a milder vaccine, that of cow pox, that inoculation against smallpox became less hazardous. John Adams called smallpox "worse than the sword!" In June 16, 1776, he wrote to Abigail saying that "small pox is ten times more terrible than Britons, Canadians and Indians, together. This was the cause of our precipitate retreat from Canada. This the cause of our disgraces at the Cedars. I don't mean that this was all. There has been want approaching to famine, as well as pestilence." *Letters of JA,* 1:119.

John B. Blake, *Public Health in the Town of Boston, 1630–1822* (Cambridge: Harvard University Press, 1959), chaps. 4–5.

"Smallpox Inoculation in Colonial Boston," *Journal of the History of Medicine,* 8 (1953): 284–300.

AA to JA, April 7, 1764, *AFC,* 1:15.

JA to his granddaughter Caroline Smith De Windt, January 1, 1820, *Journal and Correspondence,* 1:239–40: "Innoculation for smallpox was first introduced into the British Empire in the town of Boston. . . . Zabdiel Boylston, a younger brother of my grandfather, Peter Boylston of Brookline, innoculated his own children in 1720, one hundred years ago, and after he innoculated his negroes at their express desire, and carried his own family safely through the distemper. His success in the town of Boston spread to England, and produced an invitation to him to embark for that country to innoculate the royal family. He did embark, but before he arrived, the royal children had aquired courage enough to trust their own surgeons." And, "This year completes a century since my Uncle Boylston in-

troduced the practice of innoculation into English dominions; but what improvements have been made since 1720, partly by experience, but much more by the discovery of Dr. Jenner? The history of this distemper is enough to humble human pride." January 24, 1820, 1:242.

The terror of smallpox is succinctly expressed by Abigail's father. William Smith wrote in December 1763: "The small pox being in Town, I have been obliged to retire into the Country—and when I shall return is uncertain. I must therefore beg the favor of you to dispose of the Boots I spoke for, if you have made them. . . ." *Diaries of the Reverend William Smith and Cotton Tufts,* Proceedings of the Massachusetts Historical Society, vol. 42, October 1908–June 1909, p. 469.

25. JA to AA, April 11, 1764, *AFC,* 1:23.
AA to JA, April 16, 1764, *AFC,* 1:32.
Description based on Blyth pastel in Andrew Oliver, *Portraits of John and Abigail Adams* (Cambridge: Harvard University Press, The Belknap Press, 1967), p. 7. See also Henry Wilder Foote, "Benjamin Blyth of Salem," *Proceedings of the Massachusetts Historical Society,* 71 (1953–57): 69–71, 81–2.

26. JA to AA, May 7, 1764, *AFC,* 1:44–6.
27. AA to JA, May 9, 1764, *AFC,* 1:46–7.
28. JA to AA, April 11, 1764, *AFC,* 1:22.
JA to AA, September 30, 1764, *AFC,* 1:48.
Also, according to *Sibley's Harvard Graduates,* Parson Smith disliked lawyers, and didn't even want John's horse in his barn. John, therefore, had to tie his to a tree by the roadside when he came to visit. At the wedding of John and Abigail, Parson Smith preached that John "came neither eating nor drinking, & they say he hath a devil." 7:590.

29. JA to AA, September 30, 1764, *AFC,* 1:49.

30. October–December 1758, *Earliest Diary,* p. 73.

2. Mountains Arise to Hinder Me

1. November 20, 1761, *Diary and Autobiography of John Adams,* ed. L. H. Butterfield, 4 vols. (Cambridge: Harvard University Press, Atheneum, 1964), 1:225, n. 1. Also, Waldo C. Sprague, "The President John Adams and

President John Quincy Adams Birthplaces" (Quincy, Massachusetts, 1959).

January 24, 1765, *DAJA,* 1:251.

2. Before college, John Adams had broached the possibility of being a farmer

with his father. *DAJA*, 3:257. *DAJA*, 1:89, 98, 247, among others, testify repeatedly to his passion for the land.

March 18–19, 1759, *DAJA*, 1:80.

Spring 1759, *DAJA*, 1:88–9.

DAJA, 1:247, 252, n. 1.

3. AA to MC, July 15, 1766, *Adams Family Correspondence*, ed. L. H. Butterfield, 4 vols. (Cambridge: Harvard University Press, The Belknap Press, 1963–73), 1:54.

AA to AAS, May 8, 1808, De Windt Collection, the Massachusetts Historical Society, Boston.

4. JA to AA, May 27, 1776, *Letters of John Adams Addressed to his Wife*, ed. Charles Francis Adams, 2 vols. (Boston: Freeman and Bolles, 1841), 1:114.

AA to JA, June 17, 1776, *AFC*, 2:14.

5. December 27, 1760, *DAJA*, 1:185 and 1:211, n. 6.

JA to Samuel Adams, October 18, 1790, *The Works of John Adams*, ed. Charles Francis Adams, 10 vols. (Boston: Little, Brown & Co., 1850–56), 6:414–420.

January 15, 1766, *DAJA*, 1:294.

James K. Hosmer, *Samuel Adams* (New York: Chelsea House, 1980), pp. 68, 119.

AA to Isaac Smith, Jr., April 20, 1771, *AFC*, 1:76.

James Lovell to AA, May 29, 1781, *AFC*, 4:145.

James Lovell to AA, October 5, 1781, *AFC*, 4:223.

6. Abigail made no secret of her "large share of Grandmother Eves curiosity." When her "very indulgent partner [John Adams] was beyond mail pouch reach," she claimed "some small right of knowledge from others." AA to John Thaxter, February 15, 1778, *AFC*, 2:392.

For John Adams's lifelong acknowledgment of his wife's "taste for political speculations," see JA to AA, January 12, 1794, *Letters of John Adams*, 2:138.

Abigail Adams proved such an effective informant that her letters "contain more particulars then any Letters I had before received from any Body." JA to AA, July 7, 1775, *AFC*, 1:241.

AA to JA, December 30, 1773, *AFC*, 1:90.

7. AA and JA to MC, January 12, 1767, *AFC*, 1:58. The Adams's familiarity with available publications is repeatedly cited. See also JA to AA, April 15, 1776, *Letters of JA*, 1:98: "I send you every newspaper that comes out."

The Boston Gazette or Country Journal, September 1, 1755. Benjamin Edes and John Gill purchased this weekly, the colonies' second newspaper (founded in 1719), and began publishing April 7, 1755.

8. George Bancroft, *History of the United States of America*, 6 vols. (New York: D. Appleton and Company, 1897), 3:30, 34, 39.

Richard Frothingham, *The Rise of the Republic of the United States*, 10th ed. (Boston: Little, Brown & Co., 1910), p. 161.

9. Bancroft, *History*, 3:98.

Richard Morris, ed., *Encyclopedia of American History*, Bicentennial ed. (New York: Harper and Row, 1976), p. 85.

10. Bancroft, *History*, 3:59–61, 73.

11. Ibid., 3:58, 77–8, 104.

12. Ibid., 3:80–1.

Bancroft, *History*, 3:104.

13. December 20, 1765, *DAJA*, 1:265.

August 15, 1768, *DAJA*, 1:261, n. 1; also, *Braintree Town Records* (Braintree, Massachusetts), pp. 399–402, 406–7.

14. February 1765, *DAJA*, 1:255–8.

By the time the essay was reprinted in the *London Chronicle*, in November and December of 1765, it owed its title, *A Dissertation on the Feudal and Canon Law*, to Thomas Hollis. In 1804, John Adams pronounced the essay a "lamentable Bagatelle" that might have been called an "Essay upon Forefathers Rock" (meaning Plymouth Rock). *JA Works*, 10:589; *DAJA*, 3:284.

DAJA, 3:282.

JA Works, 3:464–8.

15. Four days prior to publication in *The Boston Gazette*, the instructions were printed in Richard Draper's *Massachusetts Gazette and Boston News-Letter* on October 10, 1765. *DAJA*, 1:265, n. 1.

16. December 19, 1765, *DAJA*, 1:266.

17. December 25, 1765, *DAJA*, 1:274.

DAJA, 3:282.

18. March 28, 1766, *DAJA*, 1:308.

19. May 26, 1766, *DAJA*, 1:312.

20. January 1759, *DAJA*, 1:71–2.

JA to RC, June 29, 1766, *AFC*, 1:52.

21. JA to RC, June 29, 1766, *AFC*, 1:52.

22. *DAJA*, 1:250, 272, 331.

23. AA to MC, July 15, 1766, October 13, 1766, January 31, 1767, and successive letters, *AFC*, 1:54, 57, 61.

24. April 8, 1767, *DAJA*, 1:334. January 16, 1766, *DAJA*, 1:294.

25. AA to MC, July 15, 1766, *AFC*, 1:54.

26. August [7 or 14], 1766, and November 3, 1766, *DAJA*, 1:318–20.

27. AA to MC, October 6, 1766, *AFC*, 1:55.

28. Bancroft, *History*, 3:262–3. October 19, 1769, *DAJA*, 1:344. Samuel Eliot Morison, *The Oxford History of the American People* (New York: Oxford University Press, 1965), p. 190.

29. *DAJA*, 3:288. *The Boston Gazette*, August 17, 1767; see also issues of September 21, 1767, and November 2, 1767.

Richard Frothingham, *Life and Times of Jo-seph Warren* (Boston: Little, Brown & Co., 1865), p. 79.

30. Frothingham, *Joseph Warren*, p. 29.

31. JA to RC, June 29, 1766, *AFC*, 1:52. AA to MC, July 15, 1766, *AFC*, 1:53. AA to MC, October 6, 1766, *AFC*, 1:56.

32. January 30, 1768, *DAJA*, 1:338.

33. AA to JA, September 14, 1767, *AFC*, 1:62; and *AFC*, 1:62, n. 3.

John Adams's Book: Being Notes on a Record of the Births, Marriages and Deaths of Three Generations of the Adams Family, 1734–1807, ed. Henry Adams II (Boston: Boston Atheneum, 1934).

DAJA, 1:338. AA to MC, January 31, 1767, *AFC*, 1:60.

34. AA and JA to MC, January 12, 1767, *AFC*, 1:57–8.

35. Ibid., 1:57.

3. An "Eaqual" Share of Curiosity

1. *Diary and Autobiography of John Adams*, ed. L. H. Butterfield, 4 vols. (Cambridge: Harvard University Press, Atheneum, 1964), 3:286–287.

2. Richard Frothingham, *Life and Times of Joseph Warren* (Boston: Little, Brown & Co., 1865), p. 101.

3. *DAJA*, 3:290. August 10, 1769, *DAJA*, 1:339, n. 1.

4. August 10, 1769, *DAJA*, 1:339, n. 1. *DAJA*, 3:291. *DAJA*, 2:68.

5. JA to AA, June 29, 1769, *Adams Family Correspondence*, ed. L. H. Butterfield, 4 vols. (Cambridge: Harvard University Press, The Belknap Press, 1963–73) 1:66. *DAJA*, 3:291. AA to LCA, January 30, 1813, Reel 415, Adams Papers, the Massachusetts Historical Society, Boston.

6. Frothingham, *Joseph Warren*, pp. 117–9.

7. February 26, 1770, *DAJA*, 1:350.

8. *DAJA*, 3:291. Frothingham, *Joseph Warren*, pp. 123–4.

9. *DAJA*, 3:291. Frothingham, *Joseph Warren*, pp. 127–8. The five dead were Crispus Attucks, Samuel Gray, Patrick Carr, James Caldwell, and Samuel Maverick. *The Boston Gazette*, March 12, 1770.

10. *DAJA*, 3:292.

11. *DAJA*, 3:293. Preston, aware of the vicissitudes of the case, published from the Boston jail, in the *Gazette* on March 12, 1770, his thanks "to the inhabitants in general of this Town—who throwing aside all Party and Prejudices, have with the utmost Humanity and freedom, stept forth Advocates for Truth in Defence of my injured innocence." *The Boston Gazette*, June 25, 1770, supplement. *The Essex Gazette* (Salem, Massachusetts), March 25, 1771.

12. *DAJA*, 3:294–5.

13. *DAJA*, 3:296. September 22, 1772, *DAJA*, 2:63, n. 2. John earned his living dealing with cases concerning lapsed legacies, bastardy, stolen casks of molasses, drunkenness, trespassing, assault. In a later case, tried with his friend James Otis, he won freedom, with a verdict of self-defense, for the four American sailors who had harpooned the jugular vein of a British lieutenant foolish enough to ignore warnings of dread consequences for boarding their boat, the *Pitt Packet* of Marblehead. The principal at stake was impressment, forbidden in America.

14. September 22, 1772, *DAJA*, 2:63.

15. November 28, 1772, *DAJA*, 2:68.

16. ESP to Isaac Smith, Jr., April 13, 1768, *AFC,* 1:63.

AA and JA to Isaac Smith Jr., January 4, 1770, *AFC,* 1:67–9, quoting *Hamlet,* act 3, sc. 3.

17. AA to MW, February 27, 1774, *AFC,* 1:98.

18. AA and JA to Isaac Smith, Jr., January 4, 1770, *AFC,* 1:67–8.

19. AA to Isaac Smith, Jr., April 20, 1771, *AFC,* 1:76.

20. Ibid., p. 77.

At this time, Mrs. Macaulay was writing the fifth of an eight-volume series on the *History of England, from the Accession of James I to that of the Brunswick Line* (London, 1763–1783). The first volume, *History from Accession of James I to Elevation of House of Hanover,* was reviewed in *The Boston Gazette,* September 4, 1769. The critic, John Hampden, considered the volume a "work of inexpressible merit. It is written in the true spirit of Liberty, and much more in that of the Constitution, than all the annals of the island from the landing of Julius the pirate and robber to those of Will the Norman." The book, dealing with the "diabolical" reigns of the Stuarts, proof that destruction came from the North, and that the persecuted would find asylum in the West, according to the reviewer, was recommended "to every Son and Daughter of Liberty in North-America."

21. ESP to Isaac Smith, Jr., April 13, 1768, *AFC,* 1:65.

22. Reverend James Fordyce, D.D., *Sermons to Young Women,* 4th ed. in 2 vols. (London, 1767), available at the Adams National Historic Site. Fordyce also published *The Character and Conduct of the Female Sex* (London, 1776).

AA to MC, January 31, 1767, *AFC,* 1:61.

23. John Shebbeare, *Letters on the English Nation,* 2 vols. (London, 1755).

AA to Isaac Smith, Jr., April 20, 1771, *AFC,* 1:77.

24. AA to MW, July 16, 1773, *AFC,* 1:84.

The description of Mercy Warren is based on her portrait by John Singleton Copley in the Museum of Fine Arts, Boston. The portrait is discussed and reproduced in *AFC,* 1:xiii, 240. Mercy Otis Warren was probably more fortunate than most women of her era; her education might almost be considered formal and even extensive. She was admitted to her brother James Otis's lessons with his tutor, the clergyman and Yale graduate Jonathan Russell. Mercy and James were said to have been as inseparable as George Eliot and her brother Isaac. Presumably, their reading of Pope, Dryden, and Milton as well as Raleigh's *History of the World* molded America's first female historian and playwright, who could be counted on for a baroque style and provocative opinions.

Mercy cultivated not only Abigail's but John's friendship, enlisting the latter's assistance in what amounted to research for the books she would eventually write. Once John was officially committed to the movement for independence, she planned a shrewd trade, agreeing to his offer "to draw the Character of every new Personage . . . on Condition you will do the same." Correctly, she assumed she would be the "gainer." "I expect," she wrote John, "to be made Acquainted with the Genius, the taste, and Manners, . . . of the Most Distinguished Characters in America . . . and Perhaps before the Conflict is Ended, with some of Those Dignifyed personages who have held the Regalia of Crowns And Scepters, and in the Zenith of power are the Dancing Puppets of other European Courts." *AFC,* 2:377, n. 1.

25. AA to MW, February 3, 1814, Reel 417, Adams Papers.

MW to AA, December 11, 1775, *AFC,* 1:-339.

AA to MW, December 7, 1773, *AFC,* 1:89.

AA to MW, April 13, 1774, *AFC,* 1:378.

Just as Catharine Macaulay was said to have inspired the French Madame Roland to be "La Macaulay de son pays," it is possible she may also have motivated Mercy Warren. Mrs. Macaulay sent a volume of her history to James Otis, the "great Guardian of American Liberty." Forty-two years later, Mercy produced her three-volume *History of the Rise, Progress and Termination of the American Revolution,* announcing that "the world is now viewing America, as experimenting a new system of government, a Federal Republic, to which the Kingdoms of Great Britain and Ireland bear little proportion."

26. AA to MW, December 11, 1773, *AFC*, 1:89.

27. MW to AA, January 19, 1774, *AFC*, 1:92.

28. AA to MW, December 5, 1773, *AFC*, 1:88.

The Boston Gazette, November 29, 1773.

29. Frothingham, *Joseph Warren*, p. 279.

30. AA to MW, December 5, 1773, *AFC*, 1:88–9. Nathan Hale is remembered for his reputed last words, "I only regret that I have but one life to lose for my country."

31. Ibid.

32. MW to AA, January 19, 1774, *AFC*, 1:91.

33. George Bancroft, *History of the United States of America*, 6 vols. (New York: D. Appleton and Company, 1897), 3:455–6, 6:364.

Richard Frothingham, *The Rise of the Republic of the United States*, 10th ed. (Boston: Little, Brown and Co., 1910) p. 306.

34. Bancroft, *History*, 3:450–6.

The Boston Gazette, December 20, 1773.

December 17, 1773, *DAJA*, 2:86.

"You may depend upon it they were no ordinary Mohawks," John Adams has written. "The profound secrecy in which they held their names and the total abstinence from plunder, are proofs of the character of the men. I believe they would have tarred and feathered anyone of their number who should have been detected in pocketing a pound of Hyson." JA to Hezekiah Niles, Editor of *The Weekly Register* (Baltimore), May 10, 1819, *The Works of John Adams*, ed. Charles Francis Adams, 10 vols. (Boston: Little, Brown & Co., 1850–56), 2:334.

JA to JW, December 17, 1773, ibid, 9:333. James Warren and his wife Mercy were a curious pair. Warren, nine years older than John Adams, was the latter's close friend in the early years. Unlike John Adams, Warren claimed he was "Content to Move in a small Sphere," which probably accounts for their falling out during the Revolution. He expected "no distinction but that of an honest Man who has exerted every nerve." Mercy, who would be the first to cheer Abigail on in the cause of patriotism during her lengthening separations from John, was oddly contented with her husband's refusal of major appointments and his self-imposed limitations on his involvement. Possibly, their age may explain the course they took.

It was Warren who said that though, as a general rule, the "fair" ought to be excused from the arduous cares of war and state, he certainly thought that Mercy and Abigail ("Marcia and Portia") ought to be exceptions: "I have ever ascribed to those Ladies a Share and no small one either,—in the Conduct of our American affairs." Alice Brown, *Mercy Warren*, (New York: Charles Scribner's Sons, 1896), p. 240.

35. December 17, 1773, *DAJA*, 2:85.

The Boston Gazette, January 11, 1774.

36. Ibid.

37. Ibid.

38. AA to MW, February 27, 1774, *AFC*, 1:97.

39. MW to AA, January 19, 1774, *AFC*, 1:91. AA to MW, February 27, 1774, *AFC*, 1:98.

40. AA to MW, February 27, 1774, *AFC*, 1:98.

41. Justin Winsor, ed., *The Memorial History of Boston*, 4 vols. (Boston, 1880–81), p. 52. Bancroft, *History*, 3:476–81. William Tudor, *The Life of James Otis* (Boston, 1823), pp. 437–9.

42. Bancroft, *History*, 4:6.

43. Ibid., 3:476–82. Richard B. Morris, ed., *Encyclopedia of American History*, Bicentennial ed. (New York: Harper & Row, 1976), pp. 97–8.

44. Bancroft, *History*, 3:476–82. Morris, *Encyclopedia of American History*, pp. 97–8.

45. Bancroft, *History*, 4:44.

46. *DAJA*, 2:96, n. 1. JA to AA, May 12, 1774, *AFC*, 1:107.

47. JA to AA, May 12, 1774, *AFC*, 1:107.

48. *DAJA*, 3:307. The decision of that meeting of the Boston legislature in Salem was stirring: "in Consideration of the unhappy Differences" between Great Britain and the colonies, "it is highly expedient and necessary that a Meeting of Committees from the several Colonies on this Continent be had . . . to consult upon the present State of the Colonies and the Miseries to which they are reduced by the Operation of certain Acts of Parliament respecting America." *Journals of the House of Representatives of Massachusetts* [*1715–*] (Boston, reprinted by the Massachusetts Historical Society, 1919), May–June 1774, p. 44.

June 20, 1774, *DAJA*, 2:96.

49. JA to AA, June 23 to July 9, 1774, *AFC*, 1:108–35.

50. July 1774, *AFC*, 1:136, n. 5 (re: JA conversation with Jonathan Sewall).

JA to AA, July 1, 1774, *AFC*, 1:119.

51. June 25, 1774, *DAJA*, 2:97.

52. JA to AA, July 9, 1774, *AFC*, 1:135. John mentioned on May 12 that it was expensive to keep a family in Boston. The family already seemed to have moved back to Braintree while John kept his office on Queen Street in Boston.

53. AA to JA, August 15, 1774, *AFC*, 1:140. See also *AFC*, 1:140, n. 2.

August 10, 1774, *DAJA*, 2:97–8.

54. AA to JA, August 19, 1774, *AFC*, 1:142–3.

4. The Die Is Cast

1. AA to JA, September 14–16, 1774, Abigail Adams, *Letters of Mrs. Adams*, 3rd ed. in 2 vols. (Boston: Charles C. Little and James Brown, 1841), 1:21.

AA to JA, August 19, 1774, *Letters of Mrs. Adams*, 1:13.

2. AA to JA, September 16, 1774, *Familiar Letters of John Adams and his Wife Abigail Adams, during the Revolution*, ed. Charles Francis Adams (Boston: Houghton, Mifflin and Company, 1875) p. 85.

3. AA to JA, August 19, 1774, *Letters of Mrs. Adams*, 1:14.

JA to AA, August 28, 1774, *Adams Family Correspondence*, ed. L. H. Butterfield, 4 vols. (Cambridge: Harvard University Press, The Belknap Press, 1963–73), 1:145.

4. AA to JA, September 16, 1774, *AFC*, 1:153–4.

5. AA to MW, April 13, 1776, *AFC*, 1:377.

AA to JA, April 7, 1776, *Letters of Mrs. Adams*, 1:95.

6. JA to AA, June 23, 1774, *AFC*, 1:109.

JA to AA, June 30, 1774, *AFC*, 1:117.

7. AA to MW, April 13, 1776, *AFC*, 1:377.

JW to JA, April 27, 1777, *AFC*, 2:239, n. 1.

JA to AA, August 28, 1774, *AFC*, 2:145.

On February 28, 1774, John negotiated the purchase of his father's homestead for £440 from his brother Peter Boylston Adams. This comprised a home (John's birthplace), a barn, and thirty-five acres, as well as eighteen acres of pasture in the North Common. John rationalized the latter purchase by estimating that its "numerous growth" of red cedars, perhaps 1000, would, if properly pruned, be worth a shilling each in twenty years. He also noted that this pruning would make "good fuel" after the cattle had picked the greens. In June of 1776, John agreed to buy twenty-eight additional acres of woodland, this time from his widowed sister-in-law Mrs. Elihu Adams, at a price of forty shillings per acre. In August 1787, John instructed Dr. Cotton Tufts to purchase "That Piece of land and every other, that adjoins upon me." He was referring to fifty-six acres mentioned by Tufts to Abigail. Adams's letter completely captures his ideas on the subject of property: "My view is to lay fast hold of the Town of Braintree and embrace it, with both my arms and all my might. There to live—there to die—there to lay my bones—and there to plant one of my sons, in the Profession of the Law and the practice of Agriculture, like his father.—To this end, I wish to purchase as much land there, as my utmost forces will allow that I may have farm enough to amuse me and employ me, as long as I live." JA to CT, August 27, 1787, JA Letterbook, Reel 112, Adams Papers, the Massachusetts Historical Society, Boston.

On April 24, 1796, John Adams wrote Abigail about purchasing land belonging to the Hayden family. Despite the price being "exorbitant," he said he "must have it." *Letters of John Adams Addressed to his Wife*, ed. Charles Francis Adams, 2 vols. (Boston: Freeman and Bolles, 1841), 2:225.

8. JA to AA, September 26, 1775, *AFC*, 1:286.

9. September 24, 1775, *Diary and Autobiography of John Adams*, ed. L. H. Butterfield, 4 vols. (Cambridge: Harvard University Press, Atheneum, 1964), 2:182.

10. JA to AA, October 29, 1775, *AFC*, 1:317–8.

11. Ibid.

12. JA to AA, August 28, 1774, *AFC*, 1:145.

13. JA to AA, February 18, 1776, *AFC*, 1:349.

Abigail Adams's grammar was *A New French Grammar Teaching a Person . . . to Read, Speak, and Write that Tongue* by J. E. Tandon, 3rd ed., rev., London, 1736. AA to JA, March 16, 1776, *AFC,* 1:359–60.

14. JA to AA, July 7, 1776, *AFC,* 2:39.

15. Ibid.

16. Ibid.

17. JA to AA, April 15, 1776, *AFC,* 1:384.

18. Ibid.

AA to JA, May 14, 1776, *AFC,* 1:408.

19. See JA to AA, June 29, 1774, *AFC,* 1:114: "Let us teach [our children] not only to do virtuously but to excell."

AA to MW, July 16, 1773, *AFC,* 1:85.

20. AA to MW, July 16, 1773, *AFC,* 1:85.

21. MW to AA, July 25, 1773, *AFC,* 1:86–7.

22. *DAJA,* 3:307.

AA to JA, September 14, 1774, *AFC,* 1:151.

JA to AA, August 28, 1774, *AFC,* 1:144.

23. *AFC,* 1:148, n. 3.

The Boston Gazette, October 24, 1774.

AA to JA, September 14, 1774, *AFC,* 1:151–2.

24. AA to JA, September 14, 1774, *AFC,* 1:151–2.

25. AA to JA, September 16, 1774, *AFC,* 1:152.

AFC, 1:154, n. 2.

26. MC to Isaac Smith, Jr., October 15, 1774, *AFC,* 1:171.

27. Isaac Smith, Jr., to MC, October 20, 1774, *AFC,* 1:175.

28. AA to JA, September 22, 1774, *AFC,* 1:161.

AA to JA, October 15, 1774, *AFC,* 1:170.

October 14, 1774, *DAJA,* 2:152, n. 2.

William Tudor to AA, September 3, 1774, *AFC,* 1:149.

AA to Catharine Sawbridge Macaulay, 1774, *AFC,* 1:177.

29. AA to JA, May 24, 1775, *Letters of Mrs. Adams,* Vol. I, p. 34. William Tudor to AA, September 3, 1774, *AFC,* 1:149.

30. September 2, 1774, *AFC,* 1:148, n. 6.

AA to JA, September 2, 1774, *AFC,* 1:148.

31. Richard Frothingham, *Life and Times of Joseph Warren* (Boston: Little, Brown & Co., 1865), p. 332.

32. *The Essex Gazette* (Salem, Massachusetts), September 20, 1774.

33. AA to MW, August 27, 1775, *AFC,* 1:276.

34. AA to JA, April 17, 1777, *AFC,* 2:212.

AA to JA, June 17, 1776, *AFC,* 2:13.

AA to JA, May 27, 1776, *AFC,* 1:416.

35. AA to JA, September 23, 1776, *AFC,* 2:133.

JA to AA, May 22, 1776, *AFC,* 1:412.

JA to AA, July 29, 1776, *Letters of John Adams,* 1:143.

AA to JA, July 31, 1775, *AFC,* 1:269.

AA to JA, July 25, 1775, *AFC,* 1:263.

36. JA to AA, January–October, 1776, JA Letterbook, Reel 90, Adams Papers.

37. AA to JA, October 22, 1775, *Letters of Mrs. Adams,* 1:75.

JA to AA, May 17, 1794, *Letters of John Adams,* 2:160.

38. AA to JA, September 2, 1774, *AFC,* 1:146.

39. JA to AA, July 2, 1774, *AFC,* 1:121.

AA to JA, July 5, 1775, *AFC,* 1:239.

40. JA to AA, August 28, 1774, *AFC,* 1:144. August 23, 1774, *DAJA,* 2:109.

41. JA to AA, September 29, 1774, *AFC,* 1:163.

42. JA to AA, October 7, 1774, *AFC,* 1:164.

43. August 31, 1774, *DAJA,* 2:117. September 2, 1774, *DAJA,* 2:119–20. September 3, 1774, *DAJA,* 2:121. October 11, 1774, *DAJA,* 2:151.

44. JA to AA, October 9, 1774, *AFC,* 1:166. September 14, 1774, *DAJA,* 2:134. September 22, 1774, *DAJA,* 2:136.

45. JA to AA, September 16, 1774, *AFC,* 1:156.

46. Ibid.

47. JA to AA, October 9, 1774, *AFC,* 1:166.

48. Ibid.

49. AA to JA, October 16, 1774, *AFC,* 1:172–3.

AA to MW, November [ca. 5], 1775, *AFC,* 1:323.

50. October 24 and 28, 1774, *DAJA,* 2:156–7.

51. AA to Catharine Macaulay [1774], *AFC,* 1:177.

AA to MW, January 25, 1775, *AFC,* 1:180.

The Boston Gazette, January 17 to April 17, 1775. The paper stopped publishing thereafter because of the so-called Battle of Lexington and resumed in Watertown on June 5, 1775. *AFC,* 1:195, n. 2.

52. AA to MW, January 25, 1775, *AFC,* 1:180.

53. AA to MW, February 3[?], 1775, *AFC*, 1:183–4.

54. Ibid.

55. Frothingham, *Joseph Warren*, p. 455.

Autobiography, Reminiscences and Letters of John Trumbull (New York and London: Wiley and Putnam, 1841), p. 3.

Robert A. Gross, *The Minutemen and their World* (New York: Hill and Wang, 1976), p. 130.

56. Richard Morris, ed., *Encyclopedia of American History*, Bicentennial ed. (New York: Harper & Row, 1976), p. 101.

DAJA, 3:314.

57. AA to JA, May 7, 1775, *AFC*, 1:194.

58. AA to Edward Dilly, May 22, 1775, *AFC*, 1:200.

59. AA to JA, May 24, 1775, *AFC*, 1:204–5. For day of week see *AFC*, 1:203, n. 1.

60. AA to JA, May 24, 1775, *AFC*, 1:204–5.

61. AA to JA, June 16[?], *AFC*, 1:217.

62. AA to JA, June 18, 1775, *AFC*, 1:222.

63. Ibid., 1:223.

AA to JA, July 31, 1775, *AFC*, 1:269.

AFC, 1:271, n. 2.

Frothingham, *Joseph Warren*, pp. 26, 517.

64. AA to JA, June 18, 1775, *AFC*, 1:223–4, n. 3.

Charles Francis Adams, *Three Episodes of Massachusetts History* (Boston and New York: Houghton Mifflin and Co., 1892), p. 859.

Eliza Susan (Morton) Quincy, *Memoir of the Life of Eliza S. M. Quincy* (Boston: J. Wilson and Son, 1861), p. 209. (Reminiscing during a visit on July 17, 1826, JQA told Eliza Quincy: "I remember living in the house where I was born, at the foot of Penn's Hill. The day after the battle of Lexington men came, and took the pewter spoons out of our kitchen to melt them up into bullets. On the day of the battle of Bunker Hill, I heard the cannon, and, with my mother, saw the smoke of Charlestown from Penn's Hill; and I recollect her distress on receiving intelligence of the death of Warren. During the seige of Boston, I used to go up that hill every evening to see the shells thrown by the American and British forces; which, at night, had the brilliancy of fire works."

Memoirs of John Quincy Adams, ed. Charles Francis Adams, 2 vols. (Philadelphia: J.B. Lippincott & Co., 1874–77), 1:545.

Seventy-one years after John Quincy Adams was taught these lines by his mother, he wrote to the English Quaker, Joseph Sturge, in March 1864, that he could still repeat Collins's poem by memory. *AFC*, 1:223–4, n. 3.

65. AA to JA, July 5, 1775, *AFC*, 1:240.

AA to JA, April 7 and 10, 1776, *AFC*, 1:374–5.

Julius Caesar, act 3, sc. 1, slightly adapted to AA's purpose. The complete passage reads: "Woe to the hand that shed this costly blood! /Over thy wounds now do I prophesy,— /Which, like dumb mouths, do ope their ruby lips,/To beg the voice and utterance of my tongue,—/A curse shall light upon the limbs of men;/Domestic fury and fierce civil strife/ Shall cumber all the parts of Italy."

66. AA to JA, June 22, 1775, *AFC*, 1:225–6.

67. AA to JA, June [16?], 1775, *AFC*, 1:217, 219.

AA to JA, June 25, 1775, *AFC*, 1:230.

AA to JA, July 12, 1775, *AFC*, 1:244.

AA to JA, July 5, 1775, *AFC*, 1:240.

AA to JA, July 16, 1775, *AFC*, 1:249.

68. AA to JA, June 25, 1775, *AFC*, 1:232.

69. *JQA Memoirs*, 1:5.

70. JA to AA, June 10, 1775, *AFC*, 1:213.

71. AA to James Bowdoin, June 16, 1775, *AFC*, 1:220.

72. AA to JA, June 16, 1775, *AFC*, 1:218.

73. Ibid.

JA to AA, May 29, 1775, *AFC*, 1:207.

74. JA to AA, June 17, 1775, *AFC*, 1:215.

The Boston Gazette, August 14, 1775 (extract of letter of George Washington, June 20, 1774).

DAJA, 3:323, 336.

75. AA to JA, July 16, 1775, *AFC*, 1:246–7.

76. Ibid.

77. Ibid., p. 247.

78. Ibid., pp. 249–50.

79. AA to MW, July 24, 1775, *AFC*, 1:255.

80. AA to JA, July 25, 1775, *AFC*, 1:260–1. See also JA to AA, July 7, 1775, *AFC*, 1:242.

5. Ten Thousand Difficulties

1. Elihu Adams served as captain in Colonel Benjamin Lincoln's company during the alarm of April 19, 1775, and at Grape Island off Weymouth in May. He died on August 10 or 11, 1775. *Diary and Autobiography of John Adams,* ed. L. H. Butterfield, 4 vols. (Cambridge: Harvard University Press, Atheneum, 1964), 3:326, n. 4.

AA to JA, September 16–17, 1775, *Adams Family Correspondence,* ed. L. H. Butterfield, 4 vols. (Cambridge: Harvard University Press, The Belknap Press, 1963–73), 1:278–9.

2. AA to JA, September 16–17, 1775, *AFC,* 1:279.

3. Ibid., 1:280.

4. AA to JA, September 25, 1775, *AFC,* 1:284.

AA to JA, September 29, 1775, *AFC,* 1:287–8.

Patty's last name is unknown. She was thought to be a servant or "bound girl," possibly a relation of the family who had lived in the Adams household for four years. *AFC,* 1:278, n. 2.

5. AA to JA, October 22, 1775, *AFC,* 1:309–10.

6. Ibid., 1:310.

7. AA to JA, October 25, 1775, *AFC,* 1:312. JA to AA, October 23, 1775, ibid.

8. JA to AAS, October 20, 1775, Abigail Adams Smith, *Journal and Correspondence of Miss Adams,* ed. Caroline Smith De Windt, 2 vols. (New York and London: Wiley and Putnam, 1841), 2:3–4.

9. AA to JA, October 25, 1775, *AFC,* 1:313. JA to TBA, October 20, 1775, *AFC,* 1:305.

10. AA to JA, October 9, 1775, *AFC,* 1:297. AA to JA, October 25, 1775, *AFC,* 1:313.

11. JA to AA, October 29, 1775, *AFC,* 1:316–7.

12. Ibid., 1:317.

13. AA to JA, October 25, 1775, *AFC,* 1:313.

AA to JA, November 12, 1775, *AFC,* 1:325.
AA to JA, November 5, 1775, *AFC,* 1:320.

14. *The Boston Gazette,* August 15, 1768.
AA to JA, May 4, 1775, *AFC,* 1:204–5.

15. AA to JA, July 5, 1775, *AFC,* 1:240.
AA to JA, July 23, 1775, *AFC,* 1:252–3.

16. JA to AA, July 23, 1775, *AFC,* 1:253.

By this time, John Adams was thoroughly disillusioned with John Dickinson, a fact that was to come to public attention within the next month. On August 17 *The Massachusetts Gazette* printed two letters John had written on July 24, one intended for Abigail and the other for James Warren. John's letter to Warren bared his opposition to Dickinson's motion for a second petition to the King seeking reconciliation, calling it "a measure of imbecility." John alluded to Dickinson, though not by name, as a "certain great Fortune and piddling Genius" who has "given a silly Cast to our whole Doings." John had been told that Dickinson's political sentiments were influenced by the Quakers, who intimidated his mother and his wife, both of whom were continually after Dickinson. "From my soul I pitty Mr. Dickinson," John said, admitting that if his own mother and wife expressed such sentiments he was certain that if they did not wholly unman him and make him an apostate, they would make him the most miserable man alive.

Abigail worried about the effect of these letters, but John assured her they "had no such bad Effects, as the Tories intended." Far otherwise, from what he could see and hear; he had "fresh Proofs that every Body is coming fast into every political Sentiment contained in them." He could mention compliments passed upon them, he said, and if a "serious Decision" could be made on them, he seemed positive the public voice would be found in their favor. *AFC,* 1:256, n. 1. JA to AA, October 2, 1775, *AFC,* 1:291.

17. AA to JA, November 5, 1775, *AFC,* 1:320–1.

18. AA to JA, November 12, 1775, *AFC,* 1:325.

JA to AA, November 18, 1775, *AFC,* 1:327.
JA to AA, December 3, 1775, *AFC,* 1:331–2.

19. JA to AA, December 3, 1775, *AFC,* 1:332.

AA to JA, November 27, 1775, *AFC,* 1:328–9.

20. AA to JA, November 27, 1775, *AFC,* 1:329.

21. AA to JA, November 12, 1775, *AFC,* 1:324.

22. AA to JA, November 27, 1775, *AFC,* 1:329.

23. Ibid., 1:329–30.

AA to JA, December 10, 1775, *AFC,* 1:337.

24. AA to JA, December 10, 1775, *AFC,* 1:336.

25. Ibid.

26. JA to AA, July 24, 1775, *AFC,* 1:256. JA to AA, February [13?], 1776, *AFC,* 1:347.

27. *DAJA;* 2:231; 2:232, n. 2 and 2:162, n. 1.

JA to AA, July 24, 1775, *AFC,* 1:255–6.

28. December 9, 1775, *DAJA,* 2:224, n. 1. JA to AA, February 18, 1776, *AFC,* 1:348.

Thomas Paine, *Common Sense* (Philadelphia, 1776), reprinted in *The Life and Major Writings of Thomas Paine,* ed. Philip S. Foner (Secaucus, New Jersey: The Citadel Press, 1948), pp. 3–46.

John was also eager to learn whether he was expected to remain in Congress or to assume his unsolicited appointment as Chief Justice of Massachusetts. He had accepted this office the previous November 24 and promised to fulfill it "as soon as the Circumstances of the Colonies will admit of an Adjournment of the Congress." *DAJA,* 3:359. November 18, 1775, *AFC,* 1:328.

29. JA to AA, February 18, 1776, *AFC,* 1:348.

Writings of Paine, pp. 17, 20.

30. AA to JA, February 21, 1776, *AFC,* 1:350.

AA to JA, March 2, 1776, *AFC,* 1:352.

31. JA to AA, March 19, 1776, *AFC,* 1:363.

32. Ibid.

John Adams informed Abigail on April 28, 1776, that the writer of *Common Sense* was Paine, "a Gentleman, about two Years from England." *AFC,* 1:400.

33. *Writings of Paine,* pp. ix–xliv.

David Freeman Hawke, *Paine* (New York: Harper and Row, 1974), p. 182.

34. John Adams, *Thoughts on Government: Applicable to the Present State of the American Colonies* (Philadelphia: John Dunlap, 1776), reprinted in Adrienne Koch, ed., *The American Enlightenment* (New York: George Braziller, 1965), pp. 246–50.

DAJA, 3:358–9.

35. AA to JA, May 9, 1776, *AFC,* 1:404.

36. JA to AA, May 27, 1776, *AFC,* 1:420.

37. AA to JA, February 21, 1776, *AFC,* 1:350.

AA to JA, March 2, 1776, *AFC,* 1:353.

38. AA to JA, March 3 and March 4, 1776, Abigail Adams, *Letters of Mrs. Adams,* 3rd ed. in 2 vols. (Boston: Charles C. Little and James Brown, 1841), 1:90.

39. Richard B. Morris, ed., *Encyclopedia of American History,* Bicentennial ed. (New York: Harper & Row, 1976), pp. 106–7.

AA to JA, March 10, 1776, *AFC,* 1:356, n. 3.

AA to JA, March 2–5, 1776, *AFC,* 1:353.

40. AA to JA, March 16–18, 1776, *AFC,* 1:357–8.

41. Ibid., 1:360.

42. AA to JA, March 16, 1776, *AFC,* 1:357.

43. AA to JA, March 31, 1776, *AFC,* 1:370.

44. Ibid., 1:369.

AA to JA, July 25, 1775, *AFC,* 1:261–2.

45. AA to JA, March 31–April 15, 1776, *AFC,* 1:371.

46. AA to JA, March 16, 1776, *AFC,* 1:359.

AA to JA, March 31, 1776, *AFC,* 1:370.

47. AA to JA, September 22, 1774, *AFC,* 1:162.

A few months after the death of his father, John Quincy Adams, Abigail's grandson, Charles Francis Adams, was nominated to run for Vice-President on Martin Van Buren's ticket at a convention of antislavery delegates. Later still, Henry Adams claimed that Abigail's descendants were "anti-slavery by birth, as their name was Adams and their home was Quincy." Henry Adams, *The Education of Henry Adams,* Sentry ed. (Boston: Houghton Mifflin Company, 1961), p. 25.

48. AA to JA, July 25, 1775, *AFC,* 1:263.

49. JA to AA, April 28, 1776, *AFC,* 1:400.

JA to AA, April 14, 1776, *AFC,* 1:381–2.

50. JA to AA, April 14, 1776, *AFC,* 1:382–3.

51. AA to JA, May 7, 1776, *AFC,* 1:402.

52. AA to MW, October 19, 1775, *AFC,* 1:301.

53. AA to MW, April 13, 1776, *AFC,* 1:378.

54. MW to AA, April 17, 1776, *AFC,* 1:385.

55. Ibid., 1:385–6.

56. AA to MW, April 27, 1776, *AFC,* 1:396–7.

57. MW to AA, January 28, 1775, *AFC*, 1:182.

58. AA to JA, April 27, 1776, *AFC*, 1:397.

59. JA to Joseph Palmer, May 26, 1776, JA Letterbook, Reel 89, Adams Papers, the Massachusetts Historical Society, Boston.

60. Ibid.

61. Ibid.

62. Ibid.

63. JA to AA, April 28, 1776, *AFC*, 1:401, see also *AFC*, 1:401, n. 6.

AA to JA, May 7, 1776, *AFC*, 1:402.

64. AA to JA, May 9, 1776, *AFC*, 1:405.

AA to JA, May 7, 1776, *AFC*, 1:402.

65. JA to AA, May 17, 1776, *AFC*, 1:410; and *AFC*, 1:411, n. 2.

DAJA, 3:335, 382–6.

66. JA to AA, May 17, 1776, *AFC*, 1:410–1. JA to AA, May 22, 1776, *AFC*, 1:412.

67. AA to JA, May 27, 1776, *AFC*, 1:416.

68. Ibid.

AA to JA, June 17, 1776, *AFC*, 2:13–5.

69. JA to AA, June 26, 1776, *AFC*, 2:23.

AA to John Thaxter, July 7, 1776, *AFC*, 2:37.

70. Ibid.

71. JA to AA, July 3, 1776, *AFC*, 2:27.

AA to JA, July 13, 1776, *AFC*, 2:45.

72. JA to AA, July 3, 1776, *AFC*, 2:27–8.

The motion on June 9, by Richard Henry Lee, on "certain resolutions respecting independency," directed the delegates "to propose [that Congress] declare the United Colonies free and independent states." After some debate, a committee was appointed on June 11 to draft the declaration. Its five members included Jefferson, Adams, Franklin, Sherman, and Livingston. *AFC*, 2:23, n. 2.

73. JA to Mr. Clap[?], July 1, 1776, Reel 89, Adams Papers.

JA to AA, June 26, 1776, *AFC*, 2:24.

JA to AA, July 3, 1776, *AFC*, 2:28.

74. JA to AA, July 3, 1776, *AFC*, 2:30.

75. Ibid., 2:30–1.

76. Ibid., 2:28, 31.

77. AA to JA, July 13–14, 1776, *AFC*, 2:46.

78. Ibid.

6. To Rob Me of All My Happiness

1. *The Boston Gazette*, March 3, 1777.

AA to JA, March 8, 1777, *Adams Family Correspondence*, ed. L. H. Butterfield, 4 vols. (Cambridge: Harvard University Press, The Belknap Press, 1963–73), 2:171–2.

2. JA to AA, September 6, 1776, *AFC*, 2:120–1.

For John Adams's highly personal account of one aspect of his conference with Admiral Howe, his rooming situation with Benjamin Franklin, see September 9, 1776, *Diary and Autobiography of John Adams*, ed. L. H. Butterfield, 4 vols. (Cambridge: Harvard University Press, Atheneum, 1964), 3:417–20.

"The Taverns were so full We could with difficulty obtain Entertainment. At Brunswick but one bed could be procured for Dr. Franklin and me, in a Chamber little larger than the bed, without a Chimney and with only one small Window. The Window was open, and I, who was an invalid and afraid of the Air in the night (blowing upon me), shut it close. Oh! says Franklin dont shut the Window. We shall be suffocated. I answered I was afraid of the Evening Air. Dr. Franklin replied, the Air within this Chamber will soon be, and indeed now is worse than that without Doors; come! open the Window and come to bed, and I will convince you: I believe you are not acquainted with my Theory of Colds. Opening the Window and leaping into Bed, I said I had read his letters to Dr. Cooper in which he had advanced, that Nobody ever got cold by going into a cold Church, or any other cold Air: But the Theory was so little consistent with my own experience, that I thought that I would run the risque of a cold. The Doctor then began an harrangue, upon Air and cold and Respiration and Perspiration, with which I was so much amused that I soon fell asleep . . . I remember little of the lecture, except that the Human Body, by Respiration and Perspiration, destroys a gallon of Air in a minute . . . There is much Truth I believe, in some things he advanced: but they warrant not the assertion that Cold is never taken from cold air . . . I have often asked him, whether a Person heated with Exercise, going suddenly into Cold Air, or standing still in a current of it, might not have his Pores suddenly contracted, his Perspiration stopped, and that matter thrown into the Circulations or cast upon the Lungs which he acknowledged was the Cause of Colds. To this he never could give me a satisfactory Answer. And I have heard that in the Opinion of his own Physician Dr. Jones he fell a sacrifice at last, not to the Stone but to his own Theory: having caught the violent Cold, which finally choaked him, by sitting for some hours at a Window, with the cool Air blowing upon him."

3. JA to AA, September 14, 1776, *AFC*, 2:124.

4. JA to AA, January 3, 1777, *AFC*, 2:145. *DAJA*, 2:256, n. 2.
JA to AA, March 7, 1777, *AFC*, 2:170.

5. JA to AA, April 2, 1777, *AFC*, 2:195–6. JA to AA, April 3, 1777, *AFC*, 2:197–8.

6. JA to AA, October 4, 1776, *AFC*, 2:137. JA to AA, April 2, 1777, *AFC*, 2:195.
AA to MW, [January ?, 1776], *AFC*, 1:423.
AA to JA, April 17, 1777, *AFC*, 2:211.

7. JA to AA, October 11, 1776, *AFC*, 2:141.
The Boston Gazette, November 4, 1776.
AA to JA, January 26, 1777, *AFC*, 2:147.

8. AA to JA, February 8, 1777, *AFC*, 2:157. Both "An Act to prevent Monopoly and Oppression" which was passed January 25, 1777, and a supplementary act, passed May 10, 1777, were equally unpopular and ineffective. *AFC*, 2:157, n. 1.
AA to JA, April 17, 1777, *AFC*, 2:212.
AA to JA, September 20, 1776, *AFC*, 2:128–9.
AA to JA, June 1, 1777, *AFC*, 2:251.

9. JA to AA, March 22, 1777, *AFC*, 2:181. JA to AA, June 16, 1776, *Letters of John Adams Addressed to his Wife*, ed. Charles Francis Adams, 2 vols. (Boston: Freeman and Bolles, 1841), 1:118.
JA to JQA, April 8, 1777, *AFC*, 2:204.

10. JA to JQA, March 16, 1777, *AFC*, 2:177.
JA to TBA, March 16, 1777, *AFC*, 2:178; see also *AFC*, 2:178, n. 1.
JA to CA, March 17, 1777, *AFC*, 2:180.
JA to AAS, March 17, 1777, *AFC*, 2:178–9.

11. AA to JA, August 29, 1776, *AFC*, 2:112. Virginia Woolf echoed Abigail's need in her book *A Room of One's Own* (London: Hogarth Press, 1929).

12. AA to JA, September 23, 1776, *AFC*, 2:133.
JA to AA, February 10, 1777, *AFC*, 2:159.

AA to JA, April 17, 1777, *AFC*, 2:213.

13. AA to JA, April 2, 1777, *AFC*, 2:193.
AA to JA, June 15, 1777, *AFC*, 2:266.
AA to JA, June 1, 1775, *AFC*, 2:250.

14. AA to JA, July 9, 1777, *AFC*, 2:277.
AA to JA, July 10, 1777, *AFC*, 2:279.

15. John Thaxter to JA, July 13, 1777, *AFC*, 2:282.
AA to JA, July 16, 1777, *AFC*, 2:282.
JA to AA, June 4, 1777, *AFC*, 2:255.

16. JA to AA, July 28, 1777, *AFC*, 2:292.
AA to JA, August 12, [1777?], *AFC*, 2:308.

17. AA to JA, August 5, 1777, *AFC*, 2:301.

18. AA to JA, August 22, 1777, *AFC*, 2:324.
AA to JA, September 10, 1777, *AFC*, 2:340.

19. AA to JA, July 30, 1777, *AFC*, 2:294–5.

20. JA to AA, August 30, 1777, *AFC*, 2:333–4.
JA to AA, September 1, 1777, *AFC*, 2:336.
JA to AA, October 26, 1777, *AFC*, 2:361, n. 1.

21. JA to AA, October 26, 1777, *AFC*, 2:361.

22. AA to JA, October 20, 1777, *AFC*, 2:354.
AA to JA, November 16, 1777, *AFC*, 2:367.
November 15, 1777, *DAJA*, 2:267; *DAJA*, 2:267, n. 1.
November 21, 1777, *DAJA*, 2:269, n. 1.
DAJA, 4:1.
AFC, 2:372, n. 1.
Silas Deane, who shared a joint commission with Benjamin Franklin and Arthur Lee, was recalled on November 21. *DAJA*, 2:270.

23. AA to James Lovell, December 15, 1777, *AFC*, 2:370–1; see also *AFC*, 2:371–2, n. 1.

24. Daniel Roberdeau to JA, November 28, 1777, *AFC*, 2:373, n. 1.

25. AA to Daniel Roberdeau, December 15, 1777, *AFC*, 2:372–3.

26. AA to James Lovell, December 15, 1777, *AFC*, 2:370–1.

27. Ibid., 2:371.

28. MW to AA, January 2, 1778, *AFC*, 2:376.
AFC, 2:385, n. 1.

29. *DAJA*, 4:5.
DAJA, 2:276.
AFC, 2:376, n. 3.
AA to John Thaxter, February 15, 1778, *AFC*, 2:390.
List of Stores sent on board the *Boston*, Feb-

ruary 1778, Reel 348, Adams Papers, the Massachusetts Historical Society, Boston.

James Lovell to JA, undated but around November 28, 1777, *AFC* 2:372, n. 1. *AFC,* 2:375, n. 3.

30. JA to AA, February 13, 1778, 11:30 A.M., *AFC,* 2:388.

JA to AA, February 13, 1778, 5:00 P.M., *AFC,* 2:389.

31. AA to John Thaxter, February 15, 1778, *AFC,* 2:390–1.

32. Ibid., 2:392.

James Lovell to AA, March 21, 1778, *AFC,* 2:404.

7. A Call So Honorable

1. AA to Hannah Storer, March 1, 1778, *Adams Family Correspondence,* ed. L. H. Butterfield, 4 vols. (Cambridge: Harvard University Press, The Belknap Press, 1963–73), 2:397.

AA to JA, March 8, 1778, *AFC,* 2:402.

AA to MW, December 10, 1778, *AFC,* 3:132.

Samuel Cooper to AA, March 2, 1778, *AFC,* 2:398–9.

AA to John Thaxter, May 26, 1778, *AFC,* 3:26.

2. AA to JA, September 30, 1778, *AFC,* 3:51.

AA to JQA, September 29, 1778, *AFC,* 3:97.

AA to JA, October 25, 1778, *AFC,* 3:110–1.

AA to JA, July 15, 1778, *AFC,* 3:60–2.

AA to JA, June 10, 1778, *AFC,* 3:36.

AA to Hannah Storer, March 1, 1778, *AFC,* 2:397.

3. AA to JA, June 18, 1778, *AFC,* 3:47.

Prior to Elizabeth Smith's marriage to Shaw, Abigail was plainly critical of the couple. Initially, she disapproved of her sister's seemingly flirtatious behavior. Three years later, with the wedding date set, Abigail almost boasted to John that she had never exchanged a word on the subject of the marriage with Betsy, partially, it appears, out of embarrassment. "All her acquaintance stand amazed. —An Idea of 30 years and unmarried is sufficient to make people do very unaccountable things." Somewhat sanctimoniously, she added, "Thank Heaven my Heart was early fix'd and never deviated." Abigail was incorrect about her sister's age: Betsy turned twenty-seven in April of 1777. AA to JA, March 9, 1777, *AFC,* 2:173.

4. AA to John Thaxter, September 29, 1778, *AFC,* 3:98.

AA to John Thaxter, April 9, 1778, *AFC,* 3:6.

AA to JA, July 15, 1778, *AFC,* 3:61–2.

AA to JA, September 29, 1778, *AFC,* 3:95.

The mixed use of dollars and pounds in Abigail's account of her expenses in explained by Samuel Eliot Morison in *The Oxford History of the American People* (New York: Oxford University Press, 1965) pp. 143–4 under "Currency Controversies." As no precious metals were produced in the colonies, the balance of trade with England was unfavorable. Having no metal currency, each colony, or group of colonies, established a currency of account called "lawful money" in pounds, shillings, and pence that were worth less than English sterling. The standard for this lawful money was the Spanish milled dollar or "piece of eight," eventually chosen as the standard for the United States silver dollar. Since overvaluing the Spanish dollar and undervaluing sterling did not help the colonists, they turned to paper money. Personal promissory notes and bills of exchange had long been used as currency in the colonies. These "bills of credit," from which the phrase "a dollar bill" is derived, relieved the currency shortage in time of war. Consequently, the demand grew for issuing them in time of peace.

5. AA to JA, June 30, 1778, *AFC,* 3:52.

AA to JA, July 15, 1778, *AFC,* 3:60.

6. April 8, 1778, *Diary and Autobiography of John Adams,* ed. L. H. Butterfield, 4 vols. (Cambridge: Harvard University Press, Atheneum, 1964), 2:296.

February 13–March 14, 1778, *DAJA,* 2:269–86.

February 24–26, 1778, *DAJA,* 2:15.

7. March 30–April 9, 1778, *DAJA,* 4:32–43. March 30–April 9, 1778, *DAJA,* 2:291–7; see also *DAJA,* 2:297, n. 2.

JA to AA, April 19, 1778, *AFC,* 3:14.

8. AA to JA, July 15, 1778, *AFC,* 3:60.

JA to AA, June 3, 1778, *AFC,* 3:31.
JA to AA, April 25, 1778, *AFC,* 3:31.
April 9, 1778, *DAJA,* 2:296.
JA to AA, April 12, 1778, *AFC,* 3:9–10.
9. *DAJA,* 4:118–9.
April 9, 1778, *DAJA,* 2:297.
February 9, 1779, *DAJA,* 2:346.
10. June 23, 1779, *DAJA,* 2:391–2.
DAJA, 4:69, 80–1.
JA to AA, April 25, 1778, *AFC,* 3:17.
February 9, 1779, *DAJA,* 2:346–7.
11. May 27, 1778, *DAJA,* 4:118–9.
12. May 10, 1778, *DAJA,* 2:311, n. 1.
AA to JA, June 30, 1778, *AFC,* 3:52.
May 20, 1778, *DAJA,* 2:314.
DAJA, 3:86–7.
AA to JA, July 15, 1778, *AFC,* 3:60.
13. April 21, 1778, *DAJA,* 2:304.
DAJA, 4:120.
14. February 9, 1779, *DAJA,* 2:347.
April 4–10[?], 1786, *DAJA,* 3:186.
April 16, 1778, *DAJA,* 2:302.
15. JA to Samuel Adams, May 21, 1778,
DAJA, 4:106–8.
16. April 27, 1778, *DAJA,* 4:78.
May 21, 1778, *DAJA,* 4:108–9.
JA to AA, December 3, 1778, *AFC,* 3:129.
17. JA to AA, November 27, 1778, *AFC,*
3:122–3.
18. Ibid., 3:123.
19. AA to JA, May 18, 1778, *Abigail Adams,
Letters of Mrs. Adams,* 3rd ed. in 2 vols. (Boston: Charles C. Little and James Brown,
1841). 1:122. AA to JA, November 12–13,
1778, *AFC,* 3:118–9.
20. JA to AA, December 2, 1778, *AFC,* 3:124.
21. JA to AA, December 3, 1778, *AFC,*
3:128–9.
22. AA to JA, December 27, 1778, *AFC,*
3:139–40.
23. JA to AA, December 18, 1778, *AFC,*
3:138.

24. AA to JA, December 27, 1778, *AFC,*
3:139–40.
25. AA to JA, January 2, 1779, *AFC,*
3:147.
26. JQA to AA, February 20, 1779, *AFC,*
3:175.
27. JA to AA, February 26, 1779, *AFC,*
3:179.
JA to AA, February 28, 1779, *AFC,* 3:182.
28. JA to AA, February 21, 1779, *AFC,*
3:177.
JA to AA, February 28, 1779, *AFC,* 3:182.
JA to AA [February ?, 1779], *AFC,* 3:183.
JA to AA, February 20, 1779, *AFC,* 3:174.
29. JA to AA, February 19, 1779, *AFC,*
3:173.
30. AA to James Lovell, January 4, 1779,
AFC, 3:147–8.
31. James Lovell to AA, January 19, 1779,
AFC, 3:150.
32. James Lovell to AA, March 9, 1779,
AFC, 3:187.
33. February 11, 1779, *DAJA,* 2:351–2.
34. JA to AA, February 28, 1779, *AFC,*
3:181–2.
35. JA to AA, February 20, 1779, *AFC,*
3:175.
JA to AA, [February ?, 1779], *AFC,* 3:183,
n. 1.
36. May 22, 1779, *DAJA,* 2:377.
JQA to AA, February 20, 1779, *AFC,*
3:176.
37. AA to James Lovell, June 18–26, 1779,
AFC, 3:206–7.
MW to AA, July 6, 1779, *AFC,* 3:209.
38. AA to Samuel Adams, July 30, 1779,
AFC, 3:215–6.
Samuel Adams to JA, July 31, 1779, *AFC,*
3:217, see also *AFC,* 3:217, n. 2.
39. Daniel Roberdeau to JA, November 28,
1777, *AFC,* 2:373, n. 1.
May 17, 1779, *DAJA,* 2:375.

8. This Cruel State of Separation

1. *Diary and Autobiography of John Adams,* ed.
L. H. Butterfield, 4 vols. (Cambridge: Harvard University Press, Atheneum, 1964),
4:191.
Enclosure of Samuel Huntington, November 4, 1779 *DAJA,* 4:179.
2. AA to James Lovell, November 18,
1779, *Adams Family Correspondence,* ed. L. H.

Butterfield, 4 vols. (Cambridge: Harvard University Press, The Belknap Press, 1963–73),
3:236.
JA to AA, November 14, 1779, *AFC,* 3:234.
AA to JA, November 14, 1779, *AFC,*
3:233–4.
AA to JA, October 25, 1782, *Familiar Letters
of John Adams and his Wife Abigail Adams, during*

the Revolution, ed. Charles Francis Adams (Boston: Houghton, Mifflin and Company, 1875), p. 405.

3. AA to JA, August 5, 1782, *AFC,* 4:358.

4. AA to JA, April 15, 1780, *AFC,* 3:320.
AA to JA, July 16, 1780, *AFC,* 3:377.

5. AA to JA, November 13, 1780, *AFC,* 4:-13.
AA to JQA, January 19, 1780, *AFC,* 3:268.
AA to CA, January 19, 1780, *AFC,* 3:270.

6. AA to JA, November 13, 1780, *AFC,* 4:13.
AA to JQA, January 19, 1780, *AFC,* 3:268.
AA to CA, January 19, 1780, *AFC,* 3:269.
AA to JQA, March 20, 1780, *AFC,* 3:310.

7. AA to JQA, March 20, 1780, *AFC,* 3:311-2.
AA to JQA, January 19, 1780, *AFC,* 3:268.

8. AA to CA, January 19, 1780, *AFC,* 3:270.

9. AA to JA, June [10?], 1778, *AFC,* 3:37.

10. AA to JA, January 18, 1780, *AFC,* 3:261.

11. RC to JA, January 18, 1780, *AFC,* 3:264.
AA to JA, January 18, 1780, *AFC,* 3:262; see also AA to James Lovell, December 13, 1799, *AFC,* 3:249.
AA to James Lovell, February 13, 1780, *AFC,* 3:273. For details on John Paul Jones, see Samuel Eliot Morison, *John Paul Jones: A Sailor's Biography* (Boston: Little, Brown, 1959), pp. 148-50.

12. James Lovell to AA, January 8, 1781, *AFC,* 4:61,63.
James Lovell to AA, December 15, 1777, *AFC,* 2:333.
James Lovell to AA, February 16, 1779, *AFC,* 3:172.
James Lovell to AA, December 27, 1779, *AFC,* 3:254.
James Lovell to AA, November 23, 1779, *AFC,* 3:239.
James Lovell to AA, August 19, 1778, *AFC,* 3:76.

13. AA to James Lovell, March 17, 1781, *AFC,* 4:92.
James Lovell to AA, January 13, 1780, *AFC,* 3:257.
AA to James Lovell, June 24, 1778, *AFC,* 3:48.
James Lovell to AA, June 13, 1778, *AFC,* 3:43.

14. James Lovell to AA, January 6, 1780, *AFC,* 3:256.
AA to James Lovell, February 13, 1780, *AFC,* 3:274.

15. April 21, 1778, *DAJA,* 2:304.
DAJA, 4:86-7.
AFC, 3:229.

16. June 6, 1771, *DAJA,* 2:30, n. 1.
DAJA, 2:345-6.
Julian Boyd, "Silas Deane: Death by a Kindly Teacher of Treason," *William and Mary Quarterly,* 3rd ser. 16 (April–October 1959): 165-87, 319-42, 515-50.
Edmund S. Morgan, "The Puritan Ethic and the American Revolution," *William and Mary Quarterly,* 3rd ser. 24 (January 1967):25.

17. See n. 16 above.
April 21, 1778, *DAJA,* 4:68.
May 2, 1778, *DAJA,* 4:86.
Carl Van Doren, *Benjamin Franklin* (New York: The Viking Press, 1938), p. 580.
Deane eventually wrote letters intercepted by the British and published in loyalist papers, urging Americans to reunite with Great Britain. He died in exile, on board ship, sailing from Great Britain to Canada, neither in his lifetime nor in history convincingly exonerated from his alleged crimes. But, in 1842, Congress voted for a partial restitution of $37,000 to his heirs based on finding Arthur Lee's accusations "ex parte and a gross injustice."

18. JA to William Whipple, September 11, 1779, *AFC,* 3:229-30, 232.

19. February 8, 1779, *DAJA,* 2:345; see also *DAJA,* 2:346, n. 1.
Silas Deane to John Jay, November 1780, *Deane Papers* in *Collections of the New-York Historical Society* (1886-90), 4:262.
AA to MW, January 22, 1779, *AFC,* 3:154.

20. AA to MW, February 28, 1780, *AFC,* 3:287-8.

21. Ibid.

22. AA to Elbridge Gerry, March 13, 1780, *AFC,* 3:297.

23. Ibid.

24. Ibid., 3:298-9.

25. Elbridge Gerry to AA, April 17, 1780, *AFC,* 3:323-5.

26. AA to JA, April 15, 1780, *AFC,* 3:321-2.

27. Ibid.

AA to JA, May 1, 1780, *AFC,* 3:335.

JA to AA, June 17, 1780, *AFC,* 3:366.

AA to JA, July 24, 1780, *AFC,* 3:381.

AA to JA, October 8, 1780, *AFC,* 4:2.

AA to MW, February 28, 1780, *AFC,* 3:289.

AA to JA, July 5, 1780, *AFC,* 3:371.

AA to JA, July 16, 1780, *AFC,* 3:376.

28. JA to AA, December 11, 1779, *AFC,* 3:243.

JA to AA, December 12, 1779, *AFC,* 3:245.

JA to AA, December 16, 1779, *AFC,* 3:252.

JA to AA, March 15, 1780, *AFC,* 3:301.

JA to AA, May 12, 1780, *AFC,* 3:342.

29. AA to JA, November 13, 1780, *AFC,* 4:12–3.

30. JA to AA, September 4, 1780, *AFC,* 3:410.

JA to AA, September 15, 1780, *AFC,* 3:414.

31. JA to AA, February 12, 1780, *AFC,* 3:271.

32. John A. Garraty, *The American Nation,* 2nd ed. (New York: Harper and Row, 1971), pp. 174–5.

Richard B. Morris, ed., *Encyclopedia of American History,* Bicentennial ed. (New York: Harper & Row, 1976), pp. 105, 107.

33. *Encyclopedia of American History,* pp. 116, 118.

Garraty, *American Nation,* p. 175.

Samuel Flagg Bemis, *The Diplomacy of the American Revolution: the Foundation of American Diplomacy* (New York and London: D. Appleton–Century Company, Inc., 1935), pp. 184, 186–7.

34. *AFC,* 3:391, n. 5.

July 27, 1780, *DAJA,* 2:442.

AFC, 3:394.

During this period, John championed the American cause in French, Dutch, and even British publications, wrote voluminously to his colleagues at home, incessantly to the Comte de Vergennes, who was convinced, after almost six months of correspondence, that Adams, as he told Franklin, was not endowed with "that conciliating spirit which is necessary for the important and delicate business with which he is entrusted." Nor were the "Delicacies" of the Comte de Vergennes perfectly consonant with John's way of thinking. John loathed Vergennes's insistence that he conceal powers to negotiate a treaty of commerce with the Court of London; he

yearned for a "frank and decent Communication" of his full powers. Vergennes, on his part, disputed Adams's analyses of America's financial policy and of France's disposition of its naval power. Humiliating notes informed John that in Vergennes's opinion, "toute duscution ultérieure entre nous a cet égard serois superflüe"; in another, "que le Roi n'a pas besoin de vos Sollicitations pour s'occuper des interets des Etats-unis." John's "fishing expedition" was the sort of "suitoring" for alliance that Franklin detested. He was humiliated, he said, by the "Idea of our running about from Court to Court begging for Money and Friendship, which are the more withheld the more eagerly they are sollicited, and would perhaps have been offer'd if they had not been asked." *AFC,* 3:391–2, 395.

35. JA to AA, September 25, 1780, *AFC,* 3:424.

JA to AA, December 18, 1780, *AFC,* 4:34–5.

Rector Verheyk to JA, November 10, 1780, *AFC,* 4:11–2.

36. AA to JQA, January 21, 1781, *AFC,* 4:67–8.

37. AA to JA, March 19, 1781, *AFC,* 4:93.

AA to John Thaxter, March 2, 1780, *AFC,* 3:294.

38. Alice Lee Shippen to Elizabeth Welles Shippen (Mrs. Samuel Adams), June 17, 1781, *AFC,* 4:154.

AA to James Lovell, June 30, 1781, *AFC,* 4:164.

39. Alice Lee Shippen to Elizabeth Welles Shippen, June 17, 1781, *AFC,* 4:154.

40. James Lovell to AA, June 26, 1781, *AFC,* 4:163, and see accompanying note.

JA to the Comte de Vergennes, July 17, 1780, *AFC,* 3:392, n. 5.

Bemis, *The Diplomacy of the American Revolution,* pp. 176–8.

41. James Lovell to AA, June 26, 1781, *AFC,* 4:163, and accompanying notes.

Benjamin Franklin to Robert Livingston, July 22, 1783, *The Writings of Benjamin Franklin,* ed. Albert Henry Smyth, 10 vols. (New York: The Macmillan Co., 1905–7), 9:62.

42. AA to James Lovell, June 30, 1781, *AFC,* 4:166.

43. AA to Alice Lee Shippen, June 30, 1781, *AFC,* 4:167–8.

44. AA to James Lovell, June 30, 1781, *AFC*, 4:165–6.

45. Ibid., 4:165.

James Lovell to AA, February 22, 1778, *AFC*, 2:393.

AA to Elbridge Gerry, August 4, 1781, *AFC*, 4:193.

AA to Elbridge Gerry, July 20, 1781, *AFC*, 4:183.

January 12, 1783, *DAJA*, 4:104–5, and n. 1, p. 105.

46. James Lovell to AA, July 13, 1781, *AFC*, 4:173.

James Lovell to AA, August 10, 1781, *AFC*, 4:194.

This letter, dated August 9, 1780, and sent to Congress, begins: "Mr. Adams has given Offense to the Court here, by some Sentiments and Expressions contained in several letters written to the Count de Vergennes." See *AFC*, 3:395, n. 5.

47. July 1 and July 6, 1781, *DAJA*, 2:456–7, and n. 2, p. 458.

JA to AA, July 11, 1781, *AFC*, 4:169, and n. 1, p. 170.

48. JA to AA, July 11, 1781, *AFC*, 4:169.

JA to AA, October 9, 1781, *AFC*, 4:224.

In June 1781, Congress had revoked JA's sole power to treat for peace with Great Britain by appointing him first among five joint commissioners, the others being Franklin, Jay, Laurens, and Jefferson. Their instructions were "to undertake nothing in the negotiations for peace or truce without knowledge and concurrence" of the ministers of their generous ally, the King of France. John received these papers on August 24, 1781.

49. *DAJA*, 3:4.

JA to AA, December 2, 1781, *AFC*, 4:250.

50. AA to JA, December 9, 1781, *AFC*, 4:255–7.

51. AA to JA, December 23, 1781, *AFC*, 4:271.

AA to JA, December 9, 1781, *AFC*, 4:257.

AA to JA, March 17, 1782, *AFC*, 4:295.

AA to JA, April 10, 1782, *AFC*, 4:306.

52. AA to JA, April 10, 1782, *AFC*, 4:305–6.

53. JA to AA, March 22, 1782, *AFC*, 4:300.

JA to AA, March 29, 1782, *AFC*, 4:301–2, and n. 2, p. 302.

54. AA to JA, June 17, 1782, *AFC*, 4:328.

55. AA to JA, April 10, 1782, *AFC*, 4:306.

AA to JA, March 17, 1782, *AFC*, 4:293.

AA to JA, June 17, 1782, *AFC*, 4:328.

56. JA to AA, April 1, 1782, *AFC*, 4:303, and n. 3, p. 304.

JA to Francis Dana, March 15, 1782, Dana Papers, the Massachusetts Historical Society, Boston.

DAJA, 3:9, n. 1.

Bemis, *Diplomacy of the American Revolution*, p. 169.

57. JA to AA, August 15, 1782, *AFC*, 4:361.

JA to AA, May 14, 1782, *AFC*, 4:323.

JA to AA, July 1, 1782, *AFC*, 4:337.

JA to CT, August [?] 1782, *AFC*, 4:370.

58. JA to AA, June 16, 1782, *AFC*, 4:324–5.

JA to John Boylston, July 5, 1782, *AFC*, 4:341.

John Thaxter to AA, July 27, 1782, *AFC*, 4:355.

59. Benjamin Waterhouse to AA, September 10, 1782, *AFC*, 4:380.

JA to AA, August 15, 1782, *AFC*, 4:360.

John Thaxter to AA, July 27, 1782, *AFC*, 4:355.

JA to Robert Livingston, November 8, 1782, JA Letterbook, Reel 108, Adams Papers, the Massachusetts Historical Society, Boston.

JA to Robert Livingston, November 21, 1782, JA Letterbook, Reel 108, Adams Papers.

60. JA to AA, May 14, 1782, *AFC*, 4:323.

JA to JW, June 17, 1782, *The Works of John Adams*, ed. Charles Francis Adams, 10 vols. (Boston: Little, Brown & Co., 1850–6), 9:513: "God willing, I don't want to go to Vermont. I must be within the scent of the sea."

61. AA to JA, July 17, 1782, *AFC*, 4:344–5.

62. AA to JA, August 5, 1782, *AFC*, 4:358.

AA to JA, September 3, 1782, *AFC*, 4:371–2.

AA to JA, November 13, 1782, *Familiar Letters*, p. 408.

AA to JA, November 25, 1782, ibid., p. 409.

63. AA to JA, November 13, 1782, ibid.

AA to JA, September 5, 1782, *AFC*, 4:376–7.

64. JA to AA, May 14, 1782, *AFC*, 4:323.

AA to JA, September 29, 1781, *AFC*, 4:221.

65. JA to AA, August 12, 1782, Reel 107,

Adams Papers. The next sentence reads: "It has no example in History and therefore no reasonings can be drawn from example to decide it."

JA to John Jay, September 21, 1780, JA Letterbook, Reel 102, Adams Papers.

66. November 3, 1782, *DAJA*, 3:45.
JA to AA, August 17, 1782, *AFC*, 4:364.
November 30, 1782, *DAJA*, 3:82.

67. January 20, 1783, *DAJA*, 3:106.

68. JA to AA, February 18, 1783, *Letters of John Adams Addressed to his Wife*, ed. Charles Francis Adams, 2 vols. (Boston: Freeman and Bolles, 1841), 2:89–90.
JA to AA, February 27, 1783, ibid., 2:91.

69. Ibid, 2:92.

70. JA to AA, July 1, 1782, *AFC*, 4:337.

71. JA to Robert Livingston, July 9, 1783, Reel 108, Adams Papers.

72. JA to Edmund Jennings, August 12, 1782, Reel 108, ibid.
January 11, 1783, *DAJA*, 3:102.
DAJA, 4:120.

73. Benjamin Franklin to Samuel Huntington, August 9, 1780, *Writings of BF*, 9:126–8.

74. Ibid.

75. Garraty, *American Nation*, pp. 174–5.
JA to AA, February 26, 1783, JA Letterbook, Reel 108, Adams Papers.
Charles Francis Adams, *An Autobiography* (New York: Houghton Mifflin Co., 1916), p. 30.

76. JA to Elias Boudinot, February 5, 1783, JA Letterbook, Reel 108, Adams Papers.

77. Ibid.

78. JA to Francis Dana, February 22, 1783, ibid.
JA to JW, April 9, 1783, ibid.
January 11, 1783, *DAJA*, 3:103.

79. JA to JW, April 9, 1783, JA Letterbook, Reel 108, Adams Papers.
JA to AA [after February 1783], ibid.

80. JA to Arthur Lee, April 6, 1783, ibid.

81. Ibid.

82. JA to JW, April 13, ibid.

83. JA to JW, April 9, 1783, ibid.
JA to Arthur Lee, April 12, 1783, ibid.

84. JA to JW, April 16, 1783, JA Letterbook, Reel 108, Adams Papers.

85. JA to JW, September 2, 1782, *JA Works*, 9:513–4.
JA to JW, April 9, 1783, JA Letterbook, Reel 108, Adams Papers.

86. JA to MW, January 29, 1783, JA Letterbook, Reel 108, Adams Papers.

87. September 7, 1783, *DAJA*, 3:142, n. 1.
JA to AA, May 30, 1783, *Letters of JA*, 2:93.
JA to AA, April 8—June 8, 1783, ibid., 2:95.
JA to JW, September 2, 1782, *JA Works*, 9:513–4.

88. JA to JW, September 2, 1782, *JA Works*, 9:513–4.
Samuel Adams to JA, November 4, 1783, *JA Works*, 9:520: "Your negotiation with Holland . . . is all your own, the faithful historian will do justice to your merits, perhaps not till you are dead. I would have you reconcile yourself to this thought."

89. September 7, 1783, *DAJA*, 3:141–2.
June 22, 1784, *DAJA*, 3:168, n. 1.

90. JA to JW, August 27, 1784, JA Letterbook, Reel 107, Adams Papers.
JA to Henry Knox, December 15, 1784, ibid.

91. JA to AA, September 7, 1783, *Letters of JA*, 2:100, 102.

92. September 14, 1783, *DAJA*, 3:143–4, n. 4.
Le Comte d'Antigne, *De Boulogne à Auteuil, Passy et Chaillot à Travers les Ages* (Paris: Lapina, 1922), p. 11.
JA to AA, September 7, 1783, *Letters of JA*, 2:102.

93. October 27, *DAJA*, 3:152, n. 3.

94. JA to AA, November 8, 1783, *Letters of JA*, 2:104–5.
JA to C. W. F. Dumas, May 16, 1783, JA Letterbook, Reel 108, Adams Papers.

9. A Mere American

1. AA to MC, July 6, 1784, Abigail Adams, *Letters of Mrs. Adams*, ed. Charles Francis Adams, 3rd ed. in 2 vols. (Boston: Charles C. Little and James Brown, 1841), 2:3–12.

2. AA to MC, July 6, 1784, *Letters of Mrs. Adams*, 2:9.
Abigail Adams's Diary of her voyage from Boston to Deal, 20 June–20 July 1784, *Diary*

and Autobiography of John Adams, ed. L. H. Butterfield, 4 vols. (Cambridge: Harvard University Press, Atheneum, 1964), 3:157.

3. AA to MC, July 6, 1784, *Letters of Mrs. Adams*, 2:4–5.

June 23, 1784, *DAJA*, 3:157.

4. AA to MC, July 10, 1784, *Letters of Mrs. Adams*, 2:14.

June 24, 1784, *DAJA*, 3:157–8.

5. AA to MC, July 10, 1784, *Letters of Mrs. Adams*, 2:15–6.

July 1, 1784, *DAJA*, 3:160.

AA to ESP, July 1784, Shaw Family Papers, Library of Congress, Washington, D.C.

6. AA to MC, July 6, 1784, *Letters of Mrs. Adams*, 2:10.

7. Ibid., 2:11.

AA to MC, July 8, 1784, *Letters of Mrs. Adams*, 2:13.

June 28, 1784, *DAJA*, 3:158–9.

July 9, 1784, *DAJA*, 3:165.

8. AA to MC, July 6, 1784, *Letters of Mrs. Adams*, 2:5–11.

9. AA to MC, July 8, 1784, *Letters of Mrs. Adams*, 2:13–4.

AA to JA, February 11, 1784, Reel 362, Adams Papers, the Massachusetts Historical Society, Boston.

July 18, 1784, *DAJA*, 3:166.

10. AA to MC, July 6, 1784, *Letters of Mrs. Adams*, 2:9–11.

AA to JA, December 15, 1783, *The Book of Abigail and John*, ed. L. H. Butterfield (Cambridge: Harvard University Press, 1975), p. 372.

AA to ESP [July 10? 1784], *The Book of Abigail and John*, p. 383.

11. JA to AA, October 14, 1783, *The Book of Abigail and John*, p. 365.

12. AA to JA, December 23, 1782, *The Book of Abigail and John*, pp. 333–5.

13. December 23, 1782, *The Earliest Diary of John Adams*, ed. L. H. Butterfield (Cambridge: Harvard University Press, The Belknap Press, 1966), p. 18.

14. Ibid., p. 23.

15. AAS to ESP, June 1782, *Adams Family Correspondence*, ed. L. H. Butterfield, 4 vols. (Cambridge: Harvard University Press, The Belknap Press, 1963–73), 4:335.

16. *Grandmother Tyler's Book: The Recollections of Mary Palmer Tyler* (Mrs. Royall Tyler),

1775–1866, ed. Frederick Tupper and Helen Tyler Brown (New York: G.P. Putnam's Sons, 1925), p. 74. *Earliest Diary*, p. 25.

17. Ibid, p. 77.

AA to JA, October 8, 1782, *The Book of Abigail and John*, p. 330.

Earliest Diary, p. 20.

18. AA to JA, December 23, 1782, *The Book of Abigail and John*, pp. 334–5.

19. Ibid., p. 335.

20. JA to AA, January 22, 1783, *The Book of Abigail and John*, pp. 336–8.

21. Ibid., p. 338.

22. JA to AA, January 29, 1783, *The Book of Abigail and John*, pp. 339–340.

JA to AA, February 4, 1783, *The Book of Abigail and John*, p. 340.

23. JA to Francis Dana, March 24, 1783, JA Letterbook, Reel 108, Adams Papers.

JA to Joseph Palmer, August 26, 1784, JA Letterbook, Reel 107, Adams Papers.

Joseph Palmer to JA, June 16–18, 1784, Reel 363, Adams Papers.

24. Royall Tyler to JA, January 13, 1784, Reel 362, Adams Papers.

25. Ibid.

RC to JA, January 20, 1784, Reel 362, Adams Papers.

26. JA to AA, January 25, 1784, *The Book of Abigail and John*, pp. 373–374.

JA to Royall Tyler, April 3, 1784, Reel 362, Adams Papers.

27. JA to Royall Tyler, April 3, 1784, Reel 362, Adams Papers.

28. Royall Tyler to JA, August 27, 1784, Reel 363, Adams Papers.

29. AAS to AA, January 6, 1784, Abigail Adams Smith, *Journal and Correspondence of Miss Adams*, ed. Caroline Smith De Windt, 2 vols. (New York and London: Wiley and Putnam, 1841), 2:28–9.

July 1, 1784, *DAJA*, 3:160–1.

AA to Royall Tyler, July 10, 1784, Reel 363, Adams Papers.

30. AA to Royall Tyler, July 10, 1784, Reel 363, Adams Papers.

31. Ibid.

32. Ibid.

33. AA to MC, July 16, 1784, *Letters of Mrs. Adams*, 2:17–8.

AA to MC, July 18, 1784, *Letters of Mrs. Adams*, 2:18.

34. June 20, 1784, *DAJA*, 3:154–5. July 17, 1784, *DAJA*, 3:166.

35. James Lovell to AA, February 22, 1778, *AFC*, 2:393.

AA to James Lovell, June 11, 1780, *AFC*, 3:362–4.

James Lovell to AA, June 26, 1781, *AFC*, 4:162.

AA to JA, April 28, 1783, *The Book of Abigail and John*, p. 347.

36. James Lovell to AA, June 16, 1781, *AFC*, 4:148–52.

37. AA to James Lovell, January [8?], 1782, *AFC*, 4:274.

RC to JA, July 3, 1784, Reel 363, Adams Papers.

38. AA to MC, July 20, 1784, *The Book of Abigail and John*, pp. 384–8.

39. Ibid.

10. As Happy as a Lord

1. JA to AA, July 26, 1784, *Letters of John Adams Addressed to his Wife*, ed. Charles Francis Adams, 2 vols. (Boston: Freeman and Bolles, 1841), 2:106–107.

2. Ibid.

3. TJ to JA, June 19, 1784, *The Adams-Jefferson Letters*, ed. Lester J. Cappon, 2 vols. (Chapel Hill: The University of North Carolina Press, 1959), 1:16.

JA to AA, August 1, 1784, *The Book of Abigail and John*, ed. L. H. Butterfield (Cambridge: Harvard University Press, 1975), p. 397.

4. AA to MC, July 25, 1784, The Abigail Adams Letters, American Antiquarian Society, Worcester, Massachusetts.

AA to MC, July 20, 1784, Abigail Adams, *Letters of Mrs. Adams*, 3rd ed. in 2 vols. (Boston: Little, Brown & Co., 1841), 2:26.

5. AA to MC, July 20, 1784, *Letters of Mrs. Adams*, 2:22, 24–5.

6. Ibid., 2:22–4.

7. Ibid., 2:22, 25–26.

AA to MC, July 24, 1784, *Letters of Mrs. Adams*, 2:26, 29.

AA to MC, July 26, 1784, *Letters of Mrs. Adams*, 2:37.

AA to MC, July 30, 1784, *Letters of Mrs. Adams*, 2:44.

8. *The London Chronicle*, July 22, 1784.

9. AA to MC, July 25, 1784, *Letters of Mrs. Adams*, 2:31.

10. AA to MC, July 24, 1784, *Letters of Mrs. Adams*, 2:26–30.

AA to MC, July 25, 1784, *Letters of Mrs. Adams*, 2:31–3.

AA to ESP, July 28, 1784, Shaw Family Papers, Library of Congress, Washington, D.C.

11. AA to ESP, July 28, 1784, Shaw Family Papers.

AA to MC, July 24, 1784, *Letters of Mrs. Adams*, 2:28.

AA to MC, July 25, 1784, *Letters of Mrs. Adams*, 2:33.

12. AA to ESP, July 28, 1784, Shaw Family Papers.

AA to MC, July 24, 1784, *Letters of Mrs. Adams*, 2:27–9.

AA to MC, July 26, 1784, *Letters of Mrs. Adams*, 2:38–9.

13. AA to ESP, July 28, 1784, Shaw Family Papers.

14. AA to MC, July 30, 1784, *Letters of Mrs. Adams*, 2:43.

15. Ibid., 2:43–4.

16. AAS Diary, August 7, 1784, *The Book of Abigail and John*, pp. 397–8.

17. JA to C. W. F. Dumas, August 25, 1784, JA Letterbook, Reel 107, Adams Papers, the Massachusetts Historical Society, Boston.

18. AA to MC, December 12, 1784, *Letters of Mrs. Adams*, 2:64.

11. À la Mode de Paris

1. August 8, 1784, Abigail Adams Smith, *Journal and Correspondence of Miss Adams*, ed. Caroline Smith De Windt, 2 vols. (New York and London: Wiley and Putnam, 1841), 1:7.

JA to Antoine Cerisier, December 12, 1784, JA Letterbook, Reel 107, Adams Papers, the Massachusetts Historical Society.

JA to Joseph Palmer, August 26, 1784,

JA Letterbook, Reel 107, Adams Papers.
AA to MC, September 5, 1784, Abigail Adams, *Letters of Mrs. Adams*, 3rd ed. in 2 vols. (Boston: Charles C. Little and James Brown, 1841), 2:45–6.
JA to JW, August 27, 1784, JA Letterbook, Reel 107, Adams Papers.
2. AA to Royall Tyler, September 1784, Reel 363, Adams Papers.
AA to MC, September 5, 1784, *Letters of Mrs. Adams*, 2:50.
3. AA to MC, September 5, 1784, ibid., 2:48–51.
Journal and Correspondence of Miss Adams, 1:71.
AA to Betsy Cranch, May 12, 1785, Smith-Townsend Collection, the Massachusetts Historical Society, Boston.
4. AA to MC, September 5, 1784, *Letters of Mrs. Adams*, 2:49–50.
5. Ibid., 2:46.
AA to CT, September 8, 1784, Reel 363, Adams Papers.
6. AA to ESP, December 14, 1784, *Letters of Mrs. Adams*, 2:70.
7. AA to MC, September 5, 1784, ibid., 2:48.
JA to JW, August 27, 1784, JA Letterbook, Reel 107, Adams Papers.
8. AA to Lucy Cranch, September 5, 1784, *Letters of Mrs. Adams*, 2:54–5.
AA to ESP, December 14, 1784, ibid., 2:68.
9. September 19, 1784, *Journal and Correspondence of Miss Adams*, 1:18–9.
September 5, 1784, ibid., 1:17–8.
AAS to MW, September 5, 1784, ibid., 2:31–2.
Mercure de France, September 14, 1784, September 18, 1784, November 20, 1784.
10. Andrew Oliver, *Portraits of John and Abigail Adams* (Cambridge: Harvard University Press, The Belknap Press, 1967), p. 137.
AA to ESP, May 8, 1785, *Letters of Mrs. Adams*, 2:92.
AA to MC, February 20, 1785, ibid., 2:81–3.
AA to MC, December 9, 1784, ibid., 2:60.
AA to Royall Tyler, January 4, 1785, Reel 364, Adams Papers.
11. AA to MC, February 20, 1785, *Letters of Mrs. Adams*, 2:81–3.

12. Ibid., 2:82–3.
13. April 2, 1785, *Journal and Correspondence of Miss Adams*, 1:68–9.
August 15, 1784, ibid., 1:14.
AAS to Lucy Cranch, September 4, 1784, The Abigail Adams Letters, American Antiquarian Society, Worcester, Massachusetts.
14. AA to MC, May 8, 1785, The Abigail Adams Letters.
15. AA to ESP, December 14, 1784, *Letters of Mrs. Adams*, 2:68–9.
AA to MW, September 1784, Reel 363, Adams Papers.
AA to MW, September 5, 1784, *Warren-Adams Letters*, 2 vols. (Boston: the Massachusetts Historical Society, 1925), 2:242.
16. AA to Rev. John Shaw, January 18, 1785, *Letters of Mrs. Adams*, 2:71–4.
17. Ibid.
18. AA to MC, September 5, 1784, ibid., 2:52.
AA to ESP, December 14, 1784, ibid., 2:68–9.
AA to MW, September 1784, Reel 363, Adams Papers.
19. Ibid.
20. AA to Rev. John Shaw, January 18, 1785, *Letters of Mrs. Adams*, 2:73.
21. AA to MW, September 1784, Reel 363, Adams Papers.
AA to Hannah Storer, January 20, 1785, *Letters of Mrs. Adams*, 2:75–6.
22. AA to MC, December 9, 1784, ibid., 2:60.
23. Ibid., 2:60–2.
24. Ibid., 2:61–2.
AA to Lucy Cranch, September 5, 1784, ibid., 2:55–6.
25. AA to Lucy Cranch, September 5, 1784, ibid., 2:55–6.
March 20, 1785, *Journal and Correspondence of Miss Adams*, 1:61.
May 9, ibid., 1:74–5.
26. AA to Lucy Cranch, September 5, 1784, *Letters of Mrs. Adams*, 2:55–6.
AA to CT, September 8, 1784, Reel 363, Adams Papers.
27. AA to Lucy Cranch, September 5, 1784, *Letters of Mrs. Adams*, 2:55–6.
28. AA to MC, September 5, 1784, ibid., 2:52.

AA to CT, September 8, 1784, Reel 363, Adams Papers.
29. AA to MC, September 5, 1784, *Letters of Mrs. Adams*, 2:52.
AA to CT, September 8, 1784, Reel 363, Adams Papers.
30. AA to CT, September 8, 1784, ibid.

AA to MC, September 5, 1784, *Letters of Mrs. Adams*, 2:51–2.
31. AA to CT, September 8, 1784, Reel 363, Adams Papers.
AA to MC, September 5, 1784, *Letters of Mrs. Adams*, 2:51–2.

12. A Degree of Tristeness

1. AA to MC, September 5, 1784, Abigail Adams, *Letters of Mrs. Adams*, 3rd ed. in 2 vols. (Boston: Charles C. Little and James Brown, 1841), 2:47.
AA to MW, September 1784, Reel 363, Adams Papers, the Massachusetts Historical Society, Boston.
2. AA to Royall Tyler, January 4, 1785, Reel 364, Adams Papers.
3. AA to MC, December 12, 1784, *Letters of Mrs. Adams*, 2:63.
AA to Royall Tyler, January 4, 1785, Reel 364, Adams Papers.
4. JA to Elbridge Gerry, December 12, 1784, JA Letterbook, Reel 107, Adams Papers.
JA to Thomas Cushing, August 27, 1784, JA Letterbook, Reel 107, Adams Papers.
5. JA to MW, May 6, 1785, Reel 107, Adams Papers.
6. Ibid.
7. Richard B. Morris, ed., *Encyclopedia of American History*, Bicentennial ed. (New York: Harper & Row, 1976), p. 134.
8. AA to MC, December 12, 1784, *Letters of Mrs. Adams*, 2:66.
Diary and Autobiography of John Adams, ed. L. H. Butterfield, 4 vols. (Cambridge: Harvard University Press, Atheneum, 1964), 3:180, n. 1.
JA to Samuel Adams, April 27, 1785, Reel 107, Adams Papers.
9. December 14, 1784, *Memoirs of John Quincy Adams*, ed. Charles Francis Adams, 2 vols. (Philadelphia: J.B. Lippincott & Co., 1874–77), 1:19.
AA to MC, December 12, 1784, *Letters of Mrs. Adams*, 2:66.
AA to MC, April 15, 1785, The Abigail Adams Letters, American Antiquarian Society, Worcester, Massachusetts.

10. AA to MC, April 15, 1785, ibid.
AA to ESP, January 11, 1785, Shaw Family Papers, Library of Congress, Washington, D.C.
11. AA to MC, December 12, 1784, *Letters of Mrs. Adams*, 2:66.
AAS to Lucy Cranch, June 23, 1785, The Abigail Adams Letters.
12. AA to ESP, May 8, 1785, *Letters of Mrs. Adams*, 2:90.
AA to MC, May 8, 1785, *Letters of Mrs. Adams*, 2:93–4.
AA to Lucy Cranch, May 8, 1785, The Abigail Adams Letters.
13. AA to MC, May 8, 1785, *Letters of Mrs. Adams*, 2:93–5.
14. AA to MC, May 10, 1785, *Letters of Mrs. Adams*, 2:95.
AA to MC, March 14, 1785, *Letters of Mrs. Adams*, 2:85.
November 1784, Abigail Adams Smith, *Journal and Correspondence of Miss Adams*, ed. Caroline Smith De Windt, 2 vols. (New York and London: Wiley and Putnam, 1841), 1:31–2.
February 21, 1785, ibid., 1:49.
15. October 14, 1784, ibid., 1:23.
AA to MC, May 8, 1785, *Letters of Mrs. Adams*, 2:94.
16. JA to TJ, May 22, 1785, *The Adams-Jefferson Letters*, ed. Lester J. Cappon, 2 vols. (Chapel Hill: The University of North Carolina Press, 1959), 1:21.
AA to TJ, June 6, 1785, ibid., 1:28.
17. JA to TJ, May 22, 1785, ibid., 1:21.
18. Ibid., 1:22.
19. TJ to JA, May 25, 1785, ibid., 1:23.
20. AA to TJ, June 6, 1785, ibid., 1:28.

13. In Public Character

1. AA to TJ, June 6, 1785, *The Adams-Jefferson Letters,* ed. Lester J. Cappon, 2 vols. (Chapel Hill: The University of North Carolina Press, 1959), 1:29.

2. Ibid., 1:29–30.

3. *London Chronicle,* June 4–7, 1785.

AA to MC, June 24, 1785, Abigail Adams, *Letters of Mrs. Adams,* 3rd ed. in 2 vols. (Boston: Charles C. Little and James Brown, 1841), 2:96.

London Gazette, June 4, 1785.

4. For details on early ballooning, see Vincenzo Lunardi, *An Account of the first Aerial Voyage in England in a Series of Letters* (London, 1784). With this is bound his: *An account of five aerial voyages in Scotland* (London, 1786).

AA to Betsy Cranch, September 2, 1785, Smith-Townsend Collection, the Massachusetts Historical Society, Boston.

5. AA to Lucy (Mrs. Cotton) Tufts, September 3, 1785, Reel 365, Adams Papers.

6. AA to Betsy Cranch, September 2, 1785, Smith-Townsend Collection.

AA to Isaac Smith, June 30, 1785, Smith-Carter Collection, the Massachusetts Historical Society, Boston.

7. *London Chronicle,* June 2, 1785.

8. JA to TJ, June 3, 1785, *The Adams-Jefferson Letters,* 1:27–8, and see p. 27, n. 27.

9. JA to John Jay, June 2, 1785, Reel 107, Adams Papers, the Massachusetts Historical Society, Boston.

June 1, 1785, Abigail Adams Smith, *Journal and Correspondence of Miss Adams,* ed. Caroline Smith De Windt, 2 vols. (New York and London: Wiley and Putnam, 1841), 1:78.

10. *Public Advertiser,* June 6, 1785.

Ibid., June 10, 1785.

London Chronicle, June 11, 1785.

11. TJ to AA, September 25, 1785, *The Adams-Jefferson Letters,* 1:70.

12. Ibid.

13. AA to ESP, September 15, 1785, Shaw Family Papers, Library of Congress, Washington, D.C.

ESP to AA, January 2, 1786, Reel 367, Adams Papers.

14. AA to TJ, October 19, 1785, *The Adams-Jefferson Letters,* 1:84.

JA to John Jay, May 1785–February 1786, JA Letterbook, Reel 107, Adams Papers.

AA to MC, June 24, 1785, *Letters of Mrs. Adams,* 2:98–9.

15. AA to MC, June 25, 1785, ibid., 2:102.

AA to MC, August 15, 1785, The Abigail Adams Letters, American Antiquarian Society, Worcester, Massachusetts.

AA to MC, June 24, 1785, *Letters of Mrs. Adams,* 2:100.

16. AA to MC, June 24, 1785, *Letters of Mrs. Adams,* 2:100.

17. Ibid., 2:100–1.

AA to MC, June 25, 1785, ibid., 2:101–2.

AAS to JQA, July 4, 1785, Reel 365, Adams Papers.

18. AA to MC, June 26, 1785, *Letters of Mrs. Adams,* 2:102–3.

19. Ibid., 2:103–4.

20. Ibid., 2:104–5.

AA to ESP, August 15, 1785, ibid., 2:108.

21. AA to MC, June 24, 1785, ibid., 2:96–8.

22. *Diary and Autobiography of John Adams,* ed. L. H. Butterfield, 4 vols. (Cambridge: Harvard University Press, Atheneum, 1964), 3:180–1, n. 1.

23. AA to MC, June 24, 1785, *Letters of Mrs. Adams,* 2:97.

AA to ESP, August 15, 1785, ibid., 2:106.

AA to MC, August 15, 1785, The Abigail Adams Letters.

24. AA to JQA, September 6, 1785, *Letters of Mrs. Adams,* 2:113.

AA to MC [?], 1785, Reel 366, Adams Papers.

25. AA to MC, August 15, 1785, The Abigail Adams Letters.

26. AA to Isaac Smith, June 30, 1785, Smith-Carter Collection.

AA to JQA, September 6, 1785, *Letters of Mrs. Adams,* 2:114–6.

AA to ESP, August 15, 1785, ibid., 2:108.

27. *London Chronicle,* July 1, 1785.

28. AA to JQA, September 6, 1785, *Letters of Mrs. Adams,* 2:114.

AA to ESP, September 15, 1785, Shaw Family Papers.

29. JA to TJ, January 19, 1786, *The Adams-Jefferson Letters,* 1:117.

AA to JQA, September 6, 1785, *Letters of Mrs. Adams,* 2:114–5.

DAJA, 3:180–1, n. 1.

London Chronicle, July 1, 1785.

30. AA to JQA, September 6, 1785, *Letters of Mrs. Adams,* 2:114–5.

31. JA to TJ, June 7, 1785, *The Adams-Jefferson Letters,* 1:31.

32. JA to John Jay, December 3, 1785, JA Letterbook, Reel 112, Adams Papers.

33. AA to MC, September 30, 1785, *Letters of Mrs. Adams,* 2:117–8.

34. AA to ESP, March 4, 1786, ibid., 2:124–8.

AA to Lucy Cranch, April 2, 1786, ibid., 2:129–34.

35. AAS to MC, June 22, 1785, The Abigail Adams Letters.

AAS to JQA, July 4–August 11, 1785, Reel 365, Adams Papers.

36. AA to JQA, September 6, 1785, *Letters of Mrs. Adams,* 2:113–4.

37. AAS to JQA, July 4, 1785, Reel 365, Adams Papers.

38. AAS to JQA, November 27, 1785, Reel 366, Adams Papers.

39. AAS to JQA, July 4, 1785, Reel 365, Adams Papers.

40. JQA to AAS, October 1, 1785, Reel 366, Adams Papers.

41. Ibid.

42. Ibid.

43. AAS to JQA, November 27, 1785, Reel 366, Adams Papers.

44. AAS to JQA, July 4, 1785, Reel 365, Adams Papers.

45. Ibid.

46. AAS to JQA, September 24, 1785, Reel 365, Adams Papers.

47. AAS to JQA, July 4, 1785, Reel 365, Adams Papers.

AAS to JQA, February 8–27, 1786, Reel 367, Adams Papers.

48. AA to MC, January 6, 1786, The Abigail Adams Letters.

14. Circumstances and Connections Respectable

1. AA to MC, August 2, 1784, The Abigail Adams Letters, American Antiquarian Society, Worcester, Massachusetts.

2. MC to AA, October 8, 1786, Reel 369, Adams Papers, the Massachusetts Historical Society, Boston.

3. MC to AA, January 16, 1785, Reel 364, Adams Papers.

MC to AA, January 4, 1785, ibid.

4. ESP to AA, April 30, 1785, Shaw Family Papers, Library of Congress, Washington, D.C.

5. AA to CT, May 2, 1785, Reel 365, Adams Papers.

AA to Royall Tyler, January 4, 1785, Reel 364, Adams Papers.

6. MC to AA, June 4, 1785, Reel 364, Adams Papers.

7. MC to AA, July 22, 1785, Reel 365, Adams Papers.

AA to MC, August 15, 1785, The Abigail Adams Letters.

8. Ibid.

9. Ibid.

10. Ibid.

AA to JQA, August 11, 1785, Reel 365, Adams Papers.

11. AA to JQA, February 16, 1786, Reel 367, Adams Papers.

12. Ibid.

13. Ibid.

14. Ibid.

AA to TJ, June 6, 1785, *The Adams-Jefferson Letters,* ed. Lester J. Cappon, 2 vols. (Chapel Hill: The University of North Carolina Press, 1959), 1:29.

Katharine Metcalf Roof, *Colonel William Smith and Lady* (Boston: Houghton Mifflin Company, 1929), pp. 38, 92.

15. Ibid., pp. 90, 94–5.

16. Ibid., pp. 95, 101.

17. Matthew Ridley to C. W. Livingston, September 5, 1785, Matthew Ridley Papers, the Massachusetts Historical Society, Boston.

18. AA to MC, July 4, 1786, The Abigail Adams Letters.

The Two Gentlemen of Verona, act 5, sc. 4.

19. Abigail Adams Smith, *Journal and Correspondence of Miss Adams,* ed. Caroline Smith De Windt, 2 vols. (New York: Wiley and Putnam, 1841), 1: xi.

20. AA to MC, February 26, 1786, The Abigail Adams Letters.

21. Ibid.

AA to CT, January 10, 1786, Reel 367, Adams Papers.

22. AA to CT, January 10, 1786, ibid.

CT to AA, October 12, 1785, Reel 366, Adams Papers.

23. MC to AA, November 8, 1785, Reel 366, Adams Papers.

24. MC to AA, March 22, 1786, Reel 367, Adams Papers.

MC to AA, May 7, 1786, Reel 368, Adams Papers.

MC to AA, July 2, 1786, ibid.

MC to AA, July 11, 1786, ibid.

Roof, *Col. Smith,* p. 99.

25. MC to AA, February 9, 1786, Reel 367, Adams Papers.

MC to AA, April 22, 1787, Reel 369, Adams Papers.

26. AA to MC, March 21, 1786, The Abigail Adams Letters.

AA to MC, April 24, 1786, ibid.

27. The fruits of this visit were ornamental rather than political. Jefferson sat for the portrait by Mather Brown that brought great pleasure to the Adams family. Abigail informed Jefferson that the painting "dignifies a part of our room, tho it is but a poor substitute for those pleasures which we enjoy'd some months past." AA to TJ, July 23, 1786, *The Adams-Jefferson Letters,* 1: 145.

AA to MC, April 6, 1786, Abigail Adams, *Letters of Mrs. Adams,* 3rd ed. in 2 vols. (Boston: Charles C. Little and James Brown, 1841), 2:135–6.

AA to ESP, April 24, 1786, Reel 367, Adams Papers.

28. AA to MC, March 21, 1786, The Abigail Adams Letters.

AA to MC, February 26, 1786, ibid.

29. AA to MC, May 21, 1786, ibid.

AA to MC, June 13, 1786, ibid.

AA to MC, July 4, 1786, ibid.

30. AA to MC, June 13, 1786, ibid.

AA to MC, July 4, 1786, ibid.

31. AA to MC, July 4, 1786, ibid.

AA to ESP, July 19, 1786, Shaw Family Papers.

AAS to Lucy Cranch, May 25, 1786, The Abigail Adams Letters.

AA to MC, May 25, 1786, ibid.

32. JA to RC, July 4, 1786, JA Letterbook, Reel 113, Adams Papers.

AA to MC, July 4, 1786, The Abigail Adams Letters.

33. AA to MC, June 13, 1786, ibid.

AA to MC, January 26, 1786, ibid.

34. AA to MC, May 25, 1786, ibid.

35. CT to AA, October 12, 1785, Reel 366, Adams Papers.

CT to AA, April 13, 1786, Reel 367, Adams Papers.

CT to AA, July 6, 1786, Reel 368, Adams Papers.

CT to AA, August 15, 1786, *The Earliest Diary of John Adams,* ed. L. H. Butterfield (Cambridge: Harvard University Press, The Belknap Press, 1966), p. 28, n. 76. Also Reel 368, Adams Papers.

36. AA to MC, June 13, 1786, The Abigail Adams Letters.

MC to AA, July 2, 1786, Reel 368, Adams Papers.

37. MC to AA, September 24, 1786, ibid.

MC to AA, September 28, 1786, ibid.

38. Shays, a captain during the Revolution, led a disillusioned and bitterly impoverished group, initially about five hundred, mostly former soldiers, in revolt against foreclosures on their farms and homes, against the high cost of legal defense, and against the dread servitude in debtor's prison. They also wanted taxes lowered and paper money issued. What is referred to as Shays' Rebellion lasted six months, from August 1786 to the end of February 1787, ending with almost immediate pardons for all but Shays and three other leaders, who received a delayed pardon the following year. The "Tumults" engendered by Shays were of deep concern to Abigail. She aired her views of the "ignorant wrestless desperadoes" in a candid exchange with Thomas Jefferson. AA to TJ, January 29, 1787, and TJ to AA, February 22, 1787, *The Adams-Jefferson Letters,* 1: 168–9; 1:172–3. The topic is discussed more fully in chapter fifteen.

The Earliest Diary of John Adams, pp. 28–9.

39. Royall Tyler, *The Contrast* in *Dramas From the American Theatre 1762–1909,* ed. Richard Moody (Cleveland and New York: World Publishing Co., 1966), p. 34.

40. Ibid., p. 51.

41. Ibid., pp. 33–59.

42. AA to Betsy Cranch, April 2, 1786, Smith-Townsend Collection, the Massachusetts Historical Society, Boston.

43. AA to MC, April 24, 1786, The Abigail Adams Letters.
44. AA to MC, May 25, 1786, ibid. AA to MC, April 24, 1786, ibid.

45. AA to MC, April 24, 1786, ibid. AA to MC, May 25, 1786, ibid. AA to MC, July 4, 1786, ibid.

15. One of the Choice Ones of the Earth

1. AA to TJ, June 6, 1785, *The Adams-Jefferson Letters*, ed. Lester J. Cappon, 2 vols. (Chapel Hill: The University of North Carolina Press, 1959), 1:30.
TJ to AA, June 21, 1785, ibid., 1:33.
2. *The Adams-Jefferson Letters*, thirty-five letters exchanged between TJ and AA over 32 months.
3. AA to TJ, October 7, 1785, *The Adams-Jefferson Letters*, 1:79.
TJ to AA, September 25, 1785, ibid., 1:69.
4. AA to TJ, October 7, 1785, ibid., 1:79.
TJ to AA, October 11, 1785, ibid., 1:81.
AA to TJ, February 11, 1786, ibid., 1:120.
TJ to AA, November 20, 1785, ibid., 1:98.
5. AA to TJ, June 6, 1785, ibid., 1:29.
TJ to AA, June 21, 1785, ibid., 1:33–4.
TJ to AA, August 9, 1786, ibid., 1:148.
6. AA to TJ, November 24, 1785, ibid., 1:100.
TJ to AA, August 9, 1786, ibid., 1:149.
7. AA to Isaac Smith, March 12, 1787, Smith-Carter Collection, the Massachusetts Historical Society, Boston.
8. AA to TJ, February 11, 1786, *The Adams-Jefferson Letters*, 1:119.
AA to Isaac Smith, April 8, 1786, Smith-Carter Collection.
AA to ESP, November 21, 1786, Abigail Adams, *Letters of Mrs. Adams*, 3d ed. in 2 vols. (Boston: Charles C. Little and James Brown, 1841), 2:161–2.
AA to MC, March 15, 1786, The Abigail Adams Letters, American Antiquarian Society, Worcester, Massachusetts.
9. AA to ESP, November 21, 1786, *Letters of Mrs. Adams*, 2:160.
10. *Diary and Autobiography of John Adams*, ed. L. H. Butterfield, 4 vols. (Cambridge: Harvard University Press, Atheneum, 1964), 3:201, n. 1.
AA to MC, September 12, 1786, *Letters of Mrs. Adams*, 2:145.
11. *DAJA*, 3:201–2, n. 1.

AA to MC, September 12, 1786, *Letters of Mrs. Adams*, 2:145–52.
Abigail Adams Smith, *Journal and Correspondence of Miss Adams*, ed. Caroline Smith De Windt, 2 vols. (New York and London: Wiley and Putnam, 1841), 2:53–4.
12. AA to MC, January 20, 1787, *Letters of Mrs. Adams*, 2:162.
13. Ibid., 2:162–7.
14. Ibid., 2:166–7.
15. Ibid., 2:167.
16. JA to Benjamin Hichborn, January 27, 1787, *The Works of John Adams*, ed. Charles Francis Adams, 10 vols. (Boston: Little, Brown & Co., 1850–56), 9:551.
JA to Philip Mazzei, June 12, 1787, *JA Works*, 9:552.
JA to JW, January 9, 1787, *Warren-Adams Letters*, 2 vols. (Boston: the Massachusetts Historical Society, 1925), 2:281–2.
17. R. H. Lee to JA, September 3, 1787, *JA Works*, 9:553.
AA to TJ, January 29, 1787, *The Adams-Jefferson Letters*, 1:168.
18. AA to TJ, January 29, 1787, ibid., 1:168.
About the participants in Shays' Rebellion, Abigail's grandson Charles Francis Adams would write: "They breathed the full communistic spirit of the time . . . a new set of men had come forward who could neither write English nor grasp principles of political action." Charles Francis Adams, *Three Episodes of Massachusetts History* (Boston: Houghton Mifflin and Co., 1892), p. 896.
19. TJ to AA, December 21, 1786, *The Adams-Jefferson Letters*, 1:159.
AA to TJ, January 29, 1787, ibid., 1:168–9.
20. TJ to AA, February 22, 1787, ibid., 1:173.
Jefferson wrote to John Adams on February 23, 1787, to thank him for his copy of the *Defense*. He said he had read it with "infinite satisfaction and improvement," supposed it would do "great good" in America, and

hoped its "learning and good sense" would make it "an institute for our politicians." However, he asked Adams to reconsider his statement that "Congress is not a legislative, but a diplomatic assembly." Jefferson continued: "Separating into parts the whole sovereignty of our states, some of these parts are yeilded to Congress. Upon these I should think them both legislative and executive; and that they would have been judiciary also, had not the Confederation required them for certain purposes to appoint a judiciary. It has accordingly been the decision of our courts that the Confederation is a part of the law of the land, and superior in authority to the ordinary laws, because it cannot be altered by the legislature of any one state. I doubt whether they are at all a diplomatic assembly." *The Adams-Jefferson Letters*, 1:174–5.

21. TJ to AA, December 21, 1786, ibid., 1:159.

22. AA to TJ, January 29, 1787, ibid., 1:168–9.

23. AA to ESP, January 20, 1787, Shaw Family Papers, Library of Congress, Washington, D.C.

24. AA to Lucy Cranch, April 26, 1787, The Abigail Adams Letters.

AA to MC, March 16, 1787, ibid.

25. AA to Lucy Cranch, April 26, 1787, ibid.

26. AA to MC, April 28–May 11, 1787, ibid.

27. AA to TJ, June 26, 1787, *The Adams-Jefferson Letters*, 1:178.

AA to TJ, June 27, 1787, ibid., 1:179.

AA to TJ, July 6, 1787, ibid., 1:183.

Sally Hemings was the daughter of John Wayles, Thomas Jefferson's thrice-widowed father-in-law, and the mulatto slave, Betty Hemings. This made her half-sister to Martha Jefferson, and half-aunt, if there is such a designation, to little Polly. Sally Hemings was actually only fourteen years old at the time of the crossing, though she appeared older. She is also the subject of exhaustive speculation as to whether she was Thomas Jefferson's mistress while in Paris and, subsequently, the mother of his children.

28. AA to TJ, July 6, 1787, *The Adams-Jefferson Letters*, 1:183.

AA to TJ, June 26, 1787, ibid., 1:178.

29. AA to TJ, July 6, 1787, ibid., 1:183–4.

AA to TJ, July 10, 1787, ibid., 1:186–7.

30. TJ to AA, July 1, 1787, ibid., 1:179–80.

TJ to JA, July 1, 1787, ibid., 1:180–2. Mr. Jefferson was reportedly strolling along the Seine in September of 1786 with Maria Cosway, the delicate wife of the miniature painter. He was in high spirits, fell, and dislocated his wrist. The next month, he referred to the accident in a letter to Colonel Smith as a long story, "one of those follies from which good cannot come but ill may," One possible reason that Jefferson chose not to leave Paris for Polly was his expectation of a visit from Mrs. Cosway.

AA to TJ, July 6, 1787, ibid., 1:183–4.

31. AA to TJ, July 10, 1787, ibid., 1:185.

AA to MC, July 16, 1787, *Letters of Mrs. Adams*, 2:179–80.

32. JA to TJ, July 10, 1787, *The Adams-Jefferson Letters*, 1:187.

AA to TJ, June 27, 1787, ibid., 1:179.

33. AA to Lucy Cranch, April 26, 1787, The Abigail Adams Letters.

AA to MC, September 11, 1785, ibid.

AA Diary, July 20, 1787, *DAJA*, 3:203.

34. AA Diary, July 20, 1787, ibid.

35. AA to MC, September 15, 1787, *Letters of Mrs. Adams*, 2:183–4.

36. Ibid., 2:184–5.

37. Ibid., 2:189.

38. AA to Lucy Cranch, October 3, 1787, ibid., 2:191–4.

39. Ibid., 2:192–3.

40. Ibid., 2:196–7.

JA to TJ, March 1, 1787, *The Adams-Jefferson Letters*, 1:176.

41. *DAJA*, 3:217, n. 7.

JA to CT, August 27, 1787, JA Letterbook, Reel 112, Adams Papers, the Massachusetts Historical Society, Boston.

42. AA to MC, March 8, 1787, The Abigail Adams Letters.

DAJA, 3:211, n. 2.

43. AA to MW, May 14, 1787, *Warren-Adams Letters*, 2:290.

JA to TJ, March 1, 1787, *The Adams-Jefferson Letters*, 1:176.

44. AA to TJ, September 10, 1787, ibid., 1:198.

TJ to AA, October 4, 1787, ibid., 1:201.

45. TJ to JA, August 30, 1787, ibid., 1:195.
TJ to AA, October 4, 1787, ibid., 1:201.
46. AA to TJ, December 5, 1787, ibid., 1:213.
47. TJ to JA, November 13, 1787, ibid., 1:211.
JA to CT, February 12, 1788, courtesy of The New-York Historical Society, New York.
48. AA to MC, May 11, 1787, The Abigail Adams Letters.
The Selected Writings of John and John Quincy Adams, eds. Adrienne Koch and William Peden (New York: Alfred A. Knopf, 1946), p. xix.
49. AA to MC, May 25, 1786, The Abigail Adams Letters.
AA to MC, October 20, 1787, ibid.
AA to MC, February 10, 1788, ibid.
AA to MC, September 12, 1786, ibid.
50. AA to MC, February 10, 1788, ibid.
AA to MC, September 11, 1785, ibid.
51. AA to TJ, February 26, 1788, *The Adams-Jefferson Letters,* 1:227.
52. JA to AA, March 11, 1788, *Letters of John Adams Addressed to his Wife,* ed. Charles Francis

Adams, 2 vols. (Boston: Freeman and Bolles, 1841), 2:110–1.
JA to AA, March 14, 1788, ibid., 2:111–2.
53. JA to AA, March 11, 1788, ibid., 2:110–1.
JA to AA, March 14, 1788, ibid., 2:111–2.
54. TJ to AA, February 2, 1788, *The Adams-Jefferson Letters,* 1:222.
AA to TJ, February 21, 1788, ibid., 1:226–7.
55. AA to TJ, February 21, 1788, ibid.
56. AA Diary, March 30, 1788, *DAJA,* 3:214–5. Esther Field was pregnant, apparently, at the time she married John Briesler, according to a letter from ESP to MC, May 8, 1788, Library of Congress: "I am very sorry Esther has mortified and grieved sister by her foolish conduct. Why did not the silly girl read her Bible and be married before? . . . I pity sister—for, instead of Esther's being any help, she will require herself the kindest assistance. If she should be aboard ship, it must be dreary."
AA to AAS, May 29, 1788, *Journal and Correspondence,* 2:78–9.

16. In a Flurry with Politics

1. *Massachusetts Centinel,* June 18, 1788.
Diary and Autobiography of John Adams, ed. L. H. Butterfield, 4 vols. (Cambridge: Harvard University Press, Atheneum, 1964), 3:266.
2. AA to AAS, July 7, 1788, Abigail Adams Smith, *Journal and Correspondence of Miss Adams,* ed. Caroline Smith De Windt, 2 vols. (New York and London: Wiley and Putnam, 1841), 2:84–6.
AAS to AA, August 13, 1788, ibid., 2:93.
3. AA to AAS, July 7, 1788, ibid., 2:84–6.
4. JA to Thomas Brand-Hollis, December 3, 1788, *The Works of John Adams,* ed. Charles Francis Adams, 10 vols. (Boston: Little, Brown & Co., 1850–56), 9:557.
JA to Benjamin Rush, December 2, 1788, ibid., 9:556.
5. JA to Benjamin Rush, December 2, 1788, ibid.
JA to AAS, July 16, 1788, *Journal and Correspondence,* 2:87.
AAS to AA, September 7, 1788, ibid., 2:97.
JA to AAS, November 11, 1788, ibid., 2:105.

6. JA to AAS, July 16, 1788, ibid., 2:87–9.
7. AAS to JA, July 27, 1788, ibid., 2:89–93.
8. Ibid.
AAS to AA, October 5, 1788, ibid., 2:102–3.
9. AAS to JA, July 27, 1788, ibid., 2:90–2.
JA to AAS, July 16, 1788, ibid., 2:88–9.
AAS to AA, October 5, 1788, ibid., 2:102–3.
10. JA to AA, December 2, 1788, *Letters of John Adams Addressed to his Wife,* ed. Charles Francis Adams, 2 vols. (Boston: Freeman and Bolles, 1841), 2:113–4.
11. JA to William McCreary, September 1788, JA Letterbook, Reel 93, Adams Papers, the Massachusetts Historical Society, Boston.
12. JA to Thomas Brand-Hollis, December 3, 1788, *JA Works,* 9:557.
Richard B. Morris, ed., *Encyclopedia of American History,* Bicentennial ed. (New York: Harper & Row, 1976), pp. 145–6.
13. AA to ESP, September 27, 1789, Abigail Adams, *Letters of Mrs. Adams,* 3rd ed. in 2

vols. (Boston: Charles C. Little and James Brown, 1841), 2:203.

14. AA to MC, June 28, 1789, *New Letters of Abigail Adams*, ed. Stewart Mitchell (Boston: Houghton Mifflin Company, 1947), p. 12.

AA to MC, June 19, 1789, ibid., p. 11.

15. Originally owned by Abraham Mortier, the house, called Richmond Hill, stood near what now is called Macdougal Street. John rented it from a Mrs. Jephson. It was bought on June 17, 1797, by Aaron Burr, moved, turned into a theater, and then torn down in 1849.

JA to AA, May 14, 1789, *Letters of JA,* 2:115–6.

AA to MC, January 24, 1789, *New Letters,* p. 7.

16. AA to ESP, September 27, 1789, *Letters of Mrs. Adams,* 2:201–2.

AA to Thomas Brand-Hollis, September 6, 1790, ibid., 2:204–5.

17. AA to MC, June 28, 1789, *New Letters,* pp. 12–4.

AA to MC, January 24, 1789, ibid., pp. 7–8.

AA to MC, August 9, 1789, ibid., p. 19.

AA to William Smith, August 1789, Smith-Townsend Collection, the Massachusetts Historical Society, Boston.

18. AA to MC, July 12, 1789, *New Letters,* p. 17.

AA to MC, August 9, 1789, ibid., p. 20.

AA to MC, November 3, 1789, ibid., p. 33.

19. AA to MC, August 9, 1789, ibid., p. 20.

AA to MC, November 1, 1789, ibid., p. 31.

AA to MC, November 3, 1789, ibid., p. 33.

20. AA to MC, August 9, 1789, ibid., p. 22.

AA to MC, September 1, 1789, ibid., pp. 22–3.

AA to MC, July 12, 1789, ibid., pp. 14–5.

21. AA to MC, October 11, 1789, ibid., pp. 29–30.

AA to MC, January 5, 1790, ibid., p. 35.

AA to MC, June 28, 1789, ibid., p. 13.

AA to MC, July 12, 1789, ibid., p. 15.

22. AA to MC, June 28, 1789, ibid., p. 13.

23. Description based on Wollaston's painting of Martha Washington in *The Writings of George Washington,* Jared Sparks, ed., 12 vols. (Boston: American Stationers' Company, 1837) 1:105, see facing page.

Ibid., 1:457, note, "So little remains, which is known to have come from the pen of this lady. . . ."

Janet Whitney, *Abigail Adams* (Boston: Little, Brown & Co., 1947), p. 295.

24. Martha Washington to MW, December 26, 1789, *The Writings of George Washington,* 1:457–9, n. Janet Whitney, *Abigail Adams* (Boston: Little, Brown & Co., 1947), p. 295.

AA to MC, July 12, 1789, *New Letters,* p. 15.

AA to MC, October 11, 1789, ibid., p. 30.

25. AA to MC, July 12, 1789, ibid., p. 15.

26. Ibid.

27. AA to MC, January 5, 1790, ibid., p. 35.

28. Ibid.

29. AA to MC, May 30, 1790, ibid., p. 49.

30. AA to MC, September 1, 1789, ibid., p. 23.

AA to MC, January 5, 1790, ibid., p. 36.

AA to MC, March 15, 1790, ibid., p. 41.

AA to CT, January 18, 1790, [courtesy of] The New-York Historical Society, New York.

31. AA to CT, April 18, 1790, [Courtesy of] The New-York Historical Society.

32. AA to MC, August 9, 1789, *New Letters,* pp. 19–21.

33. Ibid, pp. 20–1.

34. JA to Alexander Jardine, June 1, 1790, *JA Works,* 9:567.

JA to Richard Price, April 19, 1790, ibid., 9:563–5.

35. JA to James Sullivan, September 17, 1789, ibid., 9:562.

JA to Alexander Jardine, June 1, 1790, ibid., 9:567.

JA to Benjamin Rush, April 18, 1790, 9:565.

John Adams, "Discourses on Davila" in *The Selected Writings of John and John Quincy Adams,* ed. Adrienne Koch and William Peden (New York: Alfred A. Knopf, 1946), pp. 125–35.

36. John Adams, "A Defense of the Constitutions of Government of the United States of America" in Adrienne Koch, ed., *The American Enlightenment* (New York: George Braziller, 1965), p. 255.

37. JA to Benjamin Rush, April 18, 1790, *JA Works,* 9:565.

AA to MC, August 9, 1789, *New Letters,* p. 21.

38. AA to MC, September 1, 1789, ibid., pp. 24–6. Church's poem is reprinted in a footnote to this letter.

39. Ibid., p. 26, quoting a favorite proverb of Abigail's: "As the bird by wandering, as the

swallow by flying, so the curse causeless shall not come."

40. AA to MC, March 21, 1790, ibid., p. 43.
AA to MC, April 3, 1790, ibid., p. 44.
AA to MC, April 21, 1790, ibid., p. 46.
AA to MC, September 1, 1789, ibid., p. 23.
41. AA to MC, April 28, 1790, ibid., pp. 46–8.
AA to MC, May 30, 1790, ibid., pp. 48–9.
42. AA to CT, October 5, 1789, [Courtesy of] The New-York Historical Society.
AA to MC, June 13, 1790, *New Letters*, p. 51.
43. AA to MC, July 27, 1790, ibid., p. 55, n. 4.
AA to MC, September 1, 1789, ibid., p. 23.
Hamilton's proposal for funding debts incurred by the United States was taken up during the second session of the first Congress. Three major points of frenzied debate revolved around: 1) foreign debt of $11,710,378, due France, Holland, and Spain; 2) domestic debt, incurred by the Continental Congress, amounting to $42,414,085; and 3) state debts of $25,000,000. Agreement was reached that foreign and domestic debts be paid; state debts were assumed to the amount of $21,500,000. James Schouler, *History of the United States of America under the Constitution*, rev. ed in 7 vols. (1880–1894; reprinted, New York: Kraus Reprint Co., 1970), pp. 145, 155.
44. AA to MC, August 29, 1790, ibid., pp. 57–8.
AA to MC, August 8, 1790, *New Letters*, p. 56.
Some 25 Creek warriors, led by Andrew McGillivray, the half-breed son of a Scottish-born Tory father, arrived in New York on July 21, 1790. The next day, Washington approved an act of Congress which forbade all trade with Indian tribes without a license from the President, and prohibited purchase of Indian lands except under government authority. For further details see Schouler, *History*, 1:171–2.
45. AA to MC, October 3, 1790, *New Letters*, p. 59.
AA to CT, October 3, 1790, [Courtesy of] The New-York Historical Society.
AA to MC, October 10, 1790, *New Letters*, pp. 60–1.
46. AA to CT, October 3, 1790, [Courtesy of] The New-York Historical Society.
AA to MC, October 10, 1790, *New Letters*, p. 61.
47. AA to MC, October 10, 1790, ibid., pp. 60–1.
AA to MC, October 25, 1790, ibid., p. 63.

17. A Prospect of Calamities

1. AA to AAS, November 21, 1790, Abigail Adams, *Letters of Mrs. Adams*, 3rd ed. in 2 vols. (Boston: Charles C. Little and James Brown, 1841), 2:207–9, 213.
2. Ibid., 2:209.
AA to AAS, November 28, 1790, ibid., 2:210.
3. AA to AAS, November 21, 1790, ibid., 2:207.
AA to MC, January 9, 1791, *New Letters of Abigail Adams*, ed. Stewart Mitchell (Boston: Houghton Mifflin Company, 1947), p. 67.
4. AA to ESP, March 20, 1791, *Letters of Mrs. Adams*, 2:222.
AA to AAS, December 26, 1790, ibid., 2:211.
AA to AAS, January 8, 1791, ibid., 2:213–4.
5. AA to AAS, December 26, 1790, ibid., 2:212.
AA to ESP, March 20, 1791, ibid., 2:221–2.
6. AA to CT, March 11, 1791, [Courtesy of] The New-York Historical Society, New York.
7. Ibid.
8. AA to MC, December 12, 1790, *New Letters*, p. 67.
AA to CT, April 2, 1790, [Courtesy of] The New-York Historical Society.
AA to ESP, March 20, 1791, *Letters of Mrs. Adams*, 2:221–2.
9. AA to JQA, September 9, 1790, Reel 374, Adams Papers, the Massachusetts Historical Society, Boston.
10. Ibid.
11. JQA to JA, August 9, 1790, ibid.
12. August 14, 1756, *Diary and Autobiography of John Adams*, ed. L. H. Butterfield, 4 vols. (Cambridge: Harvard University Press, Atheneum, 1964) 1:41.
JQA to JA, August 9, 1790, Reel 374, Adams Papers.
13. JQA to JA, August 9, 1790, ibid.

JQA to AA, August 14, 1790, ibid.

14. JA to JQA, October 4, 1790, ibid.

15. AA to JQA, August 20, 1790, ibid.

16. JQA to AA, August 14, 1790, ibid.

17. AAS to JQA, June 6, 1790, Reel 373, Adams Papers.

18. James Bridges to JQA, January 28, 1790, ibid.

AAS to JQA, April 18, 1790, ibid.

19. AAS to JQA, April 18, 1790, ibid.

AAS to JQA, June 6, 1790, ibid.

20. ESP to AA, September 28, 1790, Reel 374, Adams Papers.

MC to AA, December 12, 1790, ibid.

21. JQA to AA, August 14, 1790, ibid.

AA to JQA, August 20, 1790, ibid.

AA to JQA, September 3, 1790, ibid.

Another young woman named Nancy, the future Mrs. Lyle, said to have been admired by John Quincy and his mother, was the niece of William Hamilton, from whom the Adamses rented Bush Hill in Philadelphia. Bush Hill was named and built by Andrew Hamilton, who died in 1740, one year after its completion. It was passed on to James Hamilton and then to his nephew William. *Encyclopedia of Philadelphia*, by Joseph Jackson (Harrisburg, Pennsylvania, the National Historic Association), 2:354 and Ashmead's newspaper cuttings, vol. 10, pp. 54–55.

22. AA to JQA, September 22, 1790, Reel 374, Adams Papers.

AA to JQA, August 20, 1790, ibid.

23. AA to JQA, September 22, 1790, ibid.

24. JQA to AA, August 29, 1790, ibid.

25. James Bridges to JQA, September 28, 1790, ibid.

26. AA to JQA, November 7, 1790, ibid.

JQA to AA, October 7, 1790, ibid.

27. AA to JQA, November 7, 1790, ibid.

28. Ibid.

JQA to AA, November 20, 1790, ibid.

AA to JQA, December 26, 1790, ibid.

29. JQA to AA, November 20, 1790, ibid.

AA to JQA, December 26, 1790, ibid.

30. JQA to AA, November 20, 1790, ibid.

James Bridges to JQA, April 20, 1791, ibid.

JQA to TBA, April 2, 1791, ibid.

JQA to TBA, April 20, 1791, ibid.

31. JA to JQA, June 1791, Reel 375, Adams Papers.

AA to JQA, April 18, 1791, Reel 374, Adams Papers.

32. James Bridges to JQA, September 28, 1790, ibid.

33. JQA to TBA, October 28, 1791, Reel 375, Adams Papers.

34. James Bridges to JQA, June 1791–December 1792, ibid.

James Bridges to JQA, January 23, 1792, ibid.

35. AA to MC, December 12, 1790, *New Letters*, pp. 66–7.

AA to AAS, December 26, 1790, *Letters of Mrs. Adams*, 2:211–2.

AA to JQA, December 26, 1790, Reel 374, Adams Papers.

WSS to Benjamin Walker, June 22, 1792, Katharine Metcalf Roof, *Colonel William Smith and Lady* (Boston: Houghton Mifflin Company, 1929), p. 215.

36. AA to MC, December 12, 1790, *New Letters*, pp. 67.

AA to MC, January 9, 1791, ibid., p. 68.

37. AAS to Lucy Cranch, May 6, 1785, The Abigail Adams Letters, American Antiquarian Society, Worcester, Massachusetts.

AA to AAS, January 25, 1791, *Letters of Mrs. Adams*, 2:216.

AA to AAS, February 21, 1791, ibid., 2:218.

38. AA to AAS, January 8, 1791, ibid., 2:214.

AA to AAS, February 21, 1791, ibid., 2:218–9.

39. AA to AAS, January 8, 1791, *Letters of Mrs. Adams*, 2:212–3.

40. AA to AAS, January 25, 1791, ibid., 2:216.

41. JA to WSS, March 14, 1791, Abigail Adams Smith, *Journal and Correspondence of Miss Adams*, ed. Caroline Smith De Windt, 2 vols. (New York and London: Wiley and Putnam, 1841), 2:111–2.

42. AA to WSS, March 16, 1791, ibid., 2:108–9.

43. AA to AAS, January 25, 1791, *Letters of Mrs. Adams*, 2:216.

Autobiography, January 1776, *Diary and Autobiography of John Adams*, 3:330.

44. *The Adams-Jefferson Letters*, ed. Lester J. Cappon, 2 vols. (Chapel Hill: The University of North Carolina Press, 1959), 1:240.

The Life and Major Writings of Thomas Paine, ed. Philip S. Foner (Secaucus, New Jersey: The Citadel Press, 1974), p. 244.

Thomas Paine, "Rights of Man," in *The Life and Major Writings of Thomas Paine*, p. 251.

45. *The Selected Writings of John and John Quincy Adams*, ed. Adrienne Koch and William Peden (New York: Alfred A. Knopf, 1946), p. 226.

JA to TJ, July 15, 1813, *The Adams-Jefferson Letters*, 2:357–8.

46. See chap. 16, nn. 35–39 and accompanying text.

"Rights of Man," in *The Life and Major Writings of Thomas Paine*, p. 251.

47. JA to Benjamin Rush, April 18, 1790, *The Works of John Adams*, ed. Charles Francis Adams, 10 vols. (Boston: Little, Brown & Co., 1850–56), 9:565. Also, 6:232–7; 246–8; 252; 274–7.

48. JA to Marquis de Lafayette, May 21, 1782, *JA Works*, 7:593.

49. AA to CT, June 14, 1791, [Courtesy of] The New-York Historical Society.

JA to Marquis de Lafayette, May 21, 1782, *JA Works*, 7:593.

50. JA to Benjamin Rush, April 18, 1790, *JA Works*, 9:565.

51. Ibid.

52. Ibid.

Selected Writings of JA and JQA, p. 225.

53. Ibid., p. 226.

54. Ibid.

55. John Quincy Adams and Charles Francis Adams, *The Life of John Adams*, 2 vols. (New York: Haskell House Publishers, 1968), 2:150–1.

56. TJ to JA, July 17, 1791, *The Adams-Jefferson Letters*, 1:245–6.

57. Ibid., 1:246.

58. TJ to George Washington, May 8, 1791, *The Papers of Thomas Jefferson, Princeton University*, ed. Julian Boyd, 21 vols. (Princeton, N.J.: Princeton University Press, 1950–), 20:291.

TJ to James Madison, May 9, 1791, ibid., 20:293.

TJ to Thomas Mann Randolph, July 3, 1791, *The Life and Selected Writings of Thomas Jefferson*, ed. Adrienne Koch and William Peden (New York: The Modern Library, 1972), p. 505.

59. JA to TJ, July 29, 1791, *The Adams-Jefferson Letters*, 1:247–8.

60. Ibid., 1:249.

61. Ibid., 1:248–9.

The American Enlightenment, ed. Adrienne Koch (New York: George Braziller, 1965), p. 261.

62. JA to TJ, July 29, 1791, *The Adams-Jefferson Letters*, 1:249.

63. Ibid., 1:250.

64. TJ to JA, August 30, 1791, ibid., 1:250–1.

65. Ibid., 1:251–2.

AA to TJ, May 20, 1804, ibid., 1:269.

66. AA to MC, October 30, 1791, *New Letters*, p. 74.

AA to MC, December 18, 1791, ibid., pp. 74–5.

67. AA to MC, December 12, 1790, ibid., pp. 65–6.

AA to AAS, December 26, 1790, *Letters of Mrs. Adams*, 2:210–1.

AA to ESP, March 20, 1791, ibid., 2:220–1.

AA to MC, February 5, 1792, *New Letters*, p. 77.

AA to MC, March 20, 1792, ibid., pp. 78–9.

AA to MC, April 20, 1792, ibid., pp. 81–2.

68. AA to MC, February 5, 1792, ibid., p. 77.

69. Roof, *Col. Smith*, (Boston: Houghton Mifflin Company, 1929), pp. 210–2, 232.

AA to MC, March 29, 1792, *New Letters*, p. 80.

70. JA to AA, April 15, 1794, *Letters of John Adams Addressed to his Wife*, ed. Charles Francis Adams, 2 vols. (Boston: Freeman and Bolles, 1841), 2:155–6.

71. JA to AA, January 9, 1793, ibid., 2:117–8.

JA to AA, May 17, 1794, ibid., 2:160.

JA to AA, January 5, 1795, ibid., 2:173.

72. JA to AA, April 3, 1794, ibid., 2:150–1.

JA to AA, January 22, 1794, ibid., 2:139.

JA to AA, January 24, 1793, ibid., 2:122.

73. JA to AA, December 19, 1793, ibid., 2:134.

74. JA to AAS, October 29, 1792, *Journal and Correspondence*, 2:124.

JA to AA, December 4, 1796, *Letters of JA*, 2:232–3.

JA to AAS, January 7, 1794, *Journal and Correspondence*, 2:127, 130.

JA to AA, March 2, 1794, *Letters of JA*, 2:145.

JA to AA, December 5, 1793, ibid., 2:130–1.

AA to AAS, February 3, 1794, *Letters of Mrs. Adams*, 2:224.

75. JA to AA, April 3, 1794, *Letters of JA,* 2:150.

JA to AA, January 24, 1793, ibid., 2:121.

AA to TBA, November 8, 1796, *Letters of Mrs. Adams,* 2:232.

76. Ibid.

JA to AA, March 1, 1796, *Letters of JA,* 2:206.

77. JA to AA, November 19, 1794, ibid., 2:167.

78. JA to AA, February 20, 1796, *Letters of JA,* 2:203.

79. Washington was reelected with 132 votes; George Clinton received 50 votes from the anti-Federalist opposition.

JA to AA, January 9, 1793, ibid., 2:117.

JA to AA, December 19, 1793, ibid., 2:133.

JA to AA, April 19, 1794, ibid., 2:156–7.

JA to AA, April 16, 1796, ibid., 2:221.

80. JA to AA, January 7, 1796, ibid., 2:189.

81. Ibid.

JA to AA, February 15, 1796, ibid., 2:201–2.

82. JA to AA, February 10, 1796, ibid., 2:197–8.

JA to AA, February 15, 1796, ibid., 2:202.

18. Splendid Misery

1. AA to Elbridge Gerry, December 31, 1796, *Proceedings of the Massachusetts Historical Society,* 57:499 (1923–24).

2. Richard B. Morris, ed., *Encyclopedia of American History,* Bicentennial ed. (New York: Harper & Row, 1976), p. 154.

AA to TBA, November 8, 1796, Abigail Adams, *Letters of Mrs. Adams,* 3rd ed. in 2 vols. (Boston: Charles C. Little and James Brown, 1841), 2:232.

AA to Elbridge Gerry, December 31, 1796, *MHS Proceedings,* 57:499.

3. AA to TBA, November 8, 1796, *Letters of Mrs. Adams,* 2:232.

4. JA to Thomas Welsh, March 10, 1797, JA Letterbook, Reel 117, Adams Papers, the Massachusetts Historical Society, Boston.

AA to TBA, November 8, 1796, *Letters of Mrs. Adams,* 2:231.

5. TJ to JA, December 28, 1796, *The Adams-Jefferson Letters,* ed. Lester J. Cappon, 2 vols. (Chapel Hill: The University of North Carolina Press, 1959) 1:262–3.

Jefferson, who resigned as Secretary of State on July 31, 1793, actually left office that December 31. Jefferson was pro-France, Washington less so, and inclined to consult Hamilton on foreign affairs.

6. TJ to JA, December 28, 1796, *The Adams-Jefferson Letters,* 1:263.

7. Ibid., 1:262, n. 54.

TJ to James Madison, January 1, 1797, *The Life and Selected Writings of Thomas Jefferson,* ed. Adrienne Koch and William Peden (New York: The Modern Library, 1972), p. 539.

8. TJ to James Madison, January 1, 1797, ibid., pp. 539–40.

9. AA to Elbridge Gerry, December 31, 1796, *MHS Proceedings,* 57:499.

10. JA to Henry Knox, March 30, 1797, JA Letterbook, Reel 117, Adams Papers.

11. JA to Tristram Dalton, January 19, 1797, JA Letterbook, Reel 117, Adams Papers.

JA to Elbridge Gerry, February 20, 1797, JA Letterbook, Reel 117, Adams Papers.

12. TJ to Elbridge Gerry, May 13, 1797, *Writings of Thomas Jefferson,* pp. 540–1.

13. TJ to Philip Mazzei, April 24, 1796, ibid., p. 537.

14. Ibid.

TJ to Elbridge Gerry, May 13, 1797, ibid., p. 541.

15. AA to Elbridge Gerry, December 31, 1796, *MHS Proceedings,* 57:500.

JA to Thomas Welsh, March 10, 1797, JA Letterbook, Reel 117, Adams Papers.

16. AA to Elbridge Gerry, December 31, 1796, *MHS Proceedings,* 57:500.

17. Ibid., 57:499.

AA to TBA, November 8, 1796, *Letters of Mrs. Adams,* 2:232.

18. AA to JA, February 8, 1797, ibid., 2:235–6.

19. JA to AA, February 9, 1797, *Letters of John Adams Addressed to his Wife,* ed. Charles Francis Adams, 2 vols. (Boston: Freeman and Bolles, 1841), 2:243.

JA to AA, March 5, 1797, ibid., 2:244–5.

20. JA to AA, March 5, 1797, ibid.

21. *The Works of John Adams*, ed. Charles Francis Adams, 10 vols. (Boston: Little, Brown & Co., 1850–1856), 9:105–11.

22. JA to AA, March 5, 1797, *Letters of JA,* 2:245.

JA to AA, March 9, 1797, ibid., 2:247.

JA to AA, March 17, 1797, ibid., 2:252.

23. JA to AA, March 9, 1797, ibid., 2:247.

JA to AA, March 13, 1797, ibid., 2:250.

24. JA to AA, March 17, 1797, ibid., 2:252.

25. JA to AA, March 9, 1797, ibid., 2:248.

JA to AA, March 13, 1797, ibid., 2:250.

JA to AA, April 24, 1797, ibid., 2:253.

26. AA to JA, April 26, 1797, *Letters of Mrs. Adams,* 2:236–7.

27. AA to MC, May 5, 1797, *New Letters of Abigail Adams,* ed. Stewart Mitchell (Boston: Houghton Mifflin Company, 1947), p. 88.

AA to MC, May 16, 1797, ibid., p. 89.

JA to AA, March 2, 1793, *Letters of JA,* 2:128–9.

28. JA to AA, March 2, 1793, ibid., 2:129.

29. AA to MC, May 16, 1797, *New Letters,* p. 89.

30. AA to MC, April 30, 1797, ibid., p. 87.

AA to MC, May 16, 1797, ibid., pp. 89–90.

31. AA to MC, May 16, 1797, ibid., p. 90.

AA to MC, May 24, 1797, ibid., p. 91.

32. JA to JQA, March 31, 1797, James Schouler, *History of the United States of America under the Constitution,* rev ed. in 7 vols. (1880–1894; reprint ed., New York: Kraus Reprint Co., 1970), 1: 363–7, 385.

AA to MC, May 16, 1797, *New Letters,* p. 90.

33. JA to AA, April 24, 1797, *Letters of JA,* 2:254.

AA to MC, May 24, 1797, *New Letters,* pp. 91–2.

34. Schouler, 1:356.

35. AA to TBA, November 8, 1796, *Letters of Mrs. Adams,* 2:233.

AA to MC, June 3, 1797, *New Letters,* p. 94.

36. AA to MC, June 3, 1797, ibid., pp. 94–5.

37. AA to MC, May 24, 1797, ibid., p. 92.

38. *Aurora,* May 19–20, 1797.

39. *Aurora,* May 20, 1797, June 6, 1797.

40. AA to MC, June 3, 1797, *New Letters,* p. 94.

Schouler, 1:367.

AA to MC, June 23, 1797, *New Letters,* p. 99.

41. *Aurora,* June 6, 1797.

AA to MC, June 3, 1797, *New Letters,* p. 95.

Aurora, January 30, 1797.

42. AA to MC, June 23, 1797, *New Letters,* p. 99.

AA to MC, June 6, 1797, ibid., p. 96.

AA to MC, June 3, 1797, ibid., p. 95.

43. George Washington to JA, February 20, 1797, Jared Sparks, *The Writings of George Washington,* 12 vols. (Boston: Russell, Shattuck, and Williams, 1836), 11:188.

44. JQA to AA, November 14, 1796, *Memoirs of John Quincy Adams,* ed. Charles Francis Adams, 2 vols. (Philadelphia: J.B. Lippincott & Co., 1874–77), 1:194.

45. AA to MC, June 3, 1797, *New Letters,* p. 95.

AA to William Smith, December 18, 1797, Smith-Townsend Collection, the Massachusetts Historical Society, Boston.

JA to JQA, June 2, 1797, JA Letterbook, Reel 117, Adams Papers.

46. AA to MC, June 8, 1797, *New Letters,* pp. 96–7.

47. Ibid., p. 97.

48. AA to William Smith, November 21, 1797, Smith-Townsend Collection.

AA to MC, December 26, 1797, *New Letters,* p. 120.

AA to MC (enclosed with letter of December 12, 1797), ibid., pp. 118–9.

49. AA to MC, June 23, 1797, ibid., pp. 98–9.

AA to MC, July 21, 1797, ibid., p. 104.

50. AA to MC, July 6, 1797, ibid., p. 101.

AA to MC, July 19, 1797, ibid., p. 104.

AA to MC, July 29, 1797, ibid., pp. 106–7.

AA to MC, June 23, 1797, ibid., p. 99.

AA to William Smith, July 19, 1797, Smith-Townsend Collection.

AA to William Smith, July 29, 1797, ibid.

51. Abigail was indirectly related to the Greenleafs. James Greenleaf's sister, Anna, married Abigail's nephew, William Cranch; William's sister, Lucy, married Greenleaf's brother, John.

AA to MC, June 8, 1797, *New Letters,* p. 97.

AA to MC, July 29, 1797, ibid., p. 106.

52. AA to MC, June 8, 1797, ibid., pp. 97–8.

AA to MC, February 21, 1798, ibid., pp. 134–5.

53. AA to MC, July 6, 1797, ibid., pp. 100–1.

Ibid.

Blount was expelled from Congress on July 8, 1797, found guilty "of a high misdemeanour, entirely inconsistent with his public trust and duty as a Senator." Impeachment proceedings foundered when the exiled Blount was elected to Tennessee's Senate and, as its president, declined to appear before the Senate in person. Blount was abetted further by his lawyer, who claimed his client, having already been expelled from the Senate, was no longer subject to impeachment under regulations of the federal Constitution. "And so, like most later ones, the first of federal impeachment trials in our history was lost in legal convolutions," James Schouler concluded in his *History of the United States,* dated 1880.

54. AA to MC, July 6, 1797, *New Letters,* p. 101.

AA to MC, July 11, 1797, ibid., p. 103.

AA to MC, July 19, 1797, ibid., p. 104.

55. AA to William Smith, June 10, 1797, Smith-Townsend Collection.

AA to William Smith, July 19, 1797, ibid.

56. July 26, 1797, *JQA Memoirs,* 1:199.

Henry Adams, *The Education of Henry Adams,* Sentry ed. (Boston: Houghton Mifflin Company, 1961), p. 17.

JA to JQA, October 25, 1797, JA Letterbook, Reel 119, Adams Papers.

57. *The Education of Henry Adams,* p. 17.

JQA to AA, February 28, 1796, Reel 381, Adams Papers.

58. AA to JA, March 20, 1796, Reel 381, Adams Papers.

CA to JQA, April 24, 1796, ibid.

59. AA to JQA, February 29, 1796, ibid.

60. Ibid.

61. JQA to AA, February 20, 1796, ibid.

JQA to AA, February 28, 1796, ibid.

JQA to AA, March 20, 1796, ibid.

JQA to AA, March 30, 1796, ibid.

62. JA to JQA, May 19, 1796, ibid.

AA to JQA, May 20, 1796, ibid.

63. AA to JQA, May 25, 1796, ibid.

AA to TBA, June 10, 1796, ibid.

64. JQA to AA, February 8, 1797, Reel 383, Adams Papers.

65. JQA to LCA, June 2, 1796, Reel 381, Adams Papers.

JQA to AA, June 30, 1796, ibid.

66. JQA to AA, May 5, 1796, ibid.

67. JQA to AA, January 18, 1797, Reel 383, Adams Papers.

JQA to AA, February 8, 1797, ibid.

JQA to AA, June 30, 1796, Reel 381, Adams Papers.

68. JQA to AA, May 5, 1796, Reel 383, Adams Papers.

JQA to LCA, February 7, 1797, Reel 383, ibid. See also January 20, 1797.

JQA to LCA, February 12, 1797, Reel 383, Adams Papers.

69. Joshua Johnson to JQA, November 29, 1796, Reel 382, Adams Papers.

Joshua Johnson to JQA, December 16, 1796, ibid.

JQA to Joshua Johnson, January 9, 1797, Reel 383, Adams Papers.

JQA to LCA, January 10, 1797, ibid.

JQA to LCA, January 7, 1797, ibid.

70. JQA to LCA, January 10, 1797, ibid.

71. LCA to JQA, January 17, 1797, ibid.

72. Ibid.

73. JQA to AA, January 18, 1797, ibid.

74. Ibid.

75. Ibid.

76. Ibid.

77. JQA to AA, July 6, 1797, Reel 385, Adams Papers.

JQA to JA, July 22, 1797, ibid.

AA to ESP, September 25, 1797, Shaw Family Papers, Library of Congress, Washington, D.C.

78. JQA and LCA to JA and AA, July 28, 1797, Reel 385, Adams Papers.

79. August 5, 1828, *Diary of Charles Francis Adams,* vols. 1–2 ed. Aida Dipace Donald and David Donald, 6 vols. to date (Cambridge: Harvard University Press, The Belknap Press, 1964), 2:264, n. 1.

Louisa Catherine Adams, *The Adventures of a Nobody,* Reel 269, Adams Papers.

80. Ibid.

81. AA to William Cranch, November 19, 1797, Reel 386, Adams Papers.

82. AA to MC, October 31, 1797, *New Letters,* p. 110.

AA to MC, December 12, 1797, ibid., p. 116.

83. AA to MC, November 15, 1797, *New Letters*, p. 111.

84. AA to MC, October 22, 1797, ibid., pp. 108–9.

AA to MC, November 15, 1797, ibid., pp. 110–1.

AA to MC, December 26, 1797, ibid., p. 120.

85. AA to MC, October 31, 1797, ibid., p. 109.

AA to MC, November 15, 1797, ibid., p. 111.

86. AA to MC, October 31, 1797, ibid., pp. 109–10.

AA to MC, November 15, 1797, ibid., p. 111.

AA to MC, November 28, 1797, ibid., p. 113.

AA to MC, February 6, 1798, ibid., pp. 130–1.

87. AA to MC, April 26, 1798, ibid., p. 166.

AA to MC, February 6, 1798, ibid., p. 130.

AA to MC, January 5, 1798, ibid., p. 123.

88. AA to MC, January 20, 1798, ibid., p. 124.

89. Ibid., pp. 124–5.

90. AA to MC, February [1–5], 1798, ibid., pp. 126–8.

For an example of Abigail's ardent public-relations efforts on behalf of the President, it is worth looking at her letter to Mrs. Cranch on February 28, 1798. She notes here that she had seen a copy of the *Columbian Centinel* of February 17 in which she recognizes her own writing: "I saw the centinal last Saturday and thought I knew my own Letter, but did not know whether it was an extract from one to you, or to Mr. Smith, to whom I sometimes freely scrible." The letter in the *Centinel*, signed "A Correspondent," was edited for publication, most likely, by Richard Cranch.

The letter reads: "A writer in the Chronicle of yesterday, under the signature of Plain Truth asserts 'that the President of the United States received dispatches from France *a month ago,* notwithstanding which the most profound secrecy has been maintained on this all-important subject.' Under this assertion, the writer proceeds to abuse the President and deceive the public. To prevent this incendiary from deceiving the public, you may from good authority declare the assertion of Plain Truth, to be without the least foundation. By letters from Philadelphia to the 6th February, not a word at that time had been received by the Executive from our envoys at Paris. Letters had been received from Mr. King as late as October, and from Mr. Murray, at the Hague, to the 10th November. Those gentlemen at that time were as much in the dark with respect to our Envoys, as we are here. The character of the President for patriotism and integrity is too firmly fixed with every true American, to be injured in the least by the abuse of such a vile incendiary as Plain Truth." *New Letters*, p. 136, n. 1.

91. AA to MC, February 15, 1798, *New Letters*, p. 133.

92. Ibid.

AA to MC, February 28, 1798, ibid., p. 137.

93. Ibid.

94. Ibid.

95. AA to MC, March 27, 1798, ibid., pp. 147–8.

AA to MC, March 13, 1798, ibid., pp. 143–4.

96. Ibid.

AA to MC, March 14, 1798, ibid., p. 145.

97. AA to MC, March 13, 1798, ibid., pp. 143–4.

AA to MC, March 27, 1798, ibid., p. 148.

98. AA to MC, March 13, 1798, ibid., p. 144.

19. Enough of Public and Private Anxiety

1. AA to MC, April 26, 1798, *New Letters of Abigail Adams,* ed. Stewart Mitchell (Boston: Houghton Mifflin Company, 1947), pp. 164–5.

Joseph Hopkinson, "Hail Columbia" adapted to the President's March sung at the theater by Mr. Gilbert Fox (Philadelphia: J. Ormrod, 1798).

2. AA to MC, April 26, 1798, *New Letters,* pp. 164–5.

3. AA to MC, April 26, 1798, *New Letters,* pp. 164–5.

AA to William Shaw, March 20, 1798, Shaw Family Papers, Library of Congress, Washington, D.C.

4. AA to MC, April 26, 1798, *New Letters*, p. 165.

James Schouler, *History of the United States of America under the Constitution*, rev. ed. in 7 vols. (1880–1894; reprinted, New York: Kraus Reprint Co., 1970), 1:385–93.

AA to MC, April 22, 1798, *New Letters*, p. 162.

5. AA to MC, April 4, 1798, ibid., p. 151, n. 3. (Mention has been made of a fourth agent, Madame de Villette, widow of a Royalist Colonel.)

Schouler, 1:385–93.

JA to Congress, March 19, 1798, John Adams, *The Works of John Adams*, ed. Charles Francis Adams, 10 vols. (Boston: Little, Brown and Co., 1850–1856), vol. 9:156.

AA to MC, March 20, 1798, *New Letters*, p. 196.

6. AA to MC, April 4, 1798, ibid., pp. 150–1.

7. Ibid., p. 151.

8. Ibid., p. 152.

9. Ibid.

AA to MC, July 3, 1798, ibid., p. 199.

AA to William Smith, April 8, 1798, Smith-Townsend Collection, the Massachusetts Historical Society, Boston.

AA to MC, April 7, 1798, *New Letters*, p. 154.

AA to MW, April 25, 1798, *Warren-Adams Letters*, 2 vols. (Boston: the Massachusetts Historical Society, 1925), 2:337.

10. AA to William Smith, April 8, 1798, Smith-Townsend Collection.

AA to MC, May 20, 1798, *New Letters*, p. 176.

AA to AAS, April 11, 1798, Abigail Adams Smith, *Journal and Correspondence of Miss Adams*, ed. Caroline Smith De Windt, 2 vols. (New York and London: Wiley and Putnam, 1841), 2:151–2.

11. AA to AAS, April 11, 1798, ibid., 2:152.

AA to MC, April 13, 1798, *New Letters*, p. 156.

12. AA to MC, May 18, 1798, ibid., p. 175.

AA to MC, April 22, 1798, ibid., p. 161.

AA to MC, April 13, 1798, ibid., p. 156.

AA to MC, May 10, 1798, ibid., pp. 171–2.

13. AA to AAS, April 11, 1798, *Journal and Correspondence*, 2:152.

AA to MC, March 20, 1798, *New Letters*, p. 147.

TJ to Phillip Mazzei, April 24, 1796, Adrienne Koch, ed., *The American Enlightenment* (New York: George Braziller, 1965), p. 338.

James Madison to TJ. February 1798, ibid., p. 451.

AA to AAS, April 11, 1798, *Journal and Correspondence*, 2:153.

14. AA to MC, May 18, 1798, *New Letters*, p. 175.

AA to MC, May 20, 1798, ibid., p. 176.

15. AA to MC, May 18, 1798, ibid., p. 175.

AA to MC, May 21, 1798, ibid., p. 178.

AA to MC, May 20, 1798, ibid., p. 177.

16. AA to William Shaw, June 2, 1798, Shaw Family Papers.

17. Ibid.

18. AA to MC, May 21, 1798, *New Letters*, p. 178.

AA to William Shaw, June 2, 1798, Shaw Family Papers.

AA to MC, June 8, 1798, *New Letters*, p. 190.

19. AA to MC, June 13, 1798, ibid., p. 192.

20. Ibid.

21. AA to MW, June 17, 1798, *Warren-Adams Letters*, 2:339.

22. AA to MC, January 5, 1798, *New Letters*, p. 123.

AA to MW, June 17, 1798, *Warren-Adams Letters*, 2:339.

23. AA to MC, June 19, 1798, *New Letters*, p. 193.

AA to William Smith, June 26, 1798, Smith-Townsend Collection.

AA to MC, June 25, 1798, *New Letters*, p. 196.

24. AA to MC, July 3, 1798, ibid., p. 199.

AA to Catherine Johnson, June 6, 1798, Autograph File, Houghton Library, Harvard University, Cambridge, Massachusetts.

AA to MC, June 25, 1798, *New Letters*, p. 196.

25. AA to MC, July 3, 1798, ibid., p. 199.

JA to George Washington, July 7, 1798, Dreer Collection, Historical Society of Pennsylvania, Philadelphia.

26. AA to MC, July 3, 1798, *New Letters*, p. 199.

AA to MC, July 9, 1798, ibid., p. 201.

27. AA to MC, July 17, 1798, ibid., p. 207.
28. AA to William Smith, July 17, 1798, Smith-Townsend Collection.
AA to William Smith, July 23, 1798, ibid.
29. AA to William Smith, July 23, 1798, ibid.
AA to MC, May 26, 1798, *New Letters,* p. 179.
30. AA to MC, June 19, 1798, ibid., p. 193.
AA to William Smith, July 23, 1798, Smith-Townsend Collection.
31. AA to MC, April 26, 1798, *New Letters,* p. 166.
Aurora, July 2, 1798.
32. AA to William Smith, April 8, 1798, Smith-Townsend Collection.
33. Alexander Hamilton to Jonathon Dayton, *The Papers of Alexander Hamilton,* ed. Harold C. Syrett, 26 vols. (New York: Columbia University Press, 1961–), 23:604.
Samuel Eliot Morrison, *The Life and Letters of Harrison Gray Otis,* 2 vols. (Boston and New York: Houghton Mifflin, The Riverside Press, Cambridge, 1913), Vol. 1, p. 111.
34. AA to MC, May 26, 1798, *New Letters,* p. 179.
35. The Naturalization Act, June 18, 1798, *U.S. Statutes at Large,* 1:566; also reprinted in *Documents of American History,* ed. Henry Steele Commager, 2 vols. (Englewood Clifts, New Jersey: Prentice Hall, 1973) p. 175.
36. The Alien Act, June 25, 1798, *U.S. Statutes at Large,* 1:570; reprinted in Commager, p. 176.
37. The Alien Enemies Act, July 6, 1798, *U.S. Statutes at Large,* 1:577; reprinted in Commager, p. 177.
38. AA to MC, June 19, 1798, *New Letters,* p. 193.
The Sedition Act, July 14, 1798, *U.S. Stat-utes at Large,* 1:596–7; reprinted in Commager, pp. 177–8.
39. Sedition Act, Commager, p. 178.
40. September 2, 1836, *The Diary of John Quincy Adams,* ed. Allan Nevins (New York: Longmans, Green and Co., 1929), pp. 469–70.
41. November 16, 1798, "Kentucky Resolutions" in Commager, pp. 178–9.
December 24, 1798, "Virginia Resolutions," ibid., pp. 179–80.
TJ to Elbridge Gerry, January 26, 1799, *The Life and Selected Writings of Thomas Jefferson,* ed. Adrienne Koch and William Peden (New York: The Modern Library, 1972), p. 545.
42. JA to TJ, June 14, 1813, *The Adams-Jefferson Letters,* ed. Lester J. Cappon, 2 vols. (Chapel Hill: The University of North Carolina Press, 1959), 2:329.
JA to TJ, June 25, 1813, ibid., 2:334.
43. AA to TJ, July 1, 1804, ibid., 1:273.
44. Ibid.
45. AA to MC, March 5, 1798, *New Letters,* p. 141.
AA to MC, February 6, 1798, ibid., p. 130.
AA to MC, April 22, 1798, ibid., p. 163.
AA to MC, April 26, 1798, ibid., p. 166.
46. AA to MC, April 22, 1798, ibid., p. 160.
AA to MC, April 28, 1798, ibid., p. 167.
47. AA to MC, April 22, 1798, ibid., p. 160.
AA to MC, July 12, 1798, ibid., p. 202.
48. AA to MC, July 17, 1798, ibid., pp. 206–7.
49. AA to MC, June 27, 1798, ibid., p. 198.
AA to MC, April 4, 1798, ibid., p. 152.
JA to George Washington, October 9, 1798, JA Letterbook, Reel 119, Adams Papers, the Massachusetts Historical Society, Boston.
JA to JQA, October 16, 1798, ibid.

20. Evils of a Serious Nature

1. JA to AA, November 28, 1798, *Letters of John Adams Addressed to his Wife,* ed. Charles Francis Adams, 2 vols. (Boston: Freeman and Bolles, 1841), 2:255–6.
2. AA to William Shaw, December 14, 1798, Shaw Family Papers, Library of Congress, Washington, D.C.
3. Ibid.
AA to ESP, December 30, 1798, ibid.
4. JA to AA, December 13, 1798, *Letters of JA,* 2:256–7.
JA to AA, November 28, 1798, ibid., 2:256.
5. JA to AA, December 13, 1798, ibid., 2:257.
6. AA to Catherine Johnson, June 16, 1798, Autograph File, Houghton Library, Harvard University, Cambridge, Massachusetts.

AA to William Shaw, December 14, 1798, Shaw Family Papers.

7. AA to William Shaw, March 4, 1799, ibid.

8. AA to William Smith, July 23, 1798, Smith-Townsend Collection, the Massachusetts Historical Society, Boston.

9. Ibid.

10. Ibid.

11. JA to WSS, December 19, 1798, JA Letterbook, Reel 117, Adams Papers, the Massachusetts Historical Society, Boston.

12. Ibid.

13. Ibid.

14. JA to CA, December 21, 1798, ibid.

15. JA to WSS, May 22, 1799, JA Letterbook, Reel 119, Adams Papers.

16. AA to ESP, December 30, 1798, Shaw Family Papers.

17. Ibid.

AA to William Shaw, January 6, 1799, ibid.

18. AA to William Smith, December 26, 1798, Smith-Townsend Collection.

AA to William Smith, December 30, 1798, ibid.

AA to William Shaw, January 6, 1799, Shaw Family Papers.

19. AA to MC, January 17, 1799, New Letters of Abigail Adams, ed. Stewart Mitchell (Boston: Houghton Mifflin Company, 1947), p. 208.

AA to MC, June 13, 1798, ibid., p. 191.

AA to William Smith, December 28, 1798, Smith-Townsend Collection.

AA to William Smith, December 26, 1798, ibid.

20. Janet Whitney, Abigail Adams (Boston: Little, Brown & Co., 1947), p. 286.

AA to TBA, January 23, 1799, Reel 394, Adams Papers.

AA to JQA, February 1, 1799, ibid.

JQA to AA, March 16, 1799, ibid.

AA to William Smith, December 28, 1798, Smith-Townsend Collection.

21. AA to MC, October 31, 1799, New Letters, pp. 210–1.

DAJA, 3:244–5.

TBA to JA, September 20, 1800, Reel 398, Adams Papers.

22. AA to MC, October 31, 1799, New Letters, pp. 210, 212.

23. AA to William Shaw, February 8, 1799, Shaw Family Papers.

AA to Catherine Johnson, June 16, 1798, Autograph File, Houghton Library.

24. AA to William Shaw, December 23(?), 1798, Shaw Family Papers.

25. AA to William Shaw, December 14, 1798, ibid.

AA to William Shaw, December 20, 1798, ibid.

26. AA to William Shaw, December 20, 1798, ibid.

27. AA to William Shaw, January 6, 1799, ibid.

AA to William Shaw, January 14, 1799, ibid.

28. AA to William Shaw, January 3, 1799, ibid.

AA to MC, February 15, 1798, New Letters, pp. 132, 133, n. 3.

29. AA to William Shaw, January 3, 1799, Shaw Family Papers.

30. AA to William Shaw, January 25, 1799, ibid.

31. AA to William Shaw, December 23, 1799, ibid.

32. Richard B. Morris, ed., Encyclopedia of American History, Bicentennial ed. (New York: Harper & Row, 1976) p. 154.

John Quincy Adams and Charles Francis Adams, The Life of John Adams, 2 vols. (1871; reprint ed., New York: Haskell House Publishers Ltd., 1968) 2:235, 244, 256.

See generally Ch. 23–89, 1 Stat. 547–612 (1798). An Act to establish an Executive department, to be denominated the Department of the Navy, Ch. 35, 1 Stat. 553 (1798). An Act to declare the treaties heretofore concluded with France, no longer obligatory on the United States, Ch. 67, 1 Stat. 578 (1798). An Act for an additional appropriation to provide and support a Naval Armament, Ch. 23, 1 Stat. 547 (1798). An Act to authorize the President of the United States to cause to be purchased, or built, a number of small vessels to be equipped as galleys, or otherwise, Ch. 39, 1 Stat. 556 (1798). An Act further to protect the Commerce of the United States, Ch. 68, 1 Stat. 578 (1798). An Act more effectually to protect the Commerce and Coasts of the United States, Ch. 48, 1 Stat. 561 (1798). An Act to suspend the commercial intercourse between the United States and France, and the dependencies thereof, Ch. 53, 1 Stat. 565

(1798). An Act authorizing the President of the United States to raise a Provisional Army, Ch. 47, 1 Stat. 558 (1798).

33. Alexander Hamilton to George Washington, June 2, 1798, *The Papers of Alexander Hamilton,* ed. Harold C. Syrett, 26 vols. (New York: Columbia University Press, 1961–), 21:-479.

34. Alexander Hamilton to James McHenry, June 27, 1799, ibid., 23:227.

35. AA to William Shaw, January 25, 1799, Shaw Family Papers.

36. "Du Pont and Talleyrand, 1798" *Proceedings of the Massachusetts Historical Society,* 49:63–5 (November 1915).

37. Ibid., 49:64–5, 75, n. 1.

38. Ibid., 49:65–6.

39. Ibid., 49:66–76.

40. Ibid., 49:76–8.

41. *Life of JA,* 2:260–7.

42. AA to William Shaw, December 20, 1798, Shaw Family Papers.

43. *Life of JA,* 2:271–3.

44. Ibid., 2:273–5.

Timothy Pickering to Alexander Hamilton, February 25, 1799, *Hamilton Papers,* 22:500.

Robert Liston, the British Minister to the United States to Lord Grenville, British Secretary of State of Foreign Affairs, February 22, 1799, ibid., 22:489, n. 3.

Theodore Sedgwick to Alexander Hamilton, February 19, 1799, ibid., 22:487–8.

45. *Life of JA,* 2:276–7.

46. Ibid., 2:280–1.

AA to William Shaw, March 4, 1799, Shaw Family Papers.

47. AA to William Shaw, March 9, 1799, ibid.

48. Ibid.

Life of JA, 2:282, 284.

49. AA to William Shaw, March 9, 1799, Shaw Family Papers.

50. AA to ESP, April 7, 1799, ibid.

51. Ibid.

52. *Life of JA,* 2:286, 289–290.

53. *Life of JA,* 2:286–92.

AA to MC, December 30, 1799, *New Letters,* p. 224.

54. AA to MC, December 30, 1799, ibid.

55. AA to Elizabeth Smith, January 30, 1800, Smith-Townsend Collection.

AA to MC, January 28, 1800, *New Letters,* pp. 228, 230.

21. At Least Fall with Ease

1. JA to AA, October 25, 1799, *Letters of John Adams Addressed to his Wife,* ed. Charles Francis Adams, 2 vols. (Boston: Freeman and Bolles, 1841), 2:262–3.

2. AA to MC, October 31, 1799, *New Letters of Abigail Adams,* ed. Stewart Mitchell (Boston: Houghton Mifflin Company, 1947), pp. 210–2.

AA to MC, November 26, 1799, ibid., p. 216.

AA to MC, March 18, 1800, ibid., p. 242.

AA to MC, November 15, 1799, ibid., p. 214.

3. AA to MC, December 4, 1799, ibid., pp. 218 and 207, n. 2.

4. AA to William Smith, November 19, 1799, Smith-Townsend Collection, the Massachusetts Historical Society, Boston.

AA to MC, March 15, 1800, *New Letters,* pp. 238–9.

AA to William Smith, November 22, 1799, Smith-Townsend Collection.

AA to JQA, January 5, 1800, Reel 397, Adams Papers, the Massachusetts Historical Society, Boston.

5. AA to MC, November 26, 1799, *New Letters,* pp. 216 and 213, n. 4.

AA to William Smith, November 22, 1799, Smith-Townsend Collection.

AA to William Smith, November 19, 1799, ibid.

6. *New Letters,* p. 236, n. 1

AA to MC, March 18, 1800, ibid., p. 239.

AA to William Smith, December 25, 1799, Smith-Townsend Collection.

AA to MC, December 11, 1799, *New Letters,* p. 221.

7. AA to William Smith, December 25, 1799, Smith-Townsend Collection.

AA to MC, December 30, 1799, *New Letters,* p. 225.

8. AA to MC, December 22, 1799, *New Letters,* p. 222.

9. AA to William Smith, December 25, 1799, Smith-Townsend Collection.

AA to William Smith, January 16, 1800, ibid.

AA to MC, [December] 31, [1799], *New Letters*, p. 226.

New Letters, p. 229, n. 1.

10. AA to MC, January 28, 1800, *New Letters*, p. 229.

11. Ibid, pp. 228–9.

12. Ibid., p. 229.

AA to MC, February 27, 1800, ibid, p. 235.

13. AA to MC, February 27, 1799, *New Letters*, p. 234.

14. AA to MC, March 5, 1800, ibid., p. 236.

AA to William Smith, January 16, 1800, Smith-Townsend Collection.

AA to MC, January 28, 1800, *New Letters*, p. 230.

AA to William Smith, March 3, 1800, Smith-Townsend Collection.

15. AA to MC, March 5, 1800, *New Letters*, pp. 236–7.

16. AA to MC, May 3, 1800, ibid., p. 250.

AA to MC, May 5, 1800, ibid., p. 251.

17. AA to MC, May 5, 1800, ibid.

AA to TJ, July 1, 1804, Abigail Adams, *Letters of Mrs. Adams*, 3d ed. in 2 vols. (Boston: Charles C. Little and James Brown, 1841), 2:252.

James Thomson Callender, *The Prospect Before Us*, 2 vols. Vol. 2 in 2 parts (Richmond: M. Jones, S. Pleasants and J. Lyon, 2, part 1:83, 1800–1), 1:67.

18. AA to William Smith, May 16, 1800, Smith-Townsend Collection.

John Quincy Adams and Charles Francis Adams, *The Life of John Adams*, 2 vols. (1871; reprint ed., New York: Haskell House Publishers, 1968), 2:302, 307–12.

James Schouler, *History of the United States of America under the Constitution*, rev. ed. in 7 vols. (1880–1894; reprinted, New York: Kraus Reprint Co., 1970), 1:477.

19. Samuel Eliot Morison, *The Oxford History of the American People* (New York: Oxford University Press, 1965), p. 355.

AA to MC, May 2, 1800, *New Letters*, p. 253.

20. AA to ESP, July 18, 1800, Shaw Family Papers, Library of Congress, Washington, D.C.

21. James Schouler, *History*, 1:432, 459–61, 475.

New Letters, p. 270.

Alexander Hamilton, *Papers*, 25:174, n.24.

22. AA to MC, May 5, 1800, *New Letters*, p. 252.

23. *Life of JA*, 2:314–5.

24. Ibid., 2:316–7.

25. Ibid., 2:311, 321, 325.

26. Ibid., 2:329, 337.

27. Ibid., 2:337.

Letter from Alexander Hamilton Concerning the Public Conduct and Character of John Adams, Esquire, President of the United States. October 24, 1800, *The Papers of Alexander Hamilton*, ed. Harold C. Syrett (New York: Columbia University Press, 1977), 25:169–234.

28. Letter from Hamilton, ibid, p. 190–4.

29. Ibid, p. 233–4.

30. *The Works of John Adams*, ed. Charles Francis Adams, 10 vols. (Boston: Little, Brown and Company, 1854), 9:241–311.

JA to TJ, July 12, 1813, *The Adams-Jefferson Letters*, ed. Lester J. Cappon, 2 vols. (Chapel Hill: The University of North Carolina Press, 1959), 2:352–4.

New Letters, p. 258, n. 4.

31. AA to MC, November 21, 1800, ibid., p. 258.

AA to MC, November 10, 1800, *New Letters*, p. 255.

32. AA to MC, May 26, 1800, *New Letters*, p. 253.

AA to MC, November 10, 1800, ibid., p. 255.

33. AA to MC, December 8, 1800, ibid., p. 261.

JA to TJ, March 24, 1801, *The Adams-Jefferson Letters*, 1:264.

34. ESP to William Shaw, December 27, 1800, Shaw Family Papers.

35. JQA to TBA, December 20, 1800, *The Selected Writings of John and John Quincy Adams*, ed. Adrienne Koch and William Peden (New York: Alfred A. Knopf, 1946), p. 256.

36. AA to TBA, November 13, 1800, *Letters of Mrs. Adams*, 2:237–9.

37. Ibid.

Richard B. Morris, ed., *Encyclopedia of American History*, Bicentennial ed. (New York: Harper & Row, 1976), pp. 156–7.

38. AA to TBA, November 13, 1800, *Letters of Mrs. Adams*, 2:238.

39. Ibid.

JA to AA, November 2, 1800, *Letters of JA,* 2:267.

40. Ibid.

41. AA to MC, November 10, 1800, *New Letters,* p. 255.

AA to MC, November 21, 1800, ibid., pp. 256–7.

42. AA to AAS, November 21, 1800, *Letters of Mrs. Adams,* 2:240–1.

AA to AAS, November 27, 1800, ibid., 2:243–4.

43. AA to ESP, undated fragment, probable date somewhere between November 16, 1800 and January 1801, Shaw Family Papers, Library of Congress, 2:268.

AA to AAS, November 27, 1800, *Letters of Mrs. Adams,* 2:243.

44. AA to MC, November 21, 1800, *New Letters,* p. 257.

AA to AAS, November 21, 1800, *Letters of Mrs. Adams,* 2:242.

45. AA to AAS, November 21, 1800, ibid., 2:241–2.

46. AA to MC, February 7, 1801, *New Letters,* pp. 264–5.

47. Ibid., p. 265, quoting *King John,* act 3, sc. 4.

48. Ibid., p. 266.

49. Ibid., p. 265, n. 1.

AA to William Shaw, February 14, 1801, Shaw Family Papers.

50. JA to AA, February 16, 1801, *Letters of JA.*

TJ to AA, June 13, 1804, *The Adams-Jefferson Letters,* 1:270.

The Judiciary Act reduced the Supreme Court to five members and increased the number of district judges to sixteen. Before this, Supreme Court justices traveled the circuit.

51. AA to ESP [see n. 43 above], Shaw Family Papers.

JA to CT, December 28, 1800, JA Letterbook, Reel 120, Adams Papers.

52. JA to Samuel Dexter, March 23, 1801, *JA Works,* 9:580–1.

53. AA to ESP [see n. 43 above], Shaw Family Papers.

54. Ibid.

AA to MC, January 15, 1801, *New Letters,* p. 263.

55. AA to ESP [see n. 43 above], Shaw Family Papers.

56. AA to WSS, May 3, 1801, *Letters of Mrs. Adams,* 2:245.

22. Faithful Are the Wounds

1. AA to JQA, September 23, 1801, Reel 401, Adams Papers, the Massachusetts Historical Society, Boston.

JQA to JA, September 4, 1801, ibid.

JA to JQA, September 12, 1801, JA Letterbook, Reel 118, Adams Papers.

2. AA to JQA, September 23, 1801, Reel 401, Adams Papers.

AA to TBA, July 5, 1801, ibid.

3. AA to JQA, September 23, 1801, ibid.

LCA to JQA, October 4, 1801, ibid.

4. AA to JQA, September 23, 1801, ibid.

AA to TBA, July 5, 1801, ibid.

5. JQA to JA, September 4, 1801, ibid.

JQA to LCA, September 23, 1801, ibid.

LCA to JQA, September 16, 1801, ibid.

6. JQA to LCA, September 23, 1801, ibid.

JQA to LCA, September 29, 1801, ibid.

TBA to AA, October 24, 1801, ibid.

7. LCA to JQA, September 22, 1801, ibid.

JQA to LCA, September 29, 1801, ibid.

AA to TBA, December 27, 1801, ibid.

8. AA to TBA, December 27, 1801, ibid.

9. Louisa Catherine Adams, *The Adventures of a Nobody,* Reel 269, Adams Papers.

Louisa Catherine Adams, *Record of a Life,* Reel 265, Adams Papers.

Mrs. John Quincy Adams's *Narrative of a Journey from St. Petersburg to Paris in February 1815* was published in *Scribner's* magazine in October 1903, with an introduction written by her grandson Brooks Adams.

10. *Adventures of a Nobody,* Reel 269, Adams Papers.

11. Ibid.

12. Ibid.

13. Ibid.

14. Ibid.

15. LCA to George Washington Adams, June 25, 1825, Reel 470, Adams Papers.

16. *Adventures of a Nobody*, Reel 269, Adams Papers.
Record of a Life, Reel 265, Adams Papers.
17. *Record of a Life*, ibid.
18. *Adventures of a Nobody*, Reel 269, Adams Papers.
Record of a Life, Reel 265, Adams Papers.
JQA to LCA, October 8, 1801, Reel 401, Adams Papers.
19. *Adventures of a Nobody*, Reel 269, Adams Papers.
20. AA to MC, April 16, 1800, Reel 397, Adams Papers.
AA to JQA, April 27, 1800, ibid.
AA to Catherine Johnson, March 20, 1802, Reel 401, Adams Papers.
21. *Adventures of a Nobody*, Reel 269, Adams Papers.
LCA Diary, October 25, 1812, Reel 264, Adams Papers.
22. AA to TBA, December 13, 1802, Reel 401, Adams Papers.
23. AA to TBA, November 7, 1797, Reel 386, Adams Papers.
24. AA to TBA, July 6, 1802, Reel 401, Adams Papers.
AA to TBA, December 13, 1802, ibid.
25. AA to TBA, December 13, 1802, ibid.
26. AA to TBA, February 28, 1802, ibid.
AA to ESP, July 18, 1809, Shaw Family Papers, Library of Congress, Washington, D.C.
27. AA to TBA, December 27, 1801, Reel 401, Adams Papers.
AA to TBA, February 28, 1802, ibid.
28. JQA to TBA, November 28, 1801, ibid.
29. TBA to JQA, December 7, 1801, ibid.
Edmund Quincy, *Life of Josiah Quincy* (Boston: Ticknor & Fields, 1868), p. 30.
30. TBA to JQA, January 12, 1803, Reel 402, Adams Papers.
JQA to TBA, June 20, 1803, ibid.
31. TBA to JQA, December 15, 1803, ibid.
32. JQA to AA, November 7, 1803, ibid.
33. AA to TBA, January 27, 1803, ibid.
34. AA to Ann Harrod, February 19, 1805, Reel 404, Adams Papers.
35. Ibid.
AA to Ann Harrod, March 24, 1805, ibid.
36. AA to ESP, June 10, 1801. Shaw Family Papers, Library of Congress.
AA to TBA, February 7, 1802, Reel 401, Adams Papers.

AA to AAS, July 31—August 8, 1808, Radcliffe Women's History Archives, Harvard University, Cambridge, Massachusetts.
AA to MW, January 16, 1803, *Warren-Adams Letters*, 2 vols. (Boston: the Massachusetts Historical Society, 1925), 2:342.
37. AA to MW, January 16, 1803, ibid.
38. AA to AAS, December 28, 1808, De Windt Collection, the Massachusetts Historical Society, Boston.
39. JA to TBA, September 4, 1801, JA Letterbook, Reel 118, Adams Papers.
JA to F.A. Van der Kemp, February 5, 1805, *The Works of John Adams*, ed. Charles Francis Adams, 10 vols. (Boston: Little, Brown & Co., 1850–56), 9:590.
JA to Christopher Gadsden, April 16, 1801, *JA Works*, 9:585.
October 5, 1802, *Diary and Autobiography of John Adams*, ed. L. H. Butterfield, 4 vols. (Cambridge: Harvard University Press, Atheneum, 1964), 3:253.
AA to AAS, December 28, 1808, De Windt Collection.
40. AA to AAS, December 28, 1808, ibid.
John was given a Newfoundland dog. JQA to JA, March 12, 1802, Reel 401, Adams Papers.
AA to TBA, July 6, 1802, ibid.
41. AA to Hannah Cushing, September 1, 1804, Reel 403, Adams Papers.
42. December 31, 1803, *The Diary of John Quincy Adams*, ed. Allan Nevins (New York: Longman, Green & Co., 1929), p. 21.
AA to AAS, August 29, 1808, De Windt Collection.
43. October 21, 1803, *JQA Diary*, p. 18.
October 31, 1803, ibid.
44. December 31, 1803, ibid., p. 21.
45. AA to JQA, December 18, 1803, Reel 402, Adams Papers.
AA to JQA, January 10, 1804, Reel 403, Adams Papers.
AA to JQA, December 3, 1803, Reel 402, Adams Papers.
46. AA to JQA, December 18, 1804, Reel 404, Adams Papers.
AA to LCA, December 8, 1804, Reel 403, Adams Papers.
AA to LCA, January 27, 1805, Reel 404, Adams Papers.

AA to JQA, February 15, 1806, ibid.
AA to JQA, March 24, 1806, ibid.
47. AA to LCA, December 8, 1804, Reel 403, Adams Papers.
AA to LCA, January 27, 1805, Reel 404, Adams Papers.
48. AA to Mrs. Quincy, March 24, 1806, ibid.
AA to JQA, March 24, 1806, ibid.
49. LCA to AA, December 1805, ibid.
LCA to AA, January 6, 1806, ibid.
50. AA to JQA, January 9, 1806, ibid.
51. AA to LCA, January 16, 1806, ibid.
AA to LCA, January 19, 1806, ibid.
LCA to AA, May 11, 1806, ibid.
AA to LCA, February 15, 1806, ibid.
52. AA to Mrs. Quincy, March 24, 1806, ibid.
53. JQA to LCA, May 14, 1804, ibid.
AA to TJ, May 20, 1804, *The Adams-Jefferson Letters*, ed. Lester J. Cappon, 2 vols. (Chapel Hill: The University of North Carolina Press, 1959), 1:269.
AA to TBA, May 23, 1802, Reel 401, Adams Papers.
54. AA to TJ, May 20, 1804, *The Adams-Jefferson Letters*, 1:268–9.
55. Ibid., 1:269.
56. John Eppes to TJ, June 14, 1804, Thomas Jefferson Papers, the Massachusetts Historical Society, Boston.
57. TJ to John Page, June 25, 1804, quoted in *The Adams-Jefferson Letters*, 1:265.
TJ to AA, June 13, 1804, ibid., 1:269–70.
58. TJ to AA, June 13, 1804, ibid., 1:270.

59. Ibid., 1:270–1.
60. Ibid., 1:270.
61. AA to TJ, July 1, 1804, ibid., 1:271–2.
62. Ibid., 1:272.
63. Ibid., 1:273–4.
64. Dumas Malone, *Jefferson the President: First Term* (Boston: Little, Brown & Co., 1970), chap. 12.
Fawn Brodie, *Thomas Jefferson* (New York: W.W. Norton & Company, 1974), p. 349.
AA to TJ, July 1, 1804, *The Adams-Jefferson Letters*, 1:274.
65. AA to TJ, July 1, 1804, ibid.
66. TJ to AA, July 22, 1804, ibid., 1:275–6.
67. AA to TJ, August 18, 1804, ibid., 1:276–7.
68. Ibid., 1:277.
69. AA to TJ, July 1, 1804, ibid., 1:274.
AA to TJ, August 18, 1804, ibid., 1:277–8.
70. TJ to AA, September 11, 1804, ibid., 1:278.
71. Ibid., 1:278–9.
72. AA to TJ, October 25, 1804, ibid., 1:280–1.
73. Ibid., 1:281.
74. Ibid., 1:281–2.
75. Ibid., 1:282.
AA to TJ, July 1, 1804, ibid., 1:274.
76. JA postscript to AA to TJ, October 25, 1804, ibid., 1:282.
77. TJ to Benjamin Rush, January 16, 1811, quoted in *The Adams-Jefferson Letters*, 1:268.
The Adams-Jefferson Letters, 2:284.

23. Rather Too Much than Too Little

1. Katharine Metcalf Roof, *Colonel William Smith and Lady* (Boston: Houghton Mifflin Company, 1929), p. 272.
WSS to JQA, November 28, 1805, Reel 404, Adams Papers, the Massachusetts Historical Society, Boston.
AA to JQA, November 29, 1805, ibid.
2. Roof, *Col. Smith*, pp. 268–70.
3. Roof, *Col. Smith*, pp. 266–71.
JQA to LCA, July 13, 1806, Reel 404, Adams Papers.
JQA to LCA, November 28, 1806, ibid.
4. JQA to TBA, March 19, 1806, ibid.
Roof, *Col. Smith*, p. 269.

WSS to JQA, March 23, 1806, Reel 404, Adams Papers.
WSS to JQA, March 29, 1806, ibid.
5. JQA to AA, March 14, 1806, ibid.
WSS to JQA, March 29, 1806, ibid.
6. JQA to LCA, May 4, 1806, ibid.
7. LCA, *The Adventures of a Nobody*, Reel 269, Adams Papers.
November, 1804, *Memoirs of John Quincy Adams*, ed. Charles Francis Adams, 2 vols. (Philadelphia: J.B. Lippincott & Co., 1874), pp. 316–7.
January 11, 1805, *The Diary of John Quincy*

Adams, ed. Allan Nevins (New York: Longmans, Green and Co., 1929), p. 28.

January 11–12, 1831, ibid., pp. 408–9.

8. November 25, 1805, ibid., p. 37.

November 23, 1804, ibid., p. 25.

January 11, 1805, ibid., p. 28.

JQA to LCA, July 13, 1806, Reel 404, Adams Papers.

9. ESP to AA, May 10, 1806, ibid.

ESP to AA, August 10, 1806, ibid.

10. AA to JQA, January 16, 1807, Reel 405, Adams Papers.

JQA to LCA, December 17, 1806, Reel 404, Adams Papers.

JQA to LCA, May 24, 1806, ibid.

LCA to JQA, June 2, 1806, ibid.

AA to JQA, February 27, 1807, Reel 405, Adams Papers.

11. AA to JQA, January 16, 1807, ibid.

12. AA to MW, March 9, 1807, ibid.

13. Ibid.

14. In a letter to Mercy Warren dated February 8, 1805, Thomas Jefferson enclosed his own subscription, and that of the heads of government departments, for her *History* and wrote that he had "no doubt the work she has prepared will be equally useful to our country and honourable to herself." *Warren-Adams Papers,* 2 vols. (Boston: the Massachusetts Historical Society, 1925), 2:345.

JA to MW, July–August 1807, *Warren-Adams Papers,* the Massachusetts Historical Society, Boston.

JA to MW, July 11, 1807, ibid.

15. JA to MW, July–August 1807, ibid.

JA to MW, July 11, 1807, ibid.

16. JA to MW, July 11, 1807, ibid.

JA to MW, July 20, 1807, JA Letterbook, Reel 118, Adams Papers.

17. JA to MW, July 27, 1807, *Warren-Adams Papers.*

JA to MW, July 20, 1807, JA Letterbook, Reel 118, Adams Papers.

18. JA to MW, August 2, 1807, ibid.

JA to MW, August 1, 1807, *Warren-Adams Papers.*

19. MW to JA, July 23, 1807, ibid.

MW to JA, August 27, 1807, ibid.

20. Elbridge Gerry to MW, November 1807, ibid.

MW to AA, December 28, 1807, Reel 405, Adams Papers.

21. AA to AAS, December 8, 1808, De Windt Collection, the Massachusetts Historical Society, Boston.

22. AA to ESP, June 5, 1809, *Letters of Mrs. Adams,* 3rd ed. in 2 vols. (Boston: Charles C. Little and James Brown, 1841), 2:265.

AA to AAS, May 13, 1809, Abigail Adams Smith, *Journal and Correspondence of Miss Adams,* ed. Caroline Smith De Windt, 2 vols. (New York and London: Wiley and Putnam, 1841), 2:194.

AA to Caroline Smith, February 2, 1809, ibid., 1:216.

AA to AAS, August 29, 1808, De Windt Collection.

23. AA to Caroline Smith, February 2, 1809, *Journal and Correspondence,* 1:216.

AA to AAS, May 8, 1808, De Windt Collection.

AA to AAS, July 13, 1808, Schlesinger Library, Radcliffe College, Cambridge, Massachusetts.

AA to AAS, May 13, 1809, *Journal and Correspondence,* 2:194–6.

24. December 31, 1807, *JQA Diary,* p. 50.

25. JQA to JA, December 27, 1807, Reel 405, Adams Papers.

JA to JQA, January 8, 1808, JA Letterbook, Reel 118, Adams Papers.

AA to AAS, May 8, 1808, De Windt Collection.

Richard B. Morris, ed., *Encyclopedia of American History,* Bicentennial ed. (New York: Harper & Row, 1976), p. 163.

AA to AAS, March 18, 1808, De Windt Collection.

AA to AAS, April 17, 1808, ibid.

AA to AAS, March 27, 1808, ibid.

26. *Encyclopedia,* pp. 163–4.

27. AA to AAS, March 18, 1808, De Windt Collection.

LCA to AA, January 24, 1808, Reel 405, Adams Papers.

28. JA to JQA, January 8, 1808, JA Letterbook, Reel 118, Adams Papers.

AA to JQA, February 15, 1808, Reel 405, Adams Papers.

29. AA to AAS, March 18, 1808, De Windt Collection.

30. AA to AAS, March 27, 1808, ibid.

AA to Mrs. Cushing, March 1808, Reel 405, Adams Papers.

31. June 3 and 8, 1808, *JQA Diary*, p. 57.
AA to AAS, June 19, 1808, De Windt Collection.

32. AA to AAS, August 29, 1808, ibid.

33. LCA to JQA, March 1, 1808, Reel 405, Adams Papers.
Department of State to JQA, June 29, 1809, Reel 407, Adams Papers.
July 11, 1809, *Memoirs of John Quincy Adams, 1795 to 1848*, ed. Charles Francis Adams, 12 vols. (Philadelphia: J.B. Lippincott, 1874–77), 1:550.
July 5, 1809, ibid., 1:549.

34. According to the *Cecil Textbook of Medicine*, St. Anthony disease is seen only sporadically now. It results from eating bread made from rye wheat infected with ergot fungus.

July 5, 1809, *JQA Memoirs*, 1:549.
AA to JQA, February 1809, Reel 407, Adams Papers.
LCA to JQA, February 12, 1807, ibid.
AA to ESP, June 5, 1809, *Letters of Mrs. Adams*, 2:263–6.

35. August 5, 1809, *JQA Diary*, p. 60.
AA to JQA and LCA, August 5, 1809, Reel 408, Adams Papers.

36. AA to ESP, July 18, 1809, Shaw Family Papers, Library of Congress, Washington, D.C.

37. AA to ESP, August 27, 1809, Reel 408, Adams Papers.

38. Ibid.

39. AA to Caroline Smith, November 30, 1809, *Journal and Correspondence*, 1:218.

24. The Young Shoots and Branches

1. AA to William Smith, February 20, 1816, De Windt Collection, the Massachusetts Historical Society, Boston.
AA to Caroline Smith, August 12, 1809, Reel 408, Adams Papers, the Massachusetts Historical Society, Boston.

2. October 23, 1809, *The Diary of John Quincy Adams*, ed. Allan Nevins (New York: Longmans, Green and Co., 1929), pp. 62–3.
AA to Catherine Johnson, February 23, 1810, Reel 409, Adams Papers.

3. October 23, 1809, *JQA Diary*, p. 63.
AA to Catherine Johnson, February 23, 1810, Reel 409, Adams Papers.
Robert Ker Porter, *Travelling Sketches in Russia and Sweden*, 2 vols. (London: Richard Phillips, 1809).

4. AA to JQA, March 20, 1810, Reel 409, Adams Papers.
AA to Catherine Johnson, February 23, 1810, ibid.
AA to LCA, January 21, 1811, Reel 411, Adams Papers.

5. AA to Catherine Johnson, September 13, 1810, Reel 410, Adams Papers.
AA to Catherine Johnson, November 1809, Reel 408, Adams Papers.

6. AA to Catherine Johnson, November 1809, ibid.

7. AA to AAS, April 14, 1810, *Journal and Correspondence of Miss Adams*, ed. Caroline

Smith De Windt, 2 vols. (New York and London: Wiley and Putnam, 1841), 2:208.
AA to ESP, April 23, 1810, Shaw Family Papers, Library of Congress, Washington, D.C.
AA to JQA, May 7, 1810, Reel 409, Adams Papers.

8. AA to Catherine Johnson, December 19, 1809, Reel 408, Adams Papers.
AA to Catherine Johnson, May 30, 1810, Reel 409, Adams Papers.

9. AA to Catherine Johnson, November 1809, Reel 408, Adams Papers.
AA to JQA, July 25, 1810, Reel 410, Adams Papers.

10. AA to Catherine Johnson, November 1809, Reel 408, Adams Papers.
AA to JQA, May 28, 1810, Reel 409, Adams Papers.
AA to ESP, April 23, 1810, Shaw Family Papers.

11. AA to Catherine Johnson, May 8, 1810, Reel 409, Adams Papers.

12. AA to JQA, March 20, 1810, ibid.
AA to ESP, June 13, 1810, ibid.
AA to LCA, May 15, 1810, ibid.
LCA to AA, May 13, 1810, ibid.
LCA to AA, January 4, 1810, ibid.

13. JQA to AA, February 7, 1810, ibid.
LCA to AA, May 13, 1810, ibid.
LCA to MC, June 5, 1810, ibid.

14. AA to MC, September 5, 1784, *Letters of*

Mrs. Adams, 3rd ed. in 2 vols. (Boston: Charles C. Little and James Brown, 1841), 2:48–51.

15. LCA to AA, May 13, 1810, Reel 409, Adams Papers.

AA to John Smith, February 11, 1810, ibid.

AA to Harriet Welsh, March 30, 1815, Reel 422, Adams Papers.

16. AA to Catherine Johnson, November 1809, Reel 408, Adams Papers.

17. AA to LCA, January 21, 1811, Reel 411, Adams Papers.

18. AA to LCA, May 15, 1810, Reel 409, Adams Papers.

AA to LCA, February 28, 1811, Reel 411, Adams Papers.

19. AA to Catherine Johnson, July 13, 1810, Reel 410, Adams Papers.

JA to JQA, July 3, 1816, JA Letterbook, Reel 122, Adams Papers.

AA to AAS, April 27, 1813, *Journal and Correspondence,* 2:214.

AA to AAS, April 10, 1810, ibid., 2:210.

AA to LCA, May 15, 1810, Reel 409, Adams Papers.

20. AA to Catherine Johnson, July 13, 1810, Reel 410, Adams Papers.

AA to LCA, May 15, 1810, Reel 409, Adams Papers.

James Madison to AA, August 15, 1810, Reel 410, Adams Papers.

21. AA to Catherine Johnson, September 13, 1810, ibid.

AA to ESP, November 24, 1810, Shaw Family Papers.

22. James Madison to His Imperial Majesty, October 10, 1810, Reel 410, Adams Papers.

Department of State to JQA, October 15, 1810, ibid.

23. James Madison to JQA, October 16, 1810, ibid.

24. Ibid.

25. Ibid.

26. AA to Caroline Smith, February 26, 1811, *Letters of Mrs. Adams,* 2:266.

Richard B. Morris, ed., *Encyclopedia of American History,* Bicentennial ed. (New York: Harper & Row, 1976) p. 166.

27. *Encyclopedia,* pp. 166–7.

AA to JQA, January 20, 1811, Reel 411, Adams Papers.

AA to ESP, December 29, 1811, Shaw Family Papers.

JA to Josiah Quincy, February 9, 1811, *The Selected Writings of John and John Quincy Adams,* ed. Adrienne Koch and William Peden (New York: Alfred A. Knopf, 1946), pp. 157–9.

AA to AAS, April 14, 1810, *Journal and Correspondence,* 2:208.

28. AA to LCA, January 12, 1810, Reel 409, Adams Papers.

AA to Caroline Smith, February 26, 1811, *Letters of Mrs. Adams,* 2:267.

AA to Caroline Smith, December 9, 1809, *Journal and Correspondence,* 1:318.

29. AA to Caroline Smith, January 24, 1808, *Journal and Correspondence,* 2:210–1.

30. AA to ESP, May 5, 1812, Shaw Family Papers.

AA to George Washington Adams, May 25, 1812, Reel 413, Adams Papers.

31. AA to ESP, February 28, 1811, Shaw Family Papers.

AA to George Washington Adams, January 9, 1813, Reel 415, Adams Papers.

AA to John Smith, February 11, 1810, Reel 409, Adams Papers.

32. AA to John Adams (grandson), January 5, 1812, Reel 413, Adams Papers.

33. AA to JQA, March 12, 1812, ibid.

AA to JQA, January 5, 1812, ibid.

AA to JQA, February 17, 1812, ibid.

34. AA to LCA, February 18, 1811, Reel 411, Adams Papers.

AA to LCA, March 4, 1811, ibid.

AA to LCA, February 28, 1811, ibid.

36. AA to JQA, March 4, 1811, Reel 411, Adams Papers.

37. Ibid.

38. AA to Catherine Johnson, March 5, 1811, ibid.

AA to Catherine Johnson, March 30, 1811, ibid.

AA to JQA, April 29, 1811, ibid.

39. JQA to JA, June 7, 1811, ibid.

JQA to AA, June 11, 1811, ibid.

JQA to AA, August 12, 1811, Reel 412, Adams Papers.

40. JQA to AA, June 30, 1811, Reel 411, Adams Papers.

41. AA to Catherine Johnson, July 31, 1811, Reel 412, Adams Papers.

AA to Catherine Johnson, September 22, 1811, ibid.

AA to JQA, September 24, 1811, ibid.

42. AA to Catherine Johnson, July 31, 1811, ibid.

WSS to AA, June 29, 1811, Reel 411, Adams Papers.

AA to JQA, September 24, 1811, Reel 412, Adams Papers.

AA to ESP, November 1811, Shaw Family Papers.

AA to ESP, December 29, 1811, ibid.

43. AA to JQA, November 17, 1811, Reel 412, Adams Papers.

AA to ESP, October 22, 1811, ibid.

44. AA to ESP, July 10, 1811, Shaw Family Papers.

45. AA to WSS, July 23, 1811, De Windt Collection.

46. WSS to AA, August 12, 1811, Reel 412, Adams Papers.

WSS to AA, September 15, 1811, ibid.

47. AA to WSS, August 28, 1811, De Windt Collection.

AA to WSS, September 27, 1811, ibid., 66. Katherine Metcalf Roof, *Colonel William Smith and Lady* (Boston: Houghton Mifflin Company, 1929), p. 311.

48. AA to Mrs. Benjamin Rush, September 14, 1813, Reel 412, Adams Papers.

Dr. Rush, after reading details of Abigail Smith's ailment, wrote not only to her but to her father. Dr. Rush to JA, September 20, 1811: After fifty years' experience, "I must protest against all local applications, and internal medicines for her Relief. They now and then cure, but in 19 cases out of 20 in tumour of the *breast*, they do harm, or suspend the disease until it passes beyond that time in which the only Radical Remedy is ineffectual. This Remedy is the Knife. From her account . . . it may be too late." Reel 412, Adams Papers.

AA to ESP, October 22, 1811, Shaw Family Papers.

AA to ESP, December 29, 1811, ibid.

AA to JQA, November 17, 1811, Reel 412, Adams Papers.

The full names of the doctors who operated on Mrs. Smith are Thomas Welsh, Amos Holbrook, and probably John Collins Warren.

49. AA to JQA, November 17, 1811, ibid.

AA to JQA, December 8, 1811, ibid.

AA to ESP, December 29, 1811, Shaw Family Papers.

50. John Adams wrote to Benjamin Rush on December 25, 1811: "I perceive plainly enough, Rush, that you have been teasing Jefferson to write to me, as you did me some time ago to write to him. You gravely advise me to receive the olive branch, as if there had been war; but there has never been any hostility on my part, nor that I know, on his. When there has been no war, there can be no room for negotiations of peace." *Selected Writings of JA and JQA,* pp. 164–6.

JA to TJ, January 1, 1812, *The Adams-Jefferson Letters,* ed. Lester J. Cappon, 2 vols. (Chapel Hill: The University of North Carolina Press, 1959), 2:290.

51. AA to Miss Otis, January 12, 1812, Reel 413, Adams Papers.

AA to JQA, January 5, 1812, ibid.

JQA to AA, May 28, 1812, ibid.

AA to ESP, April 20, 1812, Shaw Family Papers.

AA to JQA, April 12, 1812, Reel 412, Adams Papers.

AA to JQA, May 10, 1812, Reel 413, Adams Papers.

AA to JQA, July 29, 1812, Reel 414, Adams Papers.

52. *Encyclopedia,* p. 169.

AA to James Monroe, August 5, 1812, Reel 414, Adams Papers.

AA to JQA, July 29, 1812, ibid.

Roof, *Col. Smith,* p. 311.

53. AA to James Monroe, August 5, 1812, Reel 414, Adams Papers.

54. AA to WSS, September 6, 1812, ibid.

WSS to AA, November 30, 1812, ibid.

55. WSS to AA, January 25, 1813, Reel 415, Adams Papers.

56. AA to Caroline Smith, November 19, 1812, *Letters of Mrs. Adams,* 2:268–72.

57. Ibid.

58. AA to Caroline Smith, November 22, 1812, ibid.

59. JQA to AA, September 21, 1812, Reel 414, Adams Papers.

AA to JQA, January 25, 1813, Reel 415, Adams Papers.

LCA to George Washington Adams, June 14, 1812, Reel 413, Adams Papers.

60. AA to JQA, February 1, 1813, Reel 415, Adams Papers.

AA to George Washington Adams and John Adams (grandson), January 25, 1813, ibid.

AA to LCA, January 30, 1813, ibid.

61. AA to JQA, February 27, 1813, ibid.

62. JA to JQA, March 1, 1813, ibid.

63. AA to JQA, April 23, 1813, ibid.

LCA to AA, April 4, 1813, ibid.

64. LCA to AA, April 4, 1813, ibid.

65. Ibid.

66. JQA to AA, December 31, 1812, Reel 414, Adams Papers.

67. AA to James Monroe, April 3, 1813, Simon Gratz Collection, Historical Society of Pennsylvania, Philadelphia.

JQA to James Monroe, forwarded by AA, February 26, 1813, ibid.

68. On September 21, 1812, John Quincy noted in his *Diary* that "the Emperor was much concerned and disappointed to find the whole benefit which he expected his subjects would derive commercially from that event defeated and lost by the new war . . . between the United States and England; that he had thought there were various indications that there was on both sides a reluctance at engaging and prosecuting this war, and it had occurred to the Emperor that perhaps an amicable arrangement of the differences between the parties might be accomplished more easily and speedily by indirect than by a direct negotiation" and that the Emperor had made enquiries about whether there was "any difficulty or obstacle on the part of the Govern-

ment of the United States if he should offer his mediation for the purpose of effecting a pacification." *JQA Diary,* pp. 98–9.

James Monroe to AA, April 10, 1813, Reel 415, Adams Papers.

James Monroe to JA, April 10, 1813, ibid.

69. James Monroe to JA, April 10, 1813, ibid.

70. AA to James Monroe, April 20, 1813, ibid.

71. Ibid.

72. AA to JQA, April 23, 1813, ibid.

73. Ibid.

74. The dying captain's last words were said to be, "Don't give up the ship!" *Encyclopedia,* pp. 173–4.

AA to JQA, July 1, 1813, Reel 416, Adams Papers.

WSS to JA, July 15, 1813, Reel 416, ibid.

75. AA to JQA, August 30, 1813, Reel 416, Adams Papers.

WSS to AA, July 7, 1813, Reel 416, ibid.

AA to JQA, July 14, 1813, ibid.

76. JA to TJ, August 16, 1813, *The Adams-Jefferson Letters,* 2:366.

77. AA to TJ, postscript to JA to TJ, July 15, 1813, ibid., 2:358.

TJ to AA, August 22, 1813, ibid., 2:366–7.

78. AA to TJ, September 20, 1813, ibid., 2:377.

79. TJ to JA, October 12–13, 1813, ibid., 2:386.

80. William Cranch to AA, September 3, 1813, Reel 416, Adams Papers.

25. The Close of the Drama

1. AA to F.A. Van der Kemp, February 23, 1814, Reel 417, Adams Papers, the Massachusetts Historical Society, Boston.

AA to ESP, January 13, 1814, Shaw Family Papers, Library of Congress, Washington, D.C.

2. AA to JQA, February 10, 1816, Reel 429, Adams Papers.

3. AA to ESP, January 13, 1814, Shaw Family Papers.

AA to ESP, February 10, 1814, ibid.

4. AA to JQA, February 27, 1814, Reel 417, Adams Papers.

AA to ESP, February 10, 1814, Shaw Family Papers.

AA to LCA, December 21, 1814, Reel 421, Adams Papers.

5. AA to F.A. Van der Kemp, February 23, 1814, Reel 417, Adams Papers.

6. AA to F.A. Van der Kemp, May 26, 1815, Reel 423, Adams Papers.

AA to ESP, February 10, 1814, Shaw Family Papers.

AA to Harriet Welsh, December 8, 1814, Reel 421, Adams Papers.

7. AA to ESP, February 10, 1814, Shaw Family Papers.

AA to ESP, May 12, 1814, ibid.

AA to ESP, January 13, 1814, ibid.

8. AA to ESP, May 12, 1814, ibid.

9. Ibid.

10. WSS to AA, March 13, 1814, Reel 417, Adams Papers.

AA to ESP, February 10, 1814, Shaw Family Papers.

11. AA to Caroline Smith, October 23, 1814, Abigail Adams Smith, *Journal and Correspondence of Miss Adams,* ed. Caroline Smith De Windt, 2 vols. (New York and London: Wiley and Putnam, 1841), 1:228.

AA to ESP, September 13, 1814, Reel 419, Adams Papers.

AA to Harriet Welsh, March 18, 1814, Reel 417, Adams Papers.

AA to JQA, March 8, 1814, ibid.

12. AA to WSS, March 22, 1814, ibid.

AA to Harriet Welsh, March 18, 1814, ibid.

AA to JQA, June 12, 1814, Reel 418, Adams Papers.

AA to Harriet Welsh, March 22, 1814, Reel 417, Adams Papers.

13. AA to ESP, September 13, 1814, Reel 419, Adams Papers.

14. AA to ESP, November 20, 1814, Reel 420, Adams Papers.

15. JA to Sally Adams, October 26, 1814, JA Letterbook, Reel 122, Adams Papers.

16. AA to ESP, November 20, 1814, Reel 420, Adams Papers.

17. AA to Caroline Smith, October 23, 1814, *Journal and Correspondence,* 1:228.

AA to ESP, September 13, 1814, Reel 419, Adams Papers.

18. AA to Caroline Smith, October 23, 1814, *Journal and Correspondence,* 1:229.

19. Henry Warren to AA, October 19, 1814, Reel 420, Adams Papers.

20. JA to Benjamin Waterhouse, January 10, 1810, *Statesman and Friend: Correspondence of John Adams with Benjamin Waterhouse 1784–1822,* ed. Worthington Chauncey Ford (Boston: Little, Brown & Co., 1927), p. 47.

21. AA to MW, August 9, 1812, Reel 414, Adams Papers.

22. MW to AA, September 1, 1812, ibid.

Elbridge Gerry to MW, December 17, 1812, *Warren-Adams Letters,* 2 vols. (Boston: the Massachusetts Historical Society, 1925), 2:373–5.

23. AA to MW, December 30, 1812, is held by the New Hampshire Historical Society. Printed in Massachusetts Historical Society *Collections,* 5th series, 4 (1878), p. 501.

MW to AA, January 26, 1813, Reel 415, Adams Papers.

24. JA to Elbridge Gerry, April 17, 1813, *Warren-Adams Letters,* 2:378, 380.

25. Ibid., 2:379.

MW to JA, July 10, 1814, ibid., 2:394–5.

26. JA to MW, August 17, 1814, JA Letterbook, Reel 122, Adams Papers.

AA to Caroline Smith, October 23, 1814, *Journal and Correspondence,* 1:228.

27. AA to JQA, September 7, 1814, Reel 419, Adams Papers.

28. Ibid.

29. Ibid.

Richard B. Morris, *Encyclopedia of American History,* Bicentennial ed. (New York: Harper & Row, 1976), p. 181.

30. AA to ESP, September 13, 1814, Reel 419, Adams Papers.

AA to LCA, December 21, 1814, Reel 421, Adams Papers.

31. AA to ESP, September 13, 1814, Reel 419, Adams Papers.

32. AA to JQA, October 18, 1814, Reel 420, Adams Papers.

33. Mark Antony DeWolfe Howe, ed., *The Articulate Sisters* (Cambridge: Harvard University Press, 1946), pp. 12–3.

34. AA to ESP, February 26, 1815, Shaw Family Papers.

AA to ESP, April 10, 1815, ibid.

AA to Caroline Smith, February 19, 1815, *Journal and Correspondence,* 1:230.

AA to Harriet Welsh, February 24, 1815, Reel 422, Adams Papers.

AA to JQA, February 28, 1815, ibid.

Encyclopedia, p. 182.

35. AA to Harriet Welsh, March 5, 1815, Reel 422, Adams Papers.

AA to Caroline Smith, February 19, 1815, ibid.

JQA to AA, December 24, 1814, as copied by AA, March 5, 1815, ibid.

36. AA to JQA, March 8, 1815, ibid.

AA to ESP, February 26, 1815, Shaw Family Papers.

AA to JQA, March 10, 1815, Reel 422, Adams Papers.

37. AA to JQA, May 6, 1815, Reel 423, Adams Papers.

AA to JQA, April 11, 1815, ibid.

AA to Harriet Welsh, April 6, 1815, ibid.

38. AA to Abigail "Abbe" Shaw Felt, April 15, 1815, ibid.

AA to LCA, April 14, 1815, ibid.

AA to F.A. Van der Kemp, May 26, 1815, ibid.

39. AA to JQA, June 8, 1815, Reel 424, Adams Papers.

AA to JQA, May 6, 1815, Reel 423, Adams Papers.

AA to JQA, May 30, 1815, ibid.

40. AA to Harriet Welsh, August 6, 1815, Reel 426, Adams Papers.

41. AA to JQA, November 9, 1815, Reel 429, Adams Papers.

AA to LCA, October 20, 1815, Reel 427, Adams Papers.

42. AA to JQA, May 5, 1816, Reel 431, Adams Papers.

AA to LCA, October 20, 1815, Reel 427, Adams Papers.

AA to [?], May 10, 1815, Reel 423, Adams Papers.

43. AA to JQA, May 5, 1816, Reel 431, Adams Papers.

AA to JQA, October 12, 1815, Reel 427, Adams Papers.

AA to LCA, January 3, 1818, Reel 442, Adams Papers.

44. AA to LCA, March 1816, Reel 430, Adams Papers.

AA to F.A. Van der Kemp, April 11, 1816, ibid.

AA to F.A. Van der Kemp, April 10, 1817, Reel 437, Adams Papers.

45. AA to F.A. Van der Kemp, April 10, 1817, ibid.

AA to JQA, August 7, 1816, Reel 433, Adams Papers.

46. AA to LCA, September 2, 1815, Reel 426, Adams Papers.

AA to Harriet Welsh, October 16, 1815, Reel 427, Adams Papers.

LCA to AA, June 15, 1815, Reel 424, Adams Papers.

LCA to AA, October 2, 1815, Reel 427, Adams Papers.

AA to LCA, October 20, 1815, ibid.

47. LCA to AA, January 21, 1816, Reel 429, Adams Papers.

48. AA to LCA, March 27, 1816, Reel 430, Adams Papers.

49. JA to LCA, 1819, JA Letterbook, Reel 123, Adams Papers.

JA to JQA, 1819, ibid..

August 5, 1828, *Diary of Charles Francis Adams*, vol. 1–2 ed. Aida Dipace Donald and David Donald, 6 vols. to date (Cambridge: Harvard University Press, The Belknap Press, 1964), 2:42.

LCA, Reel 273, Adams Papers.

LCA to AA, January 21, 1816, Reel 429, Adams Papers.

Henry Adams, *The Education of Henry Adams*, Sentry ed. (Boston: Houghton Mifflin Company, 1961), pp. 18–9.

JA to LCA, April 2, 1819, JA Letterbook, Reel 123, Adams Papers.

50. AA to Harriet Welsh, September 5, 1815, Reel 426, Adams Papers.

51. LCA to AA, July 4, 1816, Reel 432, Adams Papers.

52. AA to LCA, May 20, 1815, Reel 423, Adams Papers.

AA to LCA, May 28, 1816, Reel 431, Adams Papers.

AA to LCA, September 30, 1816, Reel 434, Adams Papers.

53. AA to JQA, January 18, 1816, Reel 429, Adams Papers.

AA's Will, dated January 18, 1816, copy in her own handwriting, Reel 607, Adams Papers.

54. AA to Harriet Welsh, March 15, 1816, Reel 430, Adams Papers.

AA to Abigail "Abbe" Shaw Felt, March 30, 1816, Shaw Family Papers.

AA to JQA, March 22, 1816, Reel 430, Adams Papers.

55. AA to JA, January 1, 1797, Reel 383, Adams Papers.

AA to AAS, June 19, 1808, De Windt Collection, the Massachusetts Historical Society, Boston.

AA to John Adams (grandson), May 21, 1816, Reel 431, Adams Papers.

AA to JQA, March 22, 1816, Reel 430, Adams Papers.

56. AA to Harriet Welsh, June 7, 1816, Reel 432, Adams Papers.

57. AA to JQA, June 10, 1816, ibid.

JA to CA, June 25, 1816, JA Letterbook, Reel 122, Adams Papers.

AA to LCA, June 28, 1816, Reel 432, Adams Papers.

The colonel's son, William Steuben Smith, produced a pamphlet on his father's behalf.

Published in 1824, it was called "FACTS in Refutation of the Aspersions Against the Character and Memory of Col. Wm. Stephens Smith, as Recorded by Col. Tim. Pickering, in his Review of the Correspondence between The Hon. John Adams and the Late Wm. Cunningham, Esq."

58. JA to JQA, June 26, 1816, JA Letterbook, Reel 122, Adams Papers.

JA to JQA, July 3, 1816, ibid.

59. JA to JQA, July 18, 1816, ibid.

JA to JQA, July 26, 1816, ibid.

AA to JQA, August 27, 1816, Reel 433, Adams Papers.

AA to Harriet Welsh, August 1, 1816, ibid.

60. AA to JQA, September 30, 1816, Reel 434, Adams Papers.

AA to Richard Rush, May 20, 1816, Reel 431, Adams Papers.

Richard Rush to AA, November 11, 1816, Reel 434, Adams Papers.

AA to JQA, November 20, 1816, ibid.

61. AA to John Adams (grandson), October 24, 1816, ibid.

62. AA to JQA, November 5, 1816, ibid.

63. Ibid.

64. AA to JQA, November 20, 1816, ibid.

AA to JQA, December 6, 1816, Reel 435, Adams Papers.

AA to JQA, March 12, 1817, Reel 436, Adams Papers.

65. AA to JQA, March 17, 1817, ibid.

AA to Hannah Cushing, March 17, 1817, ibid.

JA to JQA, March 18, 1817, JA Letterbook, Reel 123, Adams Papers.

66. AA to [?], March 24, 1817, Houghton Library, Harvard University, Cambridge, Massachusetts.

AA to JQA, April 13, 1817, Reel 437, Adams Papers.

AA to JQA, May 10, 1817, ibid.

AA to JQA, March 12, 1817, Reel 436, Adams Papers.

67. AA to JQA, August 10, 1817, Reel 438, Adams Papers.

LCA to AA, August 14, 1817, ibid.

68. AA to Harriet Welsh, August 18, 1817, ibid.

Charles Francis Adams, *Charles Francis Adams* (Boston: Houghton Mifflin and Company, 1900), p. 10.

69. AA to Harriet Welsh, August 18, 1817, Reel 438, Adams Papers.

AA to Susan Boylston Adams Clark, August 26, 1817, ibid.

AA to T.B. Johnson, October 18, 1817, Reel 440, Adams Papers.

70. AA to JQA, December 14, 1817, Reel 441, Adams Papers.

AA to William Shaw, September 13, 1817, Shaw Family Papers.

AA to John Adams (grandson), September 17, 1817, Reel 439, Adams Papers.

AA to Harriet Welsh, November 18, 1817, Reel 440, Adams Papers.

71. AA to Harriet Welsh, October 17, 1817, ibid.

AA to Harriet Welsh, October 1, 1817, ibid.

AA to LCA, November 12, 1817, ibid.

AA to Harriet Welsh, November 24, 1817, ibid.

72. LCA to AA, November 12, 1817, ibid.

AA to LCA, December 12, 1817, Reel 441, Adams Papers.

73. AA to LCA, January 7, 1818, Reel 442, Adams Papers.

AA to Harriet Welsh, March 1818, Smith-Townsend Collection, the Massachusetts Historical Society, Boston.

74. AA to LCA, January 3, 1818, Reel 442, Adams Papers.

LCA to George Washington Adams, February 4, 1818, ibid.

LCA to George Washington Adams, September 23, 1817, Reel 439, Adams Papers.

75. *Articulate Sisters*, pp. 21–2.

AA to Richard Rush, July 15, 1817, Reel 438, Adams Papers.

LCA to AA, January 7, 1818, Reel 442, Adams Papers.

76. AA to LCA, January 24, 1818, ibid.

AA to Harriet Welsh, January 30, 1818, ibid.

77. AA to LCA, January 3, 1818, ibid.

AA to LCA, February 20, 1818, ibid.

AA to LCA, February 1, 1818, ibid.

78. AA to LCA, February 27, 1818, ibid.

79. AA to LCA, February 20, 1818, ibid.

John Adams's Book: Being Notes on a Record of the Births, Marriages and Deaths of Three Generations of the Adams Family, 1734–1807, ed. Henry Adams II (Boston: Boston Atheneum, 1934) p. 4.

80. AA to LCA, May 20, 1818, Reel 443, Adams Papers.

81. AA to JQA, May 30, 1818, ibid.

82. AA to LCA, May 20, 1818, ibid.

Eliza Susan Quincy, July 2, 1818, *Articulate Sisters*, pp. 27–9.

AA to LCA, August 21, 1818, Reel 444, Adams Papers.

83. LCA to AA, August 25, 1818, ibid.

Benjamin Waterhouse to JQA, October 21, 1818, ibid.

84. LCA to JA, October 31, 1818, ibid.

85. Harriet Welsh to LCA, October 22, 1818, ibid.

Harriet Welsh to LCA, October 23, 1818, ibid.

Harriet Welsh to LCA, October 26, 1818, ibid.

TBA to JQA, November 1, 1818, Reel 445, Adams Papers.

86. AA to TJ, April 29, 1817, *The Adams-Jefferson Letters*, ed. Lester J. Cappon, 2 vols. (Chapel Hill: The University of North Carolina Press, 1959), 2:511.

JA to TJ, October 20, 1818, ibid., 2:529.

TJ to JA, November 13, 1818, ibid.

87. JA to Caroline De Windt, July 12, 1820, *Journal and Correspondence*, 1:246–7.

JA refers to Rachel (Wriothesley) Vaughn, Lady Russell, see *Some Account of the Life of Rachel Wriothesley, Lady Russell . . . Followed by a series of Letters* (London, 1819).

Bibliography

In his *Diary*, Abigail Adams's grandson, Charles Francis Adams, the family editor and biographer, writes of his "mixture of feelings" as he looked over the old papers left behind by Abigail and her husband John and learned "the secret history of the lives of a single couple." By August 1, 1833, he had made out "a pretty complete set" of his grandparents' letters to one another. He found his grandfather's letters amusing "from the short concise and humorous style" in which they were written. His grandmother's interested him for their "gravity." He thought her a "thorough politician. She passed her life in the midst of one of those crises in Society," he said, "when the old work was pulled down and the new one put up."[1]

Charles Francis Adams published the first edition of Abigail's letters in 1840. Ever since, recycled or newly disclosed, her letters have appeared under varying auspices, in juxtaposition to her husband's, within her daughter's *Journal and Correspondence*, interspersed with *The Adams-Jefferson Letters*, among *New Letters* written to her sister Mary. With the comparatively recent, superbly documented ongoing publications of The Adams Papers (the monumental work of successive editors), the scope of Abigail Adams's correspondence with family, friends, and statesmen, published thus far through 1782, is increasingly illuminated.

The Adams Papers owe their origin to the Adams Manuscript Trust, which was created in 1905 by Charles Francis Adams's son and namesake to preserve as an entity the disparately owned family papers. That year they were moved from the family's Stone library, adjacent to their house in Quincy, to the Massachusetts Historical Society. Since their gift by the Trust to the Society on April 4, 1956, about one-quarter of the intended one-hundred-volume work has been published to date. A microfilm edition of The Adams Papers, 609 reels encompassing three generations who lived from 1639 to 1889, was published in four installments, from 1954 to 1959. This includes Diaries (Part I), Letterbooks (Part II), Miscellany (Part IV), Letters Received, and Other Loose Papers.

Abigail Adams's letters are embedded in the latter, "loose" category, interfiled chronologically amongst the other "loose" and disparate correspondence pertaining to the lives of all the members of the Adams family. Unlike Abigail, John purposefully copied his letters into letterbooks. As far back as July 2, 1774, John advised Abigail to keep his communications "safe, and preserve them," aware that they might "exhibit to our Posterity a kind of Picture of the Manners, Opinions, and Principles of the Times of Perplexity, Danger and Distress."[2]

Abigail, by contrast, professed "alarm" when she learned that her daughter, Nabby, not only preserved her letters but collected them for *her* daughter Caroline. Abigail was quite positive that Nabby might, due to her "affection and . . . partiality" for her mother, "stamp a value upon them which never can be felt by those less interested in them." Her letters, Abigail said, were written "without regard to style;" and as they were scarcely ever copied over, "they must be very incorrect productions, and quite unworthy preservation or perpetuity." Furthermore, Abigail cautioned Nabby; "do not let them out-live you; you may select a few perhaps worth transmitting, but in general, I fear, they are trash."[3] Again approached about her correspondence, Abigail told Francis Adrian Van der Kemp: "You terrify me my dear Sir when you ask for letters of mine to publish!"[4] Dwelling on this matter further, Abigail wrote a friend on January 28, 1818, "A pretty figure I should make . . . Heedless and inaccurate as I am, I have too much vanity to risk my reputation before the public."[5]

Despite Abigail's protests and her grandson's destruction of countless letters,[6] their abundance, both published and microfilmed, is surprising. Even more so is the existing realm of her still unpublished (and unfilmed) papers. It is these papers and companion resources that have been essential to rounding out Abigail's long, arduous, and valuable life. The following bibliography lists only principle sources, unpublished and published, for quotations and content of *Abigail Adams*.

1. July 31, 1833, *Diary of Charles Francis Adams*, 6 vols. to date, vol. 1–2 ed. Aida Dipace Donald and David Donald, vols. 3–6 ed. Marc Friedlander and L. H. Butterfield. (Cambridge: Harvard University Press, The Belknap Press, 1974), 5:137.
August 1, 1833, ibid., 5:138.
2. JA to AA, July 2, 1774, *Adams Family Correspondence*, 1:121.

3. AA to AAS, June 19, 1809, *Journal and Correspondence of Miss Adams*, 2:202.
4. AA to Francis Adrian Van der Kemp, January 24, 1818, Reel 442, Adams Papers.
5. AA to Harriet Welsh, January 28, 1818, Reel 442, Adams Papers.
6. *Adams Family Correspondence*, 1:XXVII, n. 13.

Manuscript Sources

Adams Papers, Microfilms, 1639–1889, the Massachusetts Historical Society, Boston, 1954–1959, 609 reels.

Infinitely smaller but significant collections also held by the Massachusetts Historical Society include:

The De Windt Collection: Letters from John Quincy Adams to his son George from St. Petersburg, 1811–1813, on the subject of religion. Also, letters from Abigail Adams to Abigail Adams Smith, and William Stephens Smith.

The Norton Diaries: background material on Abigail Adams's maternal forebears.

The Robert Treat Paine Collection: letters from Abigail Paine to her brother.

The Smith-Carter Collection: numerous letters from Abigail Adams to her maternal uncle, Isaac Smith, and his son Isaac Smith, Jr.

The Smith-Townsend Collection: letters from Abigail Adams to her cousin, William Smith of Boston; to her niece Betsy Cranch of Haverhill.

The Abigail Adams Letters at the American Antiquarian Society in Worcester, Massachusetts, include unpublished correspondence between Abigail Adams and her sister Mary Cranch, some especially relevant to Abigail Adams Smith's blighted romance with Royall Tyler.

The Houghton Library at Harvard University holds several letters from Abigail Adams to Mrs. Catherine Johnson, mother of Louisa Catherine Adams, among others of interest.

The New-York Historical Society has several letters from Abigail Adams to Cotton Tufts; also John Adams to Tufts and to a grandson-in-law.

The Shaw Family Papers at the Library of Congress in Washington, D.C., include Abigail Adams's correspondence with her sister, Elizabeth Shaw (later Peabody), with her nephew, William Smith Shaw, and with her niece, Abigail Adams Shaw, who married Joseph Barlow Felt.

The Simon Gratz Collection at the Historical Society of Pennsylvania in Philadelphia has Abigail Adams's letter of April 3, 1813, to James Munroe and several to Richard Rush.

Published Sources

Adams Family Correspondence. Edited by L. H. Butterfield. 4 vols. to date, Cambridge: Harvard University Press, The Belknap Press, 1963–73.

The Adams-Jefferson Letters. Edited by Lester J. Cappon. 2 vols. Chapel Hill: The University of North Carolina Press, 1959.

Adams, Abigail. *Letters of Mrs. Adams.* 3rd ed. in 2 vols. Boston: Charles C. Little and James Brown, 1841.

———. *New Letters of Abigail Adams.* Edited by Stewart Mitchell. Boston: Houghton Mifflin Company, 1947.

——— and John Adams. *The Book of Abigail and John.* Edited by L. H. Butterfield. Cambridge: Harvard University Press, 1975.

Adams, Charles Francis. *An Autobiography.* New York: Houghton Mifflin Co., 1916.

Charles Francis Adams. *Diary of Charles Francis Adams.* 6 vols. to date. Cambridge: Harvard University Press, The Belknap Press, 1964–. Vol. 1–2, edited by Aida Dipace Donald and David Donald; vols. 3–6 edited by Marc Friedlander and L. H. Butterfield (1974).

Adams, Charles Francis. *Three Episodes of Massachusetts History.* Boston and New York: Houghton Mifflin and Co., 1892.

Adams, Henry. *The Education of Henry Adams.* Boston: The Massachusetts Historical Society, 1918; Sentry ed., Boston: Houghton Mifflin Company, 1961.

———. *Mt. Saint Michel and Chartres.* Boston and New York: Houghton Mifflin Company, 1913.

Adams, Henry, II, ed. *John Adams's Book: Being Notes on a Record of the Births, Marriages and Deaths of Three Generations of the Adams Family, 1734–1807.* Boston: Boston Atheneum, 1934.

Adams, John. *Diary and Autobiography of John Adams.* Edited by L. H. Butterfield. 4 vols. Cambridge: Harvard University Press, Atheneum, 1964.

———. *The Earliest Diary of John Adams.* Edited by L. H. Butterfield. Cambridge: Harvard University Press, The Belknap Press, 1966.

———. *Letters of John Adams Addressed to his Wife.* Edited by Charles Francis Adams. 2 vols. Boston: Freeman and Bolles, 1841.

———. *The Works of John Adams.* Edited by Charles Francis Adams. 10 vols. Boston: Little, Brown & Co., 1850–1856.

———. *Statesman and Friend: Correspondence of John Adams with Benjamin Waterhouse 1784–1822.* Edited by Worthington Chauncey Ford. Boston: Little, Brown & Co., 1927.

——— and Abigail Adams. *Familiar Letters of John Adams and his Wife Abigail Adams, during the Revolution.* Edited by Charles Francis Adams. Boston: Houghton, Mifflin and Company, 1875.

——— and John Quincy Adams. *The Selected Writings of John and John Quincy Adams.* Edited by Adrienne Koch and William Peden. New York: Alfred A. Knopf, 1946.

Adams, John Quincy. *Memoirs of John Quincy Adams.* Edited by Charles Francis Adams. 2 vols. Philadelphia: J.B. Lippincott & Co., 1874–77.

———. *The Diary of John Quincy Adams.* Edited by Allan Nevins. New York: Longmans, Green and Co., 1929.

——— and Charles Francis Adams. *The Life of John Adams.* 2 vols. (1871). Reprinted, New York: Haskell House Publishers, 1968.

Adams, Mrs. John Quincy (Louisa Catherine). *Narrative of a Journey from St. Petersburg to Paris in February 1815. Scribner's Magazine,* October 1903, 34:449–463.

d'Antique, Le Comte. *De Boulogne à Auteuil, Passy et Chaillot à Travers les Ages.* Paris: Lapina, 1922.

The American Revolution: Two Centuries of Interpretation. Edited by Edmund S. Morgan. Englewood Cliffs, New Jersey: Prentice-Hall, Inc., 1965.

Aurora.

Bancroft, George. *History of the United States of America.* 6 vols. New York: D. Appleton and Company, 1897.

Bartlett, Joseph Gardner. *Henry Adams of Somersetshire, England and Braintree, Mass.* New York: privately printed, 1927.

Bemis, Samuel Flagg. *The Foundation of American Diplomacy, 1775–1823.* New York, London: D. Appleton–Century Company, Inc., 1935.

Blake, John B. *Public Health in the Town Of Boston, 1630–1822.* Cambridge: Harvard University Press, 1959.

The Boston Gazette, or Country Journal.

Brodie, Fawn. *Thomas Jefferson.* New York: W.W. Norton & Company, 1974.

Brown, Alice. *Mercy Warren* New York: Charles Scribner's Sons, 1896.

Callender, James Thomson. *The Prospect Before Us.* 2 vols., Vol. 2 in two parts. Richmond: M. Jones, S. Pleasants, Jr., and J. Lyon, 1800–1. 1:67.

Chamberlain, Mellon. *John Adams, the Statesman of the American Revolution.* Boston and New York: Houghton Mifflin and Co., 1898.

Commager, Henry Steele, ed. *Documents of American History.* 9th ed. in 2 vols. Englewood Cliffs, New Jersey: Prentice-Hall, 1973.

Crowley, John Edward. *This Sheba, Self.* Baltimore and London: The Johns Hopkins University Press, 1974.

Dickinson, John, *Letters from a farmer in Pennsylvania,* Boston. Printed by Mein and Fleming, 1768.

"Silas Deane Papers, 1774–1790." *Collections of The New-York Historical Society* 19–23. 1886–1890.

"DuPont and Talleyrand, 1798." *Proceedings of the Massachusetts Historical Society* 49:63–5. November 1915.

The Essex Gazette. Salem, Massachusetts.

Fordyce, Reverend James, D.D. *Sermons to Young Women.* 2 vols. London, 1767.

———. *The Character and Conduct of the Female Sex.* London, 1776.

Franklin, Benjamin. *The Writings of Benjamin Franklin,* edited by Albert Henry Smyth, 10 vols. New York: The Macmillan Company, 1905–07.

Frothingham, Richard. *Life and Times of Joseph Warren.* Boston: Little, Brown & Co., 1865.

———. *The Rise of the Republic of the United States.* Tenth ed. Boston: Little, Brown and Company, 1910.

Garraty, John A. *The American Nation: A History of the United States to 1877.* 2nd ed. New York: American Heritage Publishing Co., Inc., 1971.

Grandmother Tyler's Book: The Recollections of M. P. Tyler (Mrs. Royall Tyler), edited by Frederick Tupper and Helen Tyler Brown, New York: G.P. Putnam's Sons, 1925.

Gross, Robert A. *The Minutemen and their World.* New York: Hill and Wang, 1976.

Hamilton, Alexander. *The Papers of Alexander Hamilton.* Edited by Harold C. Syrett. 26 vols. New York: Columbia University Press, 1961–.

Hosmer, James K. *Samuel Adams.* New York: Chelsea House, 1980. Pp. 68, 119.

Howe, John R., Jr. *The Changing Political Thought of John Adams.* Princeton, New Jersey: Princeton University Press, 1966.

Howe, Mark Antony De Wolfe, ed. *The Articulate Sisters,* Cambridge: Harvard University Press, 1946.

Hutchinson, Thomas. *The History of the Colony and Province of Massachusetts-Bay.* Edited by Lawrence Shaw Mayo. 3 vols. Cambridge: Harvard University Press, 1936.

Jefferson, Thomas. *The Life and Selected Writings of Thomas Jefferson.* Edited by Adrienne Koch and William Peden. New York: The Modern Library, 1972.

———. *The Papers of Thomas Jefferson, Princeton University.* Edited by Julian Boyd. 21 vols. Princeton, New Jersey: Princeton University Press, 1950–. 20:291, 293.

Johnson, Allen and Dumas Malone, eds. *Dictionary of American Biography.* 20 vols. New York: Scribner, 1928–1936.

Journals of the House of Representatives of Massachusetts. 1715–. Boston. Reprinted in the Massachusetts Historical Society, 1919–.

Keller, Rosemary Skinner. *Abigail Adams and the American Revolution: A Personal History.* Ann Arbor, Michigan: University Microfilms International, 1977.

Koch, Adrienne, ed. *The American Enlightenment.* New York: George Braziller, 1965. Pp. 246–250.

London Chronicle.

London Gazette.

Lunardi, Vincenzo. *An Account of the First Aerial Voyage in England in a Series of Letters.* London, 1784.

Macaulay, Catharine Sawbridge. *History of England, from the Accession of James I to that of the Brunswick Line.* 8 vols. London, 1763–1783.

Malone, Dumas. *Jefferson the President: First Term.* Boston: Little, Brown & Co., 1970.

Massachusetts Centinel.

Massachusetts Gazette and Boston News-Letter.

Mercure de France.

Morgan, Edmund S. *The Challenge of the American Revolution.* New York: W.W. Norton, 1976.

———. "The Puritan Ethic and the American Revolution," *William and Mary Quarterly,* 3rd. series, 24 (January 1967).

Morris, Richard, ed. *Encyclopedia of American History.* Bicentennial ed. New York: Harper & Row, 1976.

Morrison, Samuel Eliot. *The Life and Letters of Harrison Gray Otis.* 2 vols. Boston and New York: The Riverside Press, Cambridge, 1913.

Musto, David F. "The Youth of John Quincy Adams." *Proceedings of the American Philosophical Society, August, 1969.* Vol. 113, no. 4, pp. 269–82.

Oliver, Andrew. *Portraits of John and Abigail Adams.* Cambridge: Harvard University Press, The Belknap Press, 1967.

Paine, Thomas. *Common Sense.* Philadelphia, 1776. Reprinted in *The Life and Major Writings of Thomas Paine.* Edited by Philip S. Foner. Secaucus, New Jersey: The Citadel Press, 1948. Pp. 3–46.

Porter, Robert Ker. *Travelling Sketches in Russia and Sweden.* 2 vols. London: Richard Phillips, 1809.

Public Advertiser.

Pulley, Judith. *The Bittersweet Friendship of Thomas Jefferson and Abigail Adams.* Essex Institute Historical Collections, Vol. 108 (July, 1972). Pp. 193–216.

Quincy, Edmund. *Life of Josiah Quincy.* Boston: Ticknor & Fields, 1868.

Quincy, Eliza Susan (Morton). *Memoir of the Life of Eliza S.M. Quincy.* Boston: J. Wilson and Son, 1861.

Quincy, Josiah. *Memoir of Josiah Quincy, Junior of Massachusetts: 1774–1775.* Edited by Eliza Susan Quincy. Boston: J. Wilson and Son, 1874.

Records of the Town of Braintree, 1640–1793. Edited by Samuel Bates. Randolph, Massachusetts: D.H. Huxford, 1886.

Report of a TRIAL:Miles Farmer, versus Dr. David Humphreys Storer, . . . Relative to the Transactions between Miss Eliza Dolph and George Washington Adams, Esq. son of the Late President of the United States. Reported by the Plaintiff, Boston. Printed for the Reporter. 1831.

Roof, Katherine Metcalf. *Colonel William Smith and Lady.* Boston: Houghton Mifflin Company, 1929.

Schouler, James. *History of the United States of America under the Constitution.* Rev. ed. in 7 vols. (1880–1894). Reprinted, New York: Kraus Reprint Co., 1970.

Sibley's Harvard Graduates. Massachusetts Historical Society. 17 vols. 1873–.

"Smallpox Inoculation in Colonial Boston." *Journal of the History of Medicine.*

Smith, Abigail Adams. *Journal and Correspondence of Miss Adams.* Edited by Caroline Smith De Windt. 2 vols. New York and London: Wiley and Putnam, 1841.

Smith, William Steuben. *FACTS in Refutation of the Aspersions Against the Character and Memory of Col. Wm. Stephens Smith, as Recorded be Col. Tim. Pickering, in his Review of the Correspondence between the Hon. John Adams and the Late Wm. Cunningham, Esq.* Washington: Davis and Forge, 1824.

Smith, William and Cotton Tufts. *Diaries of Reverend William Smith, 1734–1783, and Dr. Cotton Tufts, 1738–1784.* Proceedings of the Massachusetts Historical Society, 42:444–478. October 1908–June 1909.

Trumbull, John. *Autobiography, Reminiscences and Letters from 1756 to 1841.* New York and London: Wiley and Putnam, 1841.

Tudor, William. *Life of James Otis of Massachusetts.* Boston: Wells & Lilly, 1823.

Tyler, Royall. *The Contrast in Dramas from the American Theatre 1762–1909.* Edited by Richard Moody. Cleveland and New York: World Publishing, 1966.

Warren-Adams Letters. 2 vols. Boston: The Massachusetts Historical Society, 1925.

Warren, Mercy. *History on the Rise, Progress and Termination of the American Revolution.* 3 vols. 1805. Reprint ed., New York: AMS Press, 1970.

Washington, George. *The Writings of George Washington.* Edited by Jared Sparks. 12 vols. Boston: American Stationers' Company, 1837.

Whitney, Janet. *Abigail Adams.* Boston: Little, Brown & Co., 1947.

Winsor, Justin, ed. *The Memorial History of Boston, Including Suffolk Community, 1630–1880.* 4 vols. Boston, 1880–1881.

Wood, Gordon S. *The Creation of the American Republic, 1776–1787.* Chapel Hill: The University of North Carolina Press, 1969.

Index

The John Adams Family

JOHN ADAMS
(1691–1761)
m.
Susanna Boylston
(1709–1797)
Who married
2: John Hall
(1698–1780)

EBENEZER ADAMS
(1704–1769)
m.
Ann Boylston
(1706–1770)
Sister of
Susanna (Boylston) Adams
(1709–1797)

JOHN ADAMS
(1735–1826)
m.
Abigail Smith
(1744–1818)

ABIGAIL "NABBY" ADAMS
(1765–1813)
m.
William Stephens Smith
(1755–1816)

JOHN QUINCY ADAMS
(1767–1848)
m.
Louisa Catherine Johnson
(1775–1852)

SUSANNA ADAMS
(1768–1770)

CHARLES ADAMS
(1770–1800)
m.
Sarah "Sally" Smith
(1769–1828)

THOMAS BOYLSTON ADAMS
(1772–1832)
m.
Ann "Nancy" Harrod
(1776–1846)

PETER BOYLSTON ADAMS
(1738–1823)
m.
Mary Crosby
(1749–1823)

MARY ADAMS
(1769–1830)

BOYLSTON ADAMS
(1771–1829)
m. his cousin,
Eliza Ann Crosby

ANN ADAMS
(1773–1819)

SUSANNA ADAMS
(1777–1816)

ELIHU ADAMS
(1741–1775)
m.
Thankful White
(1747–1822)

Three children